DISCOVER AUSTRALIA

A region-by-region guide to
landscapes, wildlife and plants

READER'S DIGEST · SYDNEY

DISCOVER AUSTRALIA

A region-by-region guide to
landscapes, wildlife and plants

READER'S DIGEST · SYDNEY

Edited and designed by Reader's Digest

EXECUTIVE EDITOR	Phillip Rodwell
ASSISTANT EDITOR	Amanda David
ART EDITOR	Phillip Bush
DESIGNER	Pamela Horsnell
RESEARCH EDITOR	Vere Dodds
TEXT PROCESSOR	Karen Wain
PROJECT COORDINATOR	Robyn Hudson
PRODUCTION CONTROLLER	Louise Mitchell

Maps by Universal Press, David Carroll   Diagrams by Kim Graham

CONTRIBUTORS

Jane Calder   Barry Dowling

Milo Dunphy AM, ASTC   Jim Gasteen

Eddie Hegerl   Neil Hermes BSc (Hons)

Jim Hutchison   John McCabe

David Milledge   Michael Morcombe

Geoff Mosley BA (Hons), MA, PhD   Roger Oxley BAppSc

Margo Pfieff   Barbara Porter PhD, MSc

Peter Prineas BA, LLB   Harry F. Recher

Brian Woodward

First edition
Published by Reader's Digest (Australia) Pty Ltd (inc in NSW)
26-32 Waterloo Street, Surry Hills, NSW 2010
Copyright © 1991 Reader's Digest (Australia) Pty Ltd
Copyright © 1991 Reader's Digest Association Far East Ltd
Philippines copyright 1991 Reader's Digest Association Far East Ltd

National Library of Australia cataloguing-in-publication data:

DISCOVER AUSTRALIA

Includes index
ISBN 0 86438 135 2.

1. Landforms – Australia. 2. Australia – Description and
travel – 1976–1990. 3. Australia – Description and travel
– 1976–1990 – Guide-books.

919.40463.

Front Cover: The Twelve Apostles, Port Campbell. Back cover (top to bottom): The Olgas, central Australia; Gippsland rainforest, Victoria; Kakadu wetlands, Arnhem Land. Title page: Cliffs at Pender Bay, north of Broome, Western Australia.

Typesetting by Lettercraft Management Pty Ltd, Sydney. Colour separation by Colourscan Overseas Co. Pty Ltd, Singapore.
Printing and binding by Dai Nippon Printing Co. (HK) Ltd, Hong Kong.

INTRODUCTION

IF DAILY NEWS reports of soil erosion, clear felling of forests, pollution and spreading coastal development were taken at face value, Australia could be seen as a battle-scarred dustbowl surrounded by industrial wastelands. Two hundred years of European settlement have certainly left scars on the landscape, but compared with the rest of the world Australia is still relatively unpolluted and uncrowded.

Australia is the only nation to be the sole occupant of a continent. With large areas of the natural landscape still untouched, Australians have opportunities to avoid problems which have occurred elsewhere and to learn how to live *with* the land while making a living *from* it.

Discover Australia aims to foster an awareness of the beauty, richness and variety of the surviving and often threatened wildernesses which exist outside the cities and towns where 90 per cent of the population lives. It aims to demonstrate that a closer look at 'the bush', beyond well-known, spectacular natural wonders such as Ayers Rock and the Great Barrier Reef, is rewarded by the revelation of myriad exquisitely meshed environments where landforms, animals and plants come together in a delicately balanced harmony. The challenge to Australians in the final years of the twentieth century is to decide how far this balance can be maintained.

The first section of **Discover Australia** explains broadly how our landscapes came into being; the second section describes 40 distinctive regions in detail; the third section gives advice on how best to see Australia, with information on year-round climatic conditions.

For the sake of clarity, scientific names of animals and plants are given in brackets after common names at the first and subsequent major reference in each chapter. Common names vary from region to region and are often based misleadingly on quite different, unrelated European forms. Non-specific references are accompanied by the generic name only.

THE EDITORS

A key to the landscape regions

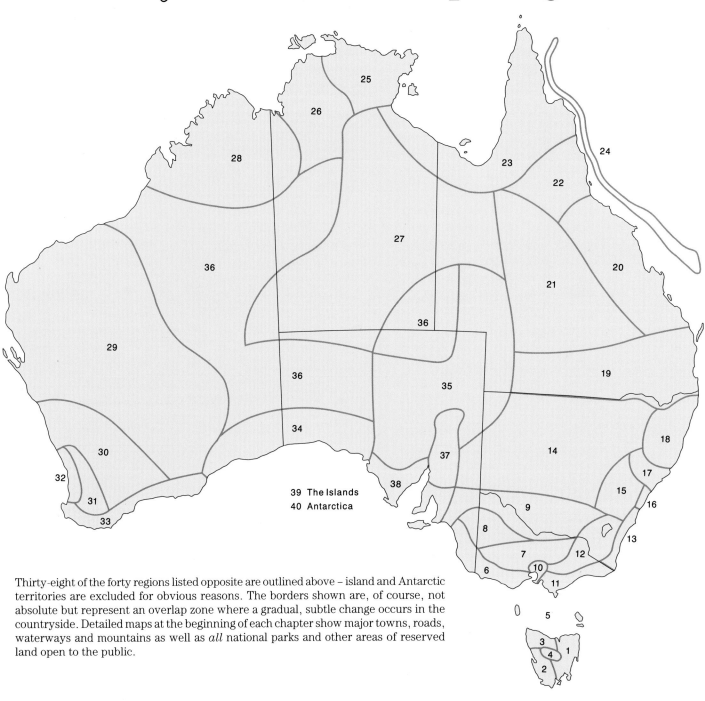

39 The Islands
40 Antarctica

Thirty-eight of the forty regions listed opposite are outlined above – island and Antarctic territories are excluded for obvious reasons. The borders shown are, of course, not absolute but represent an overlap zone where a gradual, subtle change occurs in the countryside. Detailed maps at the beginning of each chapter show major towns, roads, waterways and mountains as well as *all* national parks and other areas of reserved land open to the public.

CONTENTS

PART ONE

The shaping of the landscape *pages 8-21*

Shaped by fire, ravaged by ice, wind and water......10

The human element: a disciplined landscape........16

PART TWO

Australia: 40 contrasting regions *pages 22-377*

1 Eastern Tasmania................................24	21 Inland Queensland............................204
2 South-West Tasmania...........................34	22 Atherton Tableland Region....................210
3 North-West Tasmania...........................44	23 Cape York and the Gulf Plains................216
4 Central Tasmania................................50	24 Great Barrier Reef............................224
5 Bass Strait Islands.............................58	25 Arnhem Land..................................234
6 Geelong to the Coorong.......................62	26 Darwin and Hinterland.......................246
7 Victorian Hills.................................74	27 The Centre....................................252
8 Mallee Country................................82	28 The Kimberley.................................264
9 Murray River and Riverina.....................86	29 North-West Shoulder and Hinterland........274
10 Greater Melbourne.............................96	30 The Wheat Belt................................284
11 Gippsland 104	31 Fringe of the Plateau.........................290
12 The High Country.............................114	32 The Perth Coast...............................296
13 Southern New South Wales Coast............126	33 South-West Corner............................306
14 West of the Divide............................134	34 Nullarbor Plain................................316
15 Blue Mountains...............................144	35 Salt Lakes and Channel Country.............322
16 Greater Sydney...............................154	36 The Deserts...................................339
17 Hunter Valley.................................168	37 Flinders Ranges...............................340
18 Greater New England..........................176	38 Adelaide and the Gulf Country...............350
19 Southern Queensland.........................186	39 The Islands....................................360
20 Central Queensland Coast.....................196	40 Antarctica.....................................370

PART THREE

Seeing Australia *pages 378-389*

What does it mean?......................390

Index......................391

Acknowledgments......................400

The MacDonnell Ranges, west of Alice Springs

The shaping of the landscape

A fanciful, cross-continental walk spreads the formation of Australia along an imaginary time-line marked by momentous prehistorical milestones and where the human history of the most eroded continent begins just as the walk ends

Shaped by fire, ravaged by ice, wind and water

The enormity of time taken by the earth's landmasses and seas to assume their current familiar patterns defies the imagination. One way of comprehending it is to convert Australia's geological timescale into a modern-day journey between two cities.

The grindingly slow forces which formed today's landscapes are then reduced dramatically in scale when seen as events along an imaginary 3000-kilometre hike across the continent from Perth to Sydney. Each step of the journey represents 40 human generations and every kilometre the passage of more than a million years.

As the time-walking hikers set out from the Perth GPO in Forrest Place, the earth is still new, a shapeless swirl of cooling gasses. While the hikers are still within the city, a sphere with a molten core surrounded by a firm outer crust slowly begins to take shape.

Several million years later, the walkers reach the Swan River but there has been no visible change to the cooling, lifeless earth. As they leave Perth's metropolitan limits behind, it is difficult to believe that the first birds will not appear overhead until they reach Mittagong in the southern highlands of New South Wales, and that New Zealand and Australia will not part company until Campbelltown, on the edge of Sydney.

Even the great volcanic landforms of the Warrumbungle Range will not thrust through the earth's crust until the walkers reach suburban Sydney. The human species, *Homo sapiens*, does not enter the Australian scene until the time-walkers are almost at the steps of their goal, the Sydney GPO.

Most of the walk across Western Australia is through a lifeless place: 4.5 billion years of geological heaving, twisting and sculpting must pass before modern times are reached. It is not for a billion of these years, or after the walkers reach Norseman and the beginning of the Eyre Highway, that tiny lifeforms first appear.

REMAKING THE LANDSCAPE The granite, basalt and dolerite outcrops throughout south-eastern Australia are the legacy of the fiery volcanoes which pock-marked the landscape 360 million years ago.

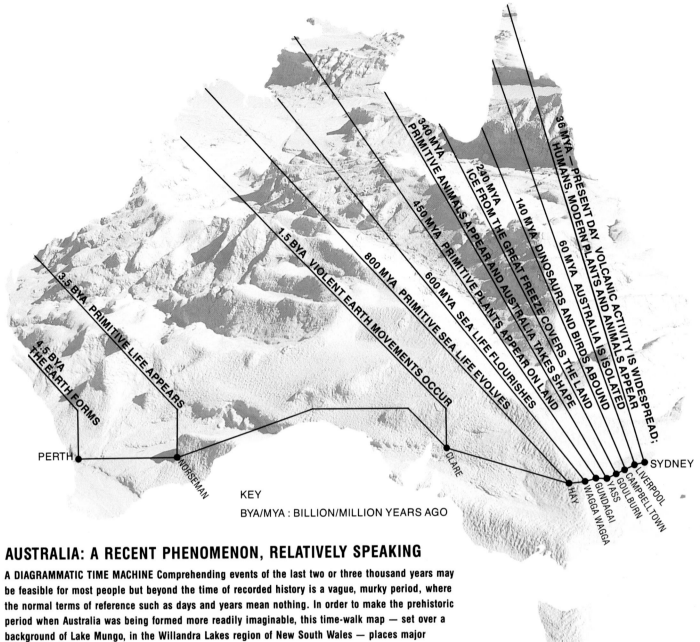

Map labels (radiating timeline from Perth to Sydney):

4.5 BYA THE EARTH FORMS
3.5 BYA PRIMITIVE LIFE APPEARS
1.5 BYA VIOLENT EARTH MOVEMENTS OCCUR
800 MYA PRIMITIVE SEA LIFE EVOLVES
600 MYA SEA LIFE FLOURISHES
450 MYA PRIMITIVE PLANTS APPEAR ON LAND
340 MYA PRIMITIVE ANIMALS APPEAR AND AUSTRALIA TAKES SHAPE
240 MYA ICE FROM THE GREAT FREEZE COVERS THE LAND
140 MYA DINOSAURS AND BIRDS ABOUND
60 MYA AUSTRALIA IS ISOLATED
30 MYA – PRESENT DAY VOLCANIC ACTIVITY IS WIDESPREAD; HUMANS, MODERN PLANTS AND ANIMALS APPEAR

PERTH
NORSEMAN
CLARE
HAY
WAGGA WAGGA
GUNDAGAI
YASS
GOULBURN
CAMPBELLTOWN
LIVERPOOL
SYDNEY

KEY
BYA/MYA : BILLION/MILLION YEARS AGO

AUSTRALIA: A RECENT PHENOMENON, RELATIVELY SPEAKING

A DIAGRAMMATIC TIME MACHINE Comprehending events of the last two or three thousand years may be feasible for most people but beyond the time of recorded history is a vague, murky period, where the normal terms of reference such as days and years mean nothing. In order to make the prehistoric period when Australia was being formed more readily imaginable, this time-walk map — set over a background of Lake Mungo, in the Willandra Lakes region of New South Wales — places major events in the earth's history along a walk from Perth to Sydney. If such a thing was possible, Australia would not become a recognisable continent until the outskirts of the eastern capital.

Here, with most of the continent still ahead, new chemicals begin to form in the first murky sea. Primitive lifeforms are already forming the composite, rock-like structures we now know as stromatolites and which still exist off the Western Australian coast (see pp. 274– 283).

As the hikers turn east and head along the Eyre Highway towards the Nullarbor Plain and the Western Australia–South Australia border, just over a billion years have passed. This represents a period when great changes occur, changes that enable higher lifeforms to evolve.

Molten iron sinks slowly below the planet's surface causing a chemical reaction that allows oxygen to be released into the atmosphere. The form

of oxygen known as ozone is also released and it forms a layer in the atmosphere which begins to screen the surface from the sun's damaging ultraviolet rays. As the walkers cross the Nullarbor Plain, protected by hats and sunscreen lotion, they are unaware of the processes occurring far overhead which would eventually allow just enough of the sun's energy onto the earth's surface to allow life to flourish.

For the time-walkers, the South Australian border represents the time when the first rock formations appear in northern Western Australia. The weathered rocks of what we know today as the Pilbara district have existed for three billion years.

By Ceduna, the midway point on the cross-continental walk, some very large

areas of what will eventually become Western Australia, the Northern Territory and South Australia have formed into a vast landmass. For the next billion years the shape of this land will change constantly as it is inundated by seas and thrust upwards in massive mountain-building processes.

One-and-a-half billion years ago, or by the time the walkers approach Clare, the beautifully coloured and twisted forms of the Flinders Ranges are forced up and folded to form mountains. This region was once a deep ocean strait and the contorted and multi-layered marine sediments which make up the bedrock of today's mountain peaks and gorges are the evidence that the material of the ranges originated under the sea.

During the same period, the worn,

11

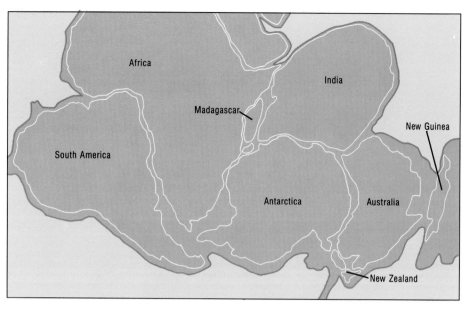

THE JIGSAW PUZZLE OF GONDWANALAND

180 MILLION YEARS AGO Below sea level, the continental shelf of each continent marks the true boundary of the landmass. Today's southern continents were once combined along their continental shelves to form a supercontinent, dubbed Gondwanaland by scientists. North America, Europe and Asia formed a second supercontinent known as Laurasia.

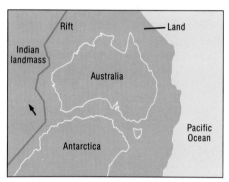

150 MILLION YEARS AGO Massive rifts, or fracture lines began to appear between 200 million and 140 million years ago, signalling the imminent breakup of Laurasia and Gondwanaland. Africa moved to the west and India moved off to the north, where the force of its collision with the new continent of Asia caused the Himalayas to be pushed up.

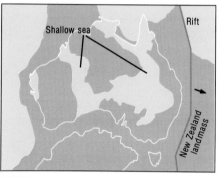

100 MILLION YEARS AGO With the breaking away of South America, Gondwanaland now incorporated the future landmasses of Australia, Antarctica and New Zealand. About 80 million years ago, the eastern fracture gave way and the Tasman Sea filled the gap as New Zealand broke away. A large part of the future Australia was covered in shallow seas.

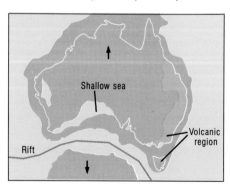

30 MILLION YEARS AGO By this time Australia had been separated from Antarctica for about 20 million years, and had started the journey northward which it continues today. As the continent passed over a fracture, volcanoes burst through the surface while the land which had once joined the continents sank beneath the sea to form continental shelves.

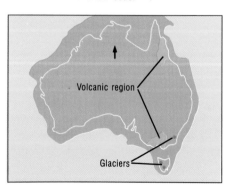

1 MILLION YEARS AGO About 25 million years ago, Australia had evolved a recognisable shape, although coastlines everywhere would fluctuate as the ice ages came and went. Australia's continental plate had long ago collided with that of New Guinea and during the last ice age, the two landmasses and Tasmania were all connected.

craggy sandstones of the Bungle Bungles in northern Western Australia and the Arnhem Land plateau in the Northern Territory also formed as layers of seabed sediments.

The birth of Uluru

Imagine the distance between the South Australia–New South Wales border and the town of Hay being equal to the 800 million years it took for a minor ice age to reshape the world's scattered landmasses. As the ice age ends, the Australian continent begins to take its present shape. The land the time-walkers see before them is still lifeless but the sea is full of primitive plant and animal forms.

As the time-walkers approach a point somewhere between Narrandera and Wagga Wagga — they are still 600 million years away from the present — an obscure bay is forming on the edge of an ancient sea. On the floor of the bay, layer upon layer of red silts and sands are deposited; over millions of years the layers will become compressed into rock.

Much later, the twisting of the earth's crust turned this gigantic sandstone rock at right angles to its original position. Today it protrudes above the surrounding plain as the monolith known as Uluru, or Ayers Rock. Like an iceberg, most of Uluru's bulk is out of sight, six kilometres below the surface of the sandy plain.

Until now, the hike across Australia has been a fairly uneventful experience coinciding only occasionally with dramatic events that have had little impact on the immediate landscape. All of a sudden, in the vicinity of Wagga Wagga, the pace of change quickens and there is a bewildering explosion in the diversity of living things.

Life in the seas that cover inland Australia is no longer confined to simple, cellular forms or shapeless, soft-bodied animals. Trilobites — tough, armour-plated, shellfish-like creatures now dominate the seas and continue to do so for 350 million years; that is from Wagga Wagga to the Goulburn region on the time-walk.

At a million years per kilometre, the hikers reach the foothills of the Great Dividing Range and the Hume Highway. This time-walk signpost is also a major signpost in the evolution of life.

Here, as the hikers turn towards Sydney, 500 million years away, some new and unusual armoured lifeforms appear beneath the waves. They are the earliest fish, jawless bottom-

feeders, and the ancestors of all the vertebrates, or animals with supporting, bony skeletons.

At the same time, countless layers of sediment are forming into sandstone on the floor of vast inland oceans — much later this would become the basement rock for much of modern south-eastern Australia. By Gundagai, the seabed sediments which now form Black Mountain in Canberra and the plains on which Melbourne is built are settling into place on the floor of an ancient sea.

Across the continent, the Kimberley region and central Australia are being split open by the uplifting of new mountain ranges, and volcanoes are erupting along the eastern coast, sending dark clouds heavy with ash to rain down on the time-walkers.

When the walkers reach the outskirts of Yass, north of Canberra, there are 340 million years yet to go. The sea now invades many parts of the eastern coastline and coral reefs develop.

These reefs give rise to limestone formations which are now part of the land and honeycombed by erosion into elaborate and beautiful cave systems. The most famous of these are at Jenolan, west of Sydney, and Chillagoe, in northern Queensland.

A mountain range appears

About 300 million years ago, a massive uplifting of Tasmania, parts of Victoria and southern New South Wales occurs. These subterranean convulsions force sea-floor fossils up into the now mountainous regions of Tasmania.

Molten rocks from deep beneath the surface are pushed through the earth's crust, bringing the Snowy Mountains into being. A period of mountain uplifting also occurs in central Australia,

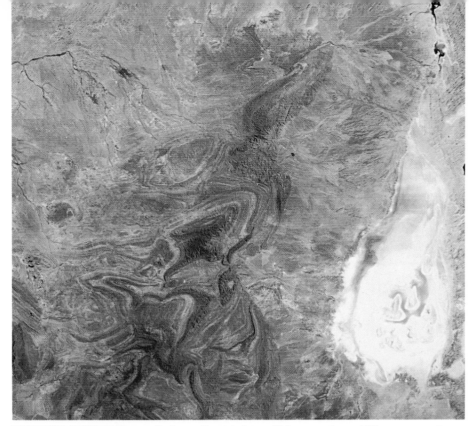

SATELLITE'S EYE VIEW The result of a continental plate collision more than a billion years ago is seen in this picture taken 70 kilometres above the earth. Salt-caked Lake Frome (right) is the result of subsidence caused by the same pressures that created the Flinders Ranges (brown, centre left).

creating the giant peaks which are the ancestors of the greatly eroded mountains known as the MacDonnell Ranges.

During this time of frigid conditions, with glaciers covering many parts of the eastern highlands, mountain building is also taking place in western Victoria as the Grampian Ranges are lifted clear of the ocean floor. Volcanic activity is widespread and the combination of volcanoes and glacial action ensures that the surface of the land undergoes dramatic changes.

At the time the walkers approach Goulburn, they are chilled by the wind off the huge ice sheet that covers much of Australia. The continent is still relatively close to the South Pole and even

such places as the Kimberley region are scoured by glaciers, while Tasmania is again underwater.

Ice action sculpts many landscapes dramatically and there is no better example of this than the rocky shore at Halletts Cove near Adelaide. Today, this carved landscape displays the scratch marks made on the rocks by the moving ice (see p. 355). Further south, a huge glacier cuts slowly through the undulating plains, separating an area of hills that are later to become Kangaroo Island.

A major event of this time that will be of great economic significance in the future is the laying down of the great coal seams along the eastern coast.

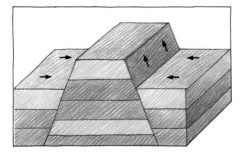

PROVIDING RELIEF

THE BIG SQUEEZE The relief, or variation in altitude of many regions occurs when enormous pressures within the earth's crust cause a fracture. With pressure from both sides, a faulted area is thrust upwards (left). This inexorable process is too slow to be observable by the naked eye but over millions of years can result in the formation of a mountain range.

From Bowen in Queensland to Newcastle and Wollongong in New South Wales, these great coal fields are forming, not in steamy, tropical rainforests, but in cold, swampy forests surrounding large, shallow lakes.

At the point where the walkers reach Marulan, Australia is largely a dry land, with the exception of a huge, freshwater sea stretching from inland Queensland to central New South Wales. An arm of this sea which is slowly filling with silt and sand eventually forms the Hawkesbury River sandstone basin. The craggy Blue Mountains and the massive sea cliffs of Sydney are part of this formation.

By Mittagong, the greatest landforming events are occurring below the surface of Tasmania: movements in the earth's molten mantle force huge rock formations up near the surface. Eventually these will be exposed to form the dramatic modern landscapes of Cradle Mountain and Mount Wellington. The same dark, dolerite rock forms the great

columnar coastal landscapes at Cape Raoul and Bruny Island on Tasmania's south-eastern coastline.

In the vicinity of Campbelltown — with Sydney on the horizon — the walk is only 135 kilometres from its end but on the comparative geological time-line, modern times are still 140 million years away. The Australian age of giant dinosaurs is at its peak and the time-walkers gasp with amazement as they see the first flowering plants appearing. Far inland, freshwater seas are flooded by the ocean as thick layers of siltstone and shale cover the porous sandstones below the surface.

The combination of impervious silt and shale settling on top of the sponge-like sandstones creates the vast artesian basins which would eventually lie under much of inland Australia. These deposits also contain mineral-rich ores which, with subsequent erosion by water percolating down from the surface, create opal-bearing rock in the regions where towns such as Lightning

Ridge, Cunnamulla, Coober Pedy and Andamooka will one day spring up.

A few kilometres beyond Campbelltown towards Sydney is equivalent to the point where the dinosaurs begin to leave a cooler landscape to more diminutive creatures — the early marsupials. The first banksia-like flowers appear and, extraordinary as it may seem, some landscapes look almost as they do today. For example, the sandplain around Ayers Rock and the Olgas in Uluru National Park has changed little in the last 65 million years.

An independent continent

On the edge of suburban Sydney, almost 3000 kilometres from the start of the time-line, the evolution of Australia's distinctive plants and animals is apace. By Liverpool, the continent finally breaks from Antarctica and is left isolated. The first gum trees appear — about 36 million years ago — and the first koalas and kangaroos decorate the landscape by Cabramatta.

CRUSHING BURDEN About 240 million years ago, rivers of ice like the Franz Josef Glacier in the Southern Alps of New Zealand, ground their way across the landscape with only the Gulf of Carpentaria region free of ice.

RECEDING COASTLINE Before the end of the last ice age — about 7000 years ago — the space between the reef of Green Island and the mainland coastal mountains would have been dry land.

Around 20 million years ago — or near the suburb of Chullora — the landscape is being moulded by a number of separate events. Molten rock from volcanoes finds its way into fissures in the rock of the Kimberley region to form some of the richest diamond deposits in the world.

To the south, the sea bites deeply into the coastline to form the Great Australian Bight. This allows coral reefs and other marine forms to flourish in the warm, shallow stretch of sea near to shore. The dead bodies of these microscopic lifeforms accumulate to such a depth that a layer of limestone is formed that eventually becomes the flat expanse of the Nullarbor Plain.

Elsewhere the foundations are being laid for what would one day be renowned as the modern world's lar-gest structure built by living creatures. The base for the Great Barrier Reef forms beneath the shallow Coral Sea as the Australian continental plate push-es northward towards the Equator.

As the time-walkers reach the loca-tion of present-day, inner suburban Leichhardt, the continent's south-eastern shore, only a few kilometres away, is buffeted by giant waves, the result of undersea convulsions caused by the eruption of the Lord Howe Island volcano. After the volcano has spent its fury and the sulphurous clouds have cleared, a large new island group is seen to break the waters of the Tasman Sea. Today, Lord Howe Island and Balls Pyramid (see pp. 360–363) are all that remain of those subtropical islands.

By George Street, the main street of central Sydney, the curious pinnacles at Nambung National Park, north of Perth, are being formed by water trick-ling through limestone a million years before the time when they would be-come tourist attractions.

Only 40 metres from the steps of the Sydney GPO in Martin Place, the time-walkers notice the sudden appearance of dark-skinned humans who have just migrated from the north of the conti-nent and who will eventually continue their migration across the land-bridge into Tasmania. The arrival of the Aborigines has its own consequences on the appearance of the land but the elements are also still at work. A great glacial period is to add the final rugged, angular touches to the Snowy Moun-tains and the Tasmanian highlands.

When the glaciers melt and the seas rise, New Guinea and Tasmania are finally separated from the Australian mainland. This occurs — about 7000 years ago — only in the last six metres of the marathon walk.

Looking to their north, the time-walkers see that Port Jackson, once a deep valley like its modern counter-parts in the Blue Mountains, is being flooded by the glacier-swollen sea to form Sydney Harbour. The last epi-sodes of volcanic activity on the conti-nent occur on the Atherton Tableland in northern Queensland and near today's South Australia–Victoria bord-er, creating lava deposits which will weather into rich, deep soil. The last known eruption is at Mount Schank, near Mount Gambier, less than 5000 years ago.

The penultimate footstep of this transcontinental hike coincides with the appearance off Sydney Heads of the weather-worn sails of the First Fleet. The final step represents the dramatic transformation which occurs across the continent as European settlers make their mark. At this time, nature reduces its firm grip on the landscape as human beings introduce their own, just as in-exorable forces for change. ☐

Of the many factors which have influenced the shaping of Australia's landscape, the hand of man has had by far the most dramatic effect while producing the most far-reaching consequences

The human element: a disciplined landscape

COEXISTENCE A sugar cane plantation near Innisfail is juxtaposed with the remains of the rainforest which once covered the hillside.

Australia, the world's most isolated inhabited continent, has been cut off from the earth's other major landmasses for millions of years. For most of this long period its landscapes, plants and animals continued to evolve in their own peculiar way without the influence or stimulation of any outside force.

It is only in the last 60 000 years or so, with the arrival of two waves of human settlers, that this evolution — the random, chance responses of vegetation and wildlife to their surroundings — has been interrupted. In that time, the landscape and its inhabitants have been subjected to varying levels of human coercion to conform to particular, imposed patterns.

Not all the changes that have occurred since the Aborigines stepped ashore somewhere along the northern coastline can be attributed to the direct or even indirect influence of humans; natural forces continued, and continue, to dictate change.

But the rate of change was amended gradually by the Aborigines and it has accelerated with such rapidity since the arrival of European settlers that the slow, once-inexorable influences of 'nature' are far overshadowed by the dramatic power of technology, whether it be in the form of axe or bulldozer.

When the first Aborigines explored their new land, the soil they walked on had never felt the tread of human feet and the rivers, mountains, plants and animals before them were observed for the first time. This was the tail-end of the ice-age epoch, a time of still frozen landscapes, when many of today's subtropical regions were clothed in cool-climate plants.

Over most of Australia the area of permanent ice was small — perhaps only fifty square kilometres — but in the south, where Tasmania was still part of the mainland, the land was dominated by glaciers. The glaciers reached their peak about 18 000 years ago after which the atmosphere began to warm up and by about 10 000 years ago the ice had turned back into water.

As the glacial water found its way into the sea, Tasmania once again became an island. To the north, the ice retreated rapidly and within a few thousand years the climate of mainland Australia was much as it is today.

During the years when the Aborigines were the sole human occupants of the continent, other major forces also shaped the landscape. Volcanoes continued to form mountains along the east coast, while inland, an immense system of lakes filled, dried out and was replaced eventually by a vast system of sand dunes.

Twenty-five thousand years ago the Murray River, already the largest in Australia and a much larger river than it is now, was dammed when subterranean movements in the earth's crust forced up part of the plain between present-day Deniliquin and Echuca, in south-western New South Wales. The ridge that was formed sliced across the Murray and forced the waters to bank up into a giant lake.

Eventually the lake filled to overflowing and the river sought out a new course to the sea, not that different to the one it follows today. The ancient lake now supports Australia's largest river red gum forest, between Echuca and Cobram.

The first intrusion

It was not long after Aboriginal settlement of Australia that deliberately set fires were introduced to the landscape. Fire was an essential tool in the daily existence of the Aborigines. They depended on it for hunting, cooking and for warmth.

Women used fire skillfully to burn the base of a dead tree and then fell it for use as campfire fuel. Fires were lit to flush out small mammals and reptiles from undergrowth and hollow logs and in regions where the bush was thick, paths were maintained by fire to enable a comfortable passage.

All over Australia, Aborigines subjected the landscape to systematic burning. Instead of infrequent, high-intensity, fires started by lightning strikes, there were frequent, low-intensity fires which cleared just the undergrowth.

Occasionally these fires were caused by camp fires which had not been doused but most fires were lit deliberately to increase the accessability and availability of plant and animal foods. The green shoots that sprang up after the fires attracted animals that could be killed and eaten.

THE BIG PICTURE In a country as large as Australia, satellite photographs are invaluable in assessing agricultural use, misuse and land degradation. The pale brown region above is cleared land just north of Gladstone, opposite Curtis Island. Red-brown indicates natural vegetation.

Aboriginal tribes walked over great distances burning the countryside in a deliberate mosaic. Sometimes the fires were set just before rain was judged to be imminent, at other times they were controlled by natural barriers such as rivers and creeks.

In the dry inland, throughout the spinifex country, the Aborigines set fires every few years, with higher rainfall areas being burned once or twice a year. These mild grass and scrub fires were nothing like the destructive bushfires of modern times and the spread of the flames would have been relatively easy to control by beating with freshly picked, leafy branches.

The second intrusion

The landscape that the first European explorers trekked through had been changed and moulded by the Aboriginal fires over many thousands of years. Compared with this, the changes wrought by Europeans occurred almost overnight, with the land taking on a new appearance with startling rapidity.

Aborigines and their firesticks were displaced; the second wave of settlers could not live off the land as had the first and after a faltering start, the new land was reshaped to support them.

The early settlers' attitude to the land and the landscapes that confronted them was based on what they had

left behind in Europe. They were ignorant of their new home and they set about wresting a living from it the best way they knew how.

There had been no major earth movements for several hundred million years and Australia's ancient soils had been exposed to the elements much longer than the soils of Europe or North America. They were generally shallow and low in nutrients and had evolved in the absence of the hard-footed, domesticated animals, such as cows and sheep, found in the Northern Hemisphere. As a result, the land was friable and rainwater easily absorbed. This was soon to change.

One early observer wrote that the sound of the timber cutter's axe echoing through the hills proclaimed the dawn of civilisation in Australia. This hardly surprising attitude was typical of a time when the interiors of several continents were ill-explored, the world's resources were regarded as infinite and nature was seen as something to be conquered.

This was the heyday of the European colonisers who set out to amend the landscapes of several continents in order to provide raw materials for the shops and factories of their homelands. In Australia's low-rainfall mallee country, one early settler noted than it was hoped to clear the

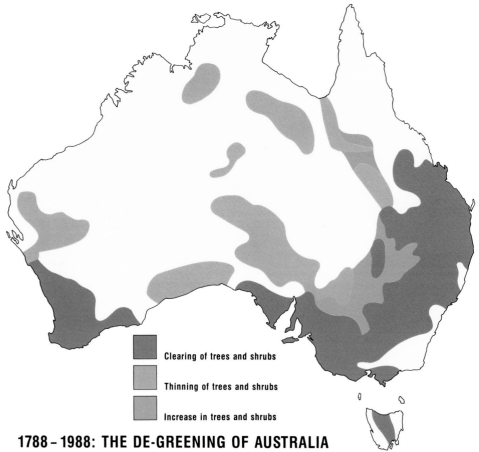

Clearing of trees and shrubs

Thinning of trees and shrubs

Increase in trees and shrubs

1788–1988: THE DE-GREENING OF AUSTRALIA

A TRIBUTE TO AXE AND CHAINSAW Satellite observations and estimates based on historical records allow scientists to form a picture of the changes that have taken place in Australia's vegetation over the last 200 years.

land and '... the face of the country from a dreary monotonous scrub to one of smiling fertility'.

Unwittingly, such pioneer farmers set about their task, demanding more of the soil than it could produce. As the first people to plough Australian soil, they were not to know that approximately 90 per cent of their new home was unsuitable for the agricultural practices they were setting in train.

The most obvious form of landscape change that has taken place in the last 200 years is the change in vegetation. There has been a progressive process of clearing the native vegetation since the beginning of white settlement. This is particularly obvious in areas which have been extensively farmed, such as the relatively fertile coastal zones.

In other regions, trees have moved in and colonised what was once scrubby grassland, and 'marginal' land, where the rainfall is unreliable, is still being denuded of trees and shrubs to make way for wheatlands. The pioneer farmers and graziers, who achieved such spectacularly successful results with wheat, sheep and cattle, would not live to learn the long-term cost of some of their enterprises as this did not become obvious for 100 years.

What was the cost? In many cases short-term economic gain was achieved at the expense of long-term land degradation. For many years technological development was seen as a substitute for ecological management.

The average 400-hectare paddock dotted with a few geriatric trees has sparked an outcry from conservation groups. Two hundred years after the establishment of the first farm on Australian soil, the concern about the way the continent's topsoil has been 'mined' has become so widespread that there are many public and private groups actively promoting and planting trees all over Australia.

Erosion, salinity and land degradation in general have forced farmers to become stewards of their land, and management rather than exploitation the aim of rural development.

The legacy of the axe

In just over 200 years, a large portion of Australia's tree cover — some estimates put it at two-thirds — has been removed. Of the 700 000 square kilometres of forest estimated to have existed two centuries ago, approximately 380 000 square kilometres remain.

The degradation of the land is often all too plain to see. In the mallee region of western Victoria, the fragile soils which were once covered in mallee eucalypts have been almost completely cleared for wheat-growing.

Extensive wind erosion creates dust which covers roads, fences and even buries buildings. Huge dust storms — such as the one which engulfed Melbourne in 250 000 tonnes of billowing topsoil in February 1983 — regularly sweep topsoil and valuable plant nutrients away.

Since European settlement, the temperate woodlands of south-eastern Australia have been the scene for a sequence of change which has been repeated in Western Australia, Queensland and Tasmania. Trees were thinned out to allow grazing and the native grasses were eaten out. Nature abhors a vacuum, and introduced pasture grasses and weeds were quick to fill the gap and become the dominant ground cover of many regions.

PADDOCK OF THE PAST? New attitudes to the use of trees in preventing erosion and sheltering stock mean that scenes such as this, on the Darling Range, may become a thing of the past.

BEFORE AND AFTER Gullies are an essential part of Australia's rural landscape which all too often become eroded into moonscapes like the one at left, near Uralla in New England. Although the causes of such erosion — overstocking, slope cultivation or overclearing — may have ceased, the landscape will renew itself only when control measures are taken. A gully near Lithgow (right) has been stabilised by strategic tree planting.

The remaining trees now suffer a very high mortality rate. This phenomenon, known as dieback, has denuded many rural landscapes.

The landscapes around Armidale, on the northern tablelands of New South Wales, are a sorry sight. Dead and dying trees stand as a testament to the widespread clearing that has occurred. Many of the remaining trees are in their death throes as a result of years of overclearing, pasture improvement, grazing and, particularly in this case, attack by insects (see p. 180).

In the days before soil conservation and controlled forestry, before anyone thought of sustainable natural resources, Australia's white pioneers innocently chopped down the rainforests. They were simply part of the bountiful cornucopia of resources in a new land.

Now, three-quarters of the rainforest is gone, the result of logging or clearing for agriculture last century and early this century. Much of this land is now unproductive, weed infested and heavily eroded.

Other relatively untouched vegetation communities have been put at risk in the latter part of the twentieth century. The mangroves along Australia's coasts and estuaries are seen as untidy growths which make the shoreline inaccessible. In fact they play a vital role in the marine food chain: mangroves form the breeding grounds and nurseries for many forms of marine life. Without them the fishing industry would not survive for long.

To many people, heathlands are like mangrove swamps, uninviting, bleak wastelands. As a result they are often the target for development and heath regions are fast disappearing.

The heathlands have not had the publicity that other ecosystems under threat have enjoyed. Environmental groups have been successful in gaining public support for the protection of spectacular forests partly because these are environments that people enjoy using. The cause of the conservation of heathlands, mangroves and many of the arid-zone plant communities is not as easy to popularise.

Upsetting the balance

Paradoxically, not all parts of Australia have suffered a loss of trees. There are regions where trees and shrubs have increased. This form of land degradation is acute in western New South Wales and south-western Queensland — in New South Wales native shrubs which are inedible to livestock have spread over 70 per cent of the west.

Before settlement, periodic fires maintained the natural balance between the trees, the shrubs and the grasses. The introduction of sheep and cattle upset this balance as grazing reduced the grass cover. Where there were no grass roots to bind the soil together, it crumbled under the hooves of stock and set rock-hard after rain.

At the same time, naturally occurring, spontaneous bushfires were suppressed whenever possible. A combination of these factors has resulted in the supremacy of the shrubs — pastoral production has declined and the soils, unbound by grass, are highly prone to erosion.

In the irrigation areas of southern New South Wales and northern Victoria, rising water tables are causing salinity on a large scale (see p. 94). Up to 3000 tonnes of dissolved salts for

FERAL PLANTS Wild tobacco (pale leaves, left and right) and lantana (orange flowers) are introduced 'exotics' which are colonising this patch of Queensland rainforest to the detriment of native plants.

each hectare are brought towards the soil surface in some regions. Vegetation is unable to survive in such conditions and a wasteland bereft of greenery is the result.

Approximately 600 000 hectares in New South Wales and Victoria have rapidly rising water tables. In Western Australia, about 138 000 hectares of agricultural land go out of production every year due to salinity.

Improving pastureland with fertiliser and legumes can eventually make the soil so acid that surface binding plants such as grasses die off, their dead roots release their hold on the soil, and when it rains the topsoil is washed away. There are estimated to be around 25 million hectares of acid soil — the area of the United Kingdom and Ireland — in Australia.

One of the less spectacular but long-standing problems of Australia's remaining bushland is the spread of exotic garden 'escapes' — decorative foreign plants that 'leap the garden fence' and are more successful in their new wild environment than elsewhere due to the lack of controls such as cold winters or animals which find them palatable. Bushland in virtually every part of Australia has been affected by introduced plants such as Paterson's curse, blackberry, lantana, clovers and medics, privet, broom and prickly pear. Such plants have changed the landscape forever.

The too-successful migrants

Land clearing — followed by competition and predation from introduced plants and animals — is the most important factor behind the decline in Australia's plants and animals.

Since 1788, eighteen species of Australian mammals have become extinct. Forty others, as well as twenty-eight species of birds, are on the endangered list. Native plants have fared little better. About one hundred species are believed to have disappeared and more than three thousand species are considered rare or threatened.

On the other side of the coin, several native animals have found their fortunes improved in the landscapes amended by human intervention. The red and grey kangaroos of the inland have been favoured by the grazing of domestic stock, especially sheep. Kangaroos like the shortly grazed grass left by the sheep and the abundant stock water points. Dingoes are their only predators and in many regions, dingo-proof fences keep kangaroos safe.

A PLAGUE UPON US

RABBIT BLUES Despite the inroads made by the fatal myxomatosis virus between the 1950s and the 1980s, rabbits continue to maintain their hold on the countryside in all but the tropical north. The diagram illustrates their steady colonisation of three-quarters of the continent.

Galahs and cockatoos too, have found the changed conditions to their liking. Huge flocks grow fat on the ample supply of grain and seed crops found around farms.

During the 1850s and 1860s, groups known as acclimatisation societies were formed in most of the Australian colonies. With the advantage of hindsight and more than a century of coping with the consequences of their actions, these well-meaning organisations can be seen

only as blissfully ignorant and appallingly short-sighted in their actions.

Acclimatisation societies were responsible for importing all kinds of exotic creatures which were thought to possess some kind of financial, sporting or aesthetic value. In some cases, nostalgia for a familiar bird sound seems to have been the importers' only motive. A veritable menagerie of creatures was shipped across the world, from silkworms, foxes, ostriches, deer

and trout to nightingales, starlings, sparrows, blackbirds and ... rabbits.

Although rabbits arrived with the First Fleet it was not until they were liberated near Geelong in 1859 that they established a foothold and commenced their invasion. The rate of spread varied from 10–15 kilometres a year in the better watered forest and coastal areas to over 100 kilometres a year in the dry interior.

By the turn of the century, rabbits had spread across almost all of southern Australia. In central Australia, they turned on the mulga and in many regions barren dustbowls were commonplace. A generation of country people grew up without ever seeing a young mulga or kurrajong tree.

In the 1950s, myxomatosis curbed the depredations of the rabbit. White cypress pines sprang up in the pilliga forest in New South Wales and graziers in Queensland saw mulga seedlings for the first time in 50 years.

Rabbits have not colonised northern Australia but cane toads and buffalos have made themselves more than at home there. Over-grazing and damage to levee banks by the south-east Asian buffalo is responsible for most of the problems in the Northern Territory's tropical waterways.

Far beyond the horizons of the average city dweller, donkeys, horses, camels, goats, pigs, foxes and cats continue to vandalise environments that evolved without an appropriate niche for any of them. Cats and foxes have thrived on a diet of native birds and small animals that originally had no natural predators, except perhaps large birds and dingoes.

The growth of awareness

Australia may occupy a whole continent but it is the driest such landmass on earth. Three-quarters of the continent is arid or semi-arid and the limitations imposed by this harsh physical environment have often been ignored.

A low and erratic rainfall and a deeply weathered terrain have combined to produce poorly structured, relatively infertile soils. Such soils are so easily eroded that land degradation has emerged as our greatest environmental problem. The deliberate and accidental introduction of plants and animals that evolved in dramatically different environments has exacerbated the situation.

In the blink of an ecological eye, Australia's human inhabitants have come dangerously close to fatally abus-

CALL OF THE WILD The descendants of domestic animals that either escaped from farms, were released when they were no longer needed or simply dumped — like cats and dogs — now run wild all over Australia. In most cases biological controls are not yet practicable and shooting and trapping are the most effective forms of control for animals such as goats and horses.

ing the land that produced such great agricultural and mineral riches. Fortunately, there is an emerging awareness and recognition of the plight of our landscapes among people in general and scientists, farmers and governments in particular.

Today, instead of acclimitisation societies there are myriad groups — from government soil, water and forestry services to the private environmental and conservation organisations — that share with farmers and foresters a concern that the land is exploited only within its limits — even if there is often loud and acrimonious public debate about what that limit is.

Whatever changes occur in the way we manage the land in the future, the landscape will never be static. If wisdom prevails, Australia in 200 years time may well look more like the land that was known as New Holland in 1788 than it does today. □

Cape Tribulation, northern Queensland

Australia: 40 contrasting regions

In contrast to the inhospitable wilderness of the west coast, the eastern portion of Tasmania is a long-farmed land of hills and dales trimmed by a rugged coastline where the natural landscape still holds sway

The ordered countryside of the Tasman coast

Although most of the countryside between Hobart and Launceston has long been given over to farming, the wilderness of Tasmania's unique landscape is still evident in the untamed areas of forests and national parks.

The ragged coastline, while marginally less rugged and more approachable than that of western Tasmania, is nevertheless punctuated by jagged crags and cliffs of dolerite lining the trail of peninsulas and islands which face the Tasman Sea.

Because of Tasmania's southerly position, the aurora australis, or southern lights, frequently lights up the night sky with coloured flames, veils and rays, adding to the mainland visitor's perception of Tasmania as a very different place. The obvious differences are those of climate, vegetation and wildlife, the last two the result of an island environment that has been isolated from the mainland for up to 12 000 years.

Because of this isolation, Tasmania's wildlife has been protected from the predations of the dingo and the fox so that some native animals extinct on the mainland have survived in the island state.

WINDSWEPT The southern headland of Pirate Bay, near the Eaglehawk Neck spit that links the Tasman Peninsula and the Forestier Peninsula, is typical of the rugged coastline of the south-east.

PASTORAL SCENE The old British town names — Perth, Campbell Town, Melton Mowbray, New Norfolk — suggest the rural nature of the Tasmanian Midlands. These hop fields are at New Norfolk.

The north of eastern Tasmania is dominated by mountains raised during geological upheavals about 165 million years ago. The plateau of Ben Lomond, capped with dolerite, is an alpine habitat surrounded by high country which is densely forested and has a high rainfall — up to 1900 millimetres in places. The plains between the mountains and the sea are blessed with a temperate climate.

South of Ben Lomond there is a loose range of mountains and hills of decreasing altitude and rainfall, with some areas south of Bothwell receiving less than 500 millimetres annually. East of this range, the Midland Highway runs through long-settled countryside. This grazing and farming region includes occasional paddocks of opium poppies — grown for use in the drug industry — which bloom pale pink and purple in late spring.

There is little left here of the native woodland which once covered the area. The planting of deciduous trees and the subdividing of land into smallholdings has resulted in the formal, managed, English-style landscape — the pretty valley of the Derwent is a good example — that is so popular with tourists.

The east coast is the warmest part of Tasmania because it is protected by hinterland mountains from the cold,

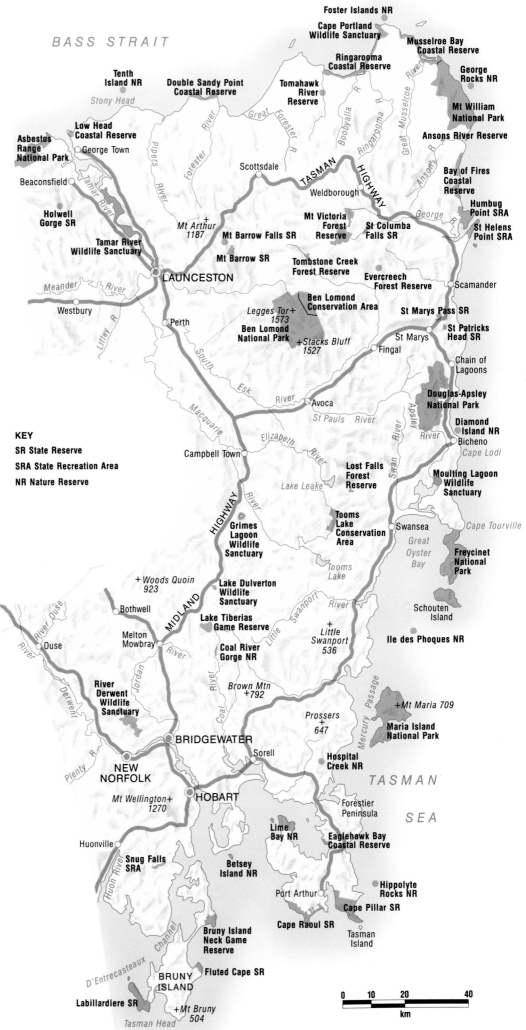

BASS STRAIT

Foster Islands NR
Cape Portland
Wildlife Sanctuary
Musselroe Bay
Coastal Reserve
Ringarooma
Coastal Reserve
George
Rocks NR
Tenth
Island NR
Double Sandy Point
Coastal Reserve
Tomahawk
River
Reserve
Mt William
National Park
Stony Head
Ansons River Reserve
Low Head
Coastal Reserve
Asbestos
Range
National Park
George Town
Scottsdale
Bay of Fires
Coastal
Reserve
Beaconsfield
Weldborough
Humbug
Point SRA
Holwell
Gorge SR
Mt Victoria
Forest
Reserve
St Columba
Falls SR
George
St Helens
Point SRA
Tamar River
Wildlife Sanctuary
Mt Arthur
1187
Mt Barrow Falls SR
Tombstone Creek
Forest Reserve
Scamander
Mt Barrow SR
Evercreech
Forest Reserve
Meander
LAUNCESTON
Ben Lomond
Conservation Area
St Marys Pass SR
Westbury
Legges Tor
1573
St Marys
St Patricks
Head SR
Perth
Ben Lomond
National Park
Stacks Bluff
1527
Fingal
Chain of
Lagoons
Douglas-Apsley
National Park
River
Avoca
Diamond
Island NR
St Pauls River
Bicheno
Campbell Town
Elizabeth
Cape Lodi
Lost Falls
Forest
Reserve
Moulting Lagoon
Wildlife
Sanctuary
Lake Leake
Tooms
Lake
Conservation
Area
Cape Tourville
Grimes
Lagoon
Wildlife
Sanctuary
Tooms
Lake
Swansea
Great
Oyster
Bay
Freycinet
National
Park
Woods Quoin
923
Lake Dulverton
Wildlife
Sanctuary
Bothwell
Schouten
Island
Lake Tiberias
Game Reserve
Little
Swanport
536
Melton
Mowbray
Coal River
Gorge NR
Ile des Phoques NR
Ouse
River
Derwent
Wildlife
Sanctuary
Brown Mtn
792
Mt Maria 709
Prossers
647
Maria Island
National Park
BRIDGEWATER
NEW
NORFOLK
Sorell
Hospital
Creek NR
TASMAN
Plenty
HOBART
Mt Wellington
1270
Forestier
Peninsula
SEA
Huonville
Lime
Bay NR
Eaglehawk Bay
Coastal Reserve
Snug Falls
SRA
Betsey
Island NR
Hippolyte
Rocks NR
Port Arthur
Cape Pillar SR
Bruny Island
Neck Game
Reserve
Cape Raoul SR
Tasman
Island
D'Entrecasteaux
BRUNY
ISLAND
Fluted Cape SR
Labillardiere SR
Mt Bruny
504
Tasman Head

KEY
SR State Reserve
SRA State Recreation Area
NR Nature Reserve

TASMAN HIGHWAY
MIDLAND HIGHWAY

0   10   20   40
km

SOUTHERN TIP The neatly eroded dolerite columns of Cape Pillar guard the windswept flanks of the Tasman Peninsula. Similar clusters occur to the west at Cape Raoul, and to the east at Cape Hauy.

NOT ALL CLIFFS The clear waters and white sand beach could almost label Wineglass Bay — on the south-eastern side of the neck of the Freycinet Peninsula — as part of a Barrier Reef island. In fact, it is one of the hundreds of coves and bays that break the cliffs of Tasmania's ruggedly uneven eastern coastline.

westerly winds and washed by a comparatively warm sea current. Much native bush and wildlife remains in forestry reserves and national parks, such as that on Freycinet Peninsula.

Behind Hobart, Mount Wellington, which rises majestically to 1270 metres, supports many different plant communities. It is capped with hard dolerite which forms the tall, vertical shapes typical of Tasmanian mountains and the coastal cliffs along the isolated Tasman Peninsula.

Ancient rises in the level of the sea drowned the lower reaches of the Derwent and Huon Rivers, creating a dramatically sculpted and indented coastline decorated by rocky islands and peninsulas that were once mountain tops.

Although the clearing of the native bush has permanently altered the region there remain many modified and some unmodified natural habitats. Dry eucalypt forest is the most common vegetation throughout the region but there are also coastal heathland and alpine environments.

Asbestos Range National Park, on the central north coast, covers 4281 hectares ranging from salt marsh on the coast to dry eucalypt forest on high hills. It is inhabited by a large number of birds and animals, many of which are easily observed.

Devil in name only

The seemingly ferocious Tasmanian devil (*Sarcophilus harrisii*) which is still found in large numbers here, has a bark much worse than its bite, despite its aggressive reputation. The dog-like devil — a mature male may measure a metre from its head to the end of its tail and weigh eight kilograms — is primarily a carrion eater which has difficulty in killing a creature as large as a rat.

This valuable scavenger will also take small prey such as corbie grubs (*Oncopera*) or roosting birds, while itself often falling easy prey to dogs. Unlike most native animals, the Tasmanian devil may have increased rather than decreased in numbers because its major food source has been augmented by the many dead animals that have been scattered along roadsides since the introduction of the motor car.

Forester or eastern grey kangaroos deserve their Latin name of *Macropus giganteus* because they are the largest kangaroos. Males may reach a head-to-tail length of up to two metres and weigh as much as 54 kilograms. They are common in the Asbestos Range National Park as is the Bennett's or red-necked wallaby (*Macropus rufogriseus*) and the small Tasmanian pademelon (*Thylogale billardierii*), which is no longer found on the mainland.

Common wombats (*Vombatus ursinus*) are sometimes still referred to as badgers in Tasmania. These thickset, roly-poly marsupials, which may weigh up to 39 kilograms, are fairly common all over Tasmania.

On Badgers Beach and Bakers Beach, thousands of vibrant red-purple soldier crabs (*Myctiris longicarpus*) carpet the sand at low tide. They feed on marine worms and snails and unlike most crabs, they propel themselves with a forward rather than a sideways movement.

The lagoon of the Asbestos Range park attracts large numbers of black swans and common waterfowl, while little penguins (*Eudyptula minor*) and migratory waders feed regularly on the

ISLAND WALLABY The Tasmanian pademelon is usually found in grassland around forests.

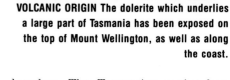

VOLCANIC ORIGIN The dolerite which underlies a large part of Tasmania has been exposed on the top of Mount Wellington, as well as along the coast.

beaches. The Tasmanian native hen (*Gallinula mortierii*) struts the lagoon banks, its hacksaw cry a common sound wherever there is water. The flightless hen has been clocked as running at fifty kilometres an hour — faster than some birds fly.

To the south-east, beyond the island's eastern 'corner', the granite headlands are separated by white, sandy beaches and clothed in eucalypt vegetation. Beyond are the flat coastal plains inhabited by a remarkably large number of mammals, particularly in the Mount William National Park (13 899 hectares) where the climate is more amenable to them than the cold west-coast region.

The parks' forester kangaroos, Bennett's wallabies, Tasmanian pademelons, wombats, devils and the graceful eastern and spotted-tail quolls (*Dasyurus viverrinus, D. maculatus*) are all in significant numbers but are more likely to be seen in the light of car headlights at night than during the day. The eastern quoll is the smaller of the two quolls and may be fawn with white spots or a very handsome near-black with white spots. Although it is common in parts of Tasmania it is rarely sighted on the mainland these days.

Tasmanian bettongs (*Bettongia gaimardi*), a type of wallaby, are also in the park and at dusk or dawn this conscientious nest-builder can be seen carrying grass and bracken for a new nest.

The coastal heathland flowers profusely in spring and summer. In the adjacent forest there are black peppermints (*Eucalyptus amygdalina*), black or swamp gum (*E. ovata*), and white gum (*E. viminalis*). The white gum's alternative name of manna — after the food which, according to the Bible, sustained the Israelites in the wilderness

TRIBUTARY The South Esk River forces its way between the dolerite walls of Cataract Gorge before joining the Tamar River at Launceston.

— was given because the edible white material which exudes from the young leaves was eaten by the Aborigines.

Gaggles of large Cape Barren geese (*Cereopsis novaehollandiae*) graze on the park's grassland while the heathland is home to many small birds, including the tawny-crowned honeyeater (*Phylidonyris melanops*) and the crescent honeyeater (*P. pyrrhoptera*).

Along the high-water mark on the beaches, fairy terns (*Sterna nereis*) and hooded plovers (*Charadrius rubricollis*) nest in shallow burrows. Offshore, George Rocks accommodates crowded rookeries of crested terns (*Sterna bergii*), Caspian terns (*Sterna caspia*), white-faced storm petrels (*Pelagodroma marina*) and prions (*Pachyptila*), as well as silver gulls which prey on the eggs and young of the other birds.

Little penguins and short-tailed shearwaters (*Puffinus tenuirostris*) are found in colonies along the east coast. The short-tailed shearwater is also called muttonbird, a name that arose from the taking of hundreds of thousands of its fat young for human consumption each year (see pp. 58–61).

The Tamar River which enters its broad estuary near Launceston, has two tributaries: the North Esk which eroded its valley relatively quickly and dropped to the level of the Tamar, and the South Esk, which had to eat its way through much harder dolerite and is higher. In the beautiful Cataract Gorge, the South Esk is confined between sheer dolerite cliffs. One side of the gorge is now a very old European garden with strutting peacocks and Victorian rotundas, while the other side defies any formality and remains native bush.

The South Esk pine (*Callitris oblonga*) is confined to the region around this river. Many native mammals live in the gorge and nine species of birds unique to Tasmania have been recorded here.

Forest around the plateau

The north-east highlands south of the Tasman Highway, from Scottsdale to Weldborough and St Helens, is state forest, much of it wet eucalyptus forest, but there are also patches of cool temperate rainforest, particularly near Weldborough and in other areas with rainfall above 1100 millimetres.

The rainforest contains impressive stands of myrtle beech (*Nothofagus cunninghamii*), southern sassafras (*Atherospermum moschatum*) — the leaves of which are fragrant when crushed — and blackwood (*Acacia melanoxylon*). Mosses and epiphytic ferns add to the lushness of these forests where the tall manferns (*Dicksonia antarctica*) grandly shelter a variety of smaller ferns.

Nearby, a complex of dolerite columns planted firmly on their broad, sandstone base soars 1213 metres into the sky to form the bulk of Mount Victoria. The surrounding 3200-hectare forest reserve contains sedgeland and rainforest where myrtle beech and celery top pine (*Phyllocladus aspleniifolius*) may grow alongside stands of woolly teatree (*Leptospermum lanigerum*) and gum-topped stringybark (*Eucalyptus delegatensis*). In the high-altitude areas, there are also areas of button-grass plain (*Gymnoschoenus sphaerocephalus*).

To the south, in the Evercreech Forest Reserve, a group of giant white gums known as the White Knights grow in deep, alluvial soil surrounded by blackwoods, myrtle, sassafras and ferns. These spectacular trees — some grow to over 90 metres — are estimated to be more than 300 years old.

EASTERN CASCADES The Cygnet River — an appropriately named tributary of the Swan River — tumbles over a steep fault in the eastern highlands to form the Meetus Falls.

BIG BEN The farm valleys of the Midlands separate the 1500-metre-high Ben Lomond Plateau from the major mountain regions to the west.

The weathered Ben Lomond plateau, like most of Tasmania's mountain regions, displays the rock formations which lie hidden beneath the farmland of the east. Erosion of the soft, overlaying rock and further uplifting by earthquakes since then has revealed huge columns of dolerite in ranked formations that are sometimes so evenly structured that it is hard to believe they were not planned and constructed to order rather than being the result of random, elemental forces.

Some of these 'organ-pipe' structures have fallen to form great piles of rubble, others have fractured and shattered forming the talus and scree which covers much of the plateau. The ice age which occurred here about 40 000 years ago has left many areas of smooth rock as evidence of its presence.

In the alpine area, snow turns the plateau into a winter ski-field. Low, slow-growing cushion plants (*Dracophyllum*, *Donatia*) and endemic mountain rocket (*Bellendena montana*) are common. Lower levels of the park are dominated by eucalyptus species including gum-topped stringybark and browntop stringybark (*Eucalyptus obliqua*) as well as Tasmania's only deciduous native tree, the tanglefoot beech (*Nothofagus gunnii*).

Other plants found only in Tasmania include the Tasmanian waratah (*Telopea truncata*), the celery-top pine and the leatherwood (*Eucryphia lucida*), famous for the honey produced from the nectar of its white flowers.

North-west of the fishing town of Bicheno lies the Douglas–Apsley National Park (16 080 hectares), bounded approximately by the Apsley and Douglas Rivers with their associated gorges and waterfalls. Fourteen species of eucalypt, including five which grow only in Tasmania, compete for space in the crowded, virgin forest between the rivers.

Almost within the small township of Bicheno are two granite outcrops where little streaked rock orchids (*Dendrobium striolatum*) grow, producing yellow flowers profusely in spring. Opposite the town wharf, a rocky island serves as a rookery to a colony of crested terns (*Sterna bergii*).

RIVERS' PARK Above the Apsley River Gorge, Tasmania's largest undisturbed dry eucalypt forest is protected in the Douglas-Apsley National Park.

VARIETY Although most Tasmanian waratahs bloom red, a rare yellow variety also exists.

South of Bicheno, the large expanse of Moulting Lagoon (512 hectares), is an important breeding ground for black swans, and is also a base for pelicans, ducks and elegant waders such as red-necked stints (*Calidris ruficollis*), red knots (*C. canutus*) and bar-tailed godwits (*Limosa lapponica*).

The Tasman coast

On the coast, the red granite cliffs and mountains rise to culminate in the Freycinet Peninsula and its national park, covering 10 010 hectares. Precipitous headlands are broken by indented bays and white, sandy beaches.

The pure white sands and startlingly blue waters are both a result of the breaking down of the crystalline granite of the cliffs. Schouten Island is a geological curiosity, its western half undulating, lightly forested dolerite, while in the east a carpet of sparse scrub overlays rugged, red granite.

Much of the park is coastal heathland and although most of the tree cover is eucalyptus, Oyster Bay pines (*Callitris rhomboidea*) are prolific together with various banksias, tea-trees, she-oaks and wattles. The white-bellied sea eagle (*Haliaeetus leucogaster*) breeds on rocky stretches of the peninsula, while yellow-tailed black cockatoos (*Calyptorhynchus funereus*) and grey butcherbirds (*Cracticus torquatus*) are found in the forest.

Despite the changes made to its environment since a convict settlement was established in the 1820s, Maria Island, further south, is a place of spectacular scenery with a great diversity of habitats and wildlife. The island — about 20 kilometres long and 13 kilometres wide — is a national park.

Sculpted cliffs of sandstone and

GRANITE PENINSULA Granite cliffs dominate the coastline of the Freycinet Peninsula — named after Louis de Freycinet, a French navigator of the early 1800s.

FROM BOTTOM TO TOP Sediments deposited on the floor of a primeval sea are displayed in the cliff faces of Maria Island.

limestone around the shore line — some of which show sediments deposited about 200 million years ago when the sea level was much higher — are complemented by a hinterland dotted with dolerite or quartzite outcrops.

The widely ranging habitats found between Maria Island's white beaches and its mountain range are home to almost 130 species of birds, including about half the known population of the rare forty-spotted pardalote (*Pardalotus quadragintus*). Along the shore, sea eagles can be seen scooping fish from the ocean while pink robins (*Petroica rodinogaster*) and swift parrots (*Lathamus discolor*) may be found in the wet gullies. Thriving populations of Cape Barren geese and mainland

emus live on the island, the latter a belated substitute for the Tasmanian emu which has been extinct since 1865.

The island's ecological balance has been upset not only by the deer and cats which came with early white settlers but by the introduction of mainland mammals such as forester kangaroos, Bennett's wallabies, bettongs and bandicoots. The waters of Maria Island support a dazzling variety of fish and shellfish, many of which are denizens of the giant kelp 'forests' which hold sway along the north-west coast of the island.

The Tasman Peninsula is a drowned mountain range. The sea rose to its present level about 6000 years ago and has been eroding and reconstructing the coastline ever since into an intriguing confusion of caves, arches, blowholes, inlets and sea stacks.

A magnificent group of sea stacks

SANDSTONE PAVING The vertical joints in the sandstone platform known as the Tessellated Pavements — on the northern side of Pirates Bay (see p. 24) — have been eroded so evenly by the action of the sea that the stone could have been laid by a mason.

BROKEN TIP The Lanterns, at the tip of Cape Hauy, are separated by needle-like dolerite spires.

which rises up from the sea near Eaglehawk Neck includes the Blowhole, the Devil's Kitchen and the Tasman Arch, which were formed by the erosion of soft sandstone capped by harder sandstone. Within the great cavity of the Arch, tree-martins (*Hirundo nigricans*) swoop to gather insects.

At the Blowhole, a great grinding and rolling of pebbles can be heard with each wave that throws itself at the rocky shoreline. At Waterfall Bay, the cliffs are so perfectly perpendicular that they could be part of a giant wall built according to the dictates of a plumb line. Stunted trees only a fraction of their normal size cling tenaciously to any available break in the cliff face.

These are significant commercial fishing waters for bluefin tuna, trevally, trumpeter and many wrasse species, as well as crayfish and abalone. Southern right whales and dolphins are sometimes seen and the Australian fur seal (*Arctocephalus pusillus*) has colonised many offshore rocks, particularly the Hippolyte Rocks, and the rock shelves and platforms below mainland cliffs.

When the blue gums of the Tasman Peninsula flower in spring the air is heavy with the heady sweetness of their scent. Their large blooms contain so much nectar that it may be scooped out on the tip of a finger. The blue gums attract many honeyeaters as well as yellow-tailed black cockatoos which are quite happy to include blossoms in their wide-ranging diet.

The butterfly and the ant

Tatnells Hill boasts many rainforest plants including ferns and cutting grass (*Gahnia psittacorum*), while here and there the large Tasmanian waratah flowers a voluptuous shade of red. The hairstreak butterfly (*Pseudalmenus chlorinda myrsilus*) of these parts has a mutually beneficial relationship with the stink ant (*Iridomyrmex foetans*).

In a bizarre but effective survival strategy, the ant guides the butterfly larvae from silver wattle (*Acacia dealbata*) to white gum to feed; it leads them to pupate in ant nests and protects them from predators, all in return for the sweet secretion from the caterpillars' backs.

In the south-east, Mount Wellington rises sharply to 1270 metres, dominating the Hobart region. It is often snow-capped in winter, with heavy falls at times lying below the 400-metre level.

THE LINK The two halves of Bruny Island are joined by a narrow sand isthmus known as The Neck. The island has sheltered anchorages and was often the first Australian landfall for early mariners after they had passed through the Roaring Forties.

The broad summit is composed of dolerite some 350 metres thick sitting on a sandstone base.

The range of habitats from Mount Wellington's base to its summit provides a microcosm of the region's environments. The dominant trees are eucalypts except in the wettest gullies where myrtles and sassafras are more abundant. Some herbaceous species including ivy-leaf violet (*Viola hederacea*), dusty daisy-bush (*Olearia phlogopappa*), and the yellow daisy (*Helichrysum scorpioides*) are found at every level.

Trees at lower levels include white gum and blue gum, white peppermint (*Eucalyptus pulchella*), black she-oak (*Allocasuarina littoralis*) and cherry ballart or native cherry (*Exocarpos cupressiformis*), a semi-parasitical plant which draws its sustenance from the roots of surrounding trees.

Above 750 metres, the urn gum (*E. urnigera*) is the dominant tree but at about 1100 metres it gives way to the hardy snow gum (*E. coccifera*). Parts of the summit untouched by bushfires have become a 'museum' of old shrubs, many of which have been growing there for over 100 years. The high, swampy areas are covered in pineapple grass (*Astelia alpina*), the *Restio australis* rush and sphagnum moss.

Bruny Island is reached by ferry and, though much of it is given over to farming or grazing, significant wild habitats remain. A tombolo, or sand barrier joins the north and south islands and this neck, which is part of the Bruny Island Neck Game Reserve (1450 hectares), is a rookery for the little penguins and muttonbirds which have colonised several areas of Bruny. The sooty shearwater (*Puffinus griseus*) also breeds on the island.

Forty-spotted pardalotes are common among the white gums, the black-backed or kelp gull (*Larus dominicanus*) is found along the shores, and the orange-bellied parrot (*Neophema chrysogaster*) is sometimes seen flitting from tree to tree.

Bruny Island's landscape completes the east-coast pattern of spectacular cliffs below broad, coastal heaths where myriad wildflowers bloom in the spring. □

GRACEFUL GUM The smooth-barked white peppermint gum is grown as a street tree in cool regions.

A primeval, rain-washed land, where quartzite peaks crown tall ranges etched by prehistoric glaciers, has come to symbolise the clash between man's material needs and the increasing pressure to preserve unique environments in their natural state

A remote world, unchanged by time

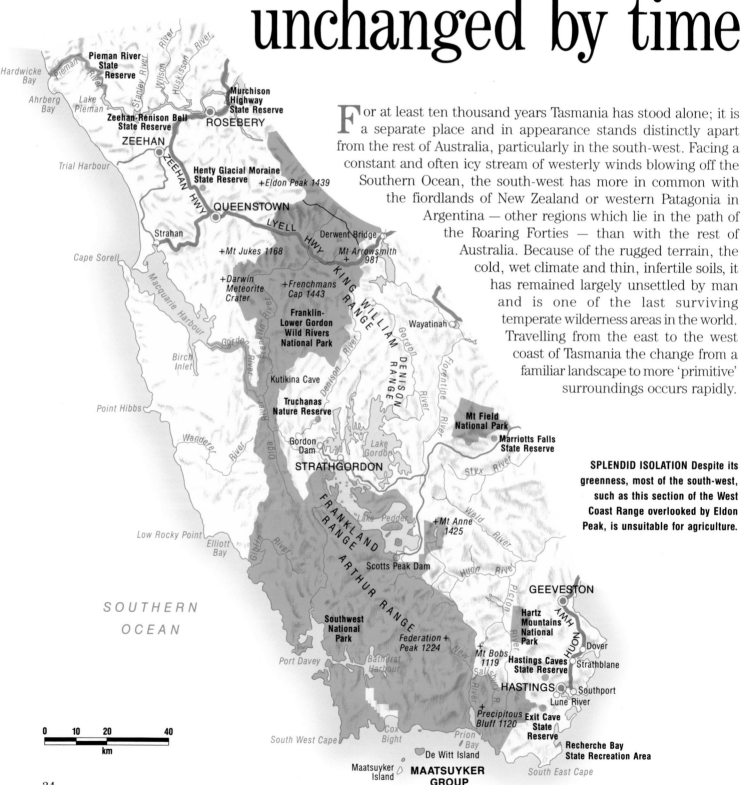

For at least ten thousand years Tasmania has stood alone; it is a separate place and in appearance stands distinctly apart from the rest of Australia, particularly in the south-west. Facing a constant and often icy stream of westerly winds blowing off the Southern Ocean, the south-west has more in common with the fiordlands of New Zealand or western Patagonia in Argentina — other regions which lie in the path of the Roaring Forties — than with the rest of Australia. Because of the rugged terrain, the cold, wet climate and thin, infertile soils, it has remained largely unsettled by man and is one of the last surviving temperate wilderness areas in the world. Travelling from the east to the west coast of Tasmania the change from a familiar landscape to more 'primitive' surroundings occurs rapidly.

SPLENDID ISOLATION Despite its greenness, most of the south-west, such as this section of the West Coast Range overlooked by Eldon Peak, is unsuitable for agriculture.

Hardwicke Bay
Ahrberg Bay
Lake Pieman
Trial Harbour
Cape Sorell
Point Hibbs
Low Rocky Point
Elliott Bay

SOUTHERN OCEAN

Pieman River State Reserve
Murchison Highway State Reserve
Zeehan-Renison Bell State Reserve
ROSEBERY
ZEEHAN
Henty Glacial Moraine State Reserve
+Eldon Peak 1439
QUEENSTOWN
Strahan
+Mt Jukes 1168
+Darwin Meteorite Crater
Franklin-Lower Gordon Wild Rivers National Park
Kutikina Cave
Truchanas Nature Reserve
Birch Inlet
Macquarie Harbour
Gordon Dam
STRATHGORDON
Derwent Bridge
Mt Arrowsmith 981
+Frenchmans Cap 1443
Wayatinah
Lake Gordon
Lake Pedder
+Mt Anne 1425
Scotts Peak Dam
Mt Field National Park
Marriotts Falls State Reserve
GEEVESTON
Hartz Mountains National Park
Dover
Strathblane
Southwest National Park
Federation + Peak 1224
+Mt Bobs 1119
Hastings Caves State Reserve
HASTINGS
Southport
Lune River
+Precipitous Bluff 1120
Exit Cave State Reserve
Recherche Bay State Recreation Area
Port Davey
Bathurst Harbour
Cox Bight
Prion Bay
De Witt Island
South West Cape
Maatsuyker Island
MAATSUYKER GROUP
South East Cape

0 10 20 40
km

At Bicheno, about midway along the east coast, the sunny open eucalypt forest, the dry climate and the rounded hills are very familiar; one could almost be anywhere in the eastern Australian bush. But beyond Derwent Bridge the scenery changes dramatically; now there are steep-sided, cloud-wrapped mountains, dark, fast-flowing rivers and dense, cool rainforests.

WORN PEAK Frenchmans Cap was carved by a glacier and eroded by the elements.

Past the white quartz cliffs of the dome-shaped mountain known as Frenchmans Cap (1443 metres) is the Franklin River and beyond that the Gordon, which thunders over rapids and bolts through wild ravines. Within this wilderness is the type of landscape seldom seen on the mainland: the cliffs, lakes and moraines produced by three different ice ages, the deepest and longest caves in Australia and the tallest forests in the southern hemisphere.

Ice Age Tasmanians

Ironically, this area, which has been largely uninhabited since the arrival of Europeans, has one of the oldest records of human settlement in Australia. Carbon dating of charcoal from a cave in the Florentine Valley shows that people have been in the region for at least thirty thousand years. Other evidence, from Kutikina Cave, located in dense rainforest on the banks of the Franklin River, shows a continuous occupation from about 20 000 to 13 000 years ago. Bones found in the cave suggest that these early inhabitants had a considerable appetite for the meat of the red-necked wallaby (*Macropus rufogriseus*) and the wombat (*Vombatus ursinus*), two animals still common in the south-west today.

The seventeen-thousand-year span between the earliest and the latest dates that humans lived in these caves

HORIZONTAL HORROR The appropriately named horizontal shrub bars the way of the most intrepid traveller as it leans towards the ground, with its branches growing almost vertically.

coincides with the last ice age. The climate was very cold and dry, there were glaciers in the mountains and most of the area was treeless. These ancient Tasmanians were the southernmost people in the world at the time.

As the climate became warmer after the end of the last ice age, dense rainforest grew back and there is little evidence of human activity in the inland part of the region after about 11 500 years ago. Movement and hunting would have been more difficult through the forests and the local tribes probably moved nearer to the coast where the sea provided them with a plentiful source of food.

When the sea level rose, following the melting of the polar ice, the coastline moved inland, reaching its present position about 6000 years ago. Large numbers of shell middens along the coast — evidence that the local people had a taste for seafood as well as red meat — testify to a long human occupation of the region.

By the time Europeans arrived, the drying of the climate, combined with frequent bushfires, had created the mosaic of contrasting vegetation that exists today — rainforest, sedgeland,

SOUTHERN EXPOSURE Not all rainforests are in the tropics; as the thick moss indicates, the temperate rainforests of Tasmania are almost as wet and lush as their Queensland counterparts.

and eucalypt forest. The sedgeland, dominated by button-grass, occupies mainly the bottom of the wet valleys. The eucalypts occur in areas periodically exposed to fire, whereas the rainforest flourishes in the moister, more sheltered sites including damp corridors along the banks of the rivers. Alpine plants crown the tops of the mountain ranges.

A fearsome reputation

After the wet tropics in northern Queensland, this area is the wettest in Australia. The frequent rain and fierce winds, combined with a rugged terrain clothed in tough, wiry undergrowth, have created such a harsh environment that it is one of the least settled regions of the country.

Early European explorers approaching from the east first had to face a broad bank of dense forest; once through this they still faced the hazards of sudden rises in river levels and belts of dense vegetation containing such botanical horrors as horizontal scrub (*Anodopetalum biglandulosum*) and bauera (*Bauera rubioides*).

The former, as its name suggests, tends to grow sideways rather than towards the sun, while the latter has wiry stems that twine inextricably among themselves and into the branches of other plants, forming an impenetrable mass of vegetation. A

37

EERIE SILENCE No human sound disturbs the fiord-like waters of Port Davey. The last Aborigines were forcibly removed in 1833 and the whalers and timber getters — their raw materials depleted — were gone by the turn of the century.

and on the mainland, the rocks of the kind that make up these ranges were buried deep beneath the surface millions of years ago by volcanic activity. Here, the veterans of constant weathering and many climatic changes, these outcrops continue to reach for the sky. What appears to be a scatter of summer snow on the summits of many of the mountain peaks is actually bare patches of hard, white quartzite.

In the breaks between the ranges, the rivers have etched their way into the softer rock. When the region was part of the seabed, limestones formed in the warm ocean and these limestones were eventually to form a large part of the Gordon, Olga, Florentine, Weld and New River Valleys.

slight misjudgement in selecting a route could mean many extra hours of struggle and the risk of exposure from pushing through the rain-drenched bush for hours on end. Not surprisingly, the newcomers soon saw the advantage in the original inhabitants' system of lighting fires to clear the way ahead.

The easiest way to the south-west, in spite of the fierce winds, is by sea. Old river valleys which were drowned when the sea level rose, provided safe havens for early mariners and Port Davey and Macquarie Harbour were soon put to use for this purpose. Port Davey was a base for whaling and transportation of Huon pine and Macquarie Harbour was a penal station.

Range upon range

The most obvious feature of the landscape of the south-west is the series of sharp-crested ranges which run roughly parallel to the western coastline. The Gordon River, the biggest in the region, cuts at right angles through the ranges and, below the Gordon Dam, flows through a spectacular gorge.

These rocky ridges and ranges provide a window onto the distant past. One of the reasons this region bears such little resemblance to the rest of Australia is that in eastern Tasmania

GLACIAL LEGACY The Frankland Range typifies the often awesome beauty of the south-west. Like the similarly high and isolated Arthur Range, this landscape was twisted and folded millions of years ago and later hewn by glaciers. A lake is stranded high amongst the peaks.

Spectacular cave systems and other un-usual examples of weathering by wind and water were to form in the lime-stone and in the adjoining countryside formed largely of dolomite. Examples of this extreme weathering are the large pinnacles and deep sinkholes high on the north-east ridge of Mount Anne, and the Anne-a-Kananda Cave, at 373 metres, the deepest cave in Australia.

Australia's longest cave is Exit Cave near Lune River, where one passage is

19 kilometres long. The cave contains gypsum needles — glass-like crystalline formations as long as knitting needles — and the strange cave feature known from its appearance as 'moonmilk'. This milky white, enigmatic material usually occurs as a pasty substance which often appears to have been poured into position. It was not until many years after its discovery that scientists were able to establish that the 'milk' was of mineral origin and not some peculiar, primitive form of animal or vegetable life.

Most of the caves in the region are home to large numbers of invertebrate creatures. Exit Cave and the nearby Entrance Cave contain more than thirty species of simple animal life. In Exit Cave there are so many glow-worms it is possible to find one's way by their soft, luminescent light.

A peculiar feature of these limestone regions is that owing to the almost per-fect drainage provided by the underly-ing rock there is very little permanent surface water. The most spectacular ex-ample of good drainage occurs where the Salisbury River plunges over the 70-metre Vanishing Falls into a pool and disappears from view to re-emerge two kilometres away.

The legacy of the ice

The reworking of the landscape by powerful glaciers resulted in far more conspicuous features than those that were formed by various forms of weathering in the limestone regions. The peculiar scalloped form of many of the ranges is the most obvious exam-ple of this glacial activity. On the Ar-thur Range in the Southwest National Park, deep armchair-like hollows follow one after the other. Most of these depressions, usually containing one or more lakes, were originally occupied by glaciers which gradually ate their way into the range, sharpening the terrain and pouring large amounts of gravelly material into the valleys as they went. Lateral moraines show where the glaciers once flowed.

The Frankland, King William and

SOUTHERN CONIFER The majestic Huon Pine, which may grow to 30 metres, is named after an eighteenth-century French naval officer.

Denison Ranges all have similar fretted features. These rugged, unyielding landscapes occur nowhere else in Australia except on a very limited scale near Mount Kosciusko. Scientists have discovered that there were at least three separate periods when glaciers were active in the south-west. Because the glaciations were less and less severe each time, relics of the early episodes were not obliterated by the later ones. The first glaciers, one million to 700 thousand years ago, reached almost the vicinity of the present sea level.

The legacy of Gondwana

It is not only the rugged, dark-coloured landforms that give the south-west its unique character. The hardy vegetation, evolved on rocky coasts and mountain slopes, contributes to the 'un-Australian' appearance. A score of plant families and more than two hundred species which are found here occur nowhere else in Australia.

The complex vegetation pattern of forest, sedge and heath is a marvel of complementary evolution. The wilderness contains all the well-known, recognisable Australian plant species, but they often look slightly at odds with their surroundings. The setting is not quite the same as that of the mainland and the familiar eucalypts and acacias are surrounded by unfamiliar company, such as the southern conifers, which are unique to Tasmania.

The conifers and the trees of the cool, temperate rainforest, are direct descendants of plants which evolved in the ancient supercontinent of Gondwana. During much of Australia's existence as a separate continent they were the dominant vegetation types. Now, because of its cool, moist climate, south-west Tasmania is the last refuge of the southern conifers.

The eucalypt-dominated forests of the region are much younger and of strictly Australian origin. Their intrusion into the south-west provides yet another window onto the past. On the mainland, the battle for dominance between the plants, which lasted for millions of years, was finally won by the eucalypts as the climate became drier and drier. Here, in a wet climate, the

EXOTIC NATIVE The pandani, botanically a peculiarly oversized heath, contrasts oddly with the other plants of the forest.

eucalypts and the conifers have each found their level and are coexisting.

Fire has been, and is still the all-important element that controls the destiny of the vegetation in this region. The eucalypts usually have an understorey of dense rainforest in the shade of which eucalypt seedlings cannot survive. If a fire, severe enough to destroy the rainforest and open the seed capsules, does not occur before the eucalypt trees have reached old age, the rainforest will gradually take over.

If a fire does occur, the eight species of conifer in this region, some occurring in rainforest and others in the subalpine areas, are readily combustible and easily destroyed. The bushfires help maintain the growth cycle of the eucalypts while preventing the conifers from becoming the dominant species.

The best known trees of the forest are the giant, slow growing Huon pine (*Lagarostrobos franklinii*) which belongs to the same family as the Californian redwoods, and the King Billy pine (*Athrotaxis selaginoides*). They are complemented by palm-like pandani or giant grass tree (*Richea pandanifolia*), which grows to nine metres and gives a peculiar tropical appearance to the cold, upland forest.

The Huon pine may live for two thousand, and possibly three thousand, years but there are few stands of mature trees left, most of them having been felled in large numbers for boat building.

Kingdom of the eucalypt

The world's largest mature, tall eucalypt forests grow in the valleys of the Weld and Picton Rivers. This broad belt of trees, part of what is usually known as the Southern Forests, acts as a kind of buffer zone between the populated area to the east and the wilderness to the west.

Although most of these forests are dominated by vast stands of messmate stringybark (*Eucalyptus obliqua*), pride of place goes to the mountain ash (*E. regnans*), which stands tallest of all. The ash may soar to 80 metres or more and is the tallest of the world's flowering plants. To the north, in the Styx Valley, one towering giant grew to 99 metres before its top was struck off by lightning.

Appropriately, for here the eucalypt reigns supreme, the trees grow just as

KING WILLIAM The numbers of the King Billy pine, here surrounded by mature pandani, are now depleted, due to its use in furniture making.

41

vigorously on the high, sub-alpine slopes where the soil is thinner and the air colder. In deference to the environment, the eucalypt has made the appropriate adaptations and in place of the messmate or the ash is the varnished gum (*E. vernicosa*), growing to all of one metre high.

The spongy plains

The wet forest of the south-west is not the only phenomenon which indicates that this is a land where the misty rain is blown across the countryside for nine months out of twelve. Sedgeland — spongy plains of peat covered with button-grass (*Gymnoschoenus sphaerocephalus*) — covers about one-third of this region.

What might from a distance look like a smooth, treeless landscape can turn out to be a succession of metre-high clumps of mature button-grass. The bushwalker has a choice of leaping awkwardly from hummock to hummock or using brute force to push between densely growing plants.

Despite the occasional discomfort caused by vegetation which is as hard and tough as its environment, the south-west is a walker's paradise. One of the longest, most arduous yet most rewarding treks in Australia is the 300-kilometre coastline route from Cockle Creek to Macquarie Harbour. The scenery ranges from broad beaches such as those at Prion Bay and Cox Bight to windswept granite peaks such as South West Cape.

For climbers, there are mountains with slopes and faces of almost every degree of difficulty, ranging from the relatively easy summer climb of Mount Anne to the giant 750-metre east wall of Frenchmans Cap — one of the country's most challenging rock climbs.

A wilderness preserved?

Paradoxically, the qualities that make the south-west attractive for development in the latter part of the twentieth century are the same qualities that ensured its survival in such a primeval state for so long. The inhospitable environment deterred all but the most intrepid prospectors and walkers until modern technology made the area's timber and hydro-electric resources relatively accessible.

In the mid-19th century attempts were made to graze sheep on the plains

AMENDED LANDSCAPE In the shadow of the Arthur Range is the 'new' Lake Pedder, beneath which lies the original, swallowed up when the Gordon River was dammed in 1971.

The difficult birth and troubled infancy of a 'heritage' area

In 1980, Australia's growing environmental movement, stimulated by the public support it received during its battle to save Lake Pedder, finally came into head-on collision with the forces of development. The battle lines were drawn indelibly when the Tasmanian Hydro-Electric Commission's plans to inundate the Franklin and Gordon River gorges were set in motion.

This second stage of the Gordon River Scheme would have blocked the main artery of the south-west wilderness and forever changed the character of the region. The shock waves from the collision continue to be felt in the 1990s as environmentalists make their voices felt all over Australia.

The first step in preventing further development was to have the south-west listed as a World Heritage Area. The list is compiled under the auspices of the United Nations Scientific and Cultural Organisation (UNESCO) in the hope that recognition by international authorities will help preserve significant natural and man-made sites (see pp. 390-91).

The first move for nomination of the area for the World Heritage list was made by the Tasmanian Labor government in December 1980. Several months before, the Southwest National Park had been extended and a new Franklin-Lower Gordon Wild Rivers National Park (see picture) proclaimed.

One of the government's aims was to prevent the damming of the Gordon River below the junction with the Franklin, a move which would inundate 114 kilometres of wild river valley as well as the important archeological site of the Kutikina Cave. The boundaries of both the national park and the World Heritage region were drawn so that an alternative dam would be possible upstream.

In November 1981, a state referendum on the question of where the dam would be built resulted in 47 per cent of voters endorsing the original scheme, 8 per cent the alternative dam, and 45 per cent simply voting informally, most of them writing the words 'no dams' across their ballot papers.

A new Liberal government took the vote as the signal to go ahead with preparations for the Gordon-below-Franklin dam and placed a large area of the national park in the hands of the Hydro Electric Commission. In December 1982, the World Heritage Committee placed what it called the 'Western Tasmanian Wilderness National Parks', an area covering 769 355 hectares and including the dam site and Cradle Mountain – Lake St Clair National Park, on the heritage list.

Preparatory work on the new dam began, resulting in a massive public protest at the site. More than 1200 people were arrested and after months of political and physical confrontation the Federal Government legislated to stop the dam. After the Commonwealth action was upheld by the High Court, a State-Commonwealth Consultative Committee was set up to coordinate management.

While the vigorous campaign for the preservation of the wild rivers was being fought and won by the conservationists, the trees of the southern forests were still being systematically logged. In 1987 the Federal Government halted logging in sections of the potential heritage area and instituted a Commonwealth Inquiry to assess the area's suitability for an eventual World Heritage listing.

A majority of the inquiry's members rejected the notion that wilderness was an attribute which alone qualified an area for Heritage listing and instead detailed individual features. Their recommendation that only five small areas qualified for World Heritage nomination was ignored by the Federal Government which instead proposed an addition to the existing heritage area of over 600 000 hectares.

Most of the south-west had been saved for posterity. The fate of the remainder continued in the balance but conservationists, cheered by the election of five 'green' candidates to the Tasmanian parliament in 1989, began campaigning for another World Heritage nomination.

near Frenchmans Cap, and at one stage plans were made for roads and settlements. Realising the unsuitability of the region for agriculture, the authorities reserved most of the land in the hands of the Crown.

Near the turn of the century the mining areas around Queenstown and Zeehan were opened up, but although small-scale mining activity — such as the alluvial tin mining which continues near Port Davey — occurred from time to time, the greater part of the south-west wilderness survived intact until the 1960s. By this time there were scenic reserves at Frenchmans Cap, Lake Pedder and Port Davey.

The concept of reserving very large areas of Tasmania in their natural state did not develop officially until 1967.

Ironically, in the same year that the decision was made to go ahead with the first stage of the Gordon River hydro-electric power scheme, thus enveloping Lake Pedder in dam waters, the Lake Pedder National Park was enlarged to form the Southwest National Park.

The new hydro-electric developments reduced the size of the wilderness by about a third. Roads were built to the Gordon and Scotts Peak Dams and two artificial lakes covering 1350 square kilometres were created. One of these lakes linked with Lake Pedder and eventually submerged it and the surrounding countryside under 15 metres of water.

Lake Pedder, a shallow lake formed between 10 000 and 12 000 years ago as a result of glacial activity, was recognised as the major scenic highlight of the south-west. Its submergence was seen by many as a clear sign that the priorities of government had swung towards economic development at the cost of conservation.

The reaction of those in favour of this dramatic re-shaping of the environment and those against any change was instant and highly polarised. Six years later the second stage of the power scheme was poised to be implemented; this would have involved flooding the gorges of the Franklin and Gordon Rivers. The heated public disagreement over the issue became known as the 'battle for the Franklin' and was not resolved until the Federal Government intervened to prevent the construction of further dams in the region. □

In a dramatic contrast to the rest of Tasmania, the north-west's high rainfall and rich, volcanic soil combine to produce a green and brown landscape of chequerboard farmland

A green and pleasant land

Tasmania's north-western corner, bordered by the Southern Ocean to the west and Bass Strait to the north, is relatively low-lying — for such a mountainous island — and has a climate marked by a high annual rainfall. Rolling plains trim the northern and western coasts; beyond are the undulating hills and minor plateaux which announce the solid barrier behind them: the escarpment fringing the vast bulk of the Central Plateau, including the western end of the ramparts of the Great Western Tiers.

The Central Plateau escarpment reaches 1226 metres at Quamby Bluff overlooking Deloraine, 1420 metres at Western Bluff behind Mole Creek and 1339 metres at Black Bluff further to the west. Other ancient, folded rocks which form peaks along this northern escarpment include the Gog Range and Mount Roland, standing alone off to the north-west.

The mountains fall away in similar fashion; behind the western coast, the Norfolk Range, which separates the Arthur and Pieman Rivers, reaches a maximum height of 759 metres at Mount Norfolk.

These low ranges and the Central Plateau rim represent ancient rocks, folded and eroded to expose tough quartzites and conglomerates — rock composed of fragments, such as pebbles, cemented together — on the ridges above valleys which have been cut through softer, more rapidly eroded limestones and schists.

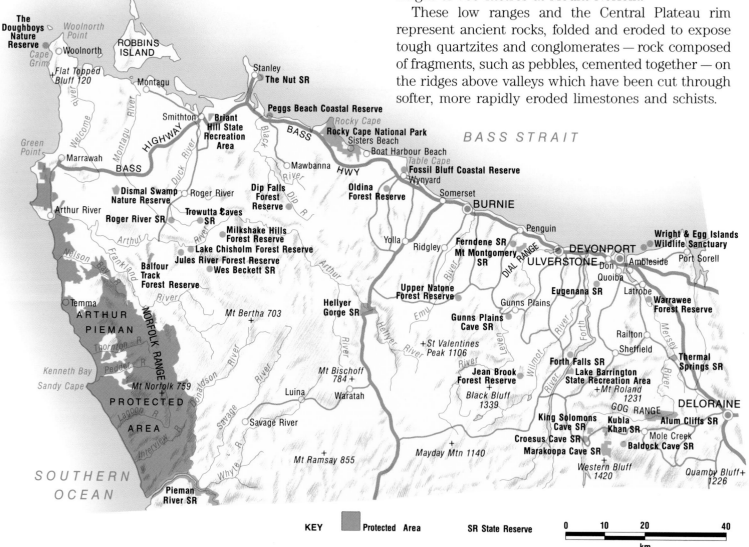

UNDER THE PLOUGH The land is farmed economically right up to the edge of Table Cape's basalt cliffs. The town of Wynyard is in the left background.

Along the Bass Strait coast, the plains have a covering of rich, mainly basalt soil on rock laid down comparatively recently. These rocks and their soil overlay represent the most extensive remnant of Tasmania's last volcanic period, some 10 to 20 million years ago.

Deep, fertile, red-brown soil is but one reminder of the area's volcanic past. The most obvious evidence is provided by the exposed lava plugs of Table Cape and the spectacular monolith known as the Nut, which rises 140 metres from the sea at Stanley. Basaltic landforms extend to the extreme north-western tip of the island in the form of the black, brooding cliffs of the appropriately named Cape Grim.

There is tin, tungsten, silver, lead, zinc, and to a lesser extent gold, in some of the ranges, and the promise of riches from these deposits was responsible for much of the early European settlement. Mount Bischoff, near Waratah, was once the world's largest tin mine, and extensive iron ore deposits are being mined at the township of Savage River.

An English landscape

Moisture-laden clouds which are swept in by westerlies, usually during the winter, empty their contents against the barriers of the western ranges and ultimately the Central Plateau. This regular rainfall from the west has produced a complex drainage network of many hundreds of creeks and rivers.

The Bass Strait hinterland, between Devonport and Smithton, is dissected by a series of parallel streams which run northwards between the Mersey and Duck Rivers. The Mersey and the Forth have their origins high up on the Central Plateau.

The Fury and Murchison Rivers, major tributaries of the extensive Pieman River system, also originate on the Central Plateau, but together with the Arthur River and its tributaries they flow west into the Southern Ocean and not into the strait.

The north-west's high rainfall is reflected in its native vegetation: wet heaths and scrubs, sedgelands and tall, moist forests share the landscape. As elsewhere, variations in soil fertility and drainage patterns are the main factors in determining where the various plants take their place in the patchwork. The 'greenness' of the north-west — often suggestive of an almost English landscape — is one of the most

distinctive features of the region and contrasts markedly with the open forests and woodlands — with their associated plants and animals — typical of eastern Tasmania and the mainland.

But along the region's eastern margin, dry sclerophyll forest intermingled with coastal heathland intrudes about Port Sorell. Port Sorell is an extensive embayment dotted with small islands which receives the waters of the Rubicon River. At low tide, a rich assemblage of wading birds can be observed probing the mud for small crustaceans and molluscs.

A farming patchwork

Most of the coastal plain and plateau from Devonport to Marrawah — particularly the areas of rich volcanic soils — has been cleared for intensive agricultural production. There are few native plants or animals left here, and the region has been colonised mainly by opportunistic, open-country birds, such as the yellow-wattled masked lapwing

OPEN-RANGE BIRDS Clearing of bushland has vastly increased the lapwing's habitat.

SURFACE IMPRESSION The peaceful, green fields of Gunns Plains overlay a network of caves.

(*Vanellus miles*) and the familiar black and white Australian magpie (*Gymnorhina tibicen*).

The migratory marsh harrier (*Circus approximans*) thrives, with its original native diet supplemented by the ubiquitous rabbit — despite the inroads made by myxomatosis, rabbits are still well established throughout northern Tasmania. Most other common birds of the north-west are introduced species, such as the starling (*Sturnus vulgaris*).

From Wynyard westwards, as far as Tasmania's north-western tip, poor soils, derived from exposed older rocks and the sands of the far north-western coastal plain, support a low cover of heath and eucalypt scrub. Coastal heathland is in its element from Boat

Harbour to Rocky Cape, and between Smithton and Woolnorth. More than 3000 hectares of heath is reserved on the ancient quartzite hills of the Rocky Cape-Sisters Beach area, as Rocky Cape National Park.

Flowers of the cape

Jutting into Bass Strait, the park is at the mercy of salt-laden winds, and the many heath plants that grow there exhibit typically tough, waxy leaves adapted to withstand the desiccating, burning effects of such exposure. Coastal heathlands, although stunted and uniform in appearance, are botanically very diverse, and close to 300 flowering plants have been listed at Rocky Cape.

There are beautiful and often spectacular sights to be seen as a result of the plants' highly evolved, sophisticated competition, in colour and form, for the attention of insect and bird pollinators during the peak autumn and spring flowering periods. At these times the honeyeaters are in keen attendance and hungrily lavish attention on their favourite blooms.

The honeyeaters range in size from the large, raucous-voiced and chestnut-winged little wattlebird (*Anthochaera lunulata*), which prefers to feed at the yellow cones of the silver banksia (*Banksia marginata*), to the delicate little red-eyed eastern spinebill (*Acanthorynchus tenuirostris*), usually observed probing for nectar in the long,

coral-pink flower tubes of the common heath (*Epacris impressa*).

Among the plants of Rocky Cape are many which grow only in Tasmania: the region's heathlands and many other plant communities of western Tasmania contain a large representation of such plants. Two such are rare ground orchids, one a leek orchid (*Prasophyllum brachystachyum*) and the other the tailed spider orchid (*Caladenia echidnachila*). The former carries between four and nine yellow-green flower heads with purple margins on a ten-centimetre-long stem, while the latter produces a single flower on a 30-centimetre-long stem, its greenish-yellow petals and sepals tapered to slender crimson points.

Rocky Cape is believed to be the only place in Tasmania where the mainland saw banksia (*Banksia serrata*) grows. An impressive, low-spreading tree, with knobbily-jointed, gnarled branches and sawtooth-edged leaves, it often attracts small flocks of Tasmania's largest and most widespread cockatoo, the yellow-tailed black cockatoo (*Calyptorhynchus funereus*).

These engaging birds, with their plaintive 'wee-la' calls, use massive bills to tear open the woody seed capsules embedded in the banksia's cones, extracting the winged seeds with remarkable dexterity. All the while they chatter busily in a series of low-pitched, squeaky, grinding noises.

Creatures of the cape

Throughout Rocky Cape National Park evidence of ground-dwelling mammals abounds although the mammals themselves may only occasionally be glimpsed on a nocturnal search. The runways and cavernous burrows of the wombat (*Vombatus ursinus*) are frequently encountered, usually advertised by the marsupial's distinctive, roughly cube-shaped droppings. The sharp-snouted southern brown bandicoot (*Isoodon obesulus*) and the long-nosed potoroo (*Potorous tridactylus*) both occur in the area, their presence given away by the conical excavations they make in the sandy soil.

The bandicoot searches mainly for insect larvae but the potoroo, one of the smallest members of the kangaroo family, supplements its diet by digging for underground fungi associated with the breakdown of organic matter. Another well-known native mammal, the short-beaked echidna (*Tachyglossus aculeatus*) also digs conically-shaped though shallower holes, in its constant search

QUARTZITE COAST These craggy bluffs facing into Bass Strait, typical of Tasmania's north-west, illustrate why Rocky Cape National Park was so named.

INEDIBLE LEEK The rare leek orchid is one of more than 50 orchids found at Rocky Cape.

for ants. It may often be encountered during daylight hours.

All three Tasmanian terrestrial snakes, the black tiger snake (*Notechis ater*), the copperhead (*Austrelaps superbus*) and the white-lippped snake (*Drysdalia coronoides*) have been observed about Rocky Cape; the attractively-patterned copperhead, with white-striped lips and flanks flecked with yellow and red, is often so docile that it will allow an observer to approach quite close as it hunts for frogs through the dense ground cover of a heathy soak.

Along the park's rocky coastline, birds are ever present. On rock platforms exposed by a receding tide, scarlet-billed, pink-legged sooty oyster-catchers (*Haematopus fuliginosus*) pick over flotsam and jetsam or probe under seaweed mats for their invertebrate food, while aloft a broad-winged, white-bellied sea eagle (*Haliaeetus leucogaster*) soars by, keen-eyed for a stranded fish.

Among the jumbled boulders and small sea caves of Rocky Cape, pearl-eyed little penguins (*Eudyptula minor*) bray a chorus of annoyance when disturbed from their nesting sites. The caves holding penguins well above the sea were formed by wave action when higher seas washed the coast during warm periods of the last ice age. Fossil beds of tropical seashells, such as those weathered away at Fossil Bluff to the east, are other indicators of higher sea levels that occurred in even earlier times, possibly up to 25 million years ago.

Underground galleries

Caves of a different nature are another important feature of Tasmania's north-west. Beneath the coastal plain, there is a network of cave systems in extensive and very ancient limestone and dolomite deposits. A number of small state reserves, in the vicinity of Mole Creek and Gunns Plains, mark some of the world's most spectacular caves, such as King Solomon, Kubla Khan and Marakoopa. These contain a breath-

taking array of extraordinary formations, some so monumentally grand and symmetrical, that they appear to have been built rather than having 'grown', drip by drip, over hundreds of thousands of years.

Despite their inhospitable ambience, the caves are inhabited by numerous specialised invertebrates such as the Tasmanian cave spider (*Hickmania troglodytes*), spider-like harvestmen or daddy long-legs, cave crickets and a variety of gnats, the larvae of which are the glow-worms which delight the popular imagination.

In the hinterland of the north-west, the high rainfall which has contributed to cave formation underground has resulted in an above-ground landscape with a dense cover of tall, moist forests.

Rainforests triumphant

Australian cool temperate rainforest reaches its peak in Tasmania. The north-west contains the only remaining large stands of such rainforest, where the massive, widely-spaced trunks of beeches reach up to provide a dense, luxuriant canopy for graceful manferns (*Dicksonia antarctica*) and a scattering of understorey shrubs and ferns. Here there is an idyllic, almost park-like atmosphere.

A profusion of lichens, liverworts, mosses and epiphytic ferns cloak the tree ferns' rough trunks and the beechs' gnarled buttresses. Fallen trunks, absorbing water like sponges, carry a dense matting of mosses and delicate filmy ferns (*Hymenophyllum*). The forest floor is carpeted with a thick layer of twigs overlaid by golden-brown beech leaves, blanketing out small ground cover plants.

The colours in this cool rainforest are usually a mixture of complementary muted greens, browns and yellows, but occasional vivid splashes of orange are created on beech trunks by the spherical fruiting bodies of a parasitic fungus known as beech oranges (*Cyttaria gunnii*). Along low river banks, colour is provided in the canopy by the cascading, creamy, purple-flushed flowers of Gunn's orchid (*Sarcochilus australis*). This species is Tasmania's only truly epiphytic orchid and the north-west is its stronghold.

The black, tannin-stained waters of north-western rivers are also a focus for wildlife, the swirling bubbles of a submerging platypus often disturbing the calm of a still backwater or a strident whistle, accompanied by an ultramarine and orange flash, announcing the

ALL LEGS The Tasmanian cave spider is a troglophile — it lives mainly in caves but sometimes ventures above ground. The species may have a leg-span of up to 120 millimetres.

PLEASURE DOMES Small chambers, such as the Jade Pool grotto, surround the giant Kubla Khan cave, like small chapels in a great cathedral. The seepage of groundwater, which eroded the subterranean limestone, is also responsible for elaborate formations such as the flowstones and stalactites shown above.

passage of the brilliant azure kingfisher (*Alcedo azurea*).

At higher elevations, in poorly-drained or less fertile areas, the rainforest canopy becomes lower and the structure more complex and tangled. Trees such as southern sassafras (*Atherosperma moschatum*), blackwood (*Acacia melanoxylon*), leatherwood (*Eucryphia lucida*), native laurel (*Anopterus glandulosus*), musk daisy bush (*Olearia argophylla*), celery top (*Phyllocladus aspleniifolius*) and King Billy pine (*Athrotaxis selaginoides*) mingle with the beech and the infamous horizontal shrub (*Anodopetalum biglandulosum*) fills gullies with a

TIGER COUNTRY? The Tasmanian tiger may still exist in the remote ranges which give rise to the Rapid River, a tributary of the Arthur River.

meshwork of stems. The large number of trees native to the region is reflected in the understorey shrubs such as the scarlet-flowered Tasmanian waratah (*Telopea truncata*), shiny-leaved whitey wood (*Acradenia franklinae*) and several species of tree-heaths (*Richea*).

Forests of the tiger?

Although the north-west's tall, moist forests are nowhere protected in national parks, there are a number of small flora reserves which conserve stands of specific interest. The Balfour Track and the Wes Beckett State Reserves and the Julius River and Lake Chisholm Forest Reserve, on tributaries of the Arthur River, all contain good examples of cool temperate rainforest.

After leaving the settlement of Roger River, travellers pass through impressive stands of rainforest and mixed forests. Further east, the 569-hectare Hellyer Gorge State Reserve, contains rainforest in a ravine cut by another tributary of the Arthur River.

On the west coast, the Pieman River State Reserve (3328 hectares) protects an 800-metre-wide strip of rainforest which hugs the banks on either side of the river. This forest contains the most northerly stands of Huon pine (*Lagarostrobos franklinii*) and one of Tasmania's rarest ferns, the graceful tree-fern (*Cyathea cunninghamii*).

The largest living marsupial carnivore — if it still exists — is the now almost legendary thylacine or tasmanian tiger (*Thylacinus cynocephalus*). The headwaters of the Arthur River may represent the last refuge of this much hunted and trapped creature. The last thylacine killed in the wild is believed to have been shot near Mawbanna in 1930. Hope for its survival in the area still persists and there have been a few reliable sightings reported in recent years.

In the Arthur River area, as elsewhere in the region, where soil nutrients decline with the outcropping of older rocks, a characteristic change in the vegetation is apparent. Rainforest grades progressively into tall wet sclerophyll forest dominated by swamp gums and then to a low forest of Smithton peppermints (*Eucalyptus nitida*). Finally, forest becomes scrub, which gradually blends in with sedgeland or buttongrass plains.

While forests occupy the major part of the north-west's remaining uncultivated land, the region's only national park is confined to a small zone of coastal heathland. Tall, moist forests which are the most visibly significant natural assets, are reserved in a few small, scattered pockets. ☐

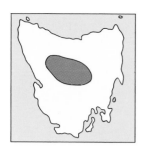
Despite the intrusion of a vast hydro-electric scheme, Australia's largest alpine region retains a brooding majesty as it looms over the world's most mountainous island

Alpine highlands haunted by the ghosts of glaciers

At the core of central Tasmania, in fact, at the core of the whole island, is the immense Central Plateau. Bounded by steep escarpments and craggy peaks, the Plateau forms the 'roof' of Tasmania; most of the island's rivers have their source in this often wet and bleak but always beautiful land.

The Central Plateau is also Lake Country; its western half alone is peppered with more than 4000 lakes. Not all these bodies of water are true lakes; while some are three to seven kilometres in length, others are mere 'tarns' or ponds. All of them are the legacy of large ice caps which have come and gone several times in this region over the last two million years, giving it an appearance usually associated with parts of northern Canada or Finland.

The western Central Plateau is the highest part of the region, rarely dropping below 1000 metres above sea level. To the south, the plateau falls away gradually to the pastoral lands of the Middle Derwent. Its northern boundary is the dramatic 800-to-1400-metre-high escarpment known as the Great Western Tiers.

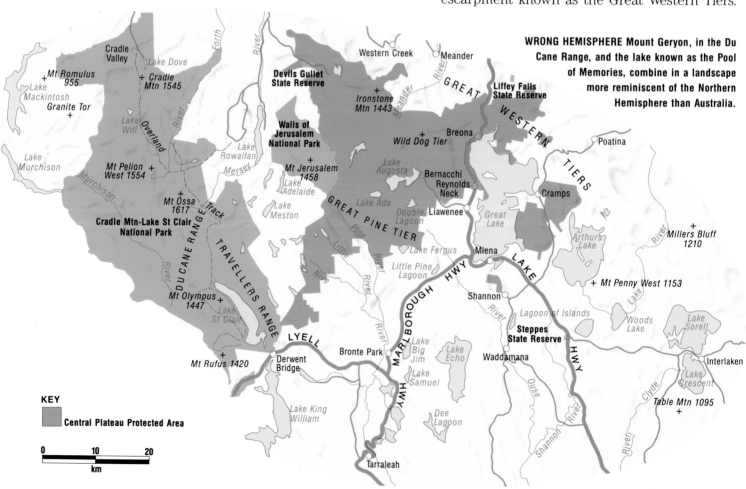

WRONG HEMISPHERE Mount Geryon, in the Du Cane Range, and the lake known as the Pool of Memories, combine in a landscape more reminiscent of the Northern Hemisphere than Australia.

KEY

Central Plateau Protected Area

0   10   20
km

AUSTRALIAN ALPS Central Tasmania includes Australia's largest alpine region; the lake within Black Bluff (top) sits in a cirque — a hollow at the head of the mountain, gouged out by a glacier. The Meander River (bottom) leaves the Central Plateau by way of the Great Western Tiers and in doing so forms the Meander Falls, shown here in the depths of winter.

To the east, bounded also by the Tiers, the plateau is relatively flat, with large, shallow lakes set amidst open eucalypt forest. To the west, beyond the plateau, are the central highlands. Here, tall peaks and deep valleys combine in the finest alpine mountain scenery in Australia.

The Antarctic connection

The rugged terrain over most of the region is made up of a fine-grained, blue-grey dolerite. The toughness of this rock and its resistance to weathering is one of the main reasons why this region is an upland. The Tasmanian dolerite deposits are probably the largest of this rock type in the world and the only example of dolerite of this age in Australia.

Studies of magnetism in the dolerite have shown that when the rock was being formed — about 165 million years ago — Tasmania was less than 1000 kilometres from the South Pole. Dolerite is also found in Antarctica and there seems little doubt, from their age and composition, that the Antarctic and Tasmanian dolerite sheets were once in close proximity, a fact which helps to confirm the theory of continental drift. Geologists believe that the formation of the Tasmanian rock was most likely a reaction to the stresses which occurred when the ancient supercontinent of Gondwana began to break up.

A land lifted high

The high, encircling cliffs of the Great Western Tiers sweep for a breathtaking 150 kilometres around the northern and eastern side of the Central Plateau. At the top of the escarpment, the cliffs are composed of the ubiquitous dolerite but lower down there are layers of sedimentary rock. The Tiers are what is known as a fault-line scarp, situated close to where a major change in the level of the land (faulting) occurred 70 to 80 million years ago.

First of all, the subterranean molten magma which was eventually to become dolerite, forced its way horizontally between layers of sedimentary rock. In some places, the layer of magma was 400 metres thick and as a result, the surface of the land often rose quite dramatically.

Subsequent earth movements caused the land to the north and the east of the Tiers to drop away, leaving the cliffs standing higher than ever. Standing on the Great Tiers, looking across the Midland Valley to Ben Lo-

SNOW CAP The dolerite peaks of the Du Cane Range may be 'tame' compared with the true alps, but in wintertime they bear a passing resemblance to their European counterparts.

MOUNTAIN LAKE One of the many valleys that funnel their icy waters into Lake St Clair here frames the classically shaped Mount Ida.

The effect of the ice on the terrain of central Tasmania was bound to be enormous: the ice cap which crowned the western part of the plateau during each ice age was probably 250 to 400 metres thick in its last incarnation. From the central area, the ice gradually filled in the surrounding valleys, at one stage reaching as far as LaTrobe.

The Derwent Glacier excavated the basin occupied by the 161-metre-deep Lake St Clair, the deepest lake in Australia. The glacier extended 30 kilometres down what is now the course of the River Derwent in the last ice age and 70 kilometres in the one before.

Moving ice and heavy frosts also had a major effect on the shape of the mountains, some of which were probably high enough to remain above the ice. The serrated peaks of the Du Cane Range are typical of these ranges their tame alpine silhouettes.

When the ice melted, the weather became warmer and thousands of lakes developed in the ice hollows gouged out of the dolerite by the action of the glaciers. Further east, well beyond the limits of the last glaciation, a group of

mond — another prehistorically 'uplifted' block — it is not difficult to imagine the magnitude of the geological forces required to frame such a breathtaking landscape.

Rivers of ice

The landscape of central Tasmania, as in many other parts of the world, was laid down amidst the heat of the fiery molten magma and later shaped by mighty glaciers. There is clear evidence of three ice ages occurring during the last two million years, and there were probably many more.

As the ice spread over the land, the evidence of earlier ice ages was buried forever, except where the previous ice had spread over a greater area. The limits of the glaciers, which moved imperceptibly but inexorably across the prehistoric landscape pushing all before them, were marked by their moraines — accumulations of debris pushed or carried by the ice which are left behind when the ice stops moving and melts away. Moraines in the Forth, Mersey and Upper Derwent Valleys, show clearly where the glaciers of this region finally came to a halt.

LAKE COUNTRY Lake Ironstone, overlooked by the mountain which bears the same name, is typical of the thousands of lakes formed after the Central Plateau's ice cap melted.

This is a misty region of heathland, low grasses and shrubs, quite unlike any landscape on the mainland. This vegetation, combined with the icy lakes and year-long snow drifts, makes for a brooding, Northern Hemisphere landscape, evocative of the vast, open tundra of the Canadian Arctic or Siberia.

The most common tree on the plateau is the pencil pine (*Athrotaxis cupressoides*); the pines usually form groves in well-drained areas sheltered from the icy winds, near streams, lakes or pools. At Dixons Kingdom, in the Walls of Jerusalem National Park (1190 hectares), a forest of nothing but pencil pine, uninterrupted by any other large plant, presents a sight which would have been common in southern Australia four million years ago. On the higher plateau, the white skeletons of dead trees and the stoney soils where the covering of peat has been burned away are mute evidence of the effects of bushfires. Seedlings sprout amongst the low undergrowth, but most are quite small as it is less than 30 years since the last major fire, and pencil pines take 55 years to grow to just a metre high.

WATER SOURCE Snow on the Great Western Tiers feeds rivers flowing to Bass Strait.

BLASTED HEATH Where the thin soils are too poor to support trees, botanical oddities such as the cushion plant grow on the alpine heaths.

large lakes, including Great Lake, Arthurs Lake, Lake Sorell and Lake Crescent, were formed by forces other than the ice. Their origin is uncertain but it appears likely that they have been caused by a slight northward tilting of the land surface. How old they are is not known, but since they are generally shallow and have not been filled with sediments, they are thought to have developed in the last 10 000 years.

The Central Plateau is littered with legacies of the ice ages, most conspicuously, the millions of boulders of every shape and size that cover large areas of the region. From a distance they give the surface the appearance of a rough, ploughed field and many of the boulder-ridden areas are known by this nickname.

The boulders are the remnants of the faces of much larger rocks or mountains, which became brittle enough to shatter when thaw followed freeze. During ice-age springs, these huge blocks — some as big as houses — moved gradually downhill, lubricated by water and snow, like huge, slow-moving rivers of rock.

The Tasmanian tundra

The largest continuous alpine area in Australia stretches for fifty kilometres west of the Great Lake, with average daily temperatures for mid-summer and mid-winter 12°C and 2°C respectively. Snow lies for extended periods, and a cold snap can glaze the trees with ice or bring a fall of snow at any season.

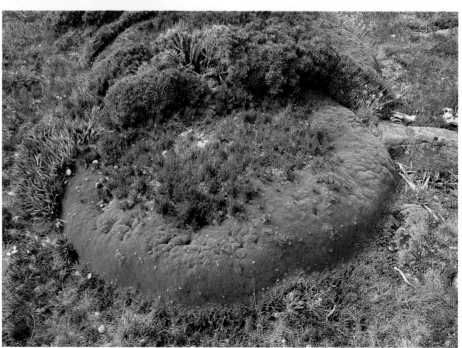

Below the Great Pine Tier to the south, the country is much more generously wooded, mainly with eucalypts such as the common and Tasmanian snow gums (*Eucalyptus pauciflora, E. coccifera*) and the cider gum (*E. gunnii*). The trees are the largest plants here, but more unusual — because of their clever adaptation to the moorland environment — are the bolster or cushion plants. A metre or more across and 30 centimetres high, they are like huge, bright green pin-cushions. They are actually composed of hundreds of tightly packed, miniature shrubs, often of several different species. They prefer damp places and sometimes invade shallow lakes and streams.

A park for all seasons

West of the Central Plateau, and taking up almost a quarter of the central Tasmania region, is the vast Cradle Mountain-Lake St Clair National Park (131 915 hectares). Plant life is more diverse here; the main native conifer is the King Billy pine (*Athrotaxis selagoinoides*) and there are some gloomy, primeval stands of Antarctic beech (*Nothofagus cunninghamii*) in the lee of the ranges and smaller rocky outcrops.

In autumn, the low, straggly shrub known as tanglefoot beech (*Nothofagus gunnii*), Tasmania's only deciduous native tree and one of the few in Australia, brings brilliant bursts of colour to the slopes as its leaves turn various shades of gold.

Despite its size and rugged terrain, the attractions of the park are readily accessible by means of the Overland Track, Australia's most famous bush-walking trail, which provides an 83-kilometre link between Cradle Mountain in the north and Lake St Clair in the south. A large part of the walk is above the 1200-metre level and in the most mountainous stretches, many tall peaks can be seen, including Tasmania's tallest, Mount Ossa (1617 metres).

The dark waters of Lake St Clair are the source of the River Derwent which faces a 160-kilometre journey to the south-west before it passes Hobart.

The wealth of clear, fresh water in the park contains an abundance of life.

GUNN'S NAMESAKES The cider gum (top), and the tanglefoot beech (*Eucalyptus gunnii, Nothogafus gunnii*) — here showing its autumn colours — are Tasmanian native plants. Both were named after Ronald Gunn, a nineteenth century official who first recorded their existence.

The most unusual species is undoubtedly the very primitive Tasmanian mountain shrimp (*Anaspides tasmaniae*). It occurs in cold steams where the temperature never rises above 15°C. Until it was found in this area in 1892, the super-order of *Syncarids* to which it belonged, was known only from 270-million-year-old fossils. Since that discovery, another species of these ancient shrimps — *Paranaspides lacustris* — has been found in the same area.

LIVING FOSSIL The mountain shrimp — unchanged for more than 200 million years — may grow up to five centimetres in length.

FISHERMAN'S PARADISE Hydro-electric installations are not the only intrusions into Tasmania's waterways. Introduced trout have flourished in lakes such as Bronte Lagoon, often at the expense of native water creatures.

The Lake Country is also famous for its trout fishing. Brown, rainbow and brook trout have all been introduced and flourish in most of the streams and lakes. While some of the best trout fishing conditions in Australia has been assured by these introductions, native fish as well as aquatic insects and crustaceans, have all suffered. The mountain shrimp, for instance, is now found only in small steams and tarns where there are no introduced fish to prey upon it.

A modified environment

Modern use of the area has wrought other severe changes to the environment. The openness of the country, even in the wooded areas, made it useful for grazing, and cattle were introduced in 1820. The Aborigines who are believed to have lived in the Lake Country for at least 31 000 years, were quickly dispossessed. By the twentieth century, there was widespread soil erosion due to overstocking, frequent burning to produce a green peat fodder for sheep, and the introduction of rabbits. The higher areas have now been withdrawn from grazing and while there are still grazing leases south of Lake Ada the sub-alpine vegetation has returned to something approaching its original state.

Native animals soon became the target of trappers, and the snaring of possums and wallabies for their skins developed into a traditional activity. The thylacine or Tasmanian tiger, (*Thylacinus cynocephalus*) and the eastern grey kangaroo (*Macropus giganteus*) were locally exterminated, but the Tasmanian devil (*Sarcophilus harrisii*) and the wombat (*Vombatus ursinus*) have survived. The inquisitive spotted-tailed quoll (*Dasyurus maculatus*) and the eastern quoll, sometimes known as the native cat (*D. viverrinus*), are a common sight around the huts and camps of the national parks.

As a high, wet region, the Central Plateau provided excellent water resources for hydro-electric power generation. The tapping of this potential for such a 'clean' source of energy was to provide great benefits for Tasmania, while having an irreversible effect on the waterways of the central highlands. In 1911, a small dam was built at the outlet of the Great Lake and within a few decades most of the water of the Central Plateau had been harnessed for electricity generation.

Increases in dam height greatly expanded the area of Great Lake and converted it from a very shallow to a deep

Tasmania's conservation heritage

Tasmanians were quick to appreciate the scenic wonders of their island state. As early as the 1890s intrepid bushwalkers who ventured into the Cradle Valley and the Lake St Clair region suggested to the Hobart authorities that it should be protected in some way from exploitation as farming land.

In 1912, an Austrian immigrant called Gustav Weindorfer, who had become enchanted by the beauty of Cradle Valley, built a chalet there called Waldheim ('forest home'). By 1913, it was attracting visitors to the region.

and Cynthia Bay, on Lake St Clair, in the 1930s and soon became a national institution amongst hikers and bushwalkers. Fortunately it was not turned into a road — mainly due to lack of funds — and today thousands annually walk the Overland Track, braving the risk of snow storms to admire the fine mountain scenery. East and west of the track, the wilderness remains.

By 1982, the Scenic Reserve had become a national park in name as well as function and was inscribed on the World Heritage list with the two other

In 1921, Weindorfer began a forceful initiative aimed at conserving the region, which had remained untouched except for some animal trapping and small-scale mineral prospecting.

With the support of tourist and scientific groups he organised the first statewide conservation campaign. The outcome was the declaration in 1922 of what was then Australia's largest national park, the 64 000-hectare Cradle Mountain – Lake St Clair Scenic Reserve. In 1940, the reserve was more than doubled in size to 131 915 hectares.

An 80-kilometre-long overland walking track was opened between Cradle Valley

Western Tasmanian wilderness parks (see pp. 34–43). Seven years later, the Walls of Jerusalem National Park (11 510 hectares; see picture), the Central Plateau Conservation Area (23 250 hectares), the Central Plateau Protected Area, and the Lemonthyme Forest — in the Forth Valley — were nominated as additions to the existing site. These cover only the far western Lakes Country, and in the spirit of Gustav Weindorfer, conservationists are campaigning for the World Heritage listing of the Central Plateau protected area to the east (see map), so that the west-to-east spectrum of the wilderness is preserved.

body of water. Even Lake St Clair, in what was then a scenic reserve, was affected when a pumping station and dam were installed. Water levels in many rivers and lakes in the central part of the plateau became subject to continual artificial raising and lowering.

Fortunately, even before these developments, the scenic delights of Tasmania had begun to inspire the early development of a conservation movement. The highly publicised environmental battles of the 1980s are a contemporary manifestation of public feeling which was already being harnessed in the early part of the century in order to prevent over-zealous development of the highlands. The World Heritage status conferred on a large part of the region in 1982 (see box) is the culmination of efforts which began seventy years ago. □

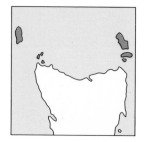

The windswept tips of ancient mountains, washed by turbulent currents from two oceans, are all that remain of the plains that once stretched between Tasmania and the mainland

Mountain peaks amid a restless sea

The Bass Strait Islands lie above the eastern and western extremities of Tasmania, guarding the approaches to the large island like lonely sentinels in the stormy strait. Buffetted by powerful westerly winds and scoured by seasonally fluctuating currents which force the waters of the Southern and Pacific Oceans together, Bass Strait can be a place of sudden and dramatic weather changes. Violent storms are common, but when they pass the strait experiences periods of serene calm, the islands appearing to float in a millpond disturbed only by the ripple of a surfacing fish or the splash of a dipping seabird.

The one hundred or so islands, islets and rocks of Bass Strait are all that remain of the land link which existed between Tasmania and the mainland until about 12 000 years ago. The eastern islands are, in fact, part of the Great Dividing Range — albeit the tips of mountains which were long ago swallowed up by the sea.

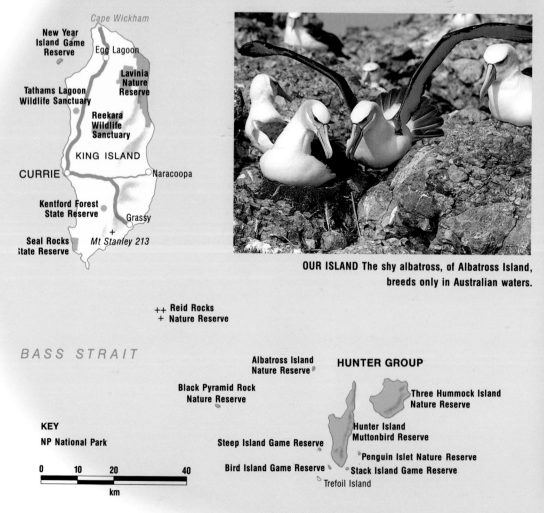

OUR ISLAND The shy albatross, of Albatross Island, breeds only in Australian waters.

Geological evidence shows that the strait has come and gone at least twice as the sea level has risen and fallen with the passage of the ice ages. The first big 'meltdown', when the sea level rose by at least 55 metres, is believed to have occurred approximately 30 million years ago.

The relatively shallow Bass Strait seabed gradually slopes upwards from west to east leaving King Island and the Hunter Group of islands, off Tasmania's north-western tip, relatively low-lying. King Island's highest point, Mount Stanley, rises to a mere 230 metres whereas to the east, the domed peaks of the Mount Strzelecki National Park on Flinders Island reach almost 760 metres.

Flinders Island is the largest of the Furneaux Group of islands which together with the much smaller Kent, Curtis and Hogan Groups form an island chain stretching from Tasmania's north-eastern corner to the mainland's southernmost point at Wilsons Promontory.

The eastern islands are composed mainly of granite; it is exposed in jagged mountain peaks and occurs very obviously as massive boulders. The western islands are older, and on King

West Moncoeur Island
Nature Reserve
Rodondo Island
Nature Reserve

North-East Islet Nature Reserve
HOGAN
GROUP

Curtis Island
Nature Reserve
CURTIS
GROUP

KENT GROUP
Deal Island
Conservation Area

Judgement Rocks
Nature Reserve

Wright Rock
Nature Reserve

Outer Sister Island
Muttonbird Reserve

Inner Sister Island
Muttonbird Reserve

Palana

FURNEAUX
GROUP

Bass Pyramid
Nature Reserve

Cape Frankland   +Mt Tanner 331

Babel Island
Muttonbird Reserve

FLINDERS
ISLAND

Cat Island
Wildlife
Sanctuary

Wybalenna Island
Wildlife Sanctuary

Patriarchs
Conservation Area

Prime Seal Island

Chalky Island
Wildlife
Sanctuary

Lackrana Wildlife
Sanctuary

Low Islets Nature Reserve

Whitemark

East Kangaroo Island
Nature Reserve

*Strzelecki
Peaks*
+756
Strzelecki
NP

Lady
Barron

Logan Lagoon
Wildlife
Sanctuary

Big Green Island
Nature Reserve

Badger Corner
Conservation Area

Chappell Islands Nature Reserve

Great Dog Island
Muttonbird Reserve

Goose Island
Conservation Area

Cape Barren
Island

+Mt Munro 687

Cape Barren

CAPE BARREN ISLAND

Gull Island
Wildlife
Sanctuary

Night Island
Wildlife Sanctuary

Clarke
Island

+ Moriarty Rocks
Nature Reserve

MOUNTAINS FROM THE SEA Though most of their bulk is beneath the sea, the Bass Strait mountains are still a forceful presence; beyond the windswept bluff is Logan Lagoon, and, in the distance, the Darling Range.

Island the ancient rocks are mined for scheelite, the source of tungsten. Close by, the small basalt islands known as Black Pyramid, Trefoil and the Steep Islands, are the eroded cones of ancient volcanoes. Striking black columns rise steeply from the pounding sea around the base of Black Pyramid.

Homing muttonbirds

The Bass Strait region contains over fifty reserves and conservation areas listed by the Tasmanian National Parks and Wildlife Service and many small islands are reserved as seabird breeding grounds. Some, such as Hunter Island and Babel, Great Dog and Little Green Islands in the Furneaux Group, are muttonbird reserves. These reserves were established to manage the breeding colonies of Bass Strait's most numerous and only commercially exploited seabird, the short-tailed shearwater (*Puffinus tenuirostris*), commonly known as the muttonbird.

These plump, sooty-brown petrels, usually about 40 centimetres long, undertake an ambitious migration each year into the North Pacific. They leave their breeding grounds at the end of March and fly across the western Pacific to the Bering Strait before returning along the Californian coast to arrive off south-eastern Australia in late September. An astonishing homing instinct directs them to return with the same mate to the same nesting burrow.

The Bass Strait mutton bird population totals about 10 million birds concentrated in the Furneaux and Hunter Groups. They spend most of the day feeding at sea and return to the densely populated rookeries at night. The air is filled with crooning and crying as the muttonbirds mate, socialise and noisily sort out disputes over nest ownership.

The muttonbird population appears well able to withstand the loss of the half-a-million chicks who are harvested each year for human consumption. The birds' numbers appear to have increased rather than dropped and twenty new rookeries have been established on King Island and offshore islets since the 1920s.

Another bird that has its stronghold on the Bass Strait Islands is the Cape Barren goose (*Cereopsis novaehollandiae*), which, despite its name, is only distantly related to the world's other geese. Cape Barren geese are stocky, pugnacious-looking birds with smoky-grey feathers, pink legs and a prominent lime-green strip across the top of the bill. The sight of a V-shaped flight

WELL-TRAVELLED The short-tailed shearwater covers 30 000 kilometres in its annual migration.

formation of geese flying over granite outcrops, accompanied by the sound of the males' deep, honking calls, creates an indelible impression.

The Cape Barren goose is a winter breeder on the small islands around Flinders and Cape Barren Islands: Goose, the Chappell Group and East Kangaroo Islands are reserved as breeding grounds. In western Bass Strait, geese also breed on Three Hummock and Hunter Islands where they were introduced in the 1960s. They build down-filled nests on the ground or in boxthorn bushes along the western sides of the islands. The attractive black and white striped young are competent swimmers from birth, plunging into the water at any sign of danger.

At the onset of summer, as waterholes on the breeding islands dry out, many geese move across to the cultivated pastures of Flinders Island where they create a nuisance to farmers by consuming crops and fouling stock waterholes with their droppings.

FAMILY GROUP Despite appearances, the Cape Barren goose is not particularly fond of water. The birds mate for life.

In order that the farmers and the geese may co-exist in peace, special reserves providing pasture and water have recently been set aside on Flinders Island at The Patriarchs and Lackrana. The nearby Logan Lagoon Wildlife Sanctuary (2155 hectares), which protects a wide range of waterfowl, also provides a summer habitat for the geese.

Many of Bass Strait's small islands and sea rocks are important breeding grounds for other seabirds besides muttonbirds and geese. Albatross Island, an elongated rock sticking out of the sea north-west of Hunter Island, is the summer home to 2000 shy albatrosses (*Diomedia cauta*), one of only three albatross colonies in Australia. Once almost wiped out by sealers who killed the birds for their feathers, the colony has taken eighty years to reach its present level.

At the height of the breeding season the colony provides an amazing spectacle. Hundreds of chicks perch upright on conical earthen nest-mounds, as the regal adults plane in on their huge wings and regurgitate meals of squid and mackerel, all of this amid a cacophony of grunting and braying calls.

Further to the west, the Black Pyramid offers a similarly impressive spectacle during the gannet breeding season. Sleek Australasian gannets (*Morus serrator*) hang in the updraft which occurs over the rock's knife-edged central ridge before gliding down to deliver catches of fish to their

blue-winged, orange-bellied and swift parrots (*Neophema chrysostoma, N. chrysogaster, Lathamus discolor*), and the tree martin (*Hirundo nigricans*) are regularly observed in passage on King Island, but such movements are seldom reported on Flinders Island.

In common with small islands throughout the world, the animal history of Bass Strait has been one of extinctions, usually occurring in two stages. The first was prehistoric and occurred in the form of natural attrition, with islands losing species progressively in relation to their size. The largest retained the greatest diversity. The second stage, after European settlement, saw the loss of many species in a short time either as the result of a physical

GRANITE PEAKS The brooding presence of Mount Strzelecki — seen here in the distance — dominates the park which bears its name.

clamouring offspring. The Black Pyramid colony of 900 birds is the third largest of the six known gannet colonies off the Australian coast.

Another Bass Strait colony, on the more accessible Cat Island, east of Flinders Island, was once the largest of all with more than 5000 birds. Tragically, this colony was reduced to fewer than ten pairs between 1900 and 1960 by fishermen seeking bait and it now seems unlikely that the population will ever recover its strength.

A biological mix

As is fitting for the remnants of the land bridge that once linked Tasmania and the mainland, the islands are home to a mixed bag of birds and plants that occur together nowhere else.

This is readily apparent from a scramble up the track to the summit of Mount Strzelecki in the south-western corner of Flinders Island. The Strzelecki National Park (4215 hectares), encompassing most of the Strzelecki Range, is forested with Tasmanian blue gums (*Eucalyptus globulus*) and Smithton peppermints (*E. nitida*) on its lower and mid slopes. In the rainforested gullies, stands of dogwood (*Pomaderris apetala*) crowd the understorey and soft tree-ferns (*Dicksonia antarctica*) branch over tannin-stained streams that swirl through granite boulders.

Noisy flocks of strong-billed and black-headed honeyeaters (*Melithreptus validirostris, M. affinis*) flit busily through the eucalypt canopy, while yellow-throated honeyeaters (*Lichen-*

ostomus flavicollis) rustle in the understorey. In the gullies, an observer is likely to catch a glimpse of the magenta-breasted pink robin (*Petroica rodinogaster*) or the sweet-voiced olive whistler (*Pachycephala olivacea*). Out of the gullies, ebony-coloured black tiger snakes (*Notechis ater*) hunt ocellated skinks (*Leiolopisma ocellatum*) that bask in patches of sunlight.

Because ten of the eleven species of birds that are exclusive to Tasmania occur on the largest Bass Strait Islands yet are unknown in Victoria, it appears that the strait operates as a barrier to the movement of many birds. Despite this, regular migrants to the mainland cross over by a westerly route where the waters are relatively open, rather than using the stepping-stone route across eastern Bass Strait. Species such as the

FURNEAUX FELLOW The ocellated skink lives only in Tasmania and the Furneaux Group of islands.

IN TRANSIT The blue-winged parrot rests in the western islands while en route to the mainland.

assault by man or indirectly by the destruction of wild habitats.

King Island has fared the worst, having lost the dwarf black King Island emu (*Dromaius minor*), the gang-gang cockatoo (*Callocephalon fimbriatum*), the eastern spinebill (*Acanthorhynchus tenuirostris*), the forty-spotted pardalote (*Pardalotus quadragintus*), the spotted-tailed quoll (*Dasyurus maculatus*) and the common wombat (*Vombatus ursinus*). The activities of nineteenth century sealers decimated a number of seal and seabird colonies.

Today, the future of Bass Strait's wild creatures looks relatively bright. Most seabird populations and the Australian fur-seal (*Arctocephalus pusillus*) appear to have recovered and stabilised and the many small island reserves ensure their future protection. □

Against the background of a ragged coastline, a combination of mountain forests, volcanic plains and heathland lagoons teeming with birdlife makes for one of Australia's most varied landscapes

Volcanic plains with a wild ocean shore

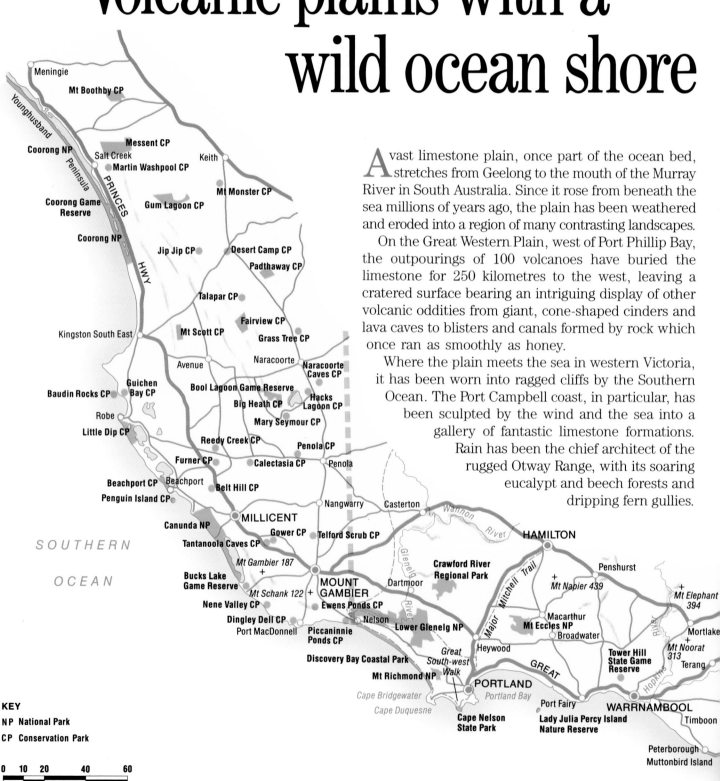

A vast limestone plain, once part of the ocean bed, stretches from Geelong to the mouth of the Murray River in South Australia. Since it rose from beneath the sea millions of years ago, the plain has been weathered and eroded into a region of many contrasting landscapes.

On the Great Western Plain, west of Port Phillip Bay, the outpourings of 100 volcanoes have buried the limestone for 250 kilometres to the west, leaving a cratered surface bearing an intriguing display of other volcanic oddities from giant, cone-shaped cinders and lava caves to blisters and canals formed by rock which once ran as smoothly as honey.

Where the plain meets the sea in western Victoria, it has been worn into ragged cliffs by the Southern Ocean. The Port Campbell coast, in particular, has been sculpted by the wind and the sea into a gallery of fantastic limestone formations. Rain has been the chief architect of the rugged Otway Range, with its soaring eucalypt and beech forests and dripping fern gullies.

KEY

N P National Park

C P Conservation Park

0 10 20   40   60
km

SUBLIME COASTLINE When the Otway Range — trimmed at the shore by the winding Great Ocean Road — meets the sea, one of Australia's most spectacular coastlines is the result.

BUSY ENVIRONMENT A gnarled tea-tree marks the merging of grass meadows and mudflats on the landward side of the Coorong. The ocean is beyond the dune scrub on the horizon.

In the south-east of South Australia, rainwater has again made its mark by gouging out a labyrinth of caves and deep, water-filled holes where it disappears into the porous limestone. Along the coast, in a great arc from Cape Bridgewater to the Murray, huge sand dunes act as a buffer to the pounding seas. Sheltering in their lee is one of the world's great wetland areas. Shallow lagoons teem with flocks of waterbirds and the surrounding heathlands are rich in native wildflowers and bush creatures. This is the Coorong.

The Otways: a wet patch

The Otway Range is a dramatic, emerald green mountain range, about 80 kilometres long, running parallel to the south-western Victorian coastline in a broad swathe from Anglesea to Cape Otway. It tumbles steeply towards its white crescent beaches or bluffs bearing colourful names like Moonlight, Rotten Point and Eagles Nest. The range rises to 650 metres and catches the full brunt of moisture-laden winds off the ocean; these bring as much as 2000 millimetres of rain a year making this region the site of the southernmost wet sclerophyll forests on the mainland.

West of Geelong the Great Ocean Road skirts heathlands rich in wildlife; at Anglesea Golf Course golfers tee off amid mobs of kangaroos lounging on the fairways. Etched into vertical cliffs on one hand with sheer drops to the ocean on the other, the road clings to the coast from Anglesea through the length of Angahook-Lorne State Park (21 000 hectares).

Westward, around the popular beach resort of Lorne, is a region of high rainfall and cool temperate rainforest. From high ridges more than a dozen waterfalls such as Phantom and Erskine Falls cascade down mossy rock faces rimmed with giant tree ferns. Swamp wallabies (*Wallabia bicolor*) are common and in the drier lowlands there are common ring-tail possums (*Pseudocheirus peregrinus*) and the eastern grey kangaroo (*Macropus giganteus*).

From the broad beach of Apollo Bay, the Great Ocean Road veers inland to the high forests of the Otway National Park (12 750 hectares) and leaves 60 kilometres of coastline from Shelly Beach to Princetown unspoiled by man. The park is the peaceful domain of the eucalypt forests.

High rainfall and rich soil support a dense cover of tall mountain ash (*Eucalyptus regnans*), alpine ash (*E. delegatensis*), Tasmanian blue gum

OTWAY LIGHT The oldest lighthouse on the mainland perches atop Cape Otway, where the coastline makes a hard right turn to the north-west.

GREEN MANSIONS The Erskine Falls are typical of the falls, cascades and rapids which fill the rainforest with the sound of running water.

PRETTY CARNIVORE The pugnacious spotted-tailed quoll has become rare in Victoria.

(*E. globulus*) and mountain grey gum (*E. cypellocarpa*). By the 1880s, the Otway Range had been systematically logged but miraculously, several stands of 65-metre-tall mountain ash were missed by loggers and are now protected within the national park.

Three million years ago great rivers of lava cut off the Otway Range from the hills to the north and a million years ago Bass Strait flooded the land bridge to Tasmania leaving the ranges to develop in isolation. Despite this isolation, scientists are still puzzled by the absence of creatures such as lyrebirds, wombats, pilotbirds, greater gliders and a host of other birds, animals and plants that are abundant in similar forests of south Gippsland and northern Tasmania. But for the long-nosed potoroo (*Potorous tridactylus*), a small member of the kangaroo family, and the spotted quoll, still sometimes known as the native cat (*Dasyurus maculatus*), the range is an important habitat.

The rare rufous bristlebird (*Dasyornis broadbenti*), now extinct in south-western Australia, is found in the coastal dune scrub at the foot of the range and as far west as the Coorong National Park in South Australia. Its

name is taken from a cluster of strong bristles curving from the base of its bill. The bristlebird seldom flies, preferring to run swiftly through the brush on long slender legs. Its call resembles a squeaking cartwheel.

The rare green ground parrot (*Pezoporus wallicus*), is another bird that seldom flies. It is one of only two ground parrot species left in Australia, and was a major reason for the establishment of the Carlisle State Park. This is 5600 hectares of grassy heathland south of Colac. It harbours the sedge

FIRE FLOWER The lizard orchid rarely flowers except after fire has swept its heathland habitat.

called button grass (*Gymnoschoenus sphaerocephalus*) on which the parrots feed, as well as a number of endangered orchids such as the lizard orchid (*Burnettia cuneata*) the swamp orchid (*Pterostylis tenuissima*) and three species of spider orchid (*Caladenia*).

A coastline in retreat

The jagged shoreline of Port Campbell National Park is retreating faster than any other part of coastal Australia. Here, where the waters of Bass Strait squeeze between Tasmania and Victoria, towering waves batter the soft limestone cliffs sending seaspray cascading over rock pinnacles and bluffs that are 160 metres high in some places. The pounding of the Southern Ocean has sculpted spectacular arches, caves and sheer gorges. Offshore a trail of rock stacks and islands stand isolated, monuments to the power of the sea.

Millimetre by millimetre, the Southern Ocean is reclaiming its old

STRANDED OFFSHORE Twelve monumental 'sea-stacks' — the Twelve Apostles — clearly indicate the former location of the Port Campbell coastline.

seabed. While rainwater worries away at vertical joints in the rock, eventually shearing off massive slabs of cliff wall, seawater, rising on the howling winds of the Roaring Forties and possessing ten times the corrosive power of freshwater, chews out caverns like The Grotto and Thunder Cave.

These caves may, in turn, become tunnels snaking inland. When a weak spot in the ground above gives way, a blowhole is formed. Near Broken Head the sea surges underground for 100 metres before spouting skyward from

succulents that cling to cliff walls. As with many coastal species, they have small pores and waxy leaves to keep out salt and retain precious freshwater.

When salt does manage to work its way into a crack in a plant's armour — usually through damage by buffeting winds — the plant automatically reacts to this irritant by growing in a leeward direction. The result is the characteristic wedge-shaped coastal heath which appears as if it has been neatly pruned with shears on the seaward side.

Seabirds, from penguins to alba-

FALLING DOWN London Bridge was cast adrift when its landward arch collapsed into the sea in 1990.

a hole almost forty metres wide. Eventually, the blowholes may collapse to form a long ravine that gradually widens into a steep gorge.

One of the sea's most impressive creations along this coast is a limestone formation called London Bridge because it once had two graceful arches. Its unique appearance is due to waves eroding the sides of a narrow headland into a pair of vaulting arches – the archway connecting to the mainland collapsed in 1990 and the remaining archway will someday collapse and leave isolated rock stacks like those making up the Twelve Apostles. Already undercut, these columns will one day crash into the sea.

Only the hardiest shrubs, such as tenacious spinifex or sea rocket that lie low and secure the sand, can live on the edge of this coast. Beaded glasswort (*Sarcocornia quinqueflora*) and pigface (*Carpobrotus rossii*) are bright green

trosses, cope with this salty environment by filtering seawater not only through their kidneys, but also through a nasal or salt gland that leaves a permanent white teardrop below the eye.

The forbidding rock stacks, islands and windy cliffs of the coast provide sanctuaries for nesting peregrine falcons (*Falco peregrinus*) that hunt from clifftops and birds such as the grey goshawk (*Accipiter novaehollandiae*), swamp harrier (*Circus approximans*), Australian kestrel (*Falco cenchroides*) and Australasian gannet (*Morus serrator*). The gannet is able to plummet like an arrow into the sea after fish, because of air sacs that cushion the impact.

One of Australia's most prolific seabirds, the short-tailed shearwaters or muttonbirds (*Puffinus tenuirostris*), arrive by the hundreds of thousands in late September to breed. They take five to seven weeks to fly approximately

14 000 kilometres from feeding grounds in the northern hemisphere as far away as Siberia. Their nesting burrows cram every available spot in the colonies on Port Campbell's rock stacks and on Muttonbird Island. Pied cormorants (*Phalacrocorax varius*) are also very much at home here and can be seen standing along cliff tops with their wings spread out to dry. Their wings absorb water to allow the birds to dive and swim deeper in search of schools of fish.

Narrow beaches at the foot of some cliffs shelter colonies of tiny fairy penguins (*Eudyptula minor*), the smallest penguin species, and the only one that breeds on the Australian mainland. Spending their days at sea the penguins scramble onto the beach at dusk seeking refuge in caves such as those near London Bridge. The birds are easy prey for foxes; although the small rookery at London Bridge has been fenced for their protection, almost one-third of the colony was lost in 1989 to a single fox that overcame the barricade.

Offshore, spouts of water signal the return of the southern right whale (*Eubalaena australis*). Every winter since May 1982 as many as nine of the whales have paused on their migration from Antarctica to the Great Australian Bight (see p. 356) to calve at Logans Beach near Warrnambool. They can be seen there frolicking with their young less than 100 metres offshore between May and August.

Land of the volcanoes

Australia is the only continent with no active volcanoes, but there are plenty of reminders of past activity on the vast lava plain that sprawls over 23 000 square kilometres from just west of Melbourne to the South Australian border. The entire region, covered one to sixty metres deep in lava flows, is peppered with cones and vents which are the remains of approximately 100 volcanoes that burst through the earth's surface in two fiery eruptions, the first about three million years ago.

The last eruption, which formed Mount Eccles, Mount Napier, Mount Gambier and Tower Hill, began 20 000 years ago, with Mount Schank the last to erupt around AD 600. Despite their long silence, some scientists are uncertain whether these volcanoes are extinct, or merely in an eerily long quiet phase between eruptions.

Most volcanoes form in one of two ways: the outpourings of lava and ash

QUIET NOW The green and peaceful setting of gently rounded Mount Leura belies its explosive, volcanic origin thousands of years ago.

VIOLENT BEGINNINGS

HILLS AND LAKES Many of the most prominent landforms of the plains mark the location of the more than 90 volcanic vents which are known to exist in this region. A conventional volcano shape is maintained when scoria, or solidified lava, piles up into a cone (top). A later eruption, or the collapse of the scoria core, results in a caldera, or enlarged crater (bottom) ringed by debris, which often fills with water, like the famous lakes at Mount Gambier.

gradually build up like layers of candle-wax to create a gently sloped mountain. Mount Schank and Mount Napier with their familiar cone shapes were formed this way. But steep-sided Mount Eccles and Mount Leura were formed by explosive eruptions that sent showers of rock into the sky in the same way that violent volcanoes like Krakatoa and Mount St Helens have erupted.

At Tower Hill near Warrnambool, the multi-coloured layers of ash that form the cliffs on the inside of the crater provide a neatly documented record of each eruption. Tower Hill — now filled with water — is a 'nested' crater where smaller volcanic cones have formed inside the main crater or caldera. Early accounts tell of the lush beauty of Tow-

er Hill which was declared Victoria's first national park in 1892, although the caldera and its islands had been cleared of trees decades before this. It is now a game reserve and, efforts are being made to return the area to its former wooded glory using as a guideline an old oil painting which shows Tower Hill as it was in the 1850s.

South Australia's best known volcano, Mount Gambier, spread ash, cinders and lava over a radius of eight kilometres when it erupted into life through the limestone. The state's second biggest city straddles the slopes of the volcano after which it is named and draws its water supply from the mysterious crater-lake. For decades scientists puzzled as to why Blue Lake turns bright turquoise every October and back to dull grey around February. The most recent theory is that as the summer sun warms the lake's surface, calcite in the water forms crystals which appear blue in the sunlight.

At Macarthur, 5112 hectares of forest on an undulating basalt landscape are preserved in Stones Faunal Reserve. To the north at Hamilton is one of Australia's few remaining strongholds for the eastern barred bandicoot (*Perameles gunnii*). Less than 300 of the endangered marsupials are thought to be left here. Once common throughout the country, most have been killed by foxes and cats. The bandicoot, which has three distinctive black bands across its

hindquarters, springs comically straight up into the air and runs off at great speed when disturbed.

The gentle slope of Mount Richmond near Portland belies its origins as a volcano born in explosive eruptions. The weathered cone has been cloaked in sand blown from the great dunes of nearby Discovery Bay Coastal Park (8590 hectares). Naturalists refer to Mount Richmond as south-west Victoria's natural botanic garden and a 1733-hectare region has been preserved as a national park because of the enormous variety of native plants that thrive in the surrounding countryside. It contains over 450 species of flowering plants such as correas, wattles and bush peas and 58 species of orchids and though spring is the wildflower season, there is always something in bloom on Mount Richmond.

Heathlands carpet the lower sandy slopes with banksias, grass trees and manna gums (*Eucalyptus viminalis*) and brown stringybarks (*E. baxteri*). In the higher reaches volcanic soils are exposed and swamp gums (*E. ovata*) grow with casuarinas and a variety of melaleucas. The wooded park is a natural aviary for the crimson rosella (*Platycercus elegans*), gang-gang cockatoo (*Callocephalon fimbriatum*), southern emu-wren (*Stipiturus malachurus*) and at least 100 other species of birdlife.

Just outside the park is a petrified forest called The Moonah. This is a grouping of hollow limestone casts of the trunks of moonah, a form of melaleuca. The casts are two metres tall and were formed by the accumulation of limestone over thousands of years; the trees themselves disappeared long ago.

Caverns, bats and bones

Beneath a landscape of pine forests and green pastures the south-east of South Australia hides a labyrinth of underground passages and chambers that would make a slice of the region look like Swiss cheese. On the surface the only visible clues to the great subterranean network are mysterious holes pockmarking farmers' paddocks or dank cave mouths carved into a hill or the side of a river gorge.

Just east of the Victoria-South Australia border, the Lower Glenelg National Park (27 300 hectares) marks the beginning of cave country. Where the Glenelg River ends its winding course from the Grampians to meet the sea at Nelson it has carved a 60-kilometre-long limestone gorge that is rarely less than 60 metres deep. All around are caves — there are at least thirty-five beneath the park.

Limestone caves are formed by rainwater: having absorbed carbon dioxide as it passes through the atmosphere and become a very mild form of carbonic acid, the water has a gently corrosive effect on the porous limestone. It flows over fissures and faults and down cracks and crevices and, like a slow-motion version of hot water poured on ice, it eventually dissolves vast areas of rock.

Many of the 173 caves so far discovered in the south-east contain a rich variety of odd and sometimes attractively shaped formations — calcite deposits left behind from the steady drip of limestone-saturated water.

Besides stalactites and stalagmites there are long hollow 'straws', massive columns and translucent rippling curtains called 'shawls'. Less common are oolites — beautiful 'pearls' formed by grains of sand that have gathered layers of calcite — and helictites — weirdly twisted tubes that sprout from walls and seem to defy gravity by growing upwards. In fact there is a thin, central tube in the helictites carrying the mineral solutions which are their building blocks.

The Bat Cave: high density living

Each spring hundreds of thousands of bent-wing bats (*Miniopterus schreibersii*) stir from winter hibernation in caves throughout south-eastern Australia and fly to the Bat Cave at Naracoorte. Here, in the largest bat colony in Australia, over 200 000 bats, mostly pregnant females, gather to give birth and raise their young.

Between November and February a dark cloud briefly fills the air every evening at dusk as the bats stream out of their cave to feed. The tiny creatures, weighing around 14 grams and with bodies about the size of a mouse, eat as much as half their weight in insects every night. The Naracoorte summer colony consumes over two tonnes of insects each evening, performing a valuable form of pest control for farmers. When insect populations drop in autumn the bats return to their winter caves, and go into hibernation.

While hibernating, the bats slow their metabolism and lower their body heat to within two degrees of the air temperature in order to conserve energy. When they are disturbed by visitors to the cave the bats are forced to quickly resume their normal temperature and flee, navigating the darkness of their caves by sending out up to 50 high frequency sonar signals per second. Such interruptions to their 'sleep' eventually deplete their fat reserves to such an extent that the sensitive creatures cannot sustain themselves for the remainder of the winter and are liable to die of starvation.

Caves such as the Bat Cave are so prevalent in the south-east that several occur in urban areas. In Mount Gambier, the entrance to Town Hall Cave is directly opposite the town hall and Umpherston and Englebrecht Caves are also within the metropolitan limits.

HOW THE DUNES FUNCTION

Coorong Salt flats and or Mobile sand dunes Low level fresh Vegetated hind dunes Inter-dune swale Fore dune Beach Ocean
grass meadows water swamps

Blow out Blow out

Fresh water soak Eucalypts Old buried
on top of old muds soil profiles Berm

Old shore lines Spinifex

Mean sea level

Muds extruded by dune Fresh water aquifer
encroachment

Salt water aquifer

WATERY ENVIRONMENT A cross-section through the sand dunes, from the Southern Ocean to the waters of the Coorong, displays the various elements which make up the Younghusband Peninsula. The sponge-like aquifers were laid down when the sea level was much higher.

70

BIRDLAND Despite its desolate appearance, the Coorong teems with wildlife, particularly waterfowl and seabirds. Beyond the mudflats are the lagoon and the ocean-side dunes.

decorations which are still in the process of forming.

In 1969 explorers squeezed through a 25-centimetre-wide passage and discovered a new chamber containing one of Australia's richest fossil beds. The remains, estimated to be 150 000 years old, included the bones of a wombat the size of a hippopotamus and a marsupial lion that hunted the giant kangaroos whose bones bear its teethmarks. The fossilised bones of more than 60 species of animals which either became trapped or simply went to the caves to die have been uncovered in this chamber.

Dunes and lagoons

'Coorong' is an Aboriginal word meaning 'narrow neck', a perfect description for the shallow lagoons stretching south for 135 kilometres from the mouth of the Murray River and protected from the Southern Ocean by the Younghusband Peninsula, a narrow strip of high sand dunes. The lagoons gradually peter out at the southern end into lakes and marshy ponds up to three times as salty as the sea. The dunes, lagoons and inland heath of this unique environment are all protected within the Coorong National Park (39 904 hectares), and the Coorong Game Reserve (6840 hectares).

The Coorong region is one of 27 Australian wetland reserves, with a total area of more than 1 250 000 hectares, which have been nominated for protection under the International Convention on Wetlands. Australia was the first nation to sign the convention.

The protected area includes six islands which are set aside as breeding habitats for a variety of seabirds including crested and fairy terns (*Sterna bergii, S. nereis*). It is the country's largest permanent nesting ground for the Australian pelican (*Pelecanus conspicillatus*). Fishing for bream, mullaway or mullet in lagoon waters, up to 4000 pelicans gather in a good breeding season and over 2000 chicks are hatched on the islands each year. Albatrosses, cormorants, ibises, gulls and grebes also nest here.

During summer or in times of inland drought, waterfowl like the grey and chestnut teal (*Anas gibberifrons, A. castanea*), Australian shelduck (*Tadorna tadornoides*) and black swan (*Cygnus atratus*) flock to the freshwater soaks that seep through the base of the sand dunes.

The lagoons are filled by a complex interaction between the Murray River,

Lower Glenelg National Park was also set aside to protect an unusual combination of at least 700 species of native plants growing on its cliffs, dunes and heaths. This region is a meeting place for the eastern and western halves of the continent. Victorian plants grow alongside Western Australian species and both eastern and western grey kangaroos (*Macropus giganteus, M. fuliginosus*) live here. A wealth of other small mammals inhabit the park including the southern brown bandicoot (*Isoodon obesulus*), and phas-

cogales (*Phascogale*) and dunnarts (*Sminthopsis*) – broad-footed and narrow-footed marsupial mice.

Some of the south-east's most spectacular caverns are in the Naracoorte Caves Conservation Park (272 hectares) near the town of Naracoorte. Only three of the 16 caves in the park are open to the public, the Victoria Fossil, Blanche and Alexandra Caves. Victoria Fossil Cave contains a honeycomb of over five kilometres of interconnecting passageways and chambers, each of them lined with elaborate limestone

HOME SWEET HOME More pelicans nest in the Coorong than anywhere else in Australia. At least 160 other species of birds live in these wetlands.

rainfall and groundwater. Although agricultural drainage projects and the construction of barrages to maintain freshwater levels in adjacent Lakes Alexandrina and Albert have disturbed the natural flow of water from the Murray River into the Coorong, the region remains a hauntingly beautiful wilderness: the pounding surf of mist-shrouded beaches and the peaceful waters of the lagoons are seldom more than two kilometres apart.

The shifting sand dunes are a delicate buffer that protects the lagoon system from the sea while also replenishing beaches cleared by wave action. When the dunes are stripped of vegetation, driven over by vehicles or even subjected to repeated pedestrian use, destructive channels called 'blowouts' are eroded by the wind.

Though wombats and emus are still common in the coastal heath, rabbits and foxes have eliminated many native plants and animals. Near Salt Creek Nature Walk, behind fences erected to keep rabbits out, native plants that used to flourish in the area only 30 years ago are regenerating. Inland, huge conservation parks such as Billiatt (59 148 hectares), Messent (12 246 hectares), Mount Rescue (28 385 hectares) are home to the malleefowl (*Leipoa ocellata*), the blue bonnet (*Northiella haematogaster*) and the eastern pygmy-possum (*Cercatetus nanus*).

Nearly half of South Australia's 4000 kilometres of coastline are beaches fringed in sand dunes. Dune and lagoon systems like the Coorong are found on the south coast all the way to Cape Bridgewater near Portland and a string

of parks protects this fragile environment. Bool Lagoon, the first game reserve in South Australia, and the adjoining Hacks Lagoon Conservation Park, south of Naracoorte are now the largest remaining wetlands in the south-east, with a combined area of 2883 hectares. More than half the eighty species of waterbirds that inhabit the wetland breed in this area, many migrating from as far north as the Bering Sea.

Three hundred brolgas — about half the entire South Australian population — breed around September when the lagoons begin to fill. The graceful, long-legged birds spend the summer at the shallow lagoon where they can be seen performing their graceful and complex dance rituals.

Here man may well be made to feel an intruder. But intrude one may. A boardwalk leads half-a-kilometre into the heart of the lagoons to a camouflaged lookout with a water bird's-eye-view of egret, spoonbill and ibis rookeries; 40 000 of these birds raise their young each year at Bool Lagoon. The best time to see and hear this almighty congress is at dawn and dusk when the trumpeting of the black swans and the raucous screeching of swamphens fills the air. □

Craters of water in place of fire

From the Red Rock Lookout on the Princes Highway near Colac there are sweeping views across more than a dozen sparkling lakes. But they are not just water-filled depressions. These are either volcanic craters or large holes caused by the collapse of volcanic lava beneath the earth's surface.

Among these craters is Lake Corangamite, three times as salty as the sea and teeming with colonies of pelicans, it is Victoria's largest lake at 234 square kilometres. Another is a tiny lake between Pirron Yallock and Camperdown which has several 'floating islands' that drift eerily from shore to shore propelled by the wind.

Although the phenomenon of such peat islands is not rare, it is unusual for them to be 30 metres across and to carry dense vegetation up to eight metres tall. During a bushfire in 1938, the peat islands caught fire and burned for several months, right through to the lake bed.

With the floods of 1952 the water level rose, the islands became mobile, and the lake's steep sides prevented them from becoming re-anchored. But conservationists are concerned about the future of the lake; since the drought of 1982-83, the water level has dropped dramatically and several of the islands seem to have not just touched bottom but run permanently aground.

A BEGINNING AND AN END The waters of the Coorong — seen here at their northern limit — stretch to the horizon, separated from the ocean by the slim Younghusband Peninsula. The narrow channel carries the waters of the Murray River to the sea (see pp. 86-95).

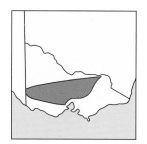
The massive Great Dividing Range, which casts a giant shadow all along Australia's east coast, sweeps westward near the New South Wales–Victoria border and peters out in an arc of gentle hills and low ranges

A gentle end for the Great Dividing Range

Hill country, with its image of rolling, rounded landscapes, is the most apt way of describing the central part of Victoria. This landscape is dominated by a great arc of hills — the hook of the giant 'J' of the Great Dividing Range.

The hills sweep across Victoria from the high country in the east, where the mountain rivers rise, to the sunset country of the Wimmera and the Mallee in the west. This gentle, almost soothing terrain, is the result of the long, steady build-up of sediments which were later compacted, eroded, and finally tilted into their present positions by a series of movements along faults in the earth's crust.

The whole cycle of these imperceptible geological processes, which continue to sculpt the landscape, is on display in the Werribee Gorge State Park (375 hectares), just over an hour's drive west of Melbourne. Here the Werribee River has carved its way through the hills to form a gorge, the walls of which provide a layer-cake cross-section of 500 million years of history.

This geological showcase begins, in reverse order, with today's hills above the gorge. These are topped by a lava capping which was spewed up from the bowels of the earth a mere one million years ago.

Around these now much eroded lava caps is a deep layer of rock dust and pebbles, left behind by retreating glaciers about 250 million years ago. Below this debris there are gently curving bands of sediment — once part of an ancient seabed — warped and compressed by enormous pressures.

Cutting through and across these sedimentary layers — like the haphazard and arbitrary shapes of colours in a marble cake — are lines of much harder basalt rock formed when molten magma was squeezed out through cracks and other weaknesses in the earth's surface crust.

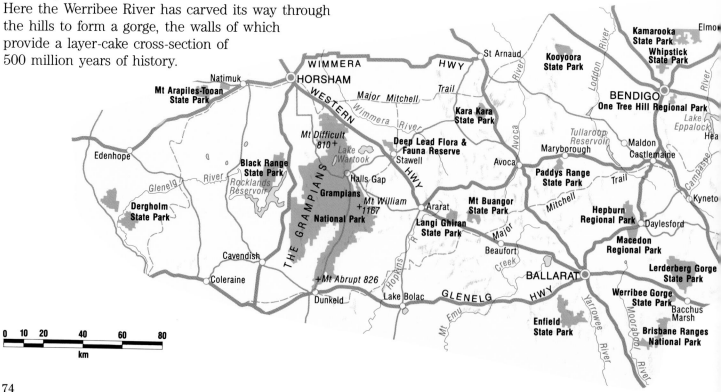

CATHEDRAL SPINE A razorback ridge, barely more than two metres wide in places, links two remote peaks in the Cathedral Range.

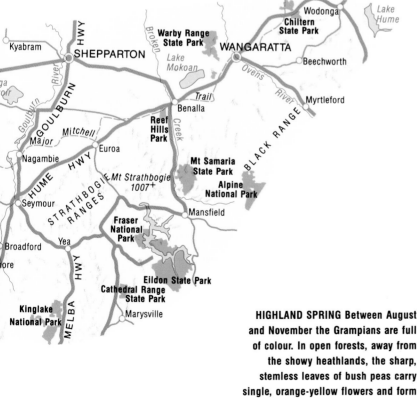

HIGHLAND SPRING Between August and November the Grampians are full of colour. In open forests, away from the showy heathlands, the sharp, stemless leaves of bush peas carry single, orange-yellow flowers and form a dense mat several centimetres thick.

Maps of Victoria's hill country often allege the presence of many 'mountains' — a not uncommon habit in a country where truly tall peaks are a rarity. The reality is more often one of bumps and protrusions on the landscape, perhaps only a few hundred metres high. Even where more dramatic interruptions appear on the horizon, they too are essentially the result of the same slow processes of sedimentation and erosion that formed the more modest hills.

The sheer age of so many hill landscapes means that much of the fertility of the soils has been leached away. Ironically, it is the poor soils that usually support the finest wildflowers.

Early white settlers were quick to realise which soils were too poor for agriculture and therefore not worth clearing. The result is areas such as the Whipstick and Brisbane Ranges — protected within the Whipstick State Park (2300 hectares) and the Brisbane Ranges National Park (7517 hectares) — which were largely passed over by farmers and graziers and are still more or less in their natural state.

Hill country isolated by broad stretches of lowland, and where the soil is harsh and relatively infertile, often gives rise to unique and specifically adapted plants. The Grampians are a particularly good example of this, with over one-third of all Victoria's

flowering plants being found there, and of these, 18 are endemic — found nowhere else in the world.

These ecologically isolated areas often display fascinating examples of what botanists call broken distribution among their plants, so that a most unexpected assortment of plants can occur in one relatively small area. At the Long Forest Flora Reserve (283 hectares), near Melbourne, much of the open country is reminiscent of the Mallee, many kilometres to the north, while down in the valleys there are

stands of blue box (*Eucalyptus bauerana*), a eucalypt more characteristic of Victoria's eastern regions.

While most of the Victorian hills were shaped by the slow accumulation of sediments deposited when the region was beneath the sea, there are some places where molten magma, deep below an insulating 'blanket' of surface rock, has been involved in the shaping of the hills.

Over time, this molten rock turned into granite which has been revealed only after millions of years of erosion have stripped away the overlying rock. Among the most unusual granite landforms and certainly those with the most spectacular origin, are the twin Acheron and Cerberean cauldrons near Marysville.

The ancient Greek names, suggesting a dark and gloomy underworld, reflect the subterranean origin of these deep hollows. Geologists believe that vast chambers of molten magma were forced up from deep within the earth, fracturing the overlying crust as they approached the surface. Finally the roofs of the chambers gave way, and violent, literally earth-shattering eruptions occurred as the molten rock burst into the atmosphere.

The round and gentle outlines of granite masses have a special appeal that is particularly evident in the inviting slopes and massive boulders of

MELVILLE MAZE On a rise in the Kooyoora State Park, a jumble of granite boulders forms a labyrinth known as Melville Caves.

NOT FARMWORTHY Although Victoria is Australia's most intensively farmed state, almost a third of its bushland is untouched due to the hilly or mountainous terrain.

Langi Ghiran and Mount Buangor State Parks (2695, 2400 hectares). Kooyoora State Park (3593 hectares), with its many caves and crevices has an enticing air of mystery even on the brightest summer day, especially since these caves were once the hideout of Captain Melville, a notorious bushranger.

The sound of birdsong

In spring, these rocky slopes are covered with a brilliant sweep of golden wattles and the boulders, still mossy from the cool, wet winter, are dotted with minute native lilies and sundews. The exuberant calls of honeyeaters, parrots and lorikeets, the confiding warbles of a magpie, or, most evocative of all, the clear, ringing call of a currawong, fill the air.

Rocky outcrops, when high enough and beyond the reach of predators, are often the favoured nesting sites of that superbly adapted bird of prey, the pere-

grine falcon (*Falco peregrinus*). This bird, which can dive down to its prey at speeds of nearly 300 kilometres an hour, uses high-speed flight not only to capture its food but also in its magnificent courting display. At the end of the breeding season the parents fly furiously at their offspring in order to drive them out of their territory.

A threat to the future of the falcon arose when rock-climbers discovered that the lofty cliffs favoured by the birds were often the most challenging to climb. The conflict has now largely been resolved by the closure of such rock faces during the breeding season.

A more easily observable avian attraction, which brings many keen birdwatchers to the hills, are the owls. A particular drawcard is the massive powerful owl (*Ninox strenua*), a majestic creature standing well over half a metre tall, its feathers handsomely barred in pale brown and white. The barking owl (*Ninox connivens*) emits an extremely loud, high-pitched cry which earned it the nickname of 'screaming-woman bird'. Both these owls have hawk-like faces and rely primarily on sight to capture their prey.

MISTLETOE BIRD The parasitic mistletoe relies on this bird to spread its seeds.

The barn owl and the sooty owl (*Tyto alba, T. tenebricosa*) which inhabit the hills, rely far more on hearing. Their faces bear the owls' characteristic disc of feathers which acts as a receiving dish, enabling the bird to pick up the sound of its prey.

A common item in the sooty owl's diet is the antechinus, a small marsupial about the size of a large mouse, and a fascinating link exists between their lifestyles. Soon after mating — a very vigorous procedure, orchestrated by

massive amounts of hormones in its blood — the male antechinus dies. After rearing the resultant young, most of the females die too.

While this annual mating drama is being played out at ground level, the sooty owls are laying their eggs, a demanding process which requires a protein-rich diet. The dead and dying male antechinuses provide a handy protein supplement for the owl nursing mothers. By the time their eggs have hatched, and the young owls are fledglings, the meat for their diets is provided by the timely deaths of large numbers of female antechinuses.

Many other birds also have highly organised breeding habits. Kookaburras, wrens and babblers share the duties of rearing the nestlings between not only the parent birds, but also the young of previous hatchings. This appears to be a simple strategy for maximising reproductive success where the climate, and therefore the food supply, may be unpredictable.

Birds are important pollinators of a surprisingly high number of Australian wildflowers. One of the most abundant plants in Victoria's hill country and one which attracts more attention than most from wild creatures are the several different genera of mistletoe.

While the plants are semi-parasites — they rely on their hosts for moisture but absorb energy from the sun by their own photosynthesis — they are a wonderfully rich source of food and shelter to a wide range of creatures.

A well-grown clump of mistletoe will be attended by honeyeaters feeding on the nectar and diminutive, but brilliantly coloured, mistletoe birds (*Dicaeum hirundinaceum*) collecting the sweet, nutritious berries for their nestlings. The caterpillars of numerous butterflies feed on these plants and occasionally even a koala seeks shade beneath their foliage.

Throughout the hills, echidnas (*Tachyglossus aculeatus*), eastern grey kangaroos (*Macropus giganteus*), swamp wallabies (*Wallabia bicolor*), and koalas (*Phascolarctos cinereus*) are quite common. Koalas spend much of the day sleeping, wedged firmly in the crook of a tree, their spines cushioned by a special pad of insulating fur along their backs.

The koala's apparent lethargy is an essential part of coping with the rather narrow niche it occupies in the natural order of things. It is a small, tree-dwelling mammal with a diet low in nutrients but high in indigestible and often toxic compounds.

The relatively small size of the koala means it has problems maintaining a stable temperature relative to the environment; the tree-dwelling habit means its size must *remain* small or it will be too heavy to climb out on slender branches to reach the youngest, most nutritious leaves; while the toxins necessitate a large liver, which adds to the animal's body weight.

Faced with such a restricted lifestyle, the koala had no choice but to evolve as a seemingly lazy creature with a low level of activity which means it needs to eat less food. In return, it is able to exploit a habitat and food source where it has few competitors.

A matter of aspect

In much of the hill country, there is a dramatic contrast between the hot, dry, northern side of the hills and the cooler, southern side. Nowhere is this better seen than in Kinglake National Park (11 430 hectares), which straddles the hills about 50 kilometres due north of Melbourne (see pp. 96–103).

On the northern slopes, the vegetation is stunted with rough-barked, narrow-leaved peppermint (*Eucalyptus radiata*) and messmate stringybark (*E. obliqua*) providing a sparse shade over colourful shrubs and smaller plants, while on the southern side are deep, shady tree-fern gullies.

On the moister southern side, the eucalypts are tall and straight, often with smooth, white bark, and the gullies frequently ring with the call of the lyrebird (*Menura novaehollandiae*). In the Cathedral Range State Park (3577 hectares), further north, one area has become known as the 'farmyard' because of the skill of the local lyrebirds at imitating the sounds of the farm animals in the valley below.

Deep down amongst the rocks and the leaf litter of the moist forests, there is a constant bustle of life as hundreds of different kinds of creeping and crawling insects and reptiles search for their daily sustenance. The forests harbour two particularly fascinating groups of animals. One of these is the peripatids, which few people have ever heard of, while the other, the leeches, are a subject of almost universal loathing.

The peripatids are small, caterpillar-

SEASONAL CONTRASTS Whipstick mallee — probably so named because bullock drivers used the thin stems as whips — is a mix of blue, green and bull mallee trees.

A STICKY END A cricket falls victim to the sticky, ensnaring threads cast by a peripatid.

like animals — there are several genera — which live among the moist, ground-level vegetation. They come into the category of 'missing links' because they have some worm-like and some insect-like characteristics, not to mention a bizarre set of courting rituals all of their own.

The leeches, on the other hand, are firmly allied with the common earthworm, and are superbly adapted to their bloodthirsty lifestyle. The anaesthetic they inject as they bite through the skin of their unfortunate host is so effective that the actual bite is seldom felt.

The hotter, northern slopes are prone to outbreaks of fire, and there are few more dramatic — or encouraging — sights in the bush than an area of regeneration after a bushfire, particularly if there are grass trees (*Xanthorrhoea*) present.

A few short months after fire, each blackened grass tree sends up a new tuft of fresh, green leaves topped by a spectacular flowering stalk up to two metres in length. The stalks bear aloft

a mass of small, creamy flowers which attract a variety of birds and insects.

A profusion of small plants racing to flower and seed — including some that may not have been seen in the area for many years — quickly cover the ground within a few weeks of a fire. This is particularly true of the ground orchids, many of which form rich carpets of colour after fire.

The timing of fire is often important — naturally occurring fires generally happen in autumn, after the summer heat has dried out the bush and many plants are dormant and better able to resist the onslaught of the heat. Deliberately lit, fuel-reduction fires are sometimes started in spring and so destroy any new growth before the plants have had time to grow new underground storage tubers, or to flower and set seed.

In some areas, such as the Whipstick State Park, the poor soils produce a profusion of colour each spring, almost regardless of what has gone before — be it fire, flood or drought.

Whipstick State Park and the nearby Kamarooka State Park (6300 hectares) are worth two annual visits: one at the end of a long, dry summer when the ground is parched and the vegetation appears to be barely holding its own against the heat and dryness, and another in spring, when winter rains have brought the whole place to life with a bewildering array of refreshed plant and animal life.

The name 'whipstick' comes from

the 'whippy', long, flexible stems that grow on the small, multi-stemmed mallee eucalypts which grow here, and which have been harvested for many years as a rich source of eucalyptus oil. Isolation from other similar vegetation has resulted in endemic species found nowhere else.

Australia Felix

Much of the western part of Victoria's hill country lies within or adjacent to the 'Australia Felix' region, named by Major Thomas Mitchell in 1836 because of his delight in coming across such a relatively felicitous landscape. Mitchell was attempting to trace the course of the Murray River south from the Murrumbidgee and his explorations had taken him through a parched, dry countryside before he reached the hills.

Certainly Australia Felix was in Mitchell's words, 'too inviting to be left unexplored', and it proved too inviting to be left uncleared. National parks and other protected lands in this part of Victoria — the only places without an agricultural future — are those areas, such as Mount Arapiles, the Grampians and Black Range, where the land developed such an incline that it was, in the words of one observer 'too steep to graze, too rocky to plough'.

AUSTRALIA FELIX This view from Mount Arapiles was first seen by Major Thomas Mitchell in July 1836. The broad plains of the Wimmera are now mostly farmland.

Early European observers, such as Sir Joseph Banks, saw a great sameness about the 'bush'. They saw vast, open forests with seemingly endless eucalypts stretching away into a blue haze. The early settlers were more hard-headed and soon came to appreciate the virtues of these forests; they valued the different timbers yielded by the versatile eucalyptus genus.

Most prized of all were the towering trunks of those monarchs of the higher, wetter high country, the mountain ash and the alpine ash (*Eucalyptus regnans, E. delegatensis*). The majestic mountain ash, with its clean, white trunk growing straight upwards for up to one hundred metres, is the dominant tree of the forest and its scientific name, derived from the Latin verb *regnare*, meaning to rule, seems more than appropriate.

Another popular timber is the messmate stringybark (*E. obliqua*), a tree of the lower hill country, which when growing in deep, moist soil produces a timber which is widely used for building and furniture. Most of the lowland eucalypts, such as stringybark, boxes, and peppermints, are more twisted and variable in their growth and so are less useful in carpentry.

The exceptions to the rule are the three lowland eucalypts which yield some of the hardest and most durable timber known. The timber of the river red gum, and the red and white ironbarks is ideal for fence posts, power poles and railway sleepers. These dense hardwoods were once much in demand for firewood and charcoal burning, especially during wartime when motor cars were run on charcoal burners.

The river red gum, with its huge, gnarled and twisted limbs, often with many hollows which provide nesting sites, is remarkably tolerant of flooding, though even it cannot withstand permanent inundation. There are many man-made lakes, where the tree's bleached remains reach up from the water.

A number of these sought-after, hill-country timbers are found in areas such as the Grampians, and the Kinglake and Cathedral Range where there is a wide range of soils and habitats. In some of these forests, reminders of the timber-cutting days can still be found, in the form of rusting machinery, or in names such as Homestead Road, in the Victoria Valley in the Grampians. This marks the site of a short-lived settlement established in the 1890s to try to provide a new life for the poor of Melbourne.

BONNIE HIGHLANDS On a misty winter's day, the view from Boroka Lookout – towards the valley of Halls Gap – illustrates why Major Thomas Mitchell named the Grampians after a Scottish range.

In recent years, there has been increasing concern about the clear-felling of forests and the destruction of habitats that results, particularly for the many birds and small marsupials which require hollows for shelter and breeding. One of these animals, Leadbeater's possum (*Gymnobelideus leadbeateri*), is a tiny gliding possum which was thought to be extinct until 1961.

The possum, which has since been found in Victoria's central highland forests, lives in the eucalypt canopy, and faces a renewed threat as logging roads carve its habitat into blocks.

Not only does this quiet, shy animal require mature trees for nesting, but it must have a varied food supply of appropriate insects, along with the fruit of the wattle gum.

Reverting to nature

On the more optimistic side, Victoria has a Flora and Fauna Guarantee Act under which habitats can be protected and which can be invoked where a species is under threat. In some places, such as Gellibrand Hill State Park (658 hectares) and Organ Pipes National Park (85 hectares) the native vegetation is reasserting itself as former farmland is taken over and managed as conservation areas.

In the Organ Pipes Park, the Victorian National Parks Service and the Friends of Organ Pipes National Park have wrought an extraordinary transformation, turning a landscape containing almost every weed known in Victoria into a park in which the native vegetation is becoming re-established.

Such revegetation projects are inevitably slow and time-consuming. First, the seed for propagating material must be gathered from the remaining plants in the area and germinated and grown in 'captivity' until it is big enough to plant in the wild. This is often a challenge in itself, especially when little is known about germination and growth requirements.

When the young plants are ready, they must be planted in a position which recreates, as close as possible, the original vegetation associations. This is painstaking work involving old photographs, field naturalists' records, early explorers' maps and whatever other evidence can be found. Planting in the bush also involves careful protection from weeds and animals.

The most telling seal of approval for all this dedicated work has come from the many different native birds which have now moved back into these revegetated areas. ☐

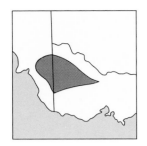

The many-stemmed mallee, so typical of a large part of western Victoria that its name was bestowed on the region, shares its semi-arid environment with the grain crops of modern agriculture

Paddocks and parks all the way to the sunset

Mallee is an Aboriginal word used to describe the shrubby eucalypts which grow over much of inland Australia. Both noun and adjective, it lends its name not only to the shrub but also to the large part of southern Australia where the plant grows.

Much of the mallee country has been cleared of the trees for which it is named, and millions of hectares of wheatfields and grazing land — still retaining the regional name — stretch across the flat plains as far as the eye can see. While the mallee land worth farming has long been under the plough, there are large tracts of typical mallee scrub protected in national parks, most notably Little Desert and Wyperfeld in Victoria and Ngarkat and Billiatt in South Australia.

Mallee country is typically flat and semi-arid, with rainfall averaging from 300 to 400 millimetres per annum, though, ironically, parts of the Little Desert are wetter. In much of the agricultural area, nature has been simplified to earth, sky and crop, all of them vast.

The mallee flora has been banished from the wheatfields and cannot be re-created; sunsets and moonrises are spectacular on these stark, flat landscapes of soil and wheat. Where cattle graze in the remaining pockets of mallee scrubland, there is almost no regeneration, so that the substantial areas of the mallee's natural ecology which remain intact are usually within the parks. Mallee eucalypts have a large, underground lignotuber which is the famous mallee root that has burned in most Victorian fireplaces. If the tree's multiple stems are broken or burnt, they regenerate from the lignotuber. This explains why large stands of mallee eucalypts are often of such an even height: having been destroyed by a bushfire, they regenerate evenly.

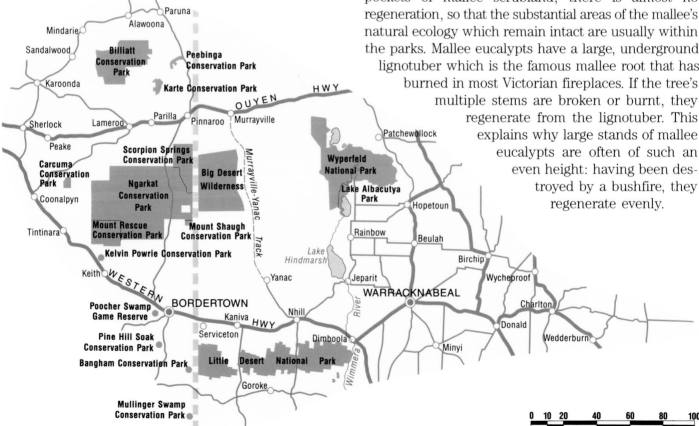

SUNSET COUNTRY The sandy Murrayville-Yanac track — winding through many kilometres of unfarmed mallee woodland in the Big Desert wilderness, north of Yanac — is a welcome respite from cultivation in the country's most intensively farmed state.

Mallees — there are several species — are low-growing, generally reaching between two and eight metres in height, depending upon age.

Although mallee eucalypts are the dominant vegetation of the area, they may be absent in grassy plains and heathlands, woodlands, sandy dunes and swales, all of these having different associated flora but still described as mallee country.

Winter and spring are the best months to visit the mallee, as high temperatures and lack of surface water make it a hazardous place for travellers in summer. In times past, Aboriginal tribes who ventured into the mallee in summer relied on the root of the oil mallee (*Eucalyptus oleosa*) for water.

'Desert' of wildflowers

Contrary to its name, Little Desert National Park (132 000 hectares), in Victoria, does not contain a desert, having an average annual rainfall of 400 millimetres, and much more in some parts of the park.

Variations in physiography, soil and rainfall produce a diversity of habitat, from low heath in the dry eastern section of the park to stands of yellow gum (*Eucalyptus leucoxylon*) on sandy clay in the swales of the west. On deeper sands, there are large areas of brown stringybark (*E. baxteri*) and coarse, open scrub.

Where the sandstone ridges are close to the surface, there are stands of mallee eucalypts and broombush (*Melaleuca uncinata*). In some swales and along the Wimmera River, there are stands of river red gum (*E. camaldulensis*) and black box (*E. largiflorens*). Mallee honey-myrtle (*M. neglecta*) is found around some claypans.

The Little Desert is renowned for its wildflowers, which bloom from mid-August until October, or as soon as the warm spring weather arrives. Colourful orchids of many species appear in profusion, though some species depend upon a particular seasonal prompting to produce of their best. Red beaks (*Lyperanthus nigricans*), for example, will flower dramatically the first year after a bushfire.

DESERT IN NAME In spring, the mallee 'desert' blooms as a bounty of wildflowers erupts almost overnight, attracting more than 200 species of native birds in the Wyperfeld National Park alone.

Other colours are found in the blue of tinsel lily (*Calectasia cyanea*), the bright white of common heath (*Epacris impressa*) and coastal tea tree (*Leptospermum laevigatum*), the gold of desert banksia (*Banksia ornata*), the pink of fringe myrtle (*Calytrix*), the red of flame heath (*Astroloma conostephioides*) and the yellow of guinea flowers (*Hibbertia*). These are just a few of the more common plants of the park's 670 species, representing about one-fifth of Victoria's plants.

Birdlife is similarly varied, with 218 species recorded, of which the malleefowl (*Leipoa ocellata*) is particularly well known. This bird is common to all the reserved areas, though its numbers appear to be dwindling.

The male malleefowl builds an incubation mound which acts like a compost heap to warm the female's eggs. Throughout the incubation period, he stands guard, and skilfully opens and closes the mound to maintain the correct temperature.

The female usually lays 15-20 eggs, of which as few as two, or even one, may reach maturity, since the eggs must survive the threat of foxes and the chicks must be strong enough to scratch their way to the surface through perhaps a metre of debris. Those that make it wander off into the scrub to grow up alone, so it is little wonder that when they mate they do so for life.

Little Desert is home to at least 23 species of honey-eaters, while other characteristic birds include the variegated fairy-wren (*Malurus lamberti*), the rufous calamanthus (*Calamanthus campestris*) and the spotted nightjar (*Caprimulgus argus*). The barking owl (*Ninox connivens*) gives vent to a quite horrific scream if it is disturbed during the day.

Among the mammals, echidnas (*Tachyglossus aculeatus*) and western grey kangaroos (*Macropus fuliginosus*) are widespread throughout the mallee. The western pygmy possum (*Cercartetus concinnus*) is occasionally found in disused birds' nests, while above the trees, the white-striped mastiff bat (*Tadarida australis*) — the largest insect-eating bat in Victoria, with a wingspan of about 40 centimetres — can be seen wheeling above the tree-tops in search of a meal.

The wide wilderness

A planned expansion of the 100 000-hectare Wyperfeld National Park by a further 218 690 hectares, would connect it with Big Desert Wilderness and Ngarkat Conservation Park in an almost unbroken 700 000 hectares of mallee parkland. This huge area of reserved land would be some 170 kilometres in length, from Dimboola in Victoria to near Tintinara in South Australia.

Much of this area, especially the Big Desert, is true wilderness — untracked, ungrazed, undisturbed by European activity. It has a sense of timelessness.

Wyperfeld is much loved by bushwalkers, field naturalists and bird watchers. Its landscape combines mallee eucalypt, slender pine (*Callitris preissii*), buloke (*Alloacasuarina luehmannii*), river red gum (*E. camaldulenses*) and black box (*E. largiflorens*). Emus and western grey kangaroos are unavoidable.

Pink cockatoos (*Cacatua leadbeateri*) are among the park's more

LIFE OF TOIL The male malleefowl works devotedly to maintain his mound.

FAMILY TIES After leaving the nest, young pink cockatoos remain with their parents as a family.

HAPPY ENDING After being driven to the point of extinction in the 1950s, malleefowls now flourish in the many-trunked forests of the Little Desert, thanks to special breeding programmes.

ostentatious creatures and adopt a modest, discreet manner only when entering or leaving their nesting hollows. The yellow and black regent parrot (*Polytelis anthopeplus*) is easily seen and contrasts with the pure blue of the splendid fairy wren (*Malurus splendens*).

Wyperfeld does not have the dramatic flowering of the Little Desert, being further north and containing fewer species of wildflowers. But there are grevilleas and riceflowers (*Pimelea*) and, beneath the stems of azure daisy-bush (*Olearis rudis*) shelter greenhoods (*Pterostylis*) and spider orchids (*Caladenia*), while rounded noon-flower or pigface (*Disphyma australe*) grows in open, sunny positions.

There are also heath-myrtles (*Micromyrtus*), the yellow flowers of grey wattles (*Acacia brachybotrya*) and the cream or white of the mallee eucalypt.

Sandy sanctuaries

The Big Desert wilderness is 113 500 hectares of infertile, often white sand, sometimes formed into large, irregular dunes, swales and plains. There is no way to drive in. Access is from the Murrayville-Yanac track and involves a five-kilometre walk across a protective strip of public land.

Vegetation is mainly heathland which may have a mallee overstorey and a variety of shrubs such as desert banksia (*Banksia ornata*), mallee pine (*Callitris preissii*), she-oak (*Allocasuarina*), coastal tea trees (*Leptospermum laevigatum*) and broombush (*Melaleuca uncinata*).

Bird species number fewer than 100, less than half the number recorded in Wyperfeld, since those depending upon permanent, open water are absent. The Big Desert is considered the best area in Victoria for reptiles, with over 50 species being recorded.

West of the border, Ngarkat Conservation Park and adjoining parks cover 270 192 hectares of low heath and mallee canopy which spreads across undulating sandhills. Aborigines of the Ngarkat tribe once ranged the area, hunting the kangaroos and brush-tailed bettongs (*Bettongia penicillata*). They complemented this diet with seed capsules gathered from the common nardoo fern (*Marsilea drummondii*) and quandong fruits (*Santalum acuminatum*).

In the heathland, desert banksia is dominant but there are stands of dwarf she-oak (*Allocasuarina pusilla*) and

FIRE-RESISTANT Dunes support many scrubby plants which regenerate after fire.

NECTAR-RICH Honeyeaters and lorikeets thrive on the nectar produced by desert banksias.

TYPICAL MALLEE The pointed, or red mallee blooms profusely in spring and summer.

broombush (*Melaleuca uncinata*). Near soaks, larger eucalypts such as brown stringybark (*E. baxteri*), manna gum (*E. viminalis*) and *Eucalyptus leucoxylon* — which is called yellow gum in Victoria but blue gum in South Australia — may be found.

Billiatt Conservation Park, which covers more than 59 000 hectares in the northernmost part of the mallee, is another wilderness park; its sandy dunefields are without tracks and support a complex mosaic of heathland, broken by outbreaks of narrow-leaved red mallee (*Eucalyptus foecunda*), pointed mallee (*E. socialis*), and gooseberry mallee (*E. calycogona*) on flats.

On the dunes, ridge-fruited mallee (*E. incrassata*) is likely to dominate along with areas of broombush (*M. uncinata*), moonah (*M. lanceolata*), mallee pine (*Callitris preissii verrucosa*) and coast tea-tree (*Leptospermum laevigatum*).

Despite the inroads of agriculture, the future of the true mallee country, the land of little trees, seems assured in the region's many national parks.□

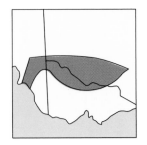

Waters from the alpine heights and outback Queensland come together as three mighty rivers and countless tributaries combine in the only truly well-watered part of the arid inland

A gathering of mighty rivers

By the time the waters of the Murray River drain into the sea, 2500 kilometres from their source, the river has collected the rainwater run-off from more than one-seventh of the continent.

The Murray and its three main tributaries, the Darling, Murrumbidgee and Lachlan Rivers, drain a huge basin stretching from central Queensland, all the way down to the northern half of Victoria. Over 80 per cent of the land surface of New South Wales drains into the Murray River system.

This vast Murray River catchment is an enormous area of land when compared with many other great river systems of the world, but its discharge to the sea is less than any other major river system.

The Indus, which drains a comparably large catchment in Pakistan, has a discharge to the sea ten times that of the Murray. Low rainfall, combined with a high evaporation rate, is the main reason for this small flow. In the last 50 years, the Murray's flow has been further reduced by the considerable amount of water that is taken out of the river and its tributaries for crop irrigation.

It is just as well that the river bed is mostly clay and relatively impermeable, for scientists have calculated that if the courses of either the Murray or Darling Rivers crossed a sandy terrain, so much of their already weak flow would be absorbed that no water would ever reach the sea.

The intricate system of interlocking channels, creeks, streams and rivers that makes up the Murray system is complex, ancient and, in its natural state, unpredictable. About 100 million years ago, a river that could well have been the ancestor of today's Murray River existed here.

No part of the modern Murray is that old, but the generally westward-flowing course of the rivers in the system has existed for millions of years. At times, the Murray River has been a raging torrent but today it is a gentle force on the landscape. Forty million years ago, as parts of the Great Dividing Range were being pushed skyward, the Murray would certainly have been as broad and swift-flowing as parts of the Amazon.

As sea levels rose and fell, the ancient Murray emptied into the sea at various localities. When the sea rose to lap shores in the vicinity of present-day Balranald, the Murray, Murrumbidgee and Darling drained separately into the ocean.

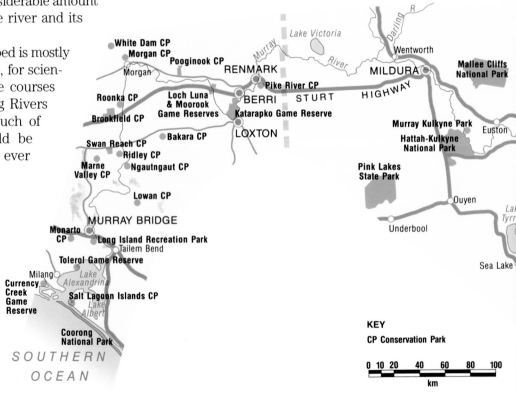

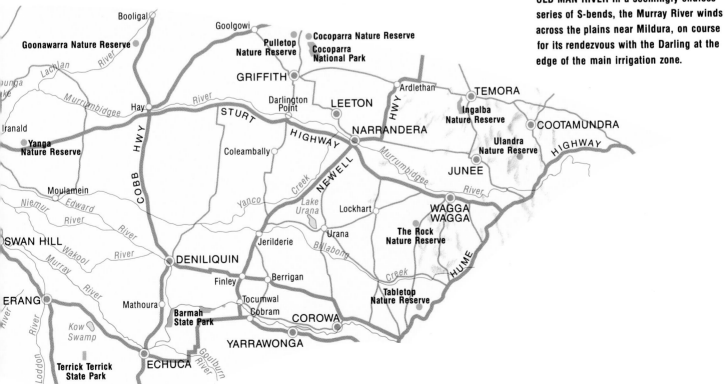

OLD MAN RIVER In a seemingly endless
series of S-bends, the Murray River winds
across the plains near Mildura, on course
for its rendezvous with the Darling at the
edge of the main irrigation zone.

At other times, the common river mouth was at Renmark or Murray Bridge. When the sea retreated from beyond today's level to way below it, the mouth was hundreds of kilometres out to sea from the current mouth, on the edge of the continental shelf.

By the time the Murray River reaches Albury, the rush of water from the Snowy Mountains has quietened with the levelling out of the landscape, and the river adopts the pace it will maintain to the sea. It meanders across the flat, dry plains of the eastern Riverina in a shallow channel cut into the alluvial deposits that have accumulated from the gradual erosion of the Eastern Highlands.

Forty kilometres north of Griffith, the unfarmed, unirrigated Riverina is on view in the Cocoparra National Park (see also pp. 134–143). The total area of reserved land within the hills and dales of the low Cocoparra Range is over 13 000 hectares. This range rises 350 metres above the flat plains of the rich Riverina district.

The range is a good example of the geological formation known as a 'hogsback'. Layers of rock over 400 million years old rise gently from the plain on one side, to be cut back at the range top by an escarpment which then falls to the plain on the same gradient on the opposite side. This conglomerate and sandstone formation has been weathered into gullies and gorges.

ROCKY RIVERINA The Riverina is renowned for its productive farming country but it would be a brave farmer who attempted to tame the rugged Cocoparra Ranges.

INFANT MURRAY The Murray takes shape as it runs in a northerly direction through the foothills of the Snowy Mountains with more than 2000 kilometres to go before it meets the sea.

The first European explorer to see this region, John Oxley, was not inspired by the country he travelled through. On his 1817 expedition, he noted '...these deserts, abandoned as they seem by every living creature capable of getting out of them'.

The cliff faces of the hogsback provide excellent nesting sites for eagles, hawks and falcons. The low ridges of the park and reserve are covered in dry eucalypt woodlands and the wide, flat valleys support dense stands of cypress pine forest.

The forests give daytime cover to large numbers of grey kangaroos. In spring, the woodlands and creek margins are a blaze of colour with bluebells (*Wahlenbergia*), Australian bugles (*Ajuga australis*), garland lilies (*Calostemma purpureum*) and a wide variety of wattles.

Large flocks of honeyeaters and parrots nest in the Cocoparra National Park and at least 150 species of birds have been recorded there. Most picnic and camping sites in the park are reached from the Witton Stock Route which marks the western side of the park. This route was first established in the late nineteenth century by Cobb & Co as part of its coach route from Melbourne to Queensland.

Patches of mallee

Another reserve — and one of some scientific importance — is also located just north of Griffith. Only 145 hectares in area, the Pulletop Nature Reserve is a patch of mallee surrounded by a sea of wheat farms.

Originally an uncleared 'back paddock' on an otherwise fully developed farm, it was left in its natural state for the use of malleefowls (*Leipoa ocellata*). This act of foresight, in the 1950s, resulted in scientific research being conducted on the birds for the first time. The reserve is now also home to dozens of species of rare inland birds and reptiles.

Thirty-five kilometres south of Wagga Wagga, the Rock Nature Reserve and its surrounding bushland encompass a stony fold of volcanic rock. The cliffs, and the grey and white box (*Eucalyptus microcarpa, E. albens*) forests at their feet, are a sanctuary for a variety of birds including many honeyeaters, thornbills (*Acanthiza*) and two birds of prey, the Australian hobby (*Falco longipennis*) and the endangered peregrine falcon (*F. peregrinus*).

Near Mathoura, the main course of

TOGETHER AT LAST The Murray and Darling — and Tuckers Creek, in the foreground — finally blend together as they flow past Wentworth.

PARROT COUNTRY As its name suggests, the mulga parrot inhabits the Murray's drier reaches.

the Murray turns sharply south, while a branch river, the Edward River, heads north. Anabranches — smaller rivers that break away from the main stream, only to rejoin the parent river further along its course — are not uncommon along the Murray and Darling. The Darling actually divides into two channels south of Menindee, so that it joins the Murray at two separate points, some 30 kilometres apart.

The Edward River is one of many anabranches along the Murray's course. Both continue on their separate ways, turning west again at Deniliquin in the north and Echuca in the south.

Upstream of Euston, the Edward and Murray Rivers eventually rejoin not far from the point where the Murrumbidgee River also flows generously into the larger river. Here the Murray, invigorated and strengthened by the contributions of its tributaries, waters the rich irrigation lands of northern Victoria's Sunraysia district, centred on Mildura.

Fruits of the semi-desert

The relatively large rivers of the continent's south-east are the arteries which provide the water for some of the world's largest dry-land irrigation developments. Irrigated lands are scattered along the Murray, the Murrumbidgee, the Lachlan and the Darling, from the Snowy Mountains to the far north-west of Victoria.

The Sunraysia region — its name is

TRANQUILITY The grey box trees of the Barmah Forest crowd the Murray's banks near Echuca.

derived from the trade name 'Sun-Raysed' — incorporates the far north-western corner of Victoria and adjacent parts of New South Wales. The region produces approximately 76 per cent of Victoria's dried fruits.

Further east, the Riverina district encompasses the lowlands of the Murray Basin, between the Lachlan River in the north and the north-west and the Murray in the south. The Murrumbidgee Irrigation Area has enabled intensive and varied cultivation to be conducted in this region.

Australia grows virtually all of its rice and apricots, 98 per cent of its dried grapes, and 70 per cent of its wine grapes, pears and peaches, on the Riverina plains. The region's wide range of temperatures means that many different crops can be grown successfully; rainfall ranges from only 200 to 400 millimetres a year and the clear skies that result bring about warm days and cool nights.

BUSH TO PADDOCK The irrigated paddocks near Robinvale, on the Victorian side of the Murray, are a dramatic contrast to the undisturbed bushland on the New South Wales side.

RURAL GEOMETRY One thousand kilometres before it joins the Murray, the Murrumbidgee River has transformed almost 3000 square kilometres of woodland into an ordered farming patchwork.

The winter cold encourages grapes, apples, pears, apricots and peaches to form. Late spring temperatures are high enough to germinate rice and cotton, while regular sunshine enables the large-scale growing of carrots, onions and other vegetables all year round. Such productivity is made possible by an extensive system of irrigation covering over one million hectares.

Silt deposited over thousands of years has covered the river plains with a variety of soils which suit a variety of crops; they vary in texture but are mainly red-brown loams. The ridge tops of ancient streams are covered with sand and surrounded by sandy loam, while the slopes carry clay loams and loams.

Between streams there is clay ranging from brown to grey. Rice is grown on these clay soils, while fruit and vegetables are planted on and near ridges, creating a landscape dominated by the regular geometry and contrasting colours of fields of crops.

Riverside reserves

Fifty kilometres south of Mildura, on the southern banks of the Murray, is the largest and most diverse region of natural bushland in the Murray basin. Hattah-Kulkyne National Park (48 000 hectares), and the adjacent Murray-Kulkyne Park (1550 hectares), incorporate majestic river red gum forests (*Eucalyptus camaldulensis*) which hug the river course, black box (*E. largiflorens*) woodlands which dot the flat

OLD MAN GUM There are few stretches of the Murray, or any other inland river for that matter, where there is not a group of mighty river red gums standing sentinel by the banks.

flood plains, and broad stretches of various scrubby mallee eucalypts well away from the river.

With this great diversity of habitats, the Hattah-Kulkyne National Park attracts an abundance of wildlife. More than 200 species of birds, including parrots, honeyeaters, numerous species of waterfowl, and pigeons, have been recorded.

Red and grey kangaroos (*Macropus rufus*, *M. giganteus*) are found in the park, the only place in Victoria where the red species occurs. The river and the park's lakes teem with golden perch (*Macquaria ambigua*), freshwater catfish (*Tandanus tandanus*) and European perch (*Perca fluvialis*).

A number of the lakes within the park, including Hattah, Arawak, Bulla and Nip Nip, are dependent on overflow from the Murray River during flood times to maintain their normal water levels. Weirs and other man-made controls on flooding — particularly large upstream water-storage dams — have interrupted the river's natural cycle of periodic flooding.

Special irrigation arrangements, such as the release of water from storage dams, are now required to ensure the survival of the lakes and their dependent plants and animals.

On the southern edge of what has come to be called the 'Sunset Country' of north-western Victoria, near the township of Underbool, an unusual group of salt lakes inspired the name of the park in which they are located. The Pink Lakes State Park covers more than 50 000 hectares of lakes, cypress pine forests and extensive sand dunes covered with mallee scrub.

During the summer months, the lakes are usually dry, their surfaces caked hard with thick, white salt. But in wintertime, water percolates up onto the lake beds and they take on the pink hue which gives the park its name.

This peculiar colour is the result of a pigment secreted by algae which, amazingly, bloom in the saline waters. These large bodies of pink-tinged water, with their various hues highlighted at dawn and dusk, are popular subjects for photography.

Upstream of Renmark, just inside the South Australian border, the Murray suddenly and unexpectedly disappears from sight as it forces its way into a shallow gorge. For the next 100 kilometres it flows between tall cliffs, sometimes more than 30 metres high.

RIGHT TURN Between Renmark and Murray Bridge the riverscape changes character as the hard limestone cliffs direct the Murray's course.

The gorge — in fact a deep channel cut into the surrounding plain — is the result of the river slowly but inexorably eroding a path through what geologists call the Pinnaroo Block. The 'block' is a large slab of limestone, sand and other marine deposits which was forced up into the river's path in prehistoric times.

The modern river has cut through the obstacle, its course through this dramatic landscape being much more rigid than on the plains, as it turns a sharp angle when it meets a limestone outcrop which has resisted the water's erosive power.

The river makes just such a sharp turn at Morgan, where it meets resistance in the form of the uplifted highlands of the Mount Lofty and Flinders Ranges. It continues through a more modest, gorge-like channel to Murray Bridge.

Finally, at Lake Alexandrina, the Murray River ends not with a bang but a whimper. Flowing along such a gentle gradient, and being tapped to the maximum for irrigation purposes, the river's strength is spent by the time it reaches the sea.

Without drama, the Murray spills gently into the vast, shallow waters of Lakes Alexandrina and Albert and slowly enters the Southern Ocean over a large, shifting sand-bar. Even at the last, the waters of the river are managed; before leaving the lakes they must pass through a series of barrages, constructed 50 years ago to prevent the ocean from backing up when the river level is low and causing flooding of the farmlands of the lower Murray Valley.

The river's red consort

The river red gum is the most widely distributed of all the eucalypts and certainly one of the best known due to its distinctive appearance. It is found in every mainland state and grows by rivers in all parts of the continent with the exception of the Nullarbor Plain, and along the eastern seaboard.

The river red gum's thickset, twisted form can reach up to 20 metres high, with some giants topping 45 metres. The tree's crown is wide and spreading, more often than not supported by a surprisingly short, thick trunk.

Trunks have been recorded up to four metres across but most of these particularly large trees, which must have been many centuries old, have long since been felled for their timber.

As its name suggests, the mature timber of the river red gum is red, with a fine texture and a waxy grain. Being hard, durable and resistant to termite attack, it is highly suitable for use as railway sleepers, flooring and fences.

UNTIDY END The Murray meanders aimlessly out of Lake Alexandrina to find an exit to the sea.

Beyond Albury, river red gums are the Murray's constant companions, growing everywhere along the banks. From Tocumwal and beyond, this narrow band widens and in places the river is flanked by a twenty-five-kilometre-wide forest of gums. The largest forests occur at Barmah, where there are 60 000 hectares of trees.

The river red gum requires regular flooding to ensure its survival. The periodic inundation of the forest floor induces seed to set and new seedlings to germinate, while permanent flooding — as sometimes occurs when damming forms artificial lakes — causes the trees to die.

Unfortunately, weirs and dams have changed the natural pattern of flooding of many of the Murray's red gum forests and regeneration of the trees is now not necessarily guaranteed. Just as water is released periodically for farm irrigation, so too do the river red gum forests require regulated inundation from water storages.

Of course it is not just the large trees that need the water. They are simply the most obvious part of the river-fringe environment.

Research at the Barmah State Forest has shown that a complex community of plants and animals not only survives periodic floods but actually requires regular inundation. Waterbirds, fish and other forms of aquatic life all require similar conditions to the water-loving gums which rely on the inland rivers to sustain them.

Forests on all sides

While the forest fringing the river from Albury to the sea is dominated by the river red gum, the plains surrounding the river have a fairly clear-cut sequence of dominant trees. Around Albury, the picturesque yellow box (*E. melliodora*) is the principal woodland tree, growing to a height of around 20 metres.

By the time the Murray reaches Echuca, with the rainfall decreasing and the river cutting through rich, red-brown soils, grey box (*E. microcarpa*) becomes the most common tree of the plains, with the attractive white cypress pine (*Cillitris glauca*) also becoming more and more evident.

Below Swan Hill, the riverlands are more often than not mallee shrublands, particularly near Boundary Bend, Red Cliffs, Merbein and Yelta. In the vicinity of the South Australian border, saltbush takes over.

These open landscapes consist of a variety of low, succulent shrubs valued commercially for sheep grazing. Despite their rather drab appearance, these semi-arid landscapes contain biological systems perfectly adapted to their harsh environment.

Within South Australia, mallee shrublands intermingle with red gum forests and saltbush plains until the flood plains surrounding Lake Alexandrina are reached. Here, where the ribbon of water which has dominated the countryside for 2500 kilometres loses its form and character in the anonymous waters of the lake, the hinterland is dominated by salt flats and melaleuca thickets.

Ribbon of life

The Murray River and its tributaries water a range of habitats which in turn support a vast number of birds and animals. Kangaroos and emus are ever present, and lazy koalas occasionally still inhabit the red gum forests. But it is the variety of birds and fish for which the region is best known. In fact, two related species of brilliantly coloured parrots are dependent on the riverine forests of the Murray and its tributaries for their breeding sites.

Superb parrots (*Polytelis swainsonii*) received their entirely worthy name because of their splendid appearance. The males are usually an iridescent green, with a bright yellow face and a splash of blood red at the throat.

The long, elegant form of these parrots was once frequently seen in the Riverina, along the Murray, and down into northern Victoria. But the superb parrot is now in decline.

SUPERB PLUMAGE The superb parrot still breeds around the Lachlan and Murrumbidgee.

Recent studies have found that the bird is concentrated at riverside sites along the Murrumbidgee between Wagga Wagga and Darlington Point. A small number of breeding sites are scattered from Cowra in the north to Barnham in the south.

DOWNSTREAM Mallees and other scrubby trees line the Murray beyond Mildura, where the tall cliffs bordering the river valley may be close at hand (opposite page) or on the horizon.

Too well watered: the unwanted salt of the riverland's earth

Over the past 70 years, water pumped from the Murray River and its tributaries has transformed vast areas of south-eastern Australia from semi-arid, eucalyptus woodlands into a patchwork of richly productive farmland producing a cornucopia of fruits and vegetables.

But in recent years the land has started to yield an unwanted and potentially devastating crop — salt. This side-effect of some of the world's most imaginative and audacious dry-land irrigation schemes has led to farmers, scientists and conservationists forming an alliance to reverse the effects of salinity.

Agricultural production in irrigation areas is worth about $450 million a year. Most of the water which makes the soil so productive is channelled from the Murray River, which is also used to supplement Adelaide's domestic water supply.

In dry years, Adelaide receives up to 80 per cent of its water from the Murray but the water is sometimes so salty that 'it is unfit for drinking by World Health Organisation standards. The Murray has always been a salty river, but, in contrast to natural fluctuations, its salinity level has risen dramatically in the last decade and stayed high.

Soil salinity usually develops in irrigation areas because of shallow water tables. The level of the water tables in the lower Murray has always been higher than the river level, so that aquifers have slowly seeped salty water into the river.

Scientists are unsure as to how the salt was originally deposited along the Murray basin. Much of the river valley was once submerged below the sea and some think the salt was left behind in marine limestones when the ocean retreated. Others argue that much of the salt comes from rainfall. The problem facing the scientists is how twentieth-century land use has accelerated the movement of salt up through the soil and into the river.

The main cause of the relatively new shallow water tables has been the replacement of the original tree of cover with shallow-rooted crops and pastures which use less water but require irrigation of the topsoil as the meagre rainfall quickly soaks beyond the reach of their short roots. The surplus irrigation moisture soaks down to the water table, which then rises.

The native trees of the Murray region, such as the mallee, have very powerful root systems which can sometimes penetrate to a depth of 18 metres. As they transpire, the trees draw up water from the depths and lose it to the atmosphere. Crops such as wheat have shallow roots and draw up very little water, while transpiring at a much lower rate than trees.

Such an increase in the amount of water in the water table causes it to rise in low-lying areas, all the way to the surface, killing off plant life (see photographs). The ground water in the Murray region is so much saltier than surface water — at a depth of five metres it is close to the salinity of sea water — that regular run-off into the river eventually makes the water unsuitable for irrigation or drinking.

State and federal authorities — including the CSIRO — have been concentrating their energies on this phenomenon for some years, and scientists are optimistic that the salt menace will eventually be controlled. Drainage channels that contain large amounts of salt are being redirected to evaporation ponds before they reach the river, and irrigation practices are constantly being improved. New water distribution systems and various ways of diluting salty water are being introduced. Annual salinity rates in a number of test sites have been substantially reduced.

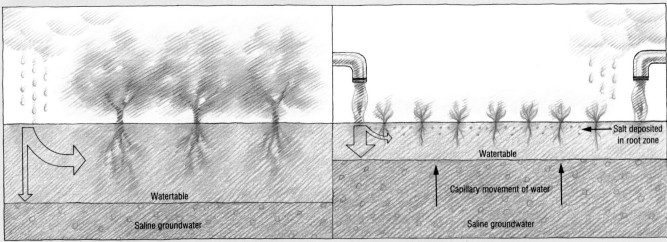

TOO MUCH OF A GOOD THING? In a natural environment most of the rainwater is taken up by roots and any excess filters down to the watertable (left). When the vegetation — particularly deep-rooted plants such as trees — is replaced by crops, and irrigation augments rainfall, much less water is absorbed by the crops' shallow roots, leaving the rest to swell the watertable. The movement of this excess water back up through the soil transfers salt to the surface, eventually killing plants and creating a saline zone where little grows (right).

The superb parrot prefers to nest in large hollows in old river red gums and the cause of its decline is believed to be the gradual disappearance of the old trees necessary for nesting. Added to this is the loss of its regular feeding grounds due to agricultural clearing and the disappearance of mature birds because of illegal trapping.

The superb parrot's close cousin, the gold and red regent parrot (*P. anthopeplus*), is also dependent on old river red gums for nesting and as a result it is also rare and declining in numbers. Regent parrots have two isolated races: one in the south-west of Western Australia and the other on the lower Murray around Mildura.

When not breeding, this beautiful long-tailed parrot spends the day feeding on the ground in farm country and in the mallee scrub. Flocks of up to 100 birds gather when a source of a favoured food, such as seeds or fruit, is discovered.

In August, matched pairs of birds return to the tall river forest along the Murray, Edward and Lower Darling Rivers. A hollow, usually 20 metres or more from the ground, is selected for the nest and four round, white eggs are laid on a deep bed of wood dust. Two months later, the fledgling parrots take to their wings.

Sharing the parrot's environment, if not its brilliant plumage, is the ground-dwelling malleefowl. Now largely confined to reserves and parks such as Pulletop near Griffith, Hattah-Kulkyne south of Mildura, and the Lowan Conservation Park (674 hectares) in South Australia, the malleefowl is one of Australia's most remarkable birds.

Toiling throughout the year, the male malleefowl maintains a huge mound of earth and leaves in which the female lays her eggs. This natural incubator may be up to five metres in diameter and over one metre high. The mound alternately insulates the eggs from the hot summer sun and warms them with the heat of fermentation when the weather is cool.

To maintain the optimum temperature of 33°C, the male malleefowl checks the temperature daily with his beak. Large amounts of sand and leaves are moved daily to keep the eggs at the correct temperature.

Another ground bird on its way to joining the national endangered species list is the quail-like and evocatively named, plains-wanderer (*Pedionomus torquatus*). The tiny bird is thought to exist now in only a few locations in south-eastern Australia. Its main habitat appears to be in the Riverina and a large research effort has been concentrated on a population in the grassy plains around Deniliquin.

Beneath the surface

The Murray River brings life not only to the countryside through which it runs; the waters themselves are full of life, despite their sometimes murky appearance. King of the Murray — albeit in greatly reduced numbers — is the giant Murray cod (*Maccullochella peeli*), Australia's largest and best known freshwater fish.

The cod, which can grow to almost two metres and weigh 100 kilograms, occurs only in the Murray-Darling river system. Silting of rivers, the introduction of foreign fish such as carp, and over-fishing mean that few large specimens are seen today.

In spring, as the river begins to rise with the alpine thaw, mature female cod deposit thousands of eggs amongst

IMPREGNABLE The fearsomely armoured Murray lobster stays in riverbed mud during drought.

submerged logs and stumps. In the warm water, the eggs soon hatch and the fry start on a steady diet of shell-fish, crayfish and other, smaller fish.

Over 20 other native freshwater fish inhabit the Murray, the most popular amongst anglers being the golden perch (*Macquarie ambigua*), silver perch (*Bidyanus bidyanus*) and river blackfish (*Gadopsis marmoratus*). Cat-fish (*Tandanus tandanus*) are also common in the middle and lower reaches of the river system.

Sharing the murky waters of the Murray and the Murrumbidgee Rivers with the Murray cod is an aquatic giant of another kind. The Murray cray is one of the largest freshwater cray-fish in the world, with heavyweights weighing in at over three kilograms.

The average crayfish measures about 20 to 30 centimetres long — about the length of a school ruler — and takes over five years to mature. Unlike yabbies, which are also common in Murray waters, the crays have ornately spined bodies and large, white claws.

Yabbies are usually active in the summer months but crays are most commonly on the move in the winter months when the females spawn. As with the Murray cod, overfishing has made them increasingly rare.

Three species of turtle frequent the waters of the Murray. The long-necked or common snake-necked turtle (*Chelodina longicollis*) is the most widespread but the Macquarie or short-necked turtle (*Emydura macquarii*) is also common. Both of these are outdone by the broad-shelled turtle (*Chelodina expansa*), weighing in at ten kilograms and with a length of about 80 centimetres. ☐

RIVER RESIDENT The broad-shelled turtle ranges from central Queensland to South Australia.

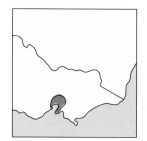

From its founding at the very head of Port Phillip Bay, Melbourne has spread to the ranges in the north and the east and along the peninsula to the south, but the city's focal point remains the broad waters, shores and islands of its blue bay

A bay city, close to nature

Since it was founded in 1835 where the Yarra River spills into Port Phillip Bay, Melbourne has gradually sprawled from the river's banks to cover more than 6100 square kilometres. Such unfettered expansion, proof of a thriving, successful city, and necessary in order to accommodate a population that has passed the three million mark, has, inevitably, had a detrimental effect on the environment of the bay and its surrounds.

In the face of a constantly growing population centre, nature has been left besieged. Victoria's animal emblem, Leadbeater's possum (*Gymnobelideus leadbeateri*), and its bird emblem, the helmeted honey-eater (*Lichenostomus leucotis*), are both endangered

species. But new attitudes and approaches have resulted in a heartening increase in the size and status of national parks and a surprising amount of wildlife can be found in urban surroundings.

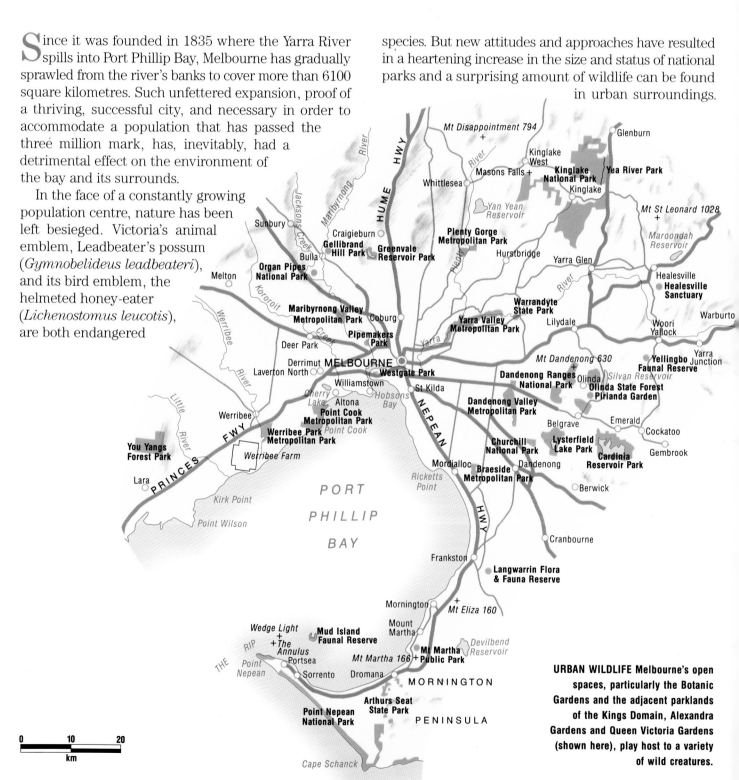

URBAN WILDLIFE Melbourne's open spaces, particularly the Botanic Gardens and the adjacent parklands of the Kings Domain, Alexandra Gardens and Queen Victoria Gardens (shown here), play host to a variety of wild creatures.

The most metropolitan of creatures are those that inhabit the Royal Botanic Gardens, a botanist's heaven containing more than 10 000 species of plants. The gardens' colony of rufous night herons (*Nycticorax caledonicus*) is believed to have existed there before the gardens were laid out. The short-finned eels (*Anguilla australis*) in its largest lake are plump and very easily observed. Like all the eels of the coastal waters of south-eastern Australia, they come from the Coral Sea as tiny creatures and will eventually obey their overpowering instincts and make the heroic return swim to spawn and die in tropical waters.

PLAYING POSSUM Leadbeater's possum was not sighted for fifty years and is still seldom seen.

PEACEFUL COEXISTENCE The sacred ibis, nothing if not adaptable, builds nests in man-made wetlands near the busy Westgate Bridge.

Long-necked tortoises (*Chelodina longicollis*), many with algae-covered shells the size of a dinner plate, sun themselves on the islands which they share with the wild waterfowl that use the lake as a refuge. Grey-headed flying-foxes (*Pteropus poliocephalus*), almost at their southernmost limit here, have established a noisy colony of up to a thousand bats and can be seen hanging from trees in the fern gully.

The feathered flyers of this inner city refuge have been recorded at more than 60 species. There are tawny frogmouths (*Podargus strigoides*), southern boobook owls (*Ninox boobook*) and the so-called 'powerful' owl (*Ninox strenua*), rare even in forest country, the sighting of which caused a ripple of excitement amongst bird-watchers.

Common ringtail and brushtail possums (*Pseudocheirus peregrinus*, *Trichosaurus vulpecula*) are still at home in many leafy suburbs, and brushtails are so plentiful in the Fitz-roy Gardens, behind Parliament House, that they have been turned into a tourist attraction. Across town, sacred and straw-necked ibises (*Threskiornis aethiopicus*, *T. spinicollis*) and pelicans (*Pelecanus conspicillatus*) now feed in newly established wetlands below the Westgate Bridge.

A thread of nature

Despite the hackneyed Sydney joke about the muddy colour of Melbourne's river, the Yarra is embroidered with many parks which help make it the link in a green corridor which threads through the suburbs and city for 193 kilometres before reaching the sea.

The Warrandyte State park (586 hectares) and Yarra Valley Metropolitan Park (450 hectares) are two of the many parks adjacent to the river which bring nature to the city and still contain some native plant and animal communities — despite the ravages of introduced plants, dogs, cats and fish.

Along the Yarra's banks some trees bearing Aboriginal markings still remain. River red gums (*Eucalyptus camaldulensis*), manna gum (*E. viminalis*), yellow box (*E. melliodora*) and red box (*E. polyanthemos*) are common, as are shrubs such as tree violet (*Hymenanthera dentata*), burgan (*Leptospermum phylicoides*), bottlebrush (*Callistemon*) and the sweet bursaria (*Bursaria spinosa*) which supports the Eltham copper butterfly (*Paralucia pyrodiscus lucida*).

Introduced fish such as brown trout (*Salmo trutta*) and European carp (*Cyprinus carpio*) have thrived in the river to the detriment of native fish, though loss of habitat is the main threat to the natives. At least nine native fish species still use the Yarra. Short-headed lampreys (*Mordacia mordax*) breed in the muddy river bed and their young migrate to sea only to return when they are sexually mature. River blackfish (*Gadopsis marmoratus*) have always

used the river, whereas Murray cod (*Maccullochella peeli*) and Macquarie perch (*Macquaria australasica*) were introduced from the inland rivers.

As the river is the major natural feature of the metropolitan area, it is not surprising that the majority of the city's wild creatures are those that live in it or along its banks. Aquatic animals and water birds abound.

Ten different kinds of frogs occur, all of which are hunted by fish, tortoises, water-rats, birds, snakes and bigger frogs. Reptiles found along the Yarra include long-necked tortoises, species of geckos and skinks, jacky lizards (*Amphibilorus muricatus*), eastern blue-tongued lizards (*Tiliqua scincoides*), the copperhead (*Austrelaps superbus*), eastern tiger (*Notechis scutatus*) and white-lipped (*Drysdalia coronoides*) snakes. Echidnas (*Tachyglossus aculeatus*) still live under the ground, possums above it, and wombats (*Vombatus ursinus*) still travel their ancestral routes in the wilder areas.

Birds, better able to escape the depredations of dogs, cats and humans than land animals, make the most visible use of the Yarra Valley and more than 180 species have been recorded there. Latham's snipe (*Gallinago hardwickii*) commute 10 000 kilometres to their breeding grounds in Japan to spend the northern winter in Australia.

Amazing as it may seem, platypuses still swim in the Yarra not far from the city; they have been there for about 60 million years and have certainly known better quality water. Koalas (*Phascolarctus cinereus*) are reported to be making their way back downstream from Warrandyte and there are various gliding possums and seven different species of bat living along the river.

City by the bay

Port Phillip Bay, stretching 60 kilometres north to south and 65 kilometres east to west, is Melbourne's major natural asset. The narrow entrance to the bay is notorious for its treacherous currents and is as dangerous as its name, 'the Rip', suggests. Beyond the Rip lies the great expanse of sheltered bay which is an important fishing and recreational area. There are many pleasant beaches strung along the eastern shore from the Yarra River mouth to Point Nepean.

This vast bay has a direct influence on Melbourne's weather as its large mass of relatively warm water affects passing cold fronts in all seasons, making forecasting difficult. Rainfall over

WILD YARRA The Yarra River, seen here upstream from its familiar city setting, is frequently bordered by park or bushland.

WHITE LIPS The white-lipped snake is venomous, but not dangerous to humans.

SWEET SURPRISE The summer flowers of the sweet bursaria conceal the sharp thorns which inspired its other common name, blackthorn.

greater Melbourne varies from about 500 millimetres annually in the western suburbs to more than 1300 millimetres in parts of the Dandenong Ranges to the east.

The bay is fished commercially for snapper (*Chrysophrys auratus*), King George whiting (*Sillaginodes punctata*) and eastern Australian salmon (*Arripis trutta*) though the biggest catch is of pilchards (*Sardinops neopilchardus*), which are used for pet food. Excessive dredging has reduced scallop beds to the point where they are no longer harvested and has altered the ecology of the bay floor by destroying some areas of seagrass — although a rich variety of seaweed grows at the southern end of the bay. Inevitably, there is pollution; this has led to high levels of mercury in some large sharks and there is a size limit on those sold for human consumption.

Friendly bottle-nosed dolphins (*Tursiops truncatus*) frequently accom-

pany the ferry which plies the waters of the Rip, between Queenscliff and Sorrento, just inside the entrance to the bay. Australian fur-seals (*Arctocephalus pusillus*) are a permanent fixture around the bases of some navigational lights and towers. They allow themselves to be scrutinised from boats and it is even possible to swim with them under the supervision of staff from the Marine Studies Centre based in Queenscliff. Closer to the city, water-rats (*Hydromys chrysogaster*) and little penguins (*Eudyptula minor*) nest and live in the rock cavities of the breakwater near St Kilda Pier.

Biologists at marine reserves such as Mud Island, Point Nepean, the Annulus and Point Cook are surveying the many species of small plants and animals within the bay which are still unnamed, but much work remains to be done. The foreshore and intertidal zones of the marine reserves are used by native plants and animals, while the

LIGHTHOUSE NURSERY Australasian gannets, which usually nest ashore, have adopted the timbered platforms of the Annulus and Wedge Lights as places to rear their chicks.

sky above the reserves provides a safe flyway for birds travelling between onshore environments around the bay.

The Mud Island Faunal Reserve, 56 hectares of saltmarsh scrub and seamarsh shallows, supports breeding colonies of Caspian terns (*Sterna caspia*), crested terns (*S. bergii*) and white-faced storm-petrels (*Pelagodroma marina*). All these suffer bravely in the face of noisy, unneighbourly competition from tens of thousands of quarrelsome silver gulls (*Larus novaehollandiae*), which find their food on Melbourne's rubbish tips and use the islands for roosting and breeding. Unfortunately, visiting humans often crush burrows and disturb nests.

The nearby Annulus and Wedge Lights are thought to be the only manmade structures where Australasian gannets (*Morus serrator*) nest. These handsome birds and their huge, fluffy, comical-looking chicks can be closely observed from boats. In their quest for fish to feed their voracious young, the adult birds make spectacular and often perpendicular dives into the sea.

Giant flocks of migratory waders use

the bay's western shores, from near Altona to the lakes, ponds and shoreline of the vast Werribee Sewage Farm. The farm's thousands of hectares, out of bounds to most humans, make it an ideal nesting place. The haven that it gives to migratory waders makes it of international significance. Common migrants are red-necked stints (*Calidris ruficollis*), eastern curlews (*Numenius madagascariensis*) and sharp-tailed sandpipers (*Calidris acuminata*) and, at times, even the rare orange-bellied parrot (*Neophema chrysogaster*) makes an appearance.

The western plains

On the flat basalt plains that lie to Melbourne's west, most former native grassland is now covered with pasture or introduced weed. Hard-edged artichoke thistle (*Cynara cardunculus*) and boxthorn (*Lycium ferocissimum*) are so predominant that in some areas it looks as though the region has been sown with dragon's teeth.

Yet, as elsewhere throughout the countryside, expanses of native vegetation survive heroically. This region is bordered on the extreme west by a brilliant burst of native greenery where the granite peaks of the You Yangs rise abruptly from the basalt. The You Yangs forest park covers 2025 hectares of mostly rocky hillsides clothed with manna gum (*E. viminalis*), red stringybark (*E. macrorhyncha*), long-leaved box (*E. goniocalyx*), blackwood (*Acacia melanoxylon*) and drooping sheoaks (*Allocasuarina verticillata*), with yellow and river red gums (*E. camaldulensis*) on the level ground.

Understorey bushes and grasses have been invaded by the prolific South African boneseed (*Chrysanthemoides monilifera*) which is able to produce 50 000 seeds on each plant. Despite this invasion of vigorous foreigners, more than 200 species of birds — about 30 per cent of all native birds — have been recorded here and kangaroos and koalas may also be seen.

The basalt plains are drained by a series of streams including the Werribee River, the Kororoit Creek and the Maribyrnong River. The Werribee River is still home to platypuses and water-rats while the hollows in the river red gums that line its banks offer nesting space to birds and mammals.

Several hundred hectares of native grassland at Derrimut and Laverton North are reserved for scientific research and here lives the endangered legless lizard known as *Demla inpar*,

A NATURAL EMBANKMENT The 'organ pipes' of Organ Pipes National Park have been revealed gradually by the erosive action of Jacksons Creek. The 'pipes' are a million-year-old lava deposit which cracked into regular columns as it cooled into basalt.

while around Cherry Lake the rare Altona skipper butterfly (*Hesperilla flavescens flavescens*) adds a decorative touch to the landscape.

The Organ Pipes National Park (85 hectares) on Jacksons Creek is named for a spectacular bank of basalt columns which stand regimented in correct organ-pipe order, tallest in the centre, shortest at either end, against a bank. Elsewhere, a pavement of what appears to be hexagonally jointed basalt tiles is actually the tops of columns that have been worn down to ground level. This park is a remarkable achievement of restoration, for its attractively wooded slopes and native grassland were once given over almost entirely to thistle and boxthorn. There are now 145 species of native plants in the park and some native creatures, such as sugar gliders, have been re-introduced.

To the brink of extinction and back again

The double-tailed orchid, the lilac and white flowers of which once peppered the Werribee Plains, is reappearing in the wild after being reduced to a lone colony of plants by a suburban railway line.

Scientists at the National Botanic Gardens in Canberra have devised a way of breeding the now rare orchid *(Diuris punctata albo-violacea)* in a 'porridge' mixture of oats and water. Dozens of species of orchids, threatened by 200 years of relentless collection by gardeners, and destruction of their habitat, may be saved by the same technique.

Paddocks of the spicily scented double-tailed orchid were recorded on the moist, grassy basalt plains that lie to the west of Melbourne by naturalists in the 1930s. But on such easily cleared, flat land, the orchid's habitat was soon taken over by agriculture. In the early 1980s, botanists discovered fifty of the by then rare plants, alongside a railway line in a suburb of Melbourne.

Specimens were taken to Canberra where the tiny orchid seeds were combined with a fungus which they require for successful germination. The seed was sown in the 'porridge' and infected with the fungus, which was extracted from the roots of an established orchid. Such plants may sprout in less than a month and can be planted in soil after six to nine months. Usually a specific fungus provides the sugars required for a specific orchid to develop, making the chance of such a relationship occurring in a small colony very slim.

TALL TIMBERS Second only to the Western Australian karri in size, the mountain ash of Victoria and Tasmania — seen here in the Dandenong Range — may soar to 90 metres.

Gellibrand Hill Park (658 hectares) is an oasis of native forest within earshot of traffic on the nearby highway; some of its river red gums are believed to be 600 years old. Wedge-tailed eagles (*Aquila audax*) soar overhead while brown falcons (*Falco berigora*) hover — still, but in motion — as they survey the ground for prey. Tree hollows are home to galahs (*Cacatua roseicapilla*), sulphur-crested cockatoos (*C. galerita*), crimson rosellas (*Platycercus elegans*), possums, jacky lizards (*Amphibolurus muricatus*) and six species of bats.

North by north-east

To the north, the broad, flat plain on which central Melbourne sits begins to undulate and sea level is left behind. Soon the foothills of the Great Dividing Range, where small-scale agriculture still rubs shoulders with the suburban fringe, make their appearance. Part of this fertile, red soil country has been reserved as a breathing space for the city dwellers to the south.

Kinglake National Park (11 430 hectares) is 65 kilometres north of Melbourne and contains at least 15 different species of eucalypt. The forest is a busy place, particularly at night, as its many inhabitants go about the bus-

WOMBELANO FALLS The Kinglake National Park is on an escarpment above the Melbourne plains.

iness of finding food. Dunnarts, antechinuses and bandicoots scurry amongst the undergrowth as possums, phascogales and gliders busy themselves in the treetops. The yellow-bellied glider (*Petaurus australis*) bites into the trunks or stems of eucalypts and feeds on the gum exuded by the tree.

Despite their reputation as shy, retiring creatures, superb lyrebirds (*Menura novaehollandiae*) are commonly seen and heard. These ground-dwellers are famous for the males' stately dancing and display, as well as for their remarkably accurate and sustained mimicry of other birds. They will allow close observation of their activities, especially in winter, when the males are bolder than usual as they search for a mate. Amongst the 90 species of birds here, are the grey currawongs (*Strepera versicolor*) and crimson rosellas (*Platycerus elegans*), which make a cheerful nuisance of themselves in the picnic ground at Masons Falls.

An urban retreat

Perhaps the most spectacular unsettled areas of natural bush near to Melbourne are those which are protected within the many reserves and parks of the Dandenong Ranges, a mere 30 kilometres east of the G.P.O.

In the Yellingbo Faunal Reserve (401 hectares), the last known colony of the helmeted honeyeater remains in a state of siege. Despite decades of concern and attempts to rehabilitate the species, its numbers have dropped from 300 birds in 1963 to around 40 — a phenomenon apparently due to the gradual shrinkage of the honeyeater's habitat.

Dandenong Ranges National Park (1920 hectares) lies almost due east of Melbourne and has been subjected to pressure from the city since the 1860s, despite being reinforced by the open spaces of the adjoining Olinda State Forest and the forest of Silvan Reservoir. When the winter cloud descends, and just the summits of Mounts Dandenong, Disappointment, Macedon and St Leonard show through, it would be easy to believe that this was part of a greater wilderness and not a vestige of the bush laid siege by suburbia.

Despite the territorial limitations, the forests of mountain ash (*Eucalyptus regnans*) in the Dandenongs are justly famous for their tall, spectacularly columnar appearance. Also spectacular amongst the thick understorey

of ferns are the rough and soft tree fern (*Cyathea australis, Dicksonia antarctica*), although there are 38 species of fern and fern-like plants recorded here.

Superb lyrebirds are often seen in the Sherbrooke Forest section of the Dandenong Ranges park, although numbers are declining due to the depredations of cats, dogs and foxes and the pressures applied by the human population. The clear mountain air often rings to the penetrating crack of the eastern whipbird (*Psophodes olivaceus*) and the powerful, single-

and wallabies and kangaroos have been reintroduced. In summer, green and golden bell frogs (*Litoria aurea*) can be seen basking in the sunshine on the banks of clear mountain streams.

At the southern limits of suburbia, Mount Martha, Mount Eliza and Arthurs Seat spring from the coastal plain as granite outcrops rising from bushland which is gradually giving way to housing. The summit of Arthurs Seat may be reached by a chairlift and there is a superb view of Port Phillip and Western Port Bays.

INTO THE STRAIT The tea-tree-covered slopes of Cape Schanck, thrusting into the wild waters of Bass Strait, mark the eastern extremity of the Point Nepean National Park.

note call of the appropriately named bell miner or bellbird (*Manorina melanophrys*).

Colourful springtime wildflower displays can be seen here. Introduced trees and flowering shrubs take full advantage of the deep soil and cool climate to add another dimension to these ranges. Rhododendrons and deciduous trees such as elm, oak and birch are juxtaposed with and sheltered by mountain ash and tree ferns. Many private gardens are open to the public in spring and autumn when the cultivated 'exotics' provide their best displays of colour.

Churchill National Park (193 hectares) is another important animal reserve where echidnas are common

The long peninsula guarding the eastern entrance to Port Phillip Bay is protected within Point Nepean National Park (2200 hectares) which includes most of the coastline from the point to Cape Schanck. The point itself is a warren of fortifications dating back to 1882 but despite these man-made intrusions, middens reveal the varied shellfish diet of the former Aboriginal inhabitants.

But it is the reefs and rock platforms around the tip of the peninsula, with the wealth of marine plants and animals they support, that make this area so significant. Unlike other reefs in the region, which have been plundered, and damaged by trampling feet, this marine reserve remains an unspoiled natural wonder. □

Broadly speaking, the continent's south-east corner provides the perfect balance for its counterpart in the west: another well-watered land of mountains, tall-timbered forests and fertile coastal plains

From the southernmost tip to the Snowy River

Gippsland is not difficult to isolate on the map, having been recognised as a distinct provincial and geographical entity for longer than most regions of Australia. This broad strip of forest and farm, taking in approximately half of Victoria's coastline, has borne its name since it was first traversed, by the Polish explorer Paul de Strzelecki, in the 1840s.

Strzelecki graciously named the region he had just crossed after the then Governor of the colony of New South Wales, George Gipps, whose domain extended to the rapidly expanding Port Phillip District. The margins of Gippsland received their final definition when the border between New South Wales and the new state of Victoria was established in 1851.

The border provides a neat cut-off line to the east, while to the north there are the ragged ranges of the Great Dividing Range and to the south, the cool, and often white-capped waters of the Tasman Sea. To the west, Gippsland peters out as town takes over from country in the gradual build-up to the urban region of greater Melbourne.

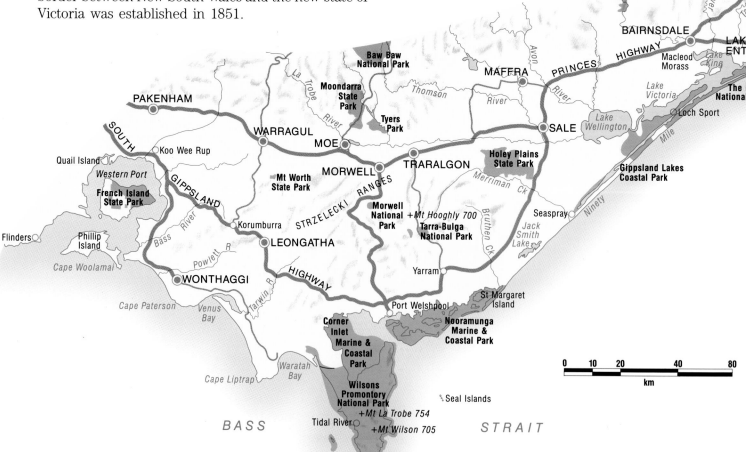

WILSONS PROMONTORY South East point is about half a kilometre short of being Australia's most southerly point; the honour goes to inaccessible South Point, four kilometres to the west.

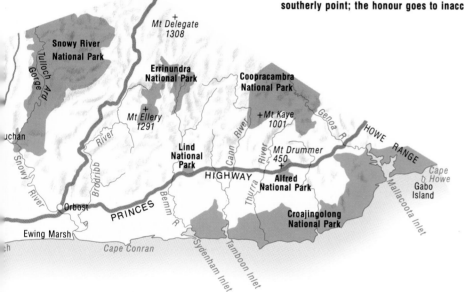

This long-settled, farming and coal-mining area encompasses the fertile river valleys flanking the southern limits of the Great Dividing Range. The narrow coastal plain is squeezed between mountain and sea in several places — particularly where the main range sweeps eastwards, and at its southern extremity, where the outlying Strzelecki Ranges reach for the very ramparts of Wilsons Promontory.

The Gippsland plain is part of the Gippsland basin which once extended all the way into Port Phillip Bay, before the major part of it was inundated by a rising sea about 10 000 years ago.

Behind Ninety Mile Beach, along the central Gippsland coast, the encroachment of the sea has been halted by a well-developed barrier of sand dunes which has been dissected into a series of barrier islands east of Corner Inlet. Further east, the dunes have dammed the waters of the La Trobe, Thomson, Avon, Mitchell and Tambo Rivers into a series of lakes which enters the sea through the opening of Lakes Entrance.

Although much of Gippsland is low-lying, the Strzelecki Ranges rise to 700 metres at Mount Hooghly, and on Wilsons Promontory, Mount La Trobe and Mount Wilson, at 754 and 705 metres respectively, provide observation posts for panoramic views out to Bass Strait.

To the north, along the margins of the Great Dividing Range, numerous peaks on spurs of the main range, such as Mount Kaye (1001 metres) and Mount Ellery (1291 metres), denote a more rugged and elevated terrain.

LAKES EXIT The approaches to the Reeve Channel — cut through the sweep of Ninety Mile Beach in 1889 to the maze of the Gippsland Lakes — are dotted with treacherous sand shoals.

Gippsland has a pleasant, fairly uniform climate, influenced by the proximity of Bass Strait but in landscape, vegetation and wildlife it is a highly diverse region mainly because of its long, narrow shape. Although the natural landscape is preserved in more than ten national parks, elsewhere the plants and animals of Gippsland have been displaced by agriculture and grazing.

After Melbourne had become an established settlement, the western half of Gippsland was subjected to intensive agricultural development, mining and logging in order to serve the needs of the growing metropolitan area. Apart from a few remote pockets in the Strzeleckis, Wilsons Promontory, the upper reaches of some rivers and isolated coastal islands, few natural areas of significant size were left undisturbed.

In the late 1800s, vast tracts of forest were cleared for dairying, and to the north of Koo-Wee-Rup a huge area of swampland was drained and converted to pasture. The cleared paddocks extend almost to Bairnsdale, with the only reminders of the original forest cover being the straggling corridors of eucalypts along roadsides or following the various watercourses.

Off the highway, in the foothills of the Dividing Range, some areas still carry a cover of native plants, although most are frequently burnt and have been disturbed by mining and logging activities.

A happier situation exists in the region's far north-western corner, where a proposed state park of 13 500 hectares will protect part of the Bunyip River catchment. Here, a mosaic of contrasting plant communities ranges from wet heaths through woodlands to wet eucalypt forest.

Two eucalypts, the white stringybark (*Eucalyptus globoidea*) and the yertchuk (*E. consideniana*), together with the southern sassafras (*Atherosperma moschatum*), are close to the western limits of their distribution here. Brickmakers sedge (*Gahnia grandis*), a tall cutting-grass growing along riverbanks, occurs in Victoria only in this area and a few places on Wilsons Promontory.

Also flanking rivers and streams is the striking gully grevillea (*Grevillea barklyana*), which is found nowhere else in the state. Its silky, pinkish-red flowers, crowded into a crested spike, contrast vividly with the velvety-white undersides of the large, pointed and

MODEST RANGE Despite their name, the Strzelecki Ranges rarely rise above 300 metres. Remnants of the original, cool rainforest remain in the Tarra-Bulga National Park.

NOT COMMON Large gully grevilleas grow only in the Bunyip River region.

HOLIDAY COAST The coastline of Croajingolong National Park, shown here near the entrance to Wingan Inlet, stretches for 100 kilometres south of the New South Wales border.

lobed leaves. The gully grevillea, which reaches up to a grand ten metres in height along Bunyip Creek, also occurs on the New South Wales south coast but there grows as a stunted coastal shrub.

Several pairs of the rare sooty owl (*Tyto tenebricosa*) live around the Bunyip River. The owl is a nocturnal predator of possums and gliders, and usually reveals its presence only by its territorial call — a loud, tremulous, drawn-out whistle like the sound of a falling bomb.

The lure of the coast

The South Gippsland Highway provides direct access from the south into the heart of Gippsland at Sale. En route it skirts the shores of Western Port, providing glimpses of the bay's islands, Quail, French and Phillip. These islands and Western Port itself are characterised by their fringing stands of grey mangroves (*Avicennia marina*), thought to be a relic from the time when this was a subtropical region.

The bay is a submerged plain with extensive shallows colonised by beds of the seagrass known as dwarf grasswrack (*Zostera muelleri*). The dead leaves of this seagrass together with those of the mangroves, provide basic nutrients for the bay's rich marine life. When exposed at low tide, the shallows become a focus for foraging flocks of wading birds and waterfowl.

About 40 species of migratory

FEEDING TIME Wading birds of all kinds flock to the productive tidal mudflats of Western Port.

wading birds from breeding grounds in northern Asia have been recorded in Western Port, one of the finest habitats for these birds in southern Australia. Great flocks of stints, sandpipers, knots (*Calidris*) and many others, probe the mud of exposed tidal flats.

At high tide, many of the waders and waterfowl retire to the broad expanses of saltmarshes which form an intermediate zone between the mangroves and dry land. The rich Western Port saltmarshes are the largest such marshes in southern Australia, extending up to a kilometre or more in width.

This muddy environment provides a habitat for birds such as the endangered orange-bellied parrot (*Neophema chrysogaster*) which seeks out the fruit of saltbushes, seablites and sea-heaths when it visits the area on winter migration from Tasmania. Below the surface of this deceptively bleak no-man's-land, the olive-brown, black-striped lizard known as the swamp skink (*Egernia coventryi*) is an uncommon creature which lives in burrows tunnelled into the bases of grass tussocks; sometimes it simply appropriates the homes of sand crabs.

The 8300-hectare French Island State Park takes in swamp forest, coastal scrub, heathlands and swamp sedgelands, which, although subjected to a history of burning and other human disturbance, remain much in their original state and rich in wildlife. Without a bridge to the mainland, human traffic and disturbance has been kept at a relatively low level.

A colony of long-nosed potoroos (*Potorous tridactylus*), one of the smallest of the kangaroos, lives in the French Island heaths, as does the rare brown- black- and white-streaked king quail (*Coturnix chinensis*).

Koalas were introduced to both French and Phillip Islands in the 1800s and flourished in the dry eucalypt forests. The thriving population has been used to re-introduce the animals to other parts of Victoria.

Phillip Island is perhaps best known for its breeding colony of the world's smallest penguin, the steely blue-plumaged little penguin (*Eudyptula minor*). The penguins have become the centre of a major tourist attraction — an evening 'penguin parade'. Each evening, people gather to watch the birds coming ashore in groups under

PINT SIZE The little penguin is the only penguin to make its base on the Australian mainland.

cover of darkness to enter their breeding burrows.

The young are in the burrows during spring and summer, which is the time of maximum activity for their parents, who bring catches of fish ashore. There are about 6000 burrows in the Phillip Island colony although recently bird numbers have dropped slightly due to their main feeding grounds, in Port Phillip Bay, being affected by over-fishing and pollution.

To the south-east, towards and beyond Wilsons Promontory, the coastal heathlands provide a habitat for two small, endangered mammals. The New Holland mouse (*Pseudomys novaehollandiae*), a native rodent of similar size and appearance to the introduced house mouse (*Mus musculus*), is known from a few localities on the western shore of Western Port.

Rediscovered near Sydney in 1967 after being presumed extinct, the New Holland mouse has been recorded from only a small number of sites throughout its range from northern New South Wales to Tasmania.

The other diminutive mammal is the swamp antechinus (*Antechinus minimus*), a similarly sized but quite unrelated marsupial, which preys on insects and other animals as large as lizards. Although not as rare as the New Holland mouse, it is restricted in its range on mainland Australia to swampy areas, mainly along the Victorian coastline. Both animals are threatened by the destruction of their most favoured habitats by frequent burning and the spread of residential development.

End of the continent

The granite bulk of Wilsons Promontory juts out into Bass Strait to define the southernmost tip of the Australian mainland. The promontory's ancient granite tors are of the same geological formation as the eastern Bass Strait islands and the peninsulas along Tasmania's east coast — all of them the last remnants of the land bridge which existed until about 12 000 years ago.

SAND BRIDGE Fierce currents and wild winds created the sandy neck known as the Yanakie Isthmus, which linked a granite island — Wilsons Promontory — to the mainland.

SUMMER SEASON Wilsons Promontory attracts so many visitors that campers have to book ahead during popular holiday periods.

Up until 4000 years ago, Wilsons Promontory itself was an island, before wind-blown and wave-washed sands created the low-lying Yanakie Isthmus. The former link with Tasmania is also reflected in the high number of plants and animals common to the island and to this southern extremity.

Much of the Yanakie Isthmus and all of the promontory, including the numerous rocks and islands off the coast, are included in the 59 000-hectare Wilsons Promontory National and Marine Parks and Marine Reserve. The strong maritime influence, high rainfall and a varied terrain result in vegetation of all types. There is dense, tough-leaved scrub on the upper slopes, wet eucalypt forest on the lower slopes and rainforest in sheltered gullies.

The promontory's mountain-side forests are dominated by eucalypts, with stands of rough-barked messmates (*Eucalyptus obliqua*) and smooth-barked southern blue gums (*E. globulus*) along ridges. Descending into the gullies, these are replaced by pale, smooth-barked mountain grey gums (*E. cypellocarpa*), fibrous-barked yellow stringybarks (*E. muellerana*) and

GULLY SCENE The lillypilly's camellia-like leaves add lushness to a eucalypt under-storey.

stands of the imposing, straight-trunked mountain ash (*E. regnans*).

In the rainforest gullies, the green luxuriance of the canopy is due almost entirely to one tree, the glossy-leaved lillypilly (*Acmena smithii*). The best example of these forests is found in Lilly Pilly Gully, to the north-west of Tidal River.

During summer and autumn, the lillypilly trees are festooned with cream-white flowers which are succeeded by crowded clusters of purplish-white berries. The national park represents the southern limit of the lillypilly as well as that of another rainforest tree, the indigo-fruited brush muttonwood (*Rapanea howittiana*).

109

Under the lillypilly canopy, the massed, spreading crowns of tree-ferns produce a second layer of greenery. Wilsons Promontory is rich in ferns with a greater density of these shade-loving plants than almost anywhere else in Victoria. In the most sheltered gullies, there are ferns upon ferns as delicate, epiphytic filmy-ferns, including the rare jungle bristle-fern (*Macroglena caudata*), cloak the hairy trunks of tall tree-ferns.

A branch range

To the north of Wilsons Promontory lie the Strzelecki Ranges, their low peaks, and plateaux cut by rivers and streams, reflecting the same history of prolonged erosion which has shaped their 'parent' range, the Great Divide. The lower slopes of the Strzeleckis were systematically cleared by early settlers and the upper slopes have been heavily logged.

Large tracts have been converted to plantations of introduced Monterey pines and the few tiny reserves in these mountains have been set aside in a last-ditch attempt to preserve a sample of the original vegetation cover.

Two small reserves — in the Tarra Valley and on the Bulga Plateau — with an area of only 1230 hectares, are nevertheless important because they contain the sole remaining, undisturbed remnants of the wet eucalypt

KING OF THE FOREST The mountain ash, which rules the temperate rainforests of the highlands, grows to 90 metres, rivalling the Western Australian karri as Australia's tallest tree.

NINETY MILE BEACH Even along Australia's sandy coastline, a beach 90 miles — or 140 kilometres — long is unusual. Along almost its entire length the beach protects a series of lakes and lagoons.

forests and cool temperate rainforests of these highlands. Here it is possible to imagine how early bushmen may have reacted to the towering old-growth forests, with their massive crowns of mountain ash towering over a dense, dark layer of dripping, moss-encrusted myrtle beech (*Nothofagus cunninghamii*) and disappearing into the mountain mist.

Tarra-Bulga National Park contains four of the state's five tree-fern species including the scarce slender tree-fern (*Cyathea cunninghamii*) and the rare skirted tree-fern (*C. marcescens*).

Descending into the wide valley of the La Trobe River, famous for its open-cut, brown coal mines, Moondarra State Park (6292 hectares), Tyers Park (1810 hectares) and Holey Plains (10 576) are state and regional parks which were established to protect remnant areas of native vegetation.

Animals of the La Trobe Valley area include the prehistoric-looking eastern water dragon (*Physignathus lesueurii*), with a toothed crest along its back and a brick-red underbelly, and the rare and beautifully marked giant burrowing frog (*Heleioporus australiacus*). The dark chocolate-brown, male giant burrowing frog gives a deep, reverberating, moaning call from its streamside burrow during the breeding season.

Eastwards, behind Ninety Mile Beach the Lakes National Park (2390 hectares) and the Gippsland Lakes Coastal Park (17 200 hectares) protect the fragile dune systems bordering Lakes Reeve, Victoria and King. These coastal lakes became tidal after being connected with the sea in 1889, and as a result cannot be regarded as fixed, static features of the landscape.

Both the Mitchell and Tambo Rivers have built extensive deltas into Lake King and barring further coastal erosion or sea-level rises, will eventually fill the lake. This has already occurred on a small scale with the formation of the

DWARF DRAGON The enigmatic Gippsland water dragon may grow to 50 centimetres long.

FERNS AND FALLS The well-watered valleys of the Tarra-Bulga National Park support tall forests and myriad species of ferns, such as those growing around the Cyathea Falls in Tarra Valley.

McLeod Morass at Bairnsdale and Ewing Marsh between Lake Tyers and the mouth of the Snowy River.

Inland from the Gippsland Lakes, on the Mitchell River, the Mitchell River National Park (11 900 hectares) contains the cave known as the Den of the Nargun. According to Aboriginal legend, the cave contains a creature called the 'nargun' which lies in wait to prey upon unwary passers-by.

Here the waters of Woolshed Creek have cut a deep, narrow, sheer-sided chasm through ancient ochre-red sandstone. Where it has seeped through the rock or dripped over ledges and the mouths of caves, the heavily mineralised water has produced massed groupings of limestone stalactites.

Beyond the river and its tributaries, on the drier upper slopes and ridges, there are dry eucalypt forests dominated by Gippsland blue gum (*Eucalyptus*

pseudoglobulus), red box (*E. polyanthemos*) and yellow box (*E. melliodora*), with occasional stands of glossy-leaved kurrajongs (*Brachychiton populneus*), recognisable in autumn and winter by their boat-shaped seed capsules. In the ravine of Woolshed Creek and its adjoining gorges, dense thickets of rainforest have developed.

Coastal corridor

Where the coastal plain becomes crowded in by mountains, east of Lakes Entrance, the climate of Gippsland becomes wetter, with rain falling all year round as moist, subtropical air moves in from the Tasman Sea. East of Orbost, tall eucalypts crowd in on both sides of the Princes Highway, with a seemingly unending line of forested hills and mountains lining the horizon.

National parks in east Gippsland conserve a wide range of environments

from coastal heathlands to high-altitude rainforests. North of the highway, on the lower slopes and in the valleys of the Dividing Range, the forests are rich in all manner of eucalypts.

The lowlands are dominated by silvertop ash (*E. sieberi*) and white stringybark with messmate stringybark (*E. obliqua*), yertchuk, yellow stringybark and mountain grey gum giving way with increasing altitude to a mosaic of wet and dry forests. On ridges, and in areas of rain shadow, the sparser dry eucalypt forest is home to silvertop ash and white stringybark with broad-leaved peppermint (*E. dives*) and red ironbark (*E. sideroxylon*), while in the gullies and areas of higher rainfall, at least ten kinds of eucalypt occur in varying combinations.

There is cool temperate rainforest at high altitudes, while lower down, following river courses or filling sheltered

pockets, warm temperate rainforest or jungle shows bright green against the olive of the surrounding eucalypts.

North-east of Lake Tyers, in the Buchan area, underground erosion of the barren, limestone landscape has formed a number of well-developed caves. The most impressive caves, Royal and Fairy, are open to tourists. This is the only locality in Victoria where the attractive Chinese brake (*Pteris vittata*) grows. The fern has specific soil requirements and grows only around outcrops of limestone.

North of Orbost, the southern section of the Snowy River National Park (95 400 hectares) protects another distinctive area of limestone outcrops in the spectacular Snowy River Gorge. The gorge's sixty-metre-high cliffs line a narrow ravine surrounding a rocky riverbed polished glassy-smooth by fast-flowing waters.

Snowy River wattles (*Acacia boormanii*), resembling gnarled bonsai trees, sprout from narrow crevices in the sheer cliffs. In the Tulloch Ard region, a colony of nimble-footed brush-tailed rock-wallabies (*Petrogale penicillata*) lives along the gorge. The rock-wallaby is an endangered animal in Victoria and the Snowy River is one of the two known places where it still exists in the state.

East of the Snowy, the broken plateau reserved in the Errinundra National Park (25 100 hectares) marks the southern margin of the Monaro Tablelands. Composed of folded and uplifted sandstones and mudstones with granite outcroppings, the Errinundra Plateau reaches over 1000 metres and is sometimes covered in snow in winter.

SUBTERRANEAN FONT This pool, in a section of Royal Cave bristling with stalactites and stalagmites, is called the Font of the Gods. The cave was opened to the public in 1913.

FOREST FLOWER The grevillea-like flowers of the Gippsland waratah open in spring.

A southern extension of the park takes in the conspicuous, conical peak of Mount Ellery the region's highest mountain, which is capped by a tor field of egg-shaped granite boulders. Interspersed among the boulders are the tough, wiry shrubs of the green- and purple-flowered monkey mint-bush (*Prostanthera walteri*) together with stunted specimens of the Gippsland waratah (*Telopea oreades*), with its scarlet flower heads.

Errinundra National Park contains the largest, cool temperate rainforest in Victoria. Plants such as the mountain plum pine (*Podocarpus lawrencei*) and mountain pepper (*Tasmannia lanceolata*), which elsewhere grow as

BEYOND THE SNOW Beyond the mountains' eastern scarp, the once-wild Snowy River flows to the sea.

shrubs, here develop into tall trees. The red-fruited plum pines may reach up to 14 metres and some of these giants have been dated as being at least 400 years old.

Beasts of the forest

Errinundra National Park is an important refuge for a number of rare animals which live in tall, wet forests; some of them are endangered species and have found a stronghold in this park. They include the vulnerable spotted-tailed quoll (*Dasyurus maculatus*) and the sooty owl (*Tyto tenebricosa*). The larger powerful owl (*Ninox strenua*) is also present where concentrations of its arboreal, marsupial prey are found.

The high rainfall along the plateau results in a multitude of rushing mountain streams which provide breeding sites for a variety of frogs. Males of both the colourfully marked black, green, brown and orange-red Blue Mountains tree frog (*Litoria citropa*) and the more subdued brown and orange Jervis Bay tree frog (*L. jervisiensis*) can be heard noisily advertising their presence on summer nights as they perch on streamside boulders waiting for a female to respond.

It is thought that one of Australia's rarest marsupials, the elusive, grey-brown long-footed potoroo (*Potorous longipes*) still scurries through the rainforest gullies of Errinundra. The only well-established colony of these shy creatures occurs about 20 kilometres to the south, in the secluded catchment of Bellbird Creek.

Closely related to the smaller, more lightly built long-nosed potoroo, the long-footed species was not properly identified until 1980. In addition to a few Victorian sightings, it is known from only one other location, just over the border in New South Wales.

In common with the long-nosed potoroo, which also lives in the Bellbird Creek area, the long-footed potoroo's diet consists mainly of various kinds of underground fungus. Because these fungi are an important part of the giant and constantly active compost heap which makes up the forest floor, the feeding activities of potoroos in dispersing its spores play an important role in maintaining the forest's food cycle.

To the west of Lind National Park and south of the highway, near the village of Cabbage Tree Creek, there is a small stand of Victoria's only palm, the graceful cabbage-tree palm (*Livistona australis*). Together with other small stands on the Brodribb River near

DRIPPING WET The atmosphere on the Errinundra Plateau is so damp that some branches are weighed down with moss.

HANDSOME CROAKER The Blue Mountains tree frog is quite at home on the ground.

Orbost and at nearby Caleys Creek, these palms represent an isolated colony more than 300 kilometres south of the nearest similar stand.

The final, northern stretch of the Gippsland coast before the New South Wales border is a wild and rugged shore not easily accessible to the casual traveller. Most coastal inlets are, in fact, ancient river valleys that have been inundated by the sea.

The dunes, coastal heaths and eucalypt woodlands of northern Gippsland are important habitats for several species of endangered birds and mammals. Secretive ground parrots forage in the heaths and sedgelands; and the coastal scrub is a popular feeding ground for the eastern bristlebird (*Dasyornis brachypterus*). Bristlebirds belong to the Australian warbler family and are characterised by their loud, clear, musical calls and a need for a low, dense, vegetation cover where they can safely search for insects and berries out of sight of predators.

Another rare bird, the masked owl (*Tyto novaehollandiae*), lives in woodland and dry eucalypt forests behind the heaths, venturing out over a more open habitat in search of prey during its nocturnal feeding forays.

In woodland, it probably encounters and may make a meal of an even rarer creature, the smoky mouse (*Pseudomys fumeus*). This large native mouse with a white-striped tail is concentrated in three widely spaced areas of Victoria, and this population, in the Croajingolong National Park (87 500 hectares), is critical to its conservation.

Coastal woodland east of Wingan Inlet contains the profusely flowering red bloodwood (*Eucalyptus gummifera*), which in autumn attracts large concentrations of dainty, nectar-eating birds and bats to its aromatic blossoms.

Flocks of honeyeaters and lorikeets may include the brilliant scarlet honeyeater (*Myzomela sanguinolenta*) and the colourful rainbow and musk lorikeets (*Trichoglossus haematodus, T. concinna*). Night visitors to the blossoms include the grey-headed flying foxes (*Pteropus poliocephalus*), from their camp at Mallacoota Inlet.

In forests and woodlands about Mallacoota, the sound of discarded casuarina cones dropping to the ground, accompanied by a soft, nasal whine is a sure sign of the presence of the larrikinish glossy black cockatoo (*Calyptorhynchus lathami*). □

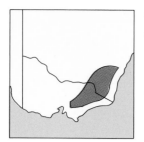

At its southern extremity, the Great Dividing Range makes a last stand for glory with a massive upthrust of blunt-topped mountains that form the roof of Australia

Misty landscapes above a sunburnt country

The high country maintains a special place in the landscape of Australia. Not only is it the highest, most mountainous part of the world's flattest continent, it is also a region of trees. In a land where thick forest generally occurs only along the narrow coastal strip, and where the remaining large tracts of these forests are the subject of dispute between loggers and conservationists, this is a terrain carpeted in a dense covering of trees.

From one end of the high country to the other — with the exception of a few areas of open alpine 'meadow' and some long fingers of cleared land along major valleys — the area is forested. A possum could travel all the way from Healesville, on the outskirts of Melbourne, to Lake Burrinjuck and almost never need to touch the ground.

There are few such large expanses of forest left in the world, and certainly no other where the eucalypt is so predominant. This forest covers a range of altitudes, from down to almost sea level to over 2000 metres. Its eucalypts have shown how versatile the common gum tree is by employing a range of clever adaptations to occupy every environment but the coolest alpine reaches.

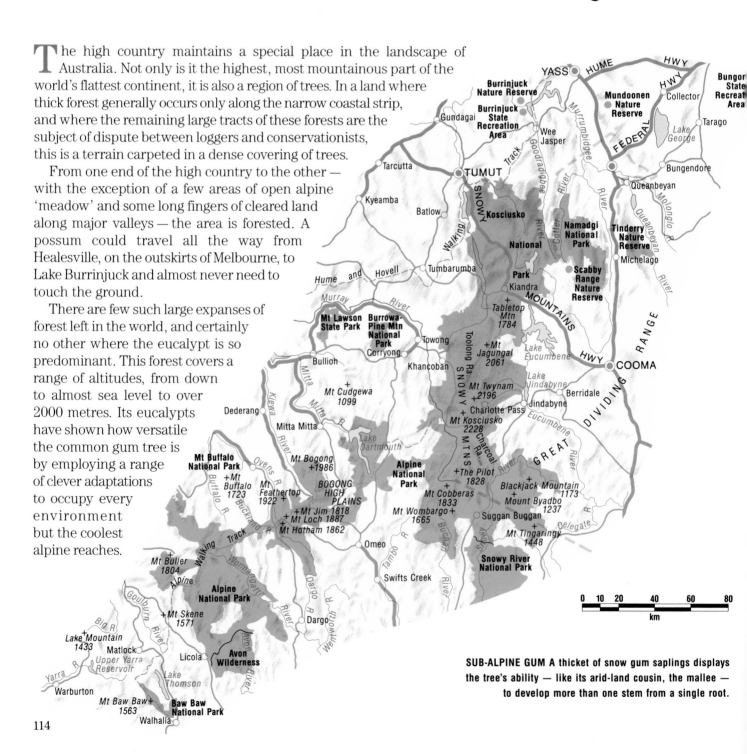

SUB-ALPINE GUM A thicket of snow gum saplings displays the tree's ability — like its arid-land cousin, the mallee — to develop more than one stem from a single root.

AFTER THE THAW At the northern edge of the Snowy Mountains, the spring thaw feeds countless streams in the alpine meadows.

The highest and most rugged part of the continent begins as steeply rising hills 50 kilometres east of Melbourne, and finally peters out 500 kilometres away in the low hills north of Canberra.

This southern section of the Great Dividing Range was lifted up by earth movements tens of millions of years ago and has been deeply dissected and smoothed down by the ravages of erosion ever since. The result is that instead of sharp mountain peaks, the highest regions are plateaux, better described as the 'high country' than the geographically flattering, accepted regional name of the Australian 'Alps'.

There may be a lack of classically shaped, inverted 'V' peaks, but the ter-rain is nevertheless very steep and rugged. Abrupt slopes erupt out of un-dulating hill country and rise, some-times almost vertically, for hundreds of metres; these are the edges of plateaux or the sides of long ridges cut into the plateaux' edges by erosion.

The alpine tops

The highest areas of the high country, covering about 400 square kilometres, are easily picked out from the air. Tree-less, they are like islands in a sea of forest. The erosion by rivers, which over millions of years has cut the deep valleys and created the steep escarp-ments of the region, has yet to reach these inner sanctums. Here, small streams meander through bogs on the undulating plains that are, in effect, the roof of Australia.

Some geologists believe that such plains may be palaeo-plains, or more or less intact remnants of the low-lying land which was uplifted to form this part of the eastern highlands between 60 and 90 million years ago. Interrup-tions to this flat alpine landscape are provided by ancient granite outcrops and more recent flows of basalt — form-ing flat-topped hills such as Mount

Loch, Mount Jim and Tabletop Mountain — which, unlike the surrounding countryside, have withstood the forces of erosion.

West of Jindabyne, the road into the Snowy Mountains rises steeply through forest and then, when the treeline is reached, on a much more gradual incline. Near Charlotte Pass, the view to the west is a grand vista of a long mountain ridge, in the winter months covered with snow. This is the Main Range, the highest land in the continent and the only part of it eroded by ice during the last glaciation.

Close inspection reveals that the ridge which forms the Main Range is fretted by a series of amphitheatre-like depressions or 'cirques'. There are 13 of them altogether, and during the last glaciation, 30 000 to 15 000 years ago, they were the source of two glaciers which extended down the valleys, one five kilometres long and the other three kilometres. The average air temperature then was 6–10°C lower than that of today. Most of the cirques are located on the eastern and southern sides of the range, the sides where the most snow accumulates.

Five glacial lakes are held aloft in this ridge, most of them in the bottom of the cirques. Four are shallow and dammed by glacial debris but the fifth and largest, Blue Lake, sits in a 28-metre-deep rock basin gouged out by a glacier. The rocky cliffs which surround Blue Lake are proof of the erosive powers of even a small glacier.

At Lake George, to the north, there is evidence of many glaciations over the last two million years but in the Snowy Mountains there is no sign of any of them except the last. Despite this, the work of hollowing out the cirques may have begun in the penultimate ice age which ended about 130 000 years ago.

The open country above the treeline is generally blanketed in snow from June to October — an average of 565 square kilometres of this country is snow-covered for over 90 days a year. Interestingly, the snow patches which occupy the cirques, often until January or February, help to maintain these relics of the ice age by counteracting the smoothing out effects of normal slope erosion.

The largest snowdrift is at 2100

FROST HARDY The showy mountain celery — named because of its succulent stalk — generally grows above 1800 metres.

metres, at the rear of the Mount Twynam cirque, where the depth can reach 30 metres. Occasionally it lasts until the next year but is always gone before the first snows of the following winter — there is no permanent snow anywhere on the mainland or in Tasmania.

Above the treeline

Trees do not grow in a region where even the warmest month of the year rarely goes above 10°C. The start of this very cold, treeless zone is called the treeline and in the Snowy Mountains, this generally occurs at about

1800 metres. Above the treeline, there are 250 square kilometres of grassland, herb field, heathland and bogs.

Wildflowers form a spectacular sight here during the spring and summer. Some plants, such as the anemone buttercup (*Ranunculus anemoneus*) and the alpine marsh-marigold (*Caltha introloba*), flower even before the snow has melted, while others, such as the mountain gentian (*Gentianella diemensis*), reach their peak in late February or March. The most spectacular displays occur in mid-summer when the silver snow daisies (*Celmisia longifolia*) and the billy buttons (*Craspedia glauca*) carpet the gently rolling slopes of the high areas.

One of the showiest individual plants is the mountain celery (*Aciphylla glacialis*) — both male and female plants have a thick, fleshy stem and sharp-tipped leaves but the male has a large, showy flower with hundreds of delicate white petals. Like many individual alpine plants, it is highly palatable to cattle and has made a good recovery in the Kosciusko National Park since grazing was banned there.

The mountain plum pine (*Podocarpus lawrencei*) is a clever exploiter of spaces between rocks, using its prostrate form to hug the boulders. Widely distributed in the high country, from Lake Mountain in the south to the Australian Capital Territory in the north, it is the only alpine conifer on the mainland. The hardiest of the shrubs, it is able to withstand temperatures of

−22°C. There are about 200 specifically alpine plants around Mount Kosciusko and at least 20 of them are found nowhere else.

The boulders which provide winter warmth for the mountain plum pine are also sought out for their summer shade by the millions of Bogong moths (*Agrotis infusa*) which migrate to above the 1400-metre level each year to escape the heat of the plains. They return to the lowlands in the autumn.

For many thousands of years, the Aborigines of this district made summer trips to the mountainside to feast on the dormant moths, which are easily gathered as they cluster under boulders and overhangs.

As the first flowers emerge from the snow in spring, the brilliantly marked corroboree frog (*Pseudophryne corroboree*) also comes out of an icy hibernation. This bright yellow and black creature, which spends its winters deep under the snow, emerging to breed in burrows in sphagnum bogs, symbolises the adaptability of the animals which are restricted to the high areas.

The cool possum

The best known animal of the cold country is the mountain pygmy-possum (*Burramys parvus*) — the only Australian mammal which lives exclusively in an alpine or sub-alpine environment. The possum was thought to be extinct and was known only from its skeletal remains until 1966, when a live animal was found sheltering in a ski hut

at Mount Hotham. The possum lives amongst the mountain plum pines, low snow gums and boulders of the alpine meadows.

In the Snowy Mountains, the pygmy-possum is found in the region of the Mount Kosciusko summit (2228 metres), and in Victoria, at five known localities in the Bogong High Plains and the Mount Hotham area. In New South Wales, the possum's total suitable habitat is estimated to be no more than eight square kilometres, while in Victoria it is thought to be a mere 1.95 square kilometres. Obviously, such a small range cannot support a very large population: the total number of pygmy-possums is estimated at 1800 adult females and 500 adult males.

The possum bones which exist in limestone caves such as Jenolan and Wombeyan, show that during the cold conditions of the ice ages the pygmy-possum was much more widespread. As the climate became warmer, it sought the comfort of higher, cooler regions; any further warming could leave it with little or no habitat.

GAUDY GLOSS Mature corroboree frogs are less than three centimetres long and, due to their webless feet, eschew regular frog practice and crawl rather than hop.

POCKET POSSUM Despite its prehensile tail, the pygmy-possum prefers the ground to the trees.

HIGH PLAINS The gently undulating country of the Victorian Alps — more tablelands than mountains — are a highlight of the vast Alpine National Park. Mount Hotham is in the foreground.

Like the better-known cold-climate creatures of the Northern Hemisphere, the possum has developed specific abilities and habits to deal with life above the 1500-metre level. It enters into a torpor, or inactive period, during the coldest months, stores seeds and fruit, and maintains an insulating layer of fat beneath its skin. Not surprisingly, it also eats Bogong moths.

The pygmy-possum has so far survived the impact of man but further development where its habitat is close to popular ski resorts may well pose a threat to its future.

Such a threat arose at the Mount Hotham resort but was averted by the use of a little imagination by the local authorities. The males' annual habit of migrating to lower altitudes after mating high in the mountains was interrupted by the construction of a road, which apparently they were unwilling to cross. A drop in fertility was the result. Life was sensibly returned to normal when an 80-metre-long 'possum tunnel' was driven under the road.

Victoria's high plains

West of the Snowy Mountains, alpine conditions persist, although the land generally drops away to a lower level. In the Bogong High Plains, the climate remains cold and the treeline drops to about 1600 metres, while on the Baw Baw Plateau the trees drop away at the 1200-metre level.

The result of this low treeline is that there are extensive meadow areas in the Victorian Alps as well as in the Snowy region. There are also open grassy landscapes in valleys 300 metres below the treeline. The extensive frost pockets which form in these semi-enclosed areas as cold air drains into them, result in a reversal of the usual sequence of vegetation; here, alpine species occur at the lowest level, on the valley bottoms.

The Victorian Alps differ from the Snowy Mountains in one important respect. The Victorian high country generally occurs in a series of isolated remnants of large plateaux, or high plains, rather than in a continuous string of ranges like those of the Snowy. These plains — the Bogong High Plains is one of the best-known examples — have rolling surfaces that are ideal for cross-country skiing. The only breaks in these undulations are the few sharp interruptions provided by basalt outcrops with names like the Ruined Castle and the Basalt Temple.

Deep soils are one of the hallmarks of the Australian alpine environment. They make for a much more fertile countryside than their rockier, more heavily eroded counterparts in places like New Zealand. Such a soft, easily eroded surface also results in a smooth, rounded topography which soothes rather than jars the senses. The deepness of the soil is the result of prehistoric glacier activity and the accumulation of dust carried from the inland and deposited by the wind. Over the last 15 000 years, airborne dust has added 20 to 1000 tonnes of soil per hectare to this landscape.

The boulders that moved

Periglacial landforms — those features formed by the freezing and thawing of material in an area adjacent to a glacier or ice sheet — include extensive screes (block fields) and river-like tongues of boulders (block streams).

The boulders, mainly of granite or

STATIONARY NOW During the last ice age, these boulders slid downhill with the spring thaw.

TRULY NATIONAL The Mount Feathertop ridge (above), seen from Mount Hotham, is part of the Alpine National Park which joins Kosciusko National Park, forming a protected alpine region of more than 1 200 000 hectares.

ALPINE AMPHIBIAN The warty Baw Baw frog has adapted to life on the upper slopes of Mount Baw Baw and is found nowhere else.

basalt, once moved down the mountain slopes every spring, lubricated by the melting ice and snow around them. In the Toolong Range, near Mount Jagungal, carbon dating of a tree stump at the base of the screes shows that this movement began about 35 000 years ago.

The boulders are now stationary, stopped in their very heavy tracks by the warming of the climate. The largest group of boulders, which started their journey higher in the mountains many thousands of years ago, are in the Mount Wombargo – Mount Cobberas area, near the state border.

In 1989, several national parks in the Victorian Alps were merged to establish the Alpine National Park, at 626 700 hectares almost as large as the vast Kosciusko National Park (646 911 hectares) in New South Wales. In practice, the Victorian park is a na-

tional park in name only because cattle are still allowed to graze over 90 per cent of its alpine meadows.

Disturbance by cattle in the past has had a profound impact on the native vegetation of the high country environment, especially in the bogs and the snow-patch herb fields. Cattle were banned from the Kosciusko National Park in 1969; before that, when grazing was allowed, the region was referred to as a state park.

Alpine islands

Baw Baw National Park (13 300 hectares) and Mount Buffalo National Park (31 000 hectares) are isolated well to the south-west of the main alpine area.

These heathlands are the home of pecularily alpine life forms, such as the Baw Baw frog (*Philoria frosti*) which lays its eggs in a foam nest in the mid-

BUFFALO'S HORN Sheer granite cliffs are commonplace in Mount Buffalo National Park. The tallest cliffs flank the 1720-metre-high Mount Buffalo, also known as the Horn.

dle of the heath, and *Richea gunnii,* a low, hardy shrub otherwise found only in the cool, upland regions of Tasmania.

Mount Buffalo is isolated from the main upland but its landscapes are those of the high country on a smaller scale. There are small grassy plains, granite tors — low, rocky hills — and woodland dominated by snow gums and the Mount Buffalo sallee (*Eucalyptus mitchelliana*) which is confined to this locality. The climb to the plateau is by a steep road which twists its way through granite slabs glistening with water which has seeped from above. The highest points — the Hump and the Horn — suggest the same imagery as they did 170 years ago when they were named by the Hume and Hovell expedition.

From the Horn, there are spectacular views of the northern face of the alps, including elegantly shaped Mount Feathertop (1922 metres), which in springtime sports a distinctive topping of snow on its summit, and Victoria's highest mountain, Mount Bogong (1986 metres), which alone amongst all the high country mountains has the shape of a true mountain and is not just the highest point of a ridge or plateau.

Sub-alpine country

Between the highest open alpine areas and the tall forests further down the slopes, is a region of approximately 4800 square kilometres which geographers refer to as 'sub-alpine' — a transitional zone where alpine plants and trees blend, as one plant community gives way to another. The snow gum is the only tree which grows above 1500 metres, the usual upper limit of the tallest forest. Despite its name, the treeline is never clearly defined and small groups of snow gums can be found on 'warm' rocky outcrops inside the alpine zone.

On similar mountainsides in the Northern Hemisphere, most of the trees growing at these altitudes are conifers resembling the traditional Christmas tree, with triangular shapes, needle-like leaves and downward-facing branches well suited to shedding snow. The snow gum, with its bulky parachute shape, upward-facing branches and broad leaves, has evolved other forms of defence against the cold and the snow.

The snow gum can withstand temperatures of −2°C, as well as maintaining the life-giving process of photosynthesis at a lower temperature than other trees. In winter, the colour of its bark changes gradually from white to yellow, pink, or even red,

providing a dramatic contrast against the ground's bright carpet of snow.

The snow gum's ligonotuber, an underground rootstock which in many eucalypts serves as regrowth insurance against damage by fire, here serves as a source of new life if a tree's above-ground growth is damaged by the crushing weight of the snow. These adaptive measures make the tree almost impervious to even the most powerful forces of nature and if the age of the lignotuber is used as a gauge, then many snow gums deserve to be described as ancient.

West of the Main Range, near Mount Kosciusko, the land slopes away ... and away and away. This is the greatest slope in Australia, where, in the space of less than 6.5 kilometres, there is a gradual drop of 1770 metres to the Geehi River.

Most of the fall is forested, although the vegetation changes character according to the altitude: from alpine plants to sub-alpine woodland at 1800 metres; to wet sclerophyll forest at 1500 metres, with alpine ash (*Eucalyptus delegatensis*), mountain gum (*E. dalrympleana*), brown barrel (*E. fastigata*) and manna gum (*E. viminalis*); to dry sclerophyll at 1300 metres with red stringy bark (*E. macrorhyncha*) and scribbly gum (*E. rossii*); and finally, at the lowest altitude, to a community of fringing woodland with river red gums (*E. camaldulensis*).

The upland forest

Temperate rainforest dominated by myrtle beech (*Nothofagus cunninghamii*) occurs at the western end of the high country around Mount Baw Baw and Lake Mountain. A stump dug up beneath the scree at 1600 metres in the Toolong Range was found to be the remains of a beech tree, indicating that before the last ice age this type of forest was more extensive.

Today, the eucalypts dominate these mountain forests. More than 50 species of eucalypt are found in the high country, making it one of the richest areas in Australia for this type of forest; there is a species and a form for almost every situation.

The mountain ash (*Eucalyptus regnans*), the dominant plant of the tall

TREE FOR ALL SEASONS The incredible adaptability of the eucalypt is illustrated by the tortured forms of the handsome snow gum. Above the 1500-metre level, other trees drop away but the snow gum survives in sheltered pockets into alpine country.

EUCALYPTUS TRIUMPHANT At the western edge of the high country, the lower slopes — such as here, along the Howqua River, near Mansfield — are carpeted with eucalypts of every shape and size.

open forest in the west of the high country, is the tallest flowering plant in the world, sometimes reaching 75 metres. It usually stands among other tall trees such as the manna gum, the alpine ash and the messmate stringy-bark (*E. obliqua*); on fertile soils, it usually has an under-storey of tree-ferns and broad-leaved shrubs.

Unlike the snow gum, the mountain ash has no lignotuber; its seeds escape fire when they are still on the tree by being firmly encased in woody cap-sules, but they need fire to break open the seed pod once it has fallen. As a group, the eucalypts have developed many other mechanisms which are either dependent on, or protection from, fire. When a bushfire occurs, it makes dramatic use of the eucalypt's volatile oils and the great amounts of flammable litter around the trees. On the other hand, to withstand the flames that they fuel, the trees have bark that is thick for insulation and pale coloured

to radiate heat, as well as the ability to resprout from a burnt stump.

The richness of the eucalypt forest is matched by the animals which are its inhabitants. There are quite dense populations of marsupials and many birds — as is to be expected in a region of trees. Their food includes leaves, flower nectars, seeds and the various gums which exude from the trunks of trees and shrubs. The wet sclerophyll forest is part of a particularly complex inter-relationship between animals and plants; the variously sized holes which occur in the mature trees which grow there are vital for the breeding of both parrots and possums.

Leadbeater's possum (*Gymno-belideus leadbeateri*), a shy, fast-moving possum of the ringtail group, lives in colonies of up to eight animals in a nest, usually in the hollow centre of dead, or very old, mountain ash trees. At night they emerge to feed on insects and gum such as that which ex-

123

udes from the silver wattle (*Acacia dealbata*). Until it was rediscovered in 1961, Leadbeater's possum was another possum thought to be extinct.

The future of the possum and some other forest animals is still uncertain because the limited areas of forest in which it occurs are scheduled to be logged on a 40–80-year rotation. The trees it needs for breeding, often up to

FURRY FLYER The feather-tail glider occurs in all the forested parts of the Dividing Range.

TAMED SNOWY These gentle, Snowy River waters north of MacKillop Bridge are the result of diversions to provide water for irrigation.

300 years old, will still survive in water catchment areas, as long as the current policy of excluding logging there is maintained. Scientists are anxious that the upland forests be fully protected, as the interaction between animals and the various plant communities is so far only partly understood.

At the other end of the high country, in the south-east, the long-footed potoroo (*Potorous longipes*) which was not described scientifically until 1980, is found in eucalypt forest with a dense under-storey of wire grass, ferns and sedges. It lives on roots, tubers, fungi and insects — all of them obtained by digging — and is particularly at home in the Snowy River National Park (95 400 hectares).

The most accessible of the mountain forests are those in the 94 000-hectare Namadgi National Park, near Canberra. In the Cotter Valley, a major water catchment area for the city, the greater glider (*Petauroides volans*), the yellow-bellied glider (*Petaurus australis*), the feather-tail glider (*Acrobates pygmaeus*), the sugar glider (*Petaurus breviceps*), numerous species of bats and the whistling tree frog (*Litoria verreauxii verreauxii*), are living evidence

of the relatively undisturbed nature of the forest. The greater glider, the largest of the gliding possums — it can glide for distances of 100 metres and make 90-degree turns — lives entirely on eucalypt leaves in the top canopy of the tall forest.

The deep valleys

Major rivers have gouged their way through these highlands, adding an additional dimension to the region. For example, the Snowy River begins as a trickle amongst the alpine meadows and snow drifts of the Snowy Mountains, then heads out across the plateau of south-eastern New South Wales towards the Tasman Sea. Suddenly, west of Bombala, it makes a great swing back towards the mountains and for 100 kilometres forces its way through a deep gorge so remote that it provides a refuge for many endangered animals and unusual plants.

On the eastern side of the Great Divide, in the southern part of Kosciusko National Park, the slopes of Charcoal Range drop 1800 metres to the Snowy River. The snow gum, alpine ash and mountain gum are familiar, but as the ridge descends still

lower there is yellow box (*Eucalyptus melliodora*) and white box (*E. albens*), and below 500 metres, a mixed white box and white cypress pine (*Callitris collumellaris*) woodland. In some places the pine occurs in extensive stands; one of the few areas in south-eastern Australia where eucalypts are not dominant.

The presence of these trees and that of common dry land grass species, usually typical of semi-arid north-western Victoria, is the result of the rainshadow which exists in the deep valley of the Snowy, creating a kind of reverse oasis. Further south, gullies on the west side of the Snowy River Valley contain pockets of warm temperate rainforest, a remnant of a forest which existed across southern Australia when the climate was wetter and warmer.

South and east of the angle formed by the Snowy River's sudden about-face, the upland around the Blackjack and Byadbo Mountains is the least-known part of Kosciusko National Park. It is also in the rainshadow of the much higher alpine country to the west.

A dry, wattle scrub, known locally as 'black jungle' because of its appearance from a distance, is actually the coastal

wattle, coast myall (*Acacia binervia*), and the rock wax-flower (*Eriostemon trachyphyllus*) growing tightly intermingled. Near the summit of Mount Tingaringy, a patch of wet mallee country with Tingaringy gum (*Eucalyptus glaucescens*) and narrow-leaved sallee (*E. moorei*) is a rare occurrence in this botanically intriguing corner of the high country.

Will o' the wisp lake

The Southern Tableland to the east of the Snowy Mountains and the forested ranges of the Australian Capital Territory are even more of a plateau than the higher areas, but most of this region's natural character has been lost.

Here and there, rocky areas still retain their native vegetation cover. One of these is Black Mountain, near the centre of Canberra; another is the 11 559-hectare Tinderry Nature Reserve, near Michelago, where there are four major vegetation formations: sub-alpine, wet sclerophyll, dry sclerophyll and wet mallee.

The most fascinating natural wonder of this area is Lake George, 25 kilometres north of Canberra on the Federal Highway. The lake is in full sight for 16 kilometres, as the highway runs between the base of the escarpment and the water's edge. The escarpment marks the Lake George Fault and the lake occupies a down-faulted area which, geographically, is a small region of inland drainage. As with Lake Eyre, its existence as a body of water and its depth depends upon the run of dry and wet years and the rate of evaporation (low in cold periods). Periodically, when it disappears altogether, fences reappear and cattle graze the lake bed.

At its deepest, Lake George is only five metres in depth but evidence of much higher lake levels — and a lake extension — can be seen in the series of gravel terraces near its northern end. Several thousand years ago the lake is believed to have reached its peak — it covered approximately twice the area it does now, was six times as deep, and overflowed into another drainage basin.

Analysis of the 134-metre-deep sediments on the lake bottom show that it has existed for 20 million years. Until six million years ago, the climate was continuously humid but then weather conditions began to vary. The sediments show change, as in modern times, from lake-full to lake-dry conditions over 750 000 years which have been correlated with eight glacial periods and eight inter-glacial periods.

Analysis of pollen grains and charcoal in the upper eight or nine metres of the lake's sediments, covering the last 350 000 years, provides the longest continuous record of vegetation history in Australia. ☐

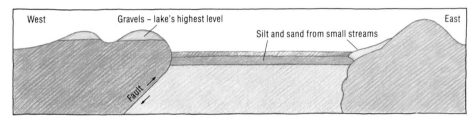

LAKE GEORGE: IT'S NO MYSTERY

NOW YOU SEE IT... To the north of the high country lies placid, and once mysterious, Lake George. The mystery, inspired by the lake's almost cyclical emptying, gave rise to many theories about underground rivers. In fact, the lake is a depression caused by a fault in the earth's surface and its contents evaporate readily due to its shallow nature.

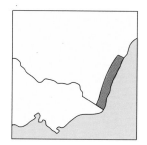

A strip of lush, green plains trimmed by bays, beaches and the blue rollers of the South Pacific provides a haven for the inhabitants of Australia's most heavily populated region

Between the cities, a green breathing space

Beyond the outskirts of Sydney's urban sprawl and its green buffer of national parks, the south coast of New South Wales begins as a narrow shelf on which the road and the railway line squeeze together as they wind their way towards Wollongong below a steep, forested escarpment.

This eastern edge of the Great Dividing Range — known here as the Southern Tablelands — runs down to the coast in the Royal National Park and hugs the shoreline closely until it reaches Stanwell Park, where it gradually recedes inland.

The widening coastal plain which is sandwiched between the hills and the sea — it is seldom more than 16 kilometres wide — has been carved out of soft shale, and forms a fertile farming region running down to the rock platforms and sandy beaches of the shore.

In a straight line, the coastline between here and Victoria measures a mere 380 kilometres, but when the shorelines of countless bays and headlands are taken into account it is almost 600 kilometres long.

In the north, the coast is marked by the largely industrial Illawarra Plain — its name taken from the

PRETTY COAST The coast is blessed with hundreds of sandy coves such as this one at the accurately named Pretty Beach, just north of Batemans Bay.

Aboriginal word meaning 'high place by the sea' — dominated by Wollongong and Port Kembla. The hills of Saddleback Mountain and its old volcanic neck, sandstone-capped Bong Bong Mountain, separate the Illawarra district from the Shoalhaven Delta where the southern New South Wales coast proper begins and extends to Cape Howe.

In marked contrast to the Illawarra, the Shoalhaven district is largely rural, with dairy farms, forests and fishing ports. A growing holiday trade means that the coastal towns are thriving while inland settlements are generally on the decline.

Illawarra's visitors come mainly from Sydney, while the 'south coast', as it is generally known, draws people from Canberra, the Southern Tablelands and Victoria, as well as the state capital.

For many Australians, this is a favourite recreational landscape. Due to its location between the Sydney–Wollongong urban region and Melbourne, with Canberra two hours' drive to the west, the south coast is only a few hours' drive from 25 per cent of the population and is readily accessible to another 25 per cent.

What in the twentieth century has become a popular holiday region for the crowded metropolitan centres of the east coast was also the first part of Australia to be examined in detail by Europeans. Captain James Cook and his crew first came in sight of Australia just south of Cape Howe, the southern-most point of New South Wales.

The sight of an Australian gannet (*Morus serrator*) on 17 April 1770, alerted Cook and his sailors that they

On the 24th, Cook named Cape St George, noted the appearance of a large bay (Jervis Bay) but did not investigate it. He named its northern point Long Nose Point.

A day later, Banks made one of the first critical assessments of the eastern Australian landscape through British eyes: 'The countrey tho in general well enough clothd appeared in some places bare; it resembled in my imagination the back of a lean Cow, covered in general with long hair, but nevertheless where her scraggy hip bones have stuck our farther than they ought accidental rubbs and knocks have entirely bard them of their share of covering'.

Below the waterline

The coast which Banks had viewed so critically was in fact a natural treasure house. The cliffs, from Old Mans Hat to the north of Jervis Bay, to St Georges Head in the south, flank underwater scenery almost as remarkable as that on view at the Great Barrier Reef.

This is one of the few places on the New South Wales coast where the 20-fathom-deep submarine contour comes so close to shore that divers and snorkellers need swim only a few metres to observe fish which would normally be much further out to sea.

Feeding along the faces of these underwater cliffs are vast schools of the slate-grey, one-spot puller or chromis (*Chromis hypsilepis*) and the dark-blotched butterfly perch (*Caesioperca lepidoptera*). The beautifully coloured eastern blue devil (*Paraplesiops bleekeri*), with its four dark cross bands and yellow fins, can occasionally be glimpsed in holes and crevices.

Huge blue wrasse (*Achoerodus viridis*), with prominent, fleshy lips, silver drummer (*Kyphosus sydneyanus*), jackass fish (*Nemadactylus macropterus*), and motley red sergeant baker (*Aulopus purpurissatus*) may also be seen around the bases of the cliffs.

Rocky reefs and grass meadows that lie just below the tide line are home to graceful anemones and colourful nudibranchs, while the intertidal rock pools, deeper water, sand bottoms, mangrove shorelines and saltmarshes, each have their own plants and animals. Eight hundred hectares of the varied marine environments of Jervis Bay are a reserve.

were about to reach the east coast of Australia. The botanist Joseph Banks recorded that the bird 'flew toward the north-west with a steady, uninterrupted flight as if he knew the road that he was going led to the shore'.

A few days later, the *Endeavour* bore on northwards past country which '...rose in gently sloping hills ... cloth'd with trees of no mean size ...' For nine days Cook sailed along the coast, carefully observing and noting detailed locations of many of the landmarks well-known to today's holidaymakers.

On 21 April the land appeared 'rather more hilly'. The next day Cook named 'a pretty high mountain' Mount Dromedary (806 metres). Another, which the observant Banks said 'much resembled those dove houses which are built four square with a small dome at the top', was named the Pigeon House (719 metres).

NO GROPER The one-metre-long blue wrasse is often referred to incorrectly as a groper.

Rugged sandstone cliffs flanking Steamers Beach, on the east of the bay, are the highest sea cliffs on the New South Wales coast, with a drop of more than 135 metres. When the south-easterlies blow, which is often, waves crash violently onto these cliffs, while in marked contrast, the low, western shoreline of Jervis Bay borders the calm, shallow waters of St Georges Basin. Here tall, graceful casuarinas line a narrow strand where pelicans, swans and cormorants feed, often in large numbers.

The wilderness chain

If a possum could travel almost all the way from the outskirts of Melbourne to the Snowy River through the tree-tops (see pp. 114–125), then the same restless animal could well continue its journey northward to the outskirts of Sydney once it discovered the chain of national parks which claim a large part of the south coast's hinterland.

A string of parks and reserves, sometimes linked, sometimes only a few kilometres apart, stretch all the way along the foothills of the Great Dividing Range, from the state border to Sydney. The coastal wilderness is, naturally, less well served as this is where agriculture and small towns — mainly on the river mouths — take precedence. But even here, numerous beaches and bays, most notably at Jervis Bay, are reserved for the future in their natural state.

LOW WATER The jointed seaweed known as Neptune's necklace adorns the rock platforms along the southern shore of Jervis Bay.

NORTH SHORE Formidable cliffs line the outer and inner shores of Beecroft Peninsula, on the northern side of Jervis Bay, where scores of Aboriginal archeological sites dot the heathland.

Pigeon House, Admiration Point and The Castle are part of one of the most picturesque wilderness regions in Australia, the 16 102-hectare Budawang National Park, inland of Ulladulla. At the heart of the park is a remote and inaccessible place ringed by pinnacles and spires, called Monolith Valley.

The valley is approached through narrow, interconnecting rainforest corridors sprouting ancient tree-ferns and giant cutting grass, and where, occasionally, tall red cedar trees grow as plentifully as they did before they were discovered by the timbergetters in the early 1800s.

At intervals, there are spectacular views across adjoining valleys. In the early morning or at dusk, when the light is diffused, the eroded hills suggest a collection of exotically shaped oriental temples.

In a region famous for a coastline

with a regular pattern of pleasant interruptions by sandy beaches, bays and headlands, some of the south coast's most spectacular scenery actually lies inland, on the eastern edge of the high country. Here, many of the rivers that rise in the Snowy Mountains begin to tumble down to the sea.

The upper reaches of the Brogo River, in the Wadbilliga National Park (76 675 hectares), are typical of the rugged mountain country above the coastal plains. Swamps and bogs surrounded by she-oak (*Casuarina*) heathland cover the hills and dales around Mount Wadbilliga.

From a craggy knoll adjacent to the mountain, a long, steep ridge drops 700 metres in a south-easterly direction over a distance of only two and a half kilometres to run into the purple, shale bed of the Brogo. In this wild, remote region, the only disturbance to the mossy banks of ferns along the river's edge are the scurryings of water rats and the careful tread of small water hens as they search for insects.

HILLS AND DALES The undulating landscape below Mount Nibelung contrasts with the mountainous terrain in the north of the vast Morton National Park.

DEEP SOUTH Red stains caused by iron deposits colour the compacted sand cliffs near Eden.

Across one run of the stream — for it is barely a river at this stage — an avenue of water gums forms a canopy across the water. These crooked, leaning trees, which may extend up to 35 metres out over waterways, are reliable indicators of a river's catchment zone.

If the gums look healthy, with whippy, thin branches, then the catchment upstream is probably in a natural state with bogs of moss releasing water slowly like giant sponges; disturbed catchment areas may result in water being released in such a volume that the gums are flooded and gradually die.

The trees of the Brogo are graceful and healthy, and they shade crystal clear pools lined with blue or purple slate and pink or grey granite. Where the river widens and tall white gums (*Eucalyptus alba*) occupy the adjacent flats, there is another steep ridge leading back up 800 metres to the she-oak heath of the tops and the headwaters of the Tuross River. Boobook owls (*Ninox boobook*) hoot along the river at night, and long-nosed bandicoots (*Perameles nasuta*) may be heard rooting round amongst the bracken.

The fanned tail of a superb lyrebird

(*Menura novaehollandiae*) may also be glimpsed here. If not seen, its throbbing call, a virtuoso imitation of every other local bird, is almost certain to be heard. Each morning and evening, yellow-tailed black cockatoos (*Calyptorhynchus funereus*) fly along the valley, wheeling overhead in what appear to be displays of sheer exuberance.

Along the shoreline

In contrast to the northern coast of New South Wales, with its long arcs of beaches often stretching for several kilometres, the beaches of the southern coast are generally small with more individual character. Their sands vary from pure, gleaming white in Jervis Bay to tawny yellow at Mimosa Rocks, while by way of a total contrast, beaches of pebbles fringe Murramarang and Mimosa Rocks National Parks. Ancient forests are preserved on view as fossilised logs in the rock platforms at Pebbly Beach in Murramarang.

Three sections of the coast — from Wonboyn to Cape Howe in the Nadgee Nature Reserve, from Merimbula to Bermagui, and from Batemans Bay to Ulladulla — display a cross-section of its varied beach and bay formations and each section can be traversed by bush tracks in about a week.

On some nights, the sea at Aragunnu Beach, in the Mimosa Rocks National Park (5181 hectares), positively sparkles. As each wave whispers up the beach, it is outlined in glittering points of phosphorescence which remain stranded on the sand at the farthest extent of the wash.

The 'lights' are sand fleas (*Noctiluca scintillans, Nyctiphaens australis*), which when approached, suddenly glow more brightly. Bats and night birds wing swiftly down to the beach to feed off the big moths which gather, seemingly mesmerised by the phosphorous in the fleas' bodies.

Further south, near Bittangabee Bay in the Ben Boyd National Park (9455 hectares), fishermen's lore has it that the fish are so greedy they will only stop biting if disturbed by a giant leopard seal (*Hydrurga leptonyx*). These giant seals, with a head disproportionately long in relation to their bodies, are grey above, pale grey to white on the underside, with light and dark grey blotches on their throat and sides.

These solitary animals, which usually inhabit the Antarctic pack-ice, often venture up the south-eastern coast — sometimes being stranded as far north as Coffs Harbour — feeding on penguins and krill. The leopard seal is the major predator of penguins and often patrols a particular stretch of coast where the penguins enter and leave the water near their nesting sites.

Dolphins also swim close inshore along this coast, sometimes frolicking in the surf amongst board riders. Occasionally a southern right whale (*Eubalaena australis*) and its calf will swim slowly past, effortlessly feeding and playing and lazily exhaling air which condenses during cold weather and gives the impression that the animal is spouting water.

This is a relaxed, friendly coast today but the ancestors of these whales would not have enjoyed such a peaceful passage. The southern right whale was the main target of early Australia's original whaling industry (see p. 321).

The whalers from the station at Eden were so efficient at slaughtering females as they entered the coast's many bays and estuaries to calve, that by the 1840s whale sightings were few and far between. After more than a century, the whales have started to return and the southern right once more introduces its new-born to its ocean environment along this coast.

On the landward side of the shoreline, behind the beaches, swamp wal-

HEADWATERS The Deua National Park runs along the eastern scarp of the Great Dividing Range and is the catchment area for the Deua River, shown here in its formative stages.

labies (*Wallabia bicolor*) loiter casually in the rush beds and bracken that grow under the tea-trees and banksias. In Murramarang National Park (1609 hectares), campers invariably share their beach camping grounds with up to a hundred eastern grey kangaroos (*Macropus giganteus*) of all sizes.

Members of this extremely tame mob have no qualms about asking for a sandwhich — a paw on the arm, a plaintive look, and a flutter of long eyelashes over huge, brown eyes is the tried and proven way of procuring a picnicker's lunch.

Back on the escarpment edges, in the Morton (154 386 hectares), Budawang, Deua (81 625 hectares) and Wadbilliga (76 675 hectares) National Parks, there are large populations of eastern greys. A big, grey male may cough a warning at intruders from its brake among the bushes. And at dusk it is not uncommon to hear the true sound of the Australian wilderness — a dingo chorus, from a nearby escarpment edge or valley.

In the Nadgee Nature Reserve (17 116 hectares), playful young dingoes sometimes come briefly onto the beaches or hunt black swans during the moulting season, when the birds are flightless and easy game for predators prepared to wade into shallow water.

Gathering of the swifts

Captain Cook did not realise how close to the mark he was when he named an isolated rocky outlier of the Great Dividing Range the Pigeon House. The 719-metre-high mountain and its surrounds are part of a busy bird habitat, but if the famous navigator had been able to conduct a closer examination, he might have named the landmark Swift House.

The white-throated needletail swift (*Hirundapus caudacutus*) spends the northern winter in these parts, as well as at other favoured locations along the east coast. At the end of March, the skies above the Little Forest Plateau, near Pigeon House, are filled with a swooping and weaving dark mass as the needletails marshal their numbers for the return to northern Asia.

CRAZY PAVING At Picnic Point, in the northern section of Mimosa Rocks National Park, the action of the sea has exposed the basalt pavement laid down during prehistoric volcanic eruptions.

Several thousand needletails, with their dark, glossy, purple-green feathers glistening in the autumn sunlight, form into a huge ball as they weave around each other, chattering noisily before their massed flight begins.

Strangely enough, it was almost 200 years before the country around Cook's 'Pigeon House' mountain was explored in detail. In the 1950s, a group of bushwalkers who witnessed a spell-binding sunset from an unnamed rocky point west of Pigeon House named it Admiration Point.

Between Admiration Point and Pigeon House the walkers explored an isolated section of mesa called The Castle, which they found to be an occasional haunt of Australia's largest bird of prey, the wedgetail eagle (*Aquila audax*). The wedgetail, with a spectacular two-and-a-half-metre wingspan, hunts by soaring high, circling up on the thermal air currents for hundreds of metres, and then swooping down onto its prey.

The equable climate and well-watered coastal plains — with an abundance of fish and shellfish in the rivers and estuaries and a variety of edible land creatures — meant that the southern coast of New South Wales attracted a large Aboriginal population long before the arrival of Europeans. At Wreck Bay, on the southern headland of Jervis Bay, shell middens — the result of an estimated 20 000 years of Aboriginal settlement — lie in piles up to three metres high.

The most favoured Aboriginal camp-sites were rock shelters in a gully beside fresh water, preferably with a plentiful supply of fuel and with the sea only a couple of hundred metres away. In such places, the Aborigines could take their choice of land or sea food and they were not deafened by the crash of waves or wet by the salt spray.

Even in the wild gorge of Tantawangalo Creek, Aboriginal chippings and spear-sharpening grooves are to be found. On a headland below Durras Mountain there are the leftover chippings of a large-scale Aboriginal stone implement 'workshop'.

Several dozen stone seats are scattered around and stone flakes are littered over several hectares. The site looks north and south along the coast and it is not difficult to imagine that the craftsmen who sat here may have watched Cook sail past.

The fate of the forests

In the south-eastern corner of the continent are Australia's largest remaining virgin eucalypt forests. Vast, pristine stands are preserved in parks and forestry reserves north and south of the state border.

These rich and valuable biological, recreational and timber resources protect the water catchments of many towns and contain a varied population of marsupials, many of them tree-dwelling creatures, such as possums and squirrel-gliders.

Several species, most notably the long-footed potoroo (*Potorous longipes*), are in danger of becoming extinct. First identified in 1980, in east Gippsland, this tiny kangaroo has only recently been confirmed as a native of the south-east forests as well.

Environmentalists are concerned that logging the forests — sometimes almost completely, in a process known as 'clearfelling' — in privately owned and state forests between Batemans Bay in New South Wales and Bairnsdale in Victoria may put the forests and their animal inhabitants at risk.

The timber industry, on the other hand, maintains that until there are enough pine plantations to supply the state's timber needs, selective logging of the southern forests will not unduly harm the environment.

In sometimes heated debates which often bear a close resemblance to the public arguments which raged for many months over the Tasmanian forests in the mid-1980s, governments, both federal and state, are trying to find a compromise which satisfies the loggers and the conservationists.

During the last century, timber-getting and dairying were the main industries of this region. In the late twentieth century, tourism has become the largest industry on the coast as the resources of the forests have become exhausted.

The history of Eden, the southernmost town of the region, on Twofold Bay, provides a typical example of the coast's economic development. It first profited from a wool and hide export market from the Monaro tablelands in the west. It then became a whaling station, until the great whale migration along the coast was virtually eliminated.

The koala-skin export trade failed next, and then the tuna fishing industry declined. Now, the collapse of the timber industry is a possibility unless the virgin forests are opened to logging or extensive eucalypt plantations are planted in the 1990s.

Conservationists believe that it is upon such development issues that the protection of much of the remaining wild parts of the southern coast of New South Wales depends.

Central to their opposition to logging forests listed in the National Estate (see pp. 90–91), such as the Coolangubra, Egan Peaks and Tantawangalo forests, is not an opposition to logging in general, but to logging areas of old growth, or undisturbed trees, such as is found in these forests. They say that the establishment of eucalypt plantations elsewhere would ensure the long-term future of the timber industry, and the ultimate fate of the forests as a happy one. □

DO NOT DISTURB? Tantawangalo is typical of the large tracts of wet eucalypt forest which still remain in the south-east due to their status as state forests.

133

Beyond the Great Dividing Range lies the vast interior of the continent. Broad plains of grass and woodland stretch for several thousand kilometres before petering out in the desert

A land of sweeping plains

Twenty-five years after establishing a settlement on the shores of Port Jackson, Australia's European settlers conquered the barrier of the Great Dividing Range and began to venture beyond the narrow coastal plain. They crossed the Blue Mountains with a particular vision in mind. The rivers beyond the mountains all flowed persistently west, so surely they must feed a great inland sea...

In 1835, Sir Thomas Mitchell allowed himself a moment of exultation at the Pink Hills, about 100 kilometres south-east of present-day Bourke: '...on the western slopes of these hills, we found some of the pinks in flower, from which they have been named. There was also an unusual verdure about the grass, and a fragrance and softness in the western breeze which seemed to welcome us to that interior region...'. But there were already many doubts about the rivers' eventual fate and

the vision, of course, was not to be realised. The only sea to be found was the one Charles Sturt spoke of metaphorically in 1844: '...the whole face of the country was covered with a gloomy scrub that extended like a sea to the very horizon'.

Sturt's sober assessment was the more accurate of the two. West of the divide it is dry more often than not. What rainfall there is varies from year to year and as the desert at the continent's heart is approached it becomes less and less reliable. Droughts are common and may last for years, killing well established trees and shrubs. The summers are hot with temperatures often climbing into the forties while the winter days may be mild, although morning frosts are common.

INLAND IMAGE The moisture beneath a dried-up tributary of the Darling River sustains a lone coolibah tree.

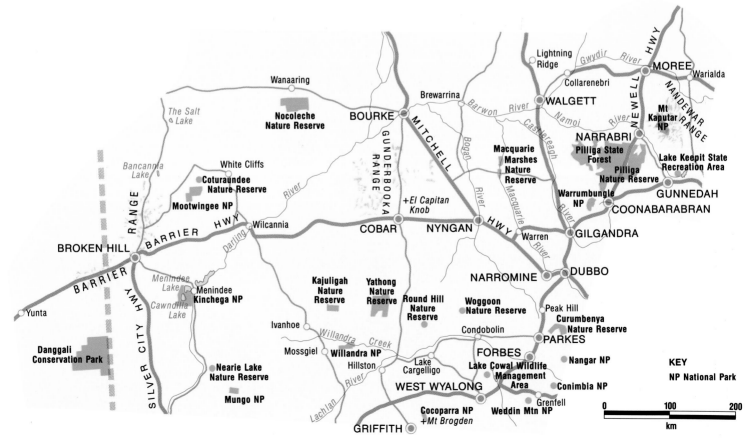

HORIZONS WEST The Warwick Hills, near White Cliffs, break the flatness of the western plains.

After the hill country of the Great Dividing Range's western slopes is left behind, the country flattens into level or slightly undulating plains. Apart from the Barrier Range near Broken Hill and the tablelands near White Cliffs, only occasional low hills or isolated peaks obstruct the view to the horizon. The flatness and aridity of the country-side is illustrated by the fact that although numerous rivers run through the region none of any size originates there; the only regular streams are those which flow from the Great Dividing Range and even some of these may be reduced to a chain of waterholes during a drought.

Most of the surplus water in this region drains into the Murray or Darling Rivers, although there are several 'local' reservoirs such as the Salt Lake and Lake Bancannia in the north-west between Tibooburra and Broken Hill. Bordering the rivers of the west are broad, alluvial flood plains veined by a complex pattern of channels which fill only after a prolonged period of heavy rain.

Plant life west of the divide is diverse and cleverly adapted to its environment. On the slopes skirting the mountain fringes and near the western plains, dense ironbark and box woodlands predominate. Here the ironbarks are firmly in their element with the silver-leaved species (*Eucalyptus melanophloia*) occurring from west of Bourke to Warialda and the mugga (*E. sideroxylon*) widespread on the

STATELY GUMS River red gums, such as these trees near Menindee, are a symbol of the inland.

central western slopes and plains — particularly on stony hillsides and gravelly ridges. The hardy ironbarks are punctuated by stands of green mallee (*E. viridis*) and wattle. Poplar (or bimble) box (*E. populnea*), grey box (*E. microcarpa*), fuzzy box (*E. conica*) and yellow box (*E. melliodora*) also grow here although not as widely as they did once; the boxes are probably the most extensively cleared plants in New South Wales.

Westwards, the box woodlands fade gradually into other woodland containing a rich variety of dry-climate trees including white cypress pine (*Callitris columellaris*), belah (*Casuarina cristata*), ironwood (*Acacia excelsa*), wilga (*Geijera parviflora*) and brigalow (*A. harpophylla*).

Oases of the west

Paradoxically, swamps are not unknown in this dry region, wetlands being a significant part of the inland scene. The swamps are most common on the floodplains accompanying the rivers but there are also large expanses of marshland around the western lakes, natural reservoirs filled periodically by the Darling and its tributaries.

The largest wetland area and one that never dries up is the Macquarie Marshes (18 000 hectares) just north of Warren. This extensive complex of channels, open lagoons and marshes fed by the Macquarie River was made a wildlife sanctuary in 1955.

Reed swamps and woodlands of river red gum (*Eucalyptus camaldulensis*), coolibah (*E. microtheca*) and black box (*E. largiflorens*) are the predominant forms of plant life here, where wide stretches of open water are tied loosely together by meandering streams breaking away and relinking with the Macquarie River. Also common in this watery environment are various sedges, spike-rushes and nardoo. The handsome red gum fringes most rivers and billabongs in the region, giving way to black box and other woodlands away from the immediate vicinity of the watercourse.

Out in the mulga

'Out in the mulga' — a time-worn variation of 'beyond the black stump' — might well have been coined especially for much of the country west of the divide. Familiar in the cities as the raw material of tourist knick-knacks, mulga (*Acacia aneura*), is the archetypal outback plant and is found throughout all but the northern and southern ex-

tremes of the arid and semi-arid areas of Australia. West of the divide it merges with bimble box in the east and bladder saltbush (*Atriplex vesicaria*) and bluebush (*Maireana brevifolia, M. sedifolia*) shrublands in the west.

Elsewhere mulga occurs as an open woodland, becoming denser to the west as the country becomes drier and providing an invaluable food for millions of sheep in time of drought.

Over much of its range mulga grows in dense stands separated by relatively bare patches of soil. The reason for

SWAMPY OASIS Almost half of the vast Macquarie Marshes — downstream of the Burrendong Dam — is a reserve for the wild creatures that breed there. The wetlands almost dried up in the 1970s when water was diverted for irrigation.

THE MULGA Like the pilliga and the mallee, the mulga — it may be a tree or a shrub depending on its habitat — has given its name to a large part of the region where it grows.

this pattern, as for the similar way in which many arid-region plants grow, is a simple matter of adaptation. The growth pattern corresponds with the contours of the terrain: the bare areas form a water catchment zone. These zones absorb a small amount of rainwater and the rest drains off into the mulga 'groves', ensuring that each plant receives adequate water when it rains. If there is very little rain, the plant's open, umbrella shape ensures that its entire surface is moistened as quickly as possible.

When rainfall is more plentiful, the plant channels nearly half of the moisture it receives down the stems to its roots. Like most acacias of the arid areas, mulga does not have true leaves. Instead it has phyllodes, which are expanded leaf stalks, and these perform the same photosynthetic duties as a

drum oleifolium) which covers a wide area of level sandplain.

Black box (*Eucalyptus largiflorens*) and coolibah (*E. microtheca*) woodlands are widespread on the clay soils of the alluvial plains near major streams. In the north, these species associate to form a woodland that dominates much of the floodplain of the upper Darling and its tributaries. Around the lower Darling, the tree cover changes with black box merging with river red gum, myall and bladder saltbush, all of these interspersed with areas of grassland.

A place to graze

The great open spaces of the western plains still support large numbers of wild grazing animals. The great red kangaroo (*Macropus rufus*) is king of the plains while lesser numbers of the eastern and western grey kangaroo (*M. giganteus, M. fuliginosus*) inhabit the woodlands and scrubs. Red and grey kangaroos are shot in large numbers for their skins and meat by government-licensed shooters. The number allowed to be slaughtered is calculated according to the estimated kangaroo population in New South Wales and the numbers on each farm property for which a licence is sought.

The emu (*Dromaius novaehollandiae*), with its long neck and dark colour, is conspicuous on the open plains. As it is not regarded as a source of meat or a threat to the fodder of sheep or cattle it has been left largely to its own devices.

The birds, which can deliver a kick hard enough to knock down a large dingo, are noted for their curiosity, a characteristic which the hunting Aborigines learnt to exploit. Seeing a flock of emus in the distance, the hunter would lie down on the ground and whistle, while waving a leg or an arm in the air. The emus, unable to ignore this, would approach to within striking distance when one of the leading birds would be killed.

While birds have survived better than mammals in the west, some species are threatened. Mallee fowl (*Leipoa ocellata*) populations have continued to decline in spite of the number of special mallee reserves established in New South Wales. This large ground-dwelling bird is an easy prey as it seems reluctant to fly, relying on its dappled camouflage and slow, deliberate movements for protection from predators.

The diminutive, quail-like plains

leaf. During long dry spells the pores in the phyllodes contract to restrict water loss and help the plant to avoid drying out.

A plain of forests

Just north of the town of Coonabarabran, at the foot of the Warrumbungle Range, stretches the vast Pilliga Scrub. The Pilliga — the name comes from an Aboriginal word meaning swamp oak or casuarina — is almost half a million hectares of forested plain, part of it the largest state forest in New South Wales and the rest nature reserve. White cypress pine, narrow-leaved red ironbark, pilliga grey box (*Eucalyptus pilligaensis*) and belah occur in the scrub.

Vast quantities of cypress pine — much of it used as floor boards — are cut here. These trees once covered millions of hectares but numbers have declined due to land being cleared for grazing and farming. Ironbark timber is also cut from the Pilliga State Forest, most of it used for railway sleepers.

One of the prettiest trees throughout the Pilliga and the rest of the western region is the leopardwood (*Flindersia maculata*), with its spotted bark and pendulous foliage. The tree, usually found on sandy flats or stony rises, was so named because it develops patchy 'spots' when it sheds its bark to reveal the pale surface beneath.

THE PILLIGA SCRUB Not all of the western plains has been cleared for agriculture. The 'scrub' is a woodland of low trees, including the winter-flowering *Acacia neriifolia* (top), and the leopardwood, with its mottled bark (bottom).

Mallee bushes, usually associated with the area of western Victoria that bears their name, are a distinctive part of the landscape of the west. These low, scrubby eucalypts stretch in a broad, patchy belt from the far south-west to Wyalong in the east and as far north as Menindee, Cobar and Nyngan. In the south-west, beyond the Darling River, the mallee fades into a patchy woodland of belah and rosewood (*Heteroden-*

wanderer (*Pedionomus torquatus*) and the much larger Australian or kori bustard (*Ardeotis kori*) are other ground-dwelling birds whose populations have declined due to extensive changes to the open plains wrought by grazing and agriculture and, in the case of the bustard (also known as the plains turkey), due to hunting.

The superb parrot (*Polytelis swainsonii*) and the regent parrot (*P. anthopeplus*) shelter and nest in hollows of old river red gums and black box trees of the river floodplains. As the number of old trees has decreased with logging, clearing, and changes in water level due to irrigation, the numbers of these parrots have declined.

The brolga (*Grus rubicundus*) is considered a seasonal visitor from the north but breeds in western river systems in times of good rain. These graceful visitors are not seen as frequently as they once were due to wild pigs having developed a taste for their eggs.

Blue hills

Despite the vastness of the plains it would be a mistake to think of the view from the Great Dividing Range as one of unrelenting flatness. Many hills break the level skyline and some of them, of no use as farmland because of their steep and rugged slopes and their

SUPERBLY COLOURED The superb parrot lives only on the western plains of New South Wales.

infertility, remain as islands of wilderness in a sea of 'tamed' countryside.

Nangar National Park (3492 hectares) north of Cowra, protects the two rugged 'headlands' of the horseshoe-shaped Nangar-Murga Range. The forested range rises from surrounding alluvial plains that have been largely cleared for agriculture. Three pairings of trees, each pair usually growing closely intermingled, dominate the woodland: red stringybark (*Eucalyptus macrorhyncha*) and black cypress pine (*Callitris endlicheri*), scribbly gum (*E. rossii*) and black cypress pine, and ironbark and black cypress pine. Many flowering shrubs are found here, in-

cluding various grevilleas, thyme spurge (*Phyllanthus thymoides*) and hop goodenia (*Goodenia ovata*), together with beautiful orchids such as the waxlip (*Glossodia major*).

The peregrine falcon (*Falco peregrinus*) and the turquoise parrot (*Neophema pulchella*) make their homes in these hills while large mammals such as grey kangaroos and red-necked wallabies and swamp wallabies (*Macropus rufogriseus, Wallabia bicolor*) are common on the slopes and in the valleys of the range.

The Nangar's ruggedness and good cover once attracted wild life of another kind: Ben Hall and other bushrangers used the range as a sanctuary from the law. The nearby Weddin Mountains and Conimbla National Parks (8361 and 7590 hectares) are similar fragments of nature in the otherwise altered landscape of the central west.

The Cocoparra Range near Griffith is composed of sandstones, shales and coarse-grained mixtures of other rock types which have been folded and subsequently eroded into a 'hogback' formation, a narrow ridge with very steep sides. Its deep, scenic gullies, and spectacular summits, such as Mount Bingar, are protected within the Cocoparra National Park (8358 hectares) and an adjoining nature reserve.

FLIGHTLESS BUT FLEET-FOOTED The nomadic emu stalks the plains in family groups or small mobs, feeding on leaves, seeds, grasses and insects.

grey kangaroos. The euros, or wallaroos (*Macropus robustus*), which once inhabited the overhangs and caves of the range in considerable numbers have been largely replaced by wild goats but national parks rangers are gradually eliminating these exotic intruders so that the natives may return. The rock faces — inaccessible to the goats — provide nesting places for wedge-tailed eagles (*Aquila audax*) and peregrine falcons (*Falco peregrinus*).

Volcanoes no more

The west's most spectacular range is the Warrumbungle, referred to by John Oxley in 1818 as a '...stupendous range of mountains, lifting their blue heads above the horizon...'. These mountains, interrupting the flat country north-east of Gilgandra with their dramatic spires and domes, are the worn-down descendants of volcanoes that were active more than 13 million years ago. Successive eruptions here caused the lava to flow repeatedly over the land until it formed many layers.

In time, when these prehistoric pressure valves were inactive, a fast-cooling lava plugged the volcanic vents; many millions of years of exposure to the elements has left these giant, weather-resistant lava stoppers to tower over the wooded ridges.

Crater Bluff, Belougery Spire and Tonduron are the names given to some of these rocky sentinels. Perhaps best known is the Breadknife, a thick blade of rock stabbing 90 metres into the air. Under this volcanic rock is sandstone which become exposed in the valleys and gorges; in most places they have been changed by intense heat and pressure into a hard quartzite.

In the Warrumbungle National Park (20 914 hectares), plants and animals of the western plains and of wetter eastern regions come together. On the sheltered southern slopes there are trees normally associated with the higher rainfall areas of the New England Tableland and in some places patches of figs and vines give a suggestion of rainforest.

On the drier northern slopes there are water-conserving plants more typical of the plains. Comparatively rich soils, formed from the weathering of volcanic rocks, support a woodland dominated by white box trees. On poorer sandy soils and rocky outcrops there is a woodland of white gum (*Eucalyptus dealbata*), narrow-leaved red ironbark (*E. crebra*) and black and white cypress pines. The higher and more

THIRTEEN MILLION YEARS OF EROSION

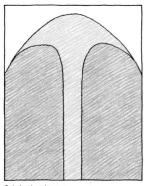

Original volcano

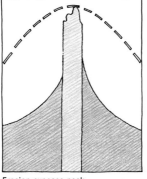

Erosion exposes neck

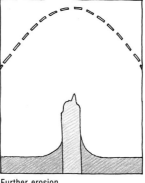

Further erosion

SKELETONS OF DEAD VOLCANOES More than 13 million years ago, the Warrumbungle Range was pitted with fiery volcanoes, generally with gentle slopes and round tops. Today's jagged, often vertical-sided peaks, were formed by the lava that solidified inside the throats and other vents of the volcanoes when they cooled down. In time, the ash and other debris of the volcanic mountainsides was eroded away, leaving the harder, cavity-filling rock, usually trachyte. These solidified volcanic plugs are called necks and dykes. The Breadknife (pictured, top), is a 100-metre-high dyke.

On the King's birthday in 1817 a member of the first European exploration party to see this range planted seeds of oak, peach, apricot and quince trees under Mount Brogden. The expedition leader, John Oxley wrote that this would '...serve to commemorate the day and situation, should these desolate plains be ever again visited by civilised man of which, however, I think there is little probability'. Ironically, the 'desolate plains' to the south were to become part of the Riverina district which produces great quantities of stone fruits of the sort that Oxley's party planted.

Dry sclerophyll forest, interspersed with cypress pine and narrow-leaved ironbark, covers the ridges and slopes of the Cocoparra Range. In the wide valleys there are fine cypress pine forests which shelter large numbers of

exposed summits are usually covered with low-growing heaths.

In late winter and spring, several species of wattle and many showy wild-flowers including wild irises (*Patersonia sericea*), pink and purple Darling peas (*Swainsona galegifolia*) and many heaths produce a spectacular display on the sandstone soils.

The varied environments of the ranges provide habitats for many animals including grey kangaroos, wallaroos, red-necked and swamp wallabies and koalas (*Phascolarctos cinereus*). The brush-tailed rock wallaby (*Petrogale penicillata*), once plentiful in these ranges, has fared badly in competition with goats and is now almost gone from the area.

Mount Exmouth, at 1206 metres, is the highest point on the range. A branch track from Dainu Gap leads up to the summit. Initially the track climbs a scree — a sloping mass of loose rock — and then continues upwards past patches of lush, bright green vegetation. Figs, vines and shrubs grow here as they are protected from bushfires and there is a regular supply of moisture from the dew that forms on the boulders at night. All over the mountain, dense clumps of sticky daisy bush (*Olearia elliptica*) are found in woodland and on the summit there are grass trees.

Nandewars: high and wet

The Nandewar Range, which reaches a height of 1508 metres at Mount Kaputar east of Narrabri is, like the Warrumbungles, of volcanic formation. Much of this dramatic mountain landscape is within the Mount Kaputar National Park (36 817 hectares). About 18 million years ago, an active volcano deposited a layer of lava here, in some places 700 metres thick. Constant erosion has worn down the softer rock to leave isolated buttes, cliff faces with columnar jointing, amphitheatre valleys and narrow canyons.

These mountains are wetter and higher than the Warrumbungles, which accounts for the wet sclerophyll forests of manna gum (*E. viminalis*), candlebark (*E. rubida*) and mountain gum (*E. dalrympleana*) on their slopes and the fine stands of snow gum (*E. pauciflora*) on their peaks. Brush-turkeys (*Alectura lathami*) frequent the wetter forests as well as greater gliders (*Petauroides volans*) and feathertail gliders (*Acrobates pygmaeus*). The park has many scenic walking tracks but otherwise much of it has been left in its natural state.

MOUNT KAPUTAR The forest eagerly colonises the well-watered volcanic slopes of the Nandewar Range, a large cross-section of which is protected within the Mount Kaputar National Park.

Jutting up from the flat, eroded landscape about 70 kilometres south of Bourke is the Gunderbooka Range, a tilted block of ancient rocks. A smaller basalt peak, El Capitan knob, lies 50 kilometres north-east of Cobar.

The best known range west of the Darling is the Barrier Range from which the mines of Broken Hill have won so much silver, lead, zinc and other minerals. Much of the original vegetation has been stripped from these ranges, but what remains indicates that they supported shrublands of wattles including the shrub known as 'dead finish' (*Acacia tetragonophylla*), allegedly named because of its ability to endure to the end of a drought when all other plants have died.

The Danggali Conservation Park (253 480 hectares), a UNESCO-designated biosphere reserve (see p. 390), protects a huge area of arid and semi-arid vegetation on the New South Wales–South Australia border. Belah (*Casuarina cristata*), false sandalwood (*Myoporum platycarpum*) and inland rosewood (*Heterodendrum oleifolium*) dominate the woodlands in the park's arid north.

No fewer than 22 native mammals, 41 reptiles and 150 birds have been counted in the park. Mammals include the little pied bat (*Chalinolobus picatus*), the greater long-eared bat (*Nyctophilus timoriensis*) and the wongai ningaui (*Ningaui ridei*), a tiny marsupial measuring a mere 60–70 mil-

limetres long and not identified by scientists until 1975. Among the rare plants are the tufted burr-daisy (*Calotis scapigera*) and wilga (*Geijera parviflora*).

The Coturaundee Range to the north-east of Broken Hill is a nature reserve of about 6700 hectares. It is an uplifted block of sandstone between

An unwelcome bicentenary

Australia's most widespread wild animal is one which conservationists and landholders alike would be happy to see wiped out. The goat, which arrived with the First Fleet and has been running wild almost ever since, now roams over all parts of the continent except the rainforest and desert regions.

In 1990, there were estimated to be 350 000 feral goats moving in herds of up to 300 animals. They eat most of the vegetation they can reach and trample what is left underfoot, breaking up the soil with their cloven hooves. The result is widespread erosion and trees stripped bare of food for native animals, sheep or cattle.

Goats were used by early settlers and miners as a handy source of milk and meat and were often allowed to range freely, many of them eventually running wild. Angora goats, imported to establish a wool industry, were set free when the scheme collapsed in the face of competition from sheep wool and these goats soon interbred and brought new vigour to the existing wild herds.

Goats are susceptible to many livestock diseases and could act as devastatingly efficient, nationwide carriers of infection if foot-and-mouth disease or rabies managed to gain a foothold in Australia. Controlling the numbers of this self-inflicted pest has proved difficult: shooting and poisoning have had some effect but trapping large numbers of the animals at waterholes, particularly during the dry season, seems to be the most effective method.

two faults, with cliffed slopes on both the eastern and western sides. The crest is relatively flat, with a few deep gorges, and bears a low open shrubland of *Acacia clivicola*, a rare wattle closely related to mulga.

A small and isolated population of the very rare yellow-footed rock wallaby (*Petrogale xanthopus*) was discovered on the Coturaundee Range in 1966, the first sighting in this area. The wallaby was originally widespread on the often rocky ranges west of the Divide, but up until the 1966 sighting it was thought to survive only in small colonies in South Australia and Queensland. The designation of this range as a nature reserve was a vital step in securing the future of this attractive creature.

Lakes of sand

Prehistoric lakes dot the plains west of the divide. Long ago, when streams ran from the foothills of the Great Dividing Range over the plains and out to sea through the Murray River, lakes formed in many places. One large chain, strung out in a north-south direction at the end of Willandra Creek, covered 1000 square kilometres between Menindee in the north and Balranald in the south.

Climatic changes over thousands of years have brought hotter, drier conditions and gradually the lakes have emptied. Now they are dry, with sand dunes on their eastern edges. Water still flows westward from the Lachlan River into Willandra Creek but long before it reaches the Murray the dry earth has drunk it completely.

The five major dry lake basins at the end of Willandra Creek have been registered as a World Heritage area, largely because of the lakes' archeological importance. Water has not reached the lakes since the end of the last glacial period, about 15 000 years ago, and consequently the landscape, particularly the high crescent-shaped sand dunes, or 'lunettes', which have formed on their eastern shores, are little changed since that time.

In the Lake Mungo lunette known as the 'Walls of China', ancient skeletons have been discovered which changed accepted theories about the physical and cultural development of Australia's earliest human inhabitants.

Skeletons and artifacts dating back 40 000 years have been found around the edges of Lake Mungo, which is now protected within Lake Mungo National Park (27 847 hectares). Archaeological investigations suggest that the ancient people who lived on the shores of the

lake when it brimmed with water and life, shared their rich environment with a number of now extinct species of giant animals, or 'megafauna', including a wombat-like creature as large as a cow, and a giant kangaroo. Fragments of Tasmanian tigers and devils have also been unearthed here.

But new lakes have formed with the help of man. Lakes Cawndilla and Menindee once filled only at flood times when the Darling overflowed, but now they are kept full by a water diversion scheme. The lakes attract a wide range of waterbirds including silver gulls, pelicans, cormorants, black swans, egrets and many species of ducks. These lakes and a section of the western bank of the Darling River are part of Kinchega National Park (44 182 hectares).

The prevailing westerly winds have built up high sand dunes on the shores of the lakes. Sandhill canegrass

ARCHEOLOGIST'S DELIGHT Dawn over Lake Mungo, an outstanding archeological site, is a bewitching time. During the last ice age, this was part of a string of abundantly rich wetlands.

INLAND 'SEA' Early explorers would have heartened at the sight of Lake Menindee, here slowly drowning an inundated river red gum.

(*Zygochloa paradoxa*) and clumps of bluebush manage to live in this unstable environment. Here, the meandering channel of the Darling River is bordered by a black soil plain with black box woodland.

Out on the red sandhill and sand plain country a shrubland of bluebush dominates. This is the home of the red kangaroo and numbers of them can be seen grazing in the morning and evening. After rain this infertile landscape is transformed by rapidly growing ephemeral plants which, in the space of a few weeks, can germinate, grow and flower profusely. ☐

The famous Blue Mountains — in fact, a collapsed plateau riven and torn by deep canyons and gorges — represent the Great Dividing Range at a most modest elevation but with a rarely matched, ruggedly spectacular terrain

A hilly plateau in retreat from the elements

In January 1836, on the Australian leg of his round-the-world journey, Charles Darwin did what many city residents have continued to do ever since — he made a trip to the Blue Mountains in order to escape the summer humidity of Sydney.

Leaving his horses to be watered at an inn near Wentworth Falls, Darwin went exploring along Jamieson Creek to the spot where it plunges over a cliff to form the falls that gave their name to the settlement. The sentiments he expressed in his diary have been echoed innumerable times by the countless tourists who have followed in his footsteps.

'It is not easy to conceive of a more magnificent spectacle than is presented to a person walking on the summit plains,' he wrote when, without any notice, he came out of the thick bush and found himself on the brink of one of the cliffs.

His diary notes summed up his impressions: '...walked mile & ¹/₂ to see Cascade: most magnificent astounding and unique view, small valley not lead to expect such scene. Certainly most stupendous cliffs I have ever seen'.

Darwin's opinion has been confirmed by the millions of tourists who continue to visit the mountains. In a broad and breathtaking sweep, the monumental sandstone plateau of the Blue Mountains dominates the landscape from the Southern Highlands to the Hunter Valley. The coastal and inland plains are firmly separated by the mountains' vast bulk, everywhere riddled with steep-sided gorges and enclosing many deep, hidden valleys.

Much of the plateau is still intact, but the many tall cliffs are simply markers of the present level of erosion; eventually the elements will widen the valleys so much that they and the plateau will virtually disappear.

The soils of the Blue Mountains are almost as infertile as it is possible for soil to be, but the eucalypts and other native plants have adapted with their customary ability to conserve as much as possible of the water

LONG VEIL Small streams on the top of the plateau feed waterfalls such as the Bridal Veil, which drops 180 metres over the eastern escarpment to find its way into the Grose River.

that they extract from the thin soils by transpiring less than trees in fertile, well-watered regions.

The forest which carpets those steep slopes and looks uniform from a distance, in fact varies as it mirrors the differences in the depth and quality of the soil cover.

As a result of its poor soil and a terrain which would test the skills of the keenest town planner, the Blue Mountains has largely escaped the impact of development. Only two roads creep across the two-hundred-and-fifteen-kilometre-long north to south sweep of the mountains — both of them still following routes plotted in the early 1800s — and its forest wilderness areas are the largest of their kind in Australia.

The Great Western Highway crosses the Blue Mountains on a narrow strip of plateau between the valleys of the Grose and Coxs Rivers. It is only a short distance from the road to the edge of the plateau where deep valleys or gorges, the chief natural wonders of the mountains, are on dramatic display.

The sides of these valleys are like cross-sections and provide windows onto geological events which occurred 230 to 190 million years ago. At that time, various kinds of material from the eroding highlands to the north and west were deposited in a great depression known as the Sydney Basin.

This displaced material became the alternating layers of shale, coal, sandstone and claystone which can be seen

145

clearly in the valley sides today, displayed like the different sections of a layer cake. Later, probably some 90 to 60 million years ago, the land containing these rocks was uplifted, and the shaping of the valleys began.

Water versus rock

South of the built-up area between Wentworth Falls and Katoomba, a long line of cliffs known as 'the southern escarpment' overlooks the Jamieson Valley and offers superb views of shales, claystones and sandstones, exposed in 200-metre-high cliffs. There are several waterfalls, the most famous of which, Wentworth Falls, is the result of an almost 300-metre plunge over the escarpment by the Jamieson Creek.

Mount Solitary is a mesa — a detached outlier of the plateau — which stands near Narrowneck Plateau. Narrowneck is only just connected to the main plateau and will one day be eroded away into a solitary mountain as well.

Also visible from the western part of the southern escarpment is the Coxs River, which has cut right through to the 'basement' granite under all the visible layers of the mountain's structure. Further north, near Capertee, Colo Creek has cut down into even older rocks, exposing 400 million years of geological history.

The nearby Pantoneys Crown is a 'butte', an isolated sandstone remnant which was once part of the main plateau. It is a stark tribute to the slow but inexorable forces of erosion which have been whittling away at the mountains since time immemorial.

On the northern edge of the central Blue Mountains plateau, the Grose River and its more powerful predecessors have cut a 750-metre-deep valley. Seen from Govetts Leap near Blackheath, the Grose Valley is almost completely walled in by giant cliffs, the most impressive being on the northern side, under Mount Banks and Mount Caley, which reach 300 metres.

At the bottom of the valley the gentler landforms around Blue Gum Forest, at the junction of the Grose River and Govetts Creek, are the product of erosion of the older, softer rocks. Here the valley is three kilometres wide. Ten kilometres downstream, the walls close in and the river runs through a narrow 500-metre-wide gorge until it reaches its end in the broad valley of the Hawkesbury.

Valleys which vary dramatically from a broad to narrow shape — they also occur in other parts of the Blue Mountains such as the Cox-Warragamba and the Capertee-Colo Valleys — have become known as 'bottleneck valleys'.

This phenomenon occurs because the rivers are still cutting through the deep layers of the tough sandstone in their lower reaches and have not yet reached the softer layers beneath. The sandstone lies mainly in the eastern part of the Blue Mountains, and becomes deeper towards the centre of the Sydney Basin.

Early scientists, including Charles Darwin, did not believe that a big enough volume of eroded material could have passed through these narrow bottlenecks to account for the wide valleys. They considered earthquakes or other alternative explanations for the excavation of the vast gorges.

Scientists now accept that the rivers are quite capable of performing this erosion, with much of the eroded material being carried away as sediment during periods of heavy rain.

LONG NECK The Narrow Neck ridge, barely 100 metres wide, punctuates the vast Jamieson Valley.

HOW TO SLICE UP A PLATEAU

WORN DOWN ... IMPERCEPTIBLY North of the Blue Mountains proper, the plateau margins of the Colo Wilderness may lack the altitude of the adjacent arms of the Great Dividing Range but they are no less rugged, being formed by the same, ceaseless action of water against rock. The mountain rivers scour their way through the sandstone and claystone layers to the underlying mudstone (left). As the softer mudstone dissolves, leaving the sandstone undermined, surface erosion takes its toll on the upper, exposed sandstone (centre). Eventually, the worn overhang collapses, creating a valley 'floor' of rubble (talus) with sheer cliffs on either side (right).

In the south-eastern part of the mountainous region, near Mittagong, the Nattai River and its tributaries run through a series of gorges with long, skirting clifflines, before breaking out into the wider Burragorang Valley, thus reversing the bottleneck shape. The valley was flooded in 1960 after a giant dam was built in the Warragamba Gorge — the neck of the bottle. The valley now contains the 88 square kilometres of Lake Burragorang, with its long arms stretching deep into the Wollondilly and Coxs River gorges.

The colossal cliffs and deep canyons of the Blue Mountains are the region's most spectacular features and they mark the chief battlelines as the worn plateau retreats in its unwinnable war against erosion. The cliffs vary in colour from red and orange to light yellow and are often marked by shallow caves.

Close inspection shows that the rock faces are made up of large, rectangular blocks bounded by horizontal bedding planes and vertical joints. Water dripping onto claystones or shales near the bottom of the cliffs causes undercutting and allows gravity to take its toll in the form of a rock fall. Once one of these blocks has been undercut beyond about one-third of its depth, its centre of gravity shifts and it breaks away to join the mass of boulders on the scree slopes below.

Occasionally, very large blocks simply slip away rather than collapsing, sliding for a short distance down the scree slope before coming to a halt. Burramoko Head, near Blackheath, is an example of this process, known as 'block gliding'.

The well-known Three Sisters formation, near Katoomba, is the result of erosion along joint planes. Normally

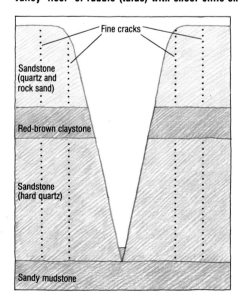

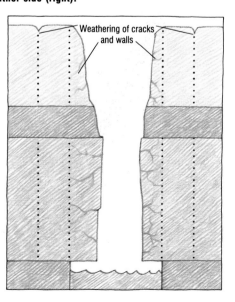

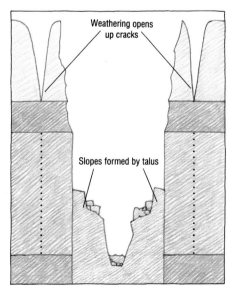

SIBLING SYMBOL The Three Sisters, against the backdrop of the Jamieson Valley, are the best known landmark of the Blue Mountains.

Fire in the readily flammable eucalypt forests is another important erosion agent. The fierce heat of summer bushfires flakes off large pieces of sandstone from exposed rocks, and weaken's the 'cement' binding the grains, leaving them loose and vulnerable to being washed away by rainwater. Ledges of ironstone are snapped off by fire and form a tough, gravelly soil highly resistant to erosion.

Hanging valleys and pagodas

Although the high-lying plateau land between the deep gorges — where the mountain towns have been built — is not about to disappear in a rush of silt, it is by no means static. It is probably in a similar condition to that of the whole Blue Mountains region when it was a 'whole', intact plateau, not sliced by the gorges.

LITTLE DIGGER Inaccessible gorges provide a fine habitat for that shy mimic, the lyrebird.

the retreat of the cliffs is extremely slow and it is rare to be able to see a recent rockfall, but coal mining under the cliffs has caused several major rockfalls in recent times.

The elements which contribute to this spectacular landscape are not restricted to the actual weathering 'elements' of wind and rain. Animals also play their small and unexpected part in this continuing drama.

The superb lyrebird (*Menura novaehollandiae*) is common in patches of tall, open eucalypt forest and rainforest on the valley sides. Lyrebirds feed on insects in the abundant litter of the forests and build large mounds for courtship display.

With their powerful legs, big, clawed feet and long toenails, they annually turn over approximately 63 tonnes of litter over each hectare of their habitat. This constant disturbance causes a movement of soil down the slopes which, over countless years, has been a considerable influence in the weathering of the valleys.

GREEN MOUNTAINS The swampy vegetation around the creek that forms Bridal Veil Falls does not stop at the cliff's edge; hanging gardens are created as it colonises every nook and cranny where the soil and seepage allow roots to form.

On those parts of the plateau that are still intact, streams flow through broad, gently sloping hollows between undulating hills of heathland or forest. These upland valleys usually have an impermeable layer of peat on a sandy base, supporting occasional boggy areas and treeless swamps.

In places, the swamps occur on the very edge of the cliffs; near Govetts Leap, for example, they create incredible hanging gardens on nearly vertical slopes.

In their lower section, the valleys change to narrow 'canyons', or 'slot valleys', such as Empress Gorge near Wentworth Falls and the Grand Canyon near Medlow Bath. The latter, 30 metres deep and only three metres wide at the top, is typical of numerous similar phenomena throughout the Blue Mountains.

The point at which a gentle, upland valley changes into a canyon, is often associated with a band of claystone within the main sandstone structure. Two claystone bands erode relatively easily, creating a 'valley in a valley' formation often with double waterfalls.

Finally, the canyons reach the plateau rim hanging above the much deeper valleys below. From a distance, these canyons appear as a mere notch in the cliffline.

The most extraordinary eroded landscape of the plateau occurs on the western escarpment between Lithgow and Nullo Mountain, about 75 kilometres to the north. Here there are pinnacles shaped like bells, domes, beehives, tabletops and many other much more peculiar shapes.

Such worn down features are usually called 'minarets' or 'pagodas'. They vary in colour — according to differences in rock type or the presence of algae — from chocolate and orange to white, grey and pink, forming a striking contrast with the olive-green bush.

In deep gullies between the rocks, the moist conditions provide a perfect habitat for ferns and green patches of wet forest. The most extensive collections of these rocks are around the cliffs of the Capertee and Wolgan Valleys and in the proposed 18 300-hectare Gardens of Stone National Park, between Glen Davis and Capertee.

These intriguing formations occur where ironstone — composed of iron which has been dissolved from overlying rocks — accumulates in bands between layers of other rock. Where these bands occur their toughness protects the strata below, which is eventually

left standing above the surrounding terrain, all around it having been eroded away.

The ironstone ledge itself finally breaks away, often as a result of fire; it is only where the slopes are steep enough to be devoid of vegetation to fuel destructive fires that the ledges progressively extend, providing more and more protection and more and more bizarre shapes.

Volcanic toppings

For about 350 million years there has been sporadic volcanic activity in the mountain area. Since volcanic material is usually more resistant to erosion than the surrounding rocks it survives as a hard capping on the hilltops.

At Yerranderie in the southern Blue Mountains, where a rich gold and silver mine attracted a population of 2000 at the end of the last century, the remains of a large volcano cover approximately 40 square kilometres.

DAMP CLOISTERS The sun's rays only occasionally penetrate this cloistral canyon which is constantly being made wider and deeper by the action of the stream and the weathering of its walls.

HARD CORE This stark piece of elemental sculpture in the Colo wilderness is the result of the rock's sandstone outer layer being eroded away, leaving a hard ironstone layer to defy the wind and rain.

This very old volcano developed before the mountains were uplifted to their present position.

At later dates, large flows of basalt from volcanic eruptions covered the sandstone in many areas, and although much of it has now been eroded away, the remnants invariably stand 100 to 300 metres above the rest of the plateau. Virtually all of the peaks of the northern Blue Mountains, such as Mount Coricudgy, Gospers Mountain and the Kekeelbons, are basalt.

These heights are the region's main landmarks. Apart from their height, they are easily identified by the richness of the vegetation which flourishes on the rich, basalt soil, compared with the much scrubbier growth on the poorer, sandstone soils.

Seen from one of these peaks, the others appear like parts of a distant archipelago. The thickness of the basalt varies: at Mount Kerry it is 230 metres, at Mount Wilson 90 metres and at Mount Bell a mere 15 metres.

Scores of 'diatremes' — the necks of old volcanoes — had quite the opposite effect on the scenery. These were the vents through which violent, volcanic eruptions actually occurred. The material that was left in these necks was relatively unresistant to erosion, and when it had been weathered away left depressions, known locally as 'holes', surrounded by cliffs in the harder sandstone.

Murphys Glen, near Bedford Creek in the central Blue Mountains, is one of these unexpected volcanic legacies, while another, in Wollemi National Park further north, is believed to have been the inspiration for the Terrible Hollow in Rolf Boldrewood's novel *Robbery Under Arms*.

The bushranger's caves

The Boyd Plateau, varying from 1100 to 1200 metres high and covering 134 square kilometres, lies at the heart of the south-western Blue Mountains. The deep valley of the Kowmung River skirts the plateau to the west and the south, but it is on its eastern edge that the steepest drops occur.

Here, the headwaters of the Coxs River's tributaries are etched deeply into its flanks. Names like Cyclops Pit and Thurat Spire reflect the rugged character of the scenery; Whalania

STONE PORTALS This archway at Wombeyan Caves, on the south-west fringe of the ranges, leads to one of the many cave systems eroded into limestone belts of the mainly sandstone mountains.

Deep and Kanangra Gorge both have almost sheer walls which soar over 900 metres from their gorge floors.

Geologically, the south-west is very different from the rest of the Blue Mountains, since it is located on the rim of the Sydney Basin and is made up mainly of basement rocks of granite and quartzite, which further north are buried beneath other layers of ancient rock. These tough rocks mean that the south-west is different in its appearance as well; being less easily eroded it has not been eaten into by river gorges in the same fashion as the plateaux to the north.

North of the Boyd, the Jenolan River and its tributaries have cut a network of caves in a belt of limestone at the bottom of a 460-metre-deep valley. These are the famous Jenolan Caves, which first became known to the world in 1838 when a bushranger was traced to his hideout in the caves. In 1866, they became one of Australia's earliest conservation reserves.

There are 300 known caves on several levels at Jenolan. Some of the most notable above-ground features are the Carlotta Arch, the 85-metre-high Devil's Coach House and the 70-metre-wide Grand Arch, through which the main access road passes. Although guided tours have been conducted for about 130 years, scientists know less about them than any similar limestone area in the country.

There are also a number of limestone caves in the remote valley of the Kowmung, free from the paraphernalia of tourism. In 1969, a public outcry prevented a proposed limestone quarry project from going ahead and the region was eventually set aside as the Kanangra-Boyd National Park (68 276 hectares).

Even further south, the Tarlo River National Park (5890 hectares) will eventually cover 12000 hectares, just north-east of Goulburn. Focusing on the Tarlo River, the rest of the park sprawls in very rugged and intricate patterns of ranges and gullies, with well developed galleries of river oak and open forests of white gum.

Waterbirds find refuge and shelter in the park — it is used as a nesting site by at least three species of wild duck — while many small mammals live along the river bank.

Spurs of the Great Dividing Range — like tributaries of great rivers — break off to the west, petering out beyond Orange and Cowra into the western plains. These smaller, branching ranges

RANGE'S RIVER The headwaters of the modest Boyd River rise on the plateau of the same name, where the eroded plateau to the north give way to a series of 'conventional' low ranges.

give this country its rolling hills, narrow plains and occasional mountain 'peaks'. The sandstone of the main range gives way to basement granite, long ago uplifted and eroded into rounded hills.

The granite soils support stands of white gum (*Eucalyptus rubida*), peppermint gum (*E. dives*) and mountain gum (*E. dalrympleana*). On the better soils, brown barrel (*E. fastigata*) appears, and above 1300 metres, the snow gum (*E. pauciflora*) is common.

Bathurst and Orange are the two major settlements in the western shadow of the Great Divide. They are surrounded by large and long-developed properties supporting cattle and sheep, and growing wheat, vegetables and fruit.

Fifty million years ago, Mount Canobolas, south-west of Orange, was an active volcano. Five separate vents each discharged a different type of lava over a long period and this is the material which has worn down to provide the rich soils for today's farms.

South-west of Cowra, the Wyangala State Recreation Area (2035 hectares) protects one of the state's largest and most attractive inland waterways — Lake Wyangala. The Wyangala Dam, on the Lachlan River, is probably the best known of the large dams in the western

PARKS' RIVER The wild Kowmung River, on the southern perimeter of the vast Blue Mountains chain of national parks, runs through a series of gorges such as this before it joins the Coxs River.

LOCAL COLOUR Spring flowers of the pultenaea shrub brighten the mountain's eucalypt forests.

ATTENTION GETTERS Like many natives, the epacris is relatively insignificent until it blooms.

Blue Mountains region. Because they were built specifically for irrigation and flood control, and not water supply, the waters of most of these dams are open to the public for recreational use.

The forest blue

Conservationists have nominated the Blue Mountains for World Heritage listing, chiefly because of its ancient gorges and cliffs, which are much older than the more famous Grand Canyon of the south-western United States. When the full history of these deep scars on the plateau is known, it will tell much about the processes which are still shaping the earth's surface.

These grand landforms are complemented perfectly by a complex pattern of plant communities, as small in its scale as the main features of the landscape are large. It seems fitting that a phenomenon caused by the main plant community — the atmospheric effect of the eucalypt forest's volatile oils — gives the area its name.

Distant landscapes in nature normally appear slighty blue because the sun's rays are scattered by contact with fine dust particles and droplets of vapour. But in the Blue Mountains, light is scattered even more effectively by fine drops of eucalyptus oil in the air, and the vegetation appears quite blue, especially from the coast.

The atmospheric blue of these mountains may not be a deeper hue than that of any other forested hills in Australia, but the extent of the forests here makes it seem so.

Open forest, dominated by eucalypts, ten to 30 metres tall, covers the whole area except for the swamps in high valleys, patches of relict rainforest,

BLACK AND BLUE The native black-eyed Susan grows all around the seaboard of the south-east.

and a few sub-alpine areas. The plant life is the richest of its type in Australia. About 100 species of orchids grow on the sands and shales, and over a thousand different species of flowering plants fill the Blue Mountains National Park alone.

Rock type is the main influence on the plants here, with many tree species being confined to a particular geological zone. At Mount Wilson for example, there is a strong contrast between the

thick rainforest on the basalt top of the mountain and the eucalypts on the dry, absorbent sandstone of the surrounding slopes.

Soils on the sandstone, which has large quartz grains, are very sandy and poor in nutrients, especially lacking in phosphorus and nitrogen. Water runs off these soils rapidly. Forests of taller trees with lush vegetation occur on the more phosphorus-rich soils.

Towards the edges of cliffs, tall trees give way to mallees and then heath. Vegetation becomes stunted on rocky outcrops — here yellow guinea flower, pink boronia and white epacris can be found. Communities of exquisite small plants grow in the moist caves and drip ledges below the cliff line. Numerous mosses and ferns couch wild violets, slender libertia and reclining epacris.

Plants of the Blue Mountains have made many adaptations to try to overcome the nutrient deficiencies of the sandstone regions. One such technique is the development of a symbiotic association between the roots of certain plants and a fungus (Mycorrhiza), which enables plants to absorb nitrogen and phosphorus more efficiently.

In another adaptive response, some casuarinas grow dense mats of very fine roots to increase the root-absorbing area, and thereby obtain the nitrogen they require. The thick, hard leaves of eucalypts may also help the trees to absorb and retain phosphorus.

Fire is a significant feature of the Blue Mountains environment and many species, particularly the eucalypts, are dependent upon it. But fires can be damaging to plants which rely on seeding for reproduction if they occur before the plants have reached maturity and produced new seed.

Most of the basalt mountains, with their deep, fertile soils, support patches of rainforest dominated by coachwood (Ceratopetalum apetalum), callicoma (Callicoma serratifolia) and sassafras (Doryphora sassafras). Dry rainforest containing red cedar (Toona australis) and silky ash (Ehretia acuminata) occurs in the valley of the Kowmung and the Kanangra Gorge, but most of the mature cedar trees were removed by the 1950s, if not long before.

The Boyd Plateau, with its elevation and moist climate, has a number of sub-alpine species such as the snow gum (Eucalyptus pauciflora) and the snow daisy (Celmisia longifolia) which also occur in the Australian Alps.

Among the more than 150 species in the Blue Mountains which are listed

as rare, endangered, or restricted in range, the best known is an endemic conifer, *Microstrobos fitzgeraldii*, a relict species from a wetter, cooler climate, which grows in the spray at the base of waterfalls.

The only other species from this genus occurs in the alpine areas of Tasmania, and in the Blue Mountains it now exists at only six wet, misty sites in cliffs above the Jamieson Valley. The largest group, which includes 90 plants at Wentworth Falls, is threatened by polluted water.

Thin on the ground

The poverty of the area's soils is reflected in the scarcity of ground-dwelling creatures. But although the population densities of mammals, reptiles and amphibians, are fairly low, in the area as a whole there is a great variety of species to match the diversity of plant life.

Amongst the common species of the open forests are the koala (*Phascolarctus cinereus*) which feeds mainly on the leaves of forest red gum (*E. terecticornis*) and grey gum (*E. punctata*), the greater glider (*Petauroides volans*) and the yellow-tailed black cockatoo

QUIET LIFE The sedentary wonga pigeon prefers the ground to the treetops.

CLASSIC CLIFFS These sheer cliffs in the Kanangra-Boyd National Park, known as the Kanangra Walls, are flanked by rubble slopes where the thin soil has been colonised eagerly by bush.

(*Callocephalon funereus*). The uncommon glossy black cockatoo (*Calyptorhynchus lathami*) relies on seeds of certain casuarina.

Regular feeders on the soft fruits of the rainforest trees include the mountain brushtail possum (*Trichosurus caninus*), the wonga pigeon (*Leucosarcia melanoleuca*) and the Australian king parrot (*Alisterus scapularis*). There are specialised birds of the swamps, such as the seed-eating tawny grassbird (*Megalurus timoriensis*) and the beautiful firetail (*Emblema bella*).

Colonies of brush-tailed rock-wallabies (*Petrogale penicillata*), which in many parts of Australia have been exterminated by habitat changes and foxes, still exist amongst the crags of the Kowmung River, Jenolan Caves and the Colo and its tributaries.

Yellow-footed skinks, blue-tongued lizards, geckoes and dragon lizards represent the lizard family, while the most common snake is the deadly red-bellied black snake, which feeds on frogs along river and creek beds.

On Sydney's doorstep

The wilderness areas which can be seen from the popular lookouts scattered around the settled areas of the central Blue Mountains stretch to the most distant horizon and beyond. The three national parks in the region — the Blue Mountains, Wollemi, and Kanangra-Boyd, covering a total area of 801 326 hectares — are mainly wilderness and remain largely as they were before white settlement.

These parks range from 60 to 160 kilometres distant from Sydney, Australia's largest population centre, and they are being managed largely for their wilderness value, complementing the older, developed parks closer to the outer suburbs.

From Katoomba, a bushwalker can trek for days along safe, well-marked tracks and see no sign of civilisation, except perhaps another hiker. In Wollemi National Park, the largest eucalypt forest wilderness in Australia, there is even more scope for enjoyment of the bush. The most popular area here is the 200-metre-deep gorge of the Colo, also a challenging canoeing river.

Starting on the Capertee near Glen Davis, there are 120 kilometres of wild, rushing river before civilisation is met with again at Upper Colo. Further north, the wilderness is little known except from the air and even in the 1990s, bushwalkers are still finding new, untrod canyons to explore. □

Despite the pressures on the environment caused by a large and growing population, Sydney remains the maritime city supreme, embracing its harbour and, in turn, itself embraced by the green belt of bushland preserved in its national parks

A maritime metropolis

Sydney is named after an eighteenth-century British politician who was largely responsible for making it a repository for his country's surplus convicts. Such an ignoble beginning could be matched only by the nobility of the setting chosen for Australia's first white settlement.

Few major cities have been lucky enough to be blessed with a location surrounded by so many handsome waterways. Sydney is situated on the central coast of New South Wales where the waves of the South Pacific Ocean break on fine beaches, crash against sandstone cliffs or enter through narrow openings to roll into the calmer waters of scores of harbours, bays and inlets.

The city has grown up around the finest of the harbours, Port Jackson, and, in time, it has developed a middle-aged spread, stretching all the way across the coastal plain to the base of the Blue Mountains.

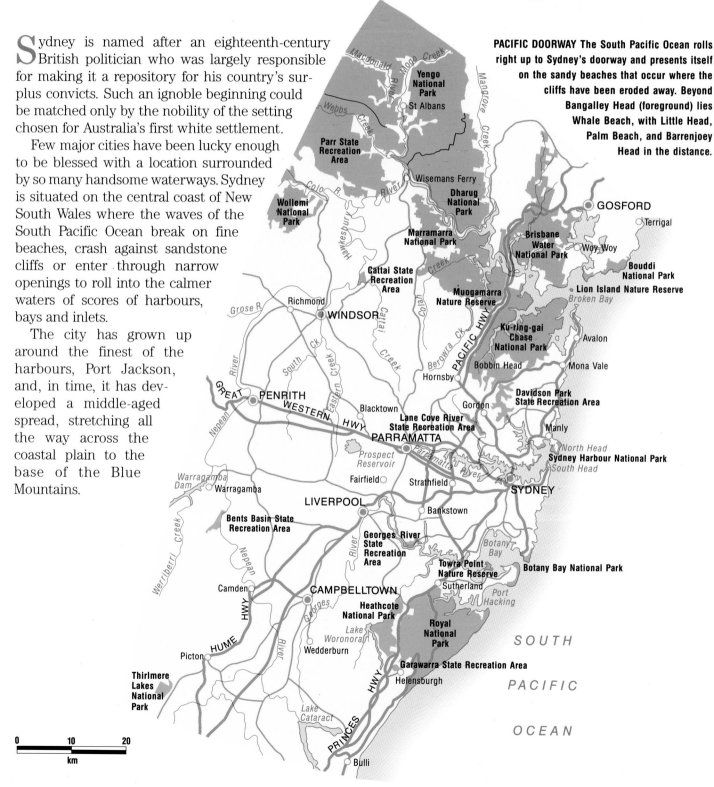

PACIFIC DOORWAY The South Pacific Ocean rolls right up to Sydney's doorway and presents itself on the sandy beaches that occur where the cliffs have been eroded away. Beyond Bangalley Head (foreground) lies Whale Beach, with Little Head, Palm Beach, and Barrenjoey Head in the distance.

CITY AND THE BUSH A view to the south-east shows the harbour entrance, South Head, Middle Head (centre, right) and Sydney's eastern suburbs. The bushland is part of the foreshore once reserved for the military but now part of Sydney Harbour National Park.

SAND GRAIN The wind and the salt spray work constantly on Sydney's soft, sandstone cliffs to form fantastic shapes and expose grain patterns as complex as any which occur in timber.

The climate verges on the subtropical, with warm, humid summers and mild, sunny winters. As a result, the citizens of this largely unplanned city have learnt to make the most of its natural advantages, cultivating a relaxed, more hedonistic lifestyle than has evolved in most other great cities.

Central Sydney is built on sandstone formed between 180 and 225 million years ago from the deep sandy sediments deposited by ancient rivers in an extensive lake or estuarine basin. Much later, a new eastern coast rose from the sea, and this elevated sandstone plateau presented an excellent medium for erosive sculpting by the water and the wind.

The 'art' of the elements is now on display: the great stained cliffs of Hawkesbury sandstone facing the sea off Vaucluse and Bondi and at the Royal National Park in the south; the massive, yellow-grey bluff at North

NORTHERN LION Lion Island, in Broken Bay, provides a protected breeding ground for seabirds.

The harbour's gateway to the Pacific Ocean is one-and-a-half kilometres wide and flanked on one side by the sandstone bluff of North Head, with its windswept cliffs almost a hundred metres high, and on the other by the less imposing South Head. Inside the heads there is a labyrinthine system of waterways where many divergent arms of deep, green water are separated by long fingers of often steep and rocky land.

Although the once brilliant waters have dimmed in recent years under the heavy pressures of the metropolis and its 3.5 million inhabitants, it is still a remarkably beautiful harbour to find within a major city. Fortunately only the modest Parramatta and Lane Cove Rivers and a few smaller streams empty into the harbour, so its waters are not subjected to a heavy silt load.

Western Sydney, flat or undulating and spreading to the Blue Mountains, is built on younger sandstone than the rest of the city. The rock is rich in shale and has broken down to form a more fertile soil than the poor ground around the harbour. Two hundred years ago, the infant colony almost starved when the first harbourside attempts at agriculture failed dismally. It was in the west, at Parramatta, that viable agriculture began and where for some years the colony's governor had his base.

A sandstone barrier

Sydney, unlike almost any other large city, is hemmed in by a belt of infertile and relatively unsettled country made up of sandstones which have been deeply dissected by the erosion of rivers. Acting as a barrier to expansion, this enclosing semi-circle of rugged plateau and ridge country was the source of frustration to early explorers.

The Surveyor-General, Sir Thomas Mitchell, travelled north in 1885 to Wisemans Ferry '... where no objects met the eye except barren rocks and stunted trees ...', and contemplated without much enjoyment the road that was to be made through this 'dreary and inhospitable scene'. Referring to the road, he commented that the 'stream of population must be confined to it, since it cannot be spread over a region so utterly unprofitable and worthless'. This crescent of wilderness is now appreciated as one of the city's great resources, providing a reservoir of natural beauty on the threshold of the crowded suburbs.

It is in this rough country, resistant to development, that an encircling

Head that guards the entrance to Sydney Harbour; Lion Island, that Sphinx-like watches the entry to Broken Bay; the many coastal headlands that divide one golden sweep of sandy beach from the next; and a thousand places around the harbour and the nearby ridges.

Everywhere the soft, granular stone has been weathered into rounded boulders, ledges, caves and potholes. The sandstone has even been built into the man-made structures of the city with its use in impressive public buildings and churches and the solid foundations of suburban homes.

Like Broken Bay in the north and Port Hacking in the south, Sydney Harbour is a drowned river valley formed during an ice age when the ocean receded and the coastal rivers cut deep valleys towards the lower sea level. When the ocean rose again, it drowned the lower reaches of these deep valleys and formed fine harbours.

chain of large parks and reserves has been established: Ku-ring-gai, Marra Marra, Bouddi, Brisbane Water, Dharug, Yengo, Wollemi, Blue Mountains, Heathcote and Royal National Parks now make up the nearest thing Sydney has to a 'green belt'.

The many exposed surfaces of soft sandstone rock in the Sydney region provided a perfect medium for the artistic expression of its Aboriginal peoples. The rock engravings which were made by them on the flat and undulating sandstone platforms and ledges are scattered from the Royal National Park in the south to the Hunter Valley in the north, and west to the Blue Mountains. More than 600 of these sites have been recorded, with the greatest concentrations north of Sydney in Warringah and the Ku-ring-gai Chase National Park (14 615 hectares) and extending across the Hawkesbury to Dharug National Park (1484 hectares).

The subjects of this rock art vary greatly: spirit beings, weapons and implements, footprints, terrestrial and marine animals are all represented. It seems likely that in some places, such as at Devils Rock in the Yengo National Park (139 861 hectares) north-west of Sydney, the engravings were associated with the spiritual life of the local people and served as a focus for a variety of ceremonies.

Phillip's choice

Botany Bay, where Captain James Cook landed in 1770, was the first choice for the first settlement in Australia. Captain Arthur Phillip brought his fleet of 11 ships into the Bay on 18 January, 1788, but found it disappointingly shallow and the surrounding country to be tidal swamps and sand dunes quite unsuitable for habitation.

Sydney Cove, which Captain Phillip chose for its deep anchorages close to shore and the presence of a stream of fresh water, remains the city's main gateway, with the potent symbols of the metropolis all in view: the distinctive sails of the Opera House on the eastern side, the great span of the Harbour Bridge arching away on the west and

GREEN EMBRACE The north-south coastal sprawl comes to an abrupt halt when it reaches the natural barriers of Broken Bay and Port Hacking, both waterways which are buffered by large areas of bushland reserved in national parks . Maitland Bay (top) is in Bouddi National Park, in the north, while the cliffs and heathland (left), are typical of the Royal National Park, in the south.

the skyscrapers of the business district towering behind. Even the stream, known as the Tank Stream, is still there, though now it flows secretly under the concrete and steel of the city.

To the west of Sydney, the Hawkesbury-Nepean river system drains 22 000 square kilometres in the hinterland extending from Goulburn in the south to Lithgow in the west and near Rylstone in the north-west. It enters the sea at Broken Bay, about 30 kilometres north of the city. The Nepean runs for many kilometres below the steep face of the Blue Mountains which rises suddenly from the western limit of the coastal plain and forms a hazy, azure backdrop, on clear days easily visible from high points in the city.

HARBOUR THRESHOLD South Head is diminutive compared with its northern counterpart and less obvious after dark. The Hornby Light has warned shipping of its presence since 1858.

159

At one stage of its journey, the Nepean River cuts into the steep slopes of the Blue Mountains and out again, forming the scenic Fairlight Gorge. At various places it is joined by mountain rivers such as the Warragamba, the Grose, the Colo and the MacDonald.

The fruitful Hawkesbury

After the Nepean becomes the Hawkesbury River, the lower reaches cut a gorge in the sandstone plateau, creating a landscape which certainly impressed the English novelist, Anthony Trollope, who visited Australia in 1872: '... on the Rhine, on the Mississippi, and on the Hawkesbury alike, there is created an idea that if the traveller would only leave the boat and wander

CITY'S WILDERNESS For about half its length, the Hawkesbury — the ocean outlet for the Nepean-Warragamba river system — flows through large national parks such as Brisbane Water (left bank) and Ku-ring-gai Chase (right).

HAWKESBURY SANDSTONE Once it reaches the tidal limits of Broken Bay, the Hawkesbury flows within the confines of a rugged, steep-sided river valley.

inland he would be paid by the revelation of marvellous beauties of nature ... the headlands are higher, the bluffs are bolder, and the turns and manoeuvres of the course which the waters have made for themselves are grander, and to me more enchanting, than those of either the European or the American river ... '.

As a drowned river valley with a full tidal range over much of its course, the Hawkesbury estuary supports a variety of fish, eels, prawns, squid, crabs, and even fairy penguins (*Eudyptula minor*), which have a colony on Lion Island. Freshwater fish such as Australian bass (*Macquaria novaemaculata*) and freshwater mullet (*Myxus petardi*) breed in the estuary and the young make their way upstream.

Perhaps most remarkable among these creatures are the short- and long-finned eels (*Anguilla australis, A. reinhardtii*) which travel great distances to maintain their life cycle. The adult eels are believed to swim from the rivers of eastern Australia to spawn in the Coral sea off New Caledonia. The eel larvae remain more than a year at sea before returning to the estuaries where they become elvers or true baby eels, and make their way upstream.

The upstream passage of the eels on the Hawkesbury-Nepean is blocked by the high wall of the Warragamba Dam, built in the late 1950s. Not to be discouraged, the five-centimetre-long elvers wriggle their way for 300 metres up the rocky bed of an adjacent small stream, cross a road, scale two concrete walls and slither another 50 metres down an embankment to reach the water. Once in the dam they grow to adulthood and complete the cycle.

From beach to marsh

Sydney's plant life is heavily influenced by the region's two main geological formations and the soils derived from them. The ubiquitous Hawkesbury sandstone produces thin soils of low fertility, and the Wiannamatta shale forms more fertile, clayey soils. Another influence is rainfall which is high near the coast and much lower inland.

In spite of their instability, dryness and exposure to salty, offshore winds, the beaches and dunes facing the ocean support a specialised native vegetation which has adapted to meet these very severe conditions. *Spinifex hirsutus*, a bluish-green grass is commonly found in these situations and with its habit of producing runners acts to bind the shifting sands. The coast wattle (*Aca-*

BANKSIA MAN The heath banksia, which may grow to seven metres, colonises poor sandstone soils along the New South Wales coast.

cia sophorae), which forms low, dark-green thickets and certain hummock grasses, such as the yellow daisy (*Senecio spathulatus*) are also found here. Behind the frontal dunes and out of the immediate blast of the wind, it is possible to find tea-trees such as the coastal species (*Leptospermum laevigatum*) in dense thickets and further landward, the hardy old man banksia (*Banksia serrata*).

Harsh conditions for plants persist on the thin soils of sandstone origin near the coast where the 'scorch' of salt-laden winds also continues to have an influence. Despite these conditions, diverse and interesting plant communities exist. There are extensive heathlands with various species of banksia including heath banksia (*Banksia ericifolia*), *Banksia asplenifolia*, the grass tree (*Xanthorrhoea media*) and smaller shrubs such as *Darwinia fascicularis, Leucopogon microphyllus* and *Epacris microphylla*.

Along creek banks and wetter areas there are sundews (*Drosera*) which use sticky, hair-covered leaves to trap insects. Coastal mallees such as *Eucalyptus obtusiflora* are often found in considerable numbers in these environments along with the dwarf apple (*Angophora hispida*).

Further inland, away from the constant influence of the sea, dry sclerophyll forests, dominated by trees of modest height such as the scribbly gum (*Eucalyptus haemastoma*) and the bloodwood (*E. gummifera*) have evolved.

In the gullies, where the soil is deeper, grow the smooth-barked apples (*Angophora costata*), bastard mahoganies (*Eucalyptus umbra*) and Sydney peppermints (*E. piperita*). A rich understorey of small, hard-leaved shrubs is usually associated with these forests. Prominent among this supporting cast

NATIVE DRUMS Drumsticks, a heath plant, is so-named because of the shape of its seed cones.

PARK DECORATION Ornamental trees such as the Moreton Bay fig — in nature, a rainforest tree — appealed to the grandiose nature of turn-of-the-century city fathers.

are grevilleas such as the red-flowering *Grevillea speciosa*, needle bushes including *Hakea sericea*, various yellow peas and Christmas bush (*Ceratopetalum gummiferum*).

In the deep, wet gullies where rivers or streams have cut through to the shales, the shale has been worn down to produce reasonably fertile soil. Here, rainforest communities may be found, with trees such as the lillypilly (*Acmena smithii*), coachwood (*Ceratopetalum apetalum*), sassafras (*Doryphora sassafras*) and various figs. Here also, as well as on the ridges above, where there is a capping of more fertile shale or basalt soils, stands of wet sclerophyll forest grow, and trees such as the roundleaf gum (*Eucalyptus deanei*) Sydney blue gum (*E. saligna*), and the blackbutt (*E. pilularis*) dominate, with fewer numbers of turpentine (*Syncarpia glomulifera*) and grey ironbark (*E. paniculata*) also present.

In the wet sclerophyll forest an extensive understorey of hard-leaved shrubs is lacking, and instead there is a cover of grasses with smaller trees such as she-oak (*Casuarina littoralis*).

Sydney's extensive coastal waterways have a fringe of distinctive aquatic vegetation, characterised most frequently by grey-green mangrove thick-

ets and occasional salt marshes, such as those at Towra Point. These are most commonly found edging bays along the Parramatta River, Middle Harbour, the Hawkesbury and Brisbane Water.

Western Sydney's Wianammata shale soils and dryer climate support archetypal 'bush': a grassy woodland consisting of grey box (*Eucalyptus hemiphloia*) and forest red gum (*E. tereticornis*), with regular scatterings of ironbarks. The trees in this region tend to be widely spaced with the ground grass-covered and lacking the profusion of flowering shrubs found in dry forests closer to the coast.

Any account of the Sydney region's vegetation which describes only native plants will of course not give the full picture, as many of the most prominent urban trees have been introduced. In the parklands of Observatory Hill, the Domain and Centennial Park and dotted throughout other parts of the inner city, the statuesque form of the Canary Island date palm (*Phoenix canariensis*) and the massive bulk and spreading branches of the Moreton Bay fig (*Ficus macrophylla*) are a very definite presence; so are the tall and formal Norfolk Island pines (*Araucaria heterophylla*) which line the beachfront at Manly as they once did at Bondi.

In suburban streets, the purple-flowering jacaranda (*Jacaranda mimosaefolia*) of South America and the brushbox (*Tristania conferta*) from the northern rainforests of New South Wales add beauty and interest to the city, although the latter rarely attains its natural shape in the city. Pruned in order to avoid snagging overhead power lines, the city brush box usually sports an unnatural 'lollipop' shape and bears little resemblance to the bush version that shoots to 20 metres before putting out a branch.

The city's bush

Compared with the older cities of the Northern Hemisphere, Sydney is not a very densely populated city due to the way it has sprawled across 4000 square kilometres. This sprawl, encouraged by the inhabitants' traditional preference for free-standing, suburban cottages has been a mixed blessing.

While suburbia has spread relentlessly in every direction except east, the rugged topography of the sandstone country to the north and south has meant that building has generally been restricted to the relatively level ridges. As a result, many kilometres of bushland in adjacent steep valleys have been left in their natural state and have often been protected by reservation in public parks.

Such islands of bush in a sea of brick and asphalt occur in the Lane Cove Valley, upper Middle Harbour and the Georges River. By a combination of good luck and good management, substantial national parks have been established close to the city at Ku-ring-gai Chase in the north, around the Sydney Harbour foreshores and at Botany Bay National Park (436 hectares) and Royal National Park (15 014 hectares) in the south. Taken together these factors account for the presence of an unusual range of native animal life within or in close proximity to the city.

The koala (*Phascolarctos cinereus*), a not terribly bright but much-loved native animal, survives in a wild state on the fringes of Sydney. Colonies of koalas can be found at Avalon on the northern beach peninsula and at Wedderburn south of Campbelltown. This slow-moving marsupial spends most of its life in eucalyptus trees, eating the leaves which form its main food.

In the outer suburbs of Sydney, the few remaining populations of wild koalas are under great pressure from urban development. The reduced availability of suitable food trees and the

SYDNEY ROCK The Hawkesbury River shoreline in Ku-ring-gai National Park shows a cross-section of shallow-soiled sandstone country. The low tide has exposed outcrops of Sydney rock oysters.

NOT A GUM TREE The smooth-barked apple, a relative of the eucalypts, thrives in well-drained gullies such as this one in Royal National Park.

threat posed by the introduction into the koala's vicinity of such things as dogs and motor cars makes their future a precarious one.

The brush-tailed possum (*Trichosurus vulpecula*) is a tree-dwelling marsupial that has adapted rather better to suburban life than the koala. It has learnt to feed on kitchen refuse and to live in the steeply gabled roofs of old houses. A muscular and able climber, the possum is well able to cope with any unwelcome interest from domestic cats and dogs.

The common ringtail possum (*Pseudocheirus peregrinus*) can also be found in Sydney but it is not as well adapted to the city as it relies on eucalyptus leaves for food and trees for shelter. The eastern pygmy-possum (*Cercartetus nanus*) which largely feeds on blossoms and insects, is also present where there are sufficient shrubs such as bottlebrushes to provide its needs. The sugar glider (*Petaurus breviceps*), a close relative of the pos-

163

sum, still occurs where forest cover remains, as does the rarely seen feathertail glider (*Acrobates pygmaeus*).

The long-nosed bandicoot (*Perameles nasuta*) lives in those parts of suburban Sydney where there are areas of bushland or large overgrown gardens. Its habit of digging up flower beds in search of the insects and grubs on which it feeds has done little to ensure its future in suburbia.

The native water rat (*Hydromys chrysogaster*) occurs in rivers and creeks throughout Sydney where it feeds on fish and other aquatic creatures. It is distinguishable from the introduced black rat, and other rodents by its thick fur and white-tipped tail.

On warm summer evenings in Sydney, the dark shapes of flying foxes can often be seen flapping awkwardly overhead. Grey-headed flying foxes or fruit bats (*Pteropus poliocephalus*) spend their days sleeping in large colonies, such as the one in the northern suburb of Gordon. At dusk they leave their camps in long columns to search for food — the fruit of the Moreton Bay fig tree is a favourite.

Juvenile bats are at first unable to fly and are carried everywhere by their mothers — even on feeding forays — until they are about a month old. The mother uses her sense of smell to find food although flying foxes — unlike other bats — have excellent vision.

Birds of a feather

Almost 400 species of birds have been recorded near Sydney if stragglers, rare migrants and those no longer present are counted. A more likely number for an experienced observer to see over a full year would be 200 species, not including some 15 or so common introduced birds.

At Towra Point in Botany Bay there are winding channels, shallow waters and mudflats which provide an important feeding ground for the migratory wading birds. These birds breed in eastern Siberia and fly south to Australia to escape the northern winter. This region is a refuge for 25 species of waders including the ruddy turnstone (*Arenaria interpres*), the red-necked stint (*Calidris ruficollis*) and eastern curlews (*Numenius madagascariensis*) that mass here in the spring and summer months. Botany Bay is also a

COMMON SKIES Rainbow lorikeets often visit Sydney gardens near areas of natural bushland. The grey-headed flying fox has also adapted to city life and feeds in Sydney's parklands.

breeding ground for the little tern (*Sterna albifrons*), a regular migrant that arrives in October and departs in April.

The mangrove swamps and samphire flats which occur here and in other coastal inlets and bays of the Sydney area support herons, cormorants and pelicans. Sea birds such as the wandering albatross (*Diomedia exulans*) — with a wingspan of well over three metres — the northern and southern giant petrels (*Macronectes halli, M. giganteus*), various skuas, and flocks of silver gulls (*Larus novaehollandiae*) and crested terns (*Sterna bergii*) are commonly seen off the coast.

In the northern suburbs, kookaburras (*Dacelo leachii*), magpies (*Gymnorhina tibicen*), the brilliantly coloured rainbow lorikeets (*Trichoglossus haematodus*) and the bold and restless noisy miner (*Manorina melanocephala*) are common.

In the sandstone forests and heathlands near the coast, such as those that occur extensively in the Royal National Park, nectar-rich banksias and grevilleas provide a rich feeding ground for honeyeaters. Yellow-faced honeyeaters (*Lichenostomus chrysops*), red wattlebirds (*Anthochaera carunculata*), noisy friarbirds (*Philemon corniculatus*) and white-naped honeyeaters (*Melithreptus lunatus*) are common visitors here. They compete for food with the New Holland, white-cheeked and white-eared honeyeaters (*Phylidonyris novaehollandiae, P. nigra, Lichenostomus leucotis*), helping to fill the bush with noise and life.

Western Sydney, with its woodlands on shale soils, supports quite a different birdlife from the sandstone areas. Here there are yellow-tinted honeyeaters (*Lichenostomus flavescens*), restless flycatchers (*Myiagra inquieta*), speckled warblers (*Sericornis sagittatus*) and yellow-rumped thornbills (*Acanthiza chrysorrhoa*), while in the wetlands and lagoons of the upper Hawkesbury, the waterfowl such as Pacific black ducks (*Anas superciliosa*), black swans (*Cygnus atratus*), Eurasian coots (*Fulica atra*), and striated herons (*Ardea striata*), are at home.

The least obvious members of the city's animal population are the reptiles which, as if aware of the general human antipathy that exists toward them, have largely maintained their presence by keeping clear of their two-legged co-inhabitants. There are about 25 species of snakes, 25 of lizards and five of turtles living around Sydney.

bush. It has the habit of laying its eggs in a hole dug into a termite mound; the termites repair the hole and in doing so cover and incubate the eggs.

Dragon lizards are also found here, the best known being the bearded dragon (*Pogona barbata*) which grows to about half a metre in length and sports a spiny 'beard' — in fact a fold of skin which it raises to frighten away its enemies. The eastern water dragon (*Physignathus lesueurii*) is of similar size but with a more slender body and a long thin tail. It sunbathes on rocks or branches by creeks until disturbed, when it drops into the water with a splash and waits on the bottom until danger has passed.

MODEST DRAGON The 'keeled' tail of the eastern waterdragon makes it an efficient swimmer; it stays under water for half an hour.

BLUE ALARM The blue-tongued lizard exposes its alarmingly coloured tongue when disturbed.

Three of the snakes are capable of inflicting a fatal bite: the death adder (*Acanthophis antarcticus*), the eastern or mainland tiger snake (*Notechis scutatus*) and the eastern brown snake (*Pseudonaja textilis*). The red-bellied black snake (*Pseudechis porphyriacus*) and the Sydney broad-headed snake (*Hoplocephalus bungaroides*) are also best given a wide berth.

Seven species of sea snake have been recorded in Sydney waters, the most common being the yellow-bellied sea-snake (*Pelamis platurus*) which grows to about 1.3 metres in length and displays the paddle-shaped tail characteristic of all sea-snakes.

The lace monitor (*Varanus varius*) is still a common sight in the urban

The long-necked turtle (*Chelodina longicollis*), which lives in creeks and swamps, is the only species of freshwater turtle to occur in the Sydney area. Many of the tropical marine turtles, including the green turtle (*Chelonia mydas*) and the loggerhead (*Caretta caretta*) visit Sydney coastal waters from time to time. These visitors from the north are easily recognised by their enormous size and swimming flippers.

The thousands of fishermen on and around the city's waters testify to the richness of its marine life. Whales and dolphins are often seen offshore and Australian fur seals (*Arctocephalus pusillus*) and leopard seals (*Hydrurga leptonyx*) are occasional visitors.

In the ocean off Sydney, cool southern waters meet a warm current from the tropics and give rise to an extraordinarily rich environment. Nearly 160 species of fish have been recorded in Sydney Harbour, many of them tropical visitors.

The Port Jackson shark (*Heterodontus portus jacksoni*), the yellow-tail kingfish (*Seriola lalandi*), the red rock cod (*Scorpaena cardinalis*) and the mulloway or jewfish (*Argyrosomus hololepidotus*) are just a few of the harbour fish familiar to Sydneysiders.

Troubled waters

Inevitably, with a large and growing population clustered around such a marine environment, the spectre of pollution has raised its head. Stormwater

up of silt has smothered many marine plants and animals and dramatically reduced water clarity in some areas.

Most things that go into the harbour eventually find their way to the bottom. Surveys have shown that sediments on the harbour floor are heavily contaminated with toxins such as various forms of refined metals and pesticides, which are washed there along with the other residues of the city's heavy industry.

The concentration of 'heavy' metals, such as lead, mercury, iron and copper, is about 100 times the natural level, especially at the head of inner harbour bays such as Darling Harbour, Blackwattle Bay and Hen and Chicken Bay.

Scientists believe that every time these sediments are stirred up in the process of dredging or waterside con-

Acclaimed as a delicacy, the oyster is grown and fattened near Sydney in extensive oyster leases in the Georges River and the Hawkesbury estuary. Oysters, being filter feeders, are easily affected by changes in water quality and pollution in the Georges River has begun to threaten the future of the oyster-growing industry there.

Hardly a Sydney summer passes without a headline about the Sydney funnelweb (*Atrax robustus*), the large, black, shiny spider most likely to elicit a response of fear and loathing in any Sydneysider. While it is found in upland areas throughout the central coast, it has become particularly associated with suburban areas such as the North Shore and the Woronora Plateau, where man has chosen to share its habitat. Since the first verified fatality in 1927, more than a dozen people have succumbed to the funnel web's venomous bite. Fortunately, the development of an effective antivenene in recent years has ended the funnel web's reign of terror.

The sounds of summer

Black prince, greengrocer, and double drummer are some of the colourful names given to Sydney's noisiest natural wonder. They are all cicadas, respectively *Psaltoda argentata*, *Cyclochila australasiae* and *Thopha saccata*. The shrill song of these large, winged insects is a feature of Sydney summers — the hotter the summer, the longer and louder the cicadas seem to continue their din.

No other insect has developed such an effective and specialised means of producing sound. Some of the larger species, such as the double drummer, produce a noise intensity in excess of 120 decibels — at close range this approaches the pain threshold of the human ear.

The song is a mating call produced by the males only. It is made by organs which are called tymbals, after a type of kettledrum. The tymbals lie at the base of the abdomen and buckle in response to the contraction of the attached muscles; the rapid buckling inwards and relaxation of the tymbals produces pulses of sound. The insect can alter the pitch of its song by expanding or contracting its abdomen which is mostly an air chamber, the tymbals occupying only a small part.

So intense is the drumming of the cicada that it actually repels birds which otherwise would feed freely on this fat insect. While the life span of the

A BAD MIX Despite stringent government regulations and stiff penalties for liquid waste dumping, oil and chemical spills, such as this one in the Georges River, continue to occur.

drains discharging into waterways and partly treated sewage flowing into the ocean have caused not only an aesthetic problem but have compromised the purity of some locally caught seafood, particularly crustaceans.

The city's roads, gutters and footpaths help create a super-efficient catchment area which collects vast amounts of water — and rubbish — every time it rains. Environmentalists believe this urban run-off is the biggest problem facing the harbour. The build-

struction work, they cause incalculable problems for marine life. Through absorption by fish and shellfish, they can easily enter the food chain and eventually affect human consumers. Other development programmes, such as filling in the heads of bays to make parks, has also had a marked effect on fish breeding patterns by removing mangrove and shallow water habitats.

One form of marine life which has suffered more than most is the Sydney rock oyster (*Crassostrea commercialis*).

cicada may be as long as seven years, nearly all of it is spent in the form of a nymph in an underground burrow, feeding on sap from roots. When it is mature the nymph works its way to the surface, sheds its skin, and emerges into a warm, summer evening to enjoy a noisy but brief adult life lasting little more than two or three weeks.

To attempt an understanding of Sydney's natural attractions in any one outing would be foolish, but there is a walk that comes close to suggesting the essence of the city's beauty. This is the Manly Scenic Walkway which covers about eight kilometres from the Spit Bridge on Middle Harbour to Dobroyd Head and then Manly. The track meanders around the Sydney Harbour National Park (388 hectares).

The walk begins in a wet gully full of rainforest trees such as lilly pilly (*Acmena smithii*), scentless rosewood (*Synoum glandulosum*) and the sweet pittosporum (*Pittosporum undulatum*). The pittosporum provided fruit to the Aborigines who once lived here and who left the midden (a refuse heap of old shell and bones) which can be seen on a rock shelf overlooking the water a little further on.

DECEMBER SONG The ear-splitting sound of the 'greengrocer' is synonymous with summer.

The track passes through eucalyptus forest and heathland and, after Grotto Point and approaching Cutler Lookout, there is a large sandstone platform bearing rock engravings depicting a giant kangaroo, fish and boomerangs. All around there is water and at Tania Park, the highest point of the walk, comes the most striking panorama, with North Harbour to the left, Middle Harbour to the right, and ahead, framed by the twin promontories of the Heads, the Pacific Ocean.

The track descends to Dobroyd Point through a tall heathland which in spring is alive with honeyeaters. From the point, seabirds such as gannets and shearwaters can often be seen and, across Manly Cove, there are the grey-green heaths of North Head and the assemblage of buildings that make up the old Quarantine Station.

A dry sclerophyll forest dominated by the smooth-barked apple (*Angophora costata*) is passed through on the way to Forty Baskets Beach and here there is an understorey of shrubs which flower impressively in late winter and spring: banksias, native fuchsias (*Epacris longiflora*), flannel flowers (*Actinotus helianthus*), the grey spider flower (*Grevillea buxifolia*) and the mountain devil (*Lambertia formosa*) are among them. The last few kilometres of the walk are through the harbourside suburbs of Fairlight and Manly and if the mood and the weather are conducive, it is worth pressing on to reach the immense, golden sweep of Manly Beach and the rolling breakers of the Pacific. ☐

The agricultural and industrial activities of the fertile Hunter Valley region are conducted against a background of some of the most extensive wilderness reserves in Australia

Fertile plains and plateaux shared with nature

The Hunter Valley is unmistakeable: a broad river valley set fair and square against the coast with a vast, fertile basin extending far into the hinterland; it is a classic example of its kind.

The valley is clearly defined north and south by mountains, westward a low rise separates it from the western slopes of New South Wales, while to the east it breaks through the Great Dividing Range to allow the Hunter River to reach the sea.

In this region, the Great Divide swings west in an expansive loop so that the valley reaches much further inland than other coastal valleys. In its climate too, the valley has links with the inland: much of its central area is quite dry for somewhere so close to the east coast.

VALLEY OF PLENTY Wine grapes thrive on the gentle, well-drained slopes of the lower Hunter Valley, overlooked by the valley's protective ranges, many of which are incorporated into national parks.

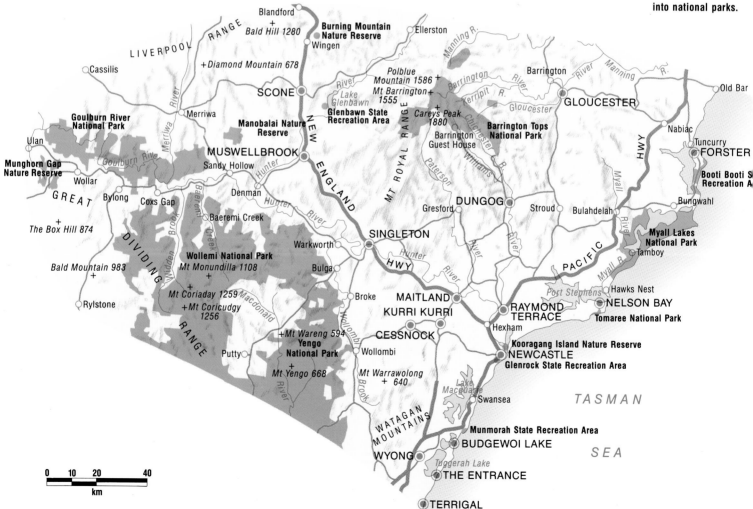

TALL CROP Many species of eucalypt, such as these ribbon gums, are harvested from the upland region fringing the Hunter Valley for use in the building trade and the manufacture of chipboard.

The central part of the Hunter Valley, from Wingen to Newcastle, tends to be undulating to hilly, with broad, fertile, flood plains along the river; this is a landscape which has been cleared and developed for grazing and the breeding of horses and cattle. Dairying, winemaking, fruit and cereal growing, and coal mining are long-established industries here.

Valley of the eucalypt

Eucalypts dominate the uncleared forest of the Hunter: the northern watershed supports large patches of wet sclerophyll forest dominated by silvertop stringybark (*Eucalyptus laevopinea*), ribbon gum (*E. viminalis*), black sallee (*E. stellulata*) and snow gum (*E. pauciflora*), while in the south, Blaxland's stringybark (*E. blaxlandii*) and Sydney blue gum (*E. Saligna*) are found.

The major wet sclerophyll forests — those which form the basis of the Valley's timber industry — are on the eastern and southern slopes of the Mount Royal Range and in the Barrington and Gloucester Tops region. Messmate stringybarks (*E. obliqua*) and tallow woods (*E. microcorys*) are common on these hills while in the Watagans, Sydney blue gum and blackbutt (*E. pilularis*) are found. The dry sclerophyll forest extends in a ragged belt from the coast as far as Mount Coricudgy, on the southern perimeter of the Hunter Valley, and contains a rich variety of trees including red bloodwood (*E. gummifera*), grey box (*E. moluccana*), spotted gum (*E. maculata*) and grey gum (*E. punctata*).

In the broad valley centre, adjacent to the flood plains, is a grassy woodland which, in the east is dominated by grey box, forested red gum (*E. tereticornis*), and broad-leaved red ironbarks (*E. fibrosa*), grading westwards into stands of white box (*E. albens*), Blakely's red gum (*E. blakelyi*), and narrow-leaved red ironbarks (*E. crebra*). Much of this central woodland has been cleared and replaced by rolling pastures of introduced grasses which dry off to a golden brown in the summer months.

In the Denman and Warkworth areas, and at Hexham, paperbark swamps are common on waterlogged ground and in the Hunter estuary there are also extensive tea-tree and mangrove swamps.

On the south- and east-facing mountain slopes, where the Pacific clouds drop their burden of moisture, pockets of rainforest flourish. Cool temperate

Where the Goulburn and Hunter Rivers meet, the rainfall is low enough for the area to be described as semi-arid. From there, in every direction, rainfall increases but nowhere more so than on the Barrington Tops with its dripping rainforests, mists and snow.

The southern part of the Hunter Valley rises into a plateau formed from ancient sandstones. There are deep valleys walled in by perpendicular cliffs and occasional basalt ridges reaching to over 1200 metres. In the west, the Goulburn River cuts through a lower sandstone plateau, while to the northwest the rolling hill country around

Merriwa runs up against the steep basalt hills and slopes of the Liverpool Range, a spur of the Great Divide.

The high and wet Mount Royal Range and the plateaux of Barrington and Gloucester Tops form the Hunter Valley's north-eastern boundary and provide, at 1586 metres, its highest summit. Along the coast, forested dunes, swampy flats and mangrove swamps run down to the sea. Lake Macquarie, Port Stephens and the Myall Lakes are closely linked to the Hunter Valley and its fortunes because of their proximity, although they are not directly part of the Hunter River system.

rainforests dominated by sassafras
(*Doryphora sassafras*) grow high up on
the slopes of the basalt mountains in
Wollemi National Park, while on the far
side of the valley, on the 'Tops'
plateaux, the rainforest is dominated
by negrohead beech (*Nothofagus
moorei*). Subtropical rainforest with red
cedar (*Toona australis*), tamarind
(*Diploglottis cunninghamii*), rosewood
(*Dysoxylum fraseranum*) and many
other species provides bursts of bright
green low down in deep valleys
beneath the 'Tops' country and the
Mount Royal Range.

There are a number of places where
an overview of the Hunter's diverse
scenery can be obtained. On the crest
of the Watagan mountains, there are
panoramas over the southern Hunter
from several lookouts in the state forest.
At Port Stephens, north of Newcastle,
the jagged coastline stretching south to
Birubi Point can be seen from the peak
of Yacaaba Head. Those who make the
climb to Careys Peak, on the southern
edge of the Barrington Tops, have views
as far east as the Stockton sand dunes
and the ocean.

An uneasy co-existence

White settlement in the Hunter Valley
began in the early 1800s and since then
industry has inflicted very obvious
marks on the landscape. There are
open-cut coal mines near Singleton and
Muswellbrook that resemble vast
craters, particularly when seen from
the air. Iron stanchions bearing electricity transmission lines radiate from power stations and march many kilometres
across the rolling hills.

There are tall smokestacks, cooling
towers and coal conveyors, and at Newcastle, a major steelworks, underground
coal mines, and all the activities of a
busy port are set within the beautiful
Hunter estuary. Nowhere is this jux-
taposition of industry and nature more
obvious than on Kooragang Island
which is shared by a nature reserve
(2926 hectares) protecting the habitat
of migratory wading birds, and an industrial complex which includes a
woodchip loader.

The swamps, mangrove forests and
mudflats of the Hunter estuary are
vital feeding and breeding grounds for
native birds, especially waders and
shore birds, as well as for migratory
birds — including ruddy turnstones
(*Arenaria interpres*) and whimbrels

SEASIDE LAKE Wallis Lake, almost a twin of Myall Lake a few kilometres to the south, is the most
northerly of the string of waterways that flank the Hunter coast.

(*Numenius phaeopus*) — which fly
thousands of kilometres from Alaska
and Siberia each year to escape the
northern winter. The estuary's intricate
web of life supports prawning and fishing industries which, like the swamps,
are threatened by industrial growth.

A park of lakes

The Myall Lakes north of Newcastle
form the largest freshwater or brackish
lake system on the New South Wales
coast. Within the Myall Lakes National
Park (31 493 hectares) are three main
lakes — Broadwater, Boolambayte and
Myall — all joined by narrow channels

and with salinity levels ranging from
close to that of seawater at Tamboy to
near freshwater at Bungwahl. The ratio of salt to fresh water depends on the
amount of rainwater running into the
lakes as there is virtually no tidal flush-
ing. The lakes have a fairly uniform
depth of about three to four metres, but
there are extensive shallows suitable
for waterfowl.

The dominant landscapes of the
park are the chain of wide lakes en-
closed on the west by forested hills and
with shorelines fringed by paperbark
trees, the extensive coastal moors and
the barrier of high, tree-covered dunes

numbers, and the waters are a breeding ground for prawns and many species of fish.

From the headlands and ocean beaches birds such as oystercatchers, gannets, terns and gulls are commonly seen. Occasionally, dolphins can be spotted riding the ocean breakers, and sometimes fairy penguins paddle their way along the rocky shore.

Subtropical to sub-alpine

East of Scone, the Mount Royal Range, a spur of the Great Divide, dips south into the Hunter Valley and broadens out, becoming the high plateau called the Barrington Tops. Here, granite once forced its way into the older sedimentary rocks, to be followed much later by volcanic outpourings that covered vast areas of country in basalt flows up to 300 metres thick. The land was then forced up into folds and eroded over many centuries to form this sub-alpine tableland which stands at the head of the Hunter and Manning Rivers.

The plateau is about 15 kilometres from east to west and 25 kilometres from north to south, and from its broad, skirting slopes ridges and streams radiate in all directions. Mount Barrington, at 1556 metres, and Careys Peak, at 1545 metres, are the highest points on the southern rim where the Paterson and Williams spurs come up to join the Mount Royal Range. Further north are the slightly higher Polblue and Brumlow Tops.

Barrington Tops National Park (39 121 hectares) is unequalled among New South Wales parks for climatic range and this is clearly reflected in its plant communities. There are lush subtropical rainforests in the deep valleys containing strangler figs, rosewood and stinging trees, and sub-alpine woodlands in the upper regions, with snow gums, grassland and sphagnum bog reminiscent of Mount Kosciusko. In between are wet sclerophyll forests of messmate stringybark, brown barrel (*Eucalyptus fastigata*) and ribbon gum, and dark patches of negrohead beech.

The subtropical and cool temperate rainforests which the park protects, together with a string of other rainforest areas distributed along the eastern highlands of New South Wales, have been accepted as World Heritage areas (see pp. 390–91). The addition to the park in 1983 of extensive subtropi-

MOUNTAIN GREENERY The Williams River rises in the Barrington-Gloucester Tops.

which separates the lakes from the sea. On the ocean side, there are long expanses of beach separated by rocky headlands. Surprisingly, some of the dunes near the coast, which rise a hundred or more metres above sea level and are covered with angophora and blackbutt forest, are no more than 2000 years old.

It was in these coastal dunes that heavy mineral sands were deposited during the stormy reworking of the coastal sand barrier after the sea's rise to its present level. These minerals are valuable in manufacturing industry, and mining of the dunes within the park for mineral sands was for many years a source of controversy between government and environmentalists. It has now ceased.

Amongst the wet sclerophyll forests of the dunes and inland hills, the moorland heaths, and the paperbark forests on the lake shores, the casual visitor may spot koalas, wallabies, possums, and gliders. Waterbirds such as black swans, ducks and egrets are attracted to the lake shallows in large

MOUNTAIN MOSS Giant mosses, such as this peat moss in the Polblue Tops, readily colonise cool, low-lying swamps in the ranges.

cal rainforests on the lower slopes of the 'Tops' country helped to make possible its promotion to a reserve of international significance.

The plateau, with its many swamps and bogs, also plays a very important role in supplying steady flows of water to the lower valleys. Unfortunately, large areas have been invaded by English broom (*Sarothamnus scoparius*), an introduced shrub which forms thickets that threaten to overwhelm many native plants and eventually upset the region's ecological balance. Efforts are now being made to find an effective biological control, possibly an insect, to eradicate this pest.

One of the popular weekend walks in the high country follows the Link Trail from Gloucester Tops along the ridge between the Chichester and Kerripit Rivers to Careys Peak, and then descends along the trail to the Barrington Guest House on the Williams River. Walkers must be equipped to deal with the sudden weather changes that occur in the high country, where a snow storm can suddenly blow in even during the warm months.

Fire down below

The casual visitor could be forgiven for thinking that one section of the upper Hunter Valley is an active volcanic region. The burning mountain at Wingen was thought to be a volcano when the first Europeans passed by it in 1828. It was soon realised that this forested hill sits over a burning coal seam.

The seam is about 30 metres below the surface and the fire is advancing slowly southwards; when it was first recorded, the fire was some 150 metres

north of its present position, indicating movement of about a metre a year. If it continues to burn at this rate, the fire could eventually burn its way out of the Burning Mountain Nature Reserve (15 hectares) which was created specifically because of its existence!

From the total length of seam known to have been burnt, it has been calculated that the fire has been burning for 5500 years and was probably started by spontaneous combustion. As the coal seam has been incinerated, the overlying rock strata have collapsed into its place causing the ground to slump and opening up cracks and fissures through which fresh air is drawn and sulphurous fumes and smoke are expelled. The surface of the ground at the active

vent area is stained by deposits of whitish quartz and iron oxide compounds, and can be very hot, reaching temperatures of 350°C in places. A walking track which winds up the slopes of Burning Mountain covers the three-and-a-half kilometres from the New England Highway to the vent area.

The Goulburn River National Park (67 897 hectares), between Sandy Hollow and Ulan, is largely a sandstone landscape dissected and eroded by many small streams and one major watercourse. The Goulburn River, a major tributary of the Hunter, has cut a 90-kilometre gorge through the park. The river flows between grass-covered banks before entering a shadowy region of cliffs honeycombed with caves.

The western plains start to show their influence on the vegetation here. The plateau country of Narrabeen sandstone supports Caley's ironbark (*Eucalyptus caleyi*), broad-leaved red ironbark, grey gum and narrow-leaved stringybark (*E. oblonga*). Trees commonly occurring near the river include yellow box (*E. melliodora*), white box, narrow-leaved red ironbark, and river oak (*Casuarina cunninghamiana*). The park supports plenty of wildlife, especially near the river, where wallabies, grey kangaroos and wombats are commonly seen.

The Goulburn River corridor is thought to have been one of the principal Aboriginal migratory routes be-

COAL-FIRED This hillside at Wingen will 'burn' as long as oxygen reaches the coal seam beneath.

COLO COUNTRY The Goulburn River, a tributary of the Hunter River, winds through the Wollemi National Park, the second largest national park in New South Wales. The park contains the vast and rugged Colo wilderness.

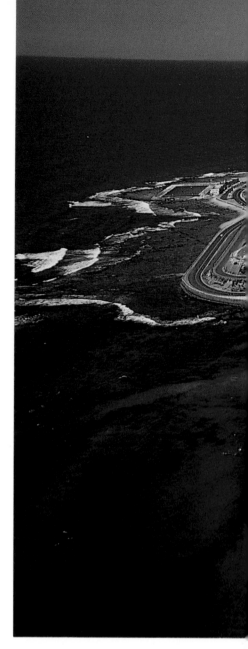

tween the central western slopes of New South Wales and the coast. Evidence of more than 250 encampments has been found scattered throughout the valley.

The Wollemi National Park (487 334 hectares) encompasses a vast sandstone wilderness extending from the Blue Mountains to the Goulburn and Hunter Valleys. The northern part of the park, which forms the south-western corner of the Hunter Valley, is a rugged plateau of Narrabeen sandstone rent by deep valleys such as Widden Brook and Baerami Creek, or punctured by deep volcanic necks.

Scattered over the plateau are dome-shaped, basalt mountains some of which, such as Mount Coricudgy and Mount Coriaday, rise to 1200 metres. The botanist R.T. Baker, collecting between Rylstone and the Goulburn River in the 1890s, found plants more like those of the western slopes of New South Wales than the tablelands. The absence of any high mountain barrier to the inland and the area's low rainfall help explain why the vegetation is such a contrast to that of the other tableland regions.

The black, and the white cypress pines (*Callitris endlicheri*, *C. glauca*) are typical trees of the west, while the two species of red ironbark are common

LAKESIDE Broad-leaf paperbarks and swamp she-oaks dominate the vegetation around coastal waterways such as Myall Lake.

in the Pilliga Scrub some 300 kilometres to the north-west. In deep, cool gullies eroded into the sandstone and on sections of the basalt mountains, rainforest has grown up.

Bushwalkers' paradise

The northern edges of Wollemi National Park are accessible at a number of places, including Baerami Creek and Coxs Gap. From many of the road-heads, the wilderness stretches away for tens of kilometres, often into national parks, and offering experienced bushwalkers opportunities for discovery and adventure.

In the south of the Hunter Valley, between Wollombi Brook and the Putty Road, the Yengo National Park (139 861 hectares), is dominated by the valley of the upper Macdonald River and the big flat-top peak of Mount Yengo. While this country is mainly pale sandstone, Yengo and the nearby Mount Wareng, are dark-coloured basalt outcrops; like the large mountains of the neighbouring Wollemi National Park, they are the remnants of the blanket of lava that welled up from the bowels of the earth and covered this part of the country in prehistoric times.

The MacDonald River and its tributaries, which flow to the Hawkesbury, have sandy beds and carry only a surface trickle of water most of the time. A low, open woodland is found here, dominated by red bloodwood, grey gum, yellow bloodwood (*Eucalyptus eximia*), and Baker's apple (*Angophora bakeri*), with an understorey of hard-leaved, spiny shrubs including grevilleas, hakeas, isopogons and native

holly (*Oxylobium ilicifolium*). At the heads of the creeks there are small paperbark swamps.

This was once part of the territory of the Darkinjang Aborigines and there is a notable religious and engraving site, known as Devil's Rock or Burragurra, on a high ridge just within the park's eastern boundary. Burragurra is thought to have been a site of Darkinjang initiations and is associated with a legend about a spirit stepping from Mount Warrawolong in the east over to Mount Yengo, using Burragurra as a stepping stone.

Walk into Newcastle

A good cross-section of the landscapes and history of the coastal Hunter Valley can be seen from the Yuelarbah Track, the last 25 kilometres of the Great North Walk from Sydney to Newcastle. It passes through part of what was once the territory of the Awabakal tribe — a region that has been occupied for at least 7800 years, according to evidence found in 1972 in an ancient food refuse heap at Swansea Heads.

The Yuelarbah Track commences at Teralba railway station and skirts the northern shore of Lake Macquarie before coming to Warners Bay — in fact, a coastal lake. The 'bay', about 22 kilometres long, is a shallow valley that has been drowned by the sea. The narrowness of the opening to the ocean at Swansea limits tidal influence, but the lake is quite salty as there is also little fresh water inflow.

After the suburb of Warners Bay is left behind, the track winds through dry eucalypt forest for about three kilometres before passing through Charlestown and Kahiba. The Glenrock State Recreation Area (150 hectares) is here, with its fine coastal scenery including sandy beaches, tree-filled valleys and a lagoon.

It was from here, in 1791, that a party of escaping convicts made the first discovery of coal on the mainland. Mining had extended down to Glenrock

by 1851 and there are plenty of signs of the old workings, including air vents, hollows caused by subsidence following a tunnel collapse, and the remains of the railway which once carried coal up the coast to Newcastle.

After traversing Merewether, Dixon and Bar Beaches, the track passes Shepherds Hill, with its fortifications built in the 1890s and strengthened during the Second World War. The ocean pool near Cooks Hill, called the Bogey Hole, was cut into the rock platform by convict labourers to make a bathing pool for the personal use of Major Morriset, who was the military commander in Newcastle from 1819 to 1822. From there, nature is left behind, and it is only a short distance down to Queens Wharf and the hubbub of Newcastle Harbour. ☐

Contrasts abound in northern New South Wales, where one of the largest continuous highland regions on the mainland is juxtaposed with a lush coastal strip washed by the waters of the South Pacific

From the highlands to the sea

Greater New England encompasses two very distinctive and climatically contrasting regions: the New England tableland and the east coast, from just north of industrial Newcastle to the glittery Gold Coast.

The tableland is the geographical heart of the region. A vast plateau, or series of plateaux, approximately 130 kilometres wide and 1000 metres above sea level, it is part of a broad, westward sweep by the Great Dividing Range. Because of its elevation, the tableland has cool winters and mild summers; it is long established as a prosperous pastoral area producing fine wool, lamb and beef.

The first sheep farmers arrived in the 1830s and named the district after their homeland. One of them, who could be suspected of having suffered from myopia, described the prospect which met his eye as 'looking precisely like an English racecourse framed in gum trees.' As in eastern Tasmania, deciduous Northern Hemisphere trees have since been planted widely, and their displays of autumn colour, together with winter snowfalls, nowadays lend some justification to the appellation chosen by the original white settlers.

Eastwards, beyond the escarpment of the Great Dividing Range, the many rivers which rise in the mountains make their way to the sea through a series of pleasant, shallow valleys and well-watered lowlands. This region of green countryside, lush forests and broad, sandy beaches is blessed with a balmy, almost tropical climate. Since the mid-1960s, it has had an irresistible attraction for city people seeking a simpler life.

In twenty years, the north coast has been transformed from a quiet agricultural region of dairy farms, banana plantations and fishing ports, into a busy tourist destination with prosperous towns stimulated by the influx of new settlers from the south.

SACRED SENTINEL Sphinx Rock, on the rugged scarp of the New England tableland, is a sacred site, one of many outcrops of significance to the large Aboriginal population which once existed here.

TO THE SEA Looking south-west from the continent's most easterly point at Cape Byron, the popular resort of Byron Bay curves away to the right. All along this coast, a series of river basins are drained by streams of various sizes, which form many swamps, lagoons and estuaries on their way to the sea.

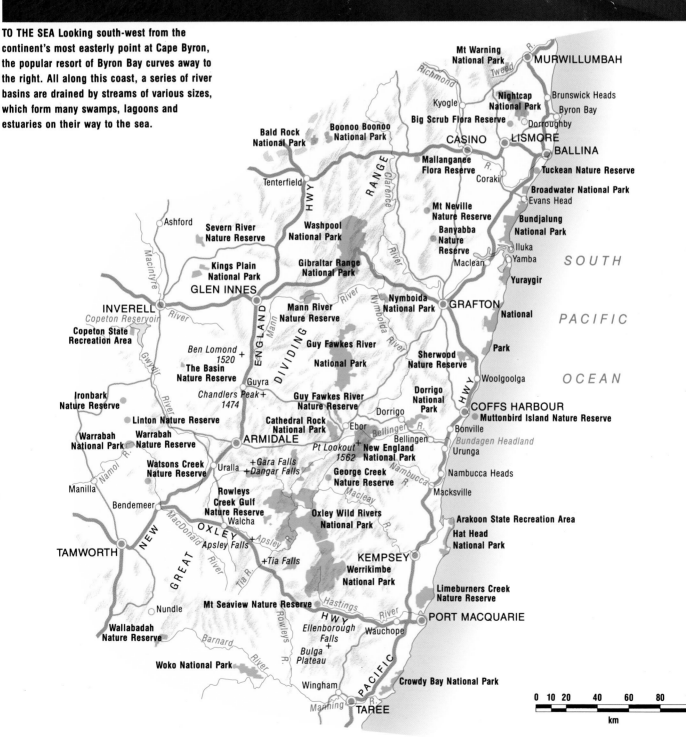

Mt Warning
National Park
MURWILLUMBAH

Richmond R.
Tweed R.

Kyogle
Nightcap
National Park
Brunswick Heads
Byron Bay

Big Scrub Flora Reserve
Dorroughby

Bald Rock
National Park
Boonoo Boonoo
National Park
CASINO
LISMORE
BALLINA

Tenterfield
Mallanganee
Flora Reserve
R.
Coraki
Tuckean Nature Reserve

Broadwater National Park
Evans Head

Ashford
Severn River
Nature Reserve
Washpool
National Park
Mt Neville
Nature Reserve
Banyabba
Nature
Reserve
Bundjalung
National Park
Iluka
Yamba

Clarence River

Maclean
SOUTH

Kings Plain
National Park
Gibraltar Range
National Park
Yuraygir

GLEN INNES
Mann River
Nature Reserve
Nymboida
National Park
GRAFTON
National

INVERELL
Copeton Reservoir
River
PACIFIC

Copeton State
Recreation Area
Mann
Park

Ben Lomond
1520
Guy Fawkes River
Sherwood
Nature Reserve

The Basin
Nature Reserve
Guyra
National Park
Woolgoolga
OCEAN

Ironbark
Nature Reserve
Chandlers Peak
1474
Guy Fawkes River
Nature Reserve
Dorrigo
National
Park
COFFS HARBOUR

Linton Nature Reserve
Cathedral Rock
National Park
Dorrigo
Bellinger R.
Bonville
Muttonbird Island Nature Reserve

Warrabah
National Park
Warrabah
Nature Reserve
ARMIDALE
Ebor
Bellingen
Bundagen Headland

Watsons Creek
Nature Reserve
Uralla
Pt Lookout
1562
New England
National Park
Urunga

Manila
Gara Falls
Dangar Falls
George Creek
Nature Reserve
Nambucca R.
Nambucca Heads

Bendemeer
Rowleys
Creek Gulf
Nature Reserve
Walcha
Oxley Wild Rivers
National Park
Macleay R.
Macksville

NEW
OXLEY
Arakoon State Recreation Area

TAMWORTH
MacDonald River
Apsley Falls
Apsley R.
KEMPSEY
Hat Head
National Park

GREAT
Tia Falls
Tia R.
Werrikimbe
National Park
Limeburners Creek
Nature Reserve

Nundle
Mt Seaview Nature Reserve
Hastings River
PORT MACQUARIE

Wallabadah
Nature Reserve
Barnard R.
HWY
Ellenborough
Falls
Bulga
Plateau
Wauchope

Woko National Park
PACIFIC
Crowdy Bay National Park

Wingham
Manning R.
TAREE

0 10 20 40 60 80 100
km

177

To travel from the coastal centres of Port Macquarie, Coffs Harbour or Ballina, across the mountains to the tableland cities of Tamworth, Armidale, and Tenterfield, and on to Inverell at the edge of the western slopes, is to take part in an environmental adventure that can be enjoyed only where mountains come close to the sea. In a short time the traveller passes through three totally contrasting environments: the coast, the mountains, and the slopes on the edge of the plains.

A landscape cross-section

From the coast, the roads inland quickly leave the plain and follow broad river valleys into the foothills of the Great Dividing Range. The river flats are given over to pasture and the grazing of cattle, while the hills are covered by dry, open eucalypt forests.

Going through the ranges, the roads narrow and twist through increasingly wet forests of tall eucalypts, and warm temperate rainforests of coachwood (*Ceratopetalum apetalum*), sassafras (*Doryphora sassasfras*), and lilly-pilly (*Acmena smithii*). A large zone of subtropical rainforest extends from the Dorrigo Plateau down into the Bellinger Valley.

Occupying the slightly drier ridges and slopes are moist forests of tall eucalypts. Flooded gum (*Eucalyptus grandis*), blackbutt (*E. pilularis*) and tallowwood (*E. microcorys*) dominate the warm, low elevations, while tallowwood occurs with Sydney blue gum (*E. saligna*) higher up. At the highest elevations, there are shining gums (*E. nitens*) and ancient forests of Antarctic beech (*Nothofagus moorei*).

Antarctic beech forests can be seen at the end of the North Plateau Road in the Werrikimbe National Park (35 178 hectares), just west of Wauchope, and at Point Lookout in the New England National Park on the road between Ebor and Armidale. An excellent walking track at the North Plateau Road picnic area passes through fine stands of beech and coachwood.

Olive whistlers (*Pachycephala olivacea*), golden whistlers (*P. pectoralis*) and rose robins (*Petroica rosea*) are common in the thick undergrowth. The same birds occur in the New England National Park (29 985 hectares), along with the spotted-tailed quoll (*Dasyurus maculatus*).

The quoll, about the size of a cat, is the largest marsupial carnivore on the mainland. Quoll numbers have been greatly reduced since European settlement and this is one of the few places where they can be seen in the wild.

The highest parts of the Dividing Range are often shrouded in mist and

ROCKS OF GIBRALTAR Many curious granite tors, shaped by erosion and encrusted with lichens, stud the forested plateau of the Gibraltar Range in between heathlands and occasional sub-alpine swamps.

ANCIENT TREES The eastern scarp ends abruptly in New England National Park where the cool temperate rainforest is dominated by negrohead beach. The plateau remains largely unspoilt by development.

rain as the warm air moving inland from the coast rises and cools, losing its moisture. Little moisture is left to fall on the tablelands beyond, and they are much drier and cooler than the coast.

The tableland is where the forest gradually fades into woodlands and grassy savannahs, most of which have been developed as pasture. There are few shrubs in these habitats, but blackthorn (*Bursaria spinosa*) is common, as are some introduced plants such as hawthorn. Introduced grasses and weeds dominate the more heavily grazed pastures.

On the poorer, granite-based soils, as in the Gibraltar Range and Cathedral Rock National Park (17 273 hectares,

6529 hectares), a dry sclerophyll forest with a dense shrub cover develops. Stringybarks (*E. caliginosa, E. youmanii*) and peppermints (*E. radiata, E. acaciiformis*) dominate these forests. There is also heathland with an abundance of flowering plants such as waratah (*Telopea speciosissima*) and Christmas bells (*Blandfordia grandiflora*) that produce spectacular displays in spring and summer.

Travelling westwards across the tablelands, the climate becomes drier and hotter and the elevation drops from over 1500 metres at Cathedral Rock to about 300 metres at Inverell on the edge of the western slopes. Open woodlands of white and yellow box (*E. albens, E. melliodora*) with rough-barked apple (*Angophora floribunda*), Blakelyi's red gum (*E. blakelyi*), and kurrajong (*Brachychiton populneus*) occur on the best soils.

On stony ridges, there is a dry sclerophyll forest dominated by ironbarks (*E. sideroxylon, E. caleyi*), and including a mixture of red stringybark (*E. macrorhyncha*), white box, she-oak (*Casuarina*) and cypress pines (*Callitris*).

Heading inland from Ballina, the roads pass through a similar array of habitats, but the climate and the vegetation change more gradually. The lower reaches of the Tweed, Clarence

and Richmond Rivers were formerly covered by an extensive tropical rainforest, known as the 'Big Scrub'. This was cleared to make way for dairy farms in the last century and only small remnants survive. Many of the farms have now been converted to growing tropical and subtropical fruits and there are extensive plantations of macadamia nuts, avocados, bananas, guavas and custard apples. Sugar cane is grown on the coastal lowlands.

The road over the mountains, from Lismore to Tenterfield, is not as steep or twisting as those further south, and passes gradually through eucalypt forest mixed with patches of dry rainforest containing tall, emergent hoop pines (*Araucaria cunninghamii*). Little of this dry rainforest has been protected in national parks, but there is a remnant in the Mallanganee Flora Reserve in the Cherry Tree North State Forest, along the highway between Casino and Tenterfield.

Blights on the land

The New England tablelands were settled by Europeans in the middle of the nineteenth century. At first, the settlers came with herds of cattle, taking advantage of the lush pastures of native grass. Eventually they set about clearing the land of trees to provide more pasture for their herds.

As the trees were felled or killed by ring-barking, the grass spread and flourished and the cattle herds increased. So too did the native herds — kangaroos, wallabies, bettongs and a host of other native mammals — which took advantage of this man-made plenty and increased to pest proportions. By the 1890s, bounties were offered to control native animals and a program of extermination began.

As it turned out, the settlers need not have bothered. Rabbits arrived on the tablelands in the 1890s and close at heel came the fox. These natives of the Old World had been introduced into Victoria thirty years earlier and spread rapidly up the east coast. Together with sheep and cattle, rabbits rapidly cleared the vegetation from the open land already cleared of trees, depriving native animals of food and shelter.

Sustained healthily by the plague of rabbits, the fox became a fierce predator of small native mammals. One after the other, the bettongs, wallabies, and quolls fell prey to something new: an efficient carnivore.

BLEAK LANDSCAPE These trees are victims of dieback, a disease with no specific cause.

By 1900, the same animals for which a bounty had been offered a mere 20 years before were declared a protected species. Despite the good intentions of the colonial legislators, the native animals of the region have never recovered from the shock of the foreign invasion.

In the latter part of the twentieth century, another form of decline appeared to complement that of the animals. Throughout the tablelands, from Victoria to Queensland and in Western Australia, the eucalypts began to die.

Across Australia, dead and dying trees threaten to become one of the most conspicuous features of the landscape, and New England is probably the most affected area. There appear to be numerous regional reasons for Rural Tree Decline, or dieback, as it is commonly known — in New England the problem was caused in large part by the repeated defoliation of the trees by Christmas beetles.

Christmas beetles have always existed in the forests and wooded areas of the tablelands; they live as larvae underground, feeding on the roots of grass. When they emerge as adults, they feed on the leaves of eucalypts. In their normal numbers they pose no threat to healthy trees, but by the 1970s, for unknown reasons, the beetles had increased to almost plague proportions.

The trees which had escaped the settler's axe were unable to withstand the loss of their leaves year after year. The huge increase in beetle numbers reflected an imbalance in nature which had its beginnings in the pattern of change begun last century. Few could have predicted the 'domino effect' that would occur when the complex interrelationship between plants and animals was upset by the region's native creatures being all but wiped out 100 years ago.

The grey skeletons that create such a stark landscape throughout the New England district today will gradually disappear as they fall and decay, or are harvested as firewood. In some areas, new trees are being planted, but these are often pines or other foreign trees which do not promote a convivial environment for native birds and animals.

Basalt: a volcanic legacy

During eastern Australia's last period of literally earth-shattering volcanic activity — some 30 million years ago, during what geologists call the oligocene period — huge flows of volcanic basalt, some as much as 300 metres thick, covered much of the region. Time has seen most of this basalt covering eroded away to form the rich, alluvial soils of the northern rivers, on which the Big Scrub developed, and of the Macintyre, Gwydir and Namoi Rivers west of the New England tableland.

RIVER WORKS The Tweed River has eroded its way through the enormous caldera of an extinct volcano, now known as Mount Warning, which was used as a navigational marker by James Cook.

A narrow band of basaltic and alluvial soils also extends north from Walcha to Glen Innes and west to Inverell. In many places, the constant erosion of the basalt soil has exposed the less fertile underlying granites and sedimentary rocks.

There are basalt caps on all the high peaks in New England — Point Lookout 1562 metres, Ben Lomond 1520 metres, and Chandlers Peak 1474 metres. This is evidence that the volcanic vents from which the basalt flowed, in the days when the earth was assuming its present state, must have been higher still.

Mount Warning (1156 metres), near Murwillumbah in the far north-east of the region, is the central vent of a volcano which was active 20 million years ago. In its prime, the immense Mount Warning volcano dominated an area of over 4000 square kilometres and was over 2500 metres in height. It extended north to Beenleigh, west to Kyogle and south to Coraki.

Remnants of this awe-inspiring physical phenomenon can still be identified as reefs in the Pacific Ocean. Caps of basalt from this primeval time account for the ruggedness of the McPherson Range to the north and Barrington Tops to the south of the region.

Mostly mountainous

The Great Dividing Range is at the heart of New England and it provides no shortage of spectacular scenery. Point Lookout, in the New England National Park, overlooks wild and rugged country where, in all directions, the forest is broken only by deep gorges, sheer cliffs and distant clearings. The lookout is in a tall woodland of snow gum (*E. pauciflora*), the trees' twisted limbs an indication of how harsh the climate can become here. In the gorges below, the eucalypt forest gradually fades into the warm, temperate rainforests of the gullies. These stand out as bright green corridors through the grey and dusty greens of the eucalypts.

The Great Divide separates those waters flowing east to the Pacific Ocean from those flowing west into the Darling and Murray River drainage systems, and ultimately into the sea through Lake Alexandrina in South Australia (see pp. 86–95). The streams and rivers flowing east have relatively small catchment areas and are only a

BALD ROCK This immense dome of granite, 750 metres long, is one of the largest pieces of exposed granite in the Southern Hemisphere.

short distance from the sea. Nonetheless, they carry huge volumes of water from the wet ranges and in places have cut deep gorges into the bedrock.

With the main range and its spurs giving rise to so many rivers, waterfalls, some of them spectacular, occur in abundance. Some falls have drops of more than 200 metres. Water flowing over Ellenborough Falls, north of Taree on the Bulga Plateau, falls 160 metres in a single drop and is one of the highest in Australia.

In the Oxley Wild Rivers National Park (92 000 hectares), there are fine waterfalls and well-maintained walking tracks at Wollomombi, Dangars Falls, and Gara Falls, just east of Armidale. The park has 13 major waterfalls ranging in height from the relatively small Bakers Creek and Moona Falls — with drops of about 30 metres — to the spectacular 220-metre plunge of Wollomombi Falls. East of Walcha, along the Oxley Highway, are the magnificent Apsley and Tia Falls.

PARADISE ALMOST LOST In the 1970s, the Washpool forest was destined to be logged; now it is one of a fragmented group of World Heritage rainforests.

Waterfalls occur elsewhere throughout the mountains, such as north of Tenterfield in the Boonoo Boonoo National Park (2692 hectares), along Rosewood Creek near Dorrigo in the Dorrigo National Park (7885 hectares) and east of Glen Innes in the Gibraltar Range National Park.

Parks: trees or timber?

Despite the changes which have been wrought over 200 years, New England's original landscapes are preserved in its many national parks. Along the coast between Taree and Evans Head there are six parks with an area of more than 54 000 hectares.

Inland, more than 260 000 hectares are reserved along the escarpment, while on the tableland proper there are state recreation areas at Copeton Reservoir (939 hectares), south-west of In-

verell, at Lake Keepit (708 hectares), near Tamworth, and the Warrabah and Kings Plain National Parks (2635 hectares, 3140 hectares), west of Armidale and Glen Innes, respectively.

Together with a multitude of smaller nature reserves, and the flora reserves and recreation areas managed by the Forestry Commission, these parks provide abundant opportunity to explore the wildlands of New England. Guy Fawkes River National Park and Oxley Wild Rivers National Park, in particular, have some of the most spectacular wild rivers scenery in the region.

The north coast of New South Wales and its hinterland had been the scene of minor skirmishes between environmentalists on one hand, and traditional land users and local authorities on the other, since the influx of new settlers began in the 1960s.

In the 1970s and early 1980s, there was bitter controversy as the conservationists clashed with loggers over the preservation of the remaining New South Wales rainforests — these scenes were to be repeated numerous times in other locations throughout Australia in the ensuing years.

In particular, the Washpool National Park (27 715 hectares) — which contains the state's largest undisturbed warm temperate rainforest — and the Nightcap National Park (4945 hectares) — where the pro- and anti-logging forces clashed physically at Terania Creek — were the focus of bitter controversy. Eventually, six separate rainforest zones — five of them within the New England district, the sixth at Barrington Tops — were placed under the protection of the National Parks and Wildlife Service.

TALL TWINS The majestic brush box of the forests, which may soar to a height of 40 metres, bears little resemblance to the modest city street tree, which is usually pruned into a relatively short, 'lollipop' shape.

As rainforest remnants — the vast, tall forests that once encompassed today's rainforest vegetation have long since disappeared — the protected areas are recognised as of particular value. As such, they were jointly declared Australia's sixth World Heritage site (see p. 391) in 1986 and are now accepted as a valuable focus for tourism and education.

Although the many coastal parks are not listed as World Heritage areas, they do protect important areas of lowland forest and heath, as well as preserving magnificent beaches and headlands from the urbanisation which is inevitable along any attractive coastline where the climate is relatively balmy. The attractions of the coast have resulted in the proliferation of resort, marina, and canal estate and other residential developments which often alter beyond recognition the interesting natural features which attracted people to the region in the first place.

Big Scrub no more

The rainforests in the New England district begin on the sandy shores of the coast and sweep inland along the river valleys, up to the Great Divide. The huge expanse of subtropical rainforest known as the Big Scrub once occupied a vast area of the lowlands along the Richmond, Tweed and Clarence Rivers. Most of it had been cleared for farms by the beginning of the century, but its grandeur and richness of life can at least be imagined by visiting some of the surviving remnants.

The best example of the Big Scrub is the Big Scrub Flora Reserve, in the Whian Whian State Forest near Doroughby. Another good example of subtropical rainforest occurs at Terania Creek near Nimbin. Some of the large brush box trees (*Tristania conferta*) destined for logging at Terania were over 1000 years old, according to Forestry Commission biologists. Examples of these trees still exist, within the Nightcap National Park.

The Big Scrub Flora Reserve is at the edge of the original Big Scrub and has been logged. Despite this, the rainforest atmosphere is almost palpable and even on a sunny day, when the light battles to reach the forest floor, the air is moist and still.

PROTEST NOTED Terania Creek (above) flows over Protestors Falls, named to commemorate the confrontations that occurred there between conservationists and loggers.

The silence is broken by the incessant calls of brown warblers or gerygones (*Gerygone mouki*), and the loud smash of wings against leaves as fruit pigeons come through the canopy. Green catbirds (*Ailuroedus crassirostris*) miaow from the canopy, and small kangaroos known as red-necked pademelons (*Thylogale thetis*), suddenly bound away.

Along the track near Rocky Creek, many of the trees and plants have been labelled for easy identification. There are towering strangler figs (*Ficus*), giant stinging trees (*Dendrocnide excelsa*), red cedars (*Toona australis*) and black beans (*Castanospermum australe*).

CAT CALL Green catbirds are bowerbirds with a surprisingly feline territorial call.

HIGH LIFE The elegant bowerbird visits the ground to build a bower and mate; otherwise it spends its life in the treetops of the rainforest.

The trees are covered in epiphytes: orchids, mosses, huge elkhorn and bird's nest ferns, which can reach the light high above the forest floor only by attaching themselves to tall trees. Waiting in the shade on the floor, are the seedlings of the forest trees themselves. As soon as one of the giants falls, the seedlings will begin a race for the sun, to be won by the swiftest and most vigorous at filling the forest gap with lush vegetation.

The sunny openings caused by these gaps in the greenery attract myriad in-

LOUD AND CLEAR As its name suggests, the noisy pitta's call is loud and continuous during the October-January breeding season.

sects and some spectacular butterflies. Colourful, nectar-rich flowers and small fruits adorn trees, this abundance of food in turn attracting birds. Grey fantails (*Rhipidura fuliginosa*), black-faced flycatchers (*Monarcha melanopsis*), and Lewin's honeyeaters (*Meliphaga lewinii*) forage in these openings for insects, nectar and fruits.

The gaps are also an avenue to the highest trees, making it possible to observe the activity of the forest canopy. There are paradise riflebirds (*Ptiloris paradiseus*), regent bowerbirds (*Sericulus chrysocephalus*), multi-coloured wompoo fruit doves (*Ptilinopus magnificus*), and the larger but less spectacular topknot pigeons (*Lopholaimus antarcticus*).

Not all of these birds are always present in the Big Scrub. Topknot and white-headed pigeons (*Columba leucomela*) travel long distances with the seasons. They move into the high country during spring and summer to nest, and return to the lowlands in autumn and winter.

White-headed pigeons are often seen feeding along roadsides where camphor laurel (*Cinnamomum camphora*), a weed tree introduced from south-east Asia, has naturalised itself. The pigeons feed on the laurel seed and assist its spread, but it does provide them with an abundance of food where there would otherwise be little.

Another rainforest bird, the noisy pitta (*Pitta versicolor*), also moves up and down the mountains with the seasons. The pitta, a large, brilliantly coloured bird of the rainforest floor, is best seen during winter in the littoral rainforests, such as at Iluka on the north shore of the broad Clarence River estuary.

Littoral rainforests develop close to the ocean, just behind the frontal dune system, as at Iluka, or on sheltered headlands, and are a feature of the north coast. Although they tend to be small, and do not have as many kinds of plants and animals as the larger areas of rainforest farther inland, they are particularly accessible and have a special attraction of their own.

Other littoral rainforests on the north coast occur at Port Macquarie (Seaview), Bundagen Headland and Bonville, just south of Coffs Harbour and at Brunswick Heads and Byron Bay. Each of these is a mini-rainforest with strangler figs, thick vines or lianas trailing up into the canopy, epiphytic ferns and orchids, huge buttress-rooted trees, and myriad birds.

HOLIDAYLAND Fingal Head, just south of Tweed Heads, interrupts a broad beach, part of an almost continuous sweep of sand from Byron Bay to the northern limits of the Gold Coast.

The cooler temperate rainforests, higher up on the Dividing Range, are not as rich as those of the Big Scrub. There are fewer kinds of trees and animals. Nonetheless, they are spectacular in their own way, and those reserved in national parks have been given World Heritage status to ensure that they are permanently protected.

A Pacific playground

In stark contrast to the dark lushness of the rainforests are the open expanses of beach and heathland, which unmistakably identify the western shores of the Pacific. Long, sandy beaches are broken only by rocky headlands. These are rich fishing grounds, and both beach and rock fishing are popular activities. The simple shellfish known as pipis can be gathered along the beaches, and limpets and snails winkled off the rocks.

Fringing the beaches are barrier dunes, usually with a scrubby forest of coast banksia (*Banksia integrifolia*). When the banksia is in bloom, it attracts flocks of nectar-feeding birds, and the braying calls of brush wattle-birds (*Anthochaera chrysoptera*) contrast with the dull roar of waves pounding on the sand.

Behind the dunes are open, dry sclerophyll forests and heathlands that are also rich in nectar. Honeyeaters and lorikeets abound in these habitats and during winter it is hard to notice anything but the movement and noise of birds. Emus (*Dromaius novaehollandiae*) are to be seen, selecting the brightest flowers for food, and the heaths are also home to the elusive ground parrot (*Pezoporus wallicus*).

Larger furry animals still exist in the protected areas of the coastal region. The cone-shaped diggings of bandicoots and the tracks of wallabies in soft sand reveal the animals' presence.

Most Australian mammals are nocturnal and those of the coast are no exception. During the day, a swamp wallaby (*Wallabia bicolor*) may be disturbed from its resting place and bound away, or a mob of eastern grey kangaroos (*Macropus giganteus*) may be seen feeding or resting in the open, but most mammals can only be found at night with the aid of a spotting light.

In the forests, squirrel gliders (*Petaurus norfolcensis*), sugar gliders

BIRDLAND Yuragir National Park, segmented into three parts, protects coastal heath and wetlands which support a large bird population.

BANKSIA BIRD The little wattlebird is one of many honeyeaters attracted by the coast banksia's brushes from autumn to spring.

(*P. breviceps*) and brushtail possums (*Trichosurus vulpecula*) are common. Fruit bats may clumsily flap their way out of the banksias where they feed on nectar.

Koala colonies occur throughout the New England region. The koala has managed to survive even in the vicinity of growing towns such as Coffs Harbour and Port Macquarie, although they too often fall prey to careless drivers and uncontrolled dogs.

Coffs Harbour has a colony of shearwaters on Muttonbird Island near the town's main jetty. These sleek, dark-grey birds can be seen just offshore, skimming over the ocean waves. They come ashore to tend their eggs or young only at night.   □

The widely contrasting terrains of southern Queensland, from sand islands to sandy semi-desert, represent a vivid cross-section of the geography of Australia's east coast

Dunes to downs: a broad slice of Australia

The three principal landscapes of eastern Australia are never more dramatically combined than in southern Queensland's threefold contrast of coast, mountains and plains. While many regions incorporate contrasting coastal and inland terrains and climates, southern Queensland has a richness within these diverse habitats that is comparable only with the adjacent New England district of New South Wales.

Off the coast, there are vast sand islands, including Fraser Island, the world's largest. On the mainland, the ranges that rise within sight of these islands are some of the highest and most scenically spectacular of the east coast. The temperate rainforest, with a character quite distinct from the far northern tropical rainforests, is at its richest along these cloud-capped ranges.

Inland there is a contrasting scene of languid rivers, winding into waterholes and billabongs, as they cross the undulating and often sparsely vegetated plains.

The first Europeans to see this coast were the mariners of the seventeenth and eighteenth centuries, who noted the volcanic spires of the Glass House Mountains rising beyond the sandy coastline. In more recent times, the sand islands off the coast have been the scene of demonstrations by conservationists campaigning to prevent any further destruction of the dunes by sand mining.

Fraser Island was the first site to be listed on the register of Australia's National Estate. It once supported a large population of Aborigines, who left evidence of their thousands of years of occupation in the form of mounds of discarded bones and shells behind the beachside dunes.

NORTH OF THE BORDER The dense growth of the heavily forested McPherson Range — often a mixture of temperate and subtropical forest, depending on altitude — is preserved in Lamington National Park.

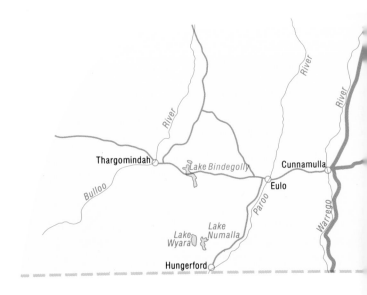

NOTHING BUT SAND The giant sand mass of
Fraser Island, the world's largest sand island,
stretches for 120 kilometres beyond its northern
tip, the appropriately named Sandy Cape.
The sand supports tall forests and, despite its
absorbent qualities, more than 40 lakes.

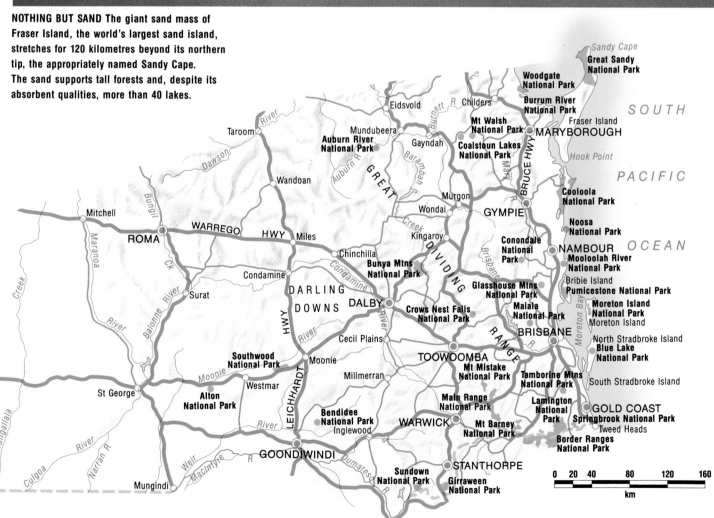

On Fraser Island, the giant sand dunes formed by coastal currents and winds rise to over 240 metres. Despite the strongly absorbent nature of sand, there are freshwater lakes in the dunes, some perched as high as 130 metres above sea level.

The lakes are maintained by vast reservoirs of rainwater within the immense, sponge-like masses of sand. Along the centre of the island there are areas of rainforest with tall trees, palms, ferns and orchids.

While Fraser Island may be the best known part of what is sometimes referred to as the 'great sandy coast', the sand islands extend south to Stradbroke Island, almost at the New South Wales border. High dunes also dominate this part of the mainland coast; like the islands, they are built up by the movement of beach sand, driven by the prevailing south-easterly winds.

Immediately inland, the sandy 'wallum' country is well known for the wildflowers of its sandy heaths. On this heathland, named wallum after the Aboriginal word for the banksia that dominates the landscape, fire is a common occurrence.

After the flames have swept by, the first good rains encourage an abundance of flowers. The most common flowering shrubs of the wallum are hakeas, grevilleas and banksias, interspersed with various species of eucalypt, leptospermum and callistemon.

SAND HILL Moreton Island's forested dunes rise to 285 metres at 'Mount' Tempest.

THE GREAT SANDY FRESHWATER LAKES

HIGH WATER High above Platypus Bay, in the Great Sandy National Park, are just a few of Fraser Island's forty-odd 'perched' lakes. The lakes, often scores of metres above sea level, are formed when rainwater is trapped between an old dune and a new dune (see diagram). Coffee rock, an impermeable layer formed when organic plant matter and minerals become cemented together, prevents the water being absorbed by the sand.

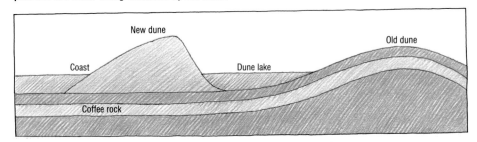

Some wildflowers, though also occurring elsewhere, have unique heathland varieties. One is the large-flowered Christmas bell (*Blandfordia grandiflora*), which occurs as a deep-yellow-flowered plant, as well as the usual orange-red, on swampy country near Cooloola.

Birdlife flourishes on the wallum heathlands in spring and early summer as nomadic honeyeaters and lorikeets are attracted by the abundant nectar of the wildflowers. The blue-faced honeyeater (*Entomyzon cyanotis*), the scarlet honeyeater (*Myzomela sanguinolenta*) and the white-cheeked honeyeater (*Phylidonyris nigra*) are regular visitors.

SAND STRAND Seventy Five Mile Beach occupies most of the long curve of Fraser Island's eastern shore. Various minerals have coloured and helped consolidate the sandcliffs, known as The Cathedrals.

Not all the coastal features of this region are sandy. At Noosa National Park (432 hectares) there are coastal headlands, cliffs, hilltop lookouts and walking tracks which overlook rocky reefs and shelves at the base of cliffs.

In the mountains' shadow

The coastal plains are dominated by the rather ominous presence of the weathered volcanic spires known as the Glass House Mountains. The nine main peaks display a variety of shapes; their great cylindrical pillars, domes and cones of rock are remnants of ancient volcanoes. Small national parks — Beerwah (245 hectares), Tibrogargan (291 hectares), Ngungun (49 hectares) and Coonowrin (113 hectares) — incorporate four of these peaks.

Further inland, the Bunya Mountains National Park (11 700 hectares) preserves a range with several peaks of around 1000 metres high, and a magnificent forest of bunya pines (*Araucaria bidwillii*), a tall conifer unique to south-eastern Queensland. Roads cross the range, and there are many kilometres of walking tracks giving access to lookouts and views of waterfalls, rainforest and the pine forests.

The Bunya Mountains were a rendezvous for many Aboriginal tribes which periodically came to collect the nuts of the bunya pine. These provided the basis for a feast after they had been roasted in the campfire. The name 'bunya' is believed to come from the local Aboriginal name for the trees, 'bon-yi'. The summits of the range carry other names of Aboriginal derivation such as Mount Kiangarow and Mount Mowbullan.

Further south, adjacent to the state border, is the Lamington Plateau, part of the McPherson Range, a massive, eastward-projecting spur of the Great Dividing Range. The spur and the main range form a spectacular arc of cliff-rimmed, rainforest-clad heights known as the Scenic Rim. Many parts of this great mountain wilderness have long been incorporated in a chain of small and large national parks.

Lamington National Park (20 200 hectares) is one such park, most parts of which are accessible by walking tracks. The gradual incline of the cliff-rimmed Lamington plateau surface reaches its maximum altitude of over

EARTH PLUG Eleven monolithic spires like the one above — the result of lava solidifying in the cores of dying volcanoes 25 million years ago — dot the Glasshouse Mountains.

1000 metres at the New South Wales border in a line of vertical cliffs. There are spectacular views south to the distant, pointed peak of Mount Warning, and the Pacific coast.

Along the precipitous, southern escarpments, the cliffs plunge to river valleys far below. Lookouts along the rim command views across valleys and lesser ranges, all set out far below like a gigantic relief map. Sometimes the valleys are blanketed in low-lying mist, while the heights are sunlit, so that the only land to be seen is the peaks of high mountains which pierce the clouds.

Although less luxuriant than the northern Queensland tropical rainforests, these subtropical and high-altitude temperate rainforests are just as thickly vegetated and contain a rich variety of plant life.

In the forests on the heights of the plateau and other parts of the Scenic Rim, there are many species of huge softwood trees growing intermingled, most of them with buttressed trunks. Their lofty crowns are lush, aerial gardens of huge staghorn and elkhorn ferns, and there are many species of epiphytic orchids.

High on the slopes of the tallest peaks, the cool, misty, often cloud-

ORCHID ALOFT The king orchid's blooms spring from the forks of rainforest trees.

enshrouded heights shelter stands of negrohead beech (*Nothofagus moorei*). Some of these trees are believed to be more than a thousand years old. Their gnarled, moss-festooned trunks, often decayed and broken, rise from a ground cover of ferns, yet slender, fresh shoots continue to emerge to form the new trunks that will last centuries into the future.

These trees belong to a genus of trees that also occurs in South America and New Zealand, and their fossilised pollen has been found in Antarctica. Northwards, similar beech forests grow on the high, cool mountains of New Guinea and New Caledonia. They are the remnants of the vegetation which once covered the ancient, southern supercontinent of Gondwana.

At a lower altitude, below the occasional cloud layer, the temperate rainforests of the peaks give way to the subtropical rainforest, with its huge buttressed trees, rising to interlocking limbs festooned with ferns and mosses. This is the habitat of the brush box (*Tristania conferta*), the hoop pine (*Araucaria cunninghamii*), the giant stinging tree, (*Dendrocnide excelsa*), as well as the heavily logged and now rare red cedar (*Toona australis*). The name — there is also a white cedar — refers to the bright crimson colour of the tree's new, spring foliage.

The scrub-bird: life at ground level

The national parks of southern Queensland are among the few remaining refuges of an elusive member of a peculiar group of birds which occur nowhere else in the world. The ground-dwelling scrub-birds are shy, secretive creatures which spend their lives not in the trees, as their ancestors did, but around them.

The rufous scrub-bird, which occurs in scattered patches of forest from mid-New South Wales to southern Queensland, scurries amongst the dense undergrowth as it searches for insects and seeds. In comical fashion, it sometimes pushes its way completely beneath the surface of the litter for several metres.

The scrub-bird's inability to make a meaningful attempt at flying means that it is an easy target for predators. As a result it is a nervous, retiring creature that is highly adept at remaining hidden, even at the closest quarters. The only time it betrays its presence is when the male utters its loud, ringing call.

Rufous scrub-birds are most easily seen in Lamington National Park, where the many tracks allow access to the thick, high-altitude forest where the bird lives. Other parks where it occurs are Mount Barney, Gibralter Range, New England, Dorrigo and Barrington Tops.

The rufous scrub-bird likes a moist environment where the undergrowth is thick and surrounded by an abundance of leaf litter. This species, and its only close relative, the noisy scrub-bird of the south coast of Western Australia, are thought to have originated in the cool, damp forests that once covered a much greater part of Australia than they do now. As the forests retreated, so did their inhabitants.

Both scrub-birds have very loud, distinctive calls: that of the rufous scrub-bird is audible for some hundreds of metres but rarely heard outside the September–December breeding season. The noisy scrub-bird, in more open country of the south-west, can be heard at least a kilometre away, in all seasons.

The male birds maintain a fairly small domain — about one or two hectares — which they defend during the breeding season with their penetrating territorial song. They have some anatomical similarities to the lyrebird and are accomplished mimics of other bird calls, but use this ability only as a response to territorial intruders.

In spring, the limbs and trunks, of trees and the mossy boulders of these coastal ranges suddenly develop bursts of colour as the various epiphytic orchids come into flower. There are at least twenty species, ranging from white to deep mauve.

Among the most common are the orange blossom orchid (*Sarcochilus falcatus*), the ravine orchid (*S. fitzgeraldii*), the olive orchid (*S. olivaceus*), and the spider orchid (*Dendrobium tetragonum*). The most spectacular displays occur around October as the golden-flowered king orchid (*Dendrobium speciosum*) comes into bloom.

Flame trees (*Brachychiton acerifolius*), are famous for the brilliant splashes of colour they bring to the green of the slopes, and in summer the deep crimson, wheel-like flowers of the fire-wheel tree (*Stenocarpus sinuatus*) are a magnet for birds and insects.

Birds and beasts

The most unusual, and seldom seen, feathered inhabitant of the forest is the rufous scrub-bird (*Atrichornis rufescens*), a secretive creature which lives in the high-altitude beech forests. The bird is a clumsy flier and spends its life at ground level, amongst the forest's thick undergrowth, betraying its presence only when it gives vent to a loud, ringing call (see box).

Much more common and widespread, although rarely seen, is the noisy pitta, (*Pitta versicolor*). Its loud, knocking call can be heard in most large areas of rainforest in this region, but it is usually only glimpsed for a moment or two before returning to its foraging deep in the undergrowth.

One of the more conspicuous birds is the rufous fantail (*Rhipidura rufifrons*). It darts about the foliage of the understorey, displaying the brilliant red-brown colours of its tail, which, as its name implies, is often spread in a graceful fan-shape.

The logrunner (*Orthonyx temminckii*), lives on the forest floor, where it fossicks about among the damp leaf-litter, often attracting attention by the rustling sounds it makes as it kicks leaves aside in its constant search for insects. Unlike most other birds, the female is more colourful than the male, with a bright orange-rufous patch at the throat, where the male has only white colouring.

The cat-like wailing calls of the green cat-bird (*Ailuroedus crassirostris*), is one of the best-known, and almost inescapable calls of the rainforests. Its

RUMMAGING RUNNER The logrunner, which rarely takes to the air, uses its stiff tail to maintain its balance while digging among the forest litter for food.

POCKET PARKS The nine 'postage-stamp' parks of Tamborine Mountain south of Brisbane, protect pockets of rainforest and bushland.

emerald-green wings and tail allow it to blend in with the foliage and they make a sighting difficult as the bird moves about the canopy.

Where creeks flow through the rainforest, beneath overhanging vegetation and bridged by the trunks of fallen trees, the shrill squeak of the azure kingfisher (*Alcedo azurea*) may be the only indication of its presence, so swiftly and unobstrusively does it dart along the waterways.

The mammals of the region are mainly nocturnal, and not easily seen. Some live in eucalypt forests, others prefer the damp rainforest. The largest, and therefore most obvious, are the mountain brushtail possum (*Trichosurus caninus*), the common ringtail (*Pseudocheirus peregrinus*), the greater glider, (*Petauroides volans*), and two pademelons, the red-legged and the red-necked species (*Thylogale stigmatica, T. thetis*).

The ranges of southern Queensland are only partly clad in rainforests; eucalypt forest covers a large part of the drier mountainsides. On the wetter eastern slopes, the forests are usually of the 'wet sclerophyll' type, with very tall trees such as the flooded gum (*Eucalyptus grandis*), with an understorey of smaller trees and shrubs. Much of this undergrowth is of rainforest species, which are able to establish themselves in the relatively moist, sheltered protection of the high canopy of the eucalypts.

Lamington ... and the rest

While Lamington National Park is the best known wilderness reserve of the mountainous part of southern Queensland, there are other national parks, with distinctive natural wonders: Main Range (11 500 hectares), Girraween (11 399 hectares), a cluster of nine small parks around Tamborine Mountain, and a chain of four parks with a total area of 2083 hectares on Springbrook Plateau.

Protecting part of the granite belt that sweeps across southern Queensland, Girraween National Park provides a contrast to the rainforested parts of the ranges. With its distinctive granitic soils, and situated further inland on the headwaters of the westward-flowing rivers, Girraween has open woodland and scrubby heaths covered with wildflowers.

GIRRAWEEN GRANITE Beyond the ranges, the granite base of the countryside is highlighted by the many boulders, such as Sphinx Rock in Girraween National Park, which dot the bushland.

SMALL BEGINNINGS The Condamine River — seen here near Dalby — was named after an aide-de-camp to Governor Darling, after whom the Downs which the river drains were named. The river's waters undergo several name changes in the early stages of their 3000-kilometre journey to the sea.

Sheer cliffs and craggy peaks of granite make for dramatic scenes; Mount Norman reaches a height of 1260 metres, and Bald Rock 1112 metres. Bare slabs of rock and piles of enormous boulders cover the upper slopes of these peaks, with uninterrupted views from the summits.

The creeks which rise in these granite ranges run into clear pools fringed with wildflower-rich heathy flats. Numerous walking tracks follow the creeks or climb to the higher parts of the park, along the way passing huge boulders that have inspired names such as 'Sphinx Rock', and 'Turtle Rock'. Some of these are quite spectacular, their rounded, pale grey granite forms piled high, sunlit against a blue sky, and dwarfing the trees growing from among their crevices.

Among these magnificent rainforests, where streams plunge over high falls and emerge from narrow gorges, are the headwaters of many of the major rivers of southern Queensland and north-eastern New South Wales. The Burnett, the Albert, the Brisbane, the Coomera and the Nerang Rivers all flow from the same region.

While the upper parts of these relatively short rivers are comprised of white-water rapids and falls — there is a fairly steep drop of about one thousand metres from their high headwaters — their lower reaches are usually tidal as they meander across the plains to their outlets into the Pacific.

Aiming for the Darling

The rivers west of the Great Dividing Range are of a very different character. The terrain falls gradually to the west, so that the rivers will eventually flow not into the Pacific, but in a south-westerly direction, and in a good year, some of their waters may even reach the Southern Ocean.

The much lower rainfall west of the ranges means that these rivers flow intermittently, being often no more than chains of waterholes during the prolonged dry seasons. The major river of this region is the Condamine, which becomes the Balonne then the Culgoa before crossing the border into New South Wales, eventually to join the Murray River.

Other seasonally significant rivers of the western plains are the MacIntyre — which rises in New South Wales and first travels north-west — the Warrego and the Paroo, all, like the Condamine, flowing to the south-west.

Southern Queensland contains the headwaters and upper reaches of many of the rivers which combine to form the Darling, and eventually flow into the Murray. Some begin in the wet forests high up in the Great Divide, where they receive fairly reliable rainfall. Despite this, it is only in the aftermath of flooding rains that their flow is not dissipated on the inland plains.

The Paroo is the principal river of the far west and is usually no more than a dry, sandy watercourse lined with gnarled gums and hardy shrubs. When it does flow, its waters are usually absorbed by lakes and marshes after a few hundred kilometres, but in flood it may break through to join the Darling. This dissipation of the waters into vast, shallow lakes, swamps and billabongs is explained by the extremely gentle gradient to the south.

When these inland rivers flow, and fill the swamps and lakes, birds converge from afar, forming huge nesting colonies. The location of the colonies varies from year to year, depending upon which river's catchment has received rain. Among the birds are likely to be three species of ibis, spoonbills, egrets, black swans, and numerous species of ducks, water hens and other small water birds.

From downs to plains

The gently undulating western slopes of the Great Divide, known as the Darling Downs, are formed of rich, basalt soils — now mostly cleared. The Darling Downs is one of the most closely settled rural areas of Australia.

With its eastern limits clearly defined by the Great Dividing Range, and with the rolling ridges and broad valleys falling away gradually to the west, the Darling Downs extend to the alluvial floodplains of the Condamine.

The natural vegetation and wildlife of the downs are protected within a number of conservation reserves. While not having the spectacular scenery of the parks of the coast or the ranges, these reserves are important in preserving the unique ecosystems of a region which reminded some early explorers of the undulating pastureland, known as 'downs', in the chalk regions of southern England.

Further inland, areas of open forest remain around the Condamine River, with mixed red ironbark (*E sideroxylon*), grey box (*E. microcarpa*), bull oak (*Casuarina luehmannii*) and black cypress pines (*Callitris endlicheri*). On the heavier soils, extensive areas of brigalow (*Acacia harpophylla*) and belah (*Casuarina cristata*), still remain despite the vast areas which have now been cleared for agriculture.

Southwood National Park, of more than 7000 hectares, south-west of Dalby, is the largest of these remnant islands of natural bushland. Its vegetation of eucalypt and acacia 'brigalow', is typical of much of the plains. Some

FOODBOWL A chequerboard of different crops at different stages of growth covers 15 000 square kilometres of rich basalt soil in the highly productive Darling Downs.

of the large animals of the plains, such as kangaroos and emus, have survived where this natural cover has remained.

The birdlife is typical of much of inland Australia, with flocks of chattery galahs, and many species of parrots. Among these are the sulphur-crested cockatoo (*Cacatua galerita*), the red-rumped parrot (*Psephotus haematonotus*), the budgerigar (*Melopsittacus undulatus*), and the cockatiel (*Leptolophus hollandicus*).

Further inland again, more than 300 kilometres from the Pacific coast, there are gently undulating, plains, with perennial Mitchell and blue grass, and across low-lying floodplains, areas of open coolibah (*E. microtheca*) woodlands. River channels and watercourses are marked out by lines of river red gums (*E. camaldulensis*), which often attain a massive size where there is permanent water.

Although lacking the spectacular scenery of the coastal plains and ranges of the eastern seaboard, these inland landscapes have a unique beauty. On the river floodplains, several extensive wetlands have evolved.

Nangram Lagoon on the Condamine, and Umbercollie Lagoon on the MacIntyre, are probably the most southerly locations of the giant, pink lotus flower (*Nelumbo speciosum*). The Aborigines used this waterlily's seeds and roots as a source of food, and are believed to have introduced the plant to these waterways from more northerly lagoons long before European settlement took place. □

Australia's two 'Great' physical features, the Dividing Range and the Barrier Reef, flank this northerly coast — one far enough to the west to keep the climate relatively dry, the second, nearby to the east, protects a shore rarely disturbed by the pounding of waves

Beyond Capricorn and behind the Reef

SUGAR COAST In north-eastern Australia, neat patches of sugar cane such as these near Proserpine dominate the coastal valleys.

Between the mountainous, rainforest-clad landscape of Queensland's wet tropics in the north and the diverse forest and coastal environments of the southern Queensland coast, lies a contrasting landscape. As can be expected from its geographical position, the region has the largest variety of plants in Australia.

The central coast of Queensland has a relatively low rainfall with a distinct dry season during which the landscape can take on a parched, brown appearance reminiscent of the inland. The two major industries of the region — cattle grazing and sugar cane production — dominate the plains and river valleys, leaving open vistas at times almost devoid of trees.

Eastwards, beyond the agricultural plains, the Great Dividing Range forms a maze of coastal ranges flanking vast lowlands that run to the coast. Having followed the New South Wales and Victorian coast quite closely, the Range veers inland once in Queensland and the mountains are quite distant from the coast.

Catchment areas for two periodically great rivers, the Fitzroy and the Burdekin, are spread over three-quarters of the region, while the remaining area is drained by short, coastal creeks and rivers. The Fitzroy and the Burdekin have annual discharges greater than any river after the Murray.

Despite this, in the dry season the lower reaches of the Burdekin are only an ankle-deep flow of water in a vast bed of sand. This sand extends for kilometres on either side of the river banks, forming a vast, underground aquifer from which the sugar- and rice-growing industries draw irrigation water.

The Fitzroy also becomes a trickle of water joining large, permanent waterholes. In the upper reaches there are fish like the spotted barramundi (*Scleropages leichhardti*), a primitive species adapted to living in water low in oxygen; sea-going barramundi (*Lates calcarifer*) live in the freshwater reaches of the lower river system along with occasional saltwater crocodiles.

BEHIND THE REEF The waves that break on the shores of Sand Bay, on the southern flanks of Cape Hillsborough, near Mackay, have been tamed by the Great Barrier Reef.

PALUMA PARK Remnants of the Paluma Range rainforest are protected in Mount Spec National Park. The western slopes water the Burdekin River catchment.

Jourama Falls National Park

Crystal Creek
– Mt Spec
National Park

Magnetic Island

TOWNSVILLE

Mt Elliot
National Park

Bowling Green Bay National Park

AYR

Cape Upstart National Park

Great
Basalt Wall
National Park

Burdekin

Creek

CHARTERS
TOWERS

HWY

BOWEN

Dryander National Park

Airlie Beach

Mt Aberdeen
National Park

Lolworth

FLINDERS

River

Proserpine

Conway National Park

Pentland

Cape River

Collinsville

Repulse
Bay

Bowen

CLARKE RANGE

Lake
Dalrymple

Mt Beatrice National Park

River

Mt Jukes, Mt Mandurana,
Mt Blackwood National Parks

Eungella
National Park

MACKAY

CORAL

Walkerston

Belyando River

Suttor

River

Glendon

Sarina

Cape Palmerston National Park

West Hill & West Hill Island National Park

Moranbah

Dipperu
National Park

BRUCE

Mazeppa
National Park

Isaac

Broad
Sound

Shoalwater Bay

SEA

Epping
Forest
National Park

Gemini
Mountains
National Park

River

HWY

Mt O'Connell
National Park

Cape
Clinton

Clermont

Peak Range
National Park

Middlemount

Byfield National Park

River

Mt Etna 283

EMERALD

BLACKWATER

Dingo

Mackenzie

River

Fitzroy Caves
National Park

Fitzroy

Yeppoon

ROCKHAMPTON

Lake
Maraboon

CAPRICORN

HWY

Curtis Island

Comet

Blackdown
Tableland
National Park

Facing Island

GLADSTONE

River

Castle Tower
National Park

Eurimbula National Park

Bustard Bay

Seventeen Seventy

Dawson R.

BILOELA

Mt Colosseum
National Park

Deepwater
National Park

Moura

Banana

Monto

Lake
Monduran

0 20 40 60 80 100

km

Isla Gorge
National Park

Wuruma
Dam

Gin Gin

BUNDABERG

The southern tributaries of the Fitzroy begin to form in the vast, sandstone curve of the Central Highlands — part of the Great Dividing Range — up to 500 kilometres inland. The Dawson River and the Nogoa River rise in the gorges and escarpments to meander across the wide valleys of the Bowen Basin, where huge, open-cut coal mines dot the landscape.

Forests of brigalow (*Acacia harpophylla*) and softwood scrubs once clothed these valleys, forming an almost impenetrable barrier to early explorers. These dense forests, relics of an era when rainforests covered much of the continent, survive in a few national parks and in narrow windbreaks and corridors along roads. The distinctive, swollen shapes of bottle trees (*Brachychiton rupestris*) still stand in many cleared paddocks.

All the rivers run

Beyond the final junction with its tributaries from the north, the lower Fitzroy is an attractive stream lined with red gums (*Eucalyptus camaldulensis*) and weeping paperbarks (*Melaleuca leucadendron*); on either side its flood plains carry coolibah woodland (*E. microtheca*), a famous and widespread inland species which grows out to the coast only in this dry corridor.

SWAGMAN'S TREE The famous coolibah tree of the inland follows the Fitzroy River to the coast.

NATURAL DAM About 150 kilometres from its estuary, near Ayr, the Burdekin River is blocked by a natural rock barrier. The cascades of the Burdekin Falls are formed when the river rises and flows over the barrier.

The Fitzroy estuary is vast; 440 square kilometres of mangrove-lined channels flooded with brown, silt-laden water. Away from the channels, wide, unvegetated salt pans shimmer in the heat. The river finally flows into the sea through an eight-kilometre-wide channel, in the lee of Curtis Island.

The southern tributaries of the Burdekin drain the northern limits of the Brigalow country, where the scrub extends through central Queensland from northern New South Wales. But the main flow of the Burdekin is from the north, where high ranges south-west of Ingham form a southern limit to the wet tropics.

West of the main river, and north around the headwaters, some of the most recent volcanic activity in Australia's history — albeit 15 000 years ago — has formed a great basalt flow

URBAN WETLANDS Only a few minutes from the centre of Townsville, a northerly portion of the coast's seasonal wetlands are protected within the Townsville Town Common Environmental Park. During the December-April wet season the swamps teem with aquatic life.

URBAN WETLANDS Only a few minutes from the centre of Townsville, a northerly portion of the coast's seasonal wetlands are protected within the Townsville Town Common Environmental Park. During the December-April wet season the swamps teem with aquatic life.

extending over hundreds of square kilometres. Craters dot the Mount Surprise basalt plateau, which now forms the divide between the Burdekin and Gulf of Carpentaria Rivers.

To the south, the great basalt wall stretches for over 100 kilometres, forming a distinct edge to one great lava flow. Waterfalls tumble over the wall, even throughout the dry season, to feed Lolworth Creek and other tributaries of the Burdekin. Further south, the river turns sharply towards the coast through ranges where a massive dam now impounds much of its water.

The Burdekin enters the sea through a classic, triangular delta with many channels. The prevailing wind sweeps sediments northwards, forming long sandspits such as Cape Bowling Green, and resulting in a complex of coastal wetlands.

Between the mouth of the river and Townsville, 90 kilometres to the north, the tidal and freshwater wetlands support the largest aggregation of water-birds in Queensland. Huge flocks of brolgas (*Grus rubicundus*), as many as 10 000 in one group, throng the sedge-covered wetlands in winter.

NATIVE CRANE The graceful brolga gathers in enormous flocks to mate and breed along the coast between Ayr and Townsville.

Cotton geese and green pygmy-geese (*Nettapus coromandelianus, N. pulchellus*), magpie geese (*Anseranas semi- palmata*), radjah shelduck (*Tadorna radjah*), and more than 200 other species have been recorded in this important coastal wetland.

The 'dry' tropics

Townsville is set in a dry, monsoonal landscape. In spring, before the storms that introduce the wet season, the grass is seared brown and many trees such as the white-trunked white gum (*Eucalyptus alba*) lose their leaves briefly before producing bright green new growth. Even the local rainforest — in fact, deciduous vine thickets — sheds leaves at the end of the 'dry'.

The surrounding hills, including those of Magnetic Island, a few kilometres offshore, are sparsely wooded outcrops except in a few moist, sheltered pockets. But just south of Townsville, Mount Elliott (1240 metres), in the Bowling Green Bay National Park (55 300 hectares), carries a lush area of true tropical rainforest — a small outlier of the wet tropics.

On the coast around Bowen, rugged, granite hills and mountains again dominate the dry, coastal lowlands. A number of these outcroppings form tiny national parks; one of them, the imposing headland of Cape Upstart (5620 hectares), is a popular destination for bushwalkers. The most exposed sites bear the spiky spinifex grass (*Triodia*) typical of the arid interior, but pockets

FOREST CREEK The rainforest on Mount Elliot, in Bowling Green Bay National Park, gives birth to Alligator Creek which cascades down to flow through this eucalypt woodland.

of coastal woodland still exist with vine thickets, through which water trickles down to unspoilt beaches.

Gloucester Island within Dryander National Park (13 400 hectares), across the harbour from Bowen, is another rugged, granite massif. The island and adjacent mainland areas are home to the rare Proserpine rock-wallaby (*Petrogale persephone*).

South of Bowen, and extending to Sarina is a high-rainfall region, usually referred to as the central coast rainforests. This Whitsunday region, a spectacular coastline of drowned valleys, is the first area where extensive rainforests are encountered south of the wet tropics. Deep, fiord-like inlets divide the coastline and beyond a narrow channel, more than 100 islands festoon the sea.

On the mainland, Mount Dryander, (820 metres), is the highest point of a rainforest-clad range overlooking the flat sugar lands of the Proserpine River valley. The Conway Range National Park (23 800 hectares) hugs the precipitous coastline, from a short distance past Airlie Beach to the mangrove-lined inlets of Repulse Bay. Open eucalypt forest on the lowlands gives way to dense rainforest along the streams and high ridges.

The dominant tree of the Whitsunday group is the hoop pine (*Araucaria cunninghamii*) which grows in thick stands on almost every hilltop. In places, its symmetrical crowns project up to 20 metres above the continuous canopy of the rainforest.

In exposed places, stunted, windswept pines cling to the ground where the soil has been eroded, surrounded

WRINKLY PINE The hoop pine has bark wrinkles which often encircle its trunk.

ISLAND PARK The forest of Gloucester Island (middleground), at the entrance to the Port of Bowen, is punctuated by granite outcrops.

by nothing more than low swards of native grasses; stock grazing, goats, fire, and the not infrequent cyclones have probably caused these grassy habitats to become more common.

The coastal rainforest is the domain of the Mackay cedar (*Albizia toona*), with its handsome, feathery crown. Paperbark trees are a feature of swamps and poorly drained soils. When they flower in autumn and winter, the woodlands are alive with parrots and honeyeaters by day and several species of flying foxes at night.

The broad-leaved paperbark (*Melaleuca viridiflora*), has greenish-cream bottlebrush flowers, but groves of trees with red or burgundy flowers are common. The tea-tree orchid (*Dendrobium canaliculatum*) finds the papery bark a good anchor from which to grow.

In moist swales just behind the beaches, and often only centimetres higher than the mangroves of the tidal zones, are spectacular forests of weeping paperbarks. These trees may be 20 to 30 metres tall with papery, white trunks over a metre in diameter and pendulous branches carrying rich-smelling, cream flowers.

The high tidal variation along the coast between Repulse Bay and Broad Sound gives the shoreline a distinct appearance. At low tide, the waterline can be 300 metres from the dunes, and in some extreme locations, up to four

WATER VIEWS The Conway Range, overlooking Repulse Bay on one side and the Whitsunday and Lindeman groups of islands on the other, runs down to the mangroves and beaches of the shoreline.

kilometres. The rippled, intertidal flats are a mixture of silt and sand with sparse seagrasses in places.

Offshore islands may be briefly connected to the mainland by a narrow spit of sand or gravel. The unwary walker who strays too far seawards may find the incoming tide moving at a fast walking pace.

The sinuous tidal estuaries are sheets of sand at low tide but soon fill with the oncoming rush of water. In the great funnel of Broad Sound, tides are pushed higher than elsewhere and a 'king' tide may have a ten-metre variation — only on the Kimberley coast in the north-west of Western Australia are there higher tides.

'Land of cloud'

The highest points of the ranges west of Mackay are incorporated within the 50 800-hectare Eungella National Park. Eungella means land of cloud — a fitting name for this 1259-metre-high tableland which is hit by a moist, south-easterly air flow that forces the clouds up the ranges, releasing mist and rain. Even when the lowlands have blue skies, clouds may be forming high on the eastern escarpment.

Most of the ranges and tableland are covered by dense rainforest and tall, moist eucalyptus forest. In the distinct rain shadow a few kilometres to the west, the tall forests give way to low, grassy woodland. Deep gorges, rutted by streams which flow west to join the Burdekin River system, carry tongues of the moist environment into the rain shadow area.

Although Eungella is geographically a tropical region, the mountain rainforest is classified as subtropical and plant and animal species similar to those in the Border Ranges — astride the Queensland–New South Wales border — are common. This is the northern limit for birds such as the regent bowerbird (*Sericulus chrysocephalus*) and the paradise riflebird (*Ptiloris paradiseus*), as well as a variety of common tree species.

Because Eungella was an isolated zone of forest for 30 000 years or more, species have evolved which are found nowhere else: the Eungella honeyeater (*Lichenostomus hindwoodi*) is found in just a few locations in the high-altitude rainforest; the Eungella gastric-brooding frog (*Rheobatrachus vitellinus*) shares with a close relative in southern Queensland the unique feature of brooding its eggs and young in its stomach.

SEA COW Warm currents lead the vegetarian dugong south to its summer feeding grounds.

The Mackay tulip oak (*Argyrodendron actinophyllum diversifolium*), with a short 'crowsfoot' buttress and shaft-like trunk, is common in areas of deep, rich soil. Red Eungella satin ash (*Acmena resa*), with its scaly, reddish bark, is a close relative of the lillypillys often found in east-coast gardens. Rainforest quandongs (*Elaeocarpus*) and laurels (*Cryptocarya*) occur everywhere and are a popular food source for flocks of fruit pigeons.

Lowland areas of the national park, such as Finch Hatton Gorge, support tropical rainforests, and the lacy crown of the tree peach (*Trema orientalis*) dominates places where cyclones have disturbed the forest. The open eucalyptus forest on the edge of the rainforest includes tall, smooth-trunked flooded gums (*Eucalyptus grandis*) and the stringybarked New England blackbutt (*E. andrewsii*).

Turtles, dugongs and others

Broad Sound and Shoalwater Bay are twin, 80-kilometre-deep indentations in the coast between Mackay and Rockhampton. The giant tides which sweep the coast twice a day rarely allow the fine, brown silt to settle in Broad Sound. Shoalwater Bay is deeper and cleaner, and sea grasses thrive in many places along the bed of the bay.

These are the grazing areas for that unusual marine mammal, the dugong (*Dugong dugon*). Although the dugong is found in other localities along the Queensland coast and in northern Australia, Shoalwater Bay is one of the most popular grazing grounds for this air-breathing herbivore that has adapted to life at sea.

Red cedar: from the forest to the antique shop

In the early 1790s, the new colony of New South Wales was desperate for building materials. Pioneer timbergetters, a resourceful and adventurous breed, were quick to set their sights on the dense forests of red cedar (*Toona australis*) that grew along the east coast from the Ulladulla region, in southern New South Wales, to the McIlwraith Range in northern Queensland.

Loggers often paved the way for early settlers as they were frequently the first explorers of this coast. Their sorties into the wild led to the first export of red cedar being made in 1795, to India; by the 1820s it was New South Wales' main export.

Cedar proved so popular that the ensuing 'cedar rush' — not as dramatic or as well-publicised as the numerous gold rushes — led to most of the large stands being cut down by the turn of the century.

Cedar-loggers cut 'drawing-roads' through the jungle of the Queensland coast, forming a network of tracks leading to a creek or the arm of a river. After being branded, the logs were cast into the shallow creeks and left there until a flood floated them into the river's main stream, from where they could be floated to the nearest township. Sometimes the logs remained in the bush or in water for as long as 15 years without showing signs of decay.

The cedar was once common on the basalt soil of the alluvial flats of large rivers, such as the Hawkesbury, but only a few pockets remain today — mainly in subtropical and riverine rainforests.

Natural regeneration is gradually occurring in some rainforests and there have been plantings by state forestry commissions but commercial cropping is unlikely; in plantation conditions groups of cedars are prone to attack by the cedar-tip moth which causes the tree to branch and grow crookedly.

The red cedar is a large, deciduous tree which may reach a height of over 40 metres, with a trunk diameter of two metres (see picture). Buttress roots spread beneath a trunk of grey or brown scaly bark, which is shed in oblong pieces. When cut through, the bark has an outer red layer and an inner whitish one; inside, the sapwood is yellowish-white and the heartwood a rich, red colour with a pleasant fragrance.

The ready nineteenth-century market for cedar is not hard to understand. The timber is light, soft, easy to work with, durable, and resistant to weather and the attacks of white ants and borers. The rich, red colour and open grain — best displayed when highly polished as in the Bendigo law courts building, above — has made red cedar the most valued Australian timber for furniture and cabinet work. Its scarcity has made it all the more sought after.

In the nineteenth century, no grand mansion was complete without cedar furniture. Today, such furniture is prized and draws high prices in antique shops.

Because of today's greatly reduced forest environment — and because it takes 90–120 years for the tree to gain its attractive, deep-red colour — it seems unlikely that red cedar will ever be plentiful again. The small supplies available mean it will remain a specialty timber for fine craftsmanship.

At least seven species of seagrass offer a rich harvest for this gentle, three-metre-long browser. Shoalwater Bay is protected from the disturbing effects of coastal agriculture and residential development as it lies within a military training reserve.

The bay is also believed to be a feeding ground for flotillas of green turtles (*Chelonia mydas*) which are thought to travel thousands of kilometres to reach this prime food source. The flatback turtle (*Chelonia depressa*), which breeds on island beaches close by, does not range as far, apparently preferring to stay in shallow, estuarine waters.

The head of Shoalwater Bay breaks up into a maze of tidal creeks, and mangrove forests, several kilometres wide in places, which trap nutrients and provide a stable breeding ground for fish and crustaceans.

Giant, sand-dune systems dominate the coastline and in some places rise to heights of 200 metres. This is the northernmost tract of the great dune environment found on Fraser Island and, further south, along the coast. The stark, volcanic headlands are covered with prostrate plants which flower profusely in late winter. Even large tree species, such as melaleucas, may be prostrated by wind, salt and the stony soils to a height of only 20 centimetres.

South of Gladstone, the coastline around Bustard Bay is still in a relatively natural state, appearing now much as it probably did on 24 May, 1770 when Captain James Cook and his party came ashore to fill their depleted water containers. The party had time to collect and make notes on the plants and animals around the Round Hill Creek estuary where the town of Seventeen Seventy and Eurimbula National Park (7830 hectares) now stand.

Just south of this point are the most northerly surf beaches in eastern Australia, for this is where the Great Barrier Reef begins to take the brunt of the Pacific rollers, leaving only small waves to lap the mainland shore.

Four species of sea turtle have been recorded nesting on these beaches; a record that no other site in the world can boast. Every year a few leathery turtles (*Dermochelys coriacea*) — at lengths of up to three metres the giants of the world's turtles — come ashore. But the main species here is the loggerhead (*Caretta caretta*).

The diverse coastal forests and sand dunes of the Bustard Bay region contain some of the southernmost examples of tropical plants. Behind the man-

groves of Eurimbula Creek, a swamp is filled with flourishing Alexandria palms (*Archtonphoenix alexandrae*).

Buff-breasted paradise kingfishers (*Tanysiptera sylvia*), a species normally found no further south than Townsville, have been found in the rainforest here. The delightful yellow-bellied sunbird (*Nectarinia jugularis*) — the females are olive and yellow, the males have an iridescent blue throat — commonly nests under the eaves of holiday cottages.

Conversely, this is the northern limit of other species, such as the noisy brush wattlebird (*Anthochaera chrysoptera*) and the nectar-rich forest and heath plants on which it feeds. The wallum banksia (*Banksia aemula*), with its fat, creamy brush and serrated leaves, is the dominant plant in the extensive 'wallum' coastal lowlands which stretch south along the coast into New South Wales.

An abundance of 'roos

Despite extensive clearing for agriculture, this coast has not yet suffered the wave of extinction of native animals which has occurred in the south and in many parts of the arid interior. There are 14 species of macropods — big-footed marsupials — in the region, but despite their numbers, this is the last refuge for some.

The eastern grey kangaroo (*Macropus giganteus*) and the common wallaroo (*M. robustus*) are among the large species that have increased in numbers since European settlement, benefiting from improved pastures and stock watering holes.

Medium-sized wallabies also remain abundant. Populations of the red-necked wallaby (*M. rufogriseus*) extend to this area from southern regions and the agile wallaby (*M. agilis*), a species ranging across northern Australia, reaches its southern limits here.

The black-striped wallaby (*M. dorsalis*) — so common along this coast that it can be a pest in some areas — and the swamp wallaby (*Wallabia bicolor*) thrive here, even though the brigalow scrubs and other dense vegetation which is the preferred habitat of both species, has been extensively cleared.

Some of the smaller animals are not faring so well. The brush-tailed bettong (*Bettongia penicillata*) is endangered and now occurs in only a few isolated pockets, appearing to prefer woodland areas with tussock grasses and dense, low shrubs. The species occurs only

HAIRY SURVIVOR The last sanctuary of the hairy-nosed wombat is fenced for its protection.

along this coast and in Western Australia, having disappeared from the other mainland states.

The bridled nailtail wallaby (*Onychogalea fraenata*) is one of the surprise stories of wildlife conservation. Once common throughout eastern Australia, all the way down to north-western Victoria, it declined rapidly and was believed extinct in the early decades of this century. Forty years after its apparent disappearance, a small colony was discovered in scrubby forest near Dingo, 160 kilometres west of Rockhampton.

NOCTURNAL FEEDER Despite its seemingly abundant numbers, the black-striped wallaby is seldom seen as it usually feeds after dark.

STRIPED SURVIVOR The bridled nailtail has a white 'bridle' stripe around its upper body.

The nailtail wallaby, called 'flashjack' by the early settlers, due to its erratic flight when flushed from cover, is in fact just as likely to lie prostrate or crawl away through dense shrubbery to avoid detection. There is still no clear-cut explanation as to why it is now found only in one area, as suitable habitats exist elsewhere.

Clearing and the effect of stock grazing have had a considerable effect on the nailtail, as with most declining marsupials, but other, less obvious factors are believed to be involved. The species is now being studied to determine its future conservation needs, which may include reintroduction back into other wild places within its once extensive range.

Two hundred and fifty kilometres north-west of the last refuge of the bridled nailtail wallaby is the home of an even rarer marsupial, the northern hairy-nosed wombat (*Lasiorhinus krefftii*). The two other wombat species in Australia have suffered some decline in range and numbers but are still listed as common, while the northern hairy-nosed is one of the most endangered of all the world's mammals.

Approximately 60 animals are believed to live in the open eucalyptus and acacia woodland in what is now the Epping Forest National Park (3160 hectares). There are indications that the population decline has been arrested and the forest is becoming a fine example of a natural landscape, free of the degrading effect of hard-hooved creatures such as sheep and cattle. ☐

The plains of inland Queensland, the birthplace of much of the lore of the traditional drover's life, have all but lost the scrub covering that gave its name to a large part of the region

Through the 'scrub' and out to Cooper Creek

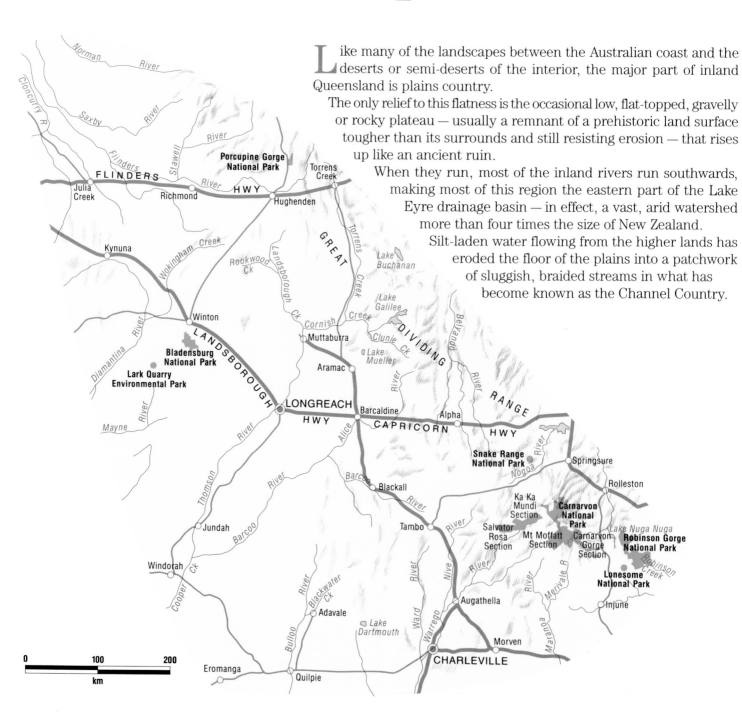

Like many of the landscapes between the Australian coast and the deserts or semi-deserts of the interior, the major part of inland Queensland is plains country.

The only relief to this flatness is the occasional low, flat-topped, gravelly or rocky plateau — usually a remnant of a prehistoric land surface tougher than its surrounds and still resisting erosion — that rises up like an ancient ruin.

When they run, most of the inland rivers run southwards, making most of this region the eastern part of the Lake Eyre drainage basin — in effect, a vast, arid watershed more than four times the size of New Zealand.

Silt-laden water flowing from the higher lands has eroded the floor of the plains into a patchwork of sluggish, braided streams in what has become known as the Channel Country.

The streams efficiently, if slowly, drain the interior as they meander for a thousand kilometres towards Lake Eyre on a gradient of about twenty centimetres to the kilometre.

The largest streams, sometimes mentioned in traditional droving stories by such authors as Henry Lawson and Banjo Paterson, are the Diamantina, Thomson and Barcoo Rivers. The Thomson and the Barcoo meet near Windorah to form Cooper Creek, a name synonymous with the harshness of the outback ever since 1861 when the two leaders of the ill-fated Burke and Wills expedition perished near their depot on the banks of the creek.

Though these streams run only during the wet season, they contain occasional permanent waterholes of enormous biological importance to the dry inland.

The Great Dividing Range forms a natural division between the coastal and inland watersheds. Rainfall tapers off after the ranges blend into the

SANDY SHORE Within a few weeks of good summer rains to the north, these dunes flanking Cooper Creek, near Windorah, will be carpeted in grass.

plains, and most of inland Queensland lies within the arid and semi-arid zones which occupy almost 70 per cent of the continent.

Low, variable rainfall and high temperatures for much of the year have encouraged the establishment of hardy and low-growing, drought-resistant plants. The scrub is a blend of familiar species such as *Acacia, Cassia, Eremophila, Grevillea* and *Eucalyptus*.

At ground level, there are wire and tussock grasses and burr-bearing plants. In the more temperate south-east, wheat and other cereals are grown intensively but the major part of inland Queensland is too dry for agriculture and is given over to grazing.

Since European settlement, the landscape has changed markedly. Over-grazing has led to the destruction of many native animal and plant habitats, while soil erosion is at a critical stage in some areas.

Many small marsupials, unable to adapt to a changing environment, with constant competition for food from domestic stock, have become extinct. Others, like the bridled nailtail walla-by (*Onychogalea fraenata*) — once a common species — the northern hairy-nosed wombat (*Lasiorhinus krefftii*) — one of the world's rarest mammals — and the yellow-footed rock-wallaby (*Petrogale xanthopus*), have retreated from their habitats and are under virtual siege in a few small, isolated areas.

As these animals take their place among the world's endangered species, much of the hardy, drought-resistant native flora survives, its resilience having been its salvation. Despite this, many species are now classified 'rare and endangered'.

Speaking geographically...

There are five major regions between the Great Dividing Range and the deserts and semi-deserts of the interior: the central highlands, the brigalow lands, the mulga lands, the Mitchell grass plains and Channel Country, and the desert uplands.

The central highlands are mainly sandstone, laid down as sediment in ancient oceans and so deeply creased and rutted by erosion that they form fifteen individual ranges. These ranges, low as they are, are Queensland's most important inland river catchment area.

The northern slopes of the highlands are drained to the coast by the Belyando, Nogoa, Comet and Dawson Rivers, while the southern run-off is into the

WATER POWER A deep gorge in the Carnarvon National Park is one of many throughout the deeply carved and rutted Carnarvon Range formed by the constantly eroding waters of highland rivers.

western headwaters of the Darling River through the Maranoa and Warrego Rivers. Rugged canyons and narrow valleys walled in by white-faced cliffs have been cut by the force of the water coming down from the 1000-metre heights, where the rainfall reaches 800 millimetres a year.

Erosion over millions of years has exposed new nutrient beds in the sedimentary layers; the complexity of soils, the terrain, and various aspects or exposures to sunlight possible in a hilly environment has enabled a great diversity of plants to evolve in one of the inland's most botanically important sites. A wealth of diverse wild creatures live here; hilly or mountainous terrains provide a more secure environment than the flat, open plains and are less amenable to farming. There are wallabies, grey kangaroos, possums, sugar gliders and koalas.

The highland's best known and most used national parks are Carnarvon

(223 000 hectares) and Blackdown Tableland (23 800 hectares), both of which have camping facilities and visitors' lodges.

Last permanent water

Two prominent landmarks of the highlands are the Minerva Hills 'volcanics' — residual, tooth-like volcanic plugs which tower above the small town of Springsure and the surrounding plains — and, further south, the Bluff and Blackdown Tableland. In the beautiful Arcadia Valley, hemmed in by the retreating scarps of the Carnarvon and Expedition Ranges, are the Arcadia wetlands. Lake Nuga Nuga with an area of 2000 hectares, often covered by the pink Undulla waterlily (*Nymphaea*), is the largest of this series of shallow lakes and swamps which nestle at the foot of the Kongabula Range — named to honour the Aboriginal tribe of the upper Comet River.

Further east where the Palm Tree

THE MOSS GARDEN Constant seepage means that native mosses and other shade-loving plants thrive
in the dark recesses of the appropriately named Violet Gorge in the Carnarvon Range.

and Robinson Creeks have laid down
deep deposits of alluvial soil at their
junction with the Dawson River, are
hundreds of small lakes fringed with
river red gums (*Eucalyptus camaldulensis*). The landscape is enhanced
by tall cabbage palms (*Livistona australis*) and red-flowering bottlebrush
(*Callistemon viminalis*) which line the
streams and blend in with the flowering heath plants and wattles.

The Brigalow ... as amended

In 1844, John Gilbert, a member of
Ludwig Leichhardt's expedition, and
one of the first Europeans to see the
brigalow country, wrote in his diary:
'One of the most beautifully picturesque and extensive scenes met our
anxious gaze. The immediate vicinity
of the hills was like park scenery —
clear undulating hills with here and
there small clumps of brigalow, while
the sides of many of the hills were dotted with single scrubs as if picked out

BRANCHED BOTTLE The distinctively shaped Queensland bottle tree does not normally grow in such splendid isolation; the surrounding brigalow scrub has been cleared to allow stock to graze.

by hand. Beyond this to the westward and round as far as we could see to the northeast was a carpet of evergreens for six or seven miles and then the high ranges rose up and formed a beautiful backdrop to the most pleasing natural picture we have seen'.

The Brigalow is an area of about six million hectares, where the early settlers followed the practice adopted in other parts of inland Australia — the Mallee, the Pilliga, the Mulga — and named the region after the plant that dominated its landscape. In this case, the region retains the name but its namesake has almost disappeared.

The acacia woodlands of the brigalow tree (*Acacia harpophylla*) have been systematically cleared since the 1880s to provide some of Queensland's prime agricultural land. Over-clearing, to provide as much wheat-growing and pasture land as possible, has resulted in a treeless landscape where only isolated clumps of the original brigalow covering remain.

The removal of the scrub's major component — the brigalow grows to about 15 metres, usually in dense clumps — inevitably had a negative effect on all the other plants in the region. With their environment changed, other plants of the Brigalow died out too.

Complex vine thickets of bottletree saplings (*Brachychiton rupestris, B. australis*), bonewood (*Macropteranthes leichhardtii*), and ooline (*Cadellia pentastylis*), once common, are now rare. The thickets provide shelter for the mound-building Australian brush-turkey (*Alectura lathami*) and many smaller birds and marsupials. The requirements of agriculture and animal husbandry, while totally detrimental to some plants and animals, have proved beneficial to others, so that the balance of nature is upset and life continues in a lopsided fashion.

Former scrub transformed into good grazing pasture by the use of introduced plants such as buffel grass (*Cenchrus ciliaris*) and artificial watering points, has allowed the kori bustard (*Ardeotis kori*) once rare, to breed prolifically, as have eastern grey kangaroos (*Macropus giganteus*), emus (*Dromaius novaehollandiae*) and the larger wallabies.

Wattle triumphant

The Mulga region, in the southwestern portion of inland Queensland, is a vast, low woodland of about twenty million hectares, making the mulga wattle (*Acacia aneura*) a much more widespread tree than its relative, the brigalow. In fact, the Mulga, the area

GUM-LIKE Due to its appearance, the native apple — also known as the apple gum — was once classified as a eucalypt.

of its greatest concentration, spreads deep into New South Wales, before sweeping westwards across all the arid and semi-arid regions of the continent.

The mulga lands are conveniently divided into 'hard' and 'soft' categories: the 'hard' mulga is confined to shallow, gravelly or hardpan, acid soils where the surface has been exposed to the elements for longer than elsewhere; the 'soft' mulga is on sandplain and acid red earths which are 'younger' and have deep soil profiles.

Though *Acacia aneura* is the most common and widespread mulga, the other mulgas, (*A. brachystachya, A. stowardii*) also grow here, though in a

more scattered fashion. These plants generally form the middle layer in shrubby, low woodlands beneath the taller eucalypts, though they may form dense to open shrublands where there are no eucalypts and occasionally, pure 'whipstick thickets' in moist hollows.

While it is often seen as a dry, rather drab, and monotonous landscape of red soil and grey foliage, the Mulga waits patiently for moisture to trigger the 'quick change' its plants are so expert at. After good rains, the countryside is transformed into a garden of flowering plants and green herbage, buzzing with bees and teeming with the wildlife which is quick to take advantage of the novel abundance of fresh, green shoots. This startling display of colour and sweet scents occurs most commonly in springtime.

Rising above the spinifex are the branches of large, spreading native apple trees (*Angophora melanoxylon*), silver-leaved ironbarks (*Eucalyptus melanophloia*), cypress pines (*Callitris*) and Kurrajongs (*Brachychiton populneus*). Grey kangaroos, emus, and, unfortunately, foxes, are numerous, with smaller numbers of red kangaroos (*Macropus rufus*) as the landscape becomes more open towards the west.

Beneath all this lies the Great Artesian Basin, first tapped in the mid-1880s, which has changed a region once deficient in permanent surface water, into one of the better-watered parts of the inland.

Sea of grass

In the arid central and northern parts of the inland, the vast treeless landscape is dominated by Mitchell grass (*Astrebla*) plains, interrupted only by occasional outbreaks of gidgee (*Acacia cambagei*), boree (*A. cana*) and coolibah (*Eucalyptus microtheca*) woodlands. Space and time take on a different dimension here, as the knee-high Mitchell grass blankets the landscape like an endless yellow wheatfield. In places, the only break on the horizon may be the punctuation of a single-lane road or the poles of a telephone line. And both of these are liable to dissolve into a heat shimmer.

North of Winton, a gentle rise in the Mitchell grass plain forms the Gulf of Carpentaria watershed, which is drained by the Flinders River. Droughts are frequent, but when they break, the lignum (*Muehlenbeckia cunninghamii*) and river red gum trees suddenly find themselves lining the

SWEEPING PLAIN Four species of Mitchell grass make up the predominant vegetation on the infertile soils of outback Queensland.

braided creeks of the Channel Country like stately willows by a perennial English stream.

When the floodwaters recede from the plains where the Barcoo and Thomson Rivers meet, a brilliant but short-lived patchwork sea of flowering plants and Cooper clover (*Trigonella suavissima*) covers the ground in every direction. The only reserve in this vast region, where such cyclical displays can be guaranteed to repeat themselves without interference, is the Bladensburg National Park (33 700 hectares) near Winton.

Scattered across the plain, as if strewn by some Dreamtime spirit, are millions of small silcrete blocks (gibbers or gidgeestones), the fractured remnants of the hard, thin crust that once paved the surface when this region was part of a series of plateaux. Mixed in with the surface rubble, are numerous chunks of petrified wood and polished quartz pebble.

Desert in name only

The desert uplands of inland Queensland, are in fact extensive, old alluvial plains supporting grassy woodlands of ironbark, bloodwoods (*Eucalyptus terminalis, E. similis, E. setosa*), ghost gum (*E. papuana*) and spinifex sandplain. These are bisected at random by low hills — fading spurs of the Great Dividing and Aramac Ranges covered by bendee (*A. catenulata*) shrubs.

There are even wetlands, of which Lake Buchanan and Lake Galilee

CALLING CARDS Millions of years ago, when inland Queensland was steamy and tropical, a herd of dinosaurs left these tracks in mudflats near present-day Winton.

(15 000 hectares) are the largest bodies of water. The wetlands are a complex of shallow, seasonally flooded salt and freshwater lakes and swamps. They are a valuable waterfowl habitat where many thousands of pelicans, black swans and spoonbills nest.

Around the shores, large flocks of brolgas dance in noisy profusion — usually before the spring breeding season, but occasionally at other times too — among grazing red and grey kangaroos. The edible, salt-tolerant shrub *Lawrencia buchananensis*, classified as an endangered species, has colonised a small area on Lake Buchanan's western beach. □

Where the mountains hug the coast and the cloud banks off the Coral Sea bring drenching rains to the lowlands, nature runs riot. The lush and complex world of the tropical rainforest is the result

The last stand of the jungle

Cloud-capped mountains, carpeted in steamy jungle and towering over narrow, coastal lowlands, bring a scenic grandeur to the Atherton Tableland region that exists in few other parts of mainland Australia. The jungle represents the largest remaining fragments of tropical rainforest in Australia.

These unique biological reservoirs, the most complex of terrestrial environments, have an instant, familiar appeal. Unlike the craggy, awe-inspiring and sometimes frightening beauty of south-west Tasmania, these forests represent the warm and lush tropical paradise of popular imagination.

The tropical rainforests, which, as the 'wet tropics', were listed as a World Heritage area (see p. 391) in 1989, now exist as a patchy belt, up to 70 kilometres wide, extending from Cooktown almost as far south as Townsville.

Despite the general concept of 'tropical' as somewhere green and lush, the description 'wet tropics' is necessary because a large part of Australia's tropics — the region north of the Tropic of Capricorn — is dry and arid.

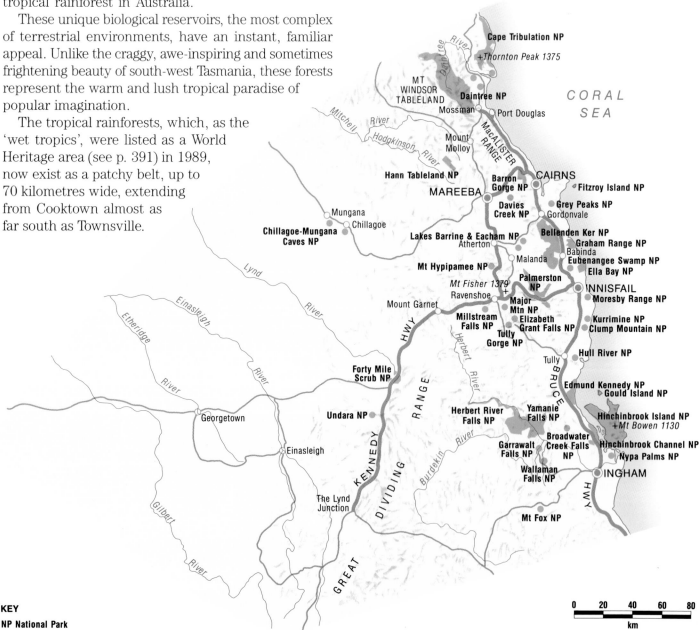

KEY

NP National Park

The uniqueness of this region is underlined by its relatively small size and the great contrast it presents to the landscapes to the north, south and west. Here the Great Dividing Range, always a brooding presence along the eastern coast of the continent, emerges from the background. The mountains curve eastward to hug the coast as in few other locations. From the shores of the Coral Sea they rise abruptly to more than 1500 metres along the Bellenden Ker Range, which includes Mount Bartle Frere, at 1622 metres Queensland's highest mountain.

To the west of the Bellenden Ker Range, the Atherton Tableland forms an undulating plateau, most of it about 750 metres above sea level, and in the south-west, the Evelyn Tableland rises to around 1000 metres, with Mt Fisher standing out at 1420 metres. The slopes rising to these tablelands and ranges are deeply dissected by many rivers and streams and these have carved a ruggedly spectacular landscape of narrow gorges and plunging waterfalls.

From the tablelands, the Herbert and Tully Rivers plunge into deep gorges which have been scoured out between ranges. Many tributary streams, in turn, plunge into the gorges to swell the waters of the larger rivers, and modest falls and cascades are common. Less than modest are the Wallaman Falls which provide one of Australia's most breathtaking sights as the riverbed of one of these tributaries meets a cliff and the waters plunge almost 300 metres in a clear drop to a new riverbed below.

Ranges by the sea

North of Cairns, between Port Douglas and Mossman, the Great Dividing Range rises to the wilderness of peaks and gorges of the Mount Windsor Tableland. At an altitude of 1000 metres, this is the source of the Daintree River. The precipitous mountain slopes, covered in thick forest, plunge to the sea without intervening coastal plains, so that the rainforest grows right to the shoreline.

Most spectacular among the coastal peaks here is Thornton Peak, capped with blackened, weathered boulders, and rising to 1374 metres. As a con-

ONLY A CREEK A rift in the Great Dividing Range turns the waters of Stony Creek, part of the Herbert River system, into the Wallaman Falls. On the coast, the rainforest near Cape Tribulation scrambles down the slopes all the way to the high-tide line (left).

necting link with the Bellenden Ker Range further south, the Macalister Range closely follows the coast between Mossman and Cairns, always dominating the landscape.

Shorter but no less spectacular spurs extend southwards from the vicinity of Atherton, forming a high blue-green wall of rainforest behind the coastal towns from Tully to Paluma, near Ingham. A parallel range, separated from the mainland by a narrow mangrove channel, rises from the sea at Hinchinbrook Island, Australia's largest island national park (39 350 hectares).

This chain of high ranges and peaks, so close to the coast, interrupts the passage of moisture-laden winds from the Pacific, so that clouds bank up like waters behind a dam. The summits are rarely without at least a trailing plume of cloud, and more often are completely enshrouded.

These north-eastern highlands have Australia's heaviest rainfall, with an annual reading of over 4000 millimetres for the Tully-Babinda strip. Some of the wettest areas of the ranges, where mist or rain are an almost constant presence, receive as much as 7600 millimetres, with readings of over 500 millimetres in one day being recorded in the most heavily drenched localities.

Most of this rain comes during the December to March wet season, often bringing floods to the coastal lowlands and turning the rivers, streams and waterfalls into rushing torrents of white water. Even through the dry season the moisture is maintained at higher altitudes by sudden storms or by the heavy clouds of mist that swirl about the peaks.

Cathedral of green

With so much rain, it is not surprising that lush jungle is the natural vegetation east of the mountain watershed. This crowded rainforest is the botanical version of high-density city living: it is vibrant with opportunistic life as plants, flourishing in the greenhouse environment, compete vigorously for light and nutrients.

The forest contains a bewildering diversity of more than 800 species of trees; in places, over a hundred species have been recorded within a hectare or two, together with an even greater number of smaller plants. Huge columnar trunks hold aloft an almost unbroken canopy of green foliage, excluding all but a few rays of sunlight from the lower levels. Here in the permanent green and brown twilight are

an array of epiphytic orchids, ferns and mosses flourishing in the rich compost provided by the leaf drop.

The character of the rainforests varies with altitude. North of Daintree the rainforest grows right to the shore, with the great trees, covered in vines and epiphytes, overhanging the waters at high tide. In most parts of the country, coastal rainforest is usually separated from the ocean by a belt of other vegetation, such as mangroves, paperbark swamps, eucalypt woodlands or heathlands.

South of Mossman, the coastal lowland rainforests on deep red, basalt soils reach the highest level of complex-

BENEATH THE CANOPY On the forest floor, gnarled buttress roots — ideal hosts for mosses and fungi — fan out beneath their trunks to grip the thin soil and provide support.

ity and richness of species, although only small patches of these forests remain. Where the coastal lowlands are swampy, there are paperbark trees and dense thickets of fan palms and vines.

On the higher slopes, the rainforest becomes cloud forest, where stunted, wind-pruned, mossy trees grow on the steep mountainsides. This is the habitat of Australia's only rhododendron, the red-flowered *Rhododendron lochae*, which flowers under grey skies during the wet season and the yellow-flowered *Agapetes meiniana*, a relative of the European heaths.

The great belt of rainforest covers the highest and most rugged ranges

and the eastern plateau escarpments, but little is left on the lower slopes or the coastal plains. These areas were long ago cleared for agriculture, so that only remnant pockets remain on the plains and the Atherton Tableland. Inland, beyond the Great Dividing Range, tropical open woodlands grow in the lower rainfall zones.

A busy, crowded place

The obvious visual magnificence of the wet tropics with their landscape of mountains, rainforests and sea, hide myriad individual natural wonders, many of which have yet to be revealed. Biologically, these and the adjoining north-eastern Queensland rainforests are of immense importance. So far scientists have only scratched the surface in their efforts to survey the full wealth of plant, insect and animal life in the region.

The diverse habitats of the Atherton region, both wet and dry, are populated by many different animals, the birds being most conspicuous. There is a great number of species unique to the region and a great many more that are similar to the flora and fauna of New Guinea. The proximity of the large island to the north and the similar tropical climate has meant that numerous plants and animals are common to both places.

While this influence of nearby New Guinea is particularly evident in the rainforests to the north, on Cape York, it has also greatly influenced the shaping of the animals further south. Creatures which are identical or very similar to those of New Guinea include kingfishers, bowerbirds, tree-kangaroos and cuscuses, and these are just a few of the animals that are found on both sides of Torres Strait.

In past ages, before the shallow straits between Cape York and New Guinea were inundated by the ocean, many species were able to move freely from one land mass to the other. While Torres Strait is a barrier to mammals, it is crossed regularly by many species of birds. Some occur on both sides as identical, or very slightly different races, while other migratory species divide their time between Australia and New Guinea.

A much lower rainfall zone, in a belt across the base of Cape York, has, for many creatures, broken the link with the rainforests of the Cape and New Guinea, isolating them in the mountainous rainforests from Cooktown south to Townsville. Separated from

A CHANGED VIEW The Atherton Tableland, looking towards the Bellenden Ker Range, displays a patch of the forest which once covered the whole region.

TWO-TONE The Herbert River ringtail possum may be black and white or fawn and white.

their northern relatives, they have evolved differences which over time have led to their classification as separate species.

In addition, the terrain, ranging from coastal lowlands to the mountain summits, has made this one of the few parts of Australia where the distribution of birds and mammals is determined mainly by altitude.

Life in the treetops

Among mammals restricted to high altitudes are the beautiful green ringtail possum (*Pseudocheirus archeri*), the shy Herbert River ringtail possum (*P. herbertensis*), the noisy lemuroid ringtail possum (*Hemibelideus lemuroides*), and the spectacular striped possum (*Dactylopsila trivirgata*). The musky rat-kangaroo (*Hypsiprymnodon moschatus*) is also unique to the rainforests between Mossman and Townsville.

Although the green ringtail possum is nocturnal, it can sometimes be seen high up in tree canopies. A combination of white, grey, yellow and black hairs gives the possum's thick fur its unusual lime-green colour. Preferring the safety of tree-tops, the possum only ventures down to the ground to cross a gap between trees.

Just after nightfall, crashing sounds in the tree foliage indicates that the lemuroid possum has begun its nightly wanderings. This woolly grey and brown possum leaps through trees, landing heavily onto cushioning clumps of leaves.

With black and white stripes along the length of head, body and tail, the striped possum resembles a skunk; its lingering pungent odour reinforces this first impression. This spectacular possum is astonishingly agile and fast, moving in a peculiar 'rowing' fashion because of its diagonally opposed limbs.

Undoubtedly the best-known bird of the upland rainforests is the golden bowerbird (*Prionodura newtoniana*), which is common at altitudes between 900 and 1500 metres. A related bird, the far less colourful tooth-billed catbird (*Ailuroedus dentirostris*), usually lives between the 600- and 1400-metre levels. The males of this rather plain, green-feathered species make a 'playground' of leaves placed face down on the ground to impress the female catbird.

Victoria's riflebird (*Ptiloris victoriae*) is one of the more imaginative rain-

SELDOM SEEN The red-necked crake prefers the ground to the air and even swims creeks.

forest birds. The black-feathered males may be seen displaying from their 'stages', which may be high stumps, or bare tree limbs. They are quite common and easily found in the national parks on the Atherton Tableland.

One of the small, high-altitude birds confined to these ranges is the grey-headed robin (*Poecilodryas albispecularis*) which is found in the forest above 200 metres. Another which prefers the uplands is Bower's shrike-thrush (*Colluricincla boweri*), an unobtrusive species which lives amongst the foliage of shrubs and small trees and in the breeding season draws attention to itself with its ringing calls.

Some other birds, while also found in parts of Cape York, are best known from, and most easily seen, in this region. The red-necked crake (*Rallina tricolor*) is most often reported from

Rainforests of the wet tropics: going...going...?

The scientific crystal ball — not to mention many years of excavation and painstaking analysis of fossils — has revealed that the predominantly dry and dusty Australian continent of today was once much wetter and covered in lush, tropical rainforest.

The distinctive eucalypts, acacias and other hardy evergreens that we call 'natives' are descended from the damp greenery that thrived in these jungles 60 million years ago.

Climatic vagaries and the material requirements of human settlement have had the rainforests in a state of constant retreat since then; all that remains is a narrow string of isolated pockets of trees that runs from Cape York to Tasmania and small patches in the Northern Territory and the northern part of Western Australia.

The world's wet tropics provide a natural glasshouse environment, with warmth and high humidity, that is ideal for plant growth. With a generally thin, but rich soil cover, that is constantly renewed as dead vegetation rots and returns to its origins as compost, plants compete vigorously for space and grow with a lushness that can only occur where their energy

is not diverted to make concessions or adaptations to accommodate a less generous climate.

Wet tropical rainforests are complex biological units that are little understood by science but in many parts of the world they have been cleared to open up land for farming, or logged in such a wholesale fashion, that they have little chance of recovery.

International concern about the preservation of what rainforest remains is prompted less by reports of the 'greenhouse effect', and the oxygen contribution trees make to our atmosphere, than by the need to preserve any unique environment that is threatened with extinction.

A closed canopy of very dense leaves, formed by broad-leaved, thin-barked trees that grow 20–30 metres high, gives the forests their distinctive character. In their pursuit of direct sunlight, massive 60-metre-high trees, such as hoop pines, emerge from the canopy and tower above. An understorey of ferns, palms and saplings thrive in the humid conditions nearer the ground, where a moist micro-climate is formed beneath the canopy.

These scientific storehouses have shown great potential for providing new staple crops and pharmaceuticals. Rice, taro and bananas came from the forest and approximately one in every four of modern drugs found its source there.

In Australia, the wet tropical area covers only 1 per cent of the continent and yet it is the country's richest animal habitat, containing 30 per cent of all marsupials, 23 per cent of the reptiles and 18 per cent of the birds. Approximately 54 vertebrate species are unique to the wet tropics and another 160 are highly dependent on it for survival.

The Daintree rainforest is the largest area of rainforest wilderness in Australia, and the last remaining sizeable tract of tropical rainforest on the coastal lowlands. Until the late 1960s, this wilderness stretched in an uninterrupted belt from the Coral Sea as far as the Mount Windsor Tableland. As such, it became the centre of a Queensland version of the battle to save the Franklin River in Tasmania (see p. 43) when a road was proposed along its coastal fringe.

The proposal came to symbolise the general threat to the forest's integrity but despite the defiance of conservationists, who conducted a vigorous protest campaign, the will of the local authority prevailed. The Cape Tribulation to Bloomfield road was built (see picture) and excluded from the World Heritage status that was conferred on the wet tropics region in 1988.

INLAND REEF Far inland from the Great Barrier Reef, the remains of another, much more ancient reef, appear in the limestone country around Chillagoe.

the coastal ranges. This secretive bird lives where the rainforest undergrowth is most dense and damp.

The odd-looking double-eyed fig-parrot (*Cyclopsitta diophthalma*) — named because of an eye-like marking near one eye — lives its life among the treetops feeding upon the seeds of native figs. The Papuan frogmouth (*Podargus papuensis*) is, within Australia, almost entirely restricted to the Cape York and Atherton Tableland regions. Here it is to be found at the edge of dense rainforest, vine thickets or mangrove forest.

Museums of nature

Fortunately, the magnificent scenery and wildlife of the mountains and tablelands can still be seen in the region's many national parks. A large number of small parks have been established on the coastal lowlands, the tablelands and on the steep slopes of the ranges. Most are easily accessible and many can be traversed by road.

Time, and sometimes patience, is required to appreciate the life of the forests. The birds can often be heard, and eventually seen, but most of the mammals require deliberate searching out, usually by torch at night.

The most famous of the Atherton region's national parks is the Daintree (58 978 hectares), where the rainforest reaches its climax in a rich and bewildering confusion of plant life (see box).

Bellenden Ker National Park (31 000 hectares), is almost entirely an undeveloped wilderness accessible only to bushwalkers. Close beside Bellenden Ker, the Palmerston National Park (14 200 hectares) includes a precipitous gorge, with lookout points along the Palmerston Highway, and has walking tracks that wind down through the rainforest to the river and its waterfalls.

On the Atherton Tableland, several small national parks preserve the pockets of the upland rainforest which were not felled by early settlers to make way for crops. These parks have walking

tracks which make their attractions more accessible than they are in the larger parks such as Bellenden Ker.

At the two volcanic crater lakes, Lake Eacham and Lake Barrine, the encircling tracks traverse rainforest where many birds, including the aggressive cassowary (*Casuarius casuarius*) may be seen. At Mount Hypipamee National Park (364 hectares), the forest comes to a sudden halt around a rocky outcrop where a steep-sided shaft drops a sheer 60 metres to the surface of a dark lake, itself more than 80 metres deep.

Inland from the Atherton Tableland, the country becomes drier, and the rainforests are replaced by eucalypt woodlands and vine-scrub thickets. In total contrast to the rich basalt soils to the east, there are outcrops of limestone and underground caves. Near the old mining town of Chillagoe, an ancient coral reef has been hollowed out into a series of caverns through which seeping water has formed chambers decorated with stalactites. □

215

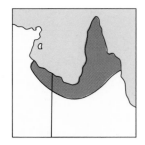
The largely untouched wilderness of Cape York, alternately lashed by monsoon rains and baked under a cloudless sky, is a last frontier for miner, pastoralist and environmentalist alike

Where the rain-drenched land runs out

The sharp tip of the broad arrowhead that is Cape York Peninsula points determinedly northward, as if it were trying to drag the continent behind it further into the tropics. In fact, Cape York is a mere ten degrees and forty-odd minutes — about 1200 kilometres — from the Equator.

The peninsula is a wild land of climatic extremes and its primitive ecosystems are largely unblurred by the impact of civilisation: it is a tropical counterpart, on a much larger scale, of the cool temperate wilderness of the south-west of Tasmania.

The area is one of the wettest in Australia but, in the perverse way of the tropics, most of the rain falls in the November–April wet season and for six months of the year drought is a major feature of the climate. The plants and animals are well adjusted to this constant cycle of feast followed by famine.

On the eastern side of the peninsula, the high land of the Great Dividing Range, the great rib of eastern Australia, persists almost all the way to the tip of Cape York. It gives up after a valiant battle, in the region of the Jardine River. The range's lush rainforests provide an avenue for the movement of birds and plants into the area from similar forests in New Guinea.

The adjacent coastline contains virtually every landform known in Australia — from the mangroves of Newcastle Bay to the dunes and lakes of Cape Flattery and the boulder-strewn slopes of Cape Melville.

TWO SEASONS The extremes of 'wet' or 'dry', with no intervening autumn or spring, govern the landscape around Mount Tozer in the Iron Range.

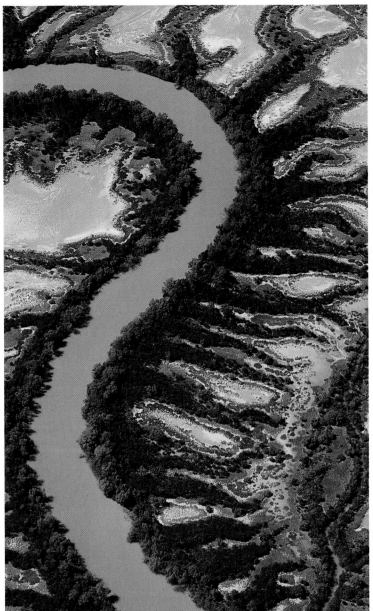

IN THE WET The Flinders River is typical of the arc of wet-season rivers that wend their way into the Gulf of Carpentaria through a muddy maze in the no-man's land of the tidal flats.

LAZY RIVER The multi-branched estuary of the Norman River is opposite Karumba, one of the few non-Aboriginal settlements on the Gulf.

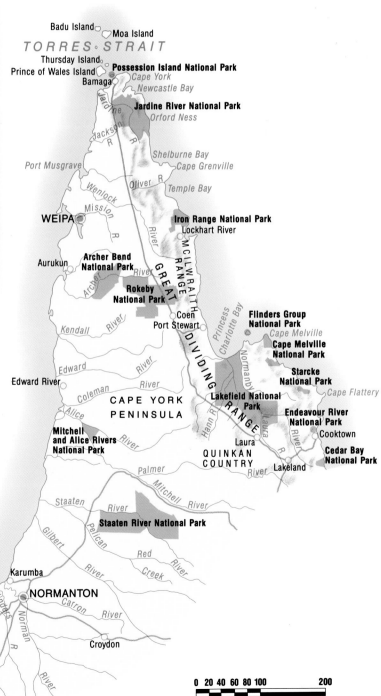

Badu Island
Moa Island
TORRES · STRAIT
Thursday Island
Prince of Wales Island
Bamaga
Possession Island National Park
Cape York
Newcastle Bay

Jardine
Jackson
R

Jardine River National Park
Orford Ness

Shelburne Bay
Cape Grenville

Port Musgrave
Wenlock
Oliver R
Temple Bay

Mission
River

WEIPA

Iron Range National Park
Lockhart River

McILWRAITH RANGE

Aurukun
Archer Bend National Park
Archer River

Rokeby National Park
Coen
Port Stewart

Kendall River

GREAT

Princess Charlotte Bay
Flinders Group National Park
Cape Melville
Cape Melville National Park

Edward River
River
Starcke National Park
Cape Flattery

Edward River
Coleman River
Alice River

CAPE YORK PENINSULA

Normanby

Lakefield National Park

DIVIDING RANGE

Endeavour River National Park
Cooktown

Mitchell and Alice Rivers National Park
River
Hann R
Laura R
Laura
QUINKAN COUNTRY
Lakeland
Cedar Bay National Park

Palmer River
Mitchell River

Staaten River
Staaten River National Park

GULF OF CARPENTARIA

SIR EDWARD PELLEW GROUP

Limmen Bight R

Borroloola

McArthur R
Foelsche R
Robinson River
Calvert R

WELLESLEY ISLANDS
Mornington Island

FORSYTH ISLANDS

SOUTH WELLESLEY ISLANDS

Gilbert River
Pelican Creek
Red Creek

Karumba
NORMANTON

Nicholson River
Doomadgee
Burketown

Gregory R
Leichhardt R
Flinders R
Norman R
Carron River

Croydon

0 20 40 60 80 100   200
km

217

West of the Great Dividing Range, the course of the rivers crossing the undulating inland plains is marked by gallery forests — narrow corridors of forest lining either side of watercourses — extending the rainforests towards the west coast.

In the south-west of the peninsula, and around the base of the Gulf of Carpentaria, the coastline is rapidly advancing into the Gulf. So gentle is the slope to the coast that every wet season the silt-bearing water spreads out from the river channels to cover all the low-lying land, and provides one of the great spectacles of the region.

The modest highlands

The highest part of the peninsula, the McIlwraith Range, rises to a height of a mere 824 metres. But what this eastern spine lacks in altitude, it makes up in the pristine character of its landscape. The mountain rainforests have never been logged and mining has barely touched the area.

The country north of Coen is the wettest part of the peninsula, as even in the dry season the ranges trap additional moisture from the south-east trade winds.

Three-quarters of the 2500 square kilometres of rainforest on the peninsula is in the McIlwraith and Iron Ranges. The semi-deciduous forests of the Iron Range are within the Iron Range National Park (34 600 hectares).

In the McIlwraith Range, an extensive plateau is covered with notophyll vineforest with emergent hoop pines (*Araucaria cunninghamii*). Here the taller mesophyll vineforests are largely confined to the corridors formed by the alluvial soils which have been deposited along the banks of rivers.

Many of the trees in the rainforest lose their leaves late in the dry season to reduce the impact of the drought, giving these forests a bare, wintry appearance which is rarely seen in the Australian countryside of evergreen trees. Fully deciduous trees include the silk cotton tree (*Bombax ceiba*) and the fig known as *Ficus alba pila*.

These forests are home to many animals which venture no further south than the peninsula and which this region shares in common with New Guinea. Among those which live on both sides of Torres Strait are the grey cuscus (*Phalanger orientalis*), the spotted cuscus (*Phalanger maculatus*), the rufous spiny bandicoot (*Echymipera rufescens*) and the Cape York melomys (*Melomys capensis*).

LEAF-DROP As the dry season progresses, this 50-metre-tall fig tree, soaring above the tangled vine thickets of the Iron Range, displays an adaptation similar to that of cool-climate, Northern Hemisphere trees — it begins to lose its leaves.

FOREST FEEDER The fig parrot is a tidy eater; the fruit never leaves the stem as it feeds.

The cinnamon antechinus (*Antechinus leo*), a voracious eater of insects, is found only in the rainforests of the Iron and McIlwraith Ranges.

These animals became isolated from New Guinea when the Arafura and Coral Seas came together to form the Torres Strait between 10 000 and 12 000 years ago. They are confined to the north-east coast of the peninsula by the arid Laura Basin, which acts as a barrier to migration southwards.

Birds of the forest that are found nowhere else in Australia include the palm cockatoo (*Probosciger aterrimus*), which uses its powerful beak to crack the hard nuts of palm trees, the eclectus or red-sided parrot (*Eclectus roratus*), and two of Australia's four birds of paradise — the magnificent riflebird (*Ptiloris magnificus*) and the trumpet manucode (*Manucodia keraudrenii*).

South of Coen, the Great Dividing Range gradually diminishes in altitude until it reaches the region between Laura and Palmerville, where it suddenly reappears as a dissected sandstone plateau. Here, the dry country covered with eucalypt woodlands contrasts markedly with the rainforest-shrouded ranges further north.

Known as the Quinkan Country, this region contains one of the world's highest concentrations of rock paintings. 'Quinkan' is the Aboriginal word

WILD-EYED The red-eyed metallic starling, Australia's only native starling, usually migrates to New Guinea during the May-October dry season.

for the spirits depicted in many of the paintings. It is estimated that there are thousands of decorated rock shelters within the 10 000 square kilometres of this rugged sandstone region.

One engraving has been dated as being at least 13 200 years old but it is believed the Aborigines decorated the walls of these caves and overhangs even before this. These very early engravings, made by chipping the rock face with a tool made of harder rock, are called 'pecked' engravings. Some of the sacred sites have large figures of cultural heroes and totemic ancestors.

Coast of contrasts

The 1000-kilometre shoreline between Cooktown and Cape York is one of Australia's greatest wilderness coasts. It is also a coastline of incredible variety.

The most surprising features are the dunefields which occur between Cape Bedford and Cape Flattery and at Cape Grenville and Orford Ness in the far north-east. The Cape Bedford-Cape Flattery dunes cover 1000 square kilometres and have been disturbed by the mining of silica sand for the Japanese glass-making industry. The extensive dunefields at Cape Grenville, between Temple and Shelburne bays, are still in their natural state.

The dunes, many of them mobile, are crescent-shaped and average 30 metres in height, occasionally reaching a maximum of 100 metres. There are scores of freshwater lakes of all shapes and sizes throughout the dunefields, their waters stained brown by rotting vegetation. In places, the lakes extend over 30 kilometres inland and they irrigate a complex mosaic of rainforest, open forest and heath.

All of the dunefields are on relatively low-lying coastlines facing south-east and are similar in character and origin to the more extensive sandmasses thousands of kilometres to the south at Fraser Island and Cooloola. They have been built up over thousands of years from sand washed into the sea by the rivers and then driven onto the shore by the south-east trade winds.

As the convex, leading edge of the dunes is blown northward, 'following' lakes are formed as the water table rises between the crescent's trailing arms. A few of the lakes are probably perched on rock layers. Just to the south of the dunefields is the Olive River, which has

a totally pristine catchment containing almost every kind of Australian wetland environment.

The contrasts in the coastline become particularly dramatic near the peninsula's tip — one of Australia's remotest regions. At Newcastle Bay, the forest of tall mangroves is one of the most extensive in Australia and is rich in marine and amphibious life.

Inland is the 110-square-kilometre Lockerbie Scrub, a rainforest area with close vegetation links with New Guinea, and to the south, the 235 000-hectare Jardine River National Park. This is a very high rainfall area and the Jardine has been estimated to carry the second greatest annual flow of any river in Queensland.

The difficulty of crossing the broad river and the swamps which accommodate its overflow long ago earned this region the name of 'wet desert'. Until a ferry began operating in 1986, many travellers experienced the frustration of being so near and yet so far from their goal of the Cape as it was impossible to take their vehicles across the Jardine.

Along the coast of the Jardine River National Park, the rainforest extends out onto the sand dunes and in places

TREE SNAKE The green python's camouflaging colour means it can rest during the day with little chance of detection by predators.

GREAT SANDY COAST AGAIN Vast coastal dune systems, broken by lakes and forests and similar to the Great Sandy Coast near Maryborough, reappear towards the tip of the Cape at Shelburne Bay.

mixes with shrubby coastal heath. The sand plains between the national park and the Cape Grenville area are largely infertile heathland.

One plant which has displayed great flexibility in adapting to this unpromising environment is the pitcher plant (*Nepenthes mirabilis*), which grows nowhere else on the continent. This tall, climbing vine compensates for the nitrogen deficiency of the region's soil by extracting the nitrogen it requires from the insects it traps in its 18-centimetre-long pitchers.

At the bottom of the pitchers is an enzyme which digests the ants, beetles and grasshoppers which fall into the trap. The plant's incredible adaptability is underlined by the fact that when grown in fertile, nitrogen-rich soils the vine does not develop its pitchers.

In boggy conditions on coastal flats, forests of broad-leaved paperbark trees (*Melaleuca viridiflora*) play host to a great number of non-parasitic aerial plants — epiphytes — that grow along their branches and in the branch forks. Perhaps the most remarkable of these are the two epiphytic species of the ant plant (*Myrmecodia*).

The ant plant deals with the problem of maintaining a year-round water supply in its exposed, sunny positions by developing a large, bulbous tuber in which water is stored for the dry season. Colonies of small ants live in tunnels in the tubers.

Rivers of the Gulf

Most of the large rivers of the peninsula run westwards from the eastern hills to the Gulf of Carpentaria. The major exceptions are the rivers of the oval-shaped Laura Basin which terminate in Princess Charlotte Bay.

The eastern boundary of the basin is the chain of hills which runs parallel to the Great Dividing Range and ends in the Cape Melville National Park (36 000 hectares). Cape Melville can be reached only by boat but the Lakefield National Park (537 000 hectares), which preserves the environments of the Laura Basin, is accessible during the dry season.

A number of large rivers, notably the Normanby, flow through the basin and are rapidly filling in Princess Charlotte Bay with silt. A ten-kilometre band of mangroves, salt pans, lagoons and marshes fringing Princess Charlotte Bay is matched by an adjacent and equally broad belt of grassy plains or savannahs which give way to melaleuca woodlands, testifying to the rapid process of soil build-up which extends the shoreline eastwards.

Further inland again, the basin is covered largely by open stringybark forest. The large gebang palm (*Corypha elata*) — which flowers and fruits only once in its lifetime and then promptly

WILD FRONTIER The largely unexplored and often impassable country of Cape York includes the Lockerbie Scrub, its largest tract of rainforest.

dies — colonises gullies and other natural drainage lines where sufficient surface water has been absorbed to maintain a ready supply of moisture during the day.

Inland, grassy plains amongst the eucalypts are the habitat of the rare and endangered golden-shouldered parrot (*Psephotus chrysopterygius*). This bird excavates a nest for its young in still active termite mounds while itself being exploited by a moth. The larvae of the *Neossiosynoeca scatophaga* moth eat the droppings of the young hatchlings and even clean the birds' feet and plumage.

The gathering of these birds for sale overseas, once common, was made relatively easy by their preference for nesting in open, cone-shaped mounds. Poaching of these and other rare bird species was one of the reasons for the establishment of Lakefield National Park (52 800 hectares).

the rainforest dominating in isolated patches. The recent expansion of these rainforests is believed to be a result of the reduction in Aboriginal burning following the movement of Aborigines to coastal reserves.

Elsewhere in the inland part of the peninsula, the most common trees are Darwin stringybarks (*Eucalyptus tetrodonta*). The gallery forests, which line the westward-flowing rivers are useful landmarks for aerial navigators crossing the generally featureless plains. This type of environment is particularly well preserved in the Rokeby-Croll and Archer Bend National Parks (457 000 hectares) and, further south, in the 470 000-hectare Staaten River National Park.

LETHAL JUG The smooth interior of the pitcher plant ensures that any insect which falls in while investigating the nectar around the rim is unlikely to get out.

TREE HOUSE Organic material deposited by its ant tenants provides nutrients for the ant plant.

In the wet, between December and March, vast areas of open water cover the plains as the various rivers spread out and join up. At this time of the year and until May or even later, such roads as there are, particularly in the northern part of the region, are impassable.

The northern limits

Between the mountains of the Great Dividing Range and the estuaries and deltas of the peninsula's west coast, the landscape lacks the high scenic drama of the ranges and the eastern coastal region. From south to north, the climate gradually becomes wetter and wetter and, in turn, the vegetation becomes more dense, culminating in the rainforests of the Jardine River and the Lockerbie scrub.

In places, north of the Wenlock River, heath mingles with vineforests,

WET WOODLANDS Swamps and other boggy regions of Cape York Peninsula are populated by densely growing paperbarks, often hosts to such epiphytic oddities as the ant plant (above left).

The park at Archer Bend has a great variety of vegetation, from tall rainforest to thorn scrub. A total of 38 species of trees have been recorded from this one area. Freshwater crocodiles (*Crocodylus johnstoni*) inhabit the large waterholes which persist during the dry season.

South of the Archer River and as far as the Coleman River, the plains are dotted with a large number of circular ponds. These depressions are not associated with any other drainage lines and their origin is unclear, although their supply of water obviously comes from the annual wet.

The Gulf plains

In the northern part of Cape York, the rivers end in a maze of coastal lagoons, mangrove swamps and a series of beach ridges covered in vineforest. Saltwater crocodiles (*Crocodylus porosus*) are common in most of the estuaries; Port Musgrave being a particular stronghold. Further south, the river systems, notably the Mitchell and the Gilbert, form large deltas.

For much of the year the land is dry and dusty, and most of the river beds

carry little or no water. Then one of the great natural events of the north occurs.

When the wet arrives, massive amounts of water move across the country spreading out from a great number of interconnected channels. As the land is only a few metres above sea level and slopes very gently seawards, the result is broad deltas of water interspersed with tidal flats. The Mitchell River which rises north-west of Cairns, has the largest discharge.

These scenes are repeated all the way across the vast marine plains which stretch towards the western end of the Gulf. But only one river, the

GREEN GALLERY A 'gallery' forest, where a ribbon of thick vegetation grows along waterways, follows the course of this Iron Range stream.

FRESH OR SALT The saltwater, or estuarine crocodile is also at home in fresh water.

Gregory, which has its source in the limestone springs on the Barkly Tableland, flows all the year round. Enough waterholes remain to provide dry-season refuges for the magpie geese (*Anseranas semipalmata*), brolgas (*Grus rubicundus*) and other northern birdlife.

During the height of the wet-season floods, stingrays, sawfish and sharks venture up the rivers and have been seen many hundreds of kilometres inland. When the rivers dry up, the bull shark (*Carcharhinus leucas*) is often stranded and has been caught in freshwater waterholes by barramundi fishermen up to seven years after a flood.

The continuous extension of the coastline seawards into the Gulf mirrors on a large scale the process occurring at Princess Charlotte Bay. Mangroves, saline mudflats and saltwater meadows extend around most of the Gulf coast and up to 40 kilometres inland.

This muddy, ill-defined coastline is one of the reasons why Burke and Wills never set eyes on the waters of the Gulf; it was probably impossible for them to walk close enough to the coast in order to see the ocean.

A cape of parks?

In the 1970s, it became obvious that many cattle stations on the peninsula could not be made profitable and the Queensland Government, anxious also to control brucellosis and tuberculosis in cattle, obliged by purchasing the leases of several stations for national parks. For a time, the government envisaged the protection of the whole peninsula as a wilderness area.

Altogether 16 300 square kilometres — about eight per cent of the peninsula — became national park during this period. The introduction of a park in the McIlwraith Range area would establish a virtually continuous chain of parks across the peninsula, incorporating examples of most of the environments which exist in this region. □

RIBBON DELTA The Carrington Channel (foreground) is one of several channels in the broad, haphazard delta of the McArthur River which enters the sea adjacent to the Sir Edward Pellew group of islands.

A dazzling chain of coral polyp colonies, spread out like a string of pearls along Australia's north-eastern coast, represents one of the few unspoiled natural wonders of the world

The irresistable allure of the coral seas

When Australia's continental shelf settled not far below the ocean's surface to be washed by the warm waters of the south-west Pacific — here shading into various alluring hues of turquoise and aquamarine — the perfect environment was created for the world's largest system of coral reefs.

The tiny creatures which found this long, shallow crescent off the Queensland coast to their liking have created a unique marine environment where the most colourful of the sea's life forms live so close to the surface that most of them can be observed by anyone able to climb aboard a glass-bottomed boat.

Beneath limpid, tropical waters that lap at the white sands of islands of dense, green vegetation there is a world of ceaseless activity as millions of tiny animals live out their sedentary lives. These microscopic coral polyps are the creators of reefs that have survived the relentless surge of the sea for at least two million years.

OUT OF THE BLUE A platform reef supports the coral cay known as Lady Musgrave Island. The blue-green streaks are caused by algae in the water.

TORRES STRAIT

Cape York

Shelburne Bay

Cape Grenville

Pandora Entrance

Raine Island Fauna Refuge

CORAL SEA

Cape Direction

GREAT

Flinders Group NP

Howick Group NP

Princess Charlotte Bay

Lizard Island NP

Cape Flattery

BARRIER

Cooktown

Cape Tribulation

Green Island NP

CAIRNS

REEF

Dunk Island NP

Hinchinbrook Island NP

Orpheus Island NP

Great Palm Island

Magnetic Island NP

MARINE

Cape Cleveland

TOWNSVILLE

Gloucester Island NP   Hayman Island

Hook Island NP

Whitsunday Island NP

Lindeman Island NP

PARK

Brampton Island NP   **Scawfell Island NP**

Mackay

Prudhoe Island NP

Middle Island NP

South Island NP

Wild Duck Island NP

Townshend Island

Great Keppel Island   **North West and Wreck Island NP**

Wilson Island NP

ROCKHAMPTON

Heron Island NP

Bunker Group

Gladstone

Lady Musgrave Island NP

Fraser Island

BUNDABERG

KEY

NP National Park

0   100   200
km

LIVING FAN The delicate but quite hard fan coral carries no algal growth so it can live in deep water beyond the reach of sunlight.

REEF ANGEL More than 1500 species of fish, including the wide-eyed blue angel, find food and shelter along the Reef.

CONTINENTAL ISLAND Lizard Island is a national park which houses a tourist resort, a marine research station — and numerous goannas.

Corals are among the most beautiful of marine organisms, and when they colonise a site they develop the colours and complex structures for which the Reef is renowned. As spectacular as the Reef itself are the plants and animals inhabiting this immense wall of coral that protects four-fifths of Queensland's eastern coast from the rollers of the South Pacific Ocean.

The Great Barrier Reef has more than 3400 individual reefs and its size and complexity is often difficult to comprehend. It is the largest and most spectacular group of reefs in the world, stretching 2300 kilometres from near Fraser Island to the Papua New Guinean coastline.

While some reefs occur directly along the shores of the Queensland coast, and others fringe the many high, or continental islands which flank the coast, the majority form a haphazard maze scattered at random across the shallow continental shelf, a submerged extension of the continent, which slopes gently offshore.

For a substantial distance south of Torres Strait, the shelf is little more than 50 kilometres wide and coral reefs are abundant here. At the shelf's narrowest point, north of Cooktown, are the Reef's narrowest crescents of coral; some are perched on the very edge of the shelf, and only a few hundred metres beyond, the water depth increases to over a kilometre. Ribbon reefs form an almost continuous outer barrier, following the outer fringe of the shelf.

South of Dunk Island, the continental shelf sweeps away from the coastline and the majority of reefs are found well away from the shore, on its outer half. Just south of Mackay, at the Reef's widest point, there are reefs up to 260 kilometres from the coast. Of all the ocean within the Great Barrier Reef region only nine per cent is actually covered by reefs.

One of the major reasons why the Reef holds such a fascination for tourists and scientists alike is its infinite variety. While there is no such thing as an 'average' reef, the average *size* of a reef is about seven square kilometres.

Some reefs are little more than a few thousand square metres in area while

OUTER EDGE Ribbon reefs, which may be up to 25 kilometres long, occur mainly north of Cairns and mark the outer limits of the continental shoreline of prehistoric times.

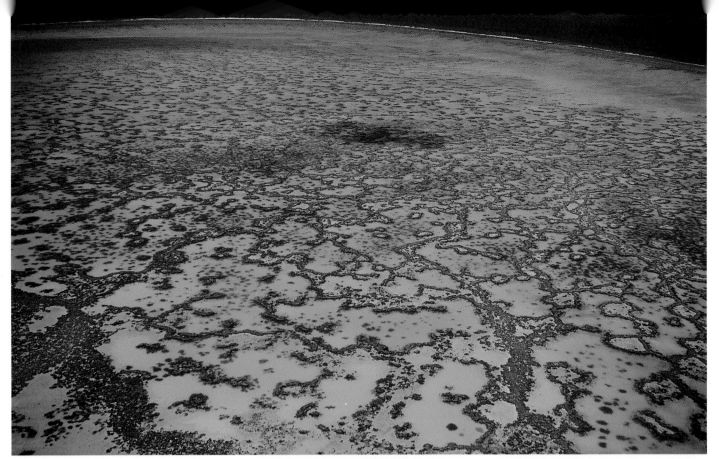

CORAL GARDENS More than 250 kilometres north-east of Rockhampton, the intricate fretwork of the Swain Reefs decorates the surface of the sea in a 200-kilometre-long band.

others may spread over 120 square kilometres. No one shape is ever repeated — many are round, oblong, or crescent shaped; others form shapes that defy description; some of the outer reefs are up to 25 kilometres long.

The only way to appreciate the true extent and variety of the Reef is to fly over it, particularly at low tide. Some reefs remain fully submerged, many others have outer ramparts that are uncovered. These ramparts form a broad, protective pavement that shelters the rest of the Reef from the full force of the South Pacific Ocean.

NIBBLING AWAY The parrotfish's hard 'beak' allows it to feed on coral and small shellfish.

TEEMING Warm reef waters provide the world's busiest, most varied marine habitats.

In some cases, only part of a reef's perimeter is exposed. Some of the most spectacularly beautiful reefs are those surrounded by a raised perimeter, which forms an exquisitely coloured turquoise lagoon containing an intricate and frequently interconnected pattern of small patch reefs — reefs within reefs.

Although it may be decades before scientists have a complete list of all of the plants and animals found on any one reef — a great many of the species are still to be identified and named — from the groups that have been studied there is clearly a staggering diversity of life.

About 1500 species of fish are known to live in the Reef region and half of these may occur on a single reef. Of the 500 or so species of reef-building corals

BRIEF EXPOSURE At low tide, the topmost growths of an outer reef show through a glassy pool.

227

found throughout the entire Indian and Pacific Oceans, about 350 are known from the Great Barrier Reef.

More than 600 species of large molluscs have been identified and it is estimated that the Reef supports at least 4000 varieties of shellfish. There are probably more than 300 different types of crabs, and even scientists were surprised when they discovered more than 250 species of coral shrimps on just one relatively small reef.

While bright colours might seem the order of the day among most reef plants and animals, many creatures survive by being heavily camouflaged and difficult to see. Another way to avoid being eaten is to hide in the rubble of dead coral or in the living coral itself: more than 100 different species of marine worms have been found in a single six-kilogram block of coral.

At the bottom of it all

Corals are simple, primitive animals that have lived in tropical seas for about 500 million years. While the size, shape and colour of coral formations varies immensely, they are all the work of one type of creature.

The individual coral animal, the polyp, is a soft-bodied creature that consists basically of a hollow cylinder crowned with a ring of tentacles. The tentacles are equipped with tiny stinging cells that can paralyse minute creatures that swim or are swept within reach. The tentacles manoeuvre the prey into the central body cavity where it is digested.

ALL SHAPES Varying light and the tug of the current help produce the myriad shapes of coral.

FAN AND FEATHERS Fan corals are a common anchoring place for delicate feather stars — relatives of the starfish known properly as crinoid echinoderms. They feed on minute organisms swept by the current into their 'arms'.

The huge coral boulders of the Great Barrier Reef all began as single coral polyps. The polyps would have grown and subdivided for a very long time, with each new subdivision resulting in the formation of two nearly identical offspring. After many generations of replication, a colony composed of individual polyps sharing both connecting tissue and a common limestone base would have formed.

This base is actually an external skeleton, formed by the secretions from special cells on the underside of each polyp. Each polyp continually secretes tiny amounts of calcium carbonate,

RICH PROFUSION Coral comes in an endless variety of shapes and sizes; these staghorn and plate corals will grow until they reach the surface.

causing the colony to expand upward and outward and, after many thousands of years, a reef is formed — the Great Barrier Reef has been growing and regenerating steadily for at least two million years.

Coral skeletons contain rings representing approximately one-year's growth, rather like the growth rings of trees. Variations in the density of the annual coral rings provide an indication of the climatic conditions during that year. By drilling into the coral and taking a core sample, growth patterns should provide information on the Reef's climate for the last thousand or more years.

The best known, and perhaps the prettiest of the corals, is the delicately structured branching coral which grows on the outer slopes. To suggest that it resembles undersea trees and shrubs is to understate its beauty.

During the day the polyps are contracted and the thin veneer of living tissue on top of each is scarcely noticeable. But at night they come into their full glory. In the darkness, the bodies and tentacles of the corals extend fully in order to trap the microscopic animals that drift across the Reef.

For a few nights each year, in late spring or summer, more than a third of the corals on the Reef undergo a syn-chronised mass spawning. Scientists are still uncertain as to why this unique event occurs the way it does.

The broadly circular, table-shaped formations supported by a central column and known as plate corals, vie with the branching corals for the attention of reef divers. Some plate corals are the size of large tables, but most are smaller. In some areas the plates form tiers, growing in closely spaced, terraced layers down the slope of a reef.

Small, colourful fish and an occasional coral trout shelter out of sight beneath the overhanging plates.

Elsewhere the Reef floor is punctuated by giant coral boulders, sometimes overshadowing much smaller outcrops of oval-shaped boulders known as brain coral because of the deep convolutions that give them an alarming resemblance to a giant, human brain.

Apart from the familiar plates and short, stubby, branching formations,

SOFT DEFLATION Not all corals are hard; soft, fleshy corals, such as this *Sarcophyton*, are able to alter their shape if disturbed by expelling seawater and 'deflating'.

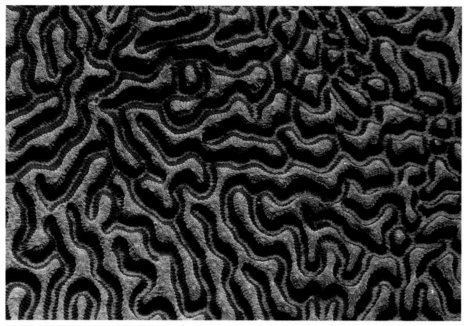

BRAIN SHAPE The maze-like, living surface of a brain coral grows over a skeleton of dead polyps.

If it was not for the vigour with which these living lawnmowers crop the Reef, its surface would be covered with dense clouds of algae, which could suffocate the living corals.

The third group of algae are unavoidably inconspicuous — they grow within the tissues of many of the lifeforms that characterise a coral reef, sharing an existence from which both benefit. Symbiotic algae have been found in the colourful mantles of giant clams and the tissues of anemones, sponges and some types of sea squirts.

The waste ammonia produced by the animal host provides the essential nutrients for the single-celled plant, and during photosynthesis the algae convert the sun's light energy into chemical energy which, in turn, supplies the animal with a vitally important source of food.

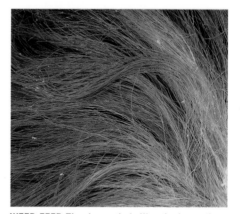

WEED FEED The dense, hair-like algal growth known as turtle weed is grazed by green turtles.

there are encrusting colonies, each one varying in appearance as a result of the differences in size and shape of the limestone cup in which the polyps reside. There is no limit to the shapes and colours adopted by these corals.

The discreet plants

To the inexperienced underwater observer, the Reef may seem to be seething with animals, but almost devoid of plants. Occasional clumps of bright green turtle weed, waving gracefully in the current, are frequently the only obvious examples of plant life.

Some reefs do support large underwater meadows of seagrass, or seasonally abundant growths of *Sargassum* and a few other conspicuous seaweeds on their shallow reef flats, but on most offshore reefs, the plant life is less than obvious. There are more than 500 known species of seaweeds on the Reef but close observation is required to find these miniature, underwater equivalents of forests and grasslands.

The seaweeds are algae — structurally simple plants that lack roots, stems and leaves, and have primitive methods of reproduction. Three groups of algae are fundamental to reef life.

Turf alga, a fine, filamentous and fleshy growth, occurs on the surfaces of most of the dead coral and rubble on any reef, while the sandy areas have their own form of sand alga.

Turf and sand algae grow very fast and in great quantities, but they are seldom very conspicuous, because they are consumed almost as quickly as they grow. The vast schools of parrot, spinefoot and surgeon fish as well as crabs and sea urchins, are dependent on algae as their main source of food.

Free meals and waste removal are not the only benefits here for the reef-building corals. In addition, the growth rate of their limestone skeletons is substantially enhanced by the algae's process of photosynthesis. While corals provide the foundations on which a reef develops, algae that produce calcium carbonate also play a vital role.

In barricade style, red coralline alga forms a type of armoured cap of encrusting growths on the shallow, outer ramparts of the Reef. In these areas most exposed to the force of the sea and where wave action is most intense, the alga forms a much more durable surface than the relatively soft limestone produced by the corals.

Fulfilling another important role in reef structures, the dead segments of some red and green algae create coral sand that fills the cracks between the individual coral colonies, while other algae and calcareous sponges help to cement the combined algal and coral framework together.

IMPRISONED The boring clam — the smallest on the reef — is usually cemented firmly into a coral pocket with just the brightly coloured, fleshy mantle around its cavity on display.

The remains of other dead reef organisms such as sea urchins, starfish, and molluscs also contribute cementing material to a reef, but the algae are the most significant producers. They are so crucial to the ecology of reefs that some scientists have suggested that the term 'coral reef' is both misleading and inappropriate and that a name such as 'tropical reef' or 'biotic reef' would suggest that more than one type of animal or plant was responsible for each living reef.

Above the waterline

When the prevailing wave patterns on a reef concentrate sandy sediments into one place, a sandbank gradually builds up. Eventually, a coral cay, or sand island may develop if enough wind-blown and wave-washed sand accumulates above the level of the highest tide.

There are about 250 coral cays on the Great Barrier Reef and like the reefs which form their foundations, no two cays are identical. Some are formed by dead coral rubble rather than sand; some are bare and barren; others support stunted plants; others shrubs; and some, forests.

Most of the cays have mixed vegetation and may even boast mangrove forests in the intertidal zone on the reef

REEFS VARIOUS, AND WHERE AND HOW THEY OCCUR

ALL SIMILAR, ALL DIFFERENT Most reefs fall into three categories (see top diagram, below): ribbon, or outer, barrier reefs which grow on the edge of the continental shelf; platform, or patch reefs which support a cay, or island formed by sedimentary debris swept onto the reef — the Hope Islands near Cooktown (above) are examples — and fringing reefs, which occur around the edges of the continental islands that were once part of the mainland. The foundations of the reefs are other, ancient reefs which were exposed for about 90 000 years (bottom diagram) and then re-inundated at the end of the ice age.

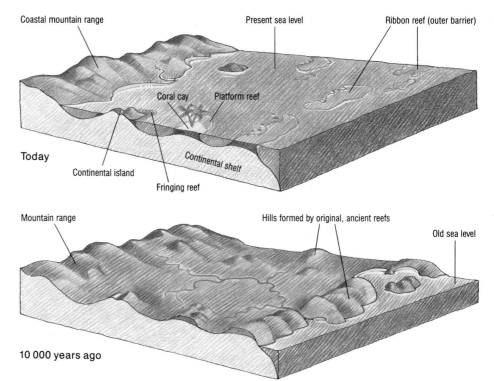

231

flat if there is sufficient shelter. The one thing the cays have in common is that they are all relatively small, their size being limited by the size of the reef below. The largest sand cay on the Great Barrier Reef has an area of little more than 100 hectares.

The most common islands throughout the chain of reefs are not the coral cays but the 950 rocky and often mountainous continental islands. As their name suggests, they are not, like the cays, a product of the cycle of life and death on a coral reef, but sections of the mainland which were isolated when the sea level rose thousands of years ago (see diagram, previous page). Continental islands vary in size from rocky protrusions the size of a suburban house to the 40 000-hectare bulk of Hinchinbrook Island.

ALL ASHORE Sea turtles need a dry environment for egg laying. These green turtles, the most common on the Reef, prefer coral cays.

While the continental islands support many of the same plants and animals as the continent which looms to their west, six thousand years of isolation has resulted in some species developing in ways that would not have been possible on the mainland with its larger range of predators and scavengers. The vegetation of these islands is as varied as that 'on shore' and some boast magnificent rainforests.

Continental islands and coral cays provide valuable nesting sites for more than one-and-a-half million seabirds which make their base in the Reef region as well as for a vast number of turtles. The world's largest rookery of green turtles (*Chelonia mydas*) is on Raine Island; and an army of female turtles, estimated at 10 000 animals, may attempt to nest on this 30-hectare island in a single night.

Sea turtles migrate up and down the coast for great distances, feeding in areas that are often far removed from their nesting beaches. These animals are so slow-growing that it may be 50 years before a green turtle reaches sexual maturity. Once breeding commences, the turtles will return to the same island every few years to nest.

Six of the world's seven species of sea turtles are found on the Reef. Of these, green, loggerhead (*Caretta caretta*) and hawksbill (*Eretmochelys imbricata*) turtles nest mainly on coral cays, while Australian flatback turtles (*Chelonia depressa*) prefer to lay their eggs on the beaches of only a few of the continental islands.

An occasional nesting visitor is the giant leathery turtle (*Dermochelys coriacea*) which at two metres or more is the biggest of the sea turtles.

WIND ASSISTED With legs so short that walking is almost impossible, the frigatebird prefers to nest on low, unsheltered islands where the wind can help it lift off the ground.

Although the leathery turtle may be seen feeding in the Reef waters it generally prefers to feed elsewhere.

As with the turtles, the seabirds are very selective about their breeding sites and only a small number of the thousands of islands available are chosen for nesting. While at least 22 species of seabirds nest on islands off the coast, all of their nesting seems to take place on a mere 78 islands, some of them little more than sand spits.

Despite this, the Reef is regarded as one of the world's richest areas for tropical and subtropical seabirds, with a few islands supporting huge populations at certain times of the year. At the peak nesting time, over 30 000 seabirds roost in an area little larger than a football field on Michaelmas Cay near Cairns, while in some years up to one million birds obliterate a square kilometre of forest on North West Island at the southern end of the Reef.

Look, but don't touch

Aborigines settled the coastline of Queensland long before the present reef system was formed. At the end of the last ice age, about 15 000 years ago, the rising sea gradually began to drown the coastal valleys. What had been the hunting grounds of many generations of tribal people became, over the next 9000 years, the shallow waters that now support the Great Barrier Reef and the coastal mountain ranges were transformed into continental islands.

Aborigines used dugout and bark canoes to fish for turtles and dugongs in reef waters, and to travel to hunting sites among the islands. Commercial exploitation of the Reef began with the bêche-de-mer industry in the 1840s. The edible sea slugs on which the industry was based were widely distributed throughout the Reef and were easily collected at low tide.

The pearl shell industry was next, with both activities heavily dependent on Aborigines and Torres Strait Islanders as the main labour force. Trochus shell fishing was developed as an industry just before World War I.

Tourism and commercial fishing are the major industries today. More than two million people visit the Reef each year and this figure is increasing at an annual rate of about ten per cent. In order to protect the Great Barrier Reef from this invasion, and the damage which could be caused by oil and mineral exploration, virtually the whole region was declared a marine park (see box) between 1979 and 1983. ☐

A truly 'national' park beneath the waves

As the second country in the world to establish a national park — the 'Royal' near Sydney, in 1879, came seven years after Yellowstone in the United States — Australia has long been at the forefront of the management of wild areas. But when a park is declared over an area of 348 700 square kilometres, only nine per cent of which is dry land — and not regular 'land' at that — then 100 years of experience goes out the window and the park managers have to develop an original approach.

When the waters of the Great Barrier Reef were declared a marine park by an Act of the Federal Parliament in 1975, a special authority was established to set up the ground rules for managing such a vast area of ocean.

allocate areas for a specific range of activities. Each section of the park was assessed for the human activities which occurred there and the biological values of the reefs it contained. This information was made available to the public so that anyone who wanted to could have a say in the Reef's future.

The marine park encompasses most of the Great Barrier Reef south of the tip of Cape York and covers an area larger than the Philippines. In this enormous, watery recreational park, scientists and rangers conduct their respective research and park management activities with boats and aqualungs, rather than horses or four-wheel-drive vehicles.

The research that has been conducted into the Reef's daily functioning and

The opportunity to maintain and conserve a unique and particularly beautiful natural phenomenon inspired the experts to respond with enthusiasm and the Reef marine park — which protects 99 per cent of the Reef system from any kind of unauthorised interference — has become one of Australia's great environmental success stories.

Previous attempts to protect coral reefs elsewhere in the world had merely set aside small areas of reef in reserves that were the equivalent of national parks on land. The marine park authority realised that to protect the Great Barrier Reef there would need to be preservation areas where human activity was restricted, while allowing a manageable range of recreational activities in the majority of reef waters.

Reef zoning plans, the equivalent of town plans on land, were developed to

growth has produced some surprises, many of them beneficial to mankind.

Investigation of coral physiology has shown that many corals have evolved a way to prevent sunburn by producing protective compounds; more efficient sun-screen products for humans may be the result. Corals have also been found to contain substances which can be used to produce drugs for the treatment of nervous and muscular disorders.

Where mainland parks are plagued by rabbits or other introduced pests, a park beneath the waves has its own special pests. The marine park seemed at one point to be in great danger from an invasion by crown-of-thorns starfish which ate the coral. Marine scientists now believe the starfish problem has receded and that its occasional appearance in great numbers may be a natural phenomenon.

On the vast Arnhem Land Plateau and its surrounding flood plains, some of the world's oldest rock paintings and one of the largest national parks in the world are guarded for posterity by the land's original inhabitants

A wild paradise, unchanged and unchanging

Arnhem Land sprawls across more than 96 000 square kilometres of the 'Top End', its landscape sculpted by the ceaseless annual cycle of heavy monsoon rains followed by months of hot, dry weather. Climatic extremes are normal here — hardly surprising in a roughly triangular, tropical region bordered north and east by the tepid waters of the Arafura Sea, while to the south, nothing breaks the monotony of the arid interior until it reaches the Southern Ocean.

The Arnhem Land landscape is dominated by the Arnhem Plateau, a giant block of quartz sandstone laid down from water-borne sediments 2000 million years ago when this region was part of the seabed. Surrounded by low woodlands and rising to 450 metres, it dominates the skyline in the west until it peters out in the hills of eastern Arnhem Land.

From its heights, Ludwig Leichhardt, the first European explorer to set eyes on the wild and beautiful land below, recorded in his journal of November 17, 1845, '...suddenly the extensive view of a magnificent valley opened before us...'

Where it breaks the plains of western Arnhem Land, from Murgenella near Van Diemen Gulf to Katherine Gorge over 1000 kilometres inland, the plateau's western front is lined with the dramatic, crumbling cliffs of the escarpment country.

Marking a retreat under the forces of erosion at about one metre every thousand years, the western edge of this sandstone plateau has left in its wake massive outliers of hard, resistant rock which have refused to give way to the constant battering of the elements. They remain stranded on the plains, often kilometres from the cliff line they were once part of.

Fretted by faulting and weathering into a maze of long, rugged crevices and gorges, the sandstone plateau

TAKING THE WATERS Come the rains of November, wetlands such as these, at Black Point Lagoon in Gurig National Park, are the first southern port of call for thousands of migratory birds.

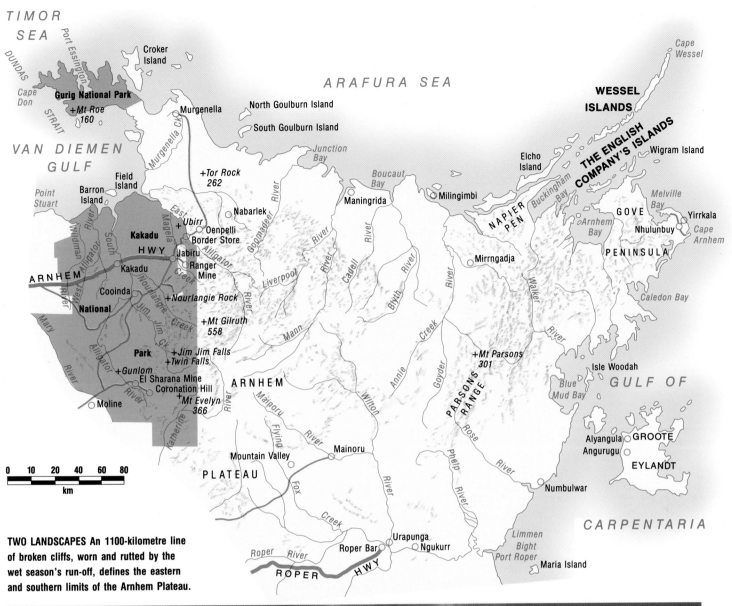

TWO LANDSCAPES An 1100-kilometre line of broken cliffs, worn and rutted by the wet season's run-off, defines the eastern and southern limits of the Arnhem Plateau.

Map labels:

TIMOR SEA

DUNDAS STRAIT

Cape Don

Port Essington

Croker Island

VAN DIEMEN GULF

Gurig National Park
+Mt Roe 160

Murgenella

ARAFURA SEA

North Goulburn Island

South Goulburn Island

WESSEL ISLANDS

Cape Wessel

THE ENGLISH COMPANY'S ISLANDS

Wigram Island

Point Stuart

Field Island

Barron Island

+Tor Rock 262

Junction Bay

Boucaut Bay

Elcho Island

Milingimbi

Maningrida

NAPIER PEN

Buckingham Bay

GOVE

Melville Bay

Yirrkala

Nabarlek

Kakadu

+Ubirr

Oenpelli
Border Store

Jabiru

Ranger Mine

Kakadu

ARNHEM

HWY

Cooinda

National

+Nourlangie Rock

+Mt Gilruth 558

Park

+Jim Jim Falls
+Twin Falls

+Gunlom

El Sharana Mine
Coronation Hill
+Mt Evelyn 366

Moline

Goomadeer River

Liverpool River

Mann River

Cadell River

Blyth River

Arnhem Bay

Nhulunbuy

Cape Arnhem

PENINSULA

Caledon Bay

Mirrngadja

Walker River

Annie Creek

Goyder River

PARSONS RANGE

+Mt Parsons 301

Isle Woodah

Blue Mud Bay

GULF OF

ARNHEM

Katherine River

Mainoru River

Flying Fox Creek

Wilton River

Rose River

Phelp River

Alyangula
Angurugu

GROOTE

EYLANDT

PLATEAU

Mountain Valley

Mainoru

Numbulwar

CARPENTARIA

Roper River

Roper Bar

Urapunga

Ngukurr

ROPER HWY

Limmen Bight
Port Roper

Maria Island

Scale: 0 10 20 40 60 80 km

ANNUAL RUN-OFF Twin Falls is but one of thousands of waterfalls that tumble over the eroded scarp to feed the vast wetland below.

is a vast catchment for the plains lower down. It channels torrential rains brought on north-west monsoon winds into major river systems of the north like the Roper, Katherine and Liverpool–Mann systems.

Within Kakadu National Park, spectacular wet-season waterfalls plunge over the rocky ramparts of the escarpment, swelling the waters of the South and East Alligator rivers. Meandering northward to Van Diemen Gulf over floodplains rich in silt, the rivers breech their banks and fan out into broad, freshwater swamps creating one of the world's most important tropical wetlands. Millions of waterbirds and an abundance of aquatic creatures — fish, turtles, frogs and crocodiles — live in the wetlands.

Arnhem Land was named after the Dutch ship the *Arnhem*, which was blown off course near this coast in 1623. To most Australians, the region remains as remote and unknown today as it was to the crew of that ship more than four hundred years ago.

Most of Arnhem Land is Aboriginal land, some of which, such as Gurig and Kakadu, is managed as national parks. Kakadu has gained international fame in recent years, not only because it is the most accessible wilderness of the Top End, but also because it offers the greatest diversity of unspoiled landscapes and rich wildlife habitats that northern Australia has to offer.

Rhythm of the six seasons

At the height of the dry season, the woodlands and plains below the plateau escarpment are brown and parched, the horizon rarely clear of the smudge of bushfire smoke. In the steamy wet season, waterfalls roar over the cliffs stimulating the vegetation of the plains into producing a riot of jungle-green growth.

Non-Aboriginal Australians acknowledge two seasons — the 'dry' from May to October and the 'wet' from November to April — but the Aborigines perceive an annual cycle of at least six distinct seasons; amendments to day-

to-day living are made as a result of the subtle signals from nature which telegraph the approach of a change.

In the hot, pre-monsoon season of October, the humidity level rises rapidly. Rumbling thunderheads and lightning fill the afternoon skies. By November, scattered showers encourage a tinge of green on the earth parched by many dry months.

In December, the rain becomes heavier and more frequent and the floodplains begin to live up to their name. Streams begin to run, linking waterholes, and the barramundi are able to move downstream to the estuaries to spawn. This is the time when the traditional Aborigines of the plains moved up into the high escarpment country to shelter in caves.

By January, the rain has set in, and day after day of incessant downpours may bring a wet-season total of up to 1600 millimetres. The heat and humidity unleash a burst of activity among plants and wildlife: this is a time of plenty, a season of hunting and mating.

Flooding flushes out goannas, snakes and a variety of burrowing creatures, sending them scurrying up trees. Roads such as the Arnhem Highway are frequently cut by up to a metre of fast-moving water.

Within a few months, plants have flowered, trees have burst into fruit and many animals have reproduced. The vast expanses of water begin to recede and streams run clear, although violent storms are still a possibility.

Waterlilies smother the surface of billabongs and waterways by April and May, when drying afternoon winds turn to the south-east, a signal to the Aborigines that it is time to begin the season of burning.

Over many thousands of years, the Aborigines evolved a complex pattern of land management using fire as a tool, based on a knowledge of seasonal changes and plant and animal life cycles. In a strategy of fighting fire with fire, they set the torch to the land in a complex pattern that encouraged fresh growth, maintained a diversity of plant life and prevented damaging, naturally occurring bushfires.

WAITING FOR THE WET Seen from the edge of the escarpment, near Ubirr, the Arnhem flood plains have become 'drylands' of scattered billabongs after almost five months without rain. Within a month of the monsoon season breaking, thick vegetation will cover the plains.

AFTER THE WET When the rains come, lagoons such as Anbangbang, are quickly inhabited by a bewildering variety of birds and aquatic creatures.

As much as 90 per cent of the lowland plains — the largest landscape in Kakadu — is burnt each year, with fire-sensitive pockets, such as the monsoon forest, protected by fire breaks. Left to a natural fire regime, plant litter accumulates and results in destructive summer fires. With or without management, fire is an inevitable part of the Arnhem Land landscape: 80 per cent of bushfires are believed to be started by lightning.

During this burning season, in the relatively cool months of June and July, fires burn during the day, but are usually doused by evening dew fall. August and September are windless but still hot and for the Aboriginal people this is an excellent season for hunting: there are geese, file snakes and long-necked turtles to be sought out in the receding billabongs. Soon the humid breezes and clapping thunder will herald the monsoon winds that will once again begin the cycle of the seasons in Arnhem Land.

The jewel in the crown

Kakadu National Park, one of the world's largest national parks, is a microcosm of Arnhem Land. A 17 552-square-kilometre wilderness that encompasses a large part of the Alligator Rivers' systems, Kakadu is one of the most biologically crowded and diverse regions in all of Australia.

Within its boundaries are found all the major land forms of the tropical north. The coastal mangroves and broad river estuaries of Van Diemen Gulf provide a buffer for extensive freshwater wetlands, while broad stretches of eucalypt woodlands lead into escarpment country, a region of soaring cliffs and rock stacks that climbs to the rocky sandstone of the Arnhem Land Plateau.

Such varied landscapes and the extremes of the wet and dry seasons have encouraged a multitude of plants and animals to flourish. The park harbours over 1200 plant species — representative of nearly all the plant communities of the Northern Territory tropics — more than 60 species of mammals, 100 of reptiles, and over 280 of birds.

Of an estimated 10 000 different insects in the park — including 1500 kinds of moths and butterflies and over 100 species of dragonfly — only half have been named by scientists.

The rivers, billabongs and swamps support at least 80 species of fish: in two creeks alone, Magela and Nourlangie, 28 freshwater species have been recorded, the same number as the entire Murray–Darling Rivers system, the largest in Australia.

It is only recently that Kakadu has revealed its treasurehouse of natural wonders to the outside world. In the 1970s, the Kakadu region was handed

SPIRITS DWELL Most of the natural features in the Kakadu landscape are significant to Aborigines as the physical manifestations of the activities of their Dreamtime ancestors.

NOW YOU SEE IT...The waters that flood the Magela flood plain in March, near the end of the wet season, soon dry out, and by July, so do the rivers that feed them.

PORT ESSINGTON For weeks after the rain stops, flooded creeks such as the Caiman continue to discharge huge volumes of water as they spread onto the tidal flats, creating channels to the sea.

back to the traditional Aboriginal owners who now lease their land to the government as a national park. To preserve the natural richness of the region as well as the many examples of Aboriginal rock art, Kakadu was inscribed on the World Heritage List in 1981, one of the few places in the world to be listed both for its natural and cultural wonders (see pp. 390–1).

The estuary coast

Along much of Arnhem Land's coast, mangroves line the shore, distinctively ranked according to each species' ability to tolerate salt water. The estuaries and tidal flats of the two major rivers in the Kakadu National Park — the South and East Alligator — are a vital transitional zone between the marine environment of Van Diemen Gulf and the freshwater floodplains so vital to the survival of wetland plants and animals.

Of the 29 species of mangrove found on Australia's tropical coastline 22 are found in Kakadu. The small-stilted or spider mangrove (*Rhizophora stylosa*) is most easily recognised by its radiating buttress roots, which are hollow in order to supply oxygen to waterlogged underground roots. The club (*Aegialitis annulata*) and red mangrove (*Brughiera exaristata*) are common and the beautiful holly-leaved mangrove (*Acanthus ilicifolius*) bears its flowers among thorny leaves.

In these strange, muddily flooded forests, where life is attuned to the cycle of the tides, are found a startling mixture of creatures. Crabs scurry about, bats flit between trees, mudskippers walk on land at low tide and several species of mangrove snakes forage among the sand for crustaceans.

The trees themselves provide roosting and breeding sites for many birds including large colonies of egrets, herons and cormorants. Honeyeaters and kingfishers frequent the mangrove

forest, and permanent inhabitants include the collared or mangrove kingfisher (*Todiramphus chloris*), the striated or mangrove heron (*Ardeola striata*), and the mangrove warbler (*Gerygone laevigaster*); colonies of flying-foxes (*Pteropus alecto*) roost in the mangroves during the day.

The waters of the tidal flats are also an important haven for the most famous fish in the Northern Territory, the barramundi (*Lates calcarifer*), which may weigh up to 40 kilograms. The barramundi leads a strange double life; the fish spawn around river mouths early in the wet season when high tides wash the fertilised eggs into coastal swamps where they develop into juveniles.

At the end of the wet season the small barramundi migrate upstream into rivers. Three to four years later, maturing males — weighing about four kilograms — move back downstream to spawn, but over the next three years these males, in a sex-changing process known as inversion, metamorphose into females and lay eggs.

On this cyclone-prone coast, tropical mangroves are the first line of defence against the enormous storm surges that sometimes lash the foreshore. Although many of the trees may not survive such storms, their sturdy roots send up new stems in time to protect the tidal flats from the next storm.

The swampy, low-lying coast and river mouths of Kakadu are inaccessible from the park itself and can only be reached by boat. In these estuaries, eight-metre tides swirl back and forth stirring turbid waters — the domain of sharks, stingrays and 40-kilogram catfish, along with large saltwater crocodiles (*Crocodylus porosus*).

In these waters and in the Arnhem Land lagoons, crocodiles are almost impossible to see when they float to the surface with only their snouts and eyes above the waterline. These giant reptiles are difficult to spot even when sunning themselves on a river bank, due to their superb camouflage, often aided by a coating of mud.

Just off the Kakadu coast lies Field Island, part of the park that remains undisturbed by feral animals and introduced weeds. The island's white beaches are nesting grounds for many sea turtles including the rare flatback turtle (*Chelonia depressa*).

In the surrounding shallows, herds of dugong (*Dugong dugon*), sometimes numbering several hundred, graze the submarine meadows of seagrass. These

gentle sea cows are the only herbivorous mammals that are completely adapted to a life at sea.

Behind the mangroves, where low swamps are inundated at high tide, salt-tolerant samphires (*Arthrocnemum*) hold the sandy soil together. On the coastal dunes and beach ridges, wattles, pandanus, palms and eugenias form open, semi-deciduous forests.

Wetlands: an annual rebirth

The almost featureless floodplains of Arnhem Land undergo a seasonal transformation probably more profound than any landscape in Australia. The coming of the wet season between December and April brings torrential downpours that swell the meandering rivers of the flat plains until they flood across hundreds of kilometres — sometimes to a depth of two to three metres.

Arnhem Land's wetlands are among the most important wildlife refuges in Australia. A sea of green grass and shining waters, they teem with life, attracting masses of waterbirds and allowing aquatic creatures like crocodiles, fish and frogs to nest among the sedges, grasses and waterlilies of the swamps. The survival of millions of birds depends on the nearly 3000 square kilometres of wetlands protected within the Kakadu National Park.

As the floodwaters recede, the plains dry out, leaving behind swamps and billabongs adorned with spectacular giant red lilies (*Nelumbo nucifera*) and mat-forming grasses (*Hymennachne acutigluma*). On the margins where drainage is poor, paperbarks thrive. Named for their layered, papery bark, the trees produce flowers rich in nectar and pollen to attract birds, bats and insects. Brightly coloured rainbow lorikeets (*Trichoglossus haematodus*) and honeyeaters dangle from the heavily scented blossoms as they feed.

The most spectacular introduction to the tropical wetlands is at Yellow Water Billabong, near Cooinda, the tourist centre of the park. At the height of the dry season, from June to October, lagoons and swamps shrink to a few billabongs and isolated waterways. As the bird habitats become smaller, the population density rockets, as millions of birds crowd around the remaining ,waters to await the next rains.

On early-morning boat trips along the twisting course of yellow water, the banks are lined with thousands of wandering whistling-ducks (*Dendrocygna arcuata*) and honking magpie geese (*Anseranas semipalmata*). Kakadu is

WOODLAND HOMES Nesting waterbirds crowd the paperbark groves which are ubiquitous throughout the marshes of Arnhem Land.

SUBMERSIBLE The lotus bird is an awkward flier, preferring to dive below the water if threatened.

the most important refuge for these geese — an estimated two-and-a-half-million of the birds congregate here to build floating nests of spike rushes. Males often mate with two females, which use the same nest and all three birds take turns at shading the eggs.

About 80 kinds of waterbird are seen in the Arnhem Land wetlands, and Kakadu is one of the first places visited by birds migrating from the north. Glossy ibis (*Plegadis falcinellus*) probe the mud with their long, curved beaks looking for frogs, spiders and aquatic insects, alongside yellow-billed spoonbills (*Platalea flavipes*) that are found only in Australia.

During the breeding season the intermediate egret (*Ardea intermedia*) develops long, delicate plumes that were highly prized a century ago as adornments for ladies' hats.

Other egrets, herons, pelicans and Australia's only stork, the two-metre-tall black-necked stork or jabiru

(*Ephippiorhynchus asiaticus*), stalk about in search of food. Some birds stand motionless in the shallows with their wings spread as if drying them. These birds are actually providing shade that attracts fish which they then scoop up.

No other bird has adapted so cleverly to life in the billabong as the red comb-crested jacana (*Irediparra gallinacea*). Nicknamed the Christbird for its apparent ability to walk on water, the jacana has the longest feet-to-body ratio of any bird.

This enables the jacana to hopscotch over the leaves of the blue lily (*Nymphaea violacea*), a floating plant with leaves as broad as a metre, thus giving the appearance of walking on the water. Alert for water pythons (*Liasis fuscus*) that may lurk underfoot, the male jacana swiftly gathers up his young under his wings at the first sign of danger and carries them to safety.

In the trees along the banks, white-bellied sea-eagles (*Haliaeetus leucogaster*) scan the waters for fish, and flying foxes squabble noisily in their daytime roosts. Down in the mud, the pitted-shelled or pig-nosed turtle (*Carettochelys insculpta*) swallows stones to aid its digestion and weigh itself down, so it can float with just its head above water. Australia's only freshwater turtle, the pig-nose was discovered in Kakadu during a search prompted by a rock painting at nearby Nourlangie which clearly depicts the creature.

The long-necked tortoise (*Chelodina longicollis*) strikes out at fish like a snake with its long neck, and escapes predators, and the dry season, by burying itself in mud.

Besides the barramundi, other fish of the billabongs and lagoons include the rare one-gilled eel (*Synbranchus bengalensis*), sharp-nosed grunter (*Syncomistes butleri*), red-tailed rainbow fish (*Melanotaenia splendida australis*), saratoga (*Scleropages jardini*) and the keen-eyed archer fish (*Toxotes chatareus*). With an archer's precision, this fish shoots down its above-water insect prey with a jet of water squirted from its mouth and accurate up to a metre and a half away.

Wetland walking tracks at Mamukala Floodplain near Kakadu Holiday Village allow visitors close-up views of thousands of magpie and green pygmy geese (*Nettapus pulchellus*), purple swamphens, and little curlews (*Numenius minutus*) that have flown all the way from breeding grounds in Siberia and Mongolia.

The wetlands are dotted with small, isolated pockets of coastal monsoon forest, dominated by trees such as milkwood (*Alstonia actinophylla*), kapok (*Bombax ceiba*) and banyans (*Ficus virens*) which support a network of

RUNNING WILD The water buffalo, which once caused great damage to the Arnhem Land environment, is one of the few feral animals to have been controlled.

climbing wild passionfruit (*Passiflora foetida*), crab's eye (*Abrus precatorius*) and loofah (*Luffa cylindrica*) vines. This jungle environment, with its dense array of flowers, is an important habitat for tropical birds like the spectacular rainbow pitta (*Pitta iris*) and the spangled drongo (*Dicrurus bracteatus*).

Pests in paradise

The sensitive wetlands are not without their pests. Water buffalos, introduced from Indonesia in the 1820s, have caused great damage by trampling the banks of waterways into quagmires. Thousands of the beasts have been removed from Kakadu, where their numbers are now thought to be under control. Sadly, the same is not true of

PRETTY PEST The *Mimosa pigra* weed is related to the sensitive plant of southern gardens.

CREATIVE LICENCE Despite their rough appearance, termite mounds are the skyscrapers of the insect world, built carefully to avoid overheating and presenting the least surface area to the midday sun.

feral pigs, which also do enormous damage to the environment by rooting in the soft ground around billabongs and creeks, destroying plant communities and fouling waterways.

Pigs also prey on small native animals and birds and have proven far more difficult to eradicate than buffalo. There are estimated to be one million pigs in the Northern Territory.

Another introduced pest that threatens Kakadu's wetlands is the sensitive *Mimosa pigra*, an introduced prickly weed that folds its leaves closed when touched. A native of South America, it is called 'the green cancer' because of its resistance to herbicides, slashing and burning.

Between the Moyle River, about 200 kilometres south-west of Darwin on the other side of the Top End, and the border of Arnhem Land, 400 square kilometres of wetlands are so impenetrably choked by the weed that even buffalo cannot force their way through.

In the war against the mimosa scien-

tists have enlisted the aid of a tiny moth called *Neurostrota gunniella*. The moth's larvae kills the plant by boring into its stem. If mimosa is not controlled it will eventually threaten the survival of many native plant and animal species.

'Twixt plains and plateau

Lowland forest covers the largest slice of Kakadu — 7000 square kilometres — and is the landscape most visible when travelling through the park. The woodlands may lack the rugged beauty of the escarpment country or the dramatic seasonal changes of the floodplains, but they support by far the greatest variety of animals and plants.

Over half of the park is open forest containing 15 species of eucalypt. In the wake of wet-season rains, three-metre-high spear grass (*Sorghum intrans*) shoots up, its crisp stalks ready to fuel dry-season fires. The yellow flowers of the kapok bush (*Cochlospermum fraseri*) grace the woodland, as do the vivid, orange flowers of the coral

tree (*Erythrina variegata*); the chocolate orchid (*Cymbidium canaliculatum*) clings to eucalypts. The red-tailed black cockatoo (*Calyptorhynchus banksii*), whistling kite (*Milvus sphenurus*) and white-cheeked rosella (*Platycercus eximius*) are permanent residents.

The most striking feature of the open woodland is the thousands of termite mounds, some of them as tall as five metres. Several species of termites construct these air-conditioned castles of clay, their interiors riddled with passages and galleries where temperatures are cool and humidity is constant.

Rearing up in the northern and eastern parts of the park are the rock walls, cliffs and outliers of the Arnhem Plateau escarpment. Within these deeply dissected cliffs and overhangs is a rich legacy of prehistoric Aboriginal rock art.

There are estimated to be 6000 rock art sites in Arnhem Land, and in Kakadu two major sites are accessible to the public at Ubirr (Obiri Rock) and

Nourlangie Rock. The rock art has been classified into seven main styles, from the simple, elegant stick figures of the 'Mimi' period — named after the spirits said to have executed this work — to exquisite and complex 'x-ray' paintings. Some rock art in the park has been dated at 22 000 years old, making it the oldest known.

The many rock shelters of the escarpment country are home to hundreds of thousands of bats, which venture out in great clouds to feed after dark.

POISED PYTHON The two-metre Oenpelli python is restricted to an area of western Arnhem Land.

Below, in the sandstone country, the huge Oenpelli python (*Morelia oenpelliensis*) was recently discovered. The beautifully marked two-metre-long snake is endemic to the area. It kills its prey, which includes small wallabies, by constriction.

The sandstone feather flower (*Pityrodia jamesii*), which grows in sandy soil, is the favoured food of another rare creature, the vivid red Leichhardt's grasshopper (*Petassida ephippigera*) which is poisonous and not eaten by any other animal. First seen by Ludwig Leichhardt in 1845, the brightly coloured insect was not identified again until 1974.

Eroded by sun, wind and rain, the sandstone country is criss-crossed by chasms and crevasses which break out along joint lines in the rock. Here, where there are permanent waters, small pockets of sandstone monsoon forest survive, a lush world of 35-metre-tall evergreen myrtle trees (*Allosyncarpia ternata*) and climbing vines spreading a luxuriant, closed canopy. Little light is allowed to reach the forest floor where mosses, lichens and ferns thrive

— a stark contrast to the aridity of the plateau surface above.

The much less rugged country of the lowlands is a more congenial environment for large animals, and dingoes (*Canis familiaris dingo*), agile wallabies (*Macropus agilis*), antilopine wallaroos (*Macropus antilopinus*), and sand monitors (*Varanus gouldii*) are among the many creatures which roam the plain. But, as elsewhere, much animal activity takes place under cover of darkness. Nocturnal woodland flyers include marsupial sugar gliders (*Petaurus breviceps*), bats and many owls, such as the masked (*Tyto novaehollandiae*) and rufous owls (*Ninox rufa*).

Peninsulas west and east

The East Alligator River, one of dozens of rivers slicing down to the sea from the Arnhem Land Plateau, draws both the eastern boundary of Kakadu National Park and the southern boundary of the 2207-square-kilometre Gurig National Park. This wild, rugged country encompasses the entire Cobourg Peninsula, and the surrounding islands that jut into Van Diemen Gulf.

Peculiarly out of place in this seemingly pristine wilderness are the pathetic remains of early attempts at European settlement. Reminders of that era linger in the ruins of the hospital, armory and other buildings of Port Essington, founded in 1838.

Thousands of bangteng cattle, water buffalo, Timor ponies and rusa deer — descendants of beasts imported from Asia to stock the colony — roam the open eucalypt woodlands. At the very tip of the peninsula, the lonely Cape Don lighthouse, built in 1916, faces across the Dundas Strait to Melville and Bathurst Islands.

Apart from occasional luxuriant patches of vine forest or paperbark swamp, the undulating terrain of the peninsula is covered in tropical eucalypt forests of Darwin stringybark (*Eucalyptus tetrodonta*) and woollybutt (*E. miniata*). Dense mangrove forests grow along the river estuaries, providing food and shelter for swarms of giant mud crabs among their tangle of roots.

The warm, sheltered tropical waters of the peninsula support such an abun-

THE FAR NORTH After the nineteenth-century military garrisons at Fort Dundas, Raffles Bay and Port Essington (above) were abandoned, the Arnhem coast remained the province of itinerant traders and missionaries until the establishment of Darwin in 1869.

EAST CROCODILE The name of the East Alligator River is a reminder that early European explorers mistook northern Australia's crocodiles for their Western Hemisphere cousins.

dance of sea life, including colourful corals, that the waters and islands surrounding Gurig National Park have been declared the Cobourg Marine Park (229 000 hectares).

As Cobourg Peninsula flanks Arnhem Land's north-western extremity, so the remote, low-lying wilderness of Gove Peninsula sweeps around Arnhem Bay to the north-east, where the Arafura Sea meets the waters of the Gulf of Carpentaria.

The bauxite mining town of Nhulunbuy, at the peninsula's eastern tip, is the stepping-off point to Wigram Island, where visitors can join in traditional Aboriginal activities, such as oyster and plant gathering, spearing fish, or gathering turtle eggs. Short-eared rock wallabies (*Petrogale brachyotis*) roam the island, and beyond its fringing coral reef pilot whales, marlin and dolphins are a frequent sight. □

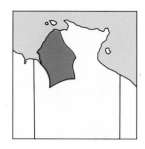

A steamy coastal plain lapped by the waters of the Timor Sea may seem an unlikely place for a modern city, but the Darwin region has survived wartime bombings and numerous cyclones to earn a permanent place on the map

On Asia's front doorstep

In many ways, the torrid 'Top End' of the Northern Territory — Darwin, its hinterland and Arnhem Land — resembles Indonesia, nearby to the north, more than it does the rest of Australia.

Darwin is much closer to Jakarta than it is to the southern capital cities not only in terms of mere distance. The region's climate is tropical, and its terrain was shaped by many of the forces that sculpted the tropical lands to the north.

The Northern Territory's mangrove-fringed shores are broken here and give way to coastal plains which stretch inland for many kilometres. In the wet season, from December to March, monsoons sweep in from the Timor Sea bringing up to 1500 millimetres of rain.

Major rivers such as the Victoria, Daly, Mary and Adelaide breach their banks to create a sprawling mosaic of wetlands, the domain of crocodiles and millions of waterbirds. When the monsoons pass, the land lies sunburnt brown and studded with billabongs, the only remnants of the wet season for the rest of the year.

On the main highway south — the Territory's lifeline with the rest of the continent — termite mounds tower metres high in roadside woodlands and pockets of monsoon rainforest cluster around permanent springs. Spectacular gorges and caves have been etched into low-lying plateau country.

Today, Darwin is an almost completely new city, having risen phoenix-like from the metaphorical ashes of Tracy, the powerful and shatteringly destructive cyclone which hit the city in 1974, destroying 5000 homes in just four hours. Within easy reach of the modern city are a variety of tropical environments.

Darwin's botanical gardens has Australia's most comprehensive collection of palms, with more than 400 species. On a nearby peninsula, the East Point Flora and Fauna Reserve has patches of rainforest. Its foreshore, fringed by stretches of white sand, is ideal for viewing the city's spectacular sunsets.

Not far from central Darwin, Casuarina Coastal Reserve (1180 hectares) encompasses dunescapes and mangroves. Ospreys and sea eagles soar above its long, wide beaches. Another 'suburban' nature park — Holmes Jungle (250 hectares), in Karama — is one of several isolated pockets of rainforest that are fed by permanent streams rather than monsoon rains.

On the banks of Palm Creek, birds such as the spectacular rainbow pitta (*Pitta iris*), which sports an iridescent blue flash on it wings, the yellow oriole (*Oriolus flavocinctus*) and the figbird (*Sphecotheres viridis*) come down to feed. All are attracted by the jungle's abundant fruit. The black whip snake (*Demansia atra*) and the olive python (*Liasis olivaceus*) are also frequently seen here.

GULF BOUND The Victoria River (left), the most substantial river in the Northern Territory, meanders through the Victoria River Valley on its 650-kilometre course to the sea. The river's fall is so slight that the tidal waters of Joseph Bonaparte Gulf reach 150 kilometres upstream.

Howard Springs, 35 kilometres 'down' the Stuart Highway is a lush patch of rainforest fringed by a permanent spring. The army dammed the spring in the 1930s to supplement Darwin's water supply. No longer needed for such a mundane purpose, it now forms a crystal-clear swimming pool.

An almost tame population of agile wallabies (*Macropus agilis*) lives at Howard Springs and the big red-tailed black cockatoos (*Calyptorhynchus banksii*), often grace the treetops.

A 1.8-kilometre walking track encircles Howard Springs Nature Park (1009 hectares). On one side, a cool, green tangle of palms and climbing swamp ferns (*Stenochlaena palustris*) thrives in the deep soils that hold moisture like a sponge; on the other, grassy eucalypt woodland is peppered with the equally green foliage of the primitive cycad (*Cycas media*), one of the few plants that may be male or female.

A fire-retarding resin in the cycad's black stalk gives it some protection against the bushfires that sweep the 'Top End' during the dry season. The

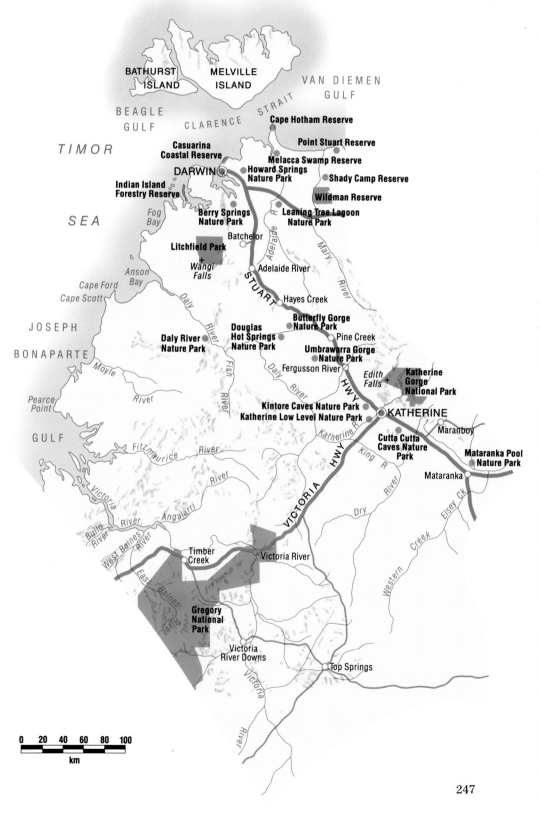

cycad, like a number of native plants, needs the stimulus of a bushfire's heat to trigger seed germination.

In this cyclone-prone land, the fine leaves and long flexible trunks of Carpentaria palms (*Carpentaria acuminata*) are well suited for survival in high winds. By contrast, the rigid, broad-leaved fan palms (*Livistona benthamii*) are usually blown over.

The wetlands and flood plains of the country which provides a backdrop for Darwin harbour a rich abundance of wildlife. During the dry season, shrinking billabongs lure birds in vast numbers; in the 'wet', the birds fan out across the lush, shallow flood plains.

Fogg Dam Conservation Reserve (1569 hectares) is a wetland only 60 kilometres south-east of Darwin, off the Arnhem Highway. Like the Howard Springs dam, this dam was built for a specific purpose — in this case to support an ill-fated rice farming project. Now, at least 60 of this region's 270-odd species of birds find it a valuable and permanent waterhole. They are best seen among the waterlilies in the pink light of dawn or dusk.

MAN-MADE LAKE Spoonbills and egrets gather to feed in the shallows of the Fogg Dam.

SANDSTONE CATCHMENT Ancient sandstone cliffs overlook sheltered pools in the main gorge at Umbrawarra Gorge National Park.

CROCODILE COUNTRY Scotts Creek, a tributary of the Mary River, south-east of Darwin, is a typical wetland watercourse.

Wildman Reserve (22 940 hectares), on the Mary River 170 kilometres east of Darwin, is a classic example of a fresh-water flood plain. Here, particularly in the paperbark forest surrounding Rockhole, a huge, winding billabong, green pygmy-geese (*Nettapus pulchellus*) and white-breasted sea eagles (*Haliaeetus leucogaster*) are a common sight.

The reserve is a major breeding ground for magpie geese (*Anseranas semipalmata*) and the black flying fox (*Pteropus alecto*). Shady Camp Reserve (678 hectares), farther north on a four-wheel-drive track along the Mary River, is another birdwatcher's haven, attracting egrets, spoonbills, herons and other wading and waterbirds.

In the dry months, Leaning Tree Lagoon Nature Park (101 hectares), on the Arnhem Highway, is a small but important refuge for waterbirds. It takes its name from a gnarled, crooked old tree beside the lagoon.

Australia's largest and most powerful wild creature, the water buffalo (*Bubalus bubalis*), which was introduced from Asia in the 1820s, has become synonymous with the 'wild' north. Despite the attractions they hold for tourists and sporting shooters, the animals are regarded as a pest, having seriously disturbed the delicate balance of nature on the flood plains.

These huge beasts create wallows in the mud, destroy native vegetation by overgrazing and cause erosion by trampling channels between fresh water streams and salt water. The increased salinity which results can mean a slow death for paperbark forests.

TABLE'S EDGE Sandy Creek — far from the torrent it becomes in the 'wet' — is one of four permanent waterfalls which irrigate patches of rainforest around the Tabletop Range.

A vigorous programme of eradication and mustering has drastically reduced buffalo herds all over the north except in the Aboriginal territory of Arnhem Land. Where the animals have been removed, the flood plains and billabongs and the wildlife they support are recovering strongly.

This region is also home to a large and powerful native animal, the crocodile. Melacca Swamp (2315 hectares), near Howard Springs, 45 kilometres north-east of Darwin, is a wetlands reserve where the saltwater crocodile (*Crocodylus porosus*) breeds prolifically. The northern estuary of the Adelaide River, east of Darwin, harbours the world's biggest population of these sole-surviving relatives of the dinosaur.

On the estuary's muddy banks, specimens up to five metres long are a common sight. In Port Darwin, which has an area greater than that of Sydney Harbour, the Conservation Commission patrols regularly to capture crocodiles. Three farms take its catch of more than 100 animals a year, and produce both skins and meat.

The Northern Territory's only crocodile farm open to the public is 40 kilometres south of Darwin. It is home to about 6500 reptiles, ranging from tiny hatchlings to four-metre long adults.

Termites down the track

One of the most distinctive features of the woodland landscapes south of the Darwin coast are the termite mounds, some of them up to seven metres tall, which stand sentinel-like shimmering in the heat. These often bizarre-looking monuments to insect ingenuity are high-rise abodes created by tiny, blind, worker termites. They mix saliva and excreta with earth to form a rock-hard cement that can last a century.

Depending on the soil, mounds range in colour from creamy white to red. Inside each mound is a humid environment where the queen produces 2000 eggs a day during her lifespan of up to 50 years.

Some mounds resemble little castles, crenellated near the top to create an airflow that helps keep the structure dry. Other mounds have a north-south aspect in order to minimise their exposure to the sun's heat and were once known as 'the bushman's compass'.

Most termites are content to eat grass but soldier termites (*Mastotermes darwiniensis*), which grow to a length of 20 millimetres, have a fierce appetite for wood and actually attack trees, hollowing out their cores or ringbarking their trunks.

Termite mounds abound along the road south-west of Darwin to Litchfield Park (65 700 hectares). The sandstone Tabletop Range, a rugged and isolated

WHITE ON BLACK The canopus butterfly spends its brief life in moist, damp gorges.

ANT INGENUITY Termite mounds on a north-south axis avoid the full impact of the midday sun.

249

ANCIENT EROSION The sheer sides of the cliffs of Katherine Gorge – some of them bearing Aboriginal paintings – preclude exploration by foot.

plateau 220 metres high, is covered in dry woodlands, and contrasts with the park's lush escarpment, which offers some of the region's best bushwalking.

On the Tabletop, springs bubble to the surface and flow as creeks down the plateau's westerly slope. All year round, a series of spectacular waterfalls — Tolmer, Wangi, Florence and Sandy Creek — plunge from the escarpment to feed deep pools fringed by palms and paperbark trees.

Colonies of the rare insect-eating orange horseshoe bat (*Rhinonicteris aurantius*) and the endangered carnivorous ghost bat (*Macroderma gigas*) inhabit the caves near Tolmer Falls. Remnants of monsoon rainforest survive in Litchfield from before the last ice age and attract fruit-eating birds such as the banded fruitdove (*Ptilinopus cinctus*), the rose-crowned fruitdove (*P. regina*) and the Torres Strait imperial pigeon (*Duculua bicolor*).

These lush pockets of vegetation are constantly under threat from fire and destructive feral animals. Pethericks Rainforest, just outside the parks and with a waterfall and thermal spring, is one such patch.

The waters of Douglas Hot Springs (3107 hectares), south of Adelaide River on the Stuart Highway, reach temperatures of up to 45°C. Where they join the colder Douglas River, the water reaches a happy medium temperature and is excellent for swimming.

Nearby is the Butterfly Gorge Nature Park (104 hectares), a moist refuge late in the dry season for thousands of black-and-white butterflies. Umbrawarra Gorge Nature Park (972 hectares), 20 kilometres south-west of Pine Creek, has a string of small waterholes and a monsoon thicket at its entrance.

The gorges of Nitmiluk

In the cool, early mornings of the dry season, canoes wend through the mist which swirls over the Katherine River and into its 13 gorges in the 180 352 hectare Nitmiluk (Katherine Gorge) National Park. The best way to explore the gorges, etched out by the river over the past 25 million years, is by boat.

The river zigzags its way through a 15-kilometre, rock-walled corridor, often turning a right-angle to trace an ancient fault line along the edge of the 1800 million-year-old Arnhem Land Plateau.

In winter, the Katherine's waterholes contract to millponds and the river is reduced to a series of rocky rapids between the gorges; in summer, the contrast could hardly be more dramatic as 1000 millimetres of rain turns the river into a thundering torrent, reaching 18 metres above its dry-season level. The swollen river sweeps away all the trees along its banks except the pandanus tree, which has a strong, extensive root system to keep it — and the banks — from toppling.

Each gorge has its own distinctive character — some wide, others tall and narrow, all except the shallowest seeing the sun only briefly at midday. The second gorge the river passes through is a spectacular canyon, its red walls rising a sheer 80 metres above the river. Spring-fed waters trickle down the cliff to nourish hanging gardens of ferns, orchids and wild passionfruit.

The windmill or fan palm (*Livistona inermis*) is found only within this gorge and on the islands in the Gulf of Carpentaria. Just above the waterline, tiny fairy martins (*Hirundo ariel*) flit busily in and out of Swallow Cave carrying mud to build their bottle-shaped

nests on the cave ceiling. Each November, floods sweep the nests away and the birds have to rebuild.

Black-and-white butterflies congregate in a crevice off the main gorge, while on rock shelves and narrow strips of sand, freshwater crocodiles (*Crocodylus johnstoni*) — commonly known as 'freshies' — sun themselves. These shy fish-eaters are harmless to humans unless disturbed during nesting. The river is home to about 30 species of fish, including barramundi, long toms, freshwater sharks and swordfish.

Atop the stony Arnhem Land Plateau, the dry season tempts out the brilliant orange flowers of the tall Darwin woollybutt (*Eucalyptus miniata*) which in turn attracts rainbow lorikeets (*Trichoglossus haematodus*) and other nectar lovers.

The gorges echo with the harsh cries of cockatoos and crows. In termite mounds in remote parts of the park, the endangered hooded parrot (*Psephotus dissimilis*) creates nesting hollows, and the stick bower of the male great bowerbird (*Chlamydera nuchalis*), assembled elaborately to attract its mate, is a common sight.

South of Katherine Gorge — only the national park has taken the region's Aboriginal name — stand gnarled towers of limestone, some of them almost mushroom-like, with large rocks balancing on their slender pinnacles. The 200-square-kilometre limestone outcrop is riddled with large and small caves, many of them unexplored.

Only the Cutta Cutta Cave, 700 metres long and containing spectacular stalactite, stalagmite and shawl

GREEN RIBBON Run-off from the Arnhem Land Plateau keeps the Roper River's banks green and lush.

formations is open to the public, but others are expected to be made accessible. Temperatures in the caves average a muggy 28–35°. This, and a relative humidity of about 100 per cent, makes them an ideal habitat for tropical bats, including the orange horseshoe bat and the ghost bat.

Two ancient types of blind, cave-dwelling shrimps found have been in pools at Cutta Cutta, a discovery which excited scientists because until then

their only known habitat was in Madagascar. The shrimps have since been discovered in other caves in the Katherine region.

Alongside the Stuart Highway, 104 kilometres south of Katherine, is Mataranka Pool, one last tropical patch before the onset of the arid terrain that stretches for thousands of kilometres to the Southern Ocean. This tiny oasis on the Roper River is fed by a thermal spring which maintains a constant temperature 31°C.

The spring is high in minerals and it creates an exquisitely clear turquoise pool, in which fish and tortoises seem suspended, as if in mid-air. At dusk, screeching flocks of sulphur-crested cockatoos (*Cacatua galerita*) wheel through the sky, then stand like tall, white candles amid the foliage of paperbark (*Melaleuca*), pandanus (*Pandanus aquaticus*) and cabbage-tree palms (*Livistona*) around the pool.

As at Katherine Low Level Nature Park and Katherine Gorge, the tumult from thousands of black flying foxes is deafening as they clamber over branches and hang in treetops preparing for their night's feeding. When different trees come into fruit in sequence, these large, flying mammals travel hundreds of kilometres around the Territory tropics on their 'fruit route' circuit.

TWO TONE The woollybutt is recognisable by its habit of dropping the bark from its upper half.

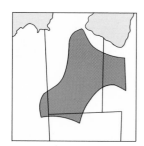

The 'dead' heart of Australia, while no more nor less arid than many other parts of the interior, and never a clear-cut geographical entity, continues to symbolise the true outback

A broad window onto the Dreamtime

Across an arid landscape, so old that it might have been worn down to dust and rock simply by the passage of time itself, odd-shaped rock formations are littered haphazardly: the comic-strip boulders of the Devils Marbles, and the shimmering domes of the Olgas and Ayers Rock. The last, the definitive symbol of the outback, rises like a rusty red blister on the plain.

This is central Australia, deep in the continent's interior, where travellers could be easily forgiven for thinking that time had stood still since the Aboriginal Dreamtime, or Alcheringa.

Despite the air-conditioned tourist buses which speed across what used to be called the 'never-never', and the bold modernity of the Ayers Rock tourist resort, the spirits of the Dreamtime are still strong here, and it is difficult for non-Aboriginal Australians not to feel at one remove from nature.

Wrinkled across the ancient face of the centre are half a dozen low ranges — really no more than tall hills. The biggest is the MacDonnell Ranges, sweeping in an arc roughly 400 kilometres from east to west and etched with river gorges and canyons throughout its length.

GREEN CENTRE The terrain of central Australia has been eroded by wind and rain longer than most parts of the earth's surface; the usually dry Finke River, the centre's longest river, is claimed by some geologists to be the world's oldest watercourse. This semi-permanent waterhole on the Finke, in the shadow of Glen Helen Gorge, is typical of the countless ponds and pools that support green patches of vegetation in the shelter of the gorge and canyon catchment areas.

WEATHER-BEATEN The MacDonnell Ranges rise up out of the very middle of central Australia, a series of parallel ridges, running east-west, that have been exposed to the elements for longer than it is possible to imagine. The scree slopes on the right-hand side of the ridges have been formed by several million years' accumulation of eroded material.

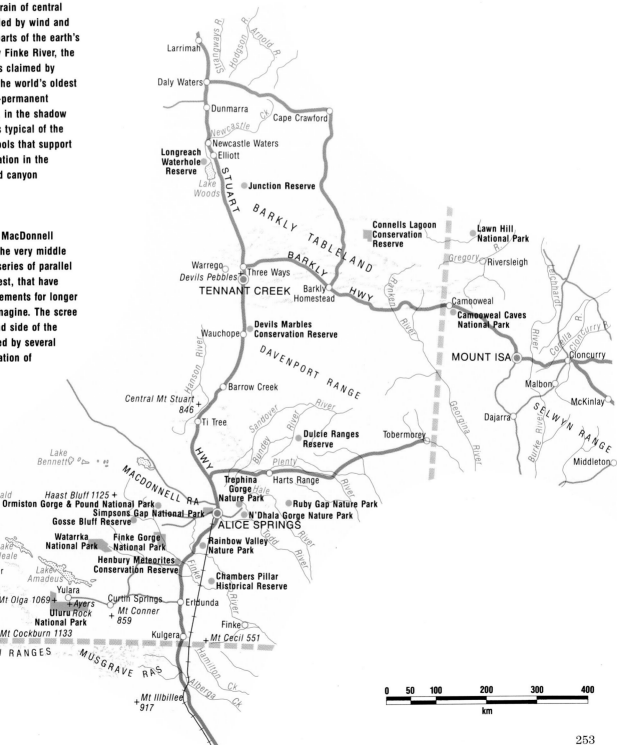

Larrimah
Daly Waters
Dunmarra
Cape Crawford
Newcastle Ck
Newcastle Waters
Longreach Waterhole Reserve
Elliott
Lake Woods
Junction Reserve
Connells Lagoon Conservation Reserve
Lawn Hill National Park
Nicholson R.
BARKLY TABLELAND
STUART
BARKLY
Gregory
Riversleigh
Warrego
Devils Pebbles
Three Ways
Ranken River
BARKLY HWY
Camooweal
Camooweal Caves National Park
TENNANT CREEK
Barkly Homestead
Leichhardt River
Devils Marbles Conservation Reserve
Georgina River
MOUNT ISA
Corella R.
Cloncurry R.
Cloncurry
Wauchope
DAVENPORT RANGE
Malbon
McKinlay
Barrow Creek
Sandover River
Dajarra
SELWYN RANGE
Central Mt Stuart 846
Ti Tree
Bundey
Plenty
Dulcie Ranges Reserve
Tobermorey
Burke River
Middleton
Hanson River
HWY
River
Georgina River
Lake Bennett
MACDONNELL RA
Trephina Gorge Nature Park
Hale
Harts Range
River
Lake Macdonald
Haast Bluff 1125
Ormiston Gorge & Pound National Park
Ruby Gap Nature Park
Lake Hopkins
Simpsons Gap National Park
Gosse Bluff Reserve
N'Dhala Gorge Nature Park
ALICE SPRINGS
Watarrka National Park
Finke Gorge National Park
Rainbow Valley Nature Park
Todd River
Henbury Meteorites Conservation Reserve
Lake Neale
Docker River
Lake Amadeus
Chambers Pillar Historical Reserve
RAWLINSON RANGE
Yulara
Finke
Mt Olga 1069
Ayers
Curtin Springs
Erldunda
Mt Conner 859
Uluru Rock National Park
Finke River
Finke
Surveyor Generals Corner
Mt Cockburn 1133
Kulgera
Mt Cecil 551
Mt Squires 705
MANN RANGES
MUSGRAVE RAS
Hamilton Ck
Alberga Ck
Mt Illbillee 917

0	50	100	200	300	400

km

253

Originally the MacDonnells would have rivalled the Himalayas, with peaks towering to 10 000 metres. Well into their middle age by the time of the dinosaurs, the relentless weathering of the 350 million years which have passed since then have eroded the ranges into mere molehills. The MacDonnells are among the oldest mountains on earth, but their highest point is Mount Zeil, at a mere 1531 metres.

These ranges, like the rest of central Australia, are dry for most of the year, but when the winter rains come they unleash an explosion of activity. Plants suddenly burst into colourful bloom, and animals mate and breed efficiently while conditions are benevolent.

The Stuart Highway is the spine and major lifeline of the Northern Territory. Running through the centre, it follows the footsteps of the early explorers and the route of the overland telegraph line, today dotted with microwave repeater stations. Travelling southwards from Darwin, the savannah woodlands fade into scrubby grasslands as the average annual rainfall drops to less than 750 millimetres.

Settlements strung out along this bitumen lifeline are few and far between, and a lonely feeling of remoteness pervades the region. Near the town of Elliott, Longreach Waterhole is an important stopover site for migratory magpie geese (*Anseranas semipalmata*) and huge numbers of waterfowl. Further south, past Tennant Creek, the jumbled profile of the Devils Marbles slides onto the horizon to announce the imminence of the centre proper.

Bigger than their cousins known as the Devils Pebbles, a short distance north of Tennant Creek, the marbles are massive, rounded granite boulders,

THE UNSTOPPABLE ALLIANCE OF SUN, WIND AND WATER

MONSTER MARBLES (above) The Devil's Marbles represent the latter stages of erosion of a single piece of granite that once sat just below the surface. As water forced its way into the natural joint lines (left), the rock separated into blocks up to seven metres square.

Gradually, as the soil covering wore away, the joint lines and corners became rounded (centre). Exposed to the atmosphere, the hardest rocks became oval or spherical as the soft rock and soil eroded away, leaving them balanced above ground (right).

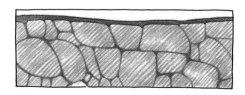
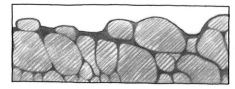
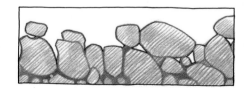

some balancing precariously atop others. At dusk, with the boulders in silhouette and the wind moaning over the yellow spinifex plain, it is a truly eerie place where the Dreamtime comes momentarily to life.

The 1500-million-year-old stones were once a single block which eroded along horizontal and vertical fault lines like a massive Rubik's Cube. In a process known as spalling, the stones shed thin 'skins' of weathered surface rock that comes away like the layers of an onion.

The true centre of Australia — the geographical midpoint of the continent — lies 189 kilometres south of the Devils Marbles at Central Mount Stuart, an 846-metre-high rounded hill west of the highway. The nearest large settlement to this imaginary central spot on the map is Alice Springs, which adopted its name in 1933 in place of the original appellation, 'Stuart'.

DESERT RELIEF A ridge at the western edge of the MacDonnell Ranges, near Alice Springs, suggests a biblical landscape as it terminates in the time-worn bluff of Mount Sonder, one of the highest points in the ranges.

GHOSTLY WHITE A multi-trunked ghost gum, clinging to a gorge wall in Kings Canyon National Park, exemplifies the stark beauty of the outback.

SHELTERED GLADE Ormiston Gorge is almost park-like where the river red gums grow.

The name originally referred to the waterhole named for the wife of the postmaster-general at the time of the overland telegraph's construction. The town sits amidst the hills of the Mac-Donnell Ranges, its southern approaches protected behind the rust-red flanks of Heavitree Gap.

Cracks in the ranges

Heavitree is one of dozens of great gashes through the MacDonnell Ranges to the east and west of Alice Springs, a series of gorges, gaps and steep-walled chasms sculpted by water-courses that are now mere rivers of sand for most of the year. It has been 20 000 years since any of central Australia's rivers flowed year-round.

The walls of the gorges, gaps and chasms glow orange and red in the harsh sunlight. A scramble to their rocky heights is well rewarded by expansive views across the ranges.

Coolibah (*Eucalyptus microtheca*) and old river red gums (*E. camaldulensis*) line dry creekbeds, their roots searching out subterranean water, while ghost gums (*E. papuana*) stand tall in open country or cling to cliff-sides. Most gorges cradle permanent waterholes at their feet, always icy cold in the shade, even in mid-summer.

Occasional billabongs sustain animal life here, and draw kangaroos and emus to drink. At twilight they become noisy watering holes for flocks of zebra finches (*Taeniopygia guttata*), pied butcherbirds (*Cracticus nigrogularis*),

NEATLY NAMED Heavitree Gap and the usually dry Todd River were named after Charles Heavitree Todd, the South Australian Postmaster-General who oversaw the overland telegraph's construction.

bright green budgerigars (*Melopsittacus undulatus*) and a riotous collection of screeching parrots.

Thousands of kilometres from the nearest large, permanent body of water, these small ponds maintain their own typical cross-section of marine creatures. On and under the water, there are frogs, crustaceans, and fish, such as the spangled perch (*Leiopotherapon unicolor*). Feral horses and cattle, unwelcome visitors that trample vegetation and foul the water, pose a serious threat to the fragile ecology of these desert oases.

The biggest ravines lie to the west

of Alice Springs, between two craggy, erosion-resistant spines of the MacDonnell Ranges. Simpsons Gap is just one of a string of jagged clefts within the popular Simpsons Gap National Park (30 950 hectares). The shy black-footed rock-wallaby (*Petrogale lateralis*) lives here amongst the witchetty bushes (*Acacia kempeana*) which harbour that most famous of Aboriginal foods, the succulent witchetty grub, in their roots. Though abundant, the wallabies are rarely seen, and a tame colony at Simpsons Gap offers a unique opportunity to observe the agile creatures around the waterholes at dusk.

Each gorge is different from the next, with its own unique character and attractions. The floor of Standley Chasm is raked by direct rays of light for only a few brief moments each day when the sun is almost directly over its closely spaced, 75-metre walls.

At enchanting Ellery Creek Big Hole Nature Park (1766 hectares), tortured folds of brilliant red rock are mirrored in the emerald waters of a pool 30 metres deep, while the narrow, winding Serpentine Gorge in the Serpentine Gorge Nature Park (518 hectares), further west, has a dark, moody character with purplish walls looming above a pair of waterholes. Kaleidoscopic veins of colour decorate the riverbank at the Ochre Pit, an important source of the pigments used in Aboriginal rock art painting.

Ormiston is the most impressive gorge within the MacDonnell Ranges. Rugged walls tower 300 metres beside Ormiston Creek, a tributary of the Finke River, as it snakes through the ranges. Also within the Ormiston Gorge and Pound National Park (4655 hectares), the biggest in the western MacDonnells, is Ormiston Pound, a ten-kilometre-wide natural amphitheatre hemmed in by ridges.

Sheltered in the moist, shady niches of Ormiston, Serpentine and Ellery Gorges, where dew and precious crops of rainwater collect, the rare cycads known as *Macrozamia macdonnellii* grow. The most primitive of all seed-producing plants, they have remained unchanged in the 200 million years since dinosaurs walked a much wetter Australia. The cycads are believed to have a lifespan of 500 years or more.

The gorges to the east of 'The Alice' are smaller in scale than those in the western MacDonnells, but those such as the gorges in Emily and Jessie Gaps Nature Park (695 hectares), carved into white quartzite and red sandstone, possess their own strange beauty. Beyond Corroboree Rock Conservation Reserve (7 hectares), named for the upright stone landmark which figures in Aboriginal lore, Trephina Gorge Nature Park (1771 hectares) contains twin chasms: quartzite-walled Trephina Gorge and the John Hayes Rock Hole, an ascending chain of pools strung along a narrow gorge.

This is lizard country, and the small, freckled monitor (*Varanus tristis*), and Australia's biggest lizard, the perentie (*Varanus giganteus*), which can grow over two metres long, are relatively common, as are tiny geckos which use

RANGES' RIFT The cleft of Standley Chasm — in some places only a few metres wide — is formed by sheer quartzite walls stained red by iron oxides that change colour as the sun passes overhead.

their tongues to clean their lidless eyes. Native fig trees (*Ficus platypoda*) struggle out of cracks in the gorge face, which also provides nesting spots for fairy martins (*Hirundo ariel*) and a refuge for many species of bat.

Uluru … the Rock

Ayers Rock (Uluru), the Olgas (Katajuta) and Mount Conner are, to all intents and purposes, recycled mountains. Six hundred million years ago a great mountain range was eroded into a sandy rubble that was deposited on the seabed and compressed into a hard, sandstone conglomerate. One hundred million years later, earth movements lifted and folded the sandstone layers above the sea. Over time, this new plain weathered away, leaving a trio of remarkable tors, or bare, rocky hills, standing on the flat plains of central Australia.

Ayers Rock and The Olgas are within the 132 538-hectare Uluru National Park, a World Heritage region since 1987. The land incorporated into the park was handed back to its traditional Aboriginal owners in 1983, and leased to the Australian National Parks and Wildlife Service, which is responsible for its day-to-day management.

Ayers Rock has always been held sacred by the Aboriginal people and has great Dreamtime significance. Areas of the rock, especially caves covered in ancient paintings, are closed to the public and still used for traditional ceremonies.

Uluru is 9.4 kilometres around its base, covers 3.33 square kilometres, and rises abruptly out of the desert to a height of 348 metres. Like an iceberg, the greater part of its bulk is buried beneath the sand and is believed to extend up to six kilometres deep underground.

The monolith is technically an 'inselberg', from the German for 'island mountain', and is composed of a hard feldspar- and quartz-rich sandstone called arkose. For the past 60 million years, it has withstood much of the weathering that has worn away the surrounding landscape. The main reason for its survival is that the rock is under compression from different directions, and this keeps the natural joints, the areas susceptible to weathering, squeezed tightly together.

Deep, parallel furrows running down the flanks clearly show that the rock has been upended from its original position and tilted by earth movements to an almost vertical 80-degree angle. These strata lines, weathering at different rates, have created the many wrinkles and grooves and are responsible for the ravaged, time-worn look that suggests that the monolith has overlooked the plains since time began.

LIFE AT THE TOP Ayers Rock, or Uluru — as important a landscape symbol to the nation as the Harbour Bridge is to Sydney — is not entirely barren. The depressions which have been eroded into its surface (top), contain the eggs of tiny shrimps (above) which are born, breed, and lay more eggs during the brief time the ephemeral rock pools are full.

Its surface is flaky and covered with thick sheets of rock curled up at the edges — like cornflakes the size of dinner plates. The flakes peel off so evenly that the rock has retained the same basic shape for millions of years and should continue to do so.

The reddish glow of sunrise and sunset strongly accentuates the characteristic terracotta hue of Ayers Rock, the cause of which was a mystery for many years. The fact is, the great monolith is rusting, as are all the red sandstones or sands typical of the centre. A dull greenish-grey when freshly exposed, the sandstone of this region quickly turns red as the iron in the rock oxidises.

As barren as the bald dome may be, the scrub around its furrowed base — well-watered by run-off from the rock — is home to common wallaroos (*Mac-*

TABLE-TOP If tilted side-on, the horizontal, sandstone rock strata of Mount Conner — shown here after rain has brought a green bounty for the brumbies in the foreground — would erode in the same fashion as Ayers Rock.

TABLE-TOP If tilted side-on, the horizontal, sandstone rock strata of Mount Conner — shown here after rain has brought a green bounty for the brumbies in the foreground — would erode in the same fashion as Ayers Rock.

ropus robustus), dingoes and rabbits, feeding on grasses in the shade of native fig trees. Australian kestrels (*Falco cenchroides*), various kites and wedge-tailed eagles (*Aquila audax*) nest on high ledges.

One intriguing creature springs to life when rain fills depressions on the top of the rock. Pale green, and about 70 millimetres long, primitive shield shrimps (*Triops*) are believed to have existed on the rock for 150 million years. Miraculously, the fertilised eggs of shield shrimps can survive years of drought and temperatures from below freezing to 55°C.

Minarets and domes

Dancing in the heat haze, 32 kilometres to the west of Uluru, is the cluster of 36 rock domes called the Olgas. To the enraptured explorer Ernest Giles, they suggested the ruins of a Middle Eastern city of '...rounded minarets, giant cupolas and monstrous domes.' From another, much earlier perspective, the Aboriginal name Katajuta means 'many heads'.

The single block that once stood on the 35 square kilometres covered by the Olgas would have dwarfed Ayers Rock. Tilted to 20 degrees off the horizontal, it was weathered along vertical joint planes into steep-sided domes separated by valleys. Unlike Ayers Rock, the Olgas are a 'pudding stone' conglomerate of pebbles and boulders cemented within sandstone.

Standing at the base of a narrow ravine called the Valley of the Winds, between two great rocky 'domes', or walking in the shadow of Mount Olga, the tallest monolith, at 546 metres high, it is not hard to understand why this site became sacred to the Aborigines.

Mount Conner has little of the mystical atmosphere of the other geological oddities which rear up from the plains, but it is still an incongruous sight on the horizon, 100 kilometres south-east of Ayers Rock. Unlike Ayers Rock and the Olgas, distinctive because of their unique, rounded resemblance to giant pebbles, Mount Conner is a flat-topped mesa. Undisturbed by earth movements, it remains an almost perfectly horizontal table-topped mountain rising 343 metres above the plain.

DREAMTIME DOMES The Olgas, once a single formation like Ayers Rock, have an air of mystery and foreboding, particularly when the wind whistles through their numerous ravines.

Although Mount Conner is part of the same geological formation as the Olgas and Ayers Rock, its rocks are even more ancient — at least 700 million years old. Topped by a hard cap of silica, it thwarts the erosive forces that have worn down the surrounding plain.

The soft sandstone escarpment below the flat top has been sculpted by wind and water into honeycombed cliffs. Chunks of the harder capping rock are constantly being undermined to become overhangs, eventually crashing down to join the slope of rubble at the mountain's feet.

A desert time capsule

South-west of Alice Springs, hidden in the recesses of the Finke River gorge, the sight of cool billabongs and gently swaying palms seems like a mirage. Palm Valley is not only an oasis but a botanical time capsule — marooned for tens of thousands of years, it is a reminder that the region was once

covered in lush tropical vegetation and inhabited by crocodiles and other creatures much larger than those which live there now.

Permanent shallow water, hoarded by the ancient sandstone of Palm Valley has allowed some of the oldest plant species in Australia to survive. As well as ferns and cycads, there is the rare red cabbage palm (*Livistona mariae*) which occurs nowhere else on earth. The nearest similar palms are more than 1000 kilometres away.

About 3000 of these living fossils with their fan-shaped fronds and straight, tall boles, some 20 metres high and 300 years old, grace the valley carved by Palm Creek. Birds like the black-faced cuckoo-shrike (*Coracina novaehollandiae*) are drawn to the trees' cream-coloured flowers and later in the year to their marble-sized seeds.

Palm Valley lies within the 45856-hectare Finke Gorge National Park; it is in a small gorge off the tortuously

winding, 150-kilometre-long Finke River Gorge where the larger gorge has cut through the Krichauff and James Ranges. The rugged, red walls of the winding Finke River are layered in terraces and are accessible only to experienced bushwalkers. The river is actually a string of waterholes lined in river red gums that are draped in orange mistletoe (*Dendrophthoe glabrescens*), a parasitic adornment, which draws sap from its host.

The Finke, which rises in the Mac-Donnell Ranges, still runs its original course, but only during the wettest of years does the ancient river reach its ultimate destination, the normally dry salt pans of Lake Eyre.

Three hundred kilometres south-west of Alice Springs, in the remote George Gill Ranges, Kings Canyon is central Australia's deepest gorge. It is part of the Watarrka National Park (106 100 hectares), named after the sandhill wattle, or umbrella bush (*Acacia ligulata*), which grows in profusion at the entrance to the canyon. The wide, valley-like gorge has steep walls rising 270 metres from Kings Creek, so flat and sheer, they might have been sliced by some great blade.

MICROCLIMATE Despite the unmistakeably Australian eucalypts, Palm Valley bears a passing resemblance to a Saharan oasis.

MAJESTIC CANYON A surrounding army of weathered sandstone knobs guards the many deep ravines and crevices of Kings Canyon.

Unlike most gorges, the finest views are on the plateau above the canyon. Wind and rain have sculpted several square kilometres of red sandstone into a cluster of beehive domes and turrets known as the Lost City. Cycads and gnarled cypress pines (*Callitris columellaris*) eke out an existence in the sparse pockets of soil, adding to a haunting atmosphere suggestive of a ruined city.

Botanically, Watarrka is one of the most diverse regions in central Australia, since it lies where the dry western plains meet well-watered range country. It contains more than 500 plant species, fully one-third of all those found in central Australia.

Moonscape in miniature

Satellite photographs of central Australia show Gosse Bluff as a perfectly round thumbprint on Missionary Plain, 160 kilometres west of Alice Springs. And like the photographs, the cause of this seemingly geological phenomenon also comes from space.

The 'bluff' is not the result of earth movements or erosion, but came into being approximately 130 million years ago when a speeding meteorite or comet — possibly as much as 600 metres in diameter — crashed into the earth. The distinct circular outline of the original shock ring — 20 kilometres across — is still visible from the air. What remains as Gosse Bluff is the four-kilometre-wide inner crater, with its 250-metre-high ramparts, which would have been twice that height at the time of impact.

Almost the same distance south of Alice Springs, is a series of 12 more craters. These were created when a meteorite weighing several thousand tonnes and travelling at more than 40 000 kilometres an hour, crashed into the earth 4700 years ago. The Aboriginal name for these Henbury Craters translates as 'sun walk fire devil rock' suggesting that the meteorite's fiery entry into the earth's atmosphere may not have gone unobserved.

The meteorite split into numerous pieces as it sped through the atmosphere, the five biggest chunks — estimated to have been the size of fuel drums — blasted out craters, while nine

MOONSCAPE The neat bowl shapes of the Henbury Craters means they collect more surface water than the surrounding countryside and generally support a variety of tough vegetation.

lighter fragments fell short and gouged out smaller depressions in line with the meteor's flight path. Now mere divots compared to Gosse Bluff — the biggest is 183 metres wide and 15 metres deep — the cluster of craters has been colonised by scrub and provides a shady refuge for wildlife in this otherwise desolate region.

Towards the sea

The north-east of this region — the direction of the nearest coastline — is bordered by the 240 000-square-kilometre expanse of the flat, mostly treeless, Barkly Tableland, which slopes gently down to the tepid waters of the Gulf of Carpentaria. With no definite drainage pattern, the rivers which form on this minor upland quickly flood their banks during the wet, as the summer rains are called.

They form vast, shallow swamps and the hard, black soil of the plains, that only moments earlier was cracked and dry or talc-fine 'bulldust', is trans-

formed by a brief shower into an impenetrable quagmire.

Predominantly clad in Mitchell (*Astrebla*) and Flinders (*Iseilema*) grass, the Barkly Tableland provides some of Australia's best grazing country for the vast cattle stations of the Northern Territory and north-western Queensland. Connells Lagoon Conservation Reserve (25 890 hectares) and the almost inaccessible Junction Reserve (19 930 hectares) have been closed off to grazing to allow the natural vegetation to regenerate.

The rich grasses of the tableland are the breeding ground for the native long-haired rat (*Rattus villosissimus*), that sometimes gathers in numbers of plague proportions to head across central Australia and sometimes into South Australia, devouring almost everything in its path. The region is also home to the kori bustard or plains turkey (*Ardeotis kori*). Once widespread, it is now able to breed in only 10 per cent of its habitat due to cattle grazing.

PLANT DEFENCE The grey cassia combats evaporation by having long, conifer-like leaves that expose only a small surface to the sun.

ALL ALONE The kori bustard was once seen in flocks but nowadays is mostly a solitary bird.

The rainbow lorikeet of eastern and northern Australia (*Trichoglossus haematodus*) and common bronze-wings (*Phaps chalcoptera*) form vast flocks from time to time. The Mitchell grasses are also a stronghold for the rare yellow chat (*Epthianura crocea*), a sparrow-sized, bright yellow bird with a narrow bill.

Every niche filled

A highly erratic annual rainfall of less than 250 millimetres means there is little cloud cover in central Australia to temper the fierce power of the sun's rays. As a result, most of the centre's ground water soon evaporates, making it one of Australia's driest regions. Plants and animals, deprived of the seasonal predictability of life in more benign climates, long ago learned to find a specific place for themselves in the environment and adapt to an almost waterless life.

Unlike Africa and the Americas, which have very ancient desert regions, Australia is a relative newcomer to aridity. Until about six million years ago, inland freshwater lakes and lush,

temperate broad-leaved forests flourished in central Australia. As the climate gradually became drier, six to three million years ago, and the continent was slowly but inexorably forced northward into warmer latitudes, plants either adapted to the changing conditions or died out.

The unique feature of the flora of central Australia is that there has not been enough time for the evolution of highly specialised desert plants like cacti; all Australia's arid-zone plants are related to species common to the other, better-watered parts of the continent. The incredible flexibility of some genera has allowed plants to accommodate themselves to any extremity of climate, be it the icy highlands of Tasmania or the parched outback.

Survival depends on capturing and conserving every drop of moisture. Some plants manage with small leaves protected by an oily or waxy skin to reduce dehydration; other leaves are fuzzy, with hairs to trap moisture and protect them from the scorching sun.

The mulga's (*Acacia aneura*) outward- and upward-pointing leaves form an efficient funnel, directing precious rainwater towards the plant's roots. During extended periods of drought the witchetty bush, mulga, ironwood (*A. estrophiolata*), spinifex (*Triodia plectrachne*) and the more than 100 species of powder-puff-flowered mulla mulla (*Ptilotus*), drop their leaves to conserve water and simply stop growing altogether. The desert oak (*Allocasuarina decaisneana*) strictly limits its above-ground growth — often for years — until it has developed roots long and probing enough to ensure its survival.

The Olive Pink Flora Park (16 hectares) on the east bank of the dry Todd River, where it passes through Alice Springs, is the country's only arid-zone botanic garden within the 250-millimetre-rainfall region. On the door of the visitor's centre is a list of plants currently flowering within the park, and during the winter months there can be 50 or more.

When rain does fall in the centre, the flora reserve — protected from the predations of plant-eating animals — comes to reflect the vast inland in microcosm. Among the 300 species of trees, flowers and shrubs in the park are desert flowers like the delightful poached egg daisy (*Myriocephalus stuartii*), paper daisies, the weeping emu-bush (*Eremophila longifolia*) and the purplish-pink broad-leaf parakeelya (*Calandrinia balonensis*), with thick, fleshy leaves and stems that store water.

Remarkable hibernating plants like the woolly cloak fern (*Cheilanthes lasiophylla*) look completely desiccated, yet sprout bright green leaves within an hour or two of rain.

DESERT EMBLEM Sturt's desert rose blooms in spring, but only in years of good rains.

The most flamboyant desert blooms belong to the annuals such as Sturt's desert rose (*Gossypium sturtianum*), the Northern Territory's floral emblem, which flaunts its mauve, hibiscus-like flowers only after a long, heavy downpour. The rose can afford extravagant, water-hungry blossoms since the plant itself does not survive the dry, instead producing seeds which can lie dormant

for up to ten years before sprouting with the first good rains.

The seeds of the showy, blood-red Sturt's desert pea (*Clianthus puniceus*) contain a growth inhibitor which will not dissolve and thus allow germination to take place until it has been inundated with enough water to see the plant through its life cycle. This prevents premature germination from taking place after rainshowers. Perennials, which strive to stay alive from year to year on the same root system, display more modest flowers, conserving some energy for the dry months.

An unpredictable 'spring'

Outback birds, particularly waterfowl, take to the skies to search out wetter regions during drought. Emus are one of the few creatures that forage in the heat of day, no matter how dry the season. Their insulating bulk of feathers keeps their temperature down. Most outback creatures are nocturnal, taking advantage of the cool of the night to search for food.

Marsupial mice are so well adapted to their arid environment that they survive without drinking at all, receiving sufficient moisture from their insect prey, and conserving it by secreting urine six times as concentrated as that of humans.

Common wallaroos can survive on dry spinifex, with no water at all, for up to 90 days, and even when water is available, go for up to 14 days without a drink. They cool off by licking their wrists and other body parts where blood vessels are near the surface.

Water-holding frogs (*Cyclorana*) swell up, with water in bladders and sacks under the skin, before digging a metre underground with their spade-shaped feet. Creating a humid burrow, they wait in hibernation for up to three years before being awakened by a change in the weather. Fish in outback billabongs must tolerate wildly varying levels of salinity as their ponds can become as salty as the sea when the water level drops. The spangled perch waits out the drought buried deep in muddy creek beds.

To give their young the best chance for survival, many creatures switch off their reproductive cycles in times of drought, then shift swiftly into high reproductive gear at the first hint of rain. The masked and black-faced woodswallows (*Leiopotherapon unicolor*) begin to pick up nesting twigs as soon as they spot a cloud on the horizon.

MAIN CHANCE Arid-land plants are able opportunists; these sunrays flower quickly after rain to ensure seeds for the next generation.

WRAP-UP An airtight membrane protects the water-holding frog against dehydration.

TANK-TOPS At first glance, the piedish beetle appears to have been overturned.

At the onset of drought, big red kangaroos can place a growing embryo in a state of suspended animation until the drought breaks. Frogs quickly mate during rain, their tadpoles developing in billabongs much faster than their cool-climate relatives. This enables them to reach maturity before their water supply disappears.

The hard shells of insects are custom-made heat shields to keep them from drying out: the odd-looking pie dish beetle (*Helaeus*) found only in central Australia, angles its coat of armour like a solar collector to deflect both heat and predators. The thorny devil (*Moloch horridus*), one of the outback's most peculiar reptiles, can change the colour of its skin to regulate body temperature. Its spiky skin channels even the smallest quantity of dew or rain directly into its mouth and if it sticks a foot into a small puddle, a network of capillaries covering its body pipes the moisture to its mouth. □

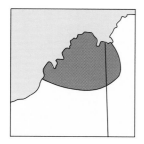
Australia's last, and possibly wildest frontier has an almost inaccessible coastline with spectacular tidal variations, and a rugged landscape ruled mercilessly by a climate of alternating extremes

Unyielding, untameable ...and unrivalled

Wild and craggy-sided gorges and spectacular waterfalls; a fretted and ragged coastline of high cliffs and mangrove-fringed tidal mudflats; rugged, multi-hued ranges of sandstone, limestone and basalt thrusting above broad plains and river valleys; all of it awesome in scale — such are the dramatic extremes of the remote, north-western wilderness known as the Kimberley.

Since this landmass rose out of the sea some 2500 million years ago, its features have been sculpted by the elements in all their forms. The north-western corner of the continent has been swept by seasonally flooded rivers which swell into torrents when the monsoon comes, then bleached and scorched by a merciless sun and blasted by fierce winds.

The terrain is clothed in a variety of subtropical grasslands and savannah woodlands and forests, studded occasionally by clear pools filled with floating water plants. Scattered tracks and a variety of non-human croaks, grunts and cries are evidence of the many wild creatures — some of which have yet to be named by scientists — inhabiting this landscape.

Not surprisingly, much is yet to be discovered about the Kimberley. Like so many parts of what was once the British Empire, it was named after a Colonial Secretary of the 1880s and is technically a statistical division of Western Australia.

The Kimberley was one of the last regions of Australia to be explored and attempts at European settlement were generally timid and tentative until the mineral discoveries of the latter part of the twentieth century. With an area of approximately 150 000 square kilometres, this remote region is as big as Victoria and Tasmania combined.

Being well within the tropics, the Kimberley has more in common geographically and biologically with the tropical north of Queensland and the Northern Territory than with the more southerly parts of Western Australia.

Flanked to the east by the Ord River Basin, and to the south by the empty wilderness of the Great Sandy Desert, the ancient Kimberley plateaux rise 300 metres above the surrounding plains.

The rugged interior is embraced by a sparse hoop of remote settlements, all of them with a unique outback character — towns like Fitzroy Crossing, Halls Creek and Turkey Creek. On the coast, Derby maintains a friendly rivalry with Broome, where a colourful history and scenic attractions have provided the basis for a growing tourist industry.

FAR REMOVED This lush patch of rainforest is at the bottom of Quail Creek Gorge, in the Regent River country, where even four-wheel drive vehicles are defeated by the terrain.

DEPTHS OF THE 'DRY' In the dry season, the King George River meanders across a remote plain between the Drysdale River and Cambridge Gulf before forking lazily in two and emptying into the sea over 80-metre sandstone cliffs.

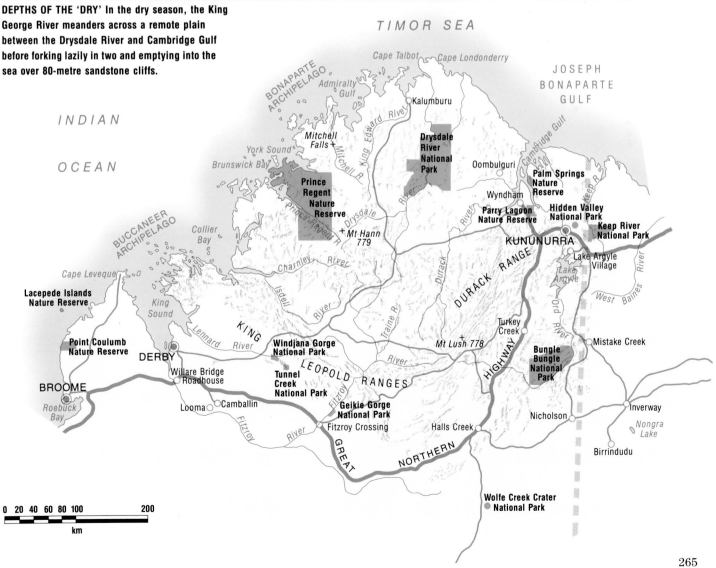

TIMOR SEA

JOSEPH BONAPARTE GULF

INDIAN

OCEAN

Cape Talbot   Cape Londonderry

BONAPARTE ARCHIPELAGO

Admiralty Gulf

Kalumburu

York Sound

Mitchell Falls +

Brunswick Bay

Drysdale River National Park

Oombulguri

Palm Springs Nature Reserve

Prince Regent Nature Reserve

Wyndham

Parry Lagoon Nature Reserve

Hidden Valley National Park

Keep River National Park

Buccaneer Archipelago

Collier Bay

+ Mt Hann 779

Charnley   River

KUNUNURRA

Lake Argyle Village

Cape Leveque

King Sound

Isdell

River

DURACK RANGE

West Baines River

Lacepede Islands Nature Reserve

Lennard   River

KING

Traine R.

Lake Argyle

Point Coulumb Nature Reserve

Windjana Gorge National Park

LEOPOLD   RANGES

River

Mt Lush 778 +

Turkey Creek

HIGHWAY

Bungle Bungle National Park

Mistake Creek

DERBY

Willare Bridge Roadhouse

Tunnel Creek National Park

BROOME

Looma   Camballin

Geikie Gorge National Park

Fitzroy Crossing

Halls Creek

Nicholson

Inverway

Roebuck Bay

Fitzroy   River

GREAT   NORTHERN

Nongra Lake

Birrindudu

Wolfe Creek Crater National Park

0 20 40 60 80 100   200

km

265

WATER CUT After countless wet seasons, the Lennard River has worn its way 80 metres down into a limestone plateau to form the Windjana Gorge.

TRACKLESS The Prince Regent River enters Brunswick Bay through St George Basin, south-east of Mount Trafalgar's monolithic mesa.

The Kimberley is an ancient, geologically stable landmass edged by a more 'mobile' zone of rock. The sandstone surface is broken frequently by outcrops of ancient, sedimentary and volcanic rocks, the oldest rocks of the region. The central plateau of the Kimberley has been heavily eroded, mainly by torrential summer rain and floodwaters which have exposed the rock strata and created a rugged and at times breathtakingly varied landscape.

The flat, domed Kimberley plateau is sliced and divided by the rivers of the northern Kimberley which radiate from its heart, near Mount Hann. With the land sloping away in all directions, the Drysdale and King Edward Rivers flow northwards, the tributaries of the Fitzroy southwards, the Isdell and Charnley westwards, and the Prince Regent to the north-west.

The tidal torrents

Where they reach the sea, the Kimberley rivers run out sluggishly onto broad, mangrove-fringed mudflats, extended by deposits of sediment eroded from riverbeds during the wet season. Between estuaries and bays, the ragged, deeply indented coastline is characterised by high sandstone cliffs and low basalt promontories.

Twice a day this wild coast is washed by phenomenal tides, where the variation between high and low may be as much as 12 metres. As the powerful tides turn, huge volumes of water sluice through narrow channels, creating a navigational nightmare of rapids, whirlpools and shifting shoals.

The gigantic tides, swirling through coastal gorges, create tidal races which sometimes resemble horizontally flowing waterfalls. There are several of these races, one of the most spectacular being at Talbot Bay, north of King Sound, where the narrowness of the gorge creates an especially fast and furious waterfall where the rushing water may reach speeds of up to 30 knots.

The incoming tide can 'run' for almost twelve hours after which there is a brief moment of calm as it peaks. The pull of the outgoing tide quickly asserts itself and for the next 12 hours Talbot Bay resounds to the roar of a torrent rushing back out to sea.

Elsewhere, the waters of narrow inlets such as George Water and Walcott Inlet are in an almost constant state of turmoil as the restless tides create an ever-changing pattern of whirlpools and eddies.

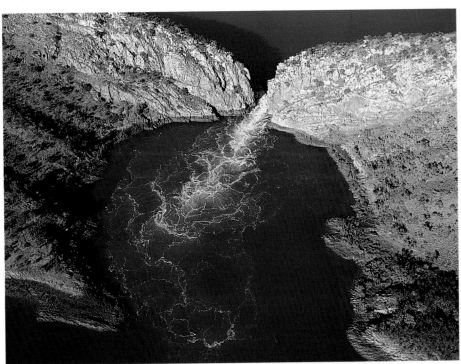

TIDAL SURGE The incoming tide forces its way into an inlet on the Buccaneer Archipelago.

The coastal zone is so wild and unformed that the actual coastline is often virtually impossible to reach by land and frequently inaccessible by sea, so formidable are its swamps and cliffs. The largest creature to inhabit this coast is as primitive as the landscape, for this is part of northern Australia's crocodile coast.

The deadly saltwater crocodile patrols the coast north of Broome and, as long as rivers are still swollen by wet-season rains, it can be found in waterways many kilometres inland.

Beasts over five metres long have been sighted floating in the inlets or mangrove swamps, with just the top of their heads and their eyes protruding above the surface. Any waterbird that swoops down in search of a meal often ends up becoming one itself.

The inoffensive freshwater crocodile, recognisable by its relatively small body and long, narrow snout, inhabits the inland waters. The banks of billabongs in semi-arid country, kilometres from any large body of water, are often decorated by groups of freshwater crocodiles, basking in the sun as they digest the previous evening's meal.

In the northern Kimberley, water — albeit here a slightly more seasonal

HOME SWEET HOME Tidal mudflats provide the perfect environment for saltwater crocodiles.

MUD STREAMS The muddy patterns which appear around King Sound at low tide are typical of the formless Kimberley estuaries where land gives way begrudgingly to sea.

phenomenon — is also a powerful force in shaping the landscape. A short way from the coast, the Mitchell River plunges 150 metres into a sandstone-walled basin, creating the spectacular Mitchell Falls. This thundering curtain of muddy water gradually diminishes to little more than a trickle as the dry season asserts its influence.

Another northern river, the Prince Regent, forces its way through some of the most rugged ranges and highest peaks of this already intimidatingly harsh countryside. Jagged sandstone scarps stand out from the gentler, eroded volcanic landscapes where cattle graze over the black, cracking clays of the valley plains.

The rocky screes of the northern Kimberley support patches of rainforest — in the form of vine thickets, usually found on the sheltered southern slopes. These low forests, with a canopy only five to ten metres above ground punctured by the crowns of mostly deciduous trees reaching up to 15 metres high, are similar to the vine thickets of the dry tropics of Queensland.

Scientists suspect that in the 25 years since these unusual 'rainforests' were discovered, they have been gradually retreating and degenerating, largely as a result of the widespread use of fire to clear land and herd cattle. Fire destroys the outer trees, pushing back the boundary of the thicket. The cattle which seek shelter in these small, shady patches trample the undergrowth, further disturbing an already threatened habitat.

In places, ancient volcanic activity resulted in flows of lava which have since vitrified into exposed outcrops of glass-like obsidian. This is the material which was used by the Kimberley Aborigines to make their almost perfectly symmetrical, serrated, leaf-shaped spearheads.

The Aborigines of the north-west were also the creators and custodians

DRAINING NORTHWARD Wet-season run-off from the Mitchell Plateau pours over the final drop of the three-stepped Mitchell Falls.

of the Wandjina — spirit figures with mouthless, stylised heads bearing helmet-like decorations. The Wandjina spirits were believed to control rain, flood and lightning; the Aborigines explain the strange, circular headdresses of the Wandjina figures as being representations of clouds and lightning.

Honeycombs and domes

In the southern Kimberley, ancient limestone reefs formed in primeval seas have endured the forces of erosion to survive as the Napier and Oscar Ranges, which extend for nearly 300 kilometres across the plains. The reefs were formed about 350 million years ago when the Kimberley was an island lapped by a shallow tropical sea which covered what is now the surrounding black soil plains. These mighty reef structures were built up by lime-secreting algae, and, to a much lesser extent, coral organisms.

Today the ranges have eroded into a spectacularly worn landscape honeycombed with caves and gorges. At Geikie Gorge, floodwaters of the Fitzroy River have exposed the jointed, fluted limestone of the old reef and undercut the vertical walls with caves. In the dry season, the banks exposed by the receding floodwaters are favourite basking sites for freshwater crocodiles.

At Windjana Gorge, the Lennard River has cut through the Napier Range to similar effect. High cliffs tower 90 metres above invitingly clear pools. Over centuries, the limestone at the base of the cliffs has dissolved and the water has carved out deep grottoes and caves.

STONE FENCE The remarkably straight natural barrier known as the Wall of China — in fact, a narrow vein of quartz stripped of its sandstone cover — marches across the hills near Halls Creek.

Where the waters of Tunnel Creek cross the Napier Range they have mined the rock to form a mighty natural tunnel 750 metres long and up to 12 metres high. Stalactites hang from the roof of the tunnel except where the overlying rock has collapsed to form a shaft which opens to the sky. Flying foxes use this shaft to gain entry to their roosting sites inside.

Most of this south-western part of the Kimberley is drained by the great Fitzroy River. From its source on the central dome of the Kimberley Plateau, the Fitzroy cuts through deep gorges before flowing southwards across the sandstones, basalts and granites of the King Leopold Ranges. After crossing the limestone belt which includes Geikie Gorge, the Fitzroy is joined by the Lennard and runs out onto a broad series of floodplains.

The eastern Kimberley is dominated by the Ord River and its extensive, rolling floodplain. When the Ord was dammed to provide irrigation water, the resulting lake became the largest man-made body of water in Australia; Lake Argyle boasts nine times the volume of water of Sydney Harbour.

Behind the lake, the terraced profile of the rugged Carr Boyd Ranges rises 450 metres above the surrounding plains. Elsewhere, boulder-strewn mesas and hills give way to jagged ridges and steep-sided ravines.

STORED WATERS The vast waters of Lake Argyle, held in check by the modest Ord River Dam (right), form the largest man-made lake in Australia, with a surface area of more than 740 square kilometres. The early promise of this remote irrigation scheme has yet to be realised.

WATERPROOF The lichen and silica 'skin' on the giant bluffs and domes of the Bungle Bungle Range protects the soft sandstone beneath from complete erosion.

It was in the midst of this rugged landscape that the world's largest known diamond deposit was discovered in the late 1970s. Within a few years of its discovery, the Argyle open-cut mine was producing almost a third of the world's diamonds, more than any other mine or any other country.

On the fringes of the desert, about 150 kilometres south of Halls Creek, is the Wolf Creek crater — the second largest crater in Australia known to have been caused by a meteor. The crater is a circular hole nearly one kilometre across and 50 metres deep. Scientists have estimated that the meteor, some fragments of which have been collected and examined, plunged to earth about 25 million years ago.

But the most remarkable feature of this ancient landscape is the Bungle Bungle Range, a rock massif tucked into the 'elbow' of the Ord River, south of Lake Argyle. This soft sandstone plateau rising 200 metres above the plains has been sculpted into a maze of fragile, beehive-shaped domes and

LUNAR LANDSCAPE The Wolfe Creek crater makes a dramatic scar on the arid plains of the southern Kimberley; enough moisture gathers in the fine sand of its centre to support a grove of scrubby trees.

chiselled gorges resembling a medieval, mud-brick city of the Middle East.

The constantly eroding 'domes' are covered in a skin of alternating bands of orange silica and black lichen. Since its discovery, this extraordinary formation has been safeguarded by the reservation of more than 300 000 hectares of surrounding land as a national park.

The southern parts of the Kimberley are generally drier than the north and on the fringes of the desert annual rainfall may sometimes be as low as 350 millimetres. In the north, the average exceeds 1500 millimetres in places, and in some years as much as 4000 millimetres of rain is estimated to drench the countryside.

Most of the rain falls in the summer, between November and April. Tropical cyclones often bring additional downpours, swelling the rivers until they become raging torrents which engrave valleys and gorges into the landscape and wash vast amounts of soil and sand further downstream. The flow rate of the large rivers at such times has been estimated to exceed 30 000 cubic metres per second.

The patient plants

The fierce, dry heat which follows the 'wet' opens up fissures in the black soil plains and exposes increasingly large areas of dry river bed. By this time, the main flush of plant growth and flowering is over because many plants flower during the wet season, disperse their seed after the rains pass and then become relatively dormant to wait out the long dry season.

Of the 1500 species of plants found in the Kimberley, about 350 are found nowhere else. As in most parts of Australia, the most common species is the eucalyptus, but it is not always the first to be noticed.

The traveller's attention is more likely to be hijacked by the exotic plants of the dry tropics: the delicious scent of the lemonwood (*Dolichandrone heterophylla*), the strange helicopter-shaped fruit of the stinkwood (*Gyrocarpus americanus*) and the swollen baobab (*Adansonia gregorii*).

All around are scrubby woodlands surrounded by tough grasses. On rocky outcrops and on the dry, southern plains the only plant hardy enough to make an impact on the landscape is the spinifex, seemingly impervious to the deprivations which would kill most plants in less than 24 hours.

Majestic and adaptable river red gums (*Eucalyptus camaldulensis*) line the 'Top End' riverbeds just as they

WELL ADAPTED Despite harsh conditions, the bridal tree may grow to ten metres tall.

do the Murray River, thousands of kilometres away to the south-east. Here they are joined by the tropical paperbark tree known as the cajeput (*Melaleuca viridiflora*).

Around river pools, screw pines or pandanus palms (*Pandanus*) thrive on the edges of thickets and the water surface may be covered with floating plants such as goodenias (*Goodenia lamprosperma*) which are superbly adapted to the changing whims of the climate. The goodenia is able to replace its floating leaves with self-supporting leaves on rigid stems as the water dries up from the pools. Here and there, jewel-like pockets of miniature jungle flourish where springs or seepages create permanent dampness.

Around the eroded hills, hardly grand enough to qualify as 'ranges', scattered trees or shrubs, such as the golden-flowered bridal tree (*Xanthostemon paradoxus*), make the most of the small amounts of accumulated soil in

---

The Kimberley's giant 'water bottles'

In 1856, when Augustus Gregory's expedition to the Kimberley came upon the strange bottle-shaped trees that were to be named after its leader, its members concluded that the baobab tree — *Adansonia gregorii* — must have been diseased. How otherwise could a tree have such a swollen trunk and such distorted, arthritic branches?

Baobabs, or boabs as they are often known in Australia, are restricted to the Kimberley region, occuring most commonly on the plains flanking the Fitzroy River and the Ord River and in the limestone hills of the Oscar and Napier Ranges.

The tree often grows specimen-like, in isolated stands, sometimes in 'family groups' with a parent encircled by its offspring. Although it is usually regarded as a plant of the semi-arid zone it is often found in wetter areas in association with rainforest plants.

The baobab tree lives up to its shape by storing huge amounts of water in the soft, fleshy, almost spongy wood of its trunk — a great advantage in the extreme climate of the north. Aborigines are said to have used this water source in times of drought by squeezing moisture out of chunks cut from the trunk.

Baobabs are thought to be very long-lived, with some trees known to be well over 100 years old. The tree's distinguishing feature, its massively bulging trunk, comes in a range of bottle shapes — from long, elegant wine bottles with tapered necks to bulbous carafes — which sometimes leads to confusion with its distant relative, the Queensland bottle tree.

The baobab can grow 20 – 40 metres high, although most trees reach about 12 metres with a girth of 3 metres.

Peculiarly gnarled and twisted branches extend from the silver-grey trunk, heightening its strange appearance, particulary at night, when the bark gleams in the moonlight. In the wet season, large, white-cream flowers spring from the tree's bare branches. The luxuriant, scented flowers are up to ten centimetres wide.

By late summer, the foliage is full grown. Later, the furry, brown fruit forms, and falls to the ground as cricketball-sized seed pods.

Elsewhere, the baobab grows only in Africa and Madagascar and its origins in Australia are difficult to explain. It is possible that baobab seed pods reached Australia by floating on ocean currents, or perhaps the tree is a living remnant of life on the ancient, southern supercontinent of Gondwana.

cracks and crevices. Below, in the valleys, groves of tropical wild almond bushes (*Terminalia*) give out a delicate fragrance.

Like broad sweeps of the Cape York and Arnhem Land coast, the shoreline along much of the Kimberley coast is low, and ill-defined — ideal mangrove country. Broad mangrove belts thrive around the estuaries of rivers like the Prince Regent, the Drysdale and the Ord. And there is not one but nearly 20 species of mangrove here, some with prop roots or buttresses, others with less spectacular knee roots.

The mangrove environment includes many aquatic animals, the numbers and activities of which fluctuate with the tides, but there are few other plants capable of surviving in such a salty zone — mainly lichens, ferns and mistletoe which live on the mangroves themselves.

The landscape of the southern Kimberley becomes progressively drier until it merges into the desert. Open forests and woodlands dominate these lowland plains, whilst the dry backblocks support characteristic scrub land. Sometimes the red sandhills flaunt startling flashes of colour, such as the deep purple flowers of the tinsel plant (*Cyanostegia cyanocalyx*).

A feathered menagerie

The Kimberley plays host to most of the mammals and reptiles that occur all over tropical Australia but its great distinction is the richness and diversity of its bird life.

The region is an ornithologist's delight with more than 200 species recorded on the Mitchell Plateau alone. The list is probably not complete as there are still vast areas of the Kimberley where the wildlife populations have yet to be investigated.

This is the domain of tropical birds — three kinds of ibis, black-necked storks or jabirus (*Ephippiorhynchus asiaticus*), magpie geese (*Anseranas semipalmata*), spoonbills and egrets are all here in noisy profusion. Amidst loud, excited trumpeting, brolgas (*Grus rubicundus*) stage impromptu ballets in celebration of courtship.

At dawn, the stately kori bustard (*Ardeotis kori*) flies out of the scrub and onto the plains where it struts through the grasslands foraging for seeds, fruits and insects. This is one of the few places in Australia where bustards still occur in groups — most of those surviving in pockets of grassland elsewhere lead a lone existence.

MOSQUITO COAST Dense bands of mangroves combine with broad tidal mudflats to discourage seaward exploration of the Kimberley coast.

Up in the trees, a bewildering variety of honeyeaters, often accompanied by silver-crowned friarbirds (*Philemon argenticeps*) — noisily feed on nectar and insects. They share the trees with rainbow lorikeets (*Trichoglossus haematodus*) orioles (*Oriolus*), great bowerbirds (*Chlamydera nuchalis*), little corellas (*Cacatua pastinator*) and cockatoos (*Cacatua galerita*).

Grass seed-heads are busily probed by a rainbow-coloured collection of pretty and inquisitive finches. On the ground, the rarely seen black grass-wren (*Amytornis housei*) runs and skips about amongst the sandstone boulders and the spinifex. White-quilled rock-pigeons (*Petrophassa albipennis*), disturbed as they feed on fallen figs, take noisy flight and return to their rock-ledge roosts.

Around streams and river pools, the purple-crowned fairy-wren (*Malurus coronatus*) lives amongst the pandanus palms together with blue-winged kookaburras (*Dacelo leachii*) and the fleet azure kingfisher (*Alcedo azurea*) which flashes its vivid colours as it darts over the water. Hollows in the riverside trees provide nesting sites for large populations of fearless and noisy red-winged parrots (*Aprosmictus erythropterus*) and striated pardalotes (*Pardalotus striatus*). □

LOVE NEST The bowerbird's bower is intended to be an irresistible attraction to females.

273

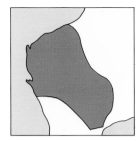

The north-west is best known for its vast mineral deposits and offshore oil, but its ancient landscape harbours many little known natural attractions, from the rock-like living fossils of Shark Bay to the lush oases of the Fortescue River

The broad, iron shoulder of the west

LIVING FOSSILS The stromatolites of Shark Bay are built up by layers of algae that have existed in this form for thousands of millions of years.

The broad shoulder of land that stretches from the north-western coast of Western Australia down to the salt lakes and goldfields deep in the interior provides a cross-section view of Australia's largest state.

At the northern extremity are the spectacular Pilbara and Carnarvon coastlines; southwards, in the region between the wheat belt and the desert country to the north-east, is the rest of the Pilbara and the Murchison and Gascoyne areas; and at the southern extremity the goldfields and the salt-lake plains reach down towards the Nullarbor.

The 'north-west', as Western Australians sometimes describe everything north of Geraldton, is used more accurately to describe the Pilbara region which sits astride the most westerly part of the continent. The Pilbara is an area larger than Victoria and stretches from the wide valley of the Fortescue River in the south to the rocky bed of the De Grey River in the north.

This is arid country, where a strong regional identity is tied to broad landscapes of gentle slopes and valley plains clothed in golden spinifex. There are scrub vistas of harsh mulga baking under sun-filled skies and deep, ochre-red gorges and ridges formed by some of the oldest exposed rock on earth.

As if this strange hinterland, mostly unknown to Europeans until a little over 100 years ago, was not enough, it is bordered by a rugged and beautiful coastline which abounds with plants and animals that scientists are just beginning to understand.

Underlying this varied landscape are ancient rocks containing huge outcrops of granite, near the Fortescue River, and covered in places with layers of soil laid down as water-borne sediments when this region was part of a primeval seabed. The older rocks are rich in minerals such as iron, manganese, asbestos, copper, tin, tantalum, and gold, while the younger soils along the western margins of the Great Western Plateau bear commercial quantities of oil.

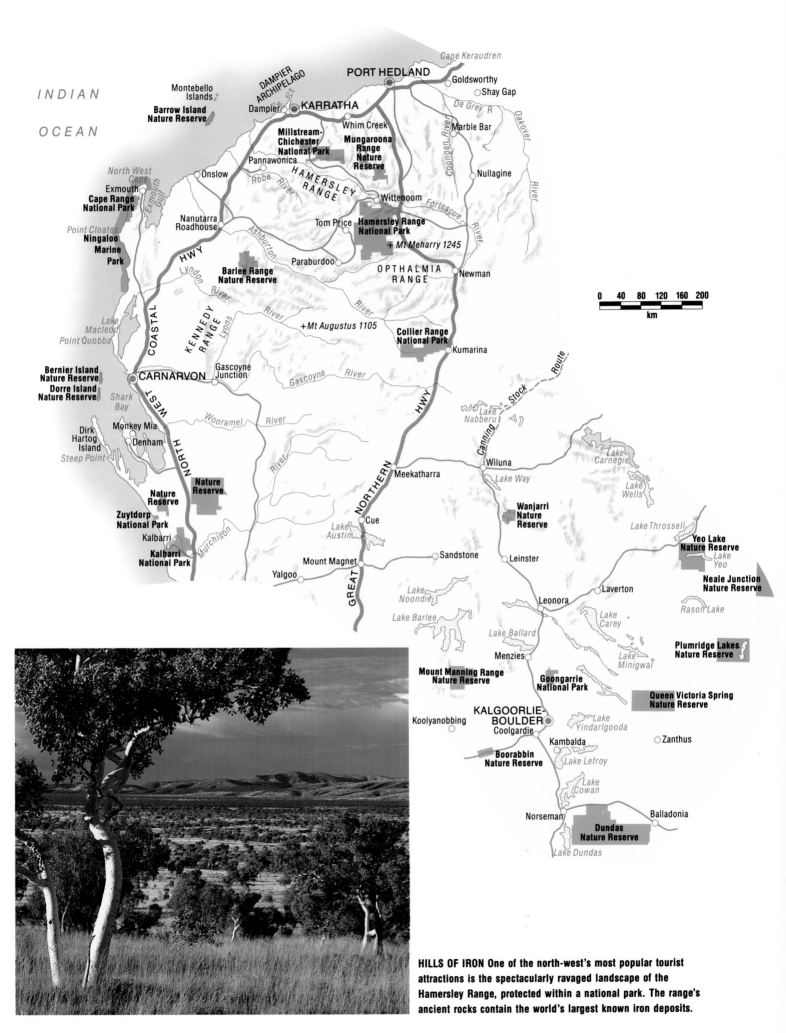

INDIAN

OCEAN

DAMPIER
ARCHIPELAGO

PORT HEDLAND

Montebello
Islands

Goldsworthy

Shay Gap

**Barrow Island
Nature Reserve**

Dampier ⊙ **KARRATHA**

De Grey R

Whim Creek

Marble Bar

Oakover River

**Millstream-
Chichester
National Park**

**Mungaroona
Range
Nature
Reserve**

Onslow

Pannawonica

HAMERSLEY
RANGE

Coongan River

Robe River

Nullagine

Wittenoom

River

North West
Cape

Exmouth

Fortescue

**Cape Range
National Park**

Nanutarra
Roadhouse

Ashburton

Tom Price

**Hamersley Range
National Park**

Point Cloates

**Ningaloo
Marine
Park**

Paraburdoo

+Mt Meharry 1245

River

**Barlee Range
Nature Reserve**

OPTHALMIA
RANGE

Newman

Lyndon River

KENNEDY
RANGE

Lyons River

+Mt Augustus 1105

Lake
Macleod

HWY

COASTAL

Point Quobba

River

**Collier Range
National Park**

0 40 80 120 160 200
km

**Bernier Island
Nature Reserve**

CARNARVON

Gascoyne
Junction

Kumarina

**Dorre Island
Nature Reserve**

Shark
Bay

Gascoyne River

Route

WEST

Wooramel River

Stock

Lake
Nabberu

Lake
Carnegie

Dirk
Hartog
Island

Monkey Mia

Denham

NORTH

Canning

Wiluna

Steep Point

River

Meekatharra

Lake Way

Lake
Wells

**Nature
Reserve**

Murchison

**Nature
Reserve**

NORTHERN

Cue

**Wanjarri
Nature
Reserve**

Lake Throssell

**Zuytdorp
National Park**

Lake
Austin

**Yeo Lake
Nature Reserve**

Kalbarri

Sandstone

Leinster

Lake
Yeo

**Kalbarri
National Park**

Mount Magnet

**Neale Junction
Nature Reserve**

Yalgoo

HWY

Laverton

Rason Lake

GREAT

Lake
Noondie

Leonora

Lake
Carey

**Plumridge Lakes
Nature Reserve**

Lake Barlee

Lake Ballard

Lake
Minigwal

Menzies

**Queen Victoria Spring
Nature Reserve**

**Mount Manning Range
Nature Reserve**

**Goongarrie
National Park**

**KALGOORLIE-
BOULDER**

Lake
Yindarlgooda

Zanthus

Koolyanobbing

Coolgardie

Kambalda

**Boorabbin
Nature Reserve**

Lake Lefroy

Lake
Cowan

Norseman

Balladonia

**Dundas
Nature Reserve**

Lake Dundas

HILLS OF IRON One of the north-west's most popular tourist
attractions is the spectacularly ravaged landscape of the
Hamersley Range, protected within a national park. The range's
ancient rocks contain the world's largest known iron deposits.

In the Pilbara, the goldfields, like those of the Kimberley to the north, include quartzite 'reefs' and the alluvial traces washed from them. At Marble Bar, where Australia's highest temperatures are recorded, the 'bar' is not of marble but quartzite-based jasper, a colourful ridge of which runs across the generally dry bed of the Coongan River.

All of the Pilbara rivers are ephemeral: after cyclonic summer rains the watercourses flood, soon bursting their banks and spreading across the plains. When the floodwaters recede, they leave debris washed into tree forks many kilometres away from the seasonal rivers.

For most of the year the riverbeds are dry, with occasional waterholes and pools within the cool, shaded gorges of the ranges which provide welcome relief for wildlife.

The Fortescue is an ancient river which winds through an almost biblical landscape, its waters soaking through the sub-soil to feed the most important aquifer in the Pilbara. At Millstream, in the Fortescue River valley, a series of pools are topped up with fresh spring-water from an underground basin of saturated limestone which extends for more than 200 square kilometres.

This natural underground reservoir

HAMERSLEY PROSPECT Mount Bruce — at 1235 metres one of the highest peaks in Western Australia — faces the main ridge of the Hamersley Range across the valley.

PILBARA WATERS During the 'wet', the Fortesque River runs muddily for 600 kilometres to the coast.

has been tapped to supply water for coastal towns and iron-ore treatment plants in the north. As with the Great Artesian Basin in the east (see p. 338), there are fears that the constant pumping of artesian water to the surface will eventually cause the Millstream 'oasis' to dry up.

The Millstream pools, in the Millstream–Chichester National Park (199 730 hectares), water a variety of habitats with vegetation ranging from spinifex hummock grassland to a dense, closed forest of magnificent cajeputs (*Melaleuca leucadendron*). Here too are river red gums, heath and sedgeland, and the Millstream fan-palm (*Livistona alfredii*). More than 100 species of birds live here, as well as flying foxes, red kangaroos, frogs and reptiles, and the air is abuzz with the jerky movement of more than 30 kinds of dragonfly.

The Fortescue is fed by streams which rise on the Hamersley Range and cut spectacular gorges into the red rock as they flow to the plains below and eventually find their way into the river. The range is the highest part of Western Australia, where the state's highest mountain, Mount Meharry (1251 metres) rises modestly above other purple, flat-topped hills.

Millions of years ago, ancient seas deposited beds of iron-bearing jaspilite and dolomite in this region, and since then these layers of material have been pushed up, folded, and finally, eroded, to produce a worn and rutted landscape with little vegetation but a great deal of grandeur. There are, of course, green patches where the water gathers.

Small, cascading waterfalls tumble into gorges to fill sheltered pools where ferns, palms and paperbarks create pockets of lush growth amidst spinifex and mulga. Near-vertical walls at Red Gorge, Knox Gorge and Joffre Falls — in the Hamersley Range National Park (617 606 hectares) — cast shadows into the cool depths for most of the day.

At Dale, Yampire and Wittenoom Gorges the weathered rock faces reveal bands of blue fibre asbestos. The fire-resistant material was mined at Wittenoom for more than twenty years before its toxic qualities became apparent.

WATER POWER The deep gorges which cut into the Hamersley Range's northern scarp are still being formed; Joffre Falls is at the head of Joffre Gorge, a 'tributary' of the Wittenoom Gorge.

The Hamersley Range provides a perfect habitat for one of the world's most unusual plants. The iron plant (*Astrotricha hamptonii*) eschews the meagre soil at the bottom of gorges and ravines and between rows of hills, choosing to put down its roots in solid rock which has a high content of high-grade iron ore. The shrub's tall, slender stems may be seen rising from inhospitable rock faces as its roots worm their way into cracks and crevices to find support and shelter from the sun.

Mulga scrub is the most common Pilbara vegetation. Scattered around beneath the mulga are various eremophilas and cassias and colourful annuals such as mullamulla (*Ptilotus exaltatus*) and the ubiquitous everlasting daisy (*Helichrysum, Helipterum*).

Cork trees (*Hakea suberea*), the aromatic sandalwood (*Santalum spicatum*) and the quandong (*S. acuminatum*) — both of which are semi-parasitic, tapping into the roots of other plants — break the monotony of the mulga vegetation. Watercourses are trimmed with narrow lines of attendant river red gums (*Eucalyptus camaldulensis*) and cajeputs (*Melaleuca leucadendron*), forming green, shady avenues; further south these trees fade into thickets of wattles (*Acacia citrinoviridis*) and shrubby melaleucas.

The spinifex which dominates the sandy areas of the north-west has its own specific population of birds and animals. The spinifex bird (*Eremiornis carteri*), the spinifex or plumed pigeon (*Geophaps plumifera*) — one of the

OFTEN DRY Yardie Creek is the major recipient of the meagre run-off from the Cape Range, along the eastern side of Exmouth Gulf.

most frequently sighted birds of the Pilbara — the jewelled gecko (*Diplodactylus elderi*) and the spinifex hopping-mouse (*Notomys alexis*) all lead lives which revolve around this particular plant and its environment.

Between spinifex clumps, the recently discovered pebble-mound mouse (*Pseudomys chapmani*) digs its shallow burrow and tops it with a mound of carefully selected small stones up to 50 centimetres high. Another mammal unknown to science until the 1980s, is the tiny Pilbara ningaui (*Ningaui timealeyi*), an aggressive and carnivorous marsupial, which, at just over five centimetres in length, is often smaller than its hapless prey.

In the mulga country of the southern Pilbara, mulga parrots (*Psephotus varius*) gather in vivid displays of

SUN DRIED On the Chichester Range — north of, and parallel to the Hamersley Range — the climate and the thin soil combine to form an environment where little other than grass hummocks will grow.

colour. Babblers, chats and treecreepers forage busily in the early morning and at dusk, while honeyeaters seek out the cascading blooms of the white dragon tree (*Sesbania formosa*) which fringes and shades the artesian soaks. Australia's largest lizard, the perentie (*Varanus giganteus*), sometimes reaching more than two metres in length, is the major predator here.

The iron-ore coast

To the north of the Fortescue River lies the Chichester Range, a volcanic tableland which overlooks vast, alluvial plains which are swept by a tide of wildflowers after good winter rains. Towards the coast, the rivers boast barramundi and mudcrabs, and the broad, coastal mudflats — the result of huge tidal variations — come alive in autumn with large flocks of visiting wading birds — sandpipers, stints, plovers, knots, tattlers, godwits and turnstones.

At Port Hedland and Dampier, huge bulk carriers load iron ore from the Newman and Tom Price mines in the Hamersleys. Karratha is another major industrial centre, one of many where growth is inextricably tied to the north-west's oil and mineral boom which began just over 30 years ago with the discovery of oil at Rough Range.

The tropical waters of the north-west coast have been little disturbed by man and abound with marlin, sailfish, Spanish mackerel, sharks and rays, turtles and sea-snakes. On the islands of the Dampier Archipelago, intriguing galleries of rock art depict the euros, rock-wallabies, jabirus, reptiles and sea creatures with which the local Aboriginal tribes co-existed.

HIGH TIDE The range of the tide along Barrow Island's limestone coastline is indicated by the section of rock discoloured by marine growths.

DOLPHIN BAY The diet of the dolphins which visit the fish-breeding grounds of Shark Bay is augmented by handouts from humans.

Other islands off the Western Australian coast now serve as the last refuge for animals and plants which became extinct on the mainland with the spread of European settlement.

One of the best known island sanctuaries is Barrow Island, the site of an active oil field and home to the widest range of animals of these islands. Further south, near Exmouth, the Cape Range peninsula, within the Cape Range National Park (50 581 hectares), and Ningaloo Reef, within the Ningaloo Marine Park (430 000 hectares), are both a biologist's treasure trove.

The rugged, waterless limestone of Cape Range shelters the shy black-footed rock-wallaby (*Petrogale lateralis*) and protects a rich fossil record, which is hidden deep within the colourful cliffs. The peninsula's sandy beaches and lagoons are flanked by the Ningaloo Reef which stretches almost unbroken for 250 kilometres just offshore (see box). This little known reef system contains more than 200 types of coral, 600 species of mollusc and 500 species of fish, and is a busy feeding ground for marine mammals such as dugongs, bottle-nosed dolphins and various whales.

Still further south, near Carnarvon, the bays, inlets and islands of Shark Bay boast many attractions which are more readily accessible to the visitor than the ranges of the inland.

DUTCH PLUCK These cliffs failed to deter the Dutchman Dirk Hartog, who sailed to the other side of the island now named after him to make the first European landing in Australia.

MARINELAND Nutrients enter the already rich waters of Shark Bay through the Gascoyne River estuary.

Dirk Hartog Island, which straddles the entrance to Shark Bay, is the site of the first recorded European landing in Australia. Its northern tip, named Cape Inscription after Dirk Hartog's famous pewter plate, nailed to a tree there in October 1616, is the mainland's westernmost extremity.

The seas of this region are home to the dugong or sea cow (*Dugong dugon*), a gentle and inquisitive vegetarian mammal which thrives on the extensive seagrass meadows of the warm coastal waters. The dugong was once exploited commercially for its oil which was considered to have special curative properties. It is now a protected species, although Aborigines may still kill the animal for food.

At Monkey Mia on the Peron Peninsula, wild bottle-nosed dolphins (*Tursiops truncatus*) make daily visits to the shore, where they mingle with tourists who wade into the shallows to feed and pat these friendly mammals with the natural grin.

The living fossils

The north-west's most unusual natural feature are enigmatic living fossils which occur in greater numbers here than anywhere else in the world. The stromatolites which live in the warm, inter-tidal waters of Hamelin Pool, the eastern branch of Shark Bay, represent a simple form of life which has remained unchanged for at least 3000 million years.

These club-shaped mounds, which resemble nothing more than lumps of volcanic rock, rise up from the sand and the mud, sometimes more than a metre tall, in colonies of several thou-

Ningaloo, or the unknown Great Western Reef

One of Australia's best kept secrets is the coral reef system off its western coast, thousands of kilometres from the famous Great Barrier Reef flanking the eastern coast.

Although only an eighth the size of the Barrier Reef, the Ningaloo Reef is still a major reef in world terms, stretching for 250 kilometres along the sandy coast between Cape Farquhar and North West Cape, near Exmouth.

Unlike its better known counterpart on the other side of the continent, Ningaloo is, to all intents and purposes, a single reef which clings modestly to the Western Australian coastline, sometimes growing only a hundred metres or so from land. This proximity is due to the edge of the continental shelf being particularly close to shore along this coast.

The reef is irresistibly accessible, especially when compared with the two-hour boat trip that separates most parts of the Great Barrier Reef from the east coast. Some of its most spectacular attractions are only a short dinghy ride from shore.

Life on the western reef is every bit as varied and abundant as in the east, with more than 200 species of coral continually building and extending a habitat that is home to at least 500 varieties of fish, more than 600 types of molluscs and 90 echinoderms (spiny-skinned creatures such as starfish).

Dugongs, hump-backed whales and other marine mammals live and feed around the reef, while rare whale sharks circle its outer reaches.

The coral colonies are positioned in the optimum place — near the edge of the continental shelf — to receive a regular and never-ending food supply of tiny, plankton-like organisms. These microscopic creatures are carried by the huge ocean swells that crash over the edge of the reef. The colourful reef system of today rests on the accumulated calcium remains of successive generations of corals and their dependent creatures.

The accessibility that makes Ningaloo so attractive, also makes the protection of its fragile environment particularly important. Ningaloo was not declared a park until 1987, by which time it was well known to tourists. As the numbers of visitors continues to increase environmentalists fear for the reef's future.

Like the Barrier Reef too, Ningaloo has its natural problems. Here the problem is not crown-of-thorns starfish but a marine snail called drupella. The same year that the marine park was declared, a survey of Ningaloo revealed extensive coral damage to at least half the reef by the snails. The explosion in the snail population is believed to be controllable and scientists hope eventually to curb their numbers.

sand. Like a coral reef, the stromatolites are built up by tiny living organisms which eventually die and are replaced by a new generation so that a columnar structure where only the surface is alive is gradually built up.

The microscopic algae which form the living surface trap similarly microscopic sediments which are washed in with the tides and bind them together with a secretion of lime. Eventually the sediment forms into a thin limestone layer and the algae begins to build a new layer on top.

At the broad entrance to Shark Bay, Bernier Island and Dorre Island provide refuges for the Western barred bandicoot (*Perameles bougainville*) and the banded hare-wallaby (*Lagostrophus fasciatus*), both of which are now extinct on the mainland. White-bellied sea eagles (*Haliaeetus leucogaster*), ospreys (*Pandion haliaetus*) and other birds of the sea ride the winds as they patrol the skies in a constant search for prey in the aquamarine waters below.

Carnarvon is the major regional centre here, where tropical fruit growing, cattle grazing, and fishing and prawning are the main industries. Carnarvon lies at the mouth of the Gascoyne River, the second largest river in the state. Like the rivers of the Channel Country, thousands of kilometres to the east, it has a vast catchment area — nearly 80 000 square kilometres — but its flow is infrequent and irregular.

The arid, sandy hinterland between the coast and the deserts of the interior supports a profusion of wildflowers among the scrub. Spinifex pigeons, zebra finches, honeyeaters and emus forage amongst the vegetation while noisy flocks of budgerigars wheel overhead, alternately flashing green and yellow as the sun's rays highlight their bright plumage.

Inland from Carnarvon, just north of the Gascoyne River, the flat and bare plateau of the Kennedy Range rises above the mulga-scrub plains. Locked within the layers of limestone and sandstone are myriad fossils from ancient seabeds, while the creatures of another age — reptiles and small marsupials — scurry above.

Further south, in the Kalbarri National Park (186 071 hectares), the Murchison River cuts through sandplains of wildflowers, carving deep gorges through multi-coloured cliffs. In many places, where the cliff faces descend in steep, narrow steps, small groups of destructive feral goats clatter over the

KALBARRI CLIFF The same sandstone that forms the massive cliffs along the Kalbarri National Park coast has been eroded into equally spectacular gorges further inland.

rocks. As they pass, they consume and trample the vegetation which binds the soil, and cause miniature landslides as their hooves dislodge stones.

Where the river runs through less rugged country, the acacias, melaleucas and grevilleas on the hills above its course contrast with the large, spreading river red gums growing along the water's edge. These gums provide vital nesting hollows for birds and possums. Branch stumps, left when branches die or break, eventually rot away inside, leaving dry nesting hollows for corellas, galahs, cockatiels and rosellas.

More than 170 species of birds have been observed in the Kalbarri park, together with at least 50 kinds of reptiles and numerous small mammals, including the delightful honey-possum (*Tarsipes rostratus*).

PLAIN'S END The size of the cliffs that erupt so abruptly to form the edge of the Kennedy Range can be judged by comparing them with the mulga trees on the plain below.

The vast, red earth plains of the Murchison River region, representing the combined drainage basins of the Gascoyne and the Murchison, measure about 500 kilometres from north to south and extend inland for nearly 700 kilometres. Low, rocky hills and intermittently flowing rivers occasionally break the even, unchanging landscape of mulga (*Acacia aneura*) vegetation.

The grey-green mulga, which may grow to seven metres in height, tends to grow in even-aged groves which regenerate in cycles after fire or drought, so that there is little variation in the height of the tree cover. Mulga has many devices to deal with drought — its leaves are tough and reflect a large percentage of the sun's heat; it stops growing during mid-summer when conditions are driest; and its foliage and rough bark channel rainfall into the soil above the roots so that the most efficient use is made of what water there is.

Mulga forms low, open woodlands over huge areas of inland Australia; in Western Australia its southern limit coincides with the 'Menzies', or mulga-eucalypt line, which extends from Shark Bay in a roughly south-easterly direction towards the town of Menzies, just north of Kalgoorlie. This imaginary line represents the transition from the erratic summer rainfall of the state's north, to the more reliable winter rainfall of the south, where the tougher mulga is replaced by eucalypt woodlands.

Salt lakes and goldfields

Between the arid, sandy deserts of the inland and the cultivated wheat belt of the south lie the salt-lake and goldfield regions. While this semi-arid landscape may, to the casual traveller, exhibit a monotonous sameness, closer scrutiny reveals more variety than might be expected. There is a host of terrains and plant communities, with the changes in the landscape and vegetation being so gradual that, at first, they may not be noticed.

Woodlands are the most widespread type of vegetation and although eucalypt trees dominate, there is usually a mixture of species. Around Kalgoorlie, where eucalypts and mulga mix, the vegetation has been thinned out considerably since settlement: timber has been cut for firewood, the salmon gum trunks felled for pit props above gold mines and the mulga used for fodder.

Plant communities throughout the region contain a mixture of wheat belt and desert species, with occasional local 'specialities' such as the bookleaf

ALMOST RIGHT On closer inspection, this 'marble' at Marble Bar was found to be an outcrop of jasper.

OCEAN BOUND Near the coast, the Murchison River makes a dramatic drop to sea level through the 80-kilometre-long Murchison Gorge.

mallee (*Eucalyptus kruseana*). The shrubby under-storey, beneath the tall eucalypts, includes species of acacia, grevillea, melaleuca and the poverty bush (*Eremophila*). Around the salt lakes, samphires (*Arthrocnemum*), saltbush (*Atriplex*) and bluebush (*Maireana*) form hardy colonies in an environment where most living organisms would soon wither and die.

The north–south chains of salt lakes which dominate local areas are sometimes connected by ill-defined channels; these are all that remain of an extinct river system which drained the plateau before it was uplifted and the climate became drier.

The flat landscape is one of broad, alluvial valley floors and weathered plains interrupted by ridges, low hills and granite outcrops. These landmarks represent erosion-resistant forms of basalt such as those that occur at Kambalda and Kalgoorlie and contain nickel and gold.

The natural aridity of the inland does not encourage a great diversity of large mammals, and, as with most such regions, reptiles and birds are the most numerous inhabitants. Species such as the western yellow robin (*Eopsaltria griseogularis*) and the elegant grass-parrot (*Neophema elegans*), are near the extremity of their range, as the country to the east is too dry to support them. □

Across the rolling plains west of the Darling Range, a rich assortment of native plants takes second place to the belt of golden grass which produces almost one-third of Australia's wheat crop

Bushland bows out to a sea of wheat

East of Perth, beyond the jarrah forests of the Darling Range, the broad, crescent-shaped wheat belt acts as a buffer between the major population centres and farming districts of the south-west and the arid lands that lie to the east.

The strongly agricultural character of the region reflects climatic conditions rather than the nature of the terrain: the seemingly endless plains which are so well-suited to the growing of wheat extend into the regions which flank the wheat belt. To the west, the high rainfall of the jarrah forest at the foot of the Darling Range disqualifies cereal crops, while the drier landscapes of the east ultimately defeat any attempt at agriculture not far short of the salt-lakes region.

As the wheat belt spread out from its beginnings on the western margins of the region, extensive clearing and cultivation removed the original vegetation to the extent that it persists only in a few reserves, on road verges, rocky outcrops and other patches of uncleared land.

The result is a mosaic where the yellow-brown background of the immense wheatfields is studded with a thriving variety of isolated plant habitats embracing woodlands, shrublands and heaths. As elsewhere in the west, they burst into spectacular displays of wildflowers in the springtime.

The richness of the plants in a region often described by scientists as one of the most remarkable expanses of impoverished soils in the entire temperate zone is yet another example of the extraordinary adaptability of Australia's native vegetation.

BUSHLAND BELT The terrain near Paynes Find is typical of the eastern wheat belt — semi-arid plains filled briefly with a flush of wildflowers after winter or early spring rains and broken occasionally by enormous outcrops of ancient, eroded granite (right).

BEFORE AND AFTER At Dongara, near Geraldton, the neat symmetry of ploughed paddocks compliments the fields where the wheat is already on its way to maturity.

The wheat belt is dominated by sand-plains which are the end result of an almost incalculable number of years of weathering of a granite plateau. Successive erosion by wind, rain and sun, together with prehistoric earth movements have resulted in a landscape with two distinct geological levels: the old granite plateau which is composed of some of the continent's most ancient rocks and is conspicuous throughout the eastern wheat belt, and the lower, 'new' plateau of younger sedimentary rocks in the north-west.

The erosion of these layers between Geraldton and Northampton — a million year's accumulation of microscopic sediments in an ancient sea — has sculpted a vast panorama of low, flat-topped hills and wide, flat valleys.

Long, hot, dry summers and warm winters are the rule here, and they are the explanation for the overwhelming success of wheat as the dominant crop. Westwards, the landscape is greener and the hills become more rugged.

In the east, the gently undulating, brown landscape is overlooked by occasional low, laterite-capped hills. Further into the interior, shallow salt lakes are all that remain of once extensive river systems. Only exceptionally heavy rains fill the complex pattern of salt

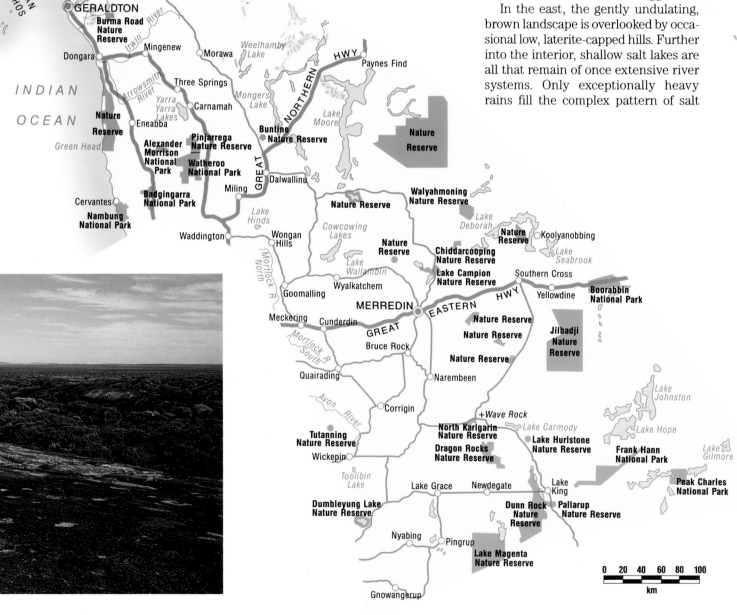

lakes, creeks and 'lost' rivers, linking them with permanent rivers such as the Moore and the Avon.

The wheat belt's annual average rainfall varies between 300 and 650 millimetres, most of it falling in the winter months. Correspondingly, the vegetation of the region has adapted with conspicuous success to low rainfall and long summer droughts.

A rich botanical mix

Although largely cleared of natural vegetation, the wheat belt still contains one of the highest concentrations of rare and localised native plants in Australia. Biologists are intrigued by this rich variety of plants and are attempting to find out why it should have occurred here.

Along the western margins of the region, the jarrah forests are gradually replaced by woodlands of wandoo (*Eucalyptus wandoo*) and York gum (*E. loxophleba*). The oddly-named raspberry jam (*Acacia acuminata*), the freshly cut wood of which has a raspberry-like aroma, often grows in company with the York gum.

Powder-bark wandoo (*E. accedens*) has colonised the gravelly hills of this area. The brown mallet (*E. astringens*) is common in the wandoo woodlands, particularly in the Dryandra State Forest, while a variety of other mallets grow throughout the wheat belt, often appearing as dense clumps of saplings after fire has destroyed the mature trees but not their seeds.

Standing above all the others — in size and attractiveness — is the salmon gum (*E. salmonophloia*) which is the most typical tree of the wheat belt. Its smooth-barked, pastel-hued trunk sup-

WANDOO DUST The outer layer of the powder-bark wandoo's bark is covered with a fine, dusty powder. The tree thrives in stony soils and dry conditions.

ports a generous canopy which may reach 25 metres above ground. Other eucalypts common throughout the wheat belt are stunted by comparison with the grand salmon gum.

Where the woodlands fade away, the mallee heaths and open heaths of the wheat belt, known locally as 'sandplain' heath, abound with low shrubs and wildflowers. Because the vegetation cover is low and unspectacular, the casual observer might dismiss these patches as barren and lacking in interest, but the botanical richness of the heaths is comparable with any other such areas in the world.

WATER DOMES The granite outcrops, or inselbergs which dot the plains are natural water catchments; early settlers built low walls to trap their run-off.

MESA MOUNT Mount Lesueur is an almost-circular mesa, but unlike the red, rocky outcrops of the outback it is covered in vegetation. Such relatively moist upland areas support plants which are extinct elsewhere.

East of Jurien Bay, on the northern sandplain between Perth and Kalbarri, the Mount Lesueur region has more than 800 plant species, a large number of which are found nowhere else and several of which are rare and endangered. This region also supports more than 120 species of birds, nearly 50 species of reptiles, and a variety of mammals and frogs which may be seen in the Mount Lesueur Reserves (13 500 hectares).

The wheat belt still rings to the cheerful but discordant screeching of noisy flocks of red-tailed and white-tailed black cockatoos (*Calyptorhynchus banksii, C. latirostris*), although their numbers are declining as the forests and woodlands which provide their food and nesting hollows are gradually cleared.

In the north, large, mixed flocks of long-billed and little corellas (*Cacatua tenuirostris, C. pastinator*) carpet the ground wherever they settle for a day's feeding. Sometimes they are accompanied by small groups of spectacularly attractive pink Major Mitchell cockatoos (*C. leadbeateri*).

The weathering of the wheat belt's old granite plateau has produced isolated outcrops of erosion-resistant rock called inselbergs. Many of these occur in groups of large granite domes, 60 metres or more high. Some stand alone as exposed platforms while others,

such as the famous Wave Rock, near Hyden, have been undercut by erosion into wave-like, overhanging cliffs.

Wave Rock, like a giant ocean wave frozen in motion, has been rendered even more watery in its appearance by colonies of tiny algae which have formed vertical streaks on the 'wave' face. The black, living algae and the brown, dead algae contribute to the continuing process of surface erosion.

The erosion of the surface of these stone outcrops has created crevices and depressions which collect moisture, dust and scraps of dead plants and other organic material, providing an environment where plants can take root. Early European settlers realised that the inselbergs acted as water catchments, and the remnants of their hand-built retaining walls can still be seen on top of granite outcrops near some settlements.

South-east of Wave Rock Reserve, the Frank Hann National Park (61 420 hectares) protects a variety of rare sandplain flowers. The spectacular red rapier feather-flower (*Verticordia mitchelliana*) is just one among those which no longer occur on the sandplains within the farming region.

Green and tough

The plants which colonise the soil pockets of inselbergs and those which grow around them have to tolerate a harsh and changeable environment. Of the wheat belt's trees, only the she-oak (*Casuarina huegeliana*) and the gungurru (*Eucalyptus caesia*) make a decent showing here.

GOLD TAIL The female red-tailed black cockatoo has no red colouring at all but is gold instead.

STILL LIFE Wave Rock's 'wave' is 15 metres high; the dome behind reaches almost 60 metres.

More modest plants such as paper-barks, bottlebrushes and wattles find themselves quite at home, while a multitude of tiny ferns, mosses, orchids, trigger plants, lichens and miniature daisies inhabit the crevices of the granite domes. Small lilies known as pin-cushions (*Borya*), which become dry and brittle during their summer dormancy, are almost instantly resurrected with soft, green leaves and white flowers when the first rains arrive.

Around the salt lakes — a chain of which are incorporated into the Lake Magenta Reserve, the largest of the wheat belt nature reserves — there are carpets of pink, white and yellow everlasting daisies, orchids, wattles, grevilleas, cassias and the uncoordinated 'committee plant'. Bluebush, salt-bush and samphire occupy the bare, salty flats, with ancient grass trees

ROCK TREE The tough gungurru eucalypt survives in the crevices of inselbergs.

HARD CUSHIONS Mossy beds of pincushions dry out in spring and are dormant in summer.

(*Xanthorrhoea*) sending up their antennae-like spikes around the shores.

During the heat of the day, clumps of shrubs or trees provide welcome shade for western grey kangaroos (*Macropus fuliginosus*) and western brush wallabies (*M. irma*) which have no fear of human competition in these parts. In the branches, the hardy, common brushtail possum (*Trichosurus vulpecula*) waits until dusk to begin its energetic foraging but the tiny pygmy-possums (*Cercartetus concinnus*) and honey-possums (*Tarsipes rostratus*) may occasionally be glimpsed darting about seeking nectar in the heat of the day while the petals of flowers are fully extended.

The Lake Grace–Lake Chinocup Nature Reserve (20 000 hectares), five kilometres south of Lake Grace, provides an oasis for thousands of water-fowl. Dumbleyung Lake, a large, saline lake, is considered one of the most im-

PLAINS FLOWER Shrubs such as the colourful *Grevillea pterosperma* replace trees on the sandplains.

portant wetlands in the south-west of Western Australia. Large rafts of ducks and diving birds occupy its open waters, while the rare freckled duck (*Stictonetta naevosa*) and the equally uncommon blue-billed duck (*Oxyura australis*) find shelter amongst dead trees and low-growing samphire plants.

Nearby Toolibin Lake provides a more sheltered habitat but its freshwater expanses disappear in dry years. When the rains have been generous, it supports large numbers of breeding waterbirds including the yellow-billed spoonbill (*Platalea flavipes*), the hardhead (*Aythya australis*) and the musk duck (*Biziura lobata*).

Towering sandstone and limestone cliffs interrupted by long stretches of sandy beach characterise the seaboard around Geraldton, where the wheat reaches the coast. The Geraldton wax tree (*Chamelaucium uncinatum*), one of the first Western Australian plants to be cultivated, grows in dense thickets in the beach dunes.

OFFSHORE The Houtman Abrolhos Islands mark the limits of the prehistoric coastline.

About sixty kilometres offshore are the Houtman Abrolhos islands, a chain of islands and reefs stretching for 80 kilometres along the edge of the Rottnest Shelf. The reefs are well out of the tropics and as such they are the world's largest coral system so far south.

The profusion of the coral reefs — there are about 80 different types of coral here — is supported by the warm water of the Leeuwin current which drifts southwards along the continental shelf. The islands have been built up from accumulations of coral fragments and sand on the underlying limestone platform which was part of the mainland before the sea level rose.

The Houtman Abrolhos are a breeding stronghold for seabirds. Huge colonies of terns, gulls, shearwaters and noddies gather here to roost. Ospreys (*Pandion haliaetus*) and white-bellied sea eagles (*Haliaeetus leucogaster*) are also seen throughout the archipelago.

Further south, in the Nambung National Park, thousands of limestone pillars up to four metres high rise out of a stark, sandy landscape like surrealistic tombstones. These peculiar shapes were formed underground when rainwater seeping from above dissolved lime in the rock and cemented shafts of sand together into columns. Only recently — in the last 200 years or so — have the columns been exposed as wind removes the overlying dunes. □

SHIFTING SANDS The winds which uncovered the pillars of the 400-hectare Pinnacles Desert continue to shift the surrounding sand and alter the shape of the landscape.

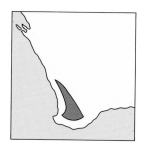
Almost parallel zones of rich eucalypt forest and woodland provide a buffer between Australia's fertile south-west corner and the increasingly dry plateau which stretches for thousands of kilometres into the interior

Twin forests along the fault line

The thickly forested Darling Range rises up behind the city of Perth, providing a backdrop to the city's setting not unlike that which occurs in Sydney, where the Blue Mountains blur the western horizon.

The 'ranges' — and the other highland regions which sweep southwards to the Porongurup Range near Albany — are in fact the southern edge, and the highest part,

of the generally low scarp of the Great Western Plateau which extends over most of Western Australia.

The Great Western Plateau rests directly on top of the thick layer of ancient rocks, laid down about 300 million years ago, which provides Australia's foundations. The south-western edge of this shield is an equally ancient fault line in the earth's surface which appears as a weathered escarpment — the Darling Range — rising up to 300 metres behind the Swan River plain and extending north-south for about 320 kilometres.

The western region of the plateau is a vast catchment area which channels its meagre resources towards the 'ranges' flanking the coast. Most of Western Australia's major rivers rise here and cut their way through the scarp to water the plains below. The bulk of the plateau is a rainshadow area and the upland regions gradually fade into the arid zone of the interior.

Millions of years of weathering have worn the western section of the Great Western Plateau down to a low relief, and as a result the rivers which run down to the sea are very modest by world standards. Most watercourses are either short streams flowing westwards from their origins on the scarp or are part of the Swan-Avon, Blackwood, or Murray river systems.

The waters of these larger rivers are too salty for human consumption or irrigation, mainly because they rise in cleared agricultural land. In general, this land is relatively well watered, receiving between 400 and 1250 millimetres a year, most of it in winter.

The plants and animals of this region — particularly the trees of the great forests — have adapted to an environment characterised by ancient, exposed rocks, infertile soils, and local variations of an otherwise Mediterranean climate.

PLATEAU'S EDGE The modest elevation of the Darling Range — a fairly constant 250 to 300 metres — makes for a gently undulating silhouette on the horizon beyond the Swan River coastal plain.

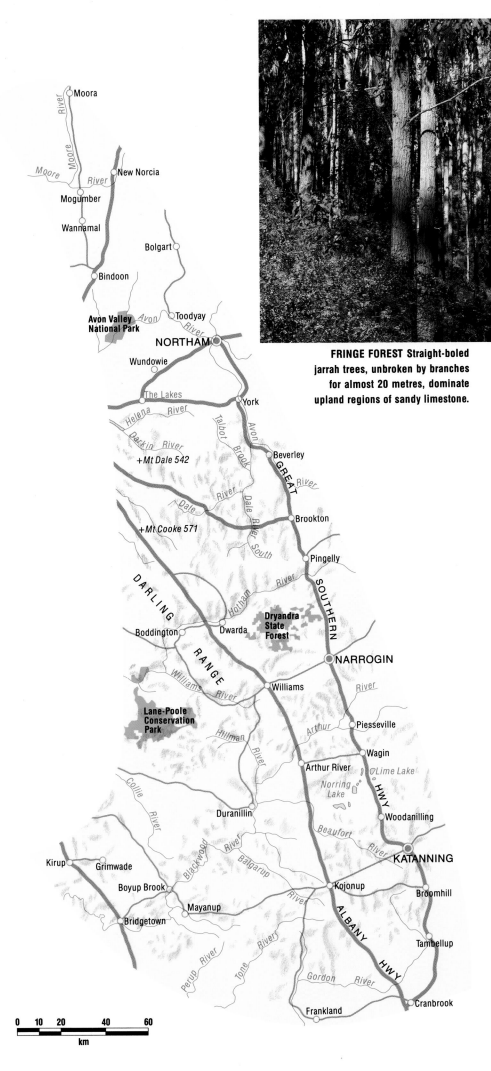

FRINGE FOREST Straight-boled jarrah trees, unbroken by branches for almost 20 metres, dominate upland regions of sandy limestone.

The upland of the plateau's edge supports a native forest dominated by the sturdy jarrah (*Eucalyptus marginata*) and the prolific marri (*E. calophylla*). Because erosion has produced a great diversity of terrain and soils, the plant life is similarly diverse and rich in species which are found nowhere else. Environmentalists are concerned that despite their size, the future of the forests is unsure because of the complex problem of dieback and the demands of forestry, mining and agriculture.

The Darling Scarp runs roughly parallel to the coast and extends from Muchea southwards to Donnybrook, beyond the region depicted on this chapter's map. It rises from a line of foothills which mark the position of what geologists call the Darling Fault.

This great fracture in the earth's surface marks the point of separation between the relatively young and soft sediments of the Perth region and the ancient, heavily eroded rocks of the Great Western Plateau, which were forged by the fire and convulsions of prehistoric volcanic activity.

The scarp, or range, extends inland in the form of gentle slopes, overlooked by occasional granite-knobbed peaks, such as Mount Vincent and Mount Cooke. These peaks, impressive in a region thousands of kilometres from a true mountain range, are remnants of an ancient, much higher plateau.

A deep mantle of weathered and leached soils overlies layers of granite and other coarse-grained rocks. Where erosion has exposed outcrops of bedrock, granite and other rock of volcanic origin is quarried; in the nearby uplands, bauxite is mined.

The hills and dales of the scarp are made up largely of gravelly sands and

hard surface rock. Red and yellow soils blanket the deep river valleys which have formed around their bases.

Farming is confined mostly to these valleys and their slopes, where the soils are more fertile than elsewhere. Further inland, where soils and permanent water tables tend to be deeper, the sands are often leached of their nutrients by heavy, seasonal rainfall.

The western forests

All over the plateau's margins, the soil and the climate have combined to produce two broad bands of tall forest. Majestic jarrahs and marris reign supreme in areas of red gravel — with woodlands on the sandier soils — while immediately to the west, the slopes of the scarp are covered with crowded woodlands of marri and wandoo (*Eucalyptus wandoo*). Along the rivers and creeks, there are flooded gums (*E. rudis*) and paperbarks (*Melaleuca*).

The Darling Scarp has been extensively cleared for farming but plants and animals of the region still exist relatively undisturbed in the Dryandra State Forest, a vast reserve of trees which covers more than 23 000 hectares.

The forest takes its name from the dryandra, a small shrub found only in Western Australia where more than 50 species grow. Even among the southwest's multitude of flowering plants, the dryandra stands out because of its variety of attractive, serrated leaf-shapes and almost iridescent flowers which resemble a cross between a banksia and a protea bloom.

PRICKLY PROTECTION The aptly named prickly dryandra has little to fear from grazing animals.

Among the jarrah and marri — and the dryandra — there is bull banksia (*Banksia grandis*) and she-oak (*Casuarina fraseriana*) in plenty. Beneath the tall, dominant trees there are zamia palms, grass trees and a variety of hardy shrubs including species of dryandra, hakea and acacia.

The mighty jarrah threatened

Jarrah is the best known of the Western Australian eucalypts and has become synonymous with the great forests of the south-west. These stringy-barked trees may grow to 40 metres in the high rainfall parts of their range; in drier areas, the trees display the eucalypt's ability for adaptation and may even grow as many-trunked mallees in the least fertile soils.

Jarrah timber is prized not only as an attractive cabinet wood — it was once known as Swan River mahogany — but its hardness, durability and

PLATEAU'S END On the escarpment slopes running down to the Swan River coastal plain, a tributary of the Helena River is bounded by woodlands of the white-barked wandoo.

resistance to insect attack make it an ideal material for flooring, fences, pylons and power poles.

The timber of the marri is also straight-grained and durable but of no commercial value. As a bloodwood, it produces generous amounts of red, resinous sap which renders it unsuitable for carpentry. But it remains a handsome tree with cream flowers and urn-shaped gumnuts which could well have been the inspiration for May Gibbs' famous gumnut babies, Snugglepot and Cuddlepie.

The majestic jarrah forests are a unique but diminishing resource. Burning and mining programmes are changing the natural balance of the complex forest environment and are helping to spread dieback, a fatal disease which

attacks mainly jarrah and some banksia species in Western Australia.

In the south-west, dieback is caused by the cinnamon soil fungus (*Phytophthora cinnamomi*) while in other parts of Australia, such as New England (see pp. 176–185), there are other causes. The microscopic, soil-borne cinnamon fungus kills the trees' fine feeding roots, causing their supply of water and nutrients to be cut off.

Banksias are one of the first trees to show the affects of dieback, and are often used by researchers to identify infected areas. Jarrah trees often do not show visible symptoms of infection for several years, until their uppermost branches start to die.

Plants growing on poorly drained, infertile soils are most at risk because the cinnamon fungus is active only in wet soils. On such sites, it grows and spreads throughout the year.

On the western edge of the scarp, where rainfall is highest, the greatest damage has occurred. Here too, intense human activity increases the spread of the fungus. Stringent forest hygiene and quarantine procedures have been introduced by the authorities where mining, logging, and other activities intrude into dieback-susceptible areas.

Fire has always been a natural part of jarrah forest development and native plants are well adapted to survive a natural fire regime. But in many areas

TREE ZONE A pocket of jarrah grows in a dryandra heathland — also known as kwongan — in the Dryandra State Forest, one of the largest areas of natural bushland in the Darling Range.

artificial burning programmes have led to the replacement of the original forest with different plants.

Changes in the vegetation have been particularly damaging where dieback-prone plants such as the bull banksia, have increased their numbers, or beneficial native legumes, such as wattles, have been eliminated. The future of the jarrah and many other trees and shrubs lies in the balance.

The wandoo-marri woodlands are a sharp contrast to the threatened forests of jarrah. These flourishing woodlands grow in the richer, deeper soils of the Darling Scarp, the trees often sharing their space with the distinctive Christmas tree (*Nuytsia floribunda*), a relatively harmless root parasite which has a brilliant, gold floral display during the summer months.

Wandoo woodlands are found mostly in the lower rainfall areas to the north and east of the jarrah forest. These forests may include the powderbark wandoo (*Eucalyptus accedens*), brown mallet (*E. astringens*), jam (*Acacia acuminata*) — so called for the raspberry-like smell of its timber — and dryandra shrubs.

The Bindoon and Toodyay regions, like so many parts of south-western Western Australia, burst into colour in the spring as the wildflowers bloom. Net bushes or one-sided bottlebrushes (*Calothamnus*), quince flowers (*Hibbertia*), *Lechenaultia* and several *Isopogon*, to name just a few, contribute to this annual profusion of blooms.

The mammals of the wandoo country are distinctive and include the woylie or brush-tailed bettong (*Bettongia penicillata*) and the rare numbat (*Myrmecobius fasciatus*), which often shelters in hollow wandoo branches which have fallen from old trees. This accommodation is often second-hand because before they fall, such branches may provide nesting hollows for owls, parrots, kingfishers or pardalotes.

The pollination game

Many of the plants which occur on the plateau, such as banksia, dryandra, eucalyptus and kangaroo paw (*Anigozanthos*) are pollinated by creatures much larger than the traditional bee, buzzing busily from flower to flower. Birds which feed on plant nectar, usually referred to as honeyeaters, distribute pollen from plant to plant, forming a mutually beneficial relationship between plant and bird.

The brown honeyeater (*Lichmera indistincta*), the western spinebill

WANDOO WOODLANDS The most extensive woodlands dominated by the wandoo eucalypts are on the shallow, sandy soils of the Darling Range foothills, below the jarrah belt.

(*Acanthorhynchus superciliosus*), the white-naped honeyeater (*Melithreptus lunatus*), and the white-cheeked honeyeater (*Phylidonyris nigra*) all play an important part in ensuring the future of new generations of shrubs and small plants.

Other, even larger creatures, help out too. In addition to the birds, some small animals provide their services as pollinating agents while they feed. The delightful western pygmy-possum (*Cercartetus concinnus*) and the tiny honey-possum (*Tarsipes rostratus*) are frequent visitors to wildflowers, where they feed on nectar and pollen and act as furred 'honeyeaters'.

Less dainty marsupials may be heard crashing through the undergrowth of forests and woodlands. The black-gloved or western brush wallaby (*Macropus irma*), the western grey kangaroo (*Macropus fuliginosus*) and

ENDANGERED SPECIES The numbat probes ant nests with a tongue half as long as its body.

the brushtail possum (*Trichosurus vulpecula*) are not hard to find.

Other animals are busy hunting and eating in this region but being diminutive compared with kangaroos or wallabies, their activities go largely unnoticed by human beings. The western quoll (*Dasyurus geoffroii*), less common than its larger cousins, is a fierce and aggressive hunter of birds, reptiles and small mammals. Its mouse-sized cousin, the fearless antechinus, is simi-

larly voracious, attacking insects and other small prey with carnivorous gusto.

Near wetlands, southern brown or short-nosed bandicoots (*Isoodon obesulus*) feed on a variety of plant material and insects. As with many other small mammals, such as dunnarts and phascogales, their numbers are declining as a result of clearing, burning, and the introduction of feral predators such as cats and dogs.

Less vulnerable because they are largely out of harm's way, are the tiny insectivorous bats, including the lesser long-eared bat, (*Nyctophilus geoffroyi*), Gould's long-eared bat (*Nyctophilus gouldi*), the King River eptesicus (*Eptesicus regulus*) and Gould's wattled bat (*Chalinolobus gouldii*), an incredibly adaptable and opportunistic creature which is found almost everywhere on the continent except Cape York.

More than fifty species of reptiles and frogs live in this relatively benign environment. The frogs are usually found around pools, or burrowed into the wet soil around streams.

Turtles were once common in the scarp's swampy wetlands, which are kept full by the generous winter rains; the long-necked turtle (*Chelodina oblonga*) is holding its own, but the western swamp turtle (*Pseudemydura umbrina*) has been rendered an endangered species by the changes which have taken place in its environment. It is now restricted to two small swamps near Bullsbrook.

Beyond the scarp, on the plateau proper, much drier scrublands are home to dragon lizards, goannas, blindsnakes and legless lizards. The venomous black tiger snake (*Notechis scutatus*) and the dugite (*Pseudonaja affinis*) are also fairly common.

Birds of the forest

A variety of birds fill the forest skies, many of them seasonal migrants to this region. In summer, the colourful rainbow bee-eater (*Merops ornatus*) migrates from the north-west to roast in an underground nest.

Other regular migrants to the plateau are the raucous flocks of red- and white-tailed black cockatoos (*Calyptorhynchus banksii, C. latirostris*), which move around the southwest of Western Australia according to season and food supply. The habitat of these birds is diminishing as a result of forest clearing, and how this will affect their long-term future is a matter of some conjecture.

NATIVE CLIMBERS In spring, patches of colour break out all over the jarrah forests as the purple pea flowers of the false sarsaparilla mingle with the white blooms of another creeper, the native clematis.

BEE FEAST The bee-eater — this one has a dragonfly — may eat several hundred bees a day.

The brilliant red-capped parrot (*Purpureicephalus spurius*) exhibits a striking adaptation to its environment; the parrot is a bird of the marri forests and its distinctively curved and elongated upper beak is perfectly shaped for extracting the seeds from large marri gumnuts. Other cheerful, gregarious parrots abound here too.

The colourful western rosella (*Platycercus icterotis*), the galah (*Cacatua roseicapilla*) and the elegant parrot (*Neophema elegans*) all find their food in the forest. Smaller and less colourful, but also less raucous and more tuneful forest birds include the splendid fairy-wren (*Malurus splendens*), the tiny southern emu-wren (*Stipiturus malachurus*), the grey fantail (*Rhipidura fuliginosa*) and the grey shrike-thrush (*Colluricincla harmonica*).

At night, the tawny frogmouth (*Podargus strigoides*) and the southern boobook or mopoke (*Ninox boobook*) emerge from their tree hollow nests to hunt silently for prey.

While logging of forest trees and general clearing for agricultural purposes have inhibited the lifestyles of some birds, others have benefited from these changes. These are mostly open-country birds such as the Australian magpie (*Gymnorhina tibicen*), the magpie-lark (*Grallina cynoleuca*) and the Australian raven (*Corvus coronoides*), whose numbers have increased as new, man-made habitats have appeared. ☐

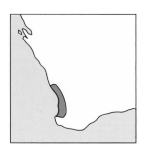

Despite the seemingly uninspiring setting of a flat, sandy plain, there are many subtle charms to be found in the untouched bushland, placid lakes and shimmering coastline of the greater Perth region

City of the dunes

PERTH WATER South of Perth's city skyscrapers — firmly embedded in the sandy coastal plain — the Swan River meanders through the southern suburbs to Fremantle.

Perth is the sunniest state capital in Australia and it sits glistening by the broad, generous waters of the Swan River estuary. A few kilometres to the south, at Perth's sister city of Fremantle, the estuary spills into the sea and interrupts a coastline of virtually continuous beaches washed by the gentle surf of the Indian Ocean.

Landward of the beaches is the sandy coastal plain, in fact, a succession of ancient, flattened sand dunes which reflect the fluctuations in sea level over the last 500 000 years. Superimposed on this very sandy environment is a pleasantly varied landscape studded with lakes, swamps and seasonal wetlands — often surprisingly close to urban areas — which support a variety of plants and animals, including migrants from far-off lands.

Close to the ocean, the coastal heathland annually bursts into drifts of the brilliant wildflowers for which this region is renowned. A distinctively Western Australian vegetation has evolved here, virtually in isolation from the rest of Australia, and is characterised by a rich and diverse variety of shrubs, most of which can be seen nowhere else in the world.

The native vegetation certainly impressed the first Europeans to explore the coast. In 1827, two years before the Swan River settlement was established, Captain James Stirling explored the site of the future city and reported most favourably on its natural attractions while noting that '...according to the testimony of an experienced person who accompanied me, the soil is admirably calculated for every species of cultivation...'.

Despite this richness of plant life and the opinion of Captain Stirling's advisor, the coastal sandplains, like sandy areas everywhere, are not a fertile medium for the cultivation of food plants. Nevertheless, the region supports a relatively intense concentration of humanity — about three-quarters of Western Australia's population lives here, on less than one per cent of the state's area. As the city's suburbs sprawl over the plain, the pressures of urban and rural development are gradually changing the natural landscape; even the offshore islands do not escape man's imprint.

HOW THE DUNES FUNCTION

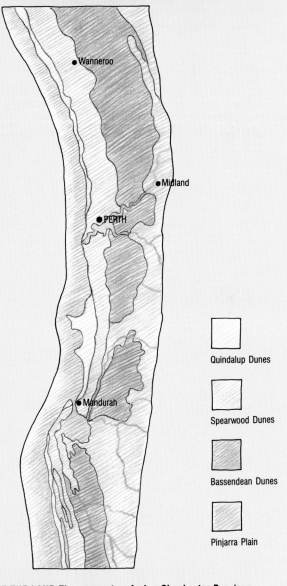

Quindalup Dunes

Spearwood Dunes

Bassendean Dunes

Pinjarra Plain

LIE OF THE LAND The promontory facing Shoalwater Bay (see photograph), which bears the houses of Rockingham (above) and Shoalwater (below), is part of the coastal, or Quindalup dune system. The soil here contains little organic matter and supports only low-growing, scrubby plants. Two other dune systems (see diagram) run the length of the region between the coastal dunes and the relatively fertile Pinjarra plain.

MODEST MURRAY The Murray River, modest compared with its eastern counterpart, brings water and silt from the Darling Plateau down to the green pastures of the Pinjarra plain.

Geographically, Perth is in some ways a mirror image of Sydney. Development inland from the city centre is limited in both cases by a mountain range and, as a result, both cities have tended to become strung out in a north-south direction.

In such a busy, metropolitan environment, where demands for more land for industrial and residential development are constant, the city is provided with breathing spaces in the form of more than a dozen national parks. These parks are spread out in an arc from the citys' northern coastal limits, inland along the western fringes of the Darling Ranges and down to the southern coast.

Some parks are set almost in the middle of suburbia and present a picture of the plain's appearance before white settlement. Neerabup National Park (1082 hectares) is one such place which preserves, cocoon-like, an environment which all around has been covered with asphalt, concrete and bricks.

This plain, like other coastal plains throughout the world, was once part of a seabed formed by sediment deposited over millions of years. The peculiar feature of the Swan River plain is that it is made up of layers of sediment of different origins, some deposited by water and some by wind, when the sea was in retreat. The tides have been turning in their present position for only the last 5000–6000 years. Before this period, fluctuations in the sea level resulted in a complex cycle of sedimentary build-up followed by shoreline erosion.

As recently as 18 000 years ago, the coastline may have extended as far as 40 kilometres out to sea from its present site, but now only the highest points of that ancient coastal plain remain above sea level, in the form of offshore islands such as Rottnest and Garden Islands.

Sand, sand, sand

The Swan coastal plain is part of the Perth Basin, an elongated rift valley covered mainly with limestone and quartz sands which in places reach depths of 12 kilometres. There are four distinct landforms, running roughly parallel to the coastline: one a smaller plain and three sand dune formations.

The most easterly landform, known as the Pinjarra plain, has the most fertile soils. These are alluvial deposits brought down by the rivers which flow from the Darling Plateau. North of Perth, the bountiful vineyards of the upper Swan are planted on the rich, red loams of the Pinjarra plain.

Immediately west of this alluvial plain is the oldest of the three sand dune systems. This 15-kilometre-wide zone of undulating, grey sand dunes has a covering of low banksia forest with a thick, shrubby under-storey. The infertile soils have little agricultural potential and large cleared areas have been turned over to pine plantations.

Many of the swamps which occurred between large dunes have now been drained or filled to accommodate the city's needs.

The second series of dunes forms hills of younger, yellow sands. In places, market gardens provide a bright splash of salad green on these marginally fertile soils. Limestone has formed beneath the surface sands and is occasionally exposed, most commonly as low cliffs and headlands along the coastline. Like the sandstone of Sydney, this limestone provided a handsome and readily available building material in colonial times and can be seen in many old buildings of the region, particularly at Fremantle.

WALYUNGA HEIGHTS Jarrah forests still stand on the steep slopes of the Walyunga National Park.

Closest to the sea, the last row of dunes is still forming behind the beaches. It is too early for trees or any tall plants to take root here, but the sand is stabilised by spinifex and low scrub, mainly wattles.

Fragments of each of these four regions are preserved in national parks, with the coastal strip being the hardest to maintain in a relatively natural state. Beachfront dunes, as is to be expected in a burgeoning metropolitan zone, are under constant recreational, residential and industrial pressure. Where the shallow-rooted dune vegetation is broken down by constant foot traffic or the tyres of recreational vehicles, the wind has free rein with the loose sand and the dunes begin to disintegrate.

A protective embrace

Despite their exposure to the vast expanse of Indian Ocean that stretches all the way to the shores of Africa, the beaches of the Perth coast face the onslaught of heavy seas only in the stormiest of conditions. The fury of the ocean is broken well offshore by a nearly continuous 'reef' — a barrier of limestone which emerges above sea level as a chain of coastal islands. Of these, Garden Island, a naval base, is closest to the mainland.

The largest of the islands (1900 hectares) is Rottnest, a popular holiday retreat and home to the endearing marsupial quokka (*Setonix brachyurus*). The smallest is Carnac Island (19 hectares), which as a conservation reserve and home to a large population of the deadly tiger snake (*Notechis scutatus*), has few visitors.

Along the Perth coast, the only large and relatively deep bay is at Cockburn Sound, south of Fremantle. Although this has traditionally been a popular area for seaside recreation, the extension of industrial and port facilities along the waterfront has created a major water pollution problem in this region. Elsewhere along the coast, the clear waters of the Indian Ocean, ranging in colour from turquoise through green to indigo, are always a refreshing sight, particularly on a hot day.

Hot days are something with which Perth is very familiar; the summers are often sweltering, with desiccating

RAT NEST Rottnest Island — the Dutch name identifies the nationality of the early explorers and their confusion of the native quokkas with rats — is surrounded by reefs and shoals.

easterly winds blowing from the arid interior. On the coast, relief is brought by the local seabreeze known as the Fremantle Doctor.

In winter, this coast, like the rest of the south-west, comes under the influence of the winds from the Roaring Forties, which bring rain off the ocean. Although on average it rains two days out of three in winter, the rain usually falls in brief, intense bursts with lengthy sunny spells in between.

Perth has more hours of sunshine than any other Australian capital except Darwin. It is also the windiest city in Australia, often being buffeted by strong winds, especially from late winter through to mid-summer.

Adapt or die

Given the little rain that falls on the coastal plain for about seven months of the year, the hot summers with their drying winds, and poor soils that do not hold moisture, this region is relatively arid and provides a fairly hostile environment for the establishment of plant life. As a result, the many unique

and diverse plants found here — several hundred species occur nowhere else — are mostly scrubby or low-growing; there are fewer than ten common tree species on the plain.

Foremost among the trees are the eucalypts — the tuart (*Eucalyptus gomphocephala*), the jarrah (*E. marginata*) and the marri (*E. calophylla*). Also common are banksias, she-oaks (*Casuarina fraserana*) and the spread-

WESTERN EUCALYPT The wandoo bears these flowers in summer and autumn.

ing wattle known as *Acacia saligna*. The Swan River peppermint (*Agonis flexuosa*) and the pricklybark (*E. todtiana*) are fairly common, while paperbarks and the Western Australian flooded gum (*E. rudis*), are found in swampy areas. Amongst the understorey plants are common bottlebrushes (*Callistemon*) and Western Australian one-sided bottlebrushes (*Calothamnus*), with their striking red or orange flower spikes.

The fertile Pinjarra plain to the east and its three adjoining dune systems each have their own distinctive vegetation pattern. The alluvial soils of the plain, sandwiched between the dunes and the Darling Scarp, support open forests and woodlands of jarrah, marri and wandoo (*Eucalyptus wandoo*), with flooded gums growing beside streams. The attractive white bark of the wandoo distinguishes this tree from the stringybarked jarrah and the marri with its abundant urn-shaped fruits, known as 'honkey nuts', which are used in children's games.

The forests of the Pinjarra plain, which gradually merge into the shorter trees and shrubs of the sandy woodland, can be seen in the many parks situated in the shadow of the Darling Ranges. The hilly Serpentine National Park (636 hectares) and the John Forrest National Park (1600 hectares) both contain two rare, protected species, the salmon gum (*E. salmonophloia*) below the scarp, and the butter gum (*E. laeliae*), on the heights. In the John Forrest park vantage points provide spectacular views across the plain and into the watery distance of the ocean.

To the north-east, the Walyunga National Park (1800 hectares) perches on the steepest slopes of the scarp. This is where the Swan River plunges over the solid, red laterite face of the scarp into smooth, granite basins — popular as swimming and boating pools — before setting its course for Perth and its meeting with the sea.

Threatened forest

Jarrah and marri trees also grow on the less fertile sands of the adjacent dune system, albeit reduced in stature, eventually being replaced by banksia woodland. The bull banksia (*Banksia grandis*), easily identified by its distinctive lobed leaves, is a problem plant — at least in large numbers — as this species is now known to be a favoured host of the fungii which threatens the jarrah forests of the south-west with

---

Why it rains in the western winter

Despite its flat, sandy terrain and relatively arid appearance, Perth enjoys a climate that broadly speaking, is more 'European' than that of most Australian population centres. The climate is Mediterranean, with hot, dry summers and mild, wet winters — wet enough, in fact,

for the annual rainfall to be greater than that of Melbourne, Hobart, Adelaide or Canberra.

Why is it that Perth is also wetter than cities in Chile, Mexico, South Africa and Morocco which occupy a similar latitude? The offshore currents are also not dissimilar: north-flowing currents run

along the western coasts of Africa, South America and Australia. The Western Australian current actually flows north, south and north again as it doubles back on itself, forming huge eddies as it does so.

But Australia has an additional current, which squeezes between the main currents and the land mass of Western Australia. This carries warm, low-salinity tropical water southwards along the continental shelf while the main currents are flowing hundreds of kilometres out to sea. Known as the Leeuwin Current, after a Dutch ship which passed this way in the seventeenth century, the 50-kilometre-wide body of water surges around the south-western corner of Australia at Cape Leeuwin (pictured) and eastwards towards the Great Australian Bight.

The current is strongest from March to July, and its arrival explains the sudden, brief appearance in autumn of tropical marine animals along the Perth coast. It also explains the generous rainfall, since the seawater, warmed by the tropical sun, releases moisture to the wintertime, low-pressure atmospheric systems as they pass eastwards on their way to the continent. When the freshly warmed oceanic air masses reach the colder land mass, the rain is released and the catchment areas around Perth provide the city with another year's water supply.

the parasitic mistletoe family, and thrives by living off the roots of other trees, shrubs and even grasses.

These trees can be seen in the undeveloped Moore River National Park (17 000 hectares) north of Perth. The park provides an excellent example of the sandy heathlands, dry dune systems and swamps of the northern coastal plain. It is the only habitat for the rose-fruited banksia (*B. laricina*).

Around swampy areas there are paperbarks, flooded gum, swamp banksia (*Banksia littoralis*) and swamp she-oak (*Casuarina obesa*). The bulrush (*Typha domingensis*) and jointed rush (*Baumea articulata*) dominate the margins of most metropolitan lakes.

The stands of banksias and eucalypts thin out towards the coastal dunes. Here the salt-laden wind and

the fatal and little-understood phenomenon known as dieback.

Dieback has spread at an alarming rate and infected forests range from the Nambung National Park north of Perth, down to the south coast and east as far as Cape Arid. The problem has reached such proportions that large quarantine areas, including a 20-kilometre-wide belt of forest to the east of the capital, have been barred to vehicles and horses in an effort to control the spread of this potentially disastrous infection.

The forest under-storey is brightened by the colourful yellow flower-heads of the narrow-leaved banksia (*Banksia attenuata*) and the pink-flowered Menzies and holly-leaved banksias (*B. menziesii, B. ilicifolia*). All provide a welcome source of nectar for honeyeaters.

The central dune system also has its own recognisable plant forms, most notably the majestic tuart which grows only here, on limestone soils, sometimes soaring to 40 metres. Generally this tree grows in mixed, open forests with jarrah and marri, but at the southern end of its range, near Busselton, it comes into its own to form the magnificent Ludlow tuart forest.

Another widespread tree of the coastal plain is the Christmas tree (*Nuytsia floribunda*). The vivid golden-orange flower clusters which cover these trees in November–December are a spectacular sight, yet the tree is a biological oddity. It is a member of

PRETTY PARASITE The roots of the Christmas tree drain nutrients from the roots of other plants.

the coarse sand combine to produce a particularly harsh and inhospitable environment. Tough spinifex binds the near-beach sands, while further back from the shore, wattle shrubs and patches of coastal heath take root in more sheltered positions. Occasionally, limestone slopes offer shelter to the Rottnest Island pine (*Callitris preissii*), or the moonah (*Melaleuca lanceolata*), although these trees are now seldom seen around Perth and are virtually restricted to Rottnest and Garden Islands.

Yalgorup National Park (11 500 hectares) south of Perth, and Neerabup National Park (1100 hectares) in the north, occupy this coastal region. More than 100 species of waterfowl have been identified in the chain of lakes and swamps that lie between parallel lines of dunes and old limestone ridges in the Yalgorup park. Short walking trails skirt some of these lakes, and beaches fringe the coastline.

Vegetable cunning

The success of the vegetation of the Perth coast, despite the less than promising soil cover, results from a clever range of adaptations. Many plants of this region endure the blistering summers by turning regular botanical 'practice' on its head and reversing the seasonal fluctuations and functions of their temperate-climate relatives: they remain dormant during the hot months and make winter their growing season. The tough, narrow leaves sported by many plants are often protected by a waxy cuticle which reflects the bright sunlight to give that hazy, peculiarly Australian quality to the light of the forest.

Banksias and eucalypts have insulating bark for protection from fire, while other genera, like the acacias, germinate in the ash left after a bushfire. Many of the eucalypts can generate new shoots from fire-ravaged trunks; even when the trees burn to ground level, new growth is generated by rootstocks (lignotubers) from below ground.

Most plants respond to the infertile soils by growing extensive root systems to draw nutrients and water from as wide an area as possible. Some, such as the zamia palm (*Macrozamia reidlei*), have special nutrient-storage organs to carry them through a dry summer. The carnivorous sundews (*Drosera*) supplement their nutrient intake with animal protein from the decaying bodies of insects caught in their sticky leaves. Native legumes, such as peas and wattles, and some

LAND OF THE BANKSIA The narrow-leaved banksia is one of more than 50 Western Australian banksias.

non-legumes, such as the she-oak, obtain extra nitrogen from nitrogen-fixing bacteria on their root nodules.

The wildlife which has evolved at the same time as these extraordinary plants is equally distinctive. The vast arid regions that separate the west coast from the east have encouraged a

ZAMIA PALM The females of the palm-like cycads are recognisable by their seed cones.

form of biological isolation, and as a result a number of unique creatures have evolved in Western Australia. While many bear close relationships to similar animals in south-eastern Australia, having had common ancestors, they are quite clearly the product of a different environment.

Bird haven

With a vast expanse of ocean to one side and a similar expanse of the arid interior to the other, the Perth coast — and the rest of the south-west — provides a vitally important habitat for birdlife. With the exception of areas in the far north of the state, the Swan coastal plain provides the only extensive system of wetlands on the western side of the continent.

These feeding grounds attract birds from far and wide: pelicans are regularly seen soaring in summer skies above the broad river estuaries at Perth and Mandurah; avocets and stilts abandon the inland salt lakes where they congregate in large numbers to breed along mudflats around Perth and on the salt lakes of Rottnest Island; and

massed flocks of stints, godwits, plovers, sandpipers, stilts, dotterels and knots include many birds which have migrated in spring from breeding grounds beyond the Arctic Circle.

The melodic call of the aptly-named clamorous reed-warbler (*Acrocephalus stentoreus*) echoes from the reed beds of most Perth lakes. The purple swamphen (*Porphyrio porphyrio*) and the Eurasian coot (*Fulica atra*) are also common inhabitants of reedy lake margins. Occasionally, there may be a glimpse of the egrets, spoonbills, ibises and herons which breed in more isolated wetlands. Secretive crakes and rails are spotted by only the most patient of birdwatchers.

Alarm calls from bushbirds and waterfowl often signal the presence of a bird of prey overhead. Wheeling above, there could be an Australian kestrel (*Falco cenchroides*) or a black-shouldered kite (*Elanus notatus*), a brown goshawk (*Accipiter fasciatus*) or the little eagle (*Hieraaetus morphnoides*) in pursuit of prey. The swamp harrier (*Circus approximans*) swoops low over lakes and swamps, scattering the waterfowl in noisy disarray.

The ducks take pride of place among the waterfowl. The most common duck of Perth's wetlands, the Pacific black duck (*Anas superciliosa*) is widely distributed throughout Australia. Many of the others are common on both the south-western and south-eastern coasts; these include the small blue-billed duck (*Oxyura australis*), the musk duck (*Biziura lobata*), with its wattled bill and strange piercing whistle, and the nomadic pink-eared duck (*Malacorhynchus membranaceus*), with its distinctive zebra stripes and flanged bill.

Complementary to the busy and sociable ducks is the slower, more dignified black swan (*Cygnus atratus*), a bird which is always associated with this coast but which in fact, is native to eastern Australia too.

The offshore islands also provide refuge for birdlife. Here, colonies of seabirds like the silver gull (*Larus novaehollandiae*) and bridled and crested terns (*Sterna anaethetus, S. bergii*), breed within sight of the mainland. Penguin Island, once a favourite holiday location, is now closed except to day visitors so that the delightful little fairy penguin (*Eudyptula minor*) may breed undisturbed. The noisy colony nests in the latter half of the year, rearing its fluffy chicks in burrows which are hidden under low vegetation.

On the mainland, flocks of larrikinish white-tailed black cockatoos (*Calyptorhynchus latirostris*), fly along the coast in raucous foraging parties, seeking the fruits of banksias, hakeas, dryandras and eucalypts. Many Perth residents have been 'sconed' by pine cones dropped in haste by black cockatoos disturbed while feeding.

Around the suburbs, magpies (*Gymnorhina tibicen*) boldly scavenge for food and defend their territories with aggressive determination. Spotted and laughing turtle-doves (*Streptopelia chinensis, S. senegalensis*), introduced to Perth from their native Asia around the turn of the century, have also become very tame around suburban gardens. The native bronzewing pigeon (*Phaps chalcoptera*) is much more timid. Suburban gardens also frequently host ring-neck parrots — both the Port Lincoln race and the local variety known as 'twenty-eights'.

The night flyers

Other creatures share the coastal skies with the birds but they are rarely heard or noticed. The high-pitched squeaks of the tiny bats which populate the night skies are often interpreted as insect sounds. Most people would be surprised at the numbers of these shy, tiny mammals which forage discreetly for moths and beetles around lights in suburban gardens. During the day they shelter in crevices and tree hollows,

TRAVELLING NORTH The reed warbler escapes the winter cold by migrating to northern Australia but always returns in the spring, to breed in the swamplands of the south-west.

TRUE COLOURS The white, outer flight feathers of the black swan are folded out of sight when the bird is on land or water. Nesting and breeding takes place throughout the year.

often becoming completely inactive if the weather is cold or if food is scarce.

Many of these tiny insect-eaters, like the King River eptesicus bat (*Eptesicus regulus*), have bodies smaller than that of a mouse, and most of the others are not much larger. Little is known of their distribution but other coastal species include two types of wattled bats and three of long-eared bats.

Much more familiar are the kangaroos and wallabies, including the western brush wallaby (*Macropus irma*) which remains fairly common in open jarrah forest and woodland. Tammar wallabies (*M. eugenii*) are now restricted to patches of coastal scrub, heath and areas of forest and woodland which provide a sufficiently dense understorey for daytime shelter.

MEAT EATER Despite its grand-sounding name, the carnivorous, yellow-footed antechinus is a mouse-like creature about 120 millimetres long. It lives mainly on a diet of mice and insects.

LITTLE WALLABY Rottnest Island's most famous resident, the small wallaby known as the quokka, is also found on the mainland.

RAT-LIKE Bandicoots, such as this southern brown variety, occur in the south-east too.

The peculiar little quokka, of Rottnest Island fame, has been a subject of both popular and scientific interest. Visitors to the island are often able to handfeed and pat the tamest individuals. The large 'captive' population on Rottnest Island has allowed the quokka to be studied in more scientific detail than most native creatures. Scientists have amassed a vast amount of information about the eating habits, temperature regulation, reproductive habits and immunology of the quokka,

and some of this may be useful in human medical research.

The coastal sandplain heaths have a varied covering of nectar-producing plants and these provide nutritious, gastronomic delights for the tiny honey-possum or noolbenger (*Tarsipes rostratus*). Its cousin, the western pygmy-possum (*Cercatetus concinnus*), searches out the flowers of banksias, grevilleas, callistemons and melaleucas wherever they form a dense understorey in a eucalypt forest.

Dunnarts (*Sminthopsis*) also scurry busily around woodlands and heathlands, searching for insects at night. The larger yellow-footed antechinus or 'mardo' (*Antechinus flavipes*), has two claims to fame: firstly these mouse-like creatures leave the inside-out skins of their prey, such as mice and birds, as a unique calling card for other animals, and secondly, the males invariably die shortly after mating — perhaps not surprising as the act is believed to sometimes last as long as 12 hours. Ash-grey

CANNIBAL Despite its size — about 90 millimetres — the bellfrog has a loud voice and is a voracious consumer of other frogs.

mice (*Pseudomys albocinereus*) have more vegetarian habits, which they pursue peacefully among the sandy heathlands.

Closer to human habitation, there are common brushtail possums (*Trichosurus vulpecula*) abundant wherever there are trees. Southern brown bandicoots or quendas (*Isoodon obesulus*) are sometimes mistaken for rats, but are in fact native marsupials which, although they may become tame if fed regularly, generally seek the protection of dense vegetation around swamps where they dig for worms, insects and bulbs.

Frogs, and their ilk

When the rains come, frog choruses erupt around the ponds, lakes and dams of the coastal plain. Moaning frogs (*Heleioporus eyrei*) carefully position themselves at just the right place in their burrows to give maximum amplification to their monotonous serenade. The call of the beautiful western green and golden bellfrog (*Litoria moorei*) sounds like a revving motorbike, whilst smaller frogs and toadlets fill in the gaps with a range of croaks, shrieks and crackles.

The frogs, together with a host of other small creatures, are the favoured food of the deadly tiger snake which is common around Perth wetlands, as is the venomous dugite (*Pseudonaja*

EMINENTLY ADAPTABLE Like many dragon lizards, the western bearded dragon can look fearsomely aggressive when disturbed, as well as varying its colour to match its surroundings.

affinis), but like most snakes they are shy and seldom seen.

Perth's most handsome reptile is the bungarra or Gould's goanna (*Varanus gouldii*), a muscular and strikingly patterned lizard growing up to two metres in length. On a smaller scale, there is the marbled gecko (*Phyllodactylus marmoratus*), a common occupant of suburban garden sheds, as well as a variety of small skink lizards. Amongst

the largest of the skinks is the bobtail or shingleback (*Tiliqua rugosa*), a placid, armour-plated fellow who makes himself at home almost anywhere along the coast. These slow-moving reptiles are often killed by motor cars, as are female oblong turtles (*Chelodina oblonga*), whose summertime search for egg-laying sites near their wetland homes often results in yet another road statistic. □

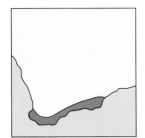

Regular winter rains help maintain the greenness of Western Australia's south-west, an isolated patch of incredible botanical diversity sandwiched between the ocean and the arid interior

Tall-timbered ranges and wildflower meadows

The constant and complex interplay between sun, sea and air currents produces such a distinctive climate for Australia's south-western corner that it occurs nowhere else on the continent on the same scale.

On the other side of Australia, the south-east is relatively well, if intermittently, watered throughout the year by the constant flow of high- and low-pressure air cells across the continent.

As each front moves towards the east, the winds swirl and change direction, bringing moist air from the Tasman Sea and the Pacific Ocean. As a result, moisture-laden clouds are in the vanguard of these weather systems and bring rain as they advance.

But in the south-west, things are different. During summer, cool fronts moving off the Indian Ocean collide with the hot air of the interior and are forced south, back over the ocean, touching only the extreme south-western corner of the continent.

As the land cools in autumn and

winter, the rain-bearing fronts are able to move straight onto the land mass and bring rain to wider, more northerly areas. The result for the south-west is a Mediterranean-type climate of dry, hot summers and cool, relatively wet winters. Only the very tip of the south-west of Western Australia receives rain throughout the year.

The dramatic contrast between the rainfall in this extreme south-western corner and the rest of the south-west is graphically illustrated by a comparison of annual figures. West of an imaginary line drawn from Cape Naturaliste through Manjimup to the coast, just east of Albany, annual rainfall exceeds 1000 millimetres. The coast west of Denmark is even wetter with more than 1270 millimetres of rain each year.

Only a short distance east, along the coast and inland, it suddenly becomes much drier: Bremer Bay and Esperance receive only half the rain of Denmark and have an average 'dry season' of five months. These are months when the amount of rain relative to temperature is insufficient to maintain plant growth.

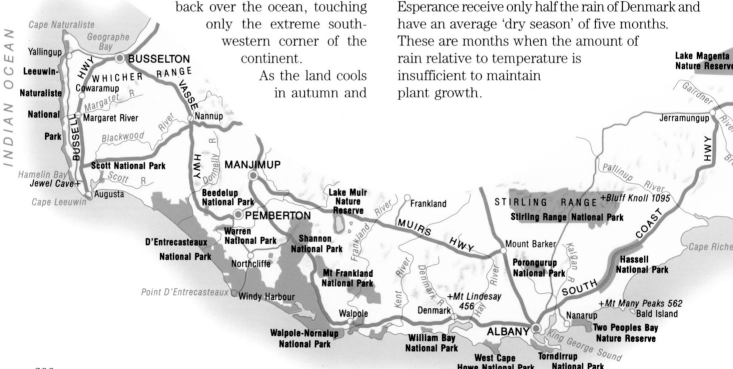

NATIVE GARDEN The botanical riches of the south-west
are best displayed in spring. Here, wattles and
kennedias bloom in a jarrah forest.

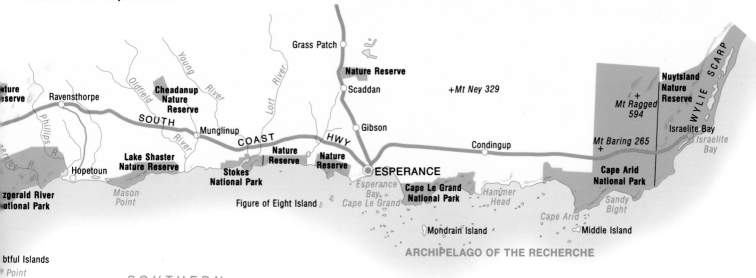

Grass Patch

Nature Reserve

ature
eserve

Ravensthorpe

**Cheadanup
Nature
Reserve**

Young River

Oldfield River

Scaddan

+Mt Ney 329

**Nuytsland
Nature
Reserve**

WYLIE SCARP

+
Mt Ragged
594

SOUTH

Munglinup

Lort River

Gibson

COAST

HWY

Condingup

Mt Baring 265
+

Israelite Bay

Phillips R

**Lake Shaster
Nature Reserve**

Hopetoun

rsley R

zgerald River
ational Park

Mason
Point

**Stokes
National Park**

**Nature
Reserve**

**Nature
Reserve**

ESPERANCE

Esperance
Bay
Cape Le Grand

**Cape Le Grand
National Park**

Israelite
Bay

**Cape Arid
National Park**

Hammer
Head

Sandy
Bight

Figure of Eight Island

Mondrain Island

Cape Arid

Middle Island

ARCHIPELAGO OF THE RECHERCHE

btful Islands
Point

SOUTHERN

OCEAN

0 10 20   40   60   80   100

km

The dry season at Denmark lasts about two months. At Israelite Bay, 650 kilometres to the east and the eastern limit of this south-west corner, the annual rainfall is less than 400 millimetres and the dry season exceeds six months.

The pattern of decreasing rainfall and increasing dry season is repeated inland from the coast. Inland from Esperance, annual precipitation declines rapidly from 600 millimetres to 500 at Gibson, 400 at Scaddan and 350 at Grass Patch — with a dry season almost eight months long.

These non-tropical wet and dry seasons, together with particular combinations of soils and landforms, determine the vegetation of the southwest corner and make it one of the most diverse landscapes in Australia.

SOUTH-EAST CORNER As its name suggests, Cape Arid is in the dry east, where sandplains and scrubby heaths encircle granite headlands.

THE GRANITE BELT Above and around the giant karri forests which clothe the Porongorup Range, the mountains' granite base shows through as bald domes or huge, weathered boulders.

Until about 45 million years ago, Australia and Antarctica were part of the same continent. A giant land fracture separated the two and Australia began a long, slow drift northward.

Soon after the separation, the southern coastline of Australia sank beneath the sea, rising five to ten million years later. During its time beneath the sea, marine sediments up to 200 metres thick were deposited on the land. Today, these make up the sandstone and siltstone parts of the landscape but there are also extensive areas of limestone, particularly in the regions south of Mount Ragged and Israelite Bay.

Underlying the marine sediments are metamorphic and granitic rocks between 1300 and 1700 million years old, with other granite rocks which intruded into these about 1100 million years ago. These hard, underlying rock layers emerge through the relatively thin marine sediments as massive, granite domes and mountains, providing some of the most spectacular scenery along the south-west coast.

'Mountains' of the south

The Recherche Archipelago islands, Mount George, Mount Lindesay, Mount Manypeaks, the Porongurup Range and the headlands of Cape Riche, Cape Le Grand and Hood Point are typical examples of the erosion-resistant outcrops which form a belt up to 40 kilometres wide along the coast. Near the coast, the outcrops seldom exceed 150 to 200 metres in height, but inland they are higher and often massive.

TOP OF THE RANGE The shale and slate core of Toolbrunup Peak, in the Stirling Range, has been uncovered by a million years' exposure to the elements.

The Porongurup Range is 650 metres above sea level and domes such as Mount Lindesay and Mount Barrow exceed 450 metres. Mount Manypeaks is 562 metres high.

The Stirling Range rises abruptly from the flat plains north of the Porongurup mountains and extends over 60 kilometres from east to west, with the highest peaks and bluffs in the southern half of Western Australia. Bluff Knoll, at 1095 metres, is the highest point.

As the air rising off the plains cools, and clouds form, the tops of the ranges are often concealed in mist. The strong winds and cool air at these relatively high altitudes, and the extra moisture provided by the mists, create a unique, cool, moist environment.

A tall, closed shrubland has developed on the mountain tops, with many species of plants restricted to small areas of particularly moist sites. Among the most spectacular of these are the mountain bells (*Darwinia*), with differ-

ent species occurring on the summits, slopes and bases of the various mounts, knolls and ranges.

The Stirling Range begins west of Cranbrook at Warriup Hill and continues east past Donnelly Peak, on to Mondurup Peak, Mounts Gog and Magog, Mount Trio and Toll Peak.

The eastern part of the range is more uniform and extends from Yungermere through Mount Success, Bluff Knoll and Isongerup to Ellen Peak, where it ends. Standing on Bluff Knoll, the mountains

QUARTZITE COAST Mid Mount Barren, appropriately midway between its East and West counterparts, overlooks Dempster Inlet on the isolated stretch of sandy coast between Hopetoun and Bremer Bay.

fall away to the distant plains over a wealth of wildflowers, and it is hard to imagine the hot, dry, flat interior that lies between here and the east coast.

The Stirling Range is formed from sedimentary rocks deposited more than 1300 million years ago and may be part of the same formation as the Barren Ranges, which stretch from north-east of Bremer Bay to the Phillips River. This ancient seabed material, now mainly quartzite, forms a rocky barrier with gently sloping sides, up to 20 kilometres wide and 90 metres above sea level.

Low mountains, such as West Mount Barren, the Whoogarup Range and the Eyre Range, jut abruptly above this barrier, while rivers, such as the Fitzgerald, cut into it, forming deep canyons. This is a most spectacular coastline, with the 90-metre-high barrier rising straight from the sea and, behind it, the Barren Ranges framed against the sky.

Botanically speaking...

The plant life of this region is as dramatically beautiful — as well as being a dramatic success of adaptation — as the spectacular landscape it inhabits. Some of the richest plant communities in the world grow here. The expanse of sand plain heaths along the Fitzgerald River provides breathtaking wildflower displays, while the flowers in their turn attract a profusion of nectar-feeding birds.

Not all of the south-west corner is

REGAL NATIVE The tough leaves of the three-metre-tall royal hakea may last for five years.

formed from ancient rocks or sediments. The rising and falling of the sea level in relatively recent times has left large areas of the coast covered in fossil sand dunes. These gently undulating deposits indicate the previous height of the ocean and can be up to six kilometres in width.

The dunes are covered by shrublands rich in wildflowers and birds. Freshwater lagoons and swamps have formed in the swales between the dunes, and where rivers cut through to the sea they have formed broad, shallow estuaries which provide rich breeding grounds for fish and waterbirds.

Between Cape Naturaliste and Cape Leeuwin, the limestone country has been eroded by time and water to form large caves — Yallingup in the north, Mammoth and Lake Caves south of Margaret River, and Jewel Cave near Augusta, are among the best.

The caves boast massive stalagmites, shawl formations and incredibly delicate stalactites. There are also many

fossils from pre-human times when the south-west was wetter and the preserve of wild beasts.

These fossils, which include the remains of the Tasmanian tiger, or thylacine, (*Thylacinus cynocephalus*), the Tasmanian devil (*Sarcophilus harrisii*), and a type of koala, are at least 40 000 years old.

Bushfires, good and bad

If land and water are the two most obvious factors shaping the vegetation of the south-west corner, fire is the third. As Australia drifted into the dry latitudes north of the fortieth parallel, naturally occurring fires became a normal event. The arrival of humans added a new dimension.

Carbon dating has confirmed that Aborigines were in the Swan Valley near Perth about 38 000 years ago, and human remains from Devils Lair, near Augusta, have been dated at 29 000 years old.

In 1829, when British colonists established the Swan River colony, the south-west corner as far east as Esperance was occupied by the Nyungar people. While relying on the abundant fish, game and wild plants of the region as staple items of their diet, the Nyungar also hunted kangaroos.

In the summer, they set the bush on fire and speared the animals as they were driven from cover by the flames. European accounts from early in the nineteenth century, indicate that these fires were often intense and burnt large areas, but that the Aborigines controlled the fires. Not only did the Aborigines extinguish flames that threatened to escape beyond the desired burning area, they had a systematic burning program: different portions of the bush were set alight in an annual sequence.

Aboriginal burning practices, it seems, produced a mosaic or patchwork of vegetation covering the spectrum from newly germinated plants to fully grown, mature bushland. This provided wildlife with an abundance of both food and cover.

The drier, more open woodlands and forests where the Aboriginal population was high were probably burnt fairly often, but the wetter heaths and forest regions would have been burnt irregularly. In contrast, modern, controlled burning practices in south-western Australia produce a more uniform pattern, with fires set early in the spring and repeated over large areas every four to six years.

CAPE TO CAPE The wild beaches and headlands of the broad, blunt sweep of limestone coast between Cape Naturaliste and Cape Leeuwin are occasionally interrupted by tall, moor-capped cliffs, such as these at Biljedup.

HANGING COLUMN For aeons, rainwater has filtered through the porous limestone around Yallingup Cave, ever-so-slowly dissolving the calcium carbonate in the rock.

It is probably too early to know the long-term effects of these new burning practices, but many biologists, concerned that they are adversely affecting Western Australia's forests and heaths, are urging practices closer to those used by the Aborigines.

The long-term effects of Aboriginal burning practices can be seen by comparing today's mainland vegetation to that on offshore islands, such as the Recherche Archipelago, which the Aborigines could not easily reach.

The long-unburnt vegetation on the Recherche islands is taller and much more dense than that on the mainland, with a greater accumulation of leaf litter and other organic matter on the ground.

Throughout the south-west corner, European burning practices have produced lower and much more open vegetation and soils with less organic matter than they contained before white settlement.

In the 160 years since the founding of the Swan River Colony, half the forests of south-western Australia have been cleared, and vast areas of mallee, heath and woodland put under crops and pasture. Native wildlife has declined dramatically, with many species becoming extinct.

Clearing of bushland for farming continues, and many of the remaining forests are affected by the introduction of different eucalypt species from eastern Australia, the woodchip industry, the establishment of pine plantations, mining, and prescription burning practices.

Despite the sacrifices required for the agricultural development necessary to feed a growing population, virgin forests remain in the large areas of the south-west corner that have been set aside as nature reserves and national parks. These protect some of the most spectacular scenery in Australia.

West of Busselton to Cape Naturaliste, and south along the coast

to Cape Leeuwin, sections of the Leeuwin-Naturaliste National Park (16 172 hectares) and some other reserves protect the region's limestone caves, coastal forest and moors. The windswept moors at Cape Leeuwin and Cape Naturaliste are covered in a carpet of wildflowers during September and October.

The tall forests in the Margaret River-Hamelin Bay area, west of the Bussel Highway, are dominated by jarrah (*Eucalyptus marginata*), mixed with stands of the marri (*E. calophylla*), blackbutt or yarri (*E. patens*), and mountain marri (*E. haematoxylon*), together with an understorey of she-oak, wattle and banksia.

To the west, there are beautiful green corridors of karri (*E. diversicolor*), but these forests are best known for their dunes, rich in the remains of marine invertebrates and land snails. These, together with the fossilised mammals recovered from the region's limestone caves, make this part of the south-west, a unique window onto the past.

Kingdom of the karri

East of Margaret River, the extensive forests are a mixture of jarrah and marri on the drier and poorer soils, and karri where it is moister and the soils richer in nutrients.

The giant karri will grow where the annual rainfall is as little as 700 millimetres, so long as the dry season does not last longer than four months. It is found as far west as the Porongurup Range, but reaches its maximum size and is most widespread where annual rainfall exceeds 1000 millimetres and the dry season is short.

The best karri forests grow near the towns of Pemberton and Manjimup — the focus of the timber industry. They are the tallest trees in Western Australia and are among the tallest in the world, sometimes reaching heights of 80–90 metres.

Throughout the forests of south-western Australia, tall trees were used until recently as fire lookouts. Ladders were spiralled around the trunk, and a platform or cabin was constructed at the top, from which fires could be spotted at long distances.

Karri and jarrah between them produce some of the finest timber in Australia. Karri is used mainly in building construction, but jarrah, considered by some to be the most beautiful wood in the world, is usually reserved for furniture making.

REACHING FOR THE SKY Forests of the tall, straight karri, which resemble an army of power poles, grow in the south-west of the south-west, where the rainfall is relatively high and regular.

Young jarrah is light in colour, almost salmon-pink, but it ages to the point of blackness. A specialty of the south-west corner is goods crafted from the hard base of grass trees (*Xanthorrhoea*). When polished, this peculiar 'timber' has a pattern not unlike snake skin.

Small areas of untouched karri forest are protected in the Beedalup (1530 hectares), Warren (1355 hectares) and Brockman (250 hectares) National Parks near Pemberton, with larger areas in Walpole-Nornalup National Park (15 877 hectares) near Walpole and in the Porongurup National Park (2572 hectares) north of Albany.

The finest examples of the tall forests of the south-west are in the Shannon National Park (52 598 hectares) east of Northcliffe. The Shannon stands were saved from logging after a long battle between timber interests and conservationists. East of Walpole, along the wettest part of the coast, are stands of red tingle (*E. jacksonii*), another south-west giant. Appropriately, the region of a mixed jarrah and tingle forest east of Walpole is called the Valley of the Giants.

In the karri's shade

In these forests it is easy to be diverted from the other natural attractions by the sheer size and beauty of the trees. A rich humus sustains a lush understorey of shrubs and fungi, where birds and insects create noise and movement.

White-breasted robins (*Eopsaltria georgiana*), brown thornbills (*Acanthiza pusilla*), and red-winged fairy-wrens (*Malurus elegans*) hunt for insects through the dense shrubbery, while parrots and lorikeets forage through the canopy. The nomadic purple-crowned lorikeet (*Glossopsitta porphyrocephala*), wanders long distances in search of nectar-rich flowers, and red-capped or king parrots (*Purpureicephalus spurius*) feed contentedly on the nutritious seeds of eucalypts using a long, hooked bill which is particularly useful for extracting the large seeds of marri gum nuts.

One of the best known birds in the south-west is the noisy scrub-bird (*Atrichornis clamosus*). Originally found in dense coastal vegetation from north of Margaret River to Albany, it was not seen from 1889 to 1961, when it was spotted at Two Peoples Bay, east of Albany.

The gullies on the slopes of Mount Gardner, where the bird survived, were part of an area designated for development but after representations to the government by conservationists it was set aside as a sanctuary. The sanctuary also protects other rare birds, including the western whipbird (*Psophodes nigrogularis*) and the western bristlebird (*Dasyornis longirostris*), as well as

BANKSIA MEN There is no such thing as a typical banksia in the south-west, where the plant displays a variety of shapes and sizes unequalled in the eastern states. This form of the scarlet banksia grows in the Stirling Ranges.

conserving extensive coastal moors inhabited by New Holland, white-cheeked and tawny-crowned honey-eaters (*Phylidonyris novaehollandiae, P. nigra, P. melanops*).

The scrub-bird, whipbird and bristlebird are all victims of the change in fire patterns introduced by Europeans. The fires have progressively changed the birds' habitats, and their frequency has meant that the birds often do not have time to re-colonise the newly maturing vegetation before the next fire sweeps through.

Small is beautiful

In total contrast to the tall-timbered forests, are the much more diminutive heaths and shrublands of the coast and plains. Known as kwongan, an Aboriginal word for low vegetation, this region is dominated by low shrubs which make the nearby forests and the bushland of most of Australia look bland by comparison.

The comparatively low stature of the banksias, hakeas, grevilleas, melaleucas and kunzeas which grow here is more than compensated for by their abundance of nectar-rich flowers. When combined with the many other small, flowering plants of the kwongan, they produce a spring floral display that is unrivalled in Australia.

STEMLESS Not a healthy crop of vegetables but the ground-hugging creeping banksia which is at the opposite end of the banksia spectrum to the tree-like specimens of more fertile zones.

SWEET BRUSH In spring, the toothbrush grevillea's blooms are irresistible to nectar-eaters.

The brilliant reds and browns of the banksias vie with the magentas, greens, yellows and whites of the grevilleas and the melaleucas. Tiny sundews (*Drosera*) send up huge, white flowers that tower centimetres above the modest, ground-level foliage. Other sundews trail over higher shrubs, their sticky insect traps like glistening beads in the sun.

Various environmental influences have combined to produce one of the richest plant communities in the world here. The ancient soils and rocks of the south-west, and the isolation of this part of Australia from the rest of the continent, have resulted in the evolution of an incredibly diverse and beautiful group of flowering plants. Of the 8000-odd species of flowering plants in Western Australia, nearly 2500 occur in the south-west and 75 per cent of these occur nowhere else in the world.

The wildflowers of the south-west are possibly Western Australia's most famous tourist attraction; they are certainly one of its greatest natural wonders. The heaths and shrublands of the Stirling Range and the Barren Ranges east of the Fitzgerald River are particularly well-endowed with flowering plants, with over 100 species restricted to the Stirling Range alone.

In contrast to the highly evolved and diverse vegetation, there are fewer

POLLINATING POSSUM Pollen is transferred from flower to flower by the honey-possum.

WESTERN MALLEE The fig-like 'fruit', or seed pod of the bell-fruited mallee inspired its name.

kinds of animals in the south-west compared to a similar-sized area in south-eastern Australia. Some animals, such as the koala, became extinct in the west long ago and others, such as the gliding possums, seem not to have found their way across to the western part of the continent.

The koala may well have migrated along the gum forests of inland river systems when the land was wetter, but possums require continuous expanses of moist forest. Birds of the eastern eucalypt forests, such as striated thornbills (*Acanthiza lineata*) and superb lyrebirds (*Menura novaehollandiae*), are also absent from the west.

The nectar-rich flowers of the kwongan attract vast numbers of honeyeaters. Along with red wattlebirds (*Anthochaera carunculata*) and western spinebills (*Acanthorhynchus superciliosus*), singing and brown honeyeaters (*Lichenostomus virescens, Lichmera indistincta*) seem to be everywhere.

With such a wealth of flowers, mammals as well as birds have adapted to take advantage of the nectar waiting to be collected. The honey-possum (*Tarsipes rostratus*), a diminutive 10–20 gram marsupial is common in the coastal heaths and shrublands. It feeds exclusively on pollen and nectar, using a long snout and a brush-tipped tongue to probe flowers. The flowers themselves benefit from the attention paid to them by birds and mammals, as many rely on them for pollination.

Living with fire

Just as the plants and animals of the south-west corner have evolved, largely in isolation, for their mutual benefit, the plants have evolved to fit the nature of the land. In a country where fire is such a pervasive force, the vegetation has developed ways to survive the recurring flames.

Whereas animals may flee the flames or take shelter beneath the ground, plants must withstand the heat. Those that are killed survive through their seed.

Many wattles require the heat of a fire to crack their seed pods open, so that water can be absorbed for germination to take place. Banksias and hakeas retain their fire-resistant seed pods and these open after the plant dies, releasing the seed onto the nutrient-rich ash bed.

IN BETWEEN Salmon gums grow most commonly in what botanists refer to as the 'transitional woodland' between the better watered parts of the south-west and the arid Nullarbor.

Other plants sprout from buds protected under tough, outer bark, or from enlarged rootstocks or lignotubers, shielded from the fire by the earth. Since fires are a frequent event throughout the south-west corner, it is possible to observe all stages of the fire process — from newly burnt to regenerated, mature vegetation — within a relatively small area like the Stirling Range National Park.

Away from the coast and mountains, where it is drier, a different vegetation appears. Inland from the karri forests, in the west of the region and on the slopes of the Stirling Range, a low jarrah and marri forest has developed with an understorey of banksia and she-oak trees. Patches of banksia woodland with Western Australian Christmas tree (*Nuytsia floribunda*) occur on sandy soils, and there are swampy areas with paperbark (*Melaleuca*) and tea-tree (*Leptospermum*).

As the land becomes drier, an open woodland of wandoo (*E. wandoo*) and marri takes over with she-oaks and banksia growing beneath. Further east, open woodlands of red mallee (*E. oleosa*), merrit (*E. flocktoniae*) and salmon gum (*E. salmonophloia*) gradually fade into a landscape of mallee heaths. Patches of bladder saltbush (*Atriplex vesicaria*) occur on compact, clay soils in this semi-arid country and as the annual rainfall drops to 300 mil-

ALL SEASONS Spring holds no special attraction for the teasel banksia which flowers at random.

FIREPROOF Like many native plants, the yellow-flowered Western Australian Christmas tree is capable of regenerating quickly after a bushfire; within weeks of a fire a new flush of flowers appears, even before the leaves.

POP-EYE The bulging eyes help the nocturnal western spiny-tailed gecko to see in the dark.

limetres, salmon gum disappears altogether and mallee becomes more extensive.

Along the coast east of Esperance, the dunes support scrubs and thickets of wattles, melaleuca, banksia and mallee eucalypts, while on the adjacent plains a heath of various banksias develops.

Many different species of animals are associated with these drier plant communities. Singing honeyeaters are still common, but other coastal species are absent. In their place are white-eared and yellow-plumed honeyeaters (*Lichenostomus leucotis, L. ornatus*), species which do not rely as heavily on nectar.

Weebills (*Smicrornis brevirostris*), chestnut-rumped thornbills (*Acanthiza uropygialis*), and red-capped robins (*Petroica goodenovii*) are abundant through the woodlands and mallee. Western grey kangaroos (*Macropus fuliginosus*) and echidnas (*Tachyglossus aculeatus*) are found here, while lizards, snakes and insects of every variety abound. □

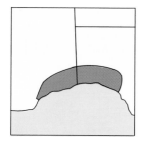
Despite its reputation, the no-man's land that links the east and the west of the continent is worthy of closer examination, both above and below its surface, and along its wild shores

An almost blank expanse on the map

The Nullarbor Plain lives up to its name as a desolate, almost treeless, and relatively waterless place. A vast, inhospitable region of almost 200 000 square kilometres, with the Southern Ocean pounding relentlessly at the cliffs along its southern extremity, it forms a formidable barrier between the population centres of the south-eastern and south-western sides of the continent.

The Nullarbor Plain's greatest feature is its very featurelessness, and it is this which inspired Alfred Delisser, in 1866, to coin its Aboriginal-sounding name from the Latin words *nulla arbor*, meaning 'no tree'. Despite the name, the Nullarbor is actually a low plateau formed by the world's largest single slab of limestone, part of which is submerged beneath the sea.

The Plain is bordered in the north by the sandy dunes of the Great Victoria Desert and to the south by the Great Australian Bight. On the eastern, South Australian side, the Plain proper is less well defined, but it begins in the vicinity of Nullarbor Homestead, near the coast.

The western approaches are marked by the gradual disappearance of the salmon gums (*Eucalyptus salmonophloia*) around Zanthus, and by the emergence of the coastal cliffs near Israelite Bay. The greatest part of the Plain lies within the borders of Western Australia.

All of the coastline fringing the Bight is marked by steep, limestone cliffs ranging from 90 to 130 metres in height. This great sea wall, almost 200 kilometres long, is believed to be the longest unbroken line of cliffs in the world.

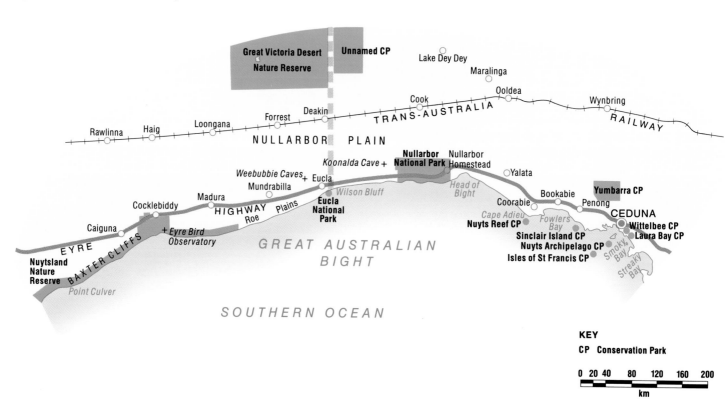

KEY

CP Conservation Park

0 20 40   80   120   160   200
km

BROAD HORIZONS This Nullarbor heathland dominated by bluebush peters out in the Great Victoria Desert, 200 kilometres to the north.

At the eastern and western ends of the Bight, these cliffs fall straight to the ocean. Access points from the Eyre Highway lead visitors to clifftop lookouts with spectacularly dramatic views of the stark coastline.

In the central region, between Cocklebiddy and Eucla, the cliffs are set back from the coast and sweep inland, creating a low-lying coastland called the Roe Plains. Here, towering sand dunes covered in dense mallee scrub separate the beaches from the limestone cliff faces to the north.

About 20 million years ago, the Nullarbor Plain of today lay beneath a large, shallow sea. This broad body of water separated south-eastern Australia from the south-west, and this long separation is one of the reasons for the differences in the modern plant communities of the two regions.

ABRUPT LAND'S END The sheer cliffs of the Bight reveal the limestone base of the Nullarbor.

Beneath this ancient sea, the remains of incalculable billions of tiny living creatures formed a thick layer of dark grey limestone. This hard, crystalline limestone, which in places is 30 metres thick, settled over an even older limestone layer which dates back about 40 million years.

When violent earth movements pushed the seabed above the surface, a limestone plateau — or plain – was born. At the centre of the modern plain the older limestone band is over 200 metres thick. Along the coastal cliffs the two limestone layers can be clearly seen, the older rocks appearing white and chalky beneath the grey, younger surface rocks.

The flat surface of the Nullarbor is little modified from the featureless surface that was raised from the sea floor millions of years ago. The limestone is so pure and porous, and the bedding plains so level, that no eroded valleys or hills stand out to give relief to the Nullarbor landscape.

Over distances of five kilometres or more, the general rise and fall of the land varies, on average, less than ten metres. Even the casual observer crossing the plain by train or car cannot help but be struck by the fact that nary creek nor stream breaks the tedium of the terrain. This surface has remained little changed by the erosive forces of wind and rain for thousands of years.

Beneath the surface is another story. This is where the erosion has occurred, in the Plain's hidden, underside. The subterranean landscape is as remarkable as the landscape above is featureless and — as any transcontinental rail traveller will attest – monotonous.

The Nullarbor underworld

Rainwater percolating through the Nullarbor limestone has formed a labyrinth of caves and waterways beneath the sands and thin soils of the surface. The technology to explore and chart these remarkable formations has been available only in the last few decades and the Nullarbor's secrets are finally being revealed.

Over a dozen large, deep caves are known from the southern parts of the plain. Aborigines knew the caves well and entered a number where they camped, quarried flint and created images on the walls.

The artwork at Koonalda Cave is the most extensive, with the majority of images being in the total darkness of the 'art passage' area of the cave. The surface of the cave is soft, and fingers or sticks were used to form parallel, meandering lines across it. The paintings are estimated to be as old as 20 000 years, and due to the deterioration that has already occurred, the cave has been closed to the public.

Many of the Nullarbor's caves are filled with lakes and streams which make exploration a hazardous and time-consuming undertaking. In scenes reminiscent of those described in a Jules Verne novel, an adventurous band of modern explorers, using climbing equipment, scuba-diving gear and aluminium boats, have begun mapping cave systems many metres below the earth's surface.

Two of the largest caves, one at Cocklebiddy and the other near Eucla, are now well explored and have become justly famous for their size and beauty. The vast caverns and lakes are often linked by flooded tunnels; at Cocklebiddy, divers have swum more than six kilometres from the entrance of the cave and still not reached the limits of the formations.

FLORAL PLAIN A spring shower on the eastern edge of the Nullarbor stimulated this flush of ephemeral wildflowers. Within a few weeks seed will be scattered to ensure the species' survival.

ANOTHER WORLD Beyond the entrance to Cocklebiddy Cave are many flooded passages — divers have so far penetrated seven kilometres.

Despite the arid environment, the Nullarbor Plain contains life of many kinds and a hike through one of its parks or reserves is liable to reveal much more of interest than might be observed by the casual traveller in a car or a train. The southern hairy-nosed wombat (*Lasiorhinus latifrons*) is the Plain's most famous inhabitant, having found its last refuge here.

Although superficially similar to the familiar forest-dwelling wombat, this desert-living marsupial is highly adapted to a dry climate. During the day, the wombats rest in extensive underground warrens, away from the desiccating effects of the desert sun. At night, they emerge to feed on the sparse vegetation.

They are physiologically adapted to survive extreme drought and can suspend their annual reproductive cycle if conditions are so dry that any young

MICROCLIMATE Protected from the wind, fruit trees thrive in the sinkhole of Koonalda Cave.

319

would be unlikely to survive. As its name suggests, the Nullarbor wombat differs from its forest cousins in having a hairy muzzle.

The Nullarbor National Park has the largest population of these unexpected desert dwellers. This unusual and highly restricted distribution of wombats suggests that they are survivors from a time when the climate was much milder and the landscape much greener. As conditions became more arid, the hairy-nosed wombat became isolated from the better watered regions to the east and west and was stranded in lonely desert refuges.

Life in the skies

Despite the lack of trees and the generally unpromising appearance of the landscape, the Nullarbor plays host to a great variety of birds. Vast, wheeling flocks of parrots, majestic wedge-tailed eagles (*Aquila audax*) and all manner of elusive bush birds attract birdwatchers from around the world.

Ironically, this region of very few trees is the site of Australia's first bird observatory, established in 1977 in the old stone building that was built as the Eyre telegraph station in 1897.

The Eyre Bird Observatory is now a centre for research into the everyday life, not only of birds but of all the other wildlife of the region as well. Resident wardens and visiting ornithologists study the habits of animals as diverse as the malleefowl, honeyeaters, seabirds, pygmy-possums and, in winter, the herds of whales that arrive off the coast each winter to calve (see box). What was once a lonely outpost of the then new telecommunications industry, is now a not-so-lonely outpost of the new science of ecology.

The wide, open spaces of the Nullarbor also contain some of Australia's most remote and least visited national parks and reserves. These combine to protect the geological, biological and historical features which give the region its special character.

The Yumbarra Conservation Park (106 189 hectares) is a large park located north of Ceduna, on the western approaches to the Nullarbor Plain. This well-wooded park does not live up to the region's name, being noted for its variety of mallee scrub species, granite outcrops and grassy glades. It contains many arid-country bird species including rufous treecreepers (*Climacteris rufa*), orange-chats (*Epthianura aurifrons*) and little button-quails (*Turnix velox*).

SOME ARBOR The Nullarbor is not entirely treeless as these tea-trees in the Hampton Tablelands show.

ENDANGERED SPECIES Agriculture has greatly reduced the range of the hairy-nosed wombat.

LITTLE NOMAD The button-quail lives in all but the coolest and most humid parts of Australia.

South Australia's third largest national park, the Nullarbor National Park, is set in unmistakeably Nullarbor country close to the Western Australian border. More than 231 000 hectares of bluebush and saltbush plain provide a thin blanket of vegetation over the underlying limestone surface.

Along this coast, the cliffs fall directly to the sea and the park's eastern boundary is close to the head of the Great Australian Bight. In addition to the desert wombats for which the park is well-known, other creatures resident here include the rare cinnamon quail-thrush (*Cinclosoma cinnamomeum*), blue bonnet (*Northiella haemogaster*) and kori bustard (*Ardeotis kori*).

The park also boasts evidence of giant, prehistoric animals that lived on the plains up to 40 000 years ago. The bones of diprotodons and other extinct creatures have been found exposed on the floors of caves.

One of the most interesting discoveries were the remains of a 2000-year-old thylacine, or Tasmanian tiger. This find was further proof that thylacines

lived on the Australian mainland until the dingo was introduced and super-seded the marsupial as the continent's main carnivore.

Situated in the centre of the Nullar-bor, just inside Western Australia, the small, coastal Eucla National Park (3342 hectares) offers spectacular views of the weather-beaten limestone cliffs from high points such as Nelson Bluff. Many rare plants are found amongst the coastal heaths including daisies, pomaderis and daisy-bush.

Some of these plants grow around the abandoned Eucla Telegraph Sta-tion, which, half submerged beneath the encroaching sand dunes, is a monu-ment to the earliest telecommunica-tions between the eastern and western sides of the continent.

At the Plain's western extremity, south of Cocklebiddy is the Nuytsland Nature Reserve (625 343 hectares). Commemorating the explorations along this coast by the sixteenth-century Dutch sailor Pieter Nuyts, this long, narrow reserve contains coastal cliffs, dunes and plains. It extends from Israe-lite Bay to near Madura and within its boundary lies the Eyre Bird Observa-tory. Nuytsland is well known for its small marsupials and its great variety of birds, especially honeyeaters.

Away from the coast, in the more arid, northern regions, the reserves are much larger; two huge reserves in particular cover a total area the size of many a small European nation. Strad-dling the Western Australian-South Australian border, they hold a vast, biological system that takes in the northern edges of the Nullarbor.

The Great Victoria Desert Nature Reserve (2 495 777 hectares) and a so-far unnamed park (2 132 600 hectares) on its eastern perimeter, form a unique arid-land reserve containing vast areas of trackless wilderness. The Plain is co-vered in grassland dominated by coarse spear-grasses punctuated by scattered herbs and small shrubs including Sturt's desert pea (*Clianthus formosus*) and swainsonas.

Here and there, small clumps of trees make a brave stand against the monotony of the grasses and the lack of water. The dead finish wattle (*Aca-cia tetragonophylla*), pittosporums and myoporums are the most common of the scrubby trees in this land of 'no trees'. To the north, the grasslands are replaced gradually by low woodlands dominated by myalls (*Acacia pendula*) set in a carpet of bluebush (*Maireana*) and other low shrubs. ☐

NULLARBOR BEACH There are beaches along the Nullarbor's arid shore as well as dramatically sheer cliffs; these eroded cliffs on the eastern edge of the Roe Plains are set back from the ocean.

'There she blows!', once more

The clifftops that fringe the head of the Great Australian Bight — known as the Head of Bight — offer views of a remarkable natural spectacle not seen in these waters for more than a century: dozens of southern right whales (*Eubalaena australis*) cavorting in the clear waters below.

Today, when the cry goes out that whales have been sighted, it is not the whalers with their harpoons who rush down to the shore, but delighted local residents and tourists, with cameras at the ready to record a sight which many thought would never occur again.

The southern right whales — fifty-tonne giants that may reach a length of eighteen metres — are returning to their traditional calving places around the bays and inlets of southern Australia after being hunted to near extinction in the nineteenth and early twentieth centuries.

Whalers are reckoned to have slaughtered at least 200 000 of the southern right species in the Southern Hemisphere; some 20 000 were taken in Australian and New Zealand waters between 1830 and 1850 alone and the huge animal was considered to be on the road to extinction until regular sightings started to occur in the whale's old haunts in the mid-1980s.

The southern right earned its name from its high blubber content, good quality baleen — the flexible, bone-like material from the whale's mouth which was used in corset manufacture — and the fact that it conveniently floated when dead. It was the 'right' whale to kill.

The whales spend the summer months in Antarctica, feeding on the minute marine organisms known as krill, before heading north with the coming of winter. Since 1982, their plumes of vapour have become an increasingly common sight off the coast from southern New South Wales to the south-west of Western Australia (see picture).

The biggest known group — about 40 creatures — migrate towards the Head of the Bight where, from June to November, they give birth, tend their young and teach the calves to swim and dive in the shallow waters. Access to the clifftops is through Aboriginal land and a permit must be obtained.

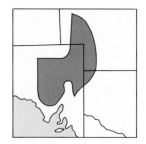

A tangled skein of wet-season rivers drains a vast catchment area but is usually defeated by the desert en route to its destination of Australia's largest — and driest — lake

Fickle rivers fall short of the empty 'sea' of salt

SEASONAL JIGSAW In a good year, the Channel Country is flushed green as excess rainwater meanders in search of a proper course.

In August 1844, an expedition of 15 men and 41 animals, led by the explorer Charles Sturt, left Adelaide with the aim of finding out whether there actually was an inland sea into which New South Wales' rivers flowed — and to reach the country's geographical centre. Sturt's expedition headed north to some of the country's most inhospitable territory, across the great stretch of gibber plains now known as Sturt's Stony Desert, and into the Simpson Desert.

The sharp edges of the gibber stones played havoc with the hooves of Sturt's horses, but it was the absence of water that finally forced him to turn back. Ironically, almost 100 years later and in the same part of the Simpson Desert, the scientist C.T. Madigan experienced such heavy rains that his party's camels had trouble making their way through the boggy plains and across the swollen rivers.

Named for its intricate patterns of river channels, the Channel Country, that vast part of outback Queensland and South Australia that lies along the south-eastern margin of the Australian arid zone, is dominated by huge, alluvial clay plains, countless salt pans and great tracts of stony desert — the gibber plains.

The focus of these channels lies in the south of this region — the biggest of all salt lakes, Lake Eyre. Despite being part of the driest region in Australia, with an annual rainfall averaging 125 millimetres, Lake Eyre and the other salt lakes are the focus of a huge river system that drains about 1.3 million square kilometres of central and north-eastern Australia. Rivers like the Finke, the Peake and the Hamilton drain arid regions, but the headwaters of larger watercourses such as the Georgina, the Diamantina, the Thompson and the Barcoo, rise on the eastern side of the Great Dividing Range and their catchments receive heavy rainfall in most years.

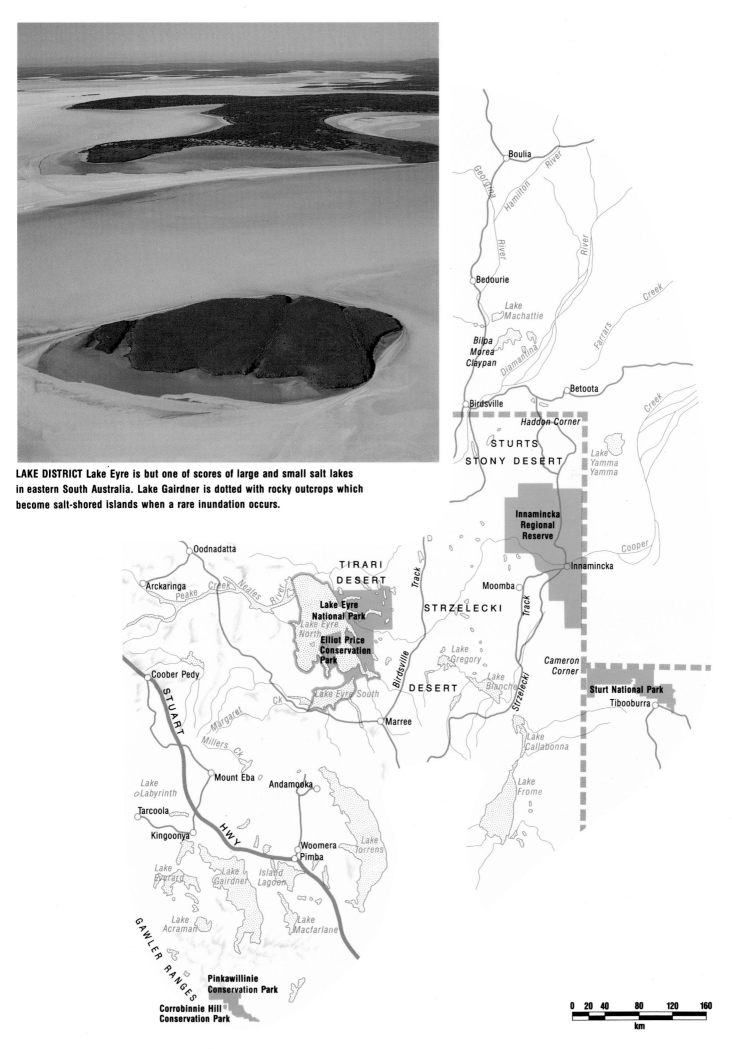

LAKE DISTRICT Lake Eyre is but one of scores of large and small salt lakes in eastern South Australia. Lake Gairdner is dotted with rocky outcrops which become salt-shored islands when a rare inundation occurs.

Boulia

Georgina River

Hamilton River

Bedourie

River

Lake Machattie

Bilpa Morea Claypan

Diamantina

Farrars Creek

Betoota

Birdsville

Haddon Corner

STURTS STONY DESERT

Lake Yamma Yamma

Creek

Innamincka Regional Reserve

Cooper

Innamincka

Moomba

Oodnadatta

TIRARI DESERT

Arckaringa

Peake Creek Neales River

Lake Eyre National Park

Lake Eyre North

Elliot Price Conservation Park

Birdsville Track

STRZELECKI

Lake Gregory

Strzelecki Track

Cameron Corner

Coober Pedy

Margaret Ck

Lake Eyre South

DESERT

Lake Blanche

Sturt National Park

Tibooburra

Millers Ck

Marree

Lake Callabonna

STUART

Mount Eba

Andamooka

Lake Labyrinth

Lake Frome

Tarcoola

HWY

Kingoonya

Woomera Pimba

Lake Torrens

Lake Everard

Lake Gairdner

Island Lagoon

Lake Acraman

Lake Macfarlane

GAWLER RANGES

Pinkawillinie Conservation Park

Corrobinnie Hill Conservation Park

0 20 40 80 120 160
km

These rivers created the wide, Channel Country flood plains: mirror-like when flooded, and channelled when dry, they display the braided patterns that are etched into the ground as the rivers divide and rejoin.

Setting course for Lake Eyre, the rivers run every summer, but their waters usually peter out in the dry, desert interior, soaked up by the sand and evaporated by the sun. On occasions when there are heavy rains in two or more consecutive years, the rivers flow as far as their lower reaches and may even reach Lake Eyre. But only three times this century has there been sufficient water to actually fill the lake; Lake Eyre was last a real lake, and far and away the biggest in Australia, in 1989.

At its lowest point, Lake Eyre lies about 16 metres below sea level. With the adjoining Lake Eyre South, it stretches over 9000 square kilometres. Most of the time it is dry — a glistening, glaring white sheet of salt, so solid in places that a heavy vehicle can be driven across it.

The rounded hills of the Gawler Ranges frame the southern border of the region. To the west is one of the bleakest and most uninviting areas in Australia — Sturt's Stony Desert. In summer it is searingly hot, its surface hard as iron, but after rain its clays and silts quickly form into a sticky mass over which travel is impossible.

The lifeless white lakes

The Channel Country does not funnel only into the vast dish of Lake Eyre. The southern extremity of the arid zone is punctuated by innumerable salt lakes or salinas, varying in size from Lakes Gairdner, Frome, Torrens and Disappointment, each several thousand square kilometres in area, to lakes of only a few square metres.

The best known of salinas, Lake Eyre was first sighted in 1840 by explorer Edward John Eyre, after whom it was named. Lake Eyre North and Lake Eyre South — linked by the 13-kilometre-long Goyder Channel — carry a crust of salt that is up to 50 centimetres thick in the south but thins to virtually nothing in the northern areas.

When it is dry, the lake bed appears completely flat. On the northern shore, mounds or lunettes rise up to 50 metres high, some greatly dissected, others still being built up by the wind — the beginning of desert dunes. The bed glitters into the distance: a vast, flat plain of salt.

DESERT SPA Mound springs, such as at this tiny oasis near Maree, occur more frequently in the Lake Eyre region than anywhere else overlaying the Great Artesian Basin (see pp. 338).

South of Lake Eyre is Lake Torrens, a D-shaped salina, about 200 kilometres long and up to 40 kilometres wide, covering about 5830 square kilometres. Standing about 34 kilometres above sea level, it is overlooked by the Arcoona Plateau on the west, a region of low-lying, dissected sandstone. Mound springs are prominent on this side, as on the eastern side of Lake Frome.

Neither lake fills often because they are large in comparison to their catchment areas. With a rare innundation of tropical rains, Lake Torrens filled early in 1989, for the first time in the twentieth century.

The most beautiful of the salinas is the dazzling Lake Gairdner. Its white, halite-encrusted bed is rimmed with red hills, red beaches and lunettes, and fringed with the shimmering pale green

On or just below the surface of the lakes, there is a crust of marine sediments, rich in silica, which is tough and resistant to weathering and erosion. The salt in the lakes has been washed out of these underlying sediments and because there is no run-off to the ocean, it has collected at the lowest points. Lake Eyre is a subsiding, asymmetrical basin.

Lake Eyre is both a great salina, or dry salt lake, and a great playa lake, a lake that is occasionally flooded. The contrast between the dry and the wet is staggering. When the rivers of the Channel Country run in torrents and the lake is flooded, it becomes Australia's biggest lake.

In the giant Lake Eyre National Park (1228 million hectares), there follows an explosion of life. Fish, carried downstream by the flooding rivers, fill the lake, and waterbirds — gulls, pelicans,

DRY CRUST Beneath Lake Eyre's dirty salt crust are many metres of grey mud. As the continent's lowest point — as much as 16 metres below sea level — the lake region is a vast drainage basin waiting to be filled.

black swans and pink ducks — flock to feed on them. Kangaroos arrive in large numbers.

But as the feeder rivers gradually dry up and the water dissolves the salt on the lake bed, it becomes increasingly salty: the fish die, and the birds and animals in turn depart. Before long the lake dries up, the salt crust sets and the landscape is once more parched and silent.

The lake was of little interest to the Aboriginal people of the region as it provided nothing in the way of sustenance, and for the European explorers it was a place of desolation. But for the modern visitor, not preoccupied with the immediate needs of survival, it can be spellbinding: its headlands and beaches look strangely naked with no water to lap their shores. The glittering sheet of snow-like salt stretches to the horizon, the heat shimmering from its surface, while gibbers and driftwood on the shoreline seem to be covered with frost.

The only signs of life in the salt lake's immediate surrounds are the inconspicuous samphire bushes (*Arthrocnemum*

of mulga and myall bushes. Its irregular shape covers 8880 square kilometres, the halite overlying saline clays and sands with gypsum crystals. Not far beneath that is the volcanic bedrock of the region.

Many rocky islands that stand above the salt crust were isolated hills which stood above the old river valley floor. The rocky shores of these islands and the main shoreline are pock-marked with strange caverns and hollows, formed by salt weathering.

Genesis of a salt lake

In the warm, humid climate that existed between 20 000 and 40 000 years ago, Lake Eyre was a massive freshwater lake brimming with life. This ancestral lake, called Lake Dieri after the Aboriginal tribe that once inhabited the region, was three times the size of Lake Eyre and at least seventeen metres deep. The luxuriant tropical vegetation that grew on its shores was grazed by many animals, including the herbivorous diprotodon, which resembled a giant wombat.

About 20 000 years ago, the climate became drier, the streams that fed the lake petered out and it began to shrink. Strings of much smaller, salty lakes gradually assumed their present shape as they were left scattered across the flat plains.

RARE SIGHT It was a rare occasion when Lake Torrens lived up to its name and was inundated in 1989. Engineers once suggested permanent inundation through a canal to Spencer Gulf.

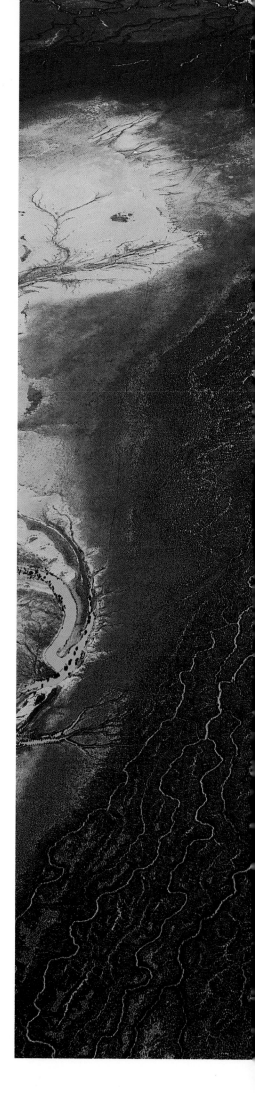

THE INLAND 'SEA' The summer rains of central and southern Queensland usually have to reach cyclonic proportions before they produce enough water to survive the 500-kilometre desert journey to Lake Eyre. When full, as here, the lake's average depth is about three metres.

halocnemoides) which dot the shore-line and the pale Lake Eyre dragon lizard (*Amphibolorus maculosus*) which makes its home there. Two tiny animals, less than a centimetre long, actually live in the lake — the salt lake louse (*Haloniscus searlei*) and the brine shrimp (*Artemia salina*).

In an environment which contains enough sodium to pickle most creatures, the louse and the shrimp withstand the salt water and miraculously survive even the drying up of the lake. When the salt encrusts the surface, the louse lives in the mud beneath the crust, while the shrimp's eggs — with a tough skin to resist desiccation — are safely stored to await the next influx of water.

Channel Country

On their way to Lake Eyre the rivers of the Channel Country flow at the gentlest of gradients — sometimes dropping as little as one metre over five kilometres. Gradually they spread over wide flood plains built by sediments they themselves have deposited over the centuries.

This huge expanse of south-western Queensland and north-eastern South Australia is a sparsely vegetated, brown land, etched with an intricate braided

DESERT FISH The five-centimetre-long desert goby, which thrives in the highly mineralised waters of mound springs, probably originated in the ocean which once covered central Australia.

pattern of riverbeds dividing and re-joining. The vegetation is adapted to withstand both drought and flood.

River red gums (*Eucalyptus camaldulensis*), coolibahs (*Eucalyptus microtheca*) and gidgees (*Acacia cambagei*), grow along creek beds, providing patches of green-grey in a brown landscape. But when rains come, the countryside is transformed to one of lush grasses and low shrubs.

The plant life in the Channel Country is vital to the entire ecosystem, because it is where the food chain begins. By providing nourishment for animals and insects, it provides also for the meat-eaters — the dingos, reptiles and birds of prey. When the rains come and the plants sprout and flower, all the creatures in the region feed and breed in a great flurry of activity, before green turns to brown once more.

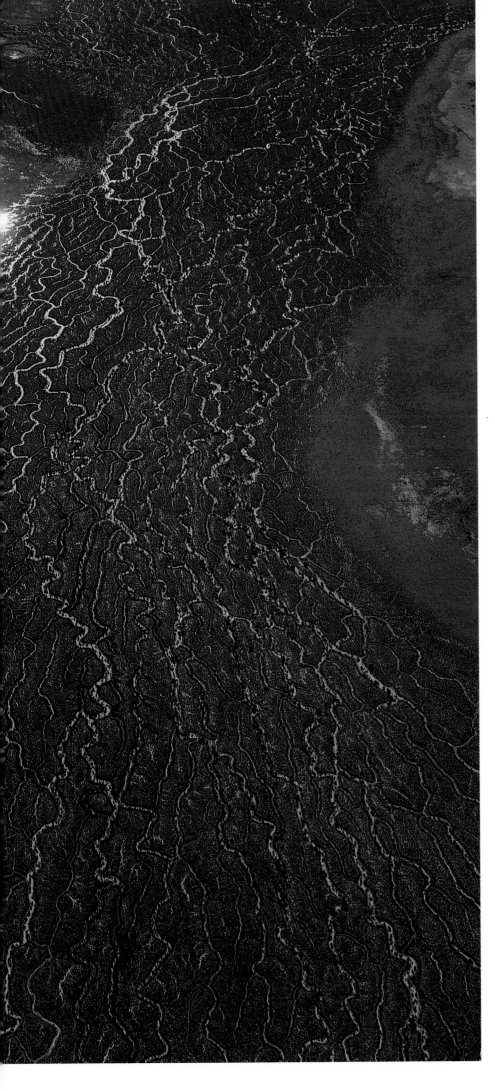

Mulgas, native fuchsias and cassias are covered with new growth and many short-lived ephemeral plants, the seeds of which may have lain dormant for years, break through the surface and bloom in profusion. Golden yellow, pink and white daisies (*Helichrysum bracteatum*, *Helipterum roseum* and *H. floribundum*), the brilliant red Sturt's desert pea, (*Clianthus formusus*), and purple and orange *Swainsona* appear in great sweeps of colour across the plains. In the mud of the many floodouts, the leaves of the nardoo water fern (*Marsilea drummondii*) appear, forming large patches of vivid green.

On the rare occasions when the rivers break their banks, the whole countryside is inundated as they merge. Not only are the various floodouts, overflows and lagoons filled with slow-moving, muddy water, but the plains are also covered. Cooper Creek, the combined waters of the Thompson and Barcoo Rivers, has reached a width of 60 kilometres south of Windorah, and the Diamantina has at times been estimated to be 50 kilometres wide below Birdsville.

DESERT'S EDGE On the edge of central Australia, the waters of Cooper Creek break up in a confusion of creeks and waterholes as the Tirari and Strzelecki Deserts (above) bar the way south.

In flood, the countryside is a spectacular sight — a sheet of water stretching as far as the eye can see. Only the strings of red gums are left above the surface to define the submerged channels. As the floods recede, the sediment carried in the water settles out and reforms the characteristic flat stretches of flood plain.

Dry rivers, 'wet' lakes

The river channels dry out first, followed by the billabongs, which occasionally break the rivers' meandering courses. Sand gathers in dry beds and billabongs, and the wind forms long, white dunes which rise incongruously from the black, silted plains.

Strange as it may seem, these rivers are crucial to the Simpson Desert. The floodwaters that flow down their channels carry sand that is eventually deposited in the lower reaches of the river valleys, in lagoons, or in Lake Eyre and other large salinas. The floodwaters sometimes even extend into the corridors between the dunes of the desert.

When the water has evaporated, the river-borne sand is picked up by the wind and shaped into the desert dunes.

NATIVE RAT The water rat, no relation to the European species, is mainly carnivorous.

Without the rivers there would be no dune fields.

While the main channel of Cooper Creek flows to Lake Eyre through the Strzelecki Desert, where its waters are soon lost forever, a second branch flows north-west into the Coongie Lakes, a region of five lakes and a series of wetlands, north of Lake Eyre. Sturt discovered this region of sparkling water in 1845, and the lakes have dried up only once in the intervening years.

The lakes provide an oasis-like home for many birds and a wide range of aquatic creatures including a variety of frogs, more than ten species of fish, and several rare or threatened animals, such as the water-rat (*Hydromys chrysogaster*), Gilbert's water dragon (*Lophognathus gilberti*), the freckled duck (*Stictonetta naevosa*) and the Cooper Creek tortoise, such a recent discovery that it has yet to be christened with a scientific name.

The 'gloomy' plain

East of the major saltpans, just north of Tibooburra, is the Sturt National Park (31 0634 hectares). Pastoral properties, acquired for the national park in the early 1970s, incorporate the flood plains on the edge of the Bulloo River overflow, and the rolling, stony downs of Mitchell grass and gibber plains which merge with the high, red sand hills of the Strzelecki Desert.

In the middle of the park, the isolated flat-topped hills of the Grey Range rise up 150 metres above the plains. Known as the 'jump-up' country, the range is a bluff formation of mesas, with deep gullies on their steeper side.

In his journal, Charles Sturt referred several times to the 'gloomy, stone-clad plain' which occupies large areas of north-eastern South Australia and adjacent parts of Queensland and New South Wales. The most prominent feature in this landscape is the layer of stones called gibbers, which covers the flat, clay surface.

The gibbers are a result of the swelling and contracting of the clay. When it swells up, after rain, fine soil or sand particles and gibbers are thrust upwards, but when the clay eventually dries up and its surface cracks, the finer materials fall down the cracks leaving a concentration of stones on the surface. Wind and water help this process as they erode the silt and the sand, leaving the stones exposed.

In spite of its 'gloomy' appearance for most of the year, this semi-desert country is quickly covered with a brightly coloured blanket of vegetation after a good fall of rain: the white and yellow of daisies, the purple of the parakeelia (*Calandrinia balonensis*) and the red of Sturt's desert pea combine in a kaleidoscope of colour. Emus

MIDDLE OF NOWHERE The skies above Birdsville, one of Australia's most isolated settlements, were once thick with the dust raised by thousands of hooves as cattle were driven southward to market.

and red and grey kangaroos quickly appear in large numbers to feast on the fresh vegetation.

The few trees of the gibber plains are confined to the watercourses. The coolibah and the river red gum grow in creek beds, and in depressions where water gathers, the red mulga (*Acacia cyperophylla*) survives, its bark peeling off and curling back on itself.

Since late in the nineteenth century, the Channel Country has been used

for cattle fattening. For many years, before the introduction of road trains, the Birdsville Track, running from the tiny Queensland town of Birdsville, across Sturt's Stony Desert to the railhead at Maree in South Australia, was one of Australia's major cattle-droving routes.

Waterholes, fed by bores sunk by the government, allowed drovers to take their animals across this inhospitable terrain even in times of drought. ☐

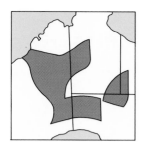

In the arid lands, where cloud rarely appears to temper the power of the sun, the wind shapes the parched surface of Australia's harshest environment

Heat, dust, and little prospect of shade

Despite the legendary aridity of the Australian continent beyond its coastal fringe, the interior is not all desert; scientifically speaking, the term 'dead heart' was an early European misnomer. But approximately one-third of the continent *is* semi-arid, while another third is *completely* arid, and a large part of this vast arid zone is generally classified as desert.

In the strictest sense, 'desert' is used to refer to a region with little or no rainfall or vegetation. Such a definition would be inappropriate here, as few areas of Australia's deserts resemble the trackless, sandy wastes of the Sahara or the Gobi. Even the most inhospitable regions of the inland receive *some* rainfall and sprout a scattered covering of formidably tenacious plants.

The word 'desert' also carries different connotations for different people. To a climatologist, a desert is a region that receives, on average, less than 250 millimetres of rainfall a year.

Such arid areas occur in polar as well as temperate regions, so that deserts can be classified as warm or cold. Within the arid lands, hyper-arid areas are defined as those with less than 125 millimetres of rain per annum, while semi-arid areas are those receiving between 250 and 380 millimetres each year.

Deserts are regions of almost perennially blue skies, where there is no insulating cloud cover to protect the earth's surface from the constant bombardment of solar radiation. This is why deserts record extraordinarily high daytime temperatures (air temperatures of 58°C and ground temperatures of 94°C have been recorded) and high daily and annual ranges.

To a biologist, deserts are regions where plants and animals have evolved features or habits that enable them to overcome a lack of water on one hand, and huge temperature ranges on the other. The ability to remain

DEVILISHLY HOT The thorny devil, militarily camouflaged and burdened with a barrage of protective devices, is master of all it surveys in the Gibson Desert.

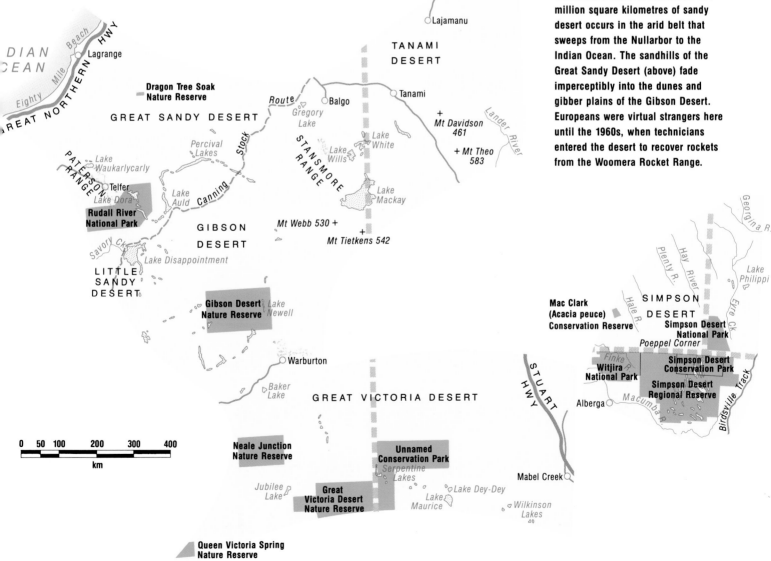

TRACKLESS Much of Australia's two million square kilometres of sandy desert occurs in the arid belt that sweeps from the Nullarbor to the Indian Ocean. The sandhills of the Great Sandy Desert (above) fade imperceptibly into the dunes and gibber plains of the Gibson Desert. Europeans were virtual strangers here until the 1960s, when technicians entered the desert to recover rockets from the Woomera Rocket Range.

INDIAN OCEAN

Eighty Mile Beach

GREAT NORTHERN HWY

Lagrange

Lajamanu

TANAMI DESERT

Dragon Tree Soak Nature Reserve

Route

Balgo

Tanami

GREAT SANDY DESERT

Gregory Lake

Stock

STANSMORE RANGE

Lander River

Mt Davidson 461

Percival Lakes

Lake White

+ Mt Theo 583

PATERSON RANGE

Lake Waukarlycarly

Lake Wills

Telfer

Lake Dora

Canning

Lake Auld

Rudall River National Park

GIBSON DESERT

Lake Mackay

Savory Ck

Mt Webb 530 +

+ Mt Tietkens 542

Lake Disappointment

LITTLE SANDY DESERT

Gibson Desert Nature Reserve

Lake Newell

Georgina R.

Plenty R.

Hay River

Lake Philippi

SIMPSON DESERT

Mac Clark (Acacia peuce) Conservation Reserve

Hale R.

Eyre Ck

Warburton

Simpson Desert National Park

Poeppel Corner

Finke

Baker Lake

GREAT VICTORIA DESERT

STUART HWY

Witjira National Park

Simpson Desert Conservation Park

Simpson Desert Regional Reserve

Alberga

Macumba R.

Birdsville Track

0 50 100 200 300 400
km

Neale Junction Nature Reserve

Unnamed Conservation Park

Serpentine Lakes

Jubilee Lake

Great Victoria Desert Nature Reserve

Lake Dey-Dey

Lake Maurice

Wilkinson Lakes

Mabel Creek

Queen Victoria Spring Nature Reserve

dormant for long periods, annual migration, well-developed cooling mechanisms (such as large ears well supplied with blood vessels), reduced leaf area, deep roots, and rapid reproduction mechanisms, are some of the methods adopted to overcome the problems of surviving in the desert.

For geologists, interested in the shape of the earth's surface, deserts are regions where the wind plays a dominant role in the shaping of the landscape, aided by occasional rains — and no desert is rainless — which generate brief floods that erode the soil and move it from one place to another.

Sand, gibbers and rock

Australia's desert areas can be broadly divided into sand deserts — roughly half of which are dunes and half gritty sand plains — stony deserts, which are largely plains of stones or 'gibbers', and deserts of a slightly higher than usual altitude where 'resistant' rock — rock which is extremely hard and almost impervious to the eroding forces of the elements — is the major feature of the landscape. But no desert region can be truly representative of one of these landscapes alone — even in dune country there are minor salt lakes and clay-pans, patches of stony desert or rocky outcrops.

The red sands of the plains come

AIR-COOLED The bilby's blood is cooled as it circulates through its large, hairless ears.

from sedimentary rock which over the centuries has been eroded by flood-waters. The wind lifts this fine dust high into the air and deposits most of it in dunes within the desert borders, but occasionally, when the atmospheric turmoil is at its most extreme, the desert topsoil can swirl over coastal cities or even fall to earth as far away as New Zealand.

Dune fields cover vast areas of the sand deserts, taking the form of parallel ridges 10 to 38 metres high, generally spaced 300 to 500 metres apart, although in some regions they may be up to two kilometres apart, with sand-plains or gibber plains between them. The strong winds of the interior have resulted in the ridge patterns of all the sandy deserts, forming the same vast, anti-clockwise whorl.

The aridity of Australia's deserts is emphasised by their position — well into the interior of a huge, compact

SHAPED BY WIND Few of Australia's sandy desert landscapes are uniform: the dunes shift with the wind and may be broken by areas of stony desert.

DUNE COUNTRY Australia's largest sand desert,
the 80 000-square-kilometre Simpson Desert,
was unexplored until the 1930s.

land mass, they are also in the rain shadow of the Great Dividing Range.

Other factors contributing to this aridity are the cold, northward-flowing current off the Western Australian coast, and, in the southern part of the continent, the nature of the underlying bedrock. The Nullarbor region is underlain by a thick mass of limestone that swallows any water that falls upon the surface.

Plains dominate these arid lands, with two major plains in particular being well-known for their stony character. Part of the Gibson Desert carries a carpet of rust-coloured stones, once described as 'a great undulating desert of gravel'. The gravel is derived from the breakdown of the iron-stone that caps the mesas of the area.

Sturt's Stony Desert, of the northeast of South Australia (see pp.332–339), on the other hand, is noted for its veneer of siliceous stones derived from the breakdown of the silcrete cappings that are preserved within the

SUN-BAKED One-third of desert country is rocky, often covered with stones known as 'gibbers'.

333

desert. The silcrete breaks into fragments with concave faces, and the edges where the faces meet are very sharp, so sharp that they played havoc with the hooves of early explorers' horses, and were commonly used by the Aborigines for making tools.

The sandy deserts, known as dune fields, are all basically similar in that they consist largely of dunes of varying shapes and lengths. The differences lie in the amount of cover given by vegetation.

The dunes of the Simpson and its associated deserts such as the Tirari, have crests essentially devoid of vegetation; the dunes fringing such areas as the Great Victoria and the Great Sandy deserts have crests that carry some vegetation; and the dunes of the Tanami, for example, are stabilised because of the density of their vegetation.

Dune country

The Great Sandy, Gibson, Great Victoria and Simpson Deserts are the major sand deserts. But even in country such as this there are few areas which resemble the endless sandhill deserts depicted in films set in North Africa or the Arabian peninsula. There is always some form of tough plant life looking for a niche in the environment.

Plants such as spindly cane grass (*Zygochloa paradoxa*), which grows thickly in the gullies along with tall, broad hummocks of the perennial desert grass called spinifex (*Triodia*), are not often put off by something as common as a drought.

Wattles, grevilleas, spotted emu bushes (*Eremophila maculata*) and numerous small trees put down roots in sheltered positions, and desert oaks (*Allocasuarina decaisneana*) grow in depressions where rain water run-off gathers and there is moisture near the surface. Low shrubs such as *Thryptomene maison-neuvii* provide cover on the dune flanks.

Even in this inhospitable environment, marble gums (*Eucalyptus gongylocarpa*) grow up to 12 metres high in the deep sand, and stands of doggedly determined river red gums (*E. camaldulensis*) grow along the edges of dry river beds, indicating the presence of underground water.

In sandplain areas, spinifex hummocks spread as far as the eye can see, and there are scattered, low woodlands of mulga and bloodwood, along with grey acacia scrub. As desert plants are constantly competing for every drop of moisture, they tend to grow far apart,

HARDY ANNUALS Sturt's desert pea enlivens arid Australia after late winter or spring rains; a long tap root ensures this annual's survival until the flowers have lured pollinating birds.

with extensive, deep root systems spreading between them. Spinifex roots may snake up to ten metres through the sand in search of water.

It is in the stony wastes of the gibber country, such as large areas of the Gibson Desert, that the plants almost give up their battle against the environment. Perennial vegetation is largely absent here, few plants managing to take root amongst the red stones, polished smooth by the elements, that carpet the ground. Little other than spinifex and stunted mulga (*Acacia aneura*), punctuated by prickly bindiis here and there, survives.

In the low ranges that occasionally occur within the deserts, there is more water for plants. At night, as the rocky soil cools rapidly, water from the air between the soil particles condenses on the rocks, forming dew.

A variety of shrubs and trees, such as white cypress pine (*Callitris columellaris*) and snappy gum (*Eucalyptus brevifolia*) grow on boulder-covered scarps where runoff

TOOTH AND CLAW A foray to the surface results in a marsupial mole — about ten centimetres long — making a meal of a gecko. The mole's silky fur eases its way through the sand.

EVER-CHANGING The usually parallel dunes in the north of the Simpson Desert are constantly being shaped and moved by the wind. This dune is gradually drifting onto the scrub corridor which separates it from the next dunefield.

PERSONAL LARDER The dunnart's tail is like a camel's hump — it stores fat for lean times.

is trapped in rocky clefts. On low hills, there is often a cover of spinifex. There are also springs fed by the Great Artesian Basin, the vast underground water store that lies beneath much of the continent.

Some keep cool...

The small mammals that live in the desert regions have developed a simple solution to the problem of living with great extremes of temperature: they spend their days underground or in deep cracks in the soil, where they are insulated from the heat, and feed by night, when it is cooler.

So well adapted to desert conditions are the spinifex hopping-mouse (*Notomys alexis*) and the fawn hopping-mouse (*N. cervinus*) that they can survive on a waterless diet of dry seeds.

Other animals emulate the camel and store food in their bodies in times of plenty for use during the inevitable lean time that will follow. The mouse-like, fat-tailed antechinus (*Pseudantechinus macdonnellensis*) and the fat-tailed dunnart (*Sminthopsis crassicaudata*) are insect-eating marsupials which eat everything available, their swollen tails serving as an energy reserve when the food runs out.

When this happens, these animals save energy by retiring to their nests and slipping into a torpor-like state. Because they obtain enough fluids from their prey they, too, do not need to drink.

One of the strangest mammals of all is the blind marsupial mole (*Notoryctes typhlops*), which, though rarely seen, is common throughout the deserts.

Little is known about this mole, which spends its life pulling its way beneath the surface of a sea of sand with its large, spade-like front claws. It feeds mainly on insect larvae, only occasionally coming to the surface.

Until the turn of the century, the bilby (*Macrotis lagotis*), a little desert bandicoot, ranged over much of the arid region. Since then, its food supplies have been depleted by the foraging of rabbits and livestock and its survival is thought to be secure only in a special sanctuary in the Tanami Desert.

The best adapted of the large mammals is the euro or common wallaroo (*Macropus robustus*). It can survive on a diet consisting largely of spinifex, with irregular access to water, providing it can find shade in which to rest during the daylight hours. It favours the rocky country of the low ranges — really no more than hills — where permanent shelter is provided by caves and permanent overhangs.

The red kangaroo (*Macropus rufus*) can also withstand desert conditions but is seldom seen where there are no trees to provide shade. Whereas the euro tends to be solitary and has a limited home range, the red kangaroo is semi-nomadic, travelling in groups through open country in search of food.

One creature not in danger of extinction is the long-haired rat (*Rattus villossisimus*), its habitat ranging from the Kimberleys to north-western New

FATAL CURIOSITY The desert death adder attracts prey by quivering the tip of its tail.

DESERT 'ROO The euro survives the desert heat by seeking the shade of rocky outcrops.

LIZARD LAND Two-thirds of the world's goannas — including the perentie — live in Australia.

South Wales. When good rains fall in the rat's arid home territory, it breeds with such vigour that a plague is often the result. All the vegetation within reach is consumed and the rats are forced to travel in search of food. Driven by hunger, they have even been known to swim across rivers.

Farms on the fringes of arid regions may be overrun by the rats, fodder stocks consumed, and houses invaded by rodents hungry enough to eat even the curtains.

For the period of the plague, predators such as birds of prey, cats and snakes, maintain full stomachs, but plant-eating animals are left with little

to sustain them in the wake of the rats. In due course, drought conditions return, the rats are reduced to cannibalism, and only a few survive to found new colonies which remain stable until the next period of rain.

... some like it hot

While many mammals in the arid regions have become rare or completely disappeared since European settlement, reptiles have fared better and are still a common sight. As reptiles lack the internal 'thermostat' of birds and mammals, their body temperature is determined by the temperature of the immediate surroundings. As a result, a

reptile's body temperature can go much higher, and lower, than that of a mammal or a bird.

To regulate their temperature, reptiles bathe in the morning sun in order to recover from the cool of the night and then retreat to the shade. Large snakes and lizards may be seen basking on rocks well into the day, as they take longer to warm up after a chilly night than less bulky creatures.

Ranging in size from tiny skinks to the largest of the lizards — the perentie (*Varanus giganteus*) can grow to over two metres — desert reptiles thrive under extreme climatic conditions. Moisture is provided mainly through their solid food, as most reptiles eat insects and other creatures with a high fluid content.

They survive the rigours of the climate by having tough, scale-covered skins which help conserve their body moisure, and which are impervious to strong, drying winds and the rasp of blown sand. Home is often a burrow which provides cool conditions in the searing heat, a degree of warmth on a cold night, when freezing to death is a distinct possibility, and sanctuary when danger threatens.

Despite their sometimes fearsome appearance most lizards are harmless and quite timid. The thorny devil (*Moloch horridus*) is a monstrous sight, bristling with spikes, but it poses a threat only to small black ants, which it consumes, one by one, in vast quantities. Not only does its medieval-looking armour deter predators, but moisture which gathers on the spikes passes into tiny capillary channels leading to its mouth, enabling it to drink whenever a night brings dew.

UNCAGED The common budgerigar, familiar to city dwellers as a solitary, caged bird, is a small parrot which roams the desert and semi-desert regions of the inland in flocks of up to 100 birds, searching for grass seeds.

The large sand goanna (*Varanus gouldii*), which is found over much of inland Australia, is common in desert country. It is fast on its feet and is capable of outstripping a human runner for at least 100 metres.

The goanna will climb a tree to evade danger if it cannot take refuge in its burrow. It has been known to mistake a stationary man for a tree, a case of shortsightedness which results in an alarming experience for both parties involved.

In sandy regions, or where the soil is not heavily compacted, the sand-swimmer skink (*Eremiascincus richardsoni*) slithers beneath the surface. These are burrowing lizards, some of which are legless and resemble snakes; they manage to move more efficiently, and more safely, beneath the surface than above ground.

A commonly sighted inhabitant of gibber plain and spinifex country is the bearded gecko (*Lucasium damaeum*), a beautifully patterned creature rarely more than seven centimetres long. There are many geckos in the arid regions, some species having a tail gland that is used to squirt attackers with a sticky fluid.

Desert-dwelling snakes are common but seldom seen as, like most snakes, they are timid and will flee when approached. The venomous mulga snake (*Pseudechis australis*), grows to three metres and is potentially very dangerous, as is the desert death adder (*Acanthophis pyrrhus*) — a metre in length — with its attractive, lacily patterned skin which helps it blend in with its environment. Bredl's python (*Morelia bredli*) is the desert form of the common carpet snake, more correctly the carpet python, as it kills its prey by constriction.

Birds without trees

Despite the arid conditions and the scarcity of trees, many small birds live in desert country, foraging for seeds and insects across the stony plains and in the sparse clumps of vegetation. Certain species have adapted to each desert habitat. The gibberbird (*Ashbyia lovensis*) lives on waterless gibber plains, an environment also frequented by the cinnamon quail-thrush (*Cinclosoma cinnamomeum*).

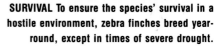

SURVIVAL To ensure the species' survival in a hostile environment, zebra finches breed year-round, except in times of severe drought.

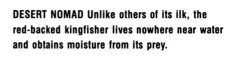

DESERT NOMAD Unlike others of its ilk, the red-backed kingfisher lives nowhere near water and obtains moisture from its prey.

In the desert grasslands, the spinifex bird (*Eremiornis carteri*) shares the spiky spinifex tussocks with the handsome, crested spinifex pigeon (*Geophaps plumifera*) and the tiny, rufous-crowned emu-wren (*Stipiturus ruficeps*). Another tiny desert bird is the nomadic black honeyeater (*Certhionyx niger*), that follows the erratic flowering of the spotted emu bush in order to feed on its nectar, and supplements its diet with insects.

When the intermittent rains come, the deserts are carpeted with vegeta-

tion as the seeds of ephemeral plants burst into life. The insect population burgeons after rain and the stimulus of a bountiful food supply provides the conditions that many birds need to breed. Several broods are commonly raised in quick succession, each taking a mere five or six weeks from nest-building to the time when young ones are tumbled out of the nest for flying lessons. At such times, the small bird population can double in two or three months.

Many desert birds, particularly the seed-eaters, can survive only if they have access to open water; early explorers were quick to note that if there were flocks of birds in the vicinity, it was a sure sign of a pool or creek. Wheeling clouds of budgerigars (*Melop-*

sittacus undulatus) are a common sight at dawn and dusk as they continue their endless search for water and seed. They descend noisily on waterholes, immersing their heads to gulp the water.

Flocks of zebra finches (*Taeniopygia guttata*) are also often seen near watering points, feeding on the ground, drinking, bathing and huddling together to preen one another. These little finches, widespread throughout the dry country, can tolerate brackish water and have a lower metabolic rate than other finches, which reduces their water 'turnover' and loss.

Unlike the other members of the kingfisher family, the nomadic red-backed kingfisher (*Todiramphus pyr-rhopygius*) lives happily well away

from permanent water and can be seen throughout the arid regions. Its diet consists of insects, small reptiles and occasionally young birds. Large birds of prey which visit the desert include the great wedge-tailed eagle (*Aquila audax*) and the black falcon (*Falco subniger*), both of which breed in large numbers in inland regions when food is plentiful.

Frogs without water

In a region where rivers, creeks or ponds disappear almost as quickly as they form, frogs spend the most part of their lives buried, either under leaf litter or in the soil. A native of sand-dune country and clay pans, and the only frog to be found in the Simpson Desert, the trilling frog (*Neobatrachus*

Mountain rains that water the inland: how a natural reservoir foils the sun

One of the world's largest and least polluted water storage systems lies beneath much of Australia's arid lands. Protected from evaporation and contamination, this invaluable water resource also magically replenishes itself.

Like a huge saucer of water, tipped on its eastern rim, the Great Artesian Basin that sits below the surface of much of central and eastern Australia is one of 19 major groundwater basins in the country.

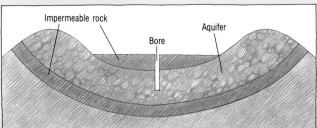

The rock that forms this vast basin was once the sandy floor of a huge, inward-draining lake system that appeared millions of years ago. Over time, these ancient sands changed to sandstone, and today are the porous rocks (aquifers) that contain underground, or artesian, water.

Sandwiched between layers of impermeable mudstones and shales, the aquifers have a remarkable sponge-like capacity for storing water in spaces between grains or fractures. These water-bearing sheets, usually deep below the surface, underlie

1.7 million square kilometres (about 22 per cent) of Australia.

With the high rim of the Great Artesian Basin rising to ground level on the western slopes of the Great Dividing Range in Queensland and New South Wales, rain which falls here soaks through the soil and straight into the main aquifers (see diagram). Travelling at a rate of about five metres per year, it gradually soaks through the surface aquifers into the bottom of the basin, deep underground.

Because some of the water has remained underground for hundreds of thousands of years, it is heavily mineralised by the time it reaches the surface and usually fit only for irrigation; but it is a vital source of water in arid and semi-arid land pastoral areas.

Artesian water comes to the surface either in natural spring outlets or man-made bores. Tapping into the aquifers brings underground water gushing up; because the level of the top of the bore is usually below the water source in the Great Dividing Range, it is already under pressure. Water from the deeper wells — some reach depths of 2000 metres — can be very hot (30-100°C) and has to be cooled before it can be used.

About 20 000 shallow bores tap water from the Basin and usually pump it to the surface using windmills. Drilling of new bores is controlled to maintain an equilibrium.

Mounds — such as at Dalhousie Springs on the edge of the Simpson Desert (see photograph) — often develop around the margins of natural spring outlets. These are formed as the heavily mineralised artesian water is evaporated, leaving its carbon and sulphur content behind as sediments. Wind-blown sand adheres to these deposits and gradually builds up into mounds. Some are 25 metres high, the result of several thousand years of evaporation and deposition.

The mound springs form valuable oases in this parched country. A variety of vegetation grows on their fringes, from seeds and grasses to stands of trees. Birds flock to the water to drink, and feed on grass seeds and desert insects, and reptiles make their homes in the surrounding rocks and low-growing vegetation.

The introduction of cattle, rabbits and more recently, tourists, has brought about the destruction of many of the fragile mound-springs. Mounds and archeological sites have been trampled, sparse plant cover has been damaged, water has been fouled, and perhaps most damaging of all, the amount of water being drawn from bores for stock has markedly reduced the flow rate of many springs, in some cases to no more than a trickle.

UP FOR AIR Spencer's burrowing frog is at home beneath a dry creek bed.

LOW-RISE The modest termite mounds of the Tanami may contain up to 100 000 ants.

centralis) can bury itself in loose soil in just a few minutes, twisting its way underground tail first, as it scrapes away the soil with its wide-toed feet.

After settling about 60 centimetres beneath the surface to wait for rain, the frog survives this dormant period by consuming its stored body fats. When soaking rain falls, the frog burrows up to the surface for a brief, busy season of eating and spawning in the temporary pools.

On the wide plains of the desert, several years can elapse before there has been enough rain for plants to grow to a size where a generation of insects can lay eggs in their shelter. The eggs will usually await the next ground-soaking rains before they hatch.

To survive in such precarious conditions, where the climate is unpredictable and fluctuating, sophisticated survival techniques are called for. Grasshoppers have become masters of disguise, one species developing a colourful camouflage which resembles a mottling of both stone and soil, while another — in the sand dunes of the Simpson — grows up with a sand-grain pattern disguise that renders it all but invisible.

Like many other desert creatures, insects burrow into the ground or shelter under stones to avoid the harsh sun; there are some grasshoppers that, in the absence of shelter, turn themselves end-on to the sun in order to expose only the minimum amount of their body surface.

Termites are usually associated with timber, but some species can live entirely on grasses, including spinifex. The nest of the spinifex termite (*Nasutitermes triodiae*) is the largest of

FULL TO BURSTING Having been fed plant nectar and insect 'honeydew' — usually after spring rains — these swollen 'storage' ants are ready to be hung up for use in drier times.

all Australian termite mounds, sometimes rising to six metres. On desert sandplains, their giant nests can be the most prominent feature.

While the termites stay hidden in their complex nests, industrious honeypot ants (*Melophorus bagoti*) can be seen busily foraging in the midday sun. The ant's name refers to its practice of using the living bodies of some of its number as food containers.

Excess supplies of nectar and 'honeydew' secreted by aphids are collected by worker ants, then force fed to so-called 'storage' ants, which swell up like small grapes. The unfortunate living larders are then hung by their forelegs from the roof of the nest. In times of drought, worker ants stroke the abdomens of the hanging 'honeypots' which then release droplets of nourishment. ☐

From the head of Spencer Gulf to the arid lands of the great salt lakes, the stark beauty of the Flinders Ranges is enhanced by the play of light on their bare peaks and slopes

The lonely moonscape of the purple hills

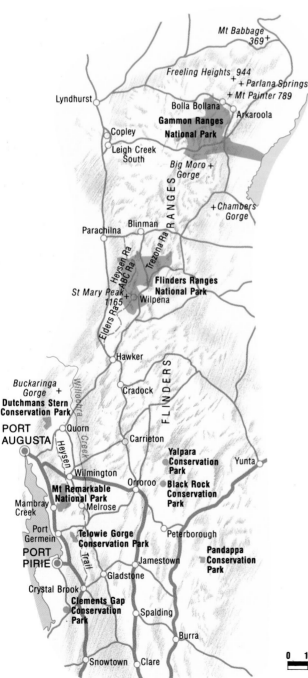

'The "bones of nature" laid bare', was the apt description applied to the Flinders Ranges by the German-born painter Sir Hans Heysen, the first man to accurately record their rugged beauty. And 'bones' they are — a 480-kilometre sweep of hard quartzite and granite outcrops which are all that remain of what was a broad plateau 70 million years ago.

More than 500 million years ago, immense geological forces buckled, squeezed and pushed up what was then part of the seafloor into a towering mountain chain which rivalled the Andes. In time, the mountains weathered to mere rounded hills. These in their turn were uplifted 70 million years ago to form a broad plateau, the ancestor of today's slowly eroding Flinders Ranges.

Rising abruptly from a vast and arid plain, the ranges are ringed in the north by the great horseshoe of Lakes Torrens, Eyre, Gregory, Blanche, Callabonna and Frome. All are splashed an inviting blue on maps, but in reality they are parched and inhospitable salt pans that rarely fill completely with water.

In contrast, the ranges, while less than modestly watered, harbour more moist pockets than might be expected. The craggy heights capture a far greater measure of rainfall than the surrounding plains and the result is tree-lined waterholes and shady gorges that provide a haven for a diversity of wildlife.

In the south, the Flinders Ranges first make their appearance as low ridges near the town of Crystal Brook, but are not particularly obvious until the dark purple profile of Mount Remarkable appears. This southernmost stretch of the ranges is a gentle introduction: velvet slopes cloaked in grass and forest, with many kilometres of low stone walls from early pastoral days snaking over the hills.

BARE BONES The early morning light and the olive-green vegetation softens the natural red-brown of Wilpena Pound's walls.

It was this southern part of the ranges that navigator and explorer Matthew Flinders sighted in 1802 when he reached the head of Spencer Gulf on his circumnavigation of Australia. In his diary he recorded seeing '...a chain of rugged mountains...', unaware that they would later bear his name.

Striking inland

Straddling the transitional zone between the relatively moist coastal climate and the aridity of central Australia, the southern Flinders are endowed with a profusion of plants and animals from both regions. The western side of the ranges is the dry side, and here bullock bush (*Heterodendrum oleifolium*) and a host of acacias typical of the dry country thrive. Parrots and cockatoos are plentiful and this is the southern limit for the desert-dwelling, narrow-nosed planigale (*Planigale tenuirostris*).

With double the rainfall, the eastern slopes are quite lush by comparison. Eucalypts, native cherries and orchids are frequented by birds of the south such as scarlet robins (*Petroica multicolor*), crimson rosellas (*Platycercus elegans*) and the superb fairy-wren (*Malurus cyaneus*).

Sugar gums (*Eucalyptus cladocalyx*), so called because their young leaves taste sweet, occur only in the southern and central Flinders, on Eyre Peninsula and Kangaroo Island. The ranges are also the westernmost limit of Australia's second largest lizard, the lace monitor (*Varanus varius*), which can reach a length of two metres.

The same marginal climate that makes for such an intriguing blend of plants and animals, caused heartbreak for those who sought to settle the Flinders after displacing the Aboriginal population. In the mid-nineteenth century, pastoralists were tempted into the ranges time and again when rains greened the landscape, only to be defeated by isolation and a highly erratic annual rainfall.

Throughout the southern ranges, from Wilmington to Hawker, the vestiges of their hopes stand in cemeteries and abandoned homesteads. Grazing and agriculture have left the landscape with deep environmental scars that are slow to heal. Cattle and sheep destroyed native ground cover

TIME-WORN The slopes of the Flinders Ranges once flanked peaks of a much grander altitude; 450 million years of erosion have resulted in one of the world's most ancient landscapes.

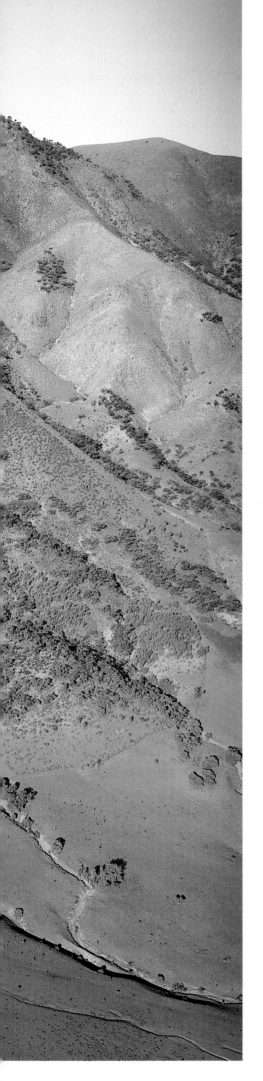

TOUGH TREE The deeply furrowed trunk of this white cypress pine in Hidden Gorge is almost as ravaged as the landscape around it. Such scenes are more typical of the northern Flinders.

and trampled the thin soil, while wheat farmers cleared the land to plant crops.

Erosion was commonplace and with the flooding that often follows drought in inland Australia, much precious topsoil was washed away. Exotic hard-hooved creatures that have run wild, such as goats and donkeys, have contributed to this erosion cycle from which the land is yet to recover.

Tracks aplenty

Within the southern Flinders lies Telowie Gorge Conservation Park (1946 hectares), the southernmost park in the Flinders, and Mount Remarkable National Park (8649 hectares), oases of native vegetation in a sea of cleared land. A four-kilometre walking track from the town of Melrose leads to the summit of Mount Remarkable, 963 metres high.

The view from the peak takes in the series of valleys and plains between the ranges that make up the Flinders. The biggest is Willochra Plain, about 60 kilometres to the north, which is a range-rimmed basin covering 100 square kilometres. The basin tips its infrequent drainage waters into the southern end of Lake Torrens, glinting bone-white on the horizon.

The ranges of Mount Remarkable park are laced with popular bushwalks that make this one of South Australia's most used parks. A walk to the summit of Mount Cavern affords a 360-degree vista revealing that this region of the southern Flinders is a basin-shaped pound formation, much like well-known Wilpena Pound to the north.

The fifteen-kilometre-long Hidden Gorge Trail traverses a cross section of Flinders' landscapes. Following Mam-

REMARKABLE MOUNT The hills and dales of the southern Flinders are gentler than the worn, craggy landscape in the more arid north. Mount Remarkable, in the distance, sits just outside the national park that bears its name.

bray Creek, the trail enters Hidden Gorge, where cypress pines (*Callitris columellaris*) crowd between stark and narrow red quartzite walls, a precursor to the rugged terrain that becomes a familiar sight towards the northern Flinders.

Amid the reed mace or cumbungi thickets of the gorge's semi-permanent waterholes, the warty-skin toadlet (*Crinia riparia*) croaks its presence. Colonies of black tiger snakes (*Notechis ater*) and carpet pythons (*Morelia spilota*) live here, relics from a wetter period. Common wallaroos (*Macropus robustus*), stocky rock-dwelling kangaroos, are often seen hopping along ledges and rock falls here, at Telowie Gorge and at nearby Dutchman's Stern Conservation Park (3532 hectares), renowned for its birdlife and orchids.

A grass tree called yakka (*Xanthorrhoea quadrangulata*) grows profusely on the gorge's rocky slopes, its fine roots seeking out moisture. To resist bushfires, like the 1988 fire that engulfed 95 per cent of the park, the yakka's stem is buried deep underground. On the return to Mambray Creek, the trail loops onto The Battery, from where the waters of Spencer Gulf can be seen in the distance.

Another track bisects the park from Mambray Creek to Alligator Gorge, a thirteen-kilometre trek that traces the courses of Mambray and Alligator Creeks through Kingfisher and Blue Gum Flats. The sheer, red cleft of Alligator Gorge narrows to the span of outspread arms, its dripping cliff faces festooned in ferns. After rain, water cascades over The Terraces, a series of broad rock steps, before churning through The Narrows.

Wilpena Pound

The Flinders' best-known feature has always been Wilpena Pound. This striking geological phenomenon is a magnificent natural amphitheatre, a vast oval encircled by a ring of steep-walled, russet-coloured ramparts.

The original inhabitants, the Adnjamathanha Aboriginal people, used the word 'wilpena' to refer to 'bent fingers of a cupped hand'. 'Pound' comes from its nineteenth century use as a stock enclosure. The formation was once a much hollower basin between

COOL RETREAT Alligator Gorge, overshadowed by sheer cliffs and containing a stream of the same name, is set within the ridges surrounding a broad, basin-like formation similar to Wilpena Pound.

500 MILLION YEARS AGO...

FLINDERS AMPHITHEATRE Despite its shape, Wilpena Pound was not formed by the impact of a giant meteorite. Its apparent symmetry is the chance result of violent earth movements approximately 450 million years ago. Sediments in an ancient sea, which compacted into rock, were pushed way above the earth's surface. Part of this new range was the original tall hills around Wilpena — formed when the rock squeezed into broad folds (see diagram). All that remains of the folds are their hardest layers which form the ripple of ridges around the pound.

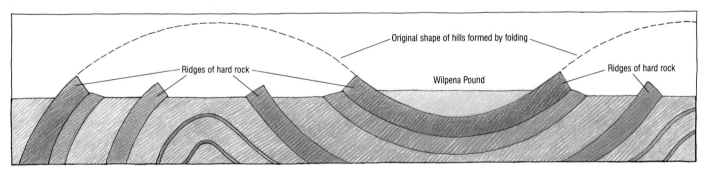

Original shape of hills formed by folding

Ridges of hard rock

Wilpena Pound

Ridges of hard rock

two ridges that gradually filled with rock and vegetation debris.

As with many such geological formations, the grandeur of this intriguing formation — once thought to be the eroded remnants of a volcano or a comet crater — is best appreciated from above. This can be done either on a scenic aeroplane flight or on the demanding but rewarding bushwalk up the outside wall of the pound to St Mary Peak, returning with an easy stroll through the level interior.

Winter is wildflower time in this semi-arid region — especially after rains — and therefore the best time'to visit. Vivid blue *Halgania dampiera* vies for attention with crimson bottlebrushes (*Callistemon teretifolius*), lilac hibiscus (*Alyogyne huegelii*), and parrotbush (*Templetonia retusa*), with its deep-red, four-centimetre-long flowers. A mauve carpet of Paterson's curse

(*Echium plantagineum*) — or salvation Jane — almost conceals the switchback trail up the outer walls.

Many of the flowering plants, like the red wild hop (*Rumex vesicarius*) — and Paterson's curse — are introduced weeds; the winged sea lavender (*Limonium thouinii*), from North Africa, arrived in the saddle bags of Afghan camel drivers. The showpiece of the endemic flowers is the dazzling, waxy-red Sturt's desert pea (*Clianthus formosus*) — South Australia's floral emblem.

Above St Mary Peak (1165 metres), magnificent wedge-tailed eagles (*Aquila audax*) and peregrine falcons (*Falco peregrinus*) hover, riding the strong updraughts gusting from the plain below. From this highest pinnacle in the Flinders Ranges, the entire 54 square kilometres of the pound is visible, with its encircling thirty-five-kilometre circumference of jagged outcrops like Fred

Knob, Pompey Pillar, Mount Ohlssen Bagge and Rawnsley Bluff.

There are other pound formations throughout the Flinders, but none as impressive or more perfectly formed as Wilpena. From St Mary Peak, rows of ranges march off into the outback haze, eventually to flatten out and merge with the gleaming white salt pans of the desert beyond.

On the floor of the pound, the track traces the meandering course of Wilpena Creek before passing out through the narrow Wilpena Creek gap at Sliding Rock, the only direct opening into the basin. Kangaroos and emus, unconcerned by passers-by, graze in the waist-deep yellow grasses amid stands of native pines and sugar gums. Although the pound was cleared for an unsuccessful attempt at wheat farming at the turn of the century, it has revegetated with a park-like lushness.

A somewhat more ambitious walk — or ride — is the two-thousand-kilometre-long Heysen Trail, named in honour of Sir Hans Heysen, which is being marked along a route from Cape Borda on Kangaroo Island all the way to the remote Freeling Heights in the northern Flinders.

A painter's landscape

The bitumen runs out at Wilpena and unsealed roads lead further into the Flinders Ranges National Park (80 578 hectares) and beyond to the range's far northern reaches. North of Wilpena Pound the landscape takes on a more rugged, inhospitable appearance with cliffs and red mountain peaks rearing up for the first time.

So skilfully did Sir Hans Heysen capture the subtle hues and shifting moods of this area in his paintings, that the western flank of the Flinders was named after him. The spectacular Moralana Scenic Route, north of Hawker, winds through the Elder Range or Hills of Arkaba, one source of Heysen's inspiration. This is what he called the '...exhilarating experience in form and colour...' that kept him in the Flinders for a third of his painting life.

On this old stock route south of Wilpena, the landscape seems to change its character not only according to weather changes, but with the time of day, as the changing light alters the colour of the hills from a ruddy red to luminescent purple and all the shades in between.

Creeks flowing towards the salt bowl of Lake Torrens, in the west, have scoured four major gorges into the Heysen Range, each containing a string of permanent waterholes and bearing its own character.

Edeowie Gorge is near Wilpena, while further north Bunyeroo, Brachina and Parachilna Gorges slice through the jagged ridges of quartzite and limestone of the Heysen and ABC Ranges — the latter so named because it has 26 sawtooth peaks in its sandstone escarpment, equal to the number of letters in the alphabet. The ABC Ranges are a commanding backdrop to the Aroona Valley, cradled between the two ranges.

Massive boulders within Brachina and Wilkawillana Gorge, in the Bunker

A TO Z POUND The evenly spaced, pyramid shapes of the 26 peaks of the ABC Ranges, sweep northward from the northern perimeter of Wilpena Pound.

Hills to the east, are peppered with tiny fossils of 500-million-year-old corals, sponges and segmented worms — among the oldest fossils ever found and clear evidence of the marine origin of the Flinders.

Life in the gorges

Sixty species of lizards, including the shingle-back or stump-tailed lizard (*Trachydosaurus rugosus*) — the biggest skink in South Australia — inhabit these gorges, together with a variety of snakes such as the venomous brown snake (*Pseudonaja textilis*) and death adder (*Acanthophis antarcticus*).

A more engaging inhabitant of the rocky country, from Telowie Gorge Conservation Park in the south throughout the northern Flinders, is the endangered yellow-footed rock-wallaby (*Petrogale xanthopus*). Once abundant throughout arid Australia, the Flinders now shelter the greatest concentration — approximately 6000 creatures — of this beautifully-marked marsupial.

WALLABY HAVEN Despite competition from rabbits and goats, rock wallabies thrive in the Flinders.

The biggest colony, numbering about 150, is seen at Buckaringa Gorge north of Quorn. The wallaby, which has yellow legs and yellow and black stripes the length of its long bushy tail, lives in cool caves and is sometimes glimpsed at waterholes at dusk.

In this northern, drier region, vegetation begins to resemble the desert plants of central Australia. There are at least five kinds of puffy pussytail (*Eucalyptus microtheca*), together with aromatic mint bushes or jockey's caps (*Prostanthera striatiflora*).

Cypress pine (*Callitris columellaris*) is one of the most common trees in the Flinders. They were once felled for jetty pilings and telegraph poles because of their resistance to termite attack. On clear mornings in late spring, the trees appear to give off smoke as they release delicate clouds of pollen. The red-flowering emu bush (*Eremophila longifolia*) is so named because emus that consume its fruit spread the seeds in their droppings.

The emu is one of the few creatures of the bush which disregards the heat of the day: efficient insulation, provided by two bushy layers of feathers, permits them the luxury of feeding while competitors are forced to seek shade. During emu courtship, the traditional roles of birds are reversed: the female develops bright blue colouring around her eyes and beak and makes a booming sound in her throat to attract the male who later hatches the eggs and attends to the young for their first two years of life.

Heading north out of the Flinders Ranges National Park, the grandly named Great Wall of China looms on the crest of the Trezona Range parallel to the unsealed road. The rock structure stretching for more than a kilometre appears to be man-made but its origin is a mystery.

A ten-kilometre side-track from the road that runs out of the park leads to Chambers Gorge, where the lofty red walls are reflected in the green billabongs in the floor of the gorge. The pools are visited by a steady stream of noisy white corellas which come to drink and bathe. In a cool, shaded section of the gorge there are Aboriginal rock carvings. Other rock art sites in the Flinders include Arkaroo Rock on the outside of Wilpena Pound's ramparts and Sacred Canyon, ten kilometres south of Wilpena.

Beyond the bitumen

In contrast to the uniform succession of undulating hills to the south, the northern Flinders are a chaotic spectacle of inaccessible ranges bounded by steep cliffs. This wild and lonely place

BILLABONG OASIS Sun-dried Chambers Gorge suggests the imminence of the arid land to the north.

IN THE DREAMING According to legend, waterholes such as this one in the far northern Flinders were carved by Arkaroo, a Dreamtime snake.

was the favourite haunt of the great Australian Antarctic explorer and geologist Sir Douglas Mawson.

Mawson saw this region as an enormous open-air museum, with the most exhaustive list of minerals found anywhere on the continent: amethysts, rubies, sapphires, garnets, tourmaline and zircon make the northern Flinders a gem hunter's paradise. But, as the ruins of smelters like those at Bolla Bollana near Arkaroola testify, commercial ore mining either petered out or proved unprofitable in the harsh environment.

The most remote regions of the northern Flinders are preserved in the ranges' largest park, the Gammon Ranges National Park (128 228 hectares) and the adjacent, private Arkaroola–Mount Painter Sanctuary (63 000 hectares). These are some of the last untouched wilderness areas left in South Australia. The Gammons are a flat quartzite plateau or 'pound' formation scored with trench-like gorges.

Apart from a few rough tracks around the park's perimeter, this is a region for experienced bushwalkers.

Big Moro Gorge, outside the national park, and Weetootla Gorge are among the most accessible gorges. At the centre of the park is Bunyip Chasm, where vertical walls little more than an arm's width apart soar upwards for 100 metres, while an eerie blue light streams downward as the sun's rays struggle to reach the bottom of the chasm.

Salt pans on the horizon

Although tall river red gums (*Eucalyptus camaldulensis*) mark strings of permanent billabongs within precipitous gorges, most of the vegetation of these arid northern ranges, with a fickle annual rainfall which averages less than 250 millimetres, is a mix of hardy acacias, cassias and mallees. Creek wattle (*Acacia rivalis*) is one of the few native plants that benefit from man's

environmental disturbances. Heavy grazing thins out its competitors and allows the tree a better foothold.

Native orange (*Capparis mitchellii*), native apricot (*Pittosporum phylliraeoides*) and quandong trees (*Santalum acuminatum*) are another living reminder of wetter times here before the passing of the last ice age.

The lovely waterholes of the Gammon Ranges — Echo Camp, Arkaroola and Stubbs — are home to the purple-spotted gudgeon (*Mogurnda mogurnda*), a small, strikingly decorated fish ten centimetres long. The waterholes are also gathering places for a noisy menagerie of little corellas (*Cacatua pastinator*), sulphur-crested cockatoos (*C. galerita*) and the flashy mallee ring-neck parrots (*Barnardius zonarius*).

The two-hundred-metre-high walls of Barraranna Gorge were once part of the seabed, and the rippled surface of some sections displays the captured ebb and flow of tides 1000 million years ago.

PALAEONTOLOGIST'S DELIGHT The outline of a prehistoric jellyfish occurs in one of the many ancient seabeds revealed in the weather-worn cliff faces of the northern Flinders.

Such ancient signposts of the past are not uncommon in the Flinders: fossils of the oldest life form ever found, those of primitive jellyfish 650 million years old, locked in Flinders Ranges sandstone and named *Ediacaria flindersi*, were uncovered in 1946 near Lake Torrens.

Arkaroo still rumbles

In 1968, the old Arkaroola sheep station was bought by the Sprigg family who created the Arkaroola–Mount Painter Sanctuary, devoted to returning the landscape to its original state. Native plants, animals and over 160 species of birds flourish, protected from the ravages of feral animals.

Arkaroola is named after an Aboriginal Dreamtime snake called Arkaroo who, according to legend, drank the nearby salty Lake Frome dry. Dragging his bloated body through the ranges, Arkaroo carved gorges, waterholes and other landmarks and now sleeps fitfully in his underground lair in the Gammon Ranges. The rumblings of his grand case of indigestion are still to be felt and heard.

Scientists explain the rumbling phenomenon a different way. Earth movements along the Paralana Fault, which spans the continent from the tip of Spencer Gulf all the way to Hughenden in central Queensland, cause minute seismic tremors almost daily. At Paralana Springs, hot water bubbles up through the fault, one of the few obvious signs of volcanic activity left in Australia. In 1926, a health spa was established at the springs, but due to its remoteness and the primitive conditions, it was abandoned soon after.

In the Mount Painter region of the northern Flinders, white granite bosses protrude above the ground. These are the hard plugs of volcanic intrusions that resisted the same

NATURE'S BOILER The waters of Hot Springs Creek were near boiling when they bubbled up through a fault line from deep beneath the earth's crust.

GLITTERING PRIZE Mount Gee is composed almost entirely of quartzite crystal.

weathering that wore down the surrounding sandstone. They protrude as rounded domes, and are colourfully named the Armchair, the Pinnacles, Giant's Head and the Needles. West of Mount Painter (790 metres) are the deepest deposits of glacial rock in the world. A five-thousand-metre thick layer of boulder conglomerate lies here, dumped by a slow-moving river of ice 500 million years ago.

Nearby Mount Gee, studded with gemstones and riddled with caverns and grottos that are lined in exquisite crystalline formations, is the only crystal quartz mountain in the world, and has been declared a geological monument by the South Australian government. The eastern edge of the ranges break away in cliffs towards the flat arid expanse of Lake Frome.

Further north, around Mount Babbage, the Flinders peter out into the parched embrace of the horseshoe of dry salt pans. Their watery mirages are so convincing that in 1840, the explorer Edward Eyre believed he stood on the shores of a vast inland lake. A later expedition, in 1857, even hauled an iron boat 700 kilometres by horse and dray from Adelaide up through these ranges in a quixotic attempt to sail a non-existent sea. □

Broad, shallow gulfs between the mouth of the Murray River and the edge of the Great Australian Bight provide South Australia with a distinctive coastline as well as a charming setting for its capital

A zig-zag coastline where the ocean strikes inland

SOUTHERN SANCTUARY The lichen-covered granite around the shores of the Flinders Chase National Park represents the southern extremity of the Mount Lofty Ranges. Most of the park has been reserved since 1919, and is one of the most significant animal sanctuaries in Australia.

The Southern Ocean has bitten two greedy, jagged chunks from the gently curving coastline of South Australia, leaving in their place two gulfs outranked in size only by the vast Gulf of Carpentaria. Embracing the deep indentations of Spencer Gulf and Gulf St Vincent are the peninsulas which give the coast its distinctive appearance: Eyre, Yorke and Fleurieu.

Situated halfway down the western side of the Fleurieu Peninsula, Adelaide benefits from the two main features of this region: gentle hills forming the limits of an undulating plain on one side and the ocean on the other, at the city's feet.

The worn Mount Lofty Ranges, sedimentary rocks laid down 1000 to 500 million years ago and among the world's oldest hills, form the spine of the Fleurieu Peninsula of which Kangaroo Island — stranded just offshore — is the lost tip. Other ancient fragments of the peninsula speckle the shallow gulf waters as much needed island havens for the many plants and animals squeezed from their vulnerable mainland habitats.

Kangaroo Island and the Yorke and Eyre Peninsulas were almost completely cleared for agriculture during the last century — except for a handful of green patches of predominantly mallee scrub — but their coastlines, ranging from peaceful mangrove swamps and quiet beaches to steep coastal cliffs ravaged by wind and waves, remain almost completely unspoiled and are their most spectacular feature.

Matthew Flinders was exaggerating somewhat when he chose the name 'lofty' for the gentle string of hills that sweep in a 4000-square-kilometre arc from Cape Jervis at the tip of the Fleurieu Peninsula to the northern end of the Barossa Valley. The Mount Lofty Ranges are, in fact, one undulating plateau bounded by scarps and rising to a maximum height of 727 metres at the summit of Mount Lofty. Here, there is a sweeping panorama over Gulf St Vincent and, at night, a fairyland effect as Adelaide's lights twinkle on the plain below.

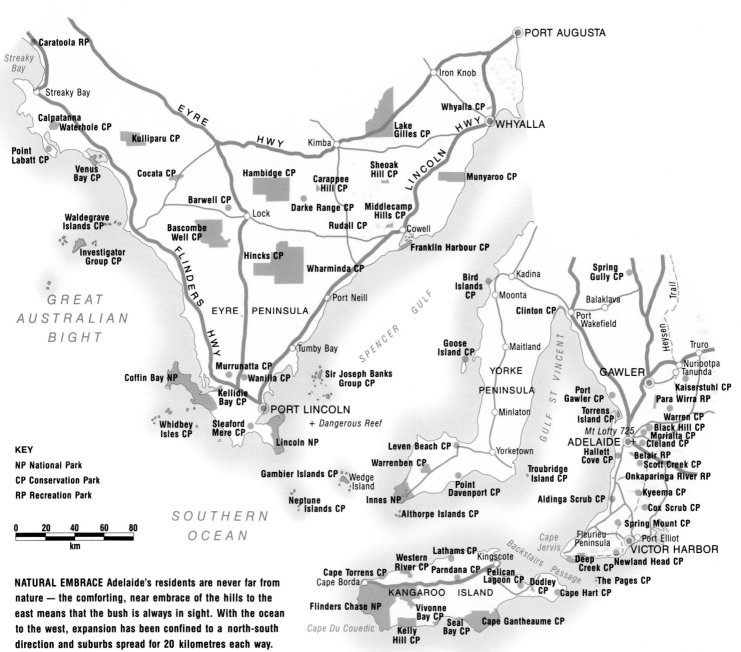

Caratoola RP
Streaky Bay
Streaky Bay
Calpatanna
Waterhole CP
Point
Labatt CP
Venus
Bay CP
Waldegrave
Islands CP
Investigator
Group CP

Kulliparu CP
Cocata CP
Barwell CP
Bascombe
Well CP
Hincks CP

PORT AUGUSTA
Iron Knob
Whyalla CP
Lake
Gilles CP
WHYALLA
Kimba
Sheoak
Hill CP
Munyaroo CP
Hambidge CP
Carappee
Hill CP
Lock
Darke Range CP
Middlecamp
Hills CP
Rudall CP
Cowell
Franklin Harbour CP
Wharminda CP

EYRE
HWY
LINCOLN
HWY

FLINDERS
HWY

GREAT
AUSTRALIAN
BIGHT

EYRE PENINSULA
Port Neill
Tumby Bay

SPENCER GULF

Bird
Islands
CP
Kadina
Moonta
Clinton CP
Goose
Island CP

Spring
Gully CP
Balaklava
Port
Wakefield

Heysen
Trail

Truro
Nuriootpa
Tanunda
Kaiserstuhl CP
Para Wirra RP

GAWLER

Murrunatta CP
Wanilla CP
Sir Joseph Banks
Group CP
Coffin Bay NP
Kellidie
Bay CP
Whidbey
Isles CP
Sleaford
Mere CP
PORT LINCOLN
+ *Dangerous Reef*
Lincoln NP

YORKE
PENINSULA
Maitland
Minlaton
Yorketown

GULF ST VINCENT

Port
Gawler CP
Torrens
Island CP
Mt Lofty 725
ADELAIDE +
Hallett
Cove CP

Warren CP
Black Hill CP
Morialta CP
Cleland CP
Belair RP
Scott Creek CP
Onkaparinga River RP
Kyeema CP
Cox Scrub CP
Spring Mount CP

Leven Beach CP
Warrenben CP
Point
Davenport CP
Troubridge
Island CP
Aldinga Scrub CP

Gambier Islands CP
Wedge
Island
Innes NP
Althorpe Islands CP
Neptune
Islands CP

Fleurieu
Peninsula
Port Elliot
VICTOR HARBOR
Deep
Creek CP
Newland Head CP
The Pages CP

*Cape
Jervis*
Backstairs Passage
Cape
Jervis

KEY
NP National Park
CP Conservation Park
RP Recreation Park

0 20 40 60 80
km

SOUTHERN
OCEAN

Lathams CP
Kingscote
Western
River CP
Parndana CP
Pelican
Lagoon CP
Dudley
CP
Cape Hart CP
Cape Torrens CP
Cape Borda
KANGAROO ISLAND
Flinders Chase NP
Vivonne
Bay CP
Seal
Bay CP
Cape Gantheaume CP
Cape Du Couedic
Kelly
Hill CP

NATURAL EMBRACE Adelaide's residents are never far from nature — the comforting, near embrace of the hills to the east means that the bush is always in sight. With the ocean to the west, expansion has been confined to a north-south direction and suburbs spread for 20 kilometres each way.

Dozens of small conservation parks are scattered throughout the Mount Lofty Ranges, preserving a patchwork of wilderness around the expanding city. The terrain varies from the open savannah woodland of Charleston Conservation Park (63 hectares) to the lush, high-rainfall forest of Spring Mount Conservation Park (199 hectares), where soaring messmate stringybarks (*Eucalyptus obliqua*) are a habitat for the yellow-tailed black cockatoo (*Calyptorhynchus funereus*). The last pockets of forest between here and the kauri and jarrah groves of Western Australia shelter in these ranges.

One of these pockets, Aldinga Scrub, the only woodland left along the southern beaches, became the centre

SEA-LION PARK The rocky coves of Seal Bay, on Kangaroo Island, provide safe breeding grounds for a large population of Australian sea-lions. About twenty-five per cent of the island's coastline is within parks or reserves.

PASTORAL SCENE Less than 10 kilometres east of the heart of Adelaide, livestock grazes the cleared areas between the reserves which dot the ranges.

of a storm of controversy when a marina was planned nearby. The project was shelved in the face of local conservation concerns and the 'Scrub' is now a 239-hectare conservation park.

Adelaide's backyard

The Fleurieu Peninsula provides the citizens of Adelaide with a close-at-hand playground and recreation area. The seaside holiday towns, such as Port Elliot and Victor Harbor, have pleasant stretches of white beach complemented by bushland reserves. From Victor Harbor a causeway leads to Granite Island, a tourist-oriented wildlife sanctuary for kangaroos, wallabies and fairy penguins.

Nearby, Hindmarsh Falls tumble in a series of cascades through thick bush rich in birdlife. To the west, in Newland Head Conservation Park (945 hectares), the endangered hooded plover (*Charadrius rubricollis*) feeds and builds its nests just above the high-tide mark on two wilderness beaches. Offshore, Pullen, West and Seal Islands are breeding grounds for sea birds.

The peninsula's biggest reserve is Deep Creek Conservation Park (4184 hectares), where tall trees line the rugged coastal cliffs. Forests once covered the entire peninsula and such pockets of the original vegetation serve as sanctuaries for the rare southern brown bandicoot (*Isoodon obesulus*) and the western pygmy-possum (*Cercatetus concinnus*). Orchids and ferns crowd the moist gullies where permanent creeks run, fed by the catchment area of the nearby hills.

The long, long trail

The Heysen Trail begins its long mainland course northward from the tip of the Fleurieu Peninsula at Cape Jervis. Named after the South Australian bush painter, Sir Hans Heysen, the trail forms a 2000-kilometre walking or riding track from Cape Borda on Kangaroo Island to the remote Freeling Heights within Gammon Ranges National Park, in the North Flinders Ranges. Throughout this scenic region the trail cleverly stitches together a series of tiny parks such as Myponga (166 hectares), Mount Magnificent (90 hectares) and Kyeema (349 hectares).

South Australia's second biggest permanent river after the Murray, the Onkaparinga, winds through a deep gorge to emerge at a broad estuary near Port Noarlunga. Despite the changes in its level due to the diversion of up to 70 per cent of its waters to the Adelaide water supply, the estuary remains a haven for herons, egrets, spoonbills and pelicans as well as an important food source for more than 20 species of fish.

The Southern Vales slope gently down the western side of the Mount Lofty Ranges towards the sea, where cool breezes create a moderate climate ideal for grape growing.

Further north, the famous winemaking region of the Barossa Valley owes its formidable reputation not only to the climate and the viticultural skills of its farmers but also to an ancient lake bed: 20 to 40 million years ago layers of sand and clay were laid down on the lake bottom, giving the valley its characteristic rich, red loamy soils.

One of the last areas of native forest in the Barossa is within Kaiserstuhl Conservation Park (397 hectares), near Tanunda. Kaiserstuhl — German for

WINE COUNTRY Most of the Clare Valley has long been under cultivation, mainly with wine grapes.

HOODED ORCHID The deciduous, banded greenhood orchid is one of many hooded orchids growing in the Mount Lofty Ranges.

MINIATURE MONSTER Although no more than 25 centimetres long, the heavily scaled shingleback lizard manages to present a fearsome appearance.

'emperor's seat' — is the name given to the largest of several granite outcrops dotting the park. Dragon lizards, skinks and geckos make their home amid the brown stringybark trees (*Eucalyptus baxteri*) which grow no further north than here. Vines were planted throughout the Barossa from the earliest days of settlement and remnants of abandoned vineyards are still visible between the regrowth of wallowa (*Acacia calamifolia*) and golden wattle (*A. pycnantha*) in Sandy Creek Conservation Park (104 hectares).

The last stand of the beautiful red stringybark (*Eucalyptus macrorhyncha*) in South Australia — a survivor from an ancient time when the region had a wetter climate — grows within the 400-hectare Spring Gully Conservation Park. The nearest similar forests are in the Grampian Ranges in Victoria. A variety of reptiles, including the shingle-back (*Trachydosaurus rugosus*), wood gecko (*Diplodactylus vittatus*) and the painted dragon (*Ctenophorus pictus*), scurry about beneath a ground cover of ferns.

Parks ... and churches

'Posterity will do me justice...' was Colonel William Light's riposte to criticism of his plan for Adelaide. In 1837, Surveyor-General Light envisioned broad boulevards and grand squares ingeniously girdled in a 688-hectare greenbelt of park and woodland; the banks of the River Torrens which meander through the city would also be public reserve. What was to become known as the city of churches, is in fact a city of parks.

Adelaide has long since outgrown its parkland perimeter but the much-loved greenbelt is still there. Australia's fourth largest city now sprawls across the Adelaide Plain, a triangle of lowland wedged between Gulf St Vincent and the horseshoe of the Adelaide Hills — part of the Mount Lofty Ranges — that form an attractive backdrop to the city.

The metropolitan parks and woodland are complemented beyond the city limits by a string of national parks in the hills and beyond. There are more than a dozen 'multi-use' parks within 45 minutes of Adelaide, some of them mere specks on the map.

The first to be established, in 1891, was Australia's second national park. This is Belair, which has expanded to 816 hectares, using the grounds of South Australia's first government house as its nucleus. The park is renowned for containing many of the 92 species of orchids found in the Mount Lofty Ranges, including the greenhood (*Pterostylis*), parson's band (*Erochilus cucullatus*) and so many others that there are orchids blooming somewhere in the park all year round.

Flocks of screeching rosellas and lorikeets, in every colour of the rainbow, decorate the branches of huge old river red and South Australian blue gums (*Eucalyptus camaldulensis, E. leucoxylon*) like Christmas ornaments. Grass-grazing, maned ducks (*Chenonetta jubata*) waddle across the park's many walking tracks, while the treetops are occupied in rather absentminded fashion by a colony of more than 50 koalas.

One of the biggest reserves of native bush in the hills is formed by the adjoining Black Hill (679 hectares) and Morialta Conservation Parks (536 hectares). Black Hill is predominantly rocky ridges and gorges heavily cloaked in eucalypt forest.

In this driest state of the driest continent, waterfalls are a rare treat. The main feature, if a seasonal one, of Morialta Park is a series of three cascades which tumble into a 30-metre-deep gorge along Fourth Creek, most predictably after rain in winter and spring.

These large parks are home to a large population of emus and kangaroos, attracted by the dams and lakes.

Eucalypt forest is dominant, with the golden wattle a favourite flowering tree of the red wattlebird (*Anthochaera carunculata*), which like other honeyeaters, uses its four-pronged, brush-tipped tongue to coax nectar and pollen from the deep reaches of the bright yellow flowers.

A stroll through Hallet Cove Conservation Park (51 hectares), on the shores of the beachside suburbs on Adelaide's southern fringe, is a journey through an ancient landscape. The shiny rock faces that slope to the sea, polished smooth by the elements, bear 'chatter marks' — deep scratches etched by the passage of glaciers. These are clear evidence of glaciation in southern Australia and this is one of the few places in the world where such markings are so well preserved. The scars were formed by the gouging action of mountains of ice 270 million years ago.

SEASONAL SURGE The waters of Fourth Creek, swollen by winter rains upstream, surge over the first of three waterfalls along its course in the Morialta Conservation Park.

PREHISTORIC COVE Debris pushed in the path of a glacier about 250 million years ago, when Australia and Antarctica were part of the same continent, so deeply scoured this rock that the 'tracks' of its movement can still be seen along this Adelaide suburban shore.

EYRE TIP The vast, limestone plain of the Eyre Peninsula comes to an end at Whalers Way, a stretch of coast at the peninsula's tip, just south of the Sleaford Mere Conservation Park, between Fishery Bay and Cape Wiles. In the nineteenth century, this was a hunting ground for southern right whales.

Erratics — rocks and debris carried along and dumped by the glaciers — still litter the beaches, some having originated as far as 50 kilometres away. Similar ice-scored rocks from this period also appear at Glacier Rock in the Inman Valley.

The 'boot' peninsula

York Peninsula, the middle peninsula which separates the two wide gulfs, resembles a boot with its toe pointing into the waters of Spencer Gulf. The landscape of the 'boot' is made up almost entirely of a narrow, tranquil plain which bears little resemblance to its original appearance, except at the very tip, in the Innes National Park (9141 hectares). The peninsula was cleared last century to make way for

waving fields of barley and wheat or neatly squared livestock paddocks. The occasional tall stone chimney of an abandoned copper smelter dots the landscape from the days when Cornish miners worked South Australia's largest copper deposits.

Nowhere on the peninsula is more than 30 kilometres from the sea; at the boomerang-shaped head of Gulf St Vincent, the shallow mangrove swamps are a haven for several species of migratory waders and colonies of cormorants. This is the ocean at its gentlest, and a stark contrast to the wild stretches of dunes and rocky limestone headlands to the south, especially fringing the tip of the peninsula.

The virgin bush of the Innes National Park is not as unsullied as it appears;

the park is in its second incarnation as bushland, having once been the site of a gypsum mine. The chain of salt lakes that pockmark over 100 square kilometres of marsh and mallee country yielded up their gypsum deposits, and when the mine closed down the land was donated to the state as a national park.

With more than 450 species of native plants in the park, there are blossoms almost year-round, with a peak season in mid- and late winter when the pea-flowers of the tall shrub known as *Templetonia retusa* erupt in a sea of red blooms.

Twenty-five of the 100 species of birds in the park are listed as rare, and the park was expanded so that one of them in particular might be better pro-

At the south-eastern tip of the Eyre Peninsula, almost separated from the mainland but for the narrow neck of land flanked by Sleaford and Boston Bays, is the 17 423-hectare Lincoln National Park, surrounded by an 11 000-hectare marine reserve. The north-facing shores of the park are well protected from the open sea and offer sheltered coves where tall coastal mallee grows right to the shoreline.

TRICOLOUR Despite its name, the Port Lincoln parrot is found all over south-western Australia.

More remote — and spectacular — is the park's craggy southern coast, where tall granite cliffs and high sand dunes predominate. In the bush there are brilliant green and blue Port Lincoln parrots (*Barnardius zonarius*) and in grassy clearings rock parrots (*Neophema petrophila*) and the rare western whipbird (*Psophodes nigrogularis*), fossick for seeds.

West of Lincoln Park is Sleaford Mere Conservation Park (688 hectares) where the main feature is a brackish coastal lake with shores lined by dark, metre-high stromatolites — rocks made up of many layers of fossilised algae. The western side of the narrow peninsula that is Coffin Bay National Park (30 380 hectares) faces the windswept Great Australian Bight and huge bald sand dunes march inland from wide, white Gunyah Beach.

Free of introduced pests such as foxes, cats and rabbits, the hundreds of islands and islets scattered off both coasts of Eyre Peninsula — some mere wave-washed rock platforms — have become havens for many endangered birds and animals, some of which have vanished completely from the mainland. The islands provide safe breeding sites for such ground-nesting birds as rock parrots, plovers and terns. The Sir Joseph Banks Group, off Tumby Bay, is the largest breeding ground in Australia of the Cape Barren goose.

Wedge Island supports introduced populations of the endangered brush-tailed bettong (*Bettongia penicillata*) that have fared so well they have been released within Venus Bay Conservation Park (1460 hectares), and on the small Baird Bay Islands (24 hectares) on the west coast. Neptune and Gambier Islands Conservation Parks (442 and 64 hectares) are home to large populations of New Zealand fur-seals (*Arctocephalus forsteri*) and the rare Australian sea-lions (*Neophoca cinerea*), both of which can also be seen basking on granite platforms at the foot of Point Labatt near Streaky Bay.

tected. The elusive olive-green western whipbird (*Psophodes nigrogularis*), discovered in 1965, is a shy, ground-dwelling bird which forages through the leaf litter in search of insects. It is recognised by its strange 'whip-crack' call.

Peninsula of parks

South Australia's most dramatic coastline occurs around the Eyre Peninsula, a great triangular wedge thrust into the Southern Ocean. The east coast, facing Spencer Gulf, is scalloped with beaches and small fishing harbours; on the more rugged west coast, the fury of the sea has hewn 100-metre cliffs along the edge of limestone plains. This is the eastern end of the Great Australian Bight and the cliffs continue in an almost unbroken line for more than one thousand kilometres.

YORKE TIP The sand dunes, salt lakes and rugged cliffs in Innes National Park, at the very toe of the Yorke Peninsula 'boot', represent one of the few uncultivated regions of the peninsula.

Inland, those parts of the Eyre Peninsula that have not been cleared for the cultivation of cereal crops and for livestock farming, have been set aside in large conservation parks for the protection of the beleaguered native plants and animals of the mallee country.

MINIATURE MONOLITH Rocky outcrops such as the granite Pildappa Rock — known properly as inselbergs — occur at random amongst the limestone of Eyre Peninsula.

These parks are mostly vast tracts of undulating dunes — some 90 metres high — cloaked in thick mallee bush. They harbour a wide variety of marsupials, including western grey and red kangaroos (*Macropus fuliginosus, M. rufus*), elusive bush rats (*Rattus fuscipes*), Mitchell's hopping mice (*Notomys mitchelli*) and fat-tailed dunnarts (*Sminthopsis crassicaudata*). Freshwater swamps support thickets of blue hibiscus and velvet bush.

The rare mallee fowl (*Leipoa ocellata*), which will only breed in large areas of untouched bush, is not uncommon here. In Hambidge Conservation Park (37 991 hectares), Gould's wattled bats (*Chalinolobus gouldii*) flit through the night while thick-tailed or barking geckos (*Underwoodisaurus milii*) scurry from cover to cover.

Across central Eyre Peninsula rises a strange collection of stone outcroppings; the biggest, Carappee Hill, is an ancient granite dome rising over the surrounding flat plains. These domed monoliths, known as 'whalebacks', are estimated to be as much as 2400 million years old. Near Streaky Bay on the west coast, the intriguing shapes of Murphy's Haystacks — more ancient granite rocks — mushroom from rolling wheatfields.

Noah's ark

Tasmania aside, Kangaroo Island is Australia's second largest island — after Melville Island, off the Northern Territory coast. Separated from the tip of the Fleurieu Peninsula by the turbulent waters of the 16-kilometre-wide Backstairs Passage — a glaciated rock basin filled with rising seas — Kangaroo Island was severed from the peninsula 9500 years ago.

Although much of the island has been cleared for agriculture, it still remains a special reserve for native wildlife and plants. The island has remained free of rabbits, foxes, cats and other European animals, as well as most introduced weeds. As a result, it is a kind of Noah's Ark where native birds and animals have never found themselves the prey of introduced carnivores or been driven to unequal competition with rapacious foragers such as rabbits.

With no natural predators except the one-metre-long Rosenberg's sand goanna (*Varanus rosenbergi*) — even the dingo failed to obtain passage here — the island's wild creatures are less timid and more relaxed than their mainland counterparts. Emus and Cape Barren geese readily snatch sandwiches from picnic tables, while the Kangaroo Island kangaroo (*Macropus fuliginosus fuliginosus*), which evolved smaller, chunkier, and built less for speed than its western grey mainland cousin, bounces along at a leisurely pace.

NATIVE HAVEN Kangaroo Island, once a convict hideout, is now an important wildlife refuge. The island's largest park, Flinders Chase, contains a variety of marsupials which thrive free of competition from rabbits or foxes.

SEA-LION BAY Sea-lions, recognisable by their external ears, are more agile than the earless seal and should be approached with caution.

KOALA COLONY Koalas were introduced to Kangaroo Island in 1923.

COASTAL GOANNA Rosenberg's sand goanna ranges from Kangaroo Island to the Perth coast.

Kangaroo Island's biggest park is the 73 662-hectare Flinders Chase National Park, which covers the entire western end of the 156-kilometre-long island. Stunted heathland clings to the park's rugged coast and inland is an undulating green sea of low, dense mallee. There are 23 species of eucalypts and more than 400 of native wildflowers, which burst into vivid colours from August to November. The Kangaroo Island narrow-leaved mallee (*Eucalyptus cneorifolia*) is found here and in isolated spots on the Fleurieu Peninsula; it is so rich in eucalyptus oil that it once fostered a thriving local industry with 50 distilleries producing folk medicine.

Since 1919 wombats, emus, platypuses, Cape Barren geese and brushturkeys (*Alectura lathami*) have been brought to the sanctuary of Kangaroo Island to ensure their survival. Koalas, completely wiped out in South Australia by the 1920s by fur hunters, were imported and now number more than 1000; a colony near Rocky River has grown so quickly that the manna gums on which it feeds are under threat. These healthy koalas are exported to help stock sanctuaries in other states.

NAMESAKE Kangaroo Island kangaroos are a sub-species of the mainland western grey.

The more than 200 species of birds on the island include South Australia's last colony of glossy black cockatoos (*Calyptorhynchus lathami*). The parrots, black with a striking band of red across their tail feathers, feed exclusively on the cones of the drooping she-oak (*Allocasuarina verticulata*).

Among the uncommon species that live in the island's swamps and marshes are the osprey (*Pandion haliaetus*), peregrine falcon (*Falco peregrinus*) and the unusual and bluntly named bush thick-knee (*Burhinus grallarius*), a ground-nesting bird decimated by foxes and almost extinct on the mainland, that wails eerily at night. Tammar wallabies (*Macropus eugenii*), also thought to be extinct on the mainland, are thriving in the absence of foxes.

At Seal Bay Conservation Park (700 hectares) visitors can stroll along a white crescent beach an arm's length from hundreds of Australian sea-lions. Against a backdrop of sand dunes, ten per cent of a population of less than 5000 sea-lions — the world's rarest — bask in the sun or ride the surf. The biggest colonies of Australian sea-lions are on a group of islands called The Pages, off the coast of the Fleurieu Peninsula, and on Dangerous Reef, off the eastern tip of Eyre Peninsula.

To the west, is Admiral's Arch, a yawning limestone sea cavern 20 metres high, rimmed in ancient stalactites. Here, at Cape du Couedic, the south-western tip of Flinders Chase National Park, New Zealand fur-seals cavort on rocky offshore sea ledges, the last visible sign of the Mount Lofty Ranges before they finally disappear beneath the sea. □

Far removed from the plains and bushland of the mainland, Australia's island territories — tropical, temperate and sub-Antarctic — have two major things in common, their isolation, and their simple but finely balanced ecological systems

By way of contrast...
offshore Australia

ADMIRALTY ISLANDS
Roach Island
Soldiers Cap
Phillip Bluff
+ Mt Eliza 148
+ Malabar 194
Permanent Park Reserve
Hells Gates
Brodies Point
Blackburn Island
Airstrip
Mutton Bird Island
CORAL REEF
Prince William Henry Bay
Mutton Bird Point
+ Intermediate Hill 250
LORD HOWE ISLAND
East Point
SOUTH
+ Mt Lidgbird 770
PACIFIC
Red Point
OCEAN
Permanent Park Reserve
+ Mt Gower 875
George Rock
King Point
Gower Island

0 1 2 4
km

The huge landmass that is the Australian continent overshadows the existence of Australia's diverse and isolated island territories which are scattered far and wide across three oceans.

These tiny specks in the world's southern seas add a new dimension to the incredible range of environments that can be experienced in Australia. From north to south, Australia's administration extends from Sabai Island, in Torres Strait, to Heard Island — a distance equivalent to the length of South America — while the east–west span, from the McDonald Islands to Norfolk Island, covers a quarter of the globe — more than the width of North America.

Because of their size, remoteness, and geological youthfulness, islands generally have a much smaller range of plants and animals than continents; on the other hand, evolving in isolation, they are often home to unusual and specifically adapted life forms. This isolation, which accounts largely for the intrigue of even the sub-Antarctic islands, is also their Achilles' heel.

ADRIFT IN AN AZURE SEA As passing clouds are snared by Mount Lidgbird and Mount Gower, Lord Howe Island — the desert island of most people's daydreams — holds its shallow lagoon in a protective embrace. Almost two-thirds of the island is reserved in its natural state.

PHILIP ISLAND

The relative simplicity of island environments and the obvious limitations that exist mean that plants and animals are highly vulnerable to intrusion into their domain by predators and aggressive competitors introduced by human beings.

Australia's six main island territories were all uninhabited at the time of European settlement of the mainland; a common theme in their history is the varying extent to which settlement has disturbed the natural environment.

A balance has occurred in the latter part of the twentieth century with the success of the many conservation measures that were introduced when it became obvious that the fragile island ecosystems were under threat. But the dawning of this awareness came too late for some plants and animals and numerous species have become extinct.

The disparate specks of land described here came under Australia's influence for various reasons, political, strategic, economic, or simply because in the days of the British Empire they came under the influence of Britain, or Britons. In time, being within Australia's general sphere of influence, they came under Australian administration.

Norfolk and Lord Howe Islands are closely associated with the Norfolk

Ridge and the Lord Howe Rise, two prominent features of the undersea landscape which were formed as the ocean floor spread out when the supercontinent Gondwana broke up about 80 million years ago. Both Lord Howe and Norfolk are the tips of prehistoric shield volcanoes.

Lord Howe and Balls Pyramid, a rock formation 29 kilometres to the south-east, were formed about 17 million years ago, and are the last remaining fragments of a chain of volcanoes, all the other 'sea mounts' having been worn down to below sea level by erosion.

Norfolk, and its smaller companion, Philip Island, were created by eruptions which began about three million years ago and ended two-and-a-half million years ago.

Both groups of islands still have a relatively substantial covering of sub-tropical rainforest. Their plants and animals have many links with Australia and New Zealand but it is the plants and animals which have developed in isolation and live nowhere else that are most intriguing.

Offshore New South Wales

Lord Howe Island, approximately 770 kilometres north-east of Sydney, is a narrow sliver of land only 12 kilometres long that is administered as part of New South Wales. To the west, between the two extremities of its crescent shape, is a six-kilometre-long lagoon protected by a coral reef — the most southerly in the world.

At its southern end, the island is dominated by the massive bulk of Mount Lidgbird (770 metres) and Mount Gower (875 metres). On the steep sides of Mount Gower, the volcanic rock of which the island is made is exposed for almost the entire height of the mountain.

Lord Howe Island's oldest rocks are in the Malabar Hills at the northern end of the island. Connecting the island's two upland areas is a region consisting of debris from the erosion of the volcano, and dune limestone — this was formed from coral blown from the lagoon area when the sea level was lower. The result is an extraordinary variety of landforms on an island of a mere 14.5 square kilometres.

As majestic and dominating as today's mountains may be the original volcano at Lord Howe Island was forty times bigger and twice as high as Mount Lidgbird or Mount Gower. The volcano's extent is indicated by the 50-metre-long submarine contour at the edge of the wave-cut platform which surrounds the island.

Balls Pyramid is at a more advanced stage of destruction than the island, but its hard volcanic rocks have helped it to retain its height and create a spire-like form. Although a mere 1100 by 400 metres at its base, it soars dizzyingly to a height of 552 metres.

The gently contrasting landforms which weld together to create the Lord Howe terrain are matched by a diverse and diverting range of vegetation, from dry forest on sheltered lowland areas to the damp, miniature cloud forest on the summit of Mount Gower. Of the island's 180 species of flowering plants, 57 are found nowhere else. There are at least 20 species of moss and 17 of ferns that are unique.

Spectacular local species include the screw pine (*Pandanus forsteri*), which is supported by ten-metre-high prop roots, and the thirteen-metre-high pumpkin flower (*Dracophyllum fitzgeraldi*), the tallest member of the heath family, which has attractive, spiky flowers. The seeds of one of the three island palms — the thatch or Kentia palm (*Howea forsteriana*) — provide the basis for the island's major export industry.

Like most small islands, where there is no place for the evolution of large land animals, Lord Howe is a haven for birds of all kinds. As might be expected, seabirds abound along its shores, but inland, the host of feathered creatures which evolved to fill every environmental niche are sadly depleted.

Curious by nature, and with virtually no natural enemies, the birds of Lord Howe Island have suffered hard at the hand of man and introduced pests such as rats and cats. After the first landings, the birds were initially so unafraid that early sailors and settlers were able to pick them straight off the branches for the cooking pot. The result is that nine of Lord Howe's original fourteen unique bird species have become extinct.

Of the survivors, the best known is the Lord Howe Island woodhen (*Tricholimnas silvestris*), a flightless rail, which by 1979 had been reduced to about 30 birds, all on Mount Gower and Mount Lidgbird. The species was saved by a highly organised programme of comprehensively poisoning rats and trapping feral cats.

PACIFIC PYRAMID The crags of Balls Pyramid rose from the sea during the same volcanic convulsions that formed Lord Howe Island.

MULTI-TRUNKED The aerial roots of the banyan eventually become subsidiary trunks.

Settlement covers only six per cent of the island and its thriving tourist industry is based on the natural attractions. A 'permanent park preserve' status protects the northern and southern parts of Lord Howe Island, Balls Pyramid and the offshore islands.

Norfolk Island

Norfolk Island, twice as far from the mainland as Lord Howe Island, is no relation to New South Wales, but a self-governing external territory of the Commonwealth. The territory of Norfolk Island, covers Norfolk, Philip and Nepean Islands, an area of 3727 hectares, two-and-a-half times the size of the Lord Howe Island group.

Like Lord Howe, these islands are mountain-top remnants, perched above the waves, of an elongated shield volcano. The shelf around the islands, 95 kilometres long, north to south, and 35 kilometres wide, east to west, marks what was the volcano's area two-and-a-half million years ago, before most of it was whittled away by wind and rain.

Most of Norfolk Island is a plateau formed from horizontal sheets of basalt. It rises to its highest point of 319 metres at Mount Bates, near the remains of one of the main volcanic vents of old. The tall cliffs which surround most of the island, and the many deep valleys cut into them are evidence that the constant action of waves has been a more powerful erosive force over the years than rain and streams.

About half a dozen freshwater streams run year round, and much of the rain which falls on the island per-

POTTED PALM The Lord Howe Island Kentia palm has become one of the most popular indoor plants in the world and thousands of seeds are exported each year — mainly to Europe.

colates through cracks and crevices in the surface to form a deep reservoir almost at sea level.

When Captain James Cook landed on Norfolk Island in 1788, it was almost completely covered by such thick subtropical forest that occasionally, exploration parties became lost. Some parts of the forest were dominated by the majestic Norfolk Island pine (*Araucaria heterophylla*) and others by various mixtures of hardwoods, palms and treeferns. Epiphytic vines were common. The Norfolk pine, which has become the island's symbol, towered above all reaching heights of over 60 metres, sometimes with a girth of 11 metres.

Between 1788 and 1814, the period of Norfolk's first settlement, forty per cent of the island was cleared. Today, only five per cent of the native forest remains undisturbed.

The disturbance caused by the invasion of European-introduced weeds, even in protected areas, is so great that eleven plant species are regarded as rare and endangered, and another five are considered vulnerable. Two species have become extinct. The Philip Island hibiscus (*Hibiscus insularis*), which grows in only two small patches, is rated by the International Union for the Conservation of Nature and Natural Resources as one of the world's ten most endangered plants.

Despite the clearing, large plants, particularly trees, still grow in the agricultural areas. Scattered Norfolk Island pines continue to add a distinctive stamp to the landscape. Groves of the shapely, pink-flowered Norfolk Island hibiscus or white oak (*Lagunaria patersonia*) can still be seen on the flat eastern section of the plateau.

Several of Norfolk Island's native trees are protected and the importation of plants and animals from overseas is strictly regulated. The Norfolk Island National Park, in the high region around Mount Bates, covers 460 hectares and protects undisturbed forest and the dramatic northern coastline where Captain Cook landed in 1774.

Neither the offshore islands, nor the area of forest which contains most of the island's surviving hardwood and vine rainforest are included in the park. This forest contains four of the island's rare, endangered plants including 20 of the few remaining broad-leaved merytas (*Meryta latifolia*) — a round-headed, small tree with large, oval, glossy leaves — growing in the wild.

The unique birdlife of Norfolk Island has been severely affected by the re-

ISLE OF PINES Steep cliffs, such as these at Anson Bay, surround most of the plateau that is Norfolk Island. The island has been settled as long as the mainland but despite widespread agricultural clearing, the famous pine tree remains a conspicuous part of its vegetation.

ANOTHER DODO? The threat of extinction that hangs over Norfolk Island's green parrots underlies the fragility of island ecosystems.

quirements of farming, particularly the clearing of land for cattle grazing. Seven of the island's original 14 native birds survive, including the green parrot (*Cyanoramphus novae-zelandiae cookii*). There are about 30 parrots left and some of these are being used in a captive breeding programme aimed at ensuring the bird's future.

The plight of another island bird, the Norfolk Island boobook owl (*Ninox undulata*), is as desperate as it can be. There is only one bird — a female — left, and male owls of a related species from New Zealand have been imported in an attempt to breed the owls in the wild. Both the green parrot and the boobook were affected by the loss of nesting sites with the decline in the number of old trees and competition from the introduced crimson rosella (*Platycercus elegans*).

Tiny Philip Island lost most of its plant cover and its soil after rabbits were introduced and it became a virtual desert. Now, with the trapping of the last rabbit in 1986, it is a heartening example of how native vegetation can regenerate even after such a massive onslaught on its resources.

As there are no rats or cats, Philip Island is a paradise for seabirds and it was not long after the elimination of the rabbits that the providence petrel (*Pterodrona solandri*) returned to the island. The bird had been exterminated during the early days of the Norfolk settlement but a colony lived on at Lord Howe Island.

Probably the most interesting of the many seabirds which base themselves on Norfolk Island are the white tern (*Gygis alba*) and the black noddy (*Anous minutus*), both of which build their nests high up in groves of Norfolk Island pines near the coast. Another bird which nests around the coastline is the red-tailed tropicbird (*Phaethon rubricaudra*).

The coastline is a focus of interest both for residents and the many tourists who are attracted to Norfolk Island. The shore's character and that of the outstandingly beautiful rural areas is thought by some observers to be threatened by the spread of residential development. As a result, a conservation plan for the whole island has been mooted but is still at the discussion stage.

In the Indian Ocean

Christmas Island, is yet another volcanic island, but far removed from Australia's Pacific possessions. This tiny Indian Ocean territory is 2300 kilometres north-west of Perth but only 300 kilometres south-west of Java. Not surprisingly, the island's natural vegetation is rainforest.

The 13 500-hectare island has a central plateau varying from 150 to 250 metres high and from here the land falls away towards the sea in a series of steep slopes and terraces. The terraces are former coral reefs — at each stage of the island's emergence from the sea a new terrace was formed.

The Christmas Island rainforest is rich in plant life, with more than 200 species of flowering plants and ferns, and, all told, about 60 plants which are found nowhere else. But it is the island's birdlife which has attracted the most attention. Christmas Island is without doubt one of the world's great seabird islands.

As there are few other specks of land in this part of the Indian Ocean, the island has become an important landfall for seabirds. It is the major breeding area for several of the distinctive seabirds of the region, the best known being the Abbotts booby (*Sula abbotti*).

Its fame is partly due to its impressive appearance and the fact that it prefers to live not along the coast but in the rainforest area of the western plateau where an enormous phosphate rock deposit has developed from thousands of years of seabird droppings.

Abbotts booby is a large bird about 80 centimetres long and weighing approximately one-and-a-half kilograms. As a long-distance flier it forages for thousands of kilometres over the ocean in its search for food but always returns to build a nest in the tall trees of the rainforest, producing at best one chick every two years.

At sea, the booby plunges deeply to take its prey of fish or squid. The bird now occurs nowhere else, having been wiped out on other islands as a result of the destruction of its forest habitat.

Although there are about 9000 boobies on Christmas Island, the bird's slow breeding habits and its inability to roost anywhere other than in the forest means that its population is relatively small. The Abbotts booby is in danger of gradually being so reduced in numbers that it will become extinct.

Mining for phosphate fertiliser commenced on Christmas Island at the end of the nineteenth century and continued until 1988. By then, much of the habitat of the boobies and other rare and endangered birds had been destroyed by the open-cut mining operations.

A 1600-hectare national park was established in 1980 but this includes

BEACH BOUND When the wet season comes, Christmas Island's land crabs return to the sea to breed.

PRISTINE Unlike the larger atoll to the south, where coconut plantations are predominant, North Keeling Island is a large seabird rookery still covered with its original rainforest.

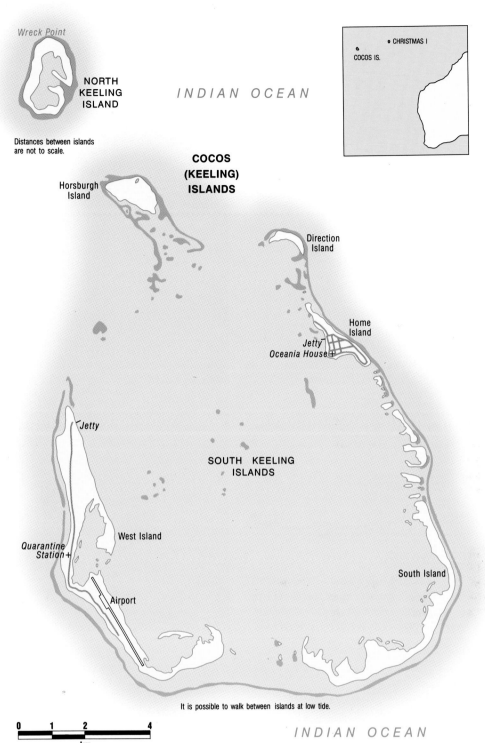

only 20 per cent of the Abbotts booby's breeding sites. A five-year moratorium on clearing in the booby's breeding areas was introduced in 1977, and after 1982 the impact of mining was minimised. It is hoped that eventually the mined areas will be re-vegetated and gradually return to something approaching their original state.

There are proposals to extend the national park — already expanded to 2370 hectares — to cover up to 70 per cent of the island but at the same time there are plans to resume mining on some areas cleared of vegetation but not yet mined.

As well as seabirds, there is a variety of other flying creatures unique to this isolated sanctuary. Three land birds — the Christmas Island imperial pigeon (*Ducula whartoni*), the Christmas Island silvereye (*Zosterops natalis*) and the Christmas Island hawk-owl (*Ninox squamipila natalis*) are natives as are the island's two species of bat.

One of Christmas Island's special sights is the annual migration of its red crabs (*Gecarcoidea natalis*), when these forest-dwelling creatures swarm from the forest to the sea to spawn. Special tunnels have been built under some roads along the major migration routes to prevent the wholesale crushing of crabs by cars and trucks.

The Cocos Islands, which were discovered by Captain William Keeling in 1609 and are officially referred to as the Cocos (Keeling) Islands in order to avoid confusion with other islands of the same name, may well have inspired many an author's idea of the idyllic tropical island tailor-made for castaways. At a distance of approximately 2770 kilometres north-west of Perth, they are one of Australia's most distant, and most recent, possessions.

Twenty-seven coral islands grouped around two atolls make up this once privately owned island group which became an Australian territory in 1955;

the descendants of John Clunies Ross, who settled the islands in the 1820s, surrendered their inherited right of ownership to the Commonwealth Government in 1978.

The main, settled atoll is a horseshoe-shaped group of islands around a lagoon, none of which rise more than six metres above sea level. The other atoll, 24 kilometres to the north, comprises a single island, known as North Keeling.

Like Christmas Island, these lonely outposts in the middle of the ocean are a base for seabirds of all kinds as well as being home to a variety of giant, land-dwelling crabs.

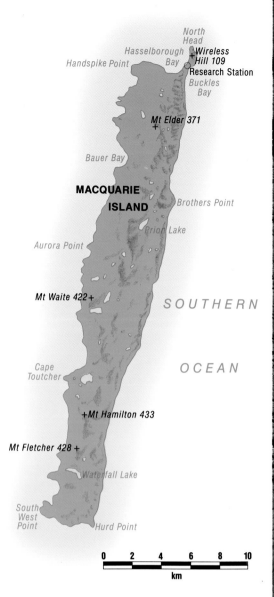

North
Head
Hasselborough Wireless
Handspike Point Bay Hill 109
Research Station
Buckles
Bay

Mt Elder 371

Bauer Bay

MACQUARIE
ISLAND Brothers Point

Prion Lake

Aurora Point

Mt Waite 422+ S O U T H E R N

O C E A N

Cape
Toutcher

+Mt Hamilton 433

Mt Fletcher 428 +

Waterfall Lake

South
West
Point Hurd Point

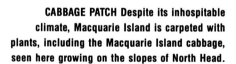

0   2   4   6   8   10
km

**CABBAGE PATCH Despite its inhospitable
climate, Macquarie Island is carpeted with
plants, including the Macquarie Island cabbage,
seen here growing on the slopes of North Head.**

**PENGUIN MEET Inscrutable and dignified, king penguins mill around on Macquarie Island's volcanic
sand beaches, impervious to the cold winds which blow for an average of 336 days a year.**

The sub-Antarctic islands

'Out of sight, out of mind' might be the attitude of most people to the ocean which encircles the earth just north of Antarctica and which contains Macquarie Island and Heard Island. There is very little land of any kind in this bleak region, a fact which makes the island landscapes and wildlife unique.

Situated south of the Roaring Forties in the 'furious fifties', these wind-blasted specks are among the few places north of the Antarctic where seals and seabirds can breed. The congregations of wildlife on the islands' teeming beaches present one of the world's great wildlife spectacles.

Although nearly 5000 kilometres apart, the west winds and currents assign these wild islands a common wildlife heritage. Even so, there is a contrast between Heard Island's landscape, which is dominated by a high volcano blanketed with ice, and low-

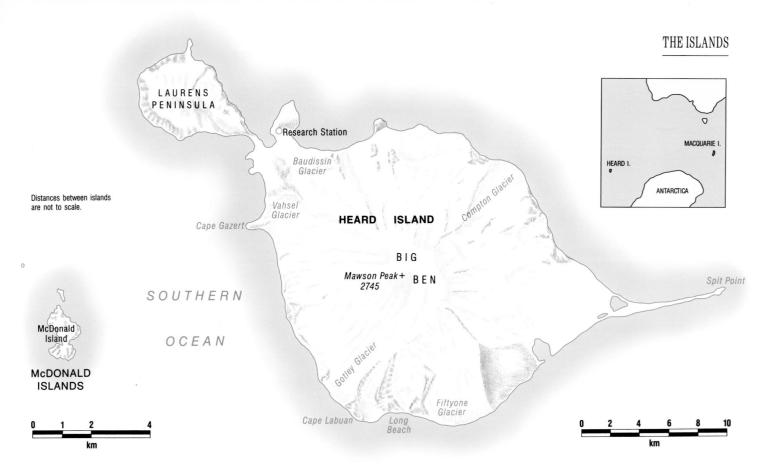

BLEAK SHORE Run-off from the mountainous spine of Macquarie Island waters the coastal plains where terrestrial and marine plant life almost merges along the tidal limits.

lying Macquarie Island which has probably never been glaciated, even during the last ice age.

The differences help explain why the natural environments of Heard Island are still intact while those of Macquarie have suffered badly from human abuse.

Macquarie Island, 5000 kilometres south-east of Tasmania, first appeared 27 million years ago when the sea floor emerged on the Macquarie Ridge. For geologists, the island provides a rare opportunity to examine something out of the ordinary — an uplifted part of the deep ocean crust, 34 kilometres long and five kilometres wide.

From a narrow coastal strip, steep slopes lead up to an undulating plateau about 150 metres above sea level. The climate is cold, wet, windy and foggy, but the temperature range is small and snow does not lie for long.

The island is too windy to support trees but there are at least 100 different lichens and 45 species of liverwort. The tallest plant is the wet tussock (*Poa foliosa*) which provides quite a luxuriant, tall, grassy cover in the more sheltered areas.

The Macquarie Island cabbage (*Stilbocarpa polaris*) is rich in vitamin C and was eaten by the early sealers to combat scurvy. It bears a large, yellow flower on a thick stalk in midsummer. Above the 200-metre level, continuous freezing and thawing has created terraces, and the vegetation

of cushion plants (*Azorella selago*) and mosses has a striped appearance.

Macquarie Island serves a similar purpose in the sub-Antarctic as Christmas Island does in the Indian Ocean. It is a vast, mid-ocean nursery for animals which derive their sustenance from the sea. At Hurd Point, half-a-million macaroni penguins (*Eudyptes chrysolophus*) spend seven months breeding and moulting in the world's largest penguin colony.

The island is also home to 200 000 king penguins (*Aptenodytes patagonicus*) and smaller numbers of gentoo penguins (*Pygoscelis papua*) and

rockhopper penguins (*Eudyptes chrysocome*). The northern giant petrel (*Macronectes halli*), the southern giant petrel (*Macronectes giganteus*) and four species of albatross breed on the island.

The wandering albatross (*Diomedea exulans*), a creature familiar to sailors far from land in the days of sail, has been reduced to 14 breeding pairs and access to its main nesting area at Caroline Bay is restricted. Some of these majestic birds have a wing span of four metres.

The beaches are shared by three species of fur seal and the southern elephant seal (*Mirounga leonina*), but

for over 100 years this was not the case. It was the fur seals which attracted men to establish a settlement in 1810. The sealers were so efficient at their task of killing seals that within ten years the animals had been exterminated; it all happened so quickly that today no-one knows if the seals which populate the beaches are of the same species as those which were slaughtered.

Exploitation of the fur seals was to be followed by the harvesting of the elephant seals for the oil content of their blubber, and then the king and macaroni penguins, which were also boiled down for their oil. Despite the reduced numbers, sealing continued sporadically until 1920.

Seals began to recolonise Macquarie Island in the 1940s and at last count there were at least 1200 non-breeding New Zealand fur seals (*Arctocephalus forsteri*) in residence. Macquarie is one of the world's most important breeding sites for the elephant seal and approximately one hundred of these huge animals, about one-sixth of the world's population, breed there.

Seals and penguins suffered most at the hands of human beings, but the general Macquarie Island environment has also not gone unscathed. Rabbits,

NEST WITH A VIEW The black-browed albatross protects its chicks from predators by building its hollow, reinforced mud nest on inaccessible cliff faces.

BEACH RETREAT A thick layer of kelp provides the perfect resting place for a group of southern elephant seals. After 100 years of being hunted, the seals disappeared from Macquarie Island for more than 20 years.

and a New Zealand bird, the weka (*Gallirallus australis*), were introduced as a source of food for the sealers, and rats and cats have escaped into the wild to wreak havoc on the countryside.

The invaders have effectively eliminated the island's two unique bird species, severely affected the breeding of several species of seabirds and reduced the area of land covered by the native tussock grass.

The island became a wildlife sanctuary in 1933 but at first the concern of the authorities was with the seals and penguins only. Macquarie has been administered by Tasmania since 1889 and became a Tasmanian Nature Reserve in 1978. An environmental management plan includes programmes for the eradication of rabbits, wekas and cats and the tussock grassland is gradually recolonising over its original terrain.

Heard and McDonald

Macquarie Island's green moorlands are reminiscent of the rolling, rounded hills of the alpine areas of Tasmania and the mainland. The Heard and McDonald Island group presents a much less welcoming appearance. It lies further south than Macquarie and, not unnaturally, has a climate which verges on the polar; to find a counterpart for these stern landscapes it is necessary to look at islands closer to the Antarctic continent, such as South Georgia.

Heard Island, 4100 kilometres southwest of Perth, is a long way from anywhere. Its 380 square kilometres are

EXTRA HARDY Green sage and the Macquarie Island cabbage (see p. 366) are the only flowering plants to break the monotony of the island's tough, tussocky grass covering.

dominated by the vast bulk of the mountain known as Big Ben. Mawson Peak (2745 metres), at Big Ben's summit, is Australia's only active volcano. The 70-metre-deep crater is like a giant pot of molten lava; the volcano was last active in 1987.

About 80 per cent of Heard Island is covered by ice in one form or another. Fifteen glaciers flow down the flanks of Big Ben, terminating in high ice cliffs which in warmer climates might come to life as rushing streams.

The glaciers are very sensitive to climatic change and since the 1940s they have retreated considerably. The ice will probably continue to retract, since the warming of the atmosphere in this region is taking place at twice the average global rate. Large, cold, coastal lagoons have been formed at a number of places where the glaciers have retreated inland.

Heard Island was claimed by Britain after a sighting by a British ship in 1833, and became an Australian territory in 1947. The absence of any introduced plants or animals has made it highly valuable to scientists interested in the study of sub-Antarctic ecosystems.

McDonald Island, much smaller than its mate, lies 40 kilometres to the west and is also volcanic. It is not often visited because its high cliffs make landing from a boat very difficult.

Because of the severe climate and the poor soils, only a few hardy species of plants exist here. On ice-free land above 200 metres, the only vegetation is mosses and lichens. Elsewhere short tussock grass (*Poa cookii*), cushion plants, and the Kerguelen cabbage (*Pringlea antiscorbutica*) are the main forms of vegetation.

Sealing was a major business in this inhospitable region from 1855 until the 1880s. Fortunately, the sealers were unable to harvest the Antarctic fur seals (*Arctocephalus gazella*) on McDonald Island, and Heard Island is being recolonised from the large colony which still exists there. Elephant seals, which were also taken from Heard Island recovered so strongly that they overpopulated the island, and are now declining to achieve a more stable population.

McDonald Island is also home to an estimated 40 000 pairs of macaroni penguins. The two-and-a-half-square-kilometre island is carpeted with chattering birds and the few visitors who make it to shore are almost overwhelmed by the odour. The macaroni penguin is the most common species on Heard Island too, with a 300 000-strong colony at Long Beach on the south coast.

Despite its name, the Heard Island shag (*Phalacrocorax atriceps*) is found only here, as is the Heard Island sheathbill (*Chionis minor nasicornis*), a sub-species of a bird which on other small islands has been exterminated by rats and cats. ☐

Australia claims a major part of the desolate yet awe-inspiring Antarctic continent, where the emptiness of the ice-encrusted interior contrasts dramatically with the myriad forms of life that thrive along its shores

An eternal winter lit by the aurora australis

Antarctica, with the least familiar shape of all the world's six continents, is hidden away, out of sight, in the earth's inhospitable nether regions.

The heavy mantle of the south polar icecap, which extends over 13.5 million square kilometres and has an average thickness of 2400 metres, ensures that the great southern continent remains permanently enshrouded in a constantly renewed blanket of white. This vast burden of ice weighs so much that it has depressed the land beneath by about 600 metres, in many places pushing it below sea level.

The icecap has helped to make the region so cold that each winter a layer of ice at least one metre thick builds up on the surface of the surrounding sea and rapidly expands to form a 20-million-square-kilometre belt of sea ice around the continent.

Two major, circular wind systems and their associated ocean currents sweep around Antarctica, cutting it off from the warmer waters of more northerly latitudes and helping to maintain the region's intense coldness. The movement of these polar waters and the marine life that exists within them is very complex.

Near the continent, the upward swell of nutrient-rich water and its exposure to the sun's rays stimulates the growth of vast amounts of single-celled plants known as phytoplankton.

SLOW THAW Icebergs are fragments that break from the edge of the Antarctic ice sheet; they may drift for four years before they melt completely.

HEAVENLY LIGHTS The bands of folded light that pulse across the night sky in the display of the aurora australis — often referred to as 'curtains' or 'drapery' because of their shape — are caused by highly energised particles from the sun which react with the earth's magnetic field, causing upper atmosphere gases to glow.

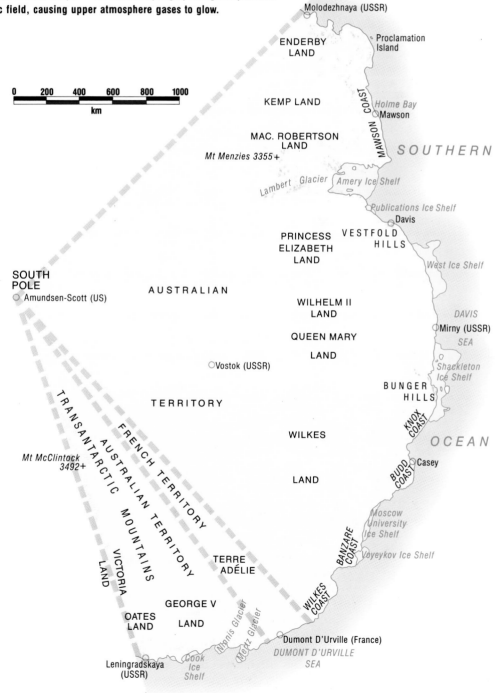

Feeding on these, and on algae which develops in the sea ice, are enormous colonies of Antarctic krill (*Euphausia superba*), a tiny crustacean.

These highly productive seas attract penguins, seals and seabirds, all of them eminently adapted to life in an intensely cold environment. Various species of great whales also make an annual pilgrimage to polar waters to feed on the rich food they produce. Although all the animal life is based on what can be produced in the sea, the small proportion of Antarctica which is not covered by ice is used by some species for breeding.

Since 1936, Australia has administered approximately six million square kilometres of the Antarctic continent — an area almost three-quarters the size of the Australian mainland. The custodial nature of Australia's 'administration' of an area which plays such a vital role in maintaining the stability of the world's climate and oceans has been underlined by its proposal that the whole of Antarctica be declared a world park.

The ice desert

The Antarctic icecap and its adjoining ice shelves contain approximately 30 million cubic kilometres of ice — about 90 per cent of the world's permanent ice by volume and about 80 per cent by area. In terms of geological time, this is an indication of how rapidly climate can change. A mere 15 000 years ago, 70 per cent of the world's ice was in the Northern Hemisphere and ice sheets covered the northern parts of North America, Europe and Asia.

Polar areas are cold mainly because

they receive very little exposure to the warming rays of the sun. Antarctica has been in its present position for between 65 and 87 million years. The icecap began to form somewhere between 35 and 40 million years ago; the cooling process was speeded up appreciably about 23 million years ago when the Drake Passage, between South America and Antarctica, opened up allowing the establishment of an insulating current all the way around the continent.

As the ice spread, it also became thicker and the region became colder still as this extended area of whiteness reflected the sun's warming rays back into the sky. The ice continued to spread until about five million years ago since when the size of the ice zone, and the closely related global sea level, have fluctuated greatly.

The continental icecap has two main divisions — East and West Antarctica — divided by the Transantarctic Mountains. Most of the Australian Antarctic Territory is covered by the East Antarctic ice sheet which is much thicker than that of the west, in places reaching a thickness of 4800 metres. Radio echo-sounding has shown that the pressure on the lowest level of ice is so enormous that it has melted and formed large 'trapped' lakes.

Surprising as it may seem, Antarctica is the driest of the continents, being to all intents and purposes a vast ice desert. The ice sheets are the product of hundreds of thousands of years of light snowfall and the annual average precipitation has a water equivalent of only three centimetres.

ICE FREE The Antarctic landmass does not emerge only around the coast; some peaks of the Transantarctic Mountains rise above 4000 metres to reveal their slopes.

GLACIER'S END Like rivers, most glaciers discharge their contents into the ocean; a tongue or 'snout' often forms where the two meet (above). The glacier ice snaps off to form icebergs.

From Casey Station in Wilkes Land to the South Pole is a distance of more than 2500 kilometres, and except for an occasional crevasse most of this is a featureless expanse of ice known as the Polar Plateau. The centre of the Plateau is the coldest area on earth. The Soviet Vostok Station, 1300 kilometres inland, has experienced −89.6°C, the lowest temperature ever recorded.

Under the force of gravity the ice is constantly spreading out towards the edge of the continent and it is around the coast that the ice movement becomes more obvious and more dramatic. The land way below the ice is not flat, and where there are valleys the ice flow is channelled into more rapidly flowing areas of ice, or glaciers.

The Lambert Glacier, in Mac. Robertson Land south of Mawson Base, is the largest glacier in the world. Four hundred kilometres long and 80 kilometres

FLOATING PLATEAU The most common icebergs are tabular — with their table-tops up to 50 metres above the sea, four-fifths of their bulk is below water.

wide, this giant river of ice is 2500 metres thick at its deepest. It discharges 35 cubic kilometres of ice into the sea every year.

At several points around the continent, the ice, 200 to 250 metres thick, extends out over the water. These 'ice shelves' are usually counted as part of the 'land' and add a total of two million square kilometres to Antarctica.

The three largest ice shelves in the Australian territory are the Shackleton, the West and the Amery. The Amery Shelf, approximately the size of Tasmania, is fed by the Lambert Glacier and extends the shoreline for 300 kilometres before the sea is reached.

At the sea edge, the ice breaks into huge, tabular icebergs; 80 per cent of Antarctica's icebergs are formed from the breaking up of the shelves by tidal forces. The fractures usually take place along the line of crevasses which have existed from the time, hundreds of years ago, when the ice was inland.

The icebergs are launched with the circum-polar currents and at first are often grounded for long spells. Eventually they move northwards into warmer waters, breaking up into smaller icebergs and sometimes turning over to reveal fantastic shapes eroded into their undersides by the ocean swell.

HIDDEN BEAUTY As it melts and changes shape, an iceberg's centre of gravity shifts, causing it to roll over. With its snowy covering washed away this iceberg reveals a jade-like surface.

BROWN ON WHITE The Vestfold Hills, along the same stretch of coast as Australia's Davis Station, are an ice-free 'oasis' where lichens and mosses grow. Further inland, they harbour freshwater lakes.

About four-fifths of the average iceberg is submerged and, like a huge, fully loaded oil tanker moving slowly through the sea, this great bulk stirs the waters bringing nutrients to the surface. Flocks of seagulls wheel around the icebergs seeking the fish which the nutrients attract.

Some icebergs are almost inconceivable in their bulk and are bigger than many large islands when they first break away. One which broke away from the Amery Ice Shelf in 1963 measured 110 kilometres long and 75 kilometres wide four years later.

The rocky margins

In the Antarctic environment, ice is so dominant that it is difficult to think of the continent without it, but about 70 million years ago the region was warm and dry with a cover of evergreen vegetation. Fifty million years ago, even though the continent had reached its polar position, it still had a forest cover.

Today ice covers all but about two per cent of Antarctica. The ice-free areas are of two main kinds: the tops of mountains projecting above the icecap and various areas close to the coast or on islands.

Along the 7500-kilometre coastline of Australia's territory there are a number of ice-free zones. Some, where snowfalls are low and where the snow which does fall blows away, are commonly referred to as oases.

SHORE BASE After spending the winter on the pack ice, which is warmer than the land, Adélie penguins return to the Antarctic shoreline to build a nest of pebbles and lay their eggs.

SEA OF ICE Pancake ice (above) is the midway point in the formation of sea ice. As the first layer of ice begins to form, the ocean swell breaks it up into roughly oval shapes which collide together, causing their edges to turn up. As the temperature drops, the ice finally freezes together. The spring thaw breaks the ice sheet up into pack ice (left).

If the icecap is the chief wonder of the Antarctic, a close second is the remarkable phenomenon of the sea ice and the way in which it spreads every winter to cover 20 million square kilometres. It is this great barrier of ice which limits sea travel to Antarctica to the summer months. Then, the ice begins to break up, covering only 2.6 million square kilometres by late February.

The expansion of the sea ice begins in March each year as the air temperature drops. At −1.8°C the surface of the sea begins to take on an oily appearance as the top layer of water starts to resemble a soupy mixture. Solid layers start to develop and gradually evolve into 'pancake' ice as the fragments are rounded by colliding with each other.

Later, the 'pancakes' freeze together, the ice thickens and snow is added. By September, the new ice is one to one-and-a-half metres thick. As the warm weather of summer approaches, it breaks up into pack ice. Where the sea ice persists for two years it reaches three metres thick.

The sea of life

Despite its smothering appearance, the thick ice actually assists the marine life which lives beneath it in several ways. It insulates the water, making it a suitable habitat for certain forms of life such as the micro-algae which grow at the base of the sea ice, staining it pink. These are released in summer for consumption by animals such as krill.

The krill, a type of zooplankton, are at the bottom of the food chain and are central to the ecosystem of the Southern Ocean, being eaten by fish, squid, Adélie penguins (*Pygoscelis adeliae*), crabeater seals (*Lobodon carcinophagus*), leopard seals (*Hydrurga leptonyx*) and several species of baleen, or whalebone whales.

Feeding mainly on the fish and squid are seabirds, emperor penguins (*Aptenodytes forsteri*), Weddell seals (*Leptonychotes weddelli*), Ross seals (*Ommatophoca rossi*) and sperm whales (*Physeter macrocephalus*).

At the opposite end of the food chain to the tiny krill are the killer whales (*Orcinus orca*), which hunt in packs and feed on seals and baleen whales, and the south polar skua (*Catharacta maccormickii*), which feeds mainly on young penguins.

The king of the polar seas is the blue whale (*Balaeoptera musculus*). This gentle giant which may weigh up to 117 tonnes and grow to 30 metres long is the largest animal that has ever lived on earth. It spends several months each summer feeding around the edge of the sea ice.

By the time international restrictions were placed on the whaling industry only a few thousand blue whales were left alive and no-one is certain whether there is enough of a breeding stock to enable it to survive. Since the blue whale lives entirely on krill when in the Antarctic, the reduction in its numbers has enabled other krill-eaters such as crabeater seals and penguins to grow in number.

SOUTHERN SEAL Weddell seals, the most common of the Antarctic seals, spend most of their time in the water, leaving the sea in spring to give birth and in summer to sunbathe.

The penguin is the creature most characteristic of Antarctic wildlife. The most common species is the Adélie, which is also the smallest, reaching a length of only 70 centimetres. During the spring, thousands of pairs of breeding Adélies come together in vast colonies on rocky outcrops to nest. In the winter, the birds retreat to the warmer conditions of the sea ice.

The emperor penguin is the only penguin species to live and breed exclusively on and around the immediate shores of Antarctica. It lives up to its name in its appearance and bearing, standing up to 1.4 metres in height, usually rigidly upright and with an air of great dignity.

Small spurs on its feet help the emperor penguin to move surely over the ice and snow. The emperor breeds mainly in large rookeries on stable sea ice near the coast.

Like the emu, the emperor penguin has turned regular sex roles on their heads and made child care a male responsibility. Eggs are incubated by the males who hold them on the top of their feet under a flap of skin which acts rather like a blanket.

During the incubation period, the male endures a 60-day fast, while the female feeds at sea. After three weeks of life, the chicks are left in a crèche of young birds while the male joins the female on feeding trips which may involve journeys of up to 100 kilometres.

TAKING THE PLUNGE Penguins have nothing to fear on the ice, but hungry seals lurk below.

All but one of the many seabirds of the Antarctic shores are migratory visitors; the Antarctic petrel (*Thalassoica antarctica*) is the only species to breed on the continent and its offshore islands. In the winter, the only seabirds that remain on the continent are the Antarctic petrel and the snow petrel (*Pagodroma nivea*).

With its pure white plumage and coal-black eyes, the snow petrel presents a striking picture as it wheels over the ice. It nests in hollows under rocks.

The animals which are most expertly adapted to a life of constant cold are the fish. Of approximately 120 species in Antarctic waters, about 90 per cent are found only here, reflecting the long period they have been isolated. Among

GET TOGETHER Penguins are nothing if not gregarious. Some summer rookeries of the Adélie species — this one is near the Australian base at Mawson — are thought to contain over one million birds.

them the majestic Antarctic cod (*Dissostichus mawsoni*), at 1.5 metres long and up to 70 kilograms in weight, is a giant among the world's fish.

The majority of the white-blooded ice fish of the *Chaenichthyidae* family are a true product of the Antarctic. The cold water of the Southern Ocean contains relatively large amounts of oxygen and species of this family, alone of all the invertebrates, have no red blood cells to carry the oxygen in their tissues but absorb it directly from the sea through capillaries in their skin.

Since this absorbtion system is not an energy-efficient way of transporting oxygen through their bodies these white-blooded fish ration their energy expenditure by moving very slowly. The juvenile fish are often almost colourless but as they grow they acquire some external colouring; the ice fish *Chaenicthys rhinoceratus* for example, is an iridescent purple colour.

The two per cent of Antarctica which is available for vegetation is so rocky and windswept that there is little scope for ordinary plants to develop. Although glacial ice has removed most of the soil, the droppings from penguin colonies contribute to almost excessive fertility in limited places.

In Australian Antarctica, there are mosses, lichens and algae, often colonising the most surprising places. Bright green stains in the cracks of rocks are not minerals but algae. If a fragment of rock is broken off, millions of microscopic algae can be found occupying minute spaces between the rock crystals just below the surface.

Blue-green algae are the most common form of plant life in Antarctica. These are very primitive plants, not dissimilar to the first plants which evolved on earth three million years ago. They grow wherever there is light, a little moisture and shelter.

The tallest plants, a mere centimetre high, are the mosses, which usually grow in sheltered places where water melts from snowbanks or the ice edge. Both mosses and lichens also benefit from the nutrients produced in the penguin colonies.

A fine balance

No country has ever 'owned' or colonised Antarctica in the usual way in which nations have sovereign control over their territories. Seven countries, including Australia, have claims over parts of Antarctica but some sections are not claimed at all.

The Antarctic Treaty of 1959 was negotiated by those countries having the closest interest in the Antarctic to prevent the region from becoming the scene of international conflict and to ensure that there was cooperation in scientific matters. Military activities were outlawed, the dumping of nuclear waste was banned and territorial claims were fixed.

HIGH SOCIETY The imposing emperor penguin is not only the largest of the penguins, it is also the only one to never venture beyond the 'shores' of the Antarctic ice sheet. The recently hatched chicks (above), still in their fluffy juvenile plumage, will be fed by their mothers for six months before fending for themselves. There are no nests, and the chicks rely on their parents' substantial bodies for protection from the elements (see left).

The convention placed great emphasis on conservation and in 1964 the Antarctic Treaty countries decided that the continent should be regarded as a 'Special Conservation Area'. It was agreed that special protection should be given to areas important for the breeding of penguins and seabirds.

A later proposal, that Antarctica become a national park open to people of all nations, was made in the hope that conservation efforts could be coordinated so that the environment was not placed at risk from activities such as mining. The idea was not taken seriously until the threat of mining became a reality. This came with the negotiation of a Convention for the Regulation of Antarctic Mineral Resource Activities in 1988.

Australia and France decided not to sign the mining convention and instead have argued for a wilderness park or reserve in which the exploitation of resources would be completely banned.

If they are successful, not only will the absolute priority of nature conservation have been established but there will almost certainly be a park or reserve authority to help coordinate the management of one of the world's great untouched natural wonders. □

POLAR TENACITY An outcrop of moss watered by a melting snowbank flourishes on an island offshore from the Vestfold Hills region.

The Arthur Range, south-west Tasmania

Seeing Australia

Before you go...

Planning ahead for trouble-free travel

Australia is a big country but the majority of its many scenic attractions are relatively easy to reach. Most regions are well served by either government or private forms of transport, and as long as certain basic precautions are taken when travelling in the outback, it is possible to visit all but the most isolated areas by motor car.

In order to ensure a relaxed, trouble-free holiday, particularly if you are visiting more than one location, it is useful to plan an itinerary, no matter how informal. Government tourist bureaux can help you plan your trip by providing up-to-date information on all aspects of travel and accommodation, as well as a free booking service.

Each state bureau has an office in its own capital city and offices in most other states, or is represented by commercial travel agents. The addresses and telephone numbers of these offices are usually listed under 'tourism' in the state government section at the front of telephone directories.

Before leaving for a holiday, cancel all home-delivery services and arrange for someone to look after your pets and plants. Local authorities usually advise householders to turn off the gas at the meter if they are leaving home for more than a week, and the electricity if leaving for more than a couple of weeks.

Holidaymakers going away for more than a few weeks should notify the local police that their house will be empty, and arrange for mail to be redirected to friends or relatives or held at the post office.

Trains and boats and 'planes

BY 'PLANE Although flying is the most expensive form of transport, off-peak fares, holiday package tours and other travel discounts have helped maintain its popularity as a way to travel, particularly when time is an important consideration. Many holidaymakers who have a set destination and a limited amount of time prefer to travel by air, often driving on from the airport in a rental car.

Major airlines provide an extensive network of flights, linking population centres across the country; commuter and charter flights service small towns and remote areas. Often it may be necessary to fly to a provincial centre with a major airline and then connect with a commuter flight, but most large airlines handle onward bookings with smaller operators.

The major airlines have discounts for children, students, groups, and those who book in advance. Fly–drive packages are offered by some airlines and car rental firms. These holidays may include accommodation, and can be booked for specified times or for an unlimited period. Some firms offer campervans as well as cars.

BY TRAIN Travelling by train is an ideal way to see a place as large as Australia, combining an impression of the vastness of the country with a finely detailed picture of the route. A network of air-conditioned rail services links the main cities, operating regularly in each direction. Many other long-distance services operate within and between states for the rail enthusiast or holidaymaker.

The major services offer a wide range of accommodation, from roomy, first-class deluxe compartments with ensuite bathrooms, to coach cars providing seated travel. There are often dining cars with licensed restaurant services, and buffet facilities for light refreshments and snacks. Major long-distance services have comfortable lounge or club cars with licensed bars, pianos and nightly showings of popular films on video tape.

Besides the standard concessions for children, students, pensioners and groups, the railways offer special travel passes for certain periods of time.

Before planning a long-distance trip, check the length of the journey and the facilities available on the train. For detailed information, contact your state government tourist bureau or railway authority.

BY COACH Private coach companies not only operate extensive and budget-priced intercapital express services, but also provide a wide range of package holidays. Large companies offer a variety of tours, from half- and full-day city or scenic sightseeing trips, to full-scale outback expeditions. The smaller companies generally specialise in unusual holidays 'off the beaten track'.

Fares on the intercapital services are usually lower than rail fares, although there is of course less freedom of movement on coaches. Different companies charge different fares and some offer pensioner, student and child discounts.

Coach travel has improved in comfort in the last few years, but it is worth finding out the length of any prospective journey. The Sydney to Melbourne service, for example takes about the same time — 13 hours — as the train service.

Large companies offer planned tours with detailed itineraries including meals and accommodation. Coaches are air-conditioned and many have toilets, video machines and stereo systems with earphones. Coach camping tours to remote outback areas have become increasingly popular with both young and old people. Most are fully serviced, with equipment and meals provided. Passengers are expected to keep their luggage to a minimum.

BY SEA The passenger and car ferry sailing between the Station Pier in Melbourne and the TT-Line terminal in Devonport is the only regularly scheduled interstate passenger ship in Australia. Taking a little more than 14 hours, the ferry sails overnight, three days a week, both ways. Reservations can be made with either the TT-Line or Station Pier.

There are a number of cruise and ferry services operating on coastal and inland waterways such as the cruise ships which ply the Murray River. Contact travel agents for information.

BY CAR Australia is almost the same size as the United States of America yet with only one-sixteenth of its population. Most of the population is centred around the coastal cities, and more than 75 per cent of people live within an hour's drive of Highway One which, in a clockwise direction, links Cairns with Darwin.

For convenience and flexibility a car is ideal, and it brings many of Australia's natural wonders within easy reach. It is possible to travel to the most remote regions and to experience the wonder and joy of new places without risking life and limb — all it takes is a little planning. Some knowledge of the safety measures it may be necesary to adopt in remote areas is useful in order to avoid danger when travelling in the outback.

It is easy to let eyes and fingers wander across a map of Australia, but another thing to know which vehicle is best suited for travelling around it. While most of Australia is accessible by conventional car, seek out the unbiased advice of the experts at your state automobile club (NRMA, RACV etc) if you plan to go off the beaten track or are thinking of buying a campervan or similar vehicle.

Highway One, which circumnavigates 15 000 kilometres of Australia's periphery, is fully sealed, and many of the highways and main roads reaching into the interior are also sealed. Those roads which are better traversed by a four-wheel drive vehicle are usually so marked on local tourist maps.

The distances between areas of interest are often so great that fly-drive packages have become more and more attractive. The trip from Melbourne to Cairns can easily take five days to a week by car, leaving the driver with little interest in *even more* driving in order to explore the Cairns region. Flying to Cairns and hiring a car immediately becomes a practical alternative.

Once the tyrannies of distance have been appreciated and accommodated into your travel plans, and when local driving conditions are understood and a suitable vehicle chosen, the most important step is to prepare the vehicle correctly (see 'Driving without tears').

Driving without tears

Always have your car fully serviced before leaving on a major trip and let the service staff know that it will be covering a large distance. Instead of ignoring a tyre which may last another 5000 kilometres, or an oil filter which will need changing at the next service, the staff should inspect the car keeping in mind the length of the trip ahead.

Will the car be more heavily laden than usual? Will the engine require servicing during the journey? Will the car be used in unfamiliar country where a cooling-system service before you leave would be prudent?

If you are planning a lengthy trip which may include travelling over long stretches of unmade roads, have new tyres fitted and install a mesh windscreen guard.

THINGS TO TAKE While many motoring organisations and well-meaning friends who have made long trips may be only too willing to advise you on what to take, you should not weigh your car down with unfamiliar equipment and spare parts.

A fine toolkit is a good companion, but useless if you have no idea how to work on your car. If you are travelling into remote areas and feel unhappy about undertaking basic mechanical repairs, ask your automobile club about beginners' courses. The underbonnet area of most modern cars is daunting. Roadside repairs to computers, electronic ignition and fuel injection are beyond even qualified mechanics.

Nevertheless, it is wise to take a toolkit that is more comprehensive than that provided with the car. Pack a set of spanners to suit your car, a hammer, a better wheelbrace than the original brace, rags, hand cleaner, oil and water (and coolant if required by your car — check the owner's manual). It is also wise to take a warning triangle, a pump or a pressurised canister of air (for emergency use only), a tow rope, a torch and jumper leads.

Only carry extra fuel if you are likely to be well away from regular supplies and if it can be carried safely outside the car or in a small, approved container in the boot.

Spare parts should be limited to those you can fit yourself. A fan belt, set of cooling system hoses, spark plugs, headlamp and light bulbs are usually sufficient unless you are very skilled. Do not forget tyre chains if visiting snow country.

Practice fitting the chains and always practice changing a wheel. There is a simple reason for this: your car's wheels may have been fitted by a tyre retailer's employee using a rattle gun. The studs or nuts may be too tight to be removed by hand. Check them all before venturing into remote country or onto unsealed roads.

Always carry enough food and drink for several days' meals if you are going into a sparsely settled area. Take plenty of water (allow a litre per person per day) and food which will not decay in the heat. Camping stores specialise in this type of food.

Good maps and the skill to read and interpret them can make or break a trip. Apart from the detailed maps available from automobile clubs, seek out those sold by each state government mapping service.

Always carry a first-aid kit authorised by a body such as the St John Ambulance Association and make sure you know how to use it.

HITTING THE ROAD City driving rarely exposes a driver to the conditions, or even the possibilities he or she will encounter on the open road. Just a few moments with a map will give you some idea of travelling times. On well-maintained highways, 500 to 750 kilometres a day may be achieved with ease.

FLINDERS RANGES The four-wheel drive vehicle has opened up even the most rugged reaches of the outback to the ordinary traveller.

In a speed-limit zone of 100 kilometres per hour, it is possible to average 80 kilometres per hour by travelling near the speed limit. If you can drive for four hours without a break, expect to have covered around 300 kilometres.

Do not be over-ambitious, and remember that this average can easily be reduced to 200 kilometres or less by lower speed limits in towns, toilet, meal and refuelling stops, and general road conditions.

When travelling with young children, plan on stopping for half an hour every two hours of travelling. The older the car's occupants, the longer they can travel without a break. Stop at least once every four hours and rest for about an hour.

Apart from the fact that you will be travelling faster than you would in the city, country and highway road conditions present many hazards. Large trucks and coaches require considerably greater passing and braking distances than ordinary vehicles. Allow these large vehicles plenty of space; if you are travelling slower than a fast-moving coach or large truck, pull over and let it pass.

In rural areas, tractors and motorised farm implements often travel very slowly. Leave plenty of space between vehicles and slow down when approaching.

Keep in mind that towards the end of the day, very early in the morning, or around hotel or club closing time, other drivers may be tired or have poor judgment.

FLOOD AND FIRES Do not drive through a swollen river or creek — deep water can appear shallow. Do not wade in to check the depth unless the water is sluggish and slow moving and there are others on hand to assist if you run into difficulties.

Do not follow a truck or coach through a flooded river. A river which is shallow enough for a large vehicle to ford may still be far too deep for a car.

If your car is washed away, wind up the windows and do not open the doors. Leave your seat belts firmly fastened and wait until the car is firmly wedged and it is safe to leave. If seat belts are loosened too early you may be injured as the vehicle is dashed about by the floodwater.

If your car's path through floodwater is relatively unimpeded and you attempt the crossing, keep the engine revs up by using first or second gear (or low gear in an automatic car). Travel slowly, and when on the other side, keep going at low speed, pressing your left foot on the brake pedal to dry out the brake pads. Do not resume normal speed until the brakes respond properly.

Do not drive into fires or towards fires which are being driven your way by the wind. Do not drive through a bushfire area if the wind is blowing across the road — it may carry the fire across your path. If fires have been reported along your planned route, seek out a local bushfire brigade worker or police officer for advice and tune into local radio broadcasts.

DRIVING IN THE OUTBACK The district where Burke and Wills died at the end of their ill-fated expedition in 1861, was, at the same time, readily supporting a large number of Aboriginal people. The Aborigines had the advantage in that they understood the country and knew where to find food.

For non-Aboriginal Australians, nothing has changed since the days of Burke and Wills. The supply depots of today are the hamlets and roadhouses scattered about the outback roads and highways. The fate of Burke and Wills could await any tourist who ignores the warnings about driving in isolated areas.

Thankfully, such incidents are uncommon and the most likely disaster to be met by the modern motorist is a broken windscreen. If your car has a laminated windscreen it will not shatter but merely crack. Have it replaced as soon as possible.

A toughened windscreen will shatter and may hinder vision. If it does, hit the section immediately in front of you to break a hole for improved vision. Stop the car, cover any adjacent air vents and remove all broken glass. Close the car's other windows and drive slowly to a town where a new windscreen can be fitted.

A flat tyre is relatively easy to fix as long as the ground where you change the wheel is smooth, flat and firm. Use a block of wood or something similar to make sure the jack does not sink into the ground and chock the car's other wheels to make sure it does not roll off the jack.

BREAKING DOWN If the car breaks down and you lack the skills to identify and fix the problem, try the following to check the fuel gauge — it may be faulty: remove the petrol cap and rock the car with the cap removed, while listening for the sound of fuel sloshing inside the tank. A car which has run out of fuel will usually misfire for a time before stopping.

Check the temperature gauge. If the cooling system has failed the engine may seize. There is little you can do about this apart from organising a tow to the nearest reputable garage.

If all the coolant has gone, the gauge may not read hot, but cold. If you have been driving for some time and the gauge reads cold, open the bonnet and check the radiator cap. Place a thick cloth over it and remove it to the safety level first so that any steam can blow off.

If there is no coolant, and the car's underbonnet area seems very hot even though the gauge reads cold, suspect the worst. When the engine has completely cooled — wait at least an hour — fill the radiator with coolant or water and look for a leak. If necessary, make a temporary patch and attempt to start the car again. Take it to a garage immediately if it does.

A major engine failure often results in coolant entering the engine's lubricant. To check this, remove the dipstick. If the oil is a light grey, cloudy colour, do not drive the car — arrange a tow.

If you intend to spend a lot of time in remote regions, it is useful to install a Citizens' Band (CB) radio. You can listen to chatter between truck drivers and others travelling the outback. More importantly, a CB radio may assist you in calling for help should the need arise.

Be aware of changing road conditions. Potholes and damaged roads do exist and can cause the car to swerve violently out of control, or break a suspension component. If the road is in poor condition, travel slowly.

Five-star or under canvas

HOTELS AND MOTELS Generally, accommodation standards and the services offered by hotels and motels vary according to price. Many leading chains offer discounts to groups. Accommodation directories are available from state government tourist bureaux, motoring associations and travel agents.

CARAVAN PARKS There are several thousand caravan parks scattered across Australia. Most have laundry, shower, toilet and shopping facilities, and some allow pets. Lists of caravan parks are available from automobile clubs and government tourist bureaux.

YOUTH HOSTELS Only members of the Australian Youth Hostels Association (AYHA) can stay at youth hostels. There is no age limit and free membership is available for children under the age of 18 whose parents are members. There are hostels in all major towns and cities and in some more out-of-the-way places as well.

CHRISTIAN ASSOCIATIONS (YMCA/YWCA) Accommodation at reasonable rates is available at YMCAs and YWCAs in some capital cities, with shared, or sometimes, private facilities. In dormitory accommodation, there is no restriction on the length of stay.

BACKPACKERS Most capital cities have commercially run hostels for backpackers. These private businesses provide hostel accommodation for travellers with photographic identification and proof that they are travelling. The style of accommodation ranges from dormitories with communal kitchen and bathroom facilities, to flats with private facilities. These hostels are usually listed under 'homes and hostels' in the yellow pages telephone directory.

UNIVERSITY COLLEGES Most colleges offer accommodation to students in holiday periods, and sometimes general accommodation is also available. For details, contact the universities.

COUNTRY PROPERTIES Some farms and sheep or cattle stations offer holiday facilities with bunk, barn or homestead accommodation. Guests are offered such diversions as bushwalking, trail-riding and fishing, and may be able to join in farm activities such as milking and cattle mustering. Information about these properties is available from government tourist bureaux.

CAMPING IN NATIONAL PARKS Caravan and camping facilities are provided in many national parks. These facilities are usually more spartan than those offered by private or municipal caravan park operations. In some parks, especially those set aside for the conservation of plants and animals, no camping is permitted.

In parks where camping is permitted, facilities and restrictions vary widely. Some allow tents but not caravans or vehicles, some require permits, and others a small fee payable on entry. Facilities can be non-existent or suprisingly comfortable. Some Tasmanian parks have huts with electricity, and bathroom and laundry facilities can be booked in advance. For the latest details of authorised camping sites, contact the relevant national park authority.

Roughing it

WALKING AND LIVING IN THE BUSH More people than ever are taking advantage of the opportunities offered by our national parks to explore the bush on foot. But it is unwise to go on long or difficult walks without a knowledge of bushcraft.

Joining a bushwalking club is probably the safest and most enjoyable way of learning bushcraft. These organisations welcome new members and provide advice, training, and supervised walks. For more information contact the federations of bushwalking clubs in Queensland, New South Wales, Victoria and Tasmania, and individual clubs in other states or territories.

Fundamental to bushcraft are the basic techniques of safety and survival. Experienced walkers should know how to light a fire under adverse conditions, how to find and prepare water for drinking, the type of food to take on trips and how to navigate by reading maps as well as using natural landmarks, the moon, sun and stars.

Codes of etiquette, accepted by all bushwalkers, minimise the impact of camping and walking on the bush, and help to preserve wild places in as unspoiled a state as possible for other walkers.

BUSH SAFETY With planning and a few basic skills, most accidents can be avoided and any that do occur can be dealt with as efficiently as possible. Before setting out on a long walk, tell a relative, friend or the local police when you expect to return.

Anyone travelling in isolated regions should know how to read a map and use a compass, but knowing how to find one's way using nature as a guide is also essential. The natural features of a terrain, the sun and the stars, are guides as useful to the experienced bush navigator as a compass or map.

FREYCINET PENINSULA The view of Wineglass Bay is one of the many delights which reward bushwalkers in Tasmania's vast national parks.

Experienced bushwalkers never rely exclusively on a map or compass — which can be lost — nor on any single natural signpost — the sun, for example may disappear behind a cloud barrier. Instead, they combine natural and man-made navigational aids, using one to check the other.

Experience and training may sharpen your ability to notice and remember the features of a region, but initially you will have to make a conscious effort to observe and memorise them. If you do get lost, either stay where you are, or retrace your steps — as long as you know you are going over familiar territory.

Avoiding — or, if the worst happens, recognising and treating — such conditions as starvation, dehydration and exposure is also vital to bushcraft. Although it is possible to survive for weeks without food, the average person cannot stay alive for more than two days without water. During summer, when more water is lost through perspiring, survival time is reduced.

Dehydration, caused by a lack of water, also occurs in very cold weather as exertion to keep warm causes the body to perspire.

CAMPING GEAR A growing interest in exploring the bush has fostered the production of lightweight camping equipment. Where tents and packs were once heavy and bulky, a modern weekend backpack and its contents can weigh as little as eleven kilograms.

A wide range of equipment of varying standards is available. Constant refinements of design and the discovery of tough, lightweight materials mean that new products appear every year. When choosing equipment, quality is important; if a badly made, cheap product fails in a remote area you could be put at risk.

Specialist bushwalking or camping shops provide the most reliable equipment for difficult or overnight walks, and experienced staff at these stores can give advice on what type of equipment is best suited to your needs.

Rules...and sound advice

FISHING REGULATIONS An amateur fisherman in New South Wales, Queensland, the Northern Territory and in most waters of South Australia, does not need a licence to fish as long as government regulations are complied with. But in Victoria, a licence is required for fresh and saltwater fishing, and in Tasmania, it is required for freshwater fishing and the fishing of abalone, scallops and crayfish in the ocean.

In Western Australia, an amateur must have a licence for netfishing or the taking of rock lobsters from the sea and marron from fresh waters. A licence is also required for freshwater fishing in the Australian Capital Territory.

There are a number of other fishing regulations, including bag limits, closed seasons, closed waters and minimum size limits for fish. Each state fishery division publishes a guide to its regulations, and this is available free of charge.

SHOOTING REGULATIONS Shooters must hold current permits and should be aware of the current state regulations. All native animals in national parks and conservation areas are protected by law, but outside these specified areas the restrictions are complex and vary from state to state and season to season.

Generally, most native birds, mammals and reptiles are protected, but the classification of protected animals changes constantly. A booklet explaining the current conditions is available free of charge from each state national park authority.

MOVEMENT OF PLANTS AND ANIMALS To prevent the spread of plant and animal pests and diseases, governments may restrict the transportation of some plant and animal matter across state borders.

To be on the safe side, it is wise not to carry any plant or animal matter across a border. Generally, the state and territory governments do not restrict the movement of household pets, but it is an offence to release dogs, cats or any other domestic animal into the wild because of the devastating effect feral animals have had on the countryside (see pp.16–21).

BEACH SAFETY For many people, holidays are synonymous with summer and visits to the beach. Keep in mind the dangers of overexposure of bare skin to the sun and swimming in unpatrolled or unenclosed waters.

NOTE *Swimming in open, coastal waters in the tropics is extremely dangerous: shark attacks have been recorded in all months of the year, and between October and May, the chironex — a deadly box jellyfish also known as the sea wasp or stinger — comes close to shore.*

If you are travelling north of Bundaberg in the east, or Port Hedland in the west, check with local authorities that the swimming season has been declared. Tune into local radio stations, as these often broadcast warnings when the chironex is sighted outside the regular 'season'.

Always carry a large bottle of vinegar. If someone is unlucky enough to be stung, do NOT touch the tentacles, but drench them with the vinegar for at least 30 seconds. Ask for assistance at the nearest lifesaving club or seek out a doctor immediately. □

Today's weather...

A cross section of conditions around the country

The wide range of climates in a country as vast as Australia means that whatever the time of year, some part of the country can be seen at its best. The weather is, of course, notoriously unpredictable but some basic background information on *average* temperature and rainfall figures can help you time your travels to coincide with what should be the most clement conditions — according to the weather bureaux' records.

In most regions, high summer is generally not a good time to travel — apart from the discomfort of travelling in the heat, the dry inland does not look its best, and tropical and subtropical coastal regions are drenched by torrential rains.

On the other hand, in the high country of the Great Dividing Range, this is a spectacular season with wildflowers blooming after the long winter. Long, mild summer days attract many visitors to Tasmania.

The best time to tour tropical northern Australia is in the winter, or dry season, since the summer, or wet season, is characterised by hot, humid days and torrential monsoon rains. During the 'dry' — in June, July and August — the days are warm, the skies cloudless, and humidity is low. Winter touring also avoids the cyclones which can occur from November to April around our northern coasts.

Winter is the most comfortable time to travel across inland Australia, where summer temperatures often exceed 38°C. Normally the winter months are dry, but occasionally heavy rains cause the rivers to flow, making the desert bloom with wildflowers that may not be seen again for decades.

Spring is the best time to visit Western Australia, when the glorious wildflowers for which the state's south-west is famous come into bloom. Touring in the cooler months is also pleasant, except perhaps in the far south-western corner where heavy rain prevails in winter. High midsummer temperatures can make travelling uncomfortable.

WHAT THE TABLES SHOW: Broad, year-round examples of the climates of the regions in this book are given here. Average monthly maximum and minimum temperatures are followed by the average monthly rainfall reading in millimetres and the number of 'clear' days a month. Where the climate varies greatly, figures for two centres are given.

'Clear' days refers to mainly cloudless days — these are defined by meteorologists as days with less than two-eighths of cloud cover at 9am, 3pm and 9pm.

SHOWERS, CLEARING A morning rainbow over Mount Wellington promises a good day's travel ahead. In a land of climatic extremes, choosing the right season to travel is all important.

1 EASTERN TASMANIA

HOBART

	Jan	Feb	Mar	Apr	May	Jun	Jul	Aug	Sep	Oct	Nov	Dec
max	21.7	21.5	20.1	17.4	14.3	12.1	11.7	13	15.1	16.9	18.3	20
min	12	12	11	9	7	5.1	4.4	5.1	6.4	7.8	9.3	10.8
mm	37	33	38	49	39	45	51	43	43	57	50	47
clear	3	3	3	2	2	3	2	2	2	1	1	1

LAUNCESTON

	Jan	Feb	Mar	Apr	May	Jun	Jul	Aug	Sep	Oct	Nov	Dec
max	23.1	23.1	20.9	17.2	13.8	11.3	10.7	12	14	16.4	18.6	21
min	10	10.2	9	6.5	4.6	2.9	2.2	3	4.2	5.5	7.1	8.7
mm	37	31	35	49	56	56	73	75	62	58	50	47
clear	4	4	4	4	3	4	4	4	3	3	2	3

2 SOUTH-WEST TASMANIA

STRATHGORDON

	Jan	Feb	Mar	Apr	May	Jun	Jul	Aug	Sep	Oct	Nov	Dec
max	19.2	19.8	17.5	14.2	11.6	9.4	8.8	9.7	11.2	13.4	15.7	17.1
min	9.5	9.7	8.6	7	5.2	3.7	2.9	3.5	4.4	5.5	6.9	8.2
mm	146	90	138	231	213	213	233	264	294	217	174	194
clear	3	3	2	1	1	1	1	1	1	2	2	3

3 NORTH-WEST TASMANIA

BURNIE

	Jan	Feb	Mar	Apr	May	Jun	Jul	Aug	Sep	Oct	Nov	Dec
max	21.4	21.7	20.3	17.9	15.4	13.4	12.7	13.2	14.5	16.4	18.1	19.6
min	12.7	13.3	12.2	9.8	8.1	6.2	5.2	5.8	6.6	7.8	9.8	10.9
mm	37	40	53	78	95	92	126	114	77	82	71	71
clear	5	5	5	5	5	5	5	5	4	4	5	3

4 CENTRAL TASMANIA

LAKE ST CLAIR

	Jan	Feb	Mar	Apr	May	Jun	Jul	Aug	Sep	Oct	Nov	Dec
max	18.4	18.9	16.2	12.7	9.7	7.6	6.6	7.8	9.7	12.2	14.4	16.1
min	7.1	7.5	6.2	4.3	2.7	1.2	0.4	0.8	1.6	3.2	4.6	6.1
mm	80	60	68	121	121	133	154	151	157	131	117	107
clear	6	5	3	2	1	1	1	1	2	3	4	4

5 BASS STRAIT ISLANDS

FLINDERS ISLAND

	Jan	Feb	Mar	Apr	May	Jun	Jul	Aug	Sep	Oct	Nov	Dec
max	21.8	22.6	21.3	18.6	16.1	13.9	13.1	13.6	14.9	16.7	18.3	19.8
min	12.9	13.4	12.7	10.7	8.9	7	5.9	6.5	7.4	8.5	9.9	11.5
mm	37	31	47	60	79	62	79	74	61	47	52	48
clear	3	3	2	2	2	3	3	3	3	3	2	2

6 GEELONG TO THE COORONG

MOUNT GAMBIER

	Jan	Feb	Mar	Apr	May	Jun	Jul	Aug	Sep	Oct	Nov	Dec
max	25.1	24.8	22.9	19.1	15.9	13.7	13	14	15.6	17.8	20	22.6
min	10.7	11.4	10.2	8.5	7.1	5.5	4.9	5.3	6	6.9	8.1	9.7
mm	17	22	27	53	68	75	96	86	72	58	50	34
clear	5	5	4	3	1	1	1	1	2	2	1	3

PORTLAND

	Jan	Feb	Mar	Apr	May	Jun	Jul	Aug	Sep	Oct	Nov	Dec
max	22.6	22.4	21.2	18.8	16.6	14.1	13.6	14.3	15.8	17.5	18.6	21
min	13.1	13.7	12.4	10.5	9.2	7.3	6.4	7	7.7	9	10.3	11.5
mm	31	23	14	58	79	90	131	118	94	89	62	44
clear	3	3	3	2	1	0	0	0	0	1	1	2

7 VICTORIAN HILLS

BENDIGO

	Jan	Feb	Mar	Apr	May	Jun	Jul	Aug	Sep	Oct	Nov	Dec
max	29	28.6	25.4	20.6	15.9	13.1	12	13.7	16.2	19.9	23.5	26.4
min	14.4	14.7	12.6	9.1	6.4	4.3	3.3	4.5	5.9	8.2	10.5	12.5
mm	27	20	23	32	51	59	53	53	50	44	30	24
clear	11	11	9	8	4	4	3	3	4	5	6	8

8 MALLEE COUNTRY

LAMEROO

	Jan	Feb	Mar	Apr	May	Jun	Jul	Aug	Sep	Oct	Nov	Dec
max	31	30.5	27.2	22.9	18.5	15.9	15.1	16.5	18.9	22.4	25.9	28.4
min	13.6	13.8	11.7	9	6.9	4.8	4.2	4.8	6	7.9	10	12.1
mm	13	13	14	25	34	36	41	42	41	39	20	17
clear	12	11	9	7	5	4	4	4	5	6	5	8

9 MURRAY RIVER AND RIVERINA

WAGGA WAGGA

	Jan	Feb	Mar	Apr	May	Jun	Jul	Aug	Sep	Oct	Nov	Dec
max	31.2	30.6	27.5	22.1	16.9	13.6	12.4	14.3	17.3	21.1	25.3	29.2
min	16.1	16.3	13.5	9.1	5.9	3.5	2.5	3.6	5.1	7.8	10.5	13.6
mm	36	26	34	31	42	39	55	57	48	49	40	32
clear	15	14	15	15	9	8	7	8	10	12	12	17

ECHUCA

	Jan	Feb	Mar	Apr	May	Jun	Jul	Aug	Sep	Oct	Nov	Dec
max	30.9	30.6	27.4	22.5	17.5	14.6	13.6	15.6	18.1	22	25.7	28.6
min	14.9	15.1	13	9.5	6.6	4.3	3.4	4.9	6.4	8.7	11.1	13.2
mm	18	14	23	27	36	42	36	40	36	34	27	19
clear	10	11	10	8	5	4	4	4	5	6	6	9

10 GREATER MELBOURNE

MELBOURNE

	Jan	Feb	Mar	Apr	May	Jun	Jul	Aug	Sep	Oct	Nov	Dec
max	25.8	25.6	23.8	20.2	16.5	13.9	13.3	14.8	17.1	19.5	21.8	24.1
min	14	14.3	13	10.6	8.4	6.7	5.7	6.5	7.7	9.3	10.9	12.7
mm	37	32	40	52	56	43	44	49	53	69	52	48
clear	6	6	5	4	3	2	2	2	3	3	3	4

11 GIPPSLAND

YALLOURN

	Jan	Feb	Mar	Apr	May	Jun	Jul	Aug	Sep	Oct	Nov	Dec
max	24.7	25	22.5	18.8	14.9	12.5	11.8	13.1	15	17.8	19.9	22.3
min	12.7	13.2	12.1	9.7	7.4	5.6	4.6	5.4	6.6	8.3	9.8	11.4
mm	46	40	50	62	85	75	84	89	99	79	82	73
clear	5	4	4	3	2	2	2	2	2	3	2	3

12 THE HIGH COUNTRY

CANBERRA

	Jan	Feb	Mar	Apr	May	Jun	Jul	Aug	Sep	Oct	Nov	Dec
max	27.7	26.9	24.5	19.7	15.1	12	11	12.8	15.9	19.2	22.5	26
min	12.9	12.9	10.7	6.5	2.9	0.8	-0.3	0.8	2.9	5.9	8.4	11.1
mm	49	57	35	40	41	29	34	47	51	53	55	36
clear	7	6	7	7	6	6	7	6	8	6	5	7

KIANDRA CHALET

	Jan	Feb	Mar	Apr	May	Jun	Jul	Aug	Sep	Oct	Nov	Dec
max	21.2	21	18.2	13.8	8.5	5.9	4	5.2	8.7	12.8	15.9	18.5
min	6.1	5.8	3.8	0.5	-2	-3.1	-4.5	-3.4	-2	0.7	2.7	4.7
mm	88	68	76	101	129	171	142	160	141	159	114	90
clear	9	9	9	8	5	6	5	5	7	5	7	7

13 SOUTHERN NEW SOUTH WALES COAST

JERVIS BAY

	Jan	Feb	Mar	Apr	May	Jun	Jul	Aug	Sep	Oct	Nov	Dec
max	23.9	24.1	23.2	21	18.3	16.2	15.2	16.1	17.8	19.7	21.4	23
min	17.5	18	17.2	14.9	12.4	10.4	9	9.7	11	13	14.6	16.2
mm	77	66	103	91	90	108	78	57	71	67	69	77
clear	6	5	6	8	8	7	9	10	7	6	5	6

14 WEST OF THE DIVIDE

BROKEN HILL

	Jan	Feb	Mar	Apr	May	Jun	Jul	Aug	Sep	Oct	Nov	Dec
max	32	31.5	28.6	23.8	18.8	15.8	15.1	16.8	20.1	24.2	27.7	30.3
min	18.7	18.5	16	12.3	8.7	6.5	5.6	6.5	8.7	11.9	14.5	16.7
mm	9	10	9	9	13	15	15	17	12	15	10	7
clear	4	3	3	4	5	6	5	5	5	5	4	4

15 BLUE MOUNTAINS

MOUNT VICTORIA

	Jan	Feb	Mar	Apr	May	Jun	Jul	Aug	Sep	Oct	Nov	Dec
max	22.6	22	19.9	16.6	12.5	9.6	8.8	10.4	13.4	16.5	19.2	21.9
min	12.3	12.6	11.1	8.3	5.4	3.2	1.9	2.8	4.5	7.2	9.1	11.1
mm	110	88	83	76	48	64	43	47	50	64	69	68
clear	6	5	5	8	7	7	8	8	8	6	6	8

BATHURST

	Jan	Feb	Mar	Apr	May	Jun	Jul	Aug	Sep	Oct	Nov	Dec
max	27.6	27.1	24.3	20.3	15.5	12.1	11.1	12.8	15.6	19.5	22.7	26
min	13.3	13.3	10.6	6.1	3.2	1.1	-0.3	0.9	2.9	6.1	8.4	10.9
mm	62	43	40	41	36	36	41	47	41	55	45	55
clear	10	8	10	10	8	5	7	8	9	7	8	10

16 GREATER SYDNEY

SYDNEY

	Jan	Feb	Mar	Apr	May	Jun	Jul	Aug	Sep	Oct	Nov	Dec
max	25.7	25.6	24.6	22.2	19.2	16.7	16	17.6	19.7	21.9	23.6	25.1
min	18.5	18.6	17.4	14.6	11.4	9.2	7.9	8.8	10.9	13.4	15.5	17.4
mm	79	89	102	95	90	102	81	55	54	57	65	56
clear	5	3	5	8	8	7	10	10	8	5	5	5

17 HUNTER VALLEY

SCONE

	Jan	Feb	Mar	Apr	May	Jun	Jul	Aug	Sep	Oct	Nov	Dec
max	31.4	30.5	28.4	25.3	20.6	17.1	16.6	18.9	21.8	25.1	28	30.9
min	17.2	16.9	14.9	10.5	6.5	4.8	3.2	4.5	7.1	10.4	13.2	15.8
mm	63	55	44	34	28	37	32	32	37	50	50	59
clear	8	6	8	10	9	7	11	11	10	8	8	9

WILLIAMTOWN

	Jan	Feb	Mar	Apr	May	Jun	Jul	Aug	Sep	Oct	Nov	Dec
max	27.5	27.2	26.3	23.6	20	17.4	16.8	18.3	20.9	23.1	25.4	27.2
min	17.9	18	16.4	13.2	9.7	7.7	6.1	6.8	8.9	12	14.2	16.4
mm	90	91	108	64	85	96	55	65	49	71	67	63
clear	6	4	6	7	7	7	10	10	9	6	5	5

18 GREATER NEW ENGLAND

ARMIDALE

	Jan	Feb	Mar	Apr	May	Jun	Jul	Aug	Sep	Oct	Nov	Dec
max	26.7	26.2	24.3	21	16.6	13.6	12.6	14.3	17.6	20.9	23.8	26.2
min	13.8	13.8	11.7	7.8	4	1.9	0.2	1.4	3.8	7.3	9.9	12.4
mm	90	73	54	40	34	49	44	42	49	62	75	76
clear	11	11	10	8	12	11	9	9	7	9	8	9

19 SOUTHERN QUEENSLAND

BRISBANE

	Jan	Feb	Mar	Apr	May	Jun	Jul	Aug	Sep	Oct	Nov	Dec
max	29.4	29	28	26.1	23.2	20.9	20.4	21.8	24	26.1	27.8	29.1
min	20.7	20.6	19.4	16.6	13.3	10.9	9.5	10.3	12.9	15.8	18.1	19.8
mm	131	116	109	60	51	44	38	29	40	64	84	116
clear	1	1	2	2	3	4	5	5	4	3	2	2

20 CENTRAL QUEENSLAND COAST

CAIRNS

	Jan	Feb	Mar	Apr	May	Jun	Jul	Aug	Sep	Oct	Nov	Dec
max	31.3	31.1	30.4	29.1	27.4	25.7	25.5	26.4	27.8	29.3	30.5	31.3
min	23.5	23.6	22.9	21.5	19.8	17.5	17	17.4	18.6	20.4	22.2	23.2
mm	374	409	396	161	85	34	20	18	19	27	65	102
clear	2	1	2	3	5	7	8	9	8	7	5	3

MACKAY

	Jan	Feb	Mar	Apr	May	Jun	Jul	Aug	Sep	Oct	Nov	Dec
max	29.7	29.3	28.4	26.6	24	21.8	21	22.5	25	27.1	28.9	29.8
min	23.3	23.1	22.1	19.9	16.8	13.4	12.4	13.8	16.3	19.4	21.7	22.8
mm	340	249	221	122	96	36	28	17	12	28	71	133
clear	2	2	4	6	8	12	15	16	12	9	6	5

21 INLAND QUEENSLAND

TAMBO

	Jan	Feb	Mar	Apr	May	Jun	Jul	Aug	Sep	Oct	Nov	Dec
max	34.3	33.9	32.1	29.1	24.4	21.4	20.9	23.2	27	30.7	35.5	34.7
min	20	19.9	17.4	12.9	8	4.5	3.1	5.2	8.6	13.4	16.6	18.9
mm	64	58	42	18	19	22	18	11	9	21	35	50
clear	9	8	10	13	14	16	20	19	19	16	12	11

22 ATHERTON TABLELAND REGION

MAREEBA

	Jan	Feb	Mar	Apr	May	Jun	Jul	Aug	Sep	Oct	Nov	Dec
max	31.1	30.7	29.8	28.4	26.7	25.2	25.1	26.3	28.1	30.4	31.8	32
min	21.1	21.3	20.2	17.7	15.3	12.3	11.1	11.7	13.6	16.1	19	20.2
mm	188	212	156	34	20	9	3	3	1	4	35	94
clear	2	1	3	3	5	8	9	10	10	10	7	4

23 CAPE YORK AND THE GULF PLAINS

COOKTOWN

	Jan	Feb	Mar	Apr	May	Jun	Jul	Aug	Sep	Oct	Nov	Dec
max	31.3	31.1	30.3	28.9	27.3	25.8	25.3	26.2	27.5	29	30.7	31.4
min	24.4	24.2	24.2	23.5	22.1	19.9	19.3	20.1	21.6	22.8	24	24.5
mm	291	334	341	177	60	39	22	20	12	14	34	119
clear	1	0	1	2	3	7	7	7	5	5	3	2

24 GREAT BARRIER REEF

HAYMAN ISLAND

	Jan	Feb	Mar	Apr	May	Jun	Jul	Aug	Sep	Oct	Nov	Dec
max	30.5	30.2	29.6	28.1	26	23.4	23.1	24.3	25.9	27.5	29.6	30.4
min	24.8	24.9	24.1	22.7	20.4	17.1	16.6	17.4	19.2	21.3	23.4	24.5
mm	203	320	271	115	112	51	36	19	9	16	55	54
clear	3	1	3	3	5	9	11	11	9	7	5	3

SPRING THAW Alpine regions are not for skiiers only; spring is a fine time for invigorating bushwalks in the Kosciusko National Park but check with rangers before setting out.

25 ARNHEM LAND

GOVE

	Jan	Feb	Mar	Apr	May	Jun	Jul	Aug	Sep	Oct	Nov	Dec
max	32.2	31.4	31	30.9	29.7	28.1	27.2	28.5	29.9	31.2	33.1	33.3
min	24.4	24.4	23.8	23.1	22.3	21	20	19.2	19.4	20.7	23	24.3
mm	277	267	267	119	55	24	14	3	0	2	1	121
clear	1	0	1	2	2	2	3	6	5	4	3	1

26 DARWIN AND HINTERLAND

DARWIN

	Jan	Feb	Mar	Apr	May	Jun	Jul	Aug	Sep	Oct	Nov	Dec
max	31.7	31.3	31.8	32.6	31.9	30.4	30.3	31.2	32.4	33	33.1	32.6
min	24.7	24.6	24.4	23.9	22	19.9	19.2	20.6	23	24.9	25.2	25.2
mm	404	336	286	75	2	0	0	0	7	55	139	199
clear	0	0	1	4	9	13	15	15	11	6	2	0

27 THE CENTRE
ALICE SPRINGS

	Jan	Feb	Mar	Apr	May	Jun	Jul	Aug	Sep	Oct	Nov	Dec
max	35.9	34.9	32.4	27.9	22.8	19.8	19.4	22.4	26.5	30.5	33.4	35.3
min	21	20.6	17.4	12.5	8.2	5	4	6.1	9.8	14.6	17.7	20.1
mm	17	17	12	2	8	4	3	2	1	20	19	21
clear	12	12	15	16	15	16	20	22	21	17	13	13

28 THE KIMBERLEY
HALLS CREEK

	Jan	Feb	Mar	Apr	May	Jun	Jul	Aug	Sep	Oct	Nov	Dec
max	36.7	35.9	35.6	33.8	29.8	27.2	26.9	29.9	33.7	37	38.3	38.2
min	24.1	23.6	22.7	20.4	16.7	13.5	12.3	14.7	18.5	22.5	24.2	24.6
mm	131	87	47	5	1	0	0	0	0	5	24	60
clear	2	3	6	11	14	17	19	19	17	13	7	3

WYNDHAM

	Jan	Feb	Mar	Apr	May	Jun	Jul	Aug	Sep	Oct	Nov	Dec
max	36.4	36.8	37	36.8	33.7	31.6	31.4	33.2	36.2	38.1	39.3	38.7
min	26.2	26.1	26.4	25.7	22.2	19.9	18.9	20.2	23.6	26.4	27.3	27.4
mm	146	155	102	10	0	0	0	0	0	4	40	109
clear	5	5	6	13	21	23	26	27	23	17	11	6

29 NORTH-WEST SHOULDER AND HINTERLAND
KALGOORLIE

	Jan	Feb	Mar	Apr	May	Jun	Jul	Aug	Sep	Oct	Nov	Dec
max	33.6	32	29.6	25	20.4	17.5	16.5	18.4	22	25.5	28.9	32.1
min	18.2	17.7	15.9	12.3	8.3	6.1	4.8	5.5	7.8	10.8	13.9	16.6
mm	6	12	9	11	22	22	21	15	11	9	11	7
clear	15	13	12	9	10	7	9	11	14	13	12	14

PORT HEDLAND

	Jan	Feb	Mar	Apr	May	Jun	Jul	Aug	Sep	Oct	Nov	Dec
max	36.3	36.1	36.7	35	30.3	27.4	26.8	28.9	32.2	34.5	36.2	36.6
min	25.4	25.3	24.3	21	17	13.7	11.9	13	15.2	17.9	21.1	23.8
mm	26	78	16	3	8	5	2	1	1	0	0	0
clear	7	6	11	13	15	17	20	23	23	24	20	15

30 THE WHEAT BELT
GERALDTON

	Jan	Feb	Mar	Apr	May	Jun	Jul	Aug	Sep	Oct	Nov	Dec
max	31.8	32.4	30.8	27.3	23.8	20.7	19.5	20	22	24.4	26.9	29.4
min	18.4	19.1	17.8	15.2	12.7	10.9	9.3	8.9	9.2	10.9	13.8	16.2
mm	1	3	5	15	62	93	93	62	29	15	5	2
clear	14	17	22	10	0	2	12	16	12	15	6	14

CHANGE EXPECTED Radio weather forecasts keep motorists aware of possible sudden changes in the weather; these thunderclouds have quickly banished the blue skies south of Alice Springs.

DALWALLINU

	Jan	Feb	Mar	Apr	May	Jun	Jul	Aug	Sep	Oct	Nov	Dec
max	35.2	34.5	31.5	26.3	21.5	18	16.9	18	21	25.2	29.1	32.9
min	18.4	18.5	16.6	13.2	10	8.1	6.6	6.7	7.8	10.2	13.2	16.1
mm	5	6	9	14	41	63	55	41	23	15	6	4
clear	16	13	14	10	10	7	8	10	12	12	13	15

31 FRINGE OF THE PLATEAU
NORTHAM

	Jan	Feb	Mar	Apr	May	Jun	Jul	Aug	Sep	Oct	Nov	Dec
max	34	33.6	30.6	25.9	20.8	17.7	16.7	17.8	20.4	23.7	28.3	32.1
min	17.1	17.1	15.4	12	8.5	6.4	5.4	5.7	7	9	12.5	15.4
mm	9	18	22	27	52	83	76	55	40	27	15	8
clear	13	11	12	7	6	4	4	5	6	7	8	14

32 THE PERTH COAST
PERTH

	Jan	Feb	Mar	Apr	May	Jun	Jul	Aug	Sep	Oct	Nov	Dec
max	30.1	30.4	28.4	24.5	21.1	18.7	17.7	18.2	19.7	21.9	24.7	27.4
min	18.3	18.6	17.2	14.4	11.8	10.3	9.2	9.3	10.2	11.8	14.1	16.4
mm	4	5	12	39	123	174	167	140	71	50	17	10
clear	10	12	12	9	8	5	5	7	9	10	11	11

33 SOUTH-WEST CORNER
ALBANY

	Jan	Feb	Mar	Apr	May	Jun	Jul	Aug	Sep	Oct	Nov	Dec
max	23.2	23.5	23	20.4	18.9	17	15.4	16.2	17.4	18.9	20.7	21.9
min	16.1	16.3	15.4	13.1	11.5	9.8	8.5	8.7	9.8	10.5	12.7	15
mm	16	14	30	65	116	125	149	117	93	72	40	25
clear	6	6	6	6	5	5	5	5	5	5	5	5

34 NULLARBOR PLAIN

RAWLINNA

	Jan	Feb	Mar	Apr	May	Jun	Jul	Aug	Sep	Oct	Nov	Dec
max	33.7	31.9	29.9	26.2	21.8	18.7	18.1	19.9	23.3	27	30	32.3
min	16.3	16.1	14.6	12	8.5	6.3	5	5.7	7.7	10.3	12.9	14.8
mm	6	5	12	8	14	13	10	10	7	11	9	9
clear	14	10	12	9	10	9	11	12	12	12	11	13

CEDUNA

	Jan	Feb	Mar	Apr	May	Jun	Jul	Aug	Sep	Oct	Nov	Dec
max	28.6	28.1	26.5	24	20.7	18.1	17.2	18.5	21.1	23.6	25.9	27.2
min	14.9	14.9	13.2	10.7	8.4	6.4	5.6	6.1	7.7	9.7	12.1	13.8
mm	6	7	4	14	29	30	38	35	20	19	20	9
clear	11	10	11	8	6	6	6	7	8	8	6	8

35 SALT LAKES AND CHANNEL COUNTRY

COOBER PEDY

	Jan	Feb	Mar	Apr	May	Jun	Jul	Aug	Sep	Oct	Nov	Dec
max	36.3	35.6	32.9	27.5	22.1	18.7	18.5	20.8	24.2	28.8	32	34.7
min	20.4	20.8	18.2	14	9.9	7	6.2	7.5	9.8	13.4	16.4	18.9
mm	5	9	3	1	6	6	3	4	3	7	5	5
clear	15	13	16	13	13	12	14	15	15	14	13	13

TIBOOBURRA

	Jan	Feb	Mar	Apr	May	Jun	Jul	Aug	Sep	Oct	Nov	Dec
max	35.7	35.3	32.3	27.1	21.8	18.4	17.7	20	23.9	28.3	32	34.7
min	22.1	21.8	18.7	14	9.3	6.2	5.2	6.8	9.9	14.1	17.5	20.3
mm	9	10	6	5	7	7	7	7	6	9	7	11
clear	18	16	18	20	18	18	19	21	21	19	18	19

36 THE DESERTS

BARROW CREEK

	Jan	Feb	Mar	Apr	May	Jun	Jul	Aug	Sep	Oct	Nov	Dec
max	36.9	35.3	33.2	30.1	25.5	22.6	22.3	25.6	29.3	32.8	35.4	37
min	23.8	23.2	21	17.1	12.7	9.2	7.9	10.6	14.2	18.2	21.5	23.2
mm	59	62	42	15	15	12	8	6	8	18	28	39
clear					not available							

37 FLINDERS RANGES

WILPENA CHALET

	Jan	Feb	Mar	Apr	May	Jun	Jul	Aug	Sep	Oct	Nov	Dec
max	31.1	31.1	27.3	23.7	16.9	13.9	12.8	15	19.5	23.7	26.6	28.9
min	15.8	16	12.7	9.1	5.5	3.7	2.9	2.9	5.3	8.6	11.4	13.5
mm	18	19	8	2	53	51	66	45	17	21	11	17
clear	18	16	17	15	9	7	9	12	17	15	14	17

PORT PIRIE

	Jan	Feb	Mar	Apr	May	Jun	Jul	Aug	Sep	Oct	Nov	Dec
max	31.6	31.6	28.9	24.6	19.9	17.1	16.2	17.7	20.4	24.1	27.2	29.4
min	17.7	18	16.1	13.4	10.7	8.4	7.7	8.3	9.6	11.9	14.4	16.2
mm	9	8	10	24	31	33	30	34	30	26	18	16
clear	13	12	13	9	6	6	5	6	7	7	8	11

38 ADELAIDE AND THE GULF COUNTRY

ADELAIDE

	Jan	Feb	Mar	Apr	May	Jun	Jul	Aug	Sep	Oct	Nov	Dec
max	28.9	29.3	26.1	22.1	18.7	15.8	14.9	16.8	18.2	21.8	24.8	27.2
min	16.8	16.9	15.1	12.1	10.1	7.6	7.2	8.3	9.3	11.3	14	15.5
mm	13	4	32	55	52	57	81	85	66	37	35	20
clear	9	9	9	6	3	2	3	3	3	6	5	7

39 THE ISLANDS

LORD HOWE ISLAND

	Jan	Feb	Mar	Apr	May	Jun	Jul	Aug	Sep	Oct	Nov	Dec
max	25.1	25.4	24.8	23.1	21	19.3	18.4	18.5	19.3	20.5	22.1	23.9
min	20.1	20.5	19.8	18.1	16.2	14.6	13.6	13.4	14.1	15.5	17	18.7
mm	93	89	109	130	143	181	174	132	119	119	101	100
clear	1	1	1	2	1	1	1	1	2	2	2	2

CHRISTMAS ISLAND

	Jan	Feb	Mar	Apr	May	Jun	Jul	Aug	Sep	Oct	Nov	Dec
max	27.8	27.9	28.2	28.3	27.7	26.8	26.2	26	26.1	26.8	27.2	27.8
min	22.4	22.3	22.7	23.3	23.4	23	22.4	22.1	22.1	22.5	22.8	22.5
mm	342	297	306	239	251	105	51	45	42	40	200	265
clear					none							

MACQUARIE ISLAND

	Jan	Feb	Mar	Apr	May	Jun	Jul	Aug	Sep	Oct	Nov	Dec
max	8.6	8.5	7.9	6.9	5.8	5	4.9	5	5.3	5.6	6.4	7.8
min	5.2	5.2	4.6	3.5	2.5	1.5	1.6	1.5	1.4	1.8	2.6	4.2
mm	84	78	88	87	78	69	63	58	73	70	65	74
clear					none							

40 ANTARCTICA

MAWSON

	Jan	Feb	Mar	Apr	May	Jun	Jul	Aug	Sep	Oct	Nov	Dec
max	2.8	-1.3	-7.3	-11.7	-13.2	-14	-15.1	-15.7	-14.4	-9.9	-2.3	2.4
min	-2.3	-7.3	-13.2	-17	-18.6	-19.7	-20.7	-21.4	-20.5	-16.4	-8.5	-2.9
mm					none							
clear	4	5	6	7	9	8	7	7	6	6	5	4

What does it mean?

Brief explanations of some common words and phrases used in this book

DIEBACK Dieback refers to a phenomenon which is responsible for the death of vast numbers of native trees across Australia. The causes are many and vary from region to region but the one common factor in tree decline appears to be the large-scale upset of natural ecosystems. In some places, the replacement of trees with crops results in increased insect populations with fewer birds to control them. Trees left in and around the farmland are soon stripped of their leaves by the insects and eventually die.

EROSION Erosion is a constant process which began the moment the earth's crust hardened. Water, wind and ice — sometimes all at once — are constantly wearing away and shifting the rock and soil of our landscapes. This 'natural' erosion often accelerates when inappropriate agricultural or grazing practices are adopted.

In Australia, inundation by the sea or major earth movements which cause the landscape to 'grow' by providing it with relief such as hills, valleys and mountains, ceased long before they did in many other parts of the world — this is why Australia is often referred to as an 'ancient' or 'old' continent. As a result, the forces of erosion have worn down much of Australia to the extent that most of the continent is flat and arid or semi-arid, with barely ten per cent being suitable for modern agriculture.

In the last 200 years, overclearing of soil-binding plants, overgrazing by hard-hooved animals and careless mining operations have resulted in so much topsoil being washed into rivers and streams, and eventually into the sea, that erosion has become the major problem facing rural Australia. Scientists have estimated that at least 50 per cent of Australia's grazing and agricultural land needs to be treated for erosion.

EXOTIC Exotics are plants or animals — but usually plants — introduced into a foreign environment from another country. Large numbers of exotic plants have been introduced into Australia in the last 200 years, often to the great detriment of the native species (see chapter two, *The human element: a disciplined landscape)*. Without the biological controls — such as insects — or the climatic restrictions — such as winter snow or frost — of their countries of origin, plants such as blackberry and lantana have colonised large areas of bush and farmland.

FERAL Feral animals are domesticated creatures which have been allowed to return to a wild state. The Australian countryside is overrun by a wide variety of feral creatures (see chapter two, *The human element: a disciplined landscape)*, the most destructive and well known being animals such as rabbits, cats, pigs and goats which either kill native wildlife or destroy its habitats and encourage erosion by their eating, foraging and burrowing habits. Other exotic but non-domesticated introductions, such as foxes, cane toads and various European freshwater fish, cause similar environmental havoc.

ICE AGE An ice age is a period of the earth's history when the polar ice sheets expand to cover large areas of land in the world's temperate zones. Ice ages are believed to be cyclical, with the present state of the world a mere pause in an ice age which could reassert itself in 30–40 000 years. The last ice age began about 15 000 years ago and ended approximately 7000 years ago, when the last glacier on the Australian mainland melted and the seas rose to isolate New Guinea and Tasmania once again.

ROCK — IGNEOUS, SEDIMENTARY AND METAMORPHIC Rocks of many varieties make up the land area of Australia but all of them belong to three basic types, igneous, sedimentary or metamorphic. Igneous rock is rock of molten origin, so in effect, it is the earth's basic building material, having formed the original surface crust when the molten lava of geological prehistory solidified.

Igneous rock forms when the molten magma — liquified rock from 15 kilometres and more below the surface — is forced up to the surface where it crystallises and solidifies. When the magma reaches the surface, usually in the form of lava spewed up in volcanic eruptions, it forms into fine-grained rock, the most common example being basalt.

When the magma does not reach the surface but cools slowly underground it forms granite. This is often later exposed by erosion. Broadly speaking, Australia's igneous rock outcrops occur in the east and the south-east along the line of the Great Dividing Range, and in isolated pockets in the central and north-western parts of the continent.

Sedimentary rock, which makes up the bulk of the exposed soil and rock surfaces of the earth, is formed when weathered and broken down particles of other rocks, together with dead organic matter — such as the sediment which accumulates on the bottom of the sea — is compressed and cemented together. Sandstone, limestone and shale are three common sedimentary rocks.

Metamorphic rock is existing rock — sedimentary or igneous — which, as the name suggests, has undergone a metamorphosis. The appearance and sometimes the chemical composition of the original rock is changed due to the action of heat and immense pressures caused by earth movements deep below the surface. Common metamorphic rocks are quartzite, marble and slate, respectively sandstone, limestone and shale before their dramatic transformation.

WORLD HERITAGE AREAS These are natural regions or cultural sites recognised by UNESCO (United Nations Educational, Scientific and Cultural Organisation) as being worthy of conservation for the world's future generations. Eight natural sites in Australia have so far been included on the World Heritage list — more than any other country except the United States which has nine.

Australia's sites are Kakadu National Park, the Great Barrier Reef, the Willandra Lakes region in New South Wales, Lord Howe Island, the Tasmanian wilderness parks, the chain of New South Wales rainforests, Uluru (Ayers Rock) and the 'wet tropics' coastal zone of northern Queensland.

About one-quarter of the places on the World Heritage list are natural 'properties', the other three-quarters being cathedrals, palaces and monuments such as the Pyramids or the Taj Mahal. According to the UNESCO convention which governs the selection of heritage sites — and which has been ratified by most members of the world body — a natural site should:
• represent a major stage of evolution (such as an ice age)
• contain habitats of threatened animals and plants
• include scenery of exceptional beauty or natural features which are found nowhere else
• represent the continuing biological and geological processes which evolve in such places as rainforests.

The Australian Heritage Commission — composed of a chairman and six members appointed by the federal Minister for the Environment — selects and proposes Australia's submissions to UNESCO in Paris. The commission also presides over the register of Australia's National Estate. The National Estate is a list of what has been called the 'places we should keep', whether natural or man made — in effect, a national heritage list. As a federal body, the commission's listings impose legal restrictions on the commonwealth government only, but its opinion is generally respected by state authorities.

Index

Bold page numbers indicate an illustration.

A

ABC Ranges 346
Aboriginal
  art 158, 167, 175, 218–19, 318, 347
  burning practices 221, 310–11
  diet 36, 83, 118, 195, **327**
  Dreamtime 239, 252
  encampments 132, 174
  middens 103, 132, 167
  migratory routes 173–4
Aborigines 36–7, 56, 98, 132, 142, 186, 190, 233, 268, 270, 272, 310, 318, 325, 342
Acacia 292, 342, 348
Acacia 206
  acuminata 286, 294
  aneura 137, 208, 262, 282, 334
  binervia 125
  boormanii 112
  brachybotrya 85
  brachystachya 208
  calamifolia 354
  cambagei 209, 326
  cana 209
  catenulata 209
  citrinoviridis 278
  clivicola 142
  cyperophylla 329
  dealbata 32, 124
  estrophiolata 262
  excelsa 137
  harpophylla 137, 195, 198, 208
  kempeana 256
  ligulata 260
  melanoxylon 29, 48, 101
  neriifolia **138**
  pendula 321
  pycnantha 354
  rivalis 348
  saligna 300
  sophorae 161
  stowardii 208
  tetragonophylla 141, 321
Acanthiza 89
  chrysorrhoa 165
  lineata 314
  pusilla 313
  uropygialis 315
Acanthophis antarcticus 165, 347
  pyrrhus 337
Acanthorhynchus superciliosus 294, 314
  tenuirostris 46, 61
Accipiter fasciatus 303
  novaehollandiae 67
Achoerodus viridis 128
Aciphylla glacialis 117
Acmena resa 201
  smithii 109, 162, 167, 178
Acradenia franklinae 49
Acrobates pygmaeus 124, 164
Acrocephalus stentoreus 303
Actinotus helianthus 167
Adansonia gregorii 272
Adelaide 94, 322, 350–9, **351**
Adelaide River 246, 249, 250
Admiral's Arch 359
Admiration Point 129, 132
Agapetes meiniana 212
Agonis flexuosa 300
Agrotis infusa 118
Ailuroedus crassirostris 184, 192
  dentirostris 213
Airlie Beach 200
Ajuga australis 88
Albany 290, 306, 312, 313
albatross 71, 367
  black-browed **368**
  shy **58**, 60
  wandering 165, 367
Albatross Island 58, 60
Albert River 194, **223**
Albizia toona 200
Albury 88, 93
Alcedo azurea 48, 193, 273
Aldinga Scrub 352
Alectura lathami 141, 208, 359
Alice Springs 255, 256, 259, 260, 261, 262, **388**
Alisterus scapularis 153
Alligator Creek **199**, 344
Alligator Gorge 344
Allocasuarina 85
  decaisneana 262, 334
  littoralis 33
  luehmannii 84
  pusilla 85

almond, wild 273
Alpine National park 120
Alyogyne huegelii 345
Amphibolurus maculosus 326
  muricatus 99
Amytornis housei 273
Anas castanea 71
  gibberifrons 71
  superciliosa 165, 303
Anaspides tasmaniae 56
Anbangbang Lagoon **237**
anemones 128, 230
Angahook-Lorne State Park 64
Anglesea 64
angophora 172
Angophora bakeri 174
  costata 161, 167
  floribunda 179
  hispida 161
  melanoxylon 209
Anguilla australis 98, 161
  reinhardtii 161
Anigozanthos 294
Anne-a-Kananda Cave 39
Anodopetalum biglandulosum 37, 48
Anopterus glandulosus 48
Anous minutus 363
Anseranas semipalmata 199, 222, 248, 254, 273
Anson Bay **363**
ant
  black 336
  honeypot 339
  stink 32
ant plant 220, **221**
Antarctica 308, 366, 368, 370– 77
antechinus 78, 103, 294
  cinnamon 218
  fat-tailed 335
  swamp 108
  yellow-footed 304
Antechinus flavipes 304
  leo 218
  minimus 108
Anthochaera carunculata 165, 314, 355
  chrysoptera 185, 203
  lunulata 46
apple 90
  Baker's 174
  dwarf 161
  native 209
  rough-barked 179
  smooth-barked 161, **163**, 167
apricot, native 348
Aprosmictus erythropterus 273
Apsley River 30, **30**
Aptenodytes forsteri 375
  patagonicus 367
Aquila audax 102, 132, 140, 259, 320, 338, 345
Arafura Sea 218
Aramac Range 209
Araucaria bidwillii 190
  cunninghamii 179, 191, 200, 218
  heterophylla 162, 363
Arawak Lake 91
Arcadia Valley 206
Arcadia wetlands 206
Archer Bend National Park 221–2
Archer River 222
Archontophoenix alexandrae 203
Arctocephalus forsteri 357, 368
  gazella 369
  pusillus 32, 61, 99, 165
Ardea striata 165
Ardeotis kori 139, 208, 261, 273, 320
Arenaria interpres 164, 171
Argyrodendron actinophyllum diversifolium 201
Argyrosomus hololepidotus 166
Arkaroola-Mount Painter Sanctuary 348, 349
Arkaroo Rock 347
Armidale 178, 181
Arnhem Land 234–46, 249
Arnhem Land Plateau 12, **235**, 250, 251
Aroona Valley 346
Arripis trutta 99
Artemia salina 326
Arthrocnemum 282
  halocnemoides 325–6
Arthur Range 39, **378–9**
Arthur River 44, 45, 49
Arthurs Lake 53
Arthurs Seat 103
Asbestos Range National Park 27, 28
ash
  alpine 64, 81, 122, 123
  Eungella satin 201
  mountain 41, 64, 81, **102**, 103, 109, 110, **110**, 122–3
  silky 152
  silvertop 111
Ashbyia lovensis 337
Astelia alpina 33
Astrebla 209, 261
Astrotricha hamptonii 278
Astroloma conostephioides 84
Atherosperma moschatum 29, 48, 106
Atherton Tableland 15, 210–15, **213**
Athrotaxis cupressoides 41
  selaginoides 41, **41**, 48, 55
Atrax robustus 166

Atrichornis clamosus 313
  rufescens 192
Atriplex 282
  vesicaria 137, 315
Aulopus purpurissatus 128
aurora australis 24, **371**
Australian Alps 152
Australian Capital Territory 117, 125
Austrelaps superbus 47, 99
Avicennia marina 107
avocets 302
Avon River 105, 286
Ayers Rock 12, 14, 252, 257, 258, **258,** 259
Aythya australis 289
Azorella selago 367

B

babbler 78
Babinda 212
Backstairs Passage 358
Badgers Beach 28
Bairnsdale 106, 111, 132
Bakers Creek Falls 181
Balaenoptera musculus 375
Bald Rock **181**, 194
Balfour Track State Reserve 49
Balls Pyramid 15, 361, 362, **362**
Balonne River 194
bandicoot 32, 103, 185, 335
  eastern barred 68–9
  long-nosed 130, 164
  rufous spiny 218
  short-nosed 295
  southern brown 47, 71, 295, 305, 353
  western barred 281
Bangalley Head **154**
banksia 31, 69, 131, 165, 167, 188, 298, 300, 303, 304, 312, 313, **313**, 314, 315
  bull 292, 294, 300
  coast 185
  creeping **313**
  desert 84, 85, **85**
  heath 161, **161**
  holly-leaved 301
  Menzies 301
  narrow-leaved 301
  old man 161
  rose-fruited 301
  saw 47
  scarlet **313**
  silver 46
  swamp 301
  teasel **315**
  wallum 203
Banksia aemula 203
  asplenifolia 161
  attenuata 301
  ericifolia 161
  grandis 292, 300
  ilicifolia 301
  integrifolia 185
  laricina 301
  littoralis 301
  marginata 46
  menziesii 301
  ornata 84, 85
  serrata 47, 161
banyan **242, 362**
baobab **272**
Barcoo River 205, 209, 322, 327
Barkly Tableland 222, 261
Barmah State Forest **89**, 93
Barnardius zonarius 348, 357
Barossa Valley 350, 353
barramundi 251
  sea-going 196
  spotted 196
Barraranna Gorge 348
barrel, brown 122, 151, 172
Barren Ranges 310, 314
Barrenjoey Head **154**
Barrier Range 136, 141
Barrington Tops 170, 171, 172, 181, 182
Barrington Tops National Park 172, 192
Barrow Island 279, **279**
Basalt Temple 119
bass, Australian 161
Bass Strait 44, 46, 58–9, 64, 105, 106, 108
  Islands 58–61
bastard mahogany 161
bat 99, 102, 124, 303–4, 365
  bent-wing 99
  fruit 164, 185
  ghost 250, 251
  Gould's long-eared 295
  Gould's wattled 295, 358
  greater long-eared 141
  King River eptesicus 295, 304
  lesser long-eared 295
  little pied 141
  long-eared 304
  mastiff 84
  orange horseshoe 250, 251
  wattled bat 304
Bat Cave 69
Batemans Bay 126, 130, 132
Bathurst 151

bauera 37
Bauera rubioides 37
Baumea articulata 301
Baw Baw National Park 120
Baw Baw Plateau 119
beaded glasswort 67
beech 191
  Antarctic 55, 178
  myrtle 29, 110, 122
  negrohead 171, 172, 191
  tanglefoot 30, 55, **55**
beech oranges 48
Beecroft Peninsula **129**
Beedalup National Park 312
Beerwah National Park 190
beetle
  Christmas 180
  pie dish 263, **263**
belah 137, 138, 141, 195
bellbird 103
Bellendena montana 30
Bellenden Ker National Park 215
Bellenden Ker Range 211, 212, **213**
Bellinger Valley 178
Belougery Spire 140
Belyando River 206
Ben Boyd National Park 131
Ben Lomond 25, 52–3, 181
Ben Lomond plateau 30, **30**
bettong 32, 180
  brush-tailed 85, 203, 294, 357
  Tasmanian 28
Bettongia gaimardi 28
  penicillata 85, 203, 294, 357
Bicheno 30, 31, 36
Bidyanus bidyanus 95
Big Ben 369, **369**
Big Desert Wilderness **83**, 84, 85
Big Moro Gorge 348
Big Scrub Flora Reserve 183
Big Scrub, the 179, 180, 183–4
bilby 335
Billiatt Conservation Park 72, 82, 85
billy buttons 117
birch 103
bird of paradise 218
Birdsville 327, 329, **329**
Birdsville Track 329
Bittangabee Bay 131
Biziura lobata 289, 303
black bean 184
blackbird 21
Black Bluff 44, **52**
blackbutt 162, 170, 172, 178, 312
  New England 201
Blackdown Tableland 206
Blackdown Tableland National Park 206
black-eyed Susan **152**
blackfish, river 98
Blackheath 146, 147
Black Hill Conservation Park 354
Blackjack Mountain 124
Black Mountain 12, 125
Black Point Lagoon **234**
Black Pyramid Island 60, 60–1
black swan 71, 131, 142, 165, 172, 195, 303, 325
blackthorn **99**, 179
blackwood 29, 48, 101
Blackwood River 290
Bladensburg National Park 209
Blandfordia grandiflora 179, 188
bloodwood 161, 209, 334
  red 113, 170, 174
  yellow 174
Bloomfield 214
Blowhole 32
blue angel **225**
bluebell 88
blue bonnet 72, 320
bluebush 137, 143, 282, 288, 320, 321
blue grass 195
Blue Gum Flat 344
Blue Gum Forest 146
Blue Lake 68, 117
Blue Mountains 14, 134, 144–53, 154, 157, 158, 159–60, **159**, 174
Blue Mountains National Park 153, 158
Bluff Knoll 309
Bogey Hole 175
Bogong High Plains 118, 119
bolster plants 55
Bombax ceiba 218
boneseed, South African 101
bonewood 208
Bong Bong Mountain 127
booby, Abbotts 364–5
Boolambayte Lake 171
Bool Lagoon 72
Boonoo Boonoo National Park 182
Border Island **232**
Border Ranges 201
boree 209
Boroka Lookout **80**
boronia 152
  pink **76**
Borya 288
Boston Bay 357
Botany Bay 158, 164
Botany Bay National Park 162

Bothwell 25
bottlebrush 98, 163, 207, 288, 294, 300
  crimson 345
  Western Australian one-sided 300
bottle tree 198, **208**, 272
Bouddi National Park 158
Bourke 134, 141
Bowen 199, 200, **200**
bowerbird 213, **273**
  golden 213
  great 251, 273
  regent 184, **184**, 201
Bowling Green Bay National Park 199, **199**
box 136
  bimble 137
  black 83, 84, 137, 138, 139, 143
  blue 77
  brush 162, 183, 191
  fuzzy 137
  grey 89, 93, 137, 170, 195
  long-leaved 101
  pilliga grey 138
  poplar 137
  red 98, 111
  white 89, 124, 140, 170, 172, 179
  yellow 93, 98, 111, 124, 137, 173, 179
box jellyfish 383
boxthorn 60, 101
Boyd Plateau 150, 152
Boyd River 151, **151**
Brachina Gorge 346
Brachychiton acerifolius 192
  australis 208
  populneus 111, 179, 209
  rupestris 198, 208
brake, Chinese 112
Breadknife 140, **140**
Bremer Bay 306, 310
bridal tree 272, **272**
Bridal Veil Falls **145, 148**
brigalow 137, 195, 198, 206–8
Brisbane 191, 193
Brisbane Ranges 76
Brisbane Ranges National Park 76
Brisbane Water National Park 158, **160**
bristlebird
  eastern 113
  rufous 64–6
  western 313
bristle-fern, jungle 110
Broad Sound 200–1
Broadwater Lake 171
Brockman National Park 312
Brodribb River 113
Broken Bay 157, **157, 158**, 159, **160**
Broken Head 67
Broken Hill 136, 141, 142
brolga 72, 139, 199, **199**, 209, 222, 273
Bronte Lagoon **56**
Broome 20, 264, 268
broom, English 173
broombush 83, 85
Brumlow Tops 172
Brunswick Bay **267**
Brunswick Heads 184
Bruny Island 14, 33, **33**
Bruny Island Neck Game Reserve 33
brush-turkey 141, 208, 359
Bubalus bubalis 248
Buccaneer Archipelago **267**
Budawang National Park 129, 131
Budawang Range **128**
budgerigar 195, 256, 338
buffel grass 208
bugle, Australian 88
Bulga Plateau 110, 181
bullock bush 342
Bulloo River 329
Bullsbrook 295
buloke 84
bulrush 301
Bungle Bungle Ranges 12, 271, **271**
Bunker Hills 346–7
Bunya Mountains 190
Bunya Mountains National Park 190
Bunyeroo Gorge 346
Bunyip Chasm 348
Bunyip Creek 107
Bunyip River 106, 107, 107
Buramoko Head 147
Burdekin Falls 198
Burdekin River 196, **197**, 198, **198**, 199, 201
Burhinus grallarius 359
Burnett River 194
Burnettia cuneata 66
Burning Mountain 173, **173**
Burning Mountain Nature Reserve 173
Burragorang Valley 147
Burramys parvus 118
bursaria, sweet 98, **99**
Bursaria spinosa 98, 179
Byron Bay 184
Busselton 301, 311
bustard, kori 139, 208, 261, **262**, 273, 320
butcherbird
  grey 31
  pied 256
buttercup, anemone 117
butterfly
  Altona skipper 101
  black-and-white 250, 251
  canopus **249**
  Eltham copper 98
  hairstreak 32
Butterfly Gorge Nature Park 250
button-grass 29, **39**, 42
button-quail 320, **320**
Bynoe River **217**
Byron Bay **177**, 185

C

cabbage
  Kerguelen 369
  Macquarie Island 367, **366, 368**
Cabbage Tree Creek 113
Cacatua galerita 102, 195, 251, 273, 348
  latirostris 287
  leadbeateri 84, 287
  pastinator 273, 287, 348
  roseicapilla 102, 295
  tenuirostris 287
Cadellia pentastylis 208
Caesioperca lepidoptera 128
Caiman Creek **240**
Cairns 211, 212, 222, 226, 233
cajeput 272, 276
Caladenia 85
  echidnachila 47
calamanthus, rufous 84
Calamanthus campestris 84
Calandrinia balonensis 262, 329
Calectasia cyanea 84
Caleys Creek 113
Calidris 107
  acuminata 101
  canutus 31
  ruficollis 31, 101, 164
callicoma 152
Callicoma serratifolia 152
Callistemon 98, 300
callistemon 188, 304
Callistemon teretifolius 345
  viminalis 207
Callitris 179, 209
  collumellaris 124, 137, 261, 334, 344, 347
  endlicheri 174, 195
  glauca 174
  oblonga 29
  preissii 84, 85, 302
  preissii verrucosa 85
  rhomboidea 31
Callocephalon fimbriatum 61, 69
  funereus 153
Calostemma purpureum 88
Calothamnus 294, 300
Calotis scapigera 142
Caltha introloba 117
Calyptorhynchus banksii 247, 295
  funereus 31, 47, 130, 352
  lathami 113, 153, 359
  latirostris 295, 303
Calytrix 84
Cambridge Gulf **265**
Campbelltown 162
Campbell Town 24
Canberra 116, 124, 125, 127
cane grass 334
  sandhill 142–3
Cape Arid 301, **308**
Cape Barren Island 60
Cape Bedford 219
Cape Borda 346, 353
Cape Bowling Green 199
Cape Bridgewater 64, 72
Cape du Couedic 359
Cape Farquhar 280
Cape Flattery 216, 219
Cape Grenville 219, 220
Cape Grim 45
Cape Hauy 27, **32**
Cape Hillsborough **197**
Cape Howe 127, 130
Cape Inscription 280
Cape Jervis 350, 353
Cape Le Grand 308
Cape Leeuwin 310, 311, 312
Cape Melville 216, 220
Cape Melville National Park 220
Cape Naturaliste 306, 310, 311, 312
Cape Otway 64, **64**
Cape Pillar **27**
Cape Range 278, 279
Cape Range National Park 279
Cape Raoul 14, 27
Cape Riche 308
Cape St George 128
Cape Schanck 103, **103**
Cape Tribulation **22–3**, **211**, 214
Cape Upstart 199
Cape York 213, 214, 215, 220
Cape York Peninsula 216–23, 221
Capparis mitchellii 348
Caprimulgus argus 84
Carappee Hill 358
Carcharhinus leucas 222
Caretta caretta 165, 202, 232
Careys Peak 171, 172, 173
Carlisle State Park 66
Carlotta Arch 151
Carnac Island 299
Carnarvon 274, 279, 281
Carnarvon National Park 206
Carnarvon Range 206
carp 95
  European 98
Carpentaria acuminata 248
Carpobrotus rossii 67
Carr Boyd Ranges 270
Carrington Channel **223**
Casey Station 372
Cassia 206
cassowary 215
Castanospermum australe 184
Castle, The 129, 132
casuarina 69, 129, 152
Casuarina 130, 179
  cristata 137, 141, 195
  cunninghamiana 173
  fraserana 292, 300
  huegeliana 287
  littoralis 162
  luehmannii 195
  obesa 301
Casuarina Coastal Reserve 247
Casuarius casuarius 215
Cataract Gorge **28**, 29
catbird
  green 184, **184**, 192–3
  tooth-billed 213
catfish 95
  freshwater 91
Catharacta maccormicki 375
Cathedral Range **75**, 81
Cathedral Range State Park 79
Cathedral Rock 179
Cathedral Rock National Park 179
Cathedrals, The **188**
Cat Island 61
cats, native 56, 64
cedar
  Mackay 200
  red 129, 152, 171, 184, 191, 202
Ceduna 320
celery, mountain 117
Celmisia longifolia 117, 152
Cenchrus ciliaris 208
Central Mount Stuart 255
Central Plateau (Tas.) 44, 45, 50–7, **52**
Central Plateau Conservation Area 57
Central Plateau Protected Area 57
Ceratopetalum apetalum 152, 162, 178
  gummiferum 162
Cercartetus concinnus 84, 288, 294, 304, 353
  nanus 72, 163
Cereopsis novaehollandiae 29, 60
Certhionyx niger 337
Chaenichthyidae 376
Chaenicthys rhinoceratus 376
Chalinolobus gouldii 295, 358
  picatus 141
Chambers Gorge 347
Chamelaucium uncinatum 289
Chandlers Peak 181
Channel Country 204, 206, 209, 322–29, **322**
Charadrius rubricollis 29, 353
Charcoal Range 124
Charleston Conservation Park 352
Charlotte Pass 117
chat, yellow 262
Charnley River 267
Cheilanthes lasiophylla 262
Chelodina expansa 95
  longicollis 95, 98, 165
  oblonga 295, 305
Chelonia depressa 202, 232
  mydas 165, 202, 232
Chenonetta jubata 354
cherry, native 33, 342
Cherry Lake 101
Cherry Tree North State Forest 179
Chichester Range **278**, 279
Chillagoe 13, 215, **215**
Chionis minor nasicornis 369
Chlamydera nuchalis 251, 273
Christmas bell 179, 188
Christmas bush 162
Christmas Island 364–5, **364**
Christmas tree 294, 301
  Western Australian 315, **315**
Chromis hypsilepis 128
Chrysanthemoides monilifera 101
Chrysophrys auratus **99**
Churchill National Park 103
cicada 166–7, **167**
Cillitris glauca 93
Cinclosoma cinnamomeum 320, 337
Cinnamomum camphora 184
cinnamon quail-thrush 320, 337
Circus approximans 46, 67, 303
clam
  boring **230**
  giant 230
Clarence River 179, 183, 184
Clare Valley **353**
Clarke Range **201**
clematis, native **295**
Clianthus formosus 321, 327, 345
  puniceus 263
Climacteris rufa 320
clover 20
  Cooper 209
coachwood 152, 162, 178
coast myall 125
cockatiel 195
cockatoo 251, 273, 342
  black 113, 359
  gang-gang 61, 69
  glossy black 153
  Major Mitchell 287
  palm 218
  pink **84**, 84–5
  red-tailed black 247, 287, **287**, 295
  sulphur-crested 102, 195, 251, 348
  white-tailed black 295, 303
  yellow-tailed black 31, 32, 47, 130, 153, 352
Cockburn Sound 299
Cocklebiddy 317, 318, 321
Cocklebiddy Cave **319**
Cockle Creek 42
Cocoparra National Park 88, 89
Cocoparra Range 88, 139, 140
Cocos (Keeling) Islands 365
cod
  Antarctic 376
  Murray 95, 99
  red rock 166
Coffin Bay National Park 357
Coffs Harbour 131, 178, 184, 185
Coleman River 222
Colluricincla boweri 214
  harmonica 295
Colo Creek 146
Colo River 153, 160
Colo Wilderness **147, 149**, 174
Columba leucomela 184
Condamine River 194, 195
Conimbla National Park 139
Connells Lagoon Conservation Reserve 261
Conway Range **200**
Conway Range National Park 200
Cook, Captain James 127–8, 131, 158, 202, 363
Cooks Hill 175
Cooktown 210, 213, 219, 226
Coolangubra State Forest 133, **133**
coolibah **134**, 137, 138, 195, 198, **198**, 209, 256, 326, 329
Coomera River 194
Coonabarabran 138
Coongan River 276
Coongie Lakes 328
Coonowrin National Park 190
Cooper Creek 204, 205, 327, **328**
Coorong 64, 71–2, **71, 72**
Coorong Game Reserve 71
Coorong National Park 64, 71
coot, Eurasian 165, 303
copper butterfly, Eltham 98
Coracina novaehollandiae 259
coral
  brain 229, **230**
  branching 229
  fan **225, 228**
  fossil 347
  plate 229, **229**
  staghorn **229**
coral reefs 215, 289, 289, 361
Coral Sea 98, 161, 211, 214, 218
corella
  little 273, 287, 348
  long-billed 287
  white 347
cork tree 278
cormorant 71, 129, 142, 165, 356
  pied 68
Corroboree Rock Conservation Reserve 257
Corvus coronoides 295
Corypha elata 220
Coturaundee Range 142
Coturnix chinensis 108
Cowra 93, 139, 151
Coxs Gap 174
Coxs River 145, 146, 147, 150, 151
Cox-Warragamba Valley 146
crab 161, **364**
  giant 365
  red 365
  soldier 28
Cracticus nigrogularis 256
  torquatus 31
Cradle Mountain 55
Cradle Mountain – Lake St Clair National
  Park 43, 55–6
Cradle Mountain – Lake St Clair Scenic
  Reserve 57
Cradle Valley 57
crake 303
  red-necked 214–15, **214**
Craspedia glauca 117
Crassostrea commercialis 166
Crater Bluff 140
crayfish 32
  Murray 95, **95**
Crinia riparia 344
Croajingolong National Park **107**, 113
crocodile 246

freshwater 222, 251, 268
saltwater 196, 222, **222**, 249, 268, **268**
Crocodylus johnstoni 222, 251
porosus 222, 249
Ctenophorus pictus 354
cuckoo-shrike, black-faced 259
Culgoa River 194
cumbungi 344
Cunnamulla 14
curlew, eastern 101, 164
currawong 77
grey 103
Curtis Island 198
cuscus 213
grey 218
spotted 218
cushion plant 30, **42**, **54**, 55, 367, 369
Cutta Cutta Cave 251
Cyanoramphus novae-zelandiae cookii 363
Cyanostegia cyanocalyx 273
Cyathea australis 103
cunninghamii 49, 110
marcescens 110
Cyathea Falls **111**
cycads 247–8, 257, 259, 261
Cycas media 247
Cyclochila australasiae 166
Cyclopsitta diophthalma 215
Cyclorana 263
Cygnet River **29**
Cygnus atratus 71, 165, 303
Cynara cardunculus 101
Cyprinus carpio 98
Cyttaria gunnii 48

D

Dacelo leachii 165, 273
Dactylopsila trivirgata 213
Daintree 212
Daintree River 211
daisy 321
everlasting 278
golden yellow 327
miniature 288
paper 262
pink 327
poached egg 262
snow 117, 152
tufted burr- 142
white 327
yellow 33, 161
daisy-bush 85, 141, 321
dusty 33
musk 48
Dalhousie Springs 338
Daly River 246
Dampier Archipelago 279
Dandenong Ranges 99, 103
Dandenong Ranges National Park 103
Dangerous Reef 359
Danggali Conservation Park 141
Darling Downs 195
Darling Plateau 298
Darling Range **59**, 284, **290**, **293**, **294**, 298, 300
Darling River 86, **87**, 89, **89**, 136, 137, 138, 142, 143, 181, 194, 195, 206
Darling Scarp 291, 294, 300
Darwin 245, 246–51, 248, 254
Darwinia 309
fascicularis 161
Dasyornis brachypterus 113
broadbenti 64–6
longirostris 313
Dasyurus geoffroii 294
maculatus 28, 56, 61, 64, 113
viverrinus 28, 56
Davis Station 374
Dawson River 198, 206, 207
Deep Creek Conservation Park 353
De Grey River 274
Demansia atra 247
Demla inpar 101
Denmark (WA) 306, 308
Dendrobium canaliculatum 200
striolatum 30
tetragonum 192
Dendrocnide excelsa 184, 191
Dendrophthoe glabrescens 260
Deniliquin 89, 95
Denison Range 40
Derwent Bridge 36
Derby 264
Dermochelys coriacea 202, 232
Derwent Glacier 53
Derwent River 25, 27, 53, 55
Derwent Valley 53
deserts 330–9, **328**
Deua National Park 131, **131**
Deua River **131**
devil
eastern blue 128
mountain 167
Tasmanian 27, 28, 56, 142, 310
thorny 263, 336
Devil's Kitchen 32
Devil's Rock 175
Devils Marbles 252, 254, **254**

Devils Pebbles 254
Devonport 45, 46
Dharug National Park 158
Diamantina River 205, 322, 327
Dicaeum hirundinaceum 78
Dicksonia antarctica 29, 48, 61, 103
dieback 19, 180, **180**, 293, 294, 300–1, 390
dingo 24, 131, 203, 259, 321, 326
Diomedea exulans 165, 367
Diplodactylus vittatus 354
Diploglottis cunninghamii 171
Dirk Hartog Island **279**
Discovery Bay Coastal Park 69
Disphyma australe 85
Dissostichus mawsoni 376
Diuris punctata albo-violacea 101
dog rose **76**
dogwood 61
dolerite 24, 27, **27**, **28**, 29, 30, **32**, 52, **53**
Dolichandrone heterophylla 272
dolphin 32, 99, 131, 165, 172, **279**, 280
bottle-nosed 99, 280
Donatia 30
Donnelly Peak 309
Doroughby 183
Dorre Island 281
Dorrigo 182
Dorrigo National Park 182, 192
Dorrigo Plateau 178
Doryphora sassafras 152, 162, 171, 178
dotterels 303
Douglas-Apsley National Park 30, **30**
Douglas Hot Springs 250
Douglas River 30, 250
Dracophyllum 30
fitzgeraldi 362
dragon 153, 165, 354
bearded 165
Lake Eyre 326
painted 354
Dromaius minor 61
novaehollandiae 138, 185, 208
Drosera 161, 302, 314
drummer, silver 128
drumsticks **161**
Dryander National Park 200
dryandra 292, **292**, 303
Dryandra State Forest 286, 292, **293**
Drysdale River **265**, 267, 273
Drysdalia coronoides 47, 99
Du Cane Range **50**, 53, **53**
duck 31, 142, 172, 303
blue-billed 289, 303
freckled 289, 329
maned 354
musk 289, 303
Pacific black 165, 303
pink 325
pink-eared 303
Duck River 45
Ducula whartoni 365
dugite 295, 305
dugong 201, **201**, 233, 280
Dugong dugon 201, 280
Dumbleyung Lake 288–9
Dunk Island 226
dunnart 71, 103, 304
fat-tailed 335, 358
Dutchman's Stern Conservation Park 344
Dysoxylum fraseranum 171

E

eagle 88
little 303
wedge-tailed 102, 132, 140, 259, 338, 345
Eaglehawk Neck **24**, 32
Eastern Highlands 88
East Point Flora and Fauna Reserve 247
echidna 78, 84, 99, 103, 315
short-beaked 47
Echium plantagineum 345
Echuca 89, 89, 93
Echymipera rufescens 218
Eclectus roratus 218
Eden 130, 131, 133
Edeowie Gorge 346
Ediacaria flindersi 349
Edward River 89, 95
eel 161
long-finned 161
short-finned 98, 161
Egan Peak State Forest 133
Egernia coventryi 107
egret 72, 142, 172, 195, 248, **248**, 303, 353
Ehretia acuminata 152
Elanus notatus 303
Elder Range 346
Eldon Peak **35**
Elephant Spit **369**
Ellenborough Falls 181, **181**
Ellery Gorge 257
Emblema bella 153
Emily and Jessie Gaps Nature Park 257
Empress Gorge 149
emu 31, 72, 84, 93, 138, **139**, 185, 195, 208, 209, 263, 329, 345, 354, 358, 359
King Island 61
Tasmanian 31

emu bush 262, 347
spotted 334, 337
emu-wren
rufous-crowned 337
southern 69, 295
Emydura macquarii 95
Englebrecht Cave 69
Entomyzon cyanotis 188
Eopsaltria georgiana 313
griseogularis 282
epacris 152, **152**
Epacris impressa 46, 84
longiflora 167
microphylla 161
Ephippiorhynchus asiaticus 273
Epping Forest National Park 203
Eptesicus regulus 295, 304
Epthianura aurifrons 320
crocea 262
Eremiascincus richardsoni 337
Eremiornis carteri 278, 337
Eremophila 206, 282
longifolia 262, 347
maculata 334
Eretmochelys imbricata 232
Eriostemon trachyphyllus 125
Erochilus cucullatus 354
Errinundra National Park 112– 13
Errinundra Plateau 112, **113**
Erskine Falls 64, **65**
Esperance 306, 308, 310, 315
Eubalaena australis 68, 131, 321
Eubalbula Creek 203
Eurimbula National Park 202
euro 140, 335
Evans Head 182
Evercreech Forest Reserve 29
Exit Cave 39
Exmouth Gulf **278**
Exocarpos cupressiformis 33
Expedition Range 206
Eyre Bird Observatory 320, 321
Eyre Peninsula 342, 350, **356**, 357, 358

oleosa 83, 315
ovata 28, 69
paniculata 162
papuana 209, 256
patens 312
pauciflora 55, 141, 151, 152, 181
pilligaensis 138
pilularis 162, 170, 178
piperita 161
polyanthemos 98, 111
populnea 137
pseudoglobulus 111
pulchella 33
punctata 153, 170
radiata 79, 179
regnans 41, 64, 81, 103, 109, 122
rossii 122, 139
rubida 141, 151
rudis 292, 300
saligna 162, 170, 178
salmonophloia 286, 300, 315, 316
setosa 209
sideroxylon 111, 136, 179, 195
sieberi 111
similis 209
socialis 85
stellulata 170
tereticornis 153, 162, 170
terminalis 209
tetrodonta 221
umbra 161
urnigera 33
vernicosa 42
viminalis 28, 69, 85, 98, 101, 122, 141, 170
viridis 137
wandoo 286, 292, 300, 315
youmanii 179
Eucla 317, 318
Eucla National Park 321
Eucryphia lucida 30, 48
Eudyptes chrysocome 367
chrysolophus 367
Eudyptula minor 28, 47, 68, 99, 108, 161, 303
Eungella National Park 201, **201**
Euphausia superba **371**
Eurimbula Creek 203
Eurimbula National Park 202
euro 140, 335
Evans Head 182
Evercreech Forest Reserve 29
Exit Cave 39
Exmouth Gulf **278**
Exocarpos cupressiformis 33
Expedition Range 206
Eyre Bird Observatory 320, 321
Eyre Peninsula 342, 350, **356**, 357, 358

Eucalyptus 206
acaciiformis 179
accedens 286, 294
alba 130, 199
albens 89, 124, 170, 179
amygdalina 28
andrewsii 201
astringens 286, 294
bauerana 77
baxteri 69, 83, 85, 354
blakelyi 170, 179
blaxlandii 170
brevifolia 334
caesia 287
caleyi 173, 179
caliginosa 179
calophylla 291, 300, 312
calycogona 85
camaldulensis 83, 84, 90, 98, 101, 122, 137, 195, 198, 207, 256, 272, 278, 326, 334, 348, 354
cladocalyx 342
cneorifolia 359
coccifera 33, 55
conica 137
consideniana 106
crebra 140, 170
cypellocarpa 64, 109
dalrympleana 122, 141, 151
dealbata 140
deanei 162
delegatensis 29, 64, 81, 122
diversicolor 312
dives 111, 151
eximia 174
fastigata 122, 151, 172
fibrosa 170
flocktoniae 315
foecunda 85
glaucescens 125
globoidea 106
globulus 61, 64, 109
gomphocephala 300
gongylocarpa 334
goniocalyx 101
grandis 178, 193, 201
gummifera 113, 161, 170
gunnii 55, **55**
haemastoma 161
haematoxylon 312
hemiphloia 162
incrassata 85
kruseana 287
laeliae 300
laevopinea 170
largiflorens 83, 84
leucoxylon 83, 85, 354
loxophleba 286
macrorhyncha 101, 122, 139, 179, 354
maculata 170
marginata 291, 300, 312
melanophloia 136, 209
melliodora 93, 98, 111, 124, 137, 173, 179
microcarpa 89, 93, 137, 195
microcorys 170, 178
microtheca 137, 138, 195, 209, 256, 326, 347
miniata 251
mitchelliana 121
moluccana 170
moorei 125
muellerana 109
nitens 178
nitida 49, 61
obliqua 30, 41, 79, 81, 109, 111, 123, 170, 352
oblonga 173
pauciflora 170
obtusiflora 161

F

Fairy Cave 112
fairy wren, purple-crowned 273
red-winged 313
splendid 85, 295
superb 84
variegated 84
Falco berigora 102
cenchroides 67, 259, 303
longipennis 89
peregrinus 67, 78, 89, 139, 140, 345, 359
subniger 338
falcon 88
black 338
brown 102
peregrine 67, 89, 139, 140, 345, 359
false sandalwood 141
false sarsaparilla **295**
fantail
grey 184, 295
rufous 192
feather star **228**
feather-flower 287
fern 48, 184, 212, 250, 259, 288, 353, 354
bird's nest 184
cloak 262
elkhorn 191
nardoo 85, 137, 327
staghorn 191
swamp 247
Ficus 184
alba pila 218
macrophylla 162
platypoda 257
fig 140, 141, 162
deciduous 218, **218**
Moreton Bay 162, **162**
native 215, 257, 259
strangler 172, 184
figbird 247
finch, zebra 256, 281, 338
Fingal Head **185**
Finke Gorge National Park 259
Finke River **253**, 257, 259, 260, 322
Finke River Gorge 260
fire 41, 268, 310–11
plants' adaptation to 123, 302, 314–15, 344
firetail, beautiful 153
fire-wheel tree 192
Fitzgerald River 270, 310, 314
Fitzroy Crossing 264

Fitzroy Gardens 98
Fitzroy River 196, 198, 267, 272
flame tree 192
flannel flower 167
flea, sand 131
Fleurieu Peninsula 350, 353, **353**, 358, 359
Flinders Chase National Park **350, 358**, 359
Flinders grass 261
Flinders Island 59, **59**, 60
Flinders Ranges 11, 13, 92, 340–49, **341, 381**
Flinders Ranges National Park 346, 347
Flinders River 209
Flindersia maculata 138
Florence Falls 250
Florentine Valley 36, 38
flycatcher
    black-faced 184
    restless 165
flying fox 164, 200
    black 248, 251
    grey-headed 98, 113, 164, **164**
Fogg Dam **248**
Fogg Dam Conservation Reserve 248
Forestier Peninsula **24**
Fortescue River 274, 276, **276,** 279
Forth River 45
Forth Valley 53, 57
Fossil Bluff 47
Fourth Creek 354, **355**
fox 20, 21, 24, 68, 72, 84, 103, 180, 209, 359
Frank Hann National Park 287
Frankland Range 39–40, **38**
Franklin-Lower Gordon Wild Rivers National
    Park 43
Franklin River 36, 43
Franz Joseph Glacier **14**
Fraser Island 186–8, **187, 188**, 202, 226
Freeling Heights 346, 353
Fremantle 296, 298, 299
French Island 107, 108
French Island State Park 108
Frenchmans Cap 36, **36**, 42, 43
Freshwater Beach **167**
Freycinet Peninsula 27, **27**, 31, **31, 383**
friarbird
    noisy 165
    silver-crowned 273
frigatebird **232**
fringe myrtle 84
frog 99, 153, 305, 329, 338
    Baw Baw 120–1
    bell 103
    corroboree 118
    Eungella 201
    giant burrowing 111
    moaning 305
    trilling 338–9
    tree 113, **113**, 124
    water-holding 263, **263**
frogmouth owl
    Papuan 215
    tawny 98, 295
fruitdove
    banded 250
    native 327
    rose-crowned 250
    wompoo 184
fuchsia, native 167, 327
Fulica atra 165, 303
fur seal 367–8
    Antarctic 369, **369**
    Australian 32, 165
    New Zealand 368

G

Gadopsis marmoratus 95, 98
Gahnia grandis 106
    psittacorum 32
galah 102, 195, 295
Gallinago hardwickii 99
Gallinula mortierii 28
Gallirallus australis 368
Gambier Island Conservation Park 357
Gammon Ranges 348, 349
Gammon Ranges National Park 348, 353
gannet 60–1, 167, 172
    Australasian 67, 100, **100**, 127
Garden Island 298, 299, 302
Gardens of Stone National Park 149
Gascoyne River **280**, 281, 282
Gawler Ranges 324
Gecarcoidea natalis 365
gecko 99, 153, 257, 337, 354
    barking 358
    bearded 337
    jewelled 278
    marbled 305
    thick-tailed 358
    western spiny-tailed **315**
    wood 354
Geelong 62, 64
Geijera parviflora 137, 142
Geikie Gorge 270
Gellibrand Hill Park 81, 102
gentian, mountain 117
Gentianella diemensis 117
Geophaps plumifera 278, 337
Georges River 162, 166, **166**

Geraldton 274, 285, 285, 289
gerygone 184
Gerygone mouki 184
gibberbird 337
gibbers 209, 329, 332
Gibraltar Range 179, **179**
Gibraltar Range National Park 182
Gibson Desert 333, 334
gidgee 209, 326
Gippsland 104–13
Gippsland Lakes **105**
Gippsland Lakes Coastal Park 111
Girraween National Park 193–4
glaciation **14**, 39–40, 53, 117, 349, 355–6, **355, 372**
Gladstone 17, 202
Glass House Mountains 186, 190, **190**
glasswort, beaded 67
Glen Helen Gorge **253**
Glenelg River 69
Glenrock State Recreation Area 175
glider 103, 107, 172, 314
    feathertail 124, 141, 164
    greater 124, 141, 153, 193
    squirrel 185
    sugar 101, 124, 163, 185
    yellow-bellied 103, 124
Glossodia major 139
Glossopsitta porphyrocephala 313
Gloucester Island 200, **200**
Gloucester Tops 170, 173
glow-worms 39, 48
goanna 226
    Gould's 305
    Rosenberg's sand 358, **359**
    sand 337
goat 21, **21**, 140, 141, 343
goby, desert **326**
godwit 303
    bar-tailed 31
Gog Range 44
goodenia 272
Goodenia lamprosperma 272
    ovata 139
goose
    Cape Barren 29, 31, 60, **60**, 357
    cotton 199
    magpie 199, 222, 248, 254, 273
    pygmy, green 199, 248
Gordon Dam 38, 43
Gordon River 36, 38, 43
goshawk
    brown 303
    grey 67
Gosse Bluff 261, **261**
Gossypium sturtianum 262
Goulburn 151, 159
Goulburn River 170, 173, 174, **174**
Goulburn River National Park 173
Goulburn Valley 174
Govetts Creek 146
Govetts Leap 146, 149
Grallina cynoleuca 295
Grampian Ranges 69, **75**, 76, **76**, 80–1, **80**, 354
Grand Arch 151
granite 59, **59, 61**, 108, **179, 181**, 194, 354, 358
Granite Island 353, **353**
grassbird 193
grass tree 41, 69, 79, 161, 288, 292, 312, **354**
grass-wrack, dwarf 107
grasshopper 339
grass tree 41, 69, 79, 161, 288, 292, 312, **354**
Great Artesian Basin 209, 276, 324, 335, 338
Great Australian Bight 15, 316, 317, **317**, 320, 321, 350, 357
Great Barrier Reef 15, 196, 197, 202, 224–33
Great Lake 53, 54, 56
Great North Walk 175
Great Ocean Road 63, 64
Great Pine Tier 55
Great Sandy Desert 264, 334
Great Sandy National Park **188**
Great Victoria Desert 316, **317**, 334
Great Victoria Desert Nature Reserve 321
Great Wall of China 347
Great Western Highway 145
Great Western Plain 62
Great Western Plateau 274, 290, 291
Great Western Tiers 44, 50, 52, **52, 54**
grebe 71
Green Island **15**
grevillea 85, 139, 162, 165, 174, 188, 304, 313, 314, 334
    gully 106–7, **107**
    toothbrush **313**
Grevillea 206
    barklyana 106
    buxifolia 167
    pterosperma **288**
    speciosa 162
Grey Range 329, **329**
Griffith 88, 89, 95, 139
'groper' **128**
Grose River 145, 146, 160
Grose Valley **145**, 146
Grotto, The 67
Grus rubicundus 139, 199, 222, 273
gudgeon 348
guinea flower 84, 152
Gulf of Carpentaria **14**, 209, **217**, 218, 220, 250, 261

Gulf St Vincent 350, 354, 356
gull 71, 172, 289, 325
    black-backed 33
    kelp 33
    silver 29, 100, 142, 165, 303
gum
    black 28
    Blakely's red 170, 179
    blue 32, 33, 85
    butter 300
    cider **55**
    flooded 178, 201, 292, 300, 301
    forest red 153, 162, 170
    ghost 209, **255**, 256
    Gippsland blue 111
    grey 153, 170, 173, 174
    manna 28–9, 69, 85, 98, 101, 122, 123, 141
    marble 334
    mountain 122, 141, 151
    mountain grey 64, 109, 111
    peppermint 151
    ribbon 170, **170**, 172
    river red 81, 83, 84, 90, 92–3, 95, 98, 101, 102, 122, **136**, 137, 138, 139, **143**, 195, 209, 256, **256**, 260, 272, 278, 326, 334,
    roundleaf 162
    salmon 286, 300, **314**, 315, 316
    scribbly 122, 139, 161, 178
    shining 178
    snappy 334
    snow 33, 55, 121–2, 141, 151–2, 170, 172, 181
    South Australian blue 354
    spotted 170
    sugar 342, 345
    swamp 28, 69
    Sydney blue 178, 162, 170
    Tasmanian blue 61, 64
    Tasmanian snow 55
    Tingaringy 125
    urn 33
    varnished 42
    Western Australian flooded 300
    white 28, 32, 33, 130, 140, 151, 199
    white peppermint **33**
    yellow 83, 85, 101
    York 286
Gunderbooka Range 141
gungurru 287, **288**
Gurig National Park **234**
Guy Fawkes River National Park 182
Gygis alba 363
Gymnobelideus leadbeateri 81, 96, 123
Gymnorhina tibicen 46, 165, 295, 303
Gymnoschoenus sphaerocephalus 29, 42, 66
Gyrocarpus americanus 272

H

Hacks Lagoon Conservation Park 72
Haematopus fuliginosus 47
hakea 174, 188, 292, 303, 313, 314
    royal **310**
Hakea suberea 278
    sericea 162
Halgania dampiera 345
Haliaeetus leucogaster 31, 47, 248, 281, 289
Halletts Cove 13
Halls Creek 264, 270, **271**
Halls Gap **80**
Haloniscus searlei 326
Hambidge Conservation Park 358
Hamelin Bay 312
Hamelin Pool 280
Hamersley Range **275–77**, 276, 278, 279
Hamersley Range National Park 276
Hamilton River 322
Hampton Tablelands **320**
hardhead 289
harrier
    marsh 46
    swamp 67, 303
Hattah-Kulkyne National Park 90, 91, 95
Hattah Lake 91
Hawker 342, 346
Hawkesbury River 14, 146, 158, 160–1, **160**, 162, **163**, 165, 174, 202
Hawkesbury-Nepean river system 159, 161
hawk-owl, Christmas Island 365
Head of Bight 321
Heard Island 360, 366–7, 368–9, **369**
heath 141
    coastal 67
    common 46, 84
    flame 84
Heathcote National Park 158
heath-myrtles 85
Heavitree Gap **256**
Helaeus 263
Heleioporus australiacus 111
    eyrei 305
Helichrysum 278
    bracteatum 327
    scorpoides 33
Heliopterum 278
    floribundum 327
    roseum 327
Hellyer Gorge State Reserve 49
Hemibelideus lemuroides 213

hen, Tasmanian native 28
Henbury Craters 261, **261**
Herbert River 211, **211**
heron 165, 248, 303, 353
    rufous night 98
    striated 165
Hesperilla flavescens flavescens 101
Heterodendrum oleifolium 138, 141, 342
Heterodontus portus jacksoni 166
Heysen Range 346
Heysen Trail 346, 353
Hibbertia 84, 294
hibiscus
    blue 358
    lilac 345
    Norfolk Island 363
    Philip Island 363
Hibiscus insularis 363
Hickmania troglodytes 48
Hieraaetus morphnoides 303
Hinchinbrook Island 212, 232
Hindmarsh Falls 353
Hippolyte Rocks 32
Hirundapus caudacutus 131
Hirundo ariel 250, 257
    nigricans 32, 61
Hobart 24, 27, 32
hobby, Australian 89
Holey Plains 110
holly, native 174–5
honeyeater 32, 46, 77, 78, 84, 89, 91, 113, 165, 167, 185, 188, 200, 301, 314, 320, 355
    black 337
    black-headed 61
    blue-faced 188
    brown 294, 314
    crested 29
    Eungella 201
    helmeted 96, 103
    Lewin's 184
    New Holland 165, 313
    scarlet 113, 188
    singing 314, 315
    strong-billed 61
    tawny-crowned 29, 313
    white-cheeked 165, 188, 294, 313
    white-eared 165, 315
    white-naped 165, 294
    yellow-faced 165
    yellow-plumed 315
    yellow-throated 61
    yellow-tinted 165
honey-myrtle, mallee 83
Hook Island **232**
hop **24**
    wild 345
Hope Islands **231**
hop goodenia 139
Hoplocephalus bungaroides 165
horizontal shrub 37, **37**, 48
horseshoe bat, orange 250
Horseshoe Beach **175**
Houtman Abrolhos Islands 289, **289**
Howard Springs 247, 249
Howard Springs Nature Park 247
Howea forsteriana 362
Hunter River 168, 172, 173, **175**
Hunter Valley 144, 158, 168–75, **168**
Huon River 27
Hydromys chrysogaster 99, 164, 329
Hydrurga leptonyx 131, 165, 375
Hymenanthera dentata 98
Hypsiprymnodon moschatus 213

I

ibis 71, 72, 195, 303
    sacred 98, **98**
    straw-necked 98
ice age 36, 53–4, 117, 118, 390
icebergs **370, 372, 373**
ice fish 376
igneous rock 390
Illawarra Plain 126–7
Indian Ocean 296, 299, 364
Inman Valley 356
Innes National Park 356, **357**
inselbergs 258, **286**, 287, 288, **358**
Inverell 178, 179, 180, 182
iris, wild 141
ironbark 136–7, 138, 139, 162, 179, 209
    Caley's 173
    broad-leaved red 170, 173
    grey 162
    narrow-leaved 140
    narrow-leaved red 138, 140, 170, 173
    red 81, 111, 174, 195
    silver-leaved 209
    white 81
iron plant 278
Iron Range **216**, 218, **218, 222**
Iron Range National Park 218
Ironstone Mountain **54**
ironwood 137, 262
Isdell River 267
Isoodon obesulus 47, 71, 295, 305, 353
Isopogon 174, 294
Israelite Bay 308, 316, 321

J

jabiru 273
Jacaranda mimosaefolia 162
jackass fish 128
Jacksons Creek 101, **101**
James Range 260
Jamieson Creek 144, 146, **146**
Jamieson Valley 146, **146**, **148**, 153
Jardine River 216, 219, 221
Jardine River National Park 219
jarrah 284, 286, 290–292, **291**, 293, **293**, **294**, 300, 304, **307**, 312, 315, 352
Jenolan Caves 13, 118, 151, 153
Jenolan River 151
Jervis Bay 128–130, **129**, 132
Jewel Cave 310
jewfish 166
jockey's cap 347
Joffre Falls 276, **277**
Joffre Gorge **277**
John Forrest National Park 300
jointed rush 301
Joseph Bonaparte Gulf 247
Julius River and Lake Chisholm State Reserve 49
Junction Reserve 261

K

Kaiserstuhl Conservation Park 353
Kakadu **239**
Kalbarri 287
Kalbarri National Park 281, **281**
Kalgoorlie 282
Kamarooka State Park 79
Kanangra-Boyd National Park 151, 153, **153**
Kanangra Gorge 151, 152
Kanangra Walls **153**
kangaroo 20, 64, 93, 101, 103, 138, 180, 195, 304, 325, 344, 345, 353, 354
  eastern grey 28, 56, 64, 71, 78, 131, 138, 185, 203, 208
  forester 28, 32
  giant 142
  great red 138
  grey 20, 88, 91, 139, 140, 141, 206, 209, 329
  red 20, 91, 143, 209, 263, 329, 335, 358
  western grey 71, 84, 138, 288, 294, 315, 358
Kangaroo Island 13, 342, 346, 350, 353, 358–9, **358**, 359
kangaroo paw 294
Karratha 279
karri **308**, 312, **312**
Karumba **217**
Katajuta 257, 259
Katherine Gorge **250**, 251
Katherine Gorge National Park 250
Katherine Low Level Nature Park 251
Katherine River 250
Katoomba 146, 147, 153
kauri 352
kelp 32, **368**
kennedia **307**
Kennedy Range 281, **281**
kestrel, Australian 67, 259, 303
Kimberley, The 13, 15, 201, 264–73, 335
Kinchega National Park 142
kingfish, yellow-tail 166
kingfisher 213
  azure 48, 193, 273
  paradise 203
  red-backed 338
Kingfisher Flat 344
King Edward River 267
King George River **265**
King Island 59, 60
Kinglake National Park **78**, 79, 102, **102**
Kinglake Range 81
King Leopold Ranges 270
Kings Canyon 260, **260**
King Sound 267, **268**
Kings Plain National Park 182
King William Range 39–40
kite 259
  black-shouldered 303
knot 107, 303
  red 31
koala 78–9, 93, 99, 101, 108, 133, 141, 153, 162, 172, 173, 185, 206, 310, 314, 354, 359, **359**
Kongabula Range 206
kookaburra 78, 165
  blue-winged 273
Koonalda Cave 318, **319**
Kooragang Island 171, **175**
Kooyoora State Park 77, **77**
Kosciusko National Park 117, 120, 124, **387**
Kowmung River 150, 151, **151**, 152, 153
Krichauff Range 260
krill 321, 371, 375
Kubla Khan Cave 47
kunzeas 313
Ku-ring-gai Chase National Park **160**, 162, **163**
kurrajong 111, 179, 209
Kutikina Cave 36, 43
kwongan **293**, 313, 314
Kyphosus sydneyanus 128

L

Lachlan River 86, 89, 90, 142, 151
Lady Musgrave Island **224**
Lagarostrobos franklinii 41, 49
lagoons 71–2, 165
Lagunaria patersonia 363
Lake Ada 56
Lake Albert 72, 92
Lake Alexandrina 72, 92, **92**, 181
Lake Argyle 270, **270**, 271
Lake Bancannia 136
Lake Barrine 215
Lake Blanche 340
Lake Buchanan 209
Lake Burragorang 147
Lake Burrinjuck 114
Lake Callabonna 340
Lake Cave 310
Lake Cawndilla 142
Lake Corangamite 72
Lake Crescent 53
Lake Dieri 325
Lake Disappointment 324
Lake Eacham 215
Lake Eyre 125, 204, 205, 260, 322–6, **323**, **324**, **326**, 328, 340
Lake Eyre National Park 325
Lake Eyre North 324
Lake Eyre South 324
Lakefield National Park 220, 221
Lake Frome **13**, 324, 340, 349
Lake Gairdner **323**, 324–5
Lake Galilee 209
Lake George 117, 125
Lake Grace 288
Lake Gregory 340
Lake Ironstone **54**
Lake Keepit 182
Lake King 111
Lake Macquarie 170, 175
Lake Menindee **143**
Lake Mountain 117, 122
Lake Mungo 142, **143**
Lake Mungo National Park 142
Lake Nuga Nuga 206
Lake Pedder **42**, 43
Lake Pedder National Park 43
Lake Reeve 111
Lake St Clair 53, **53**, 55, 57
Lakes Entrance 105, 111
Lakes National Park 111
Lake Sorell 53
Lake Torrens 324, **325**, 340, 343, 346, 349
Lake Tyers 111, 112
Lake Victoria 111
Lake Wyangala 151
Lambert Glacier 372, 373
Lambertia formosa 167
Lamington National Park **186**, 190–2, **191**, 193
Lamington Plateau 190–1, **191**
lamprey, short-headed 98
Lane Cove River 157
Langi Ghiran State Park 77
Lanterns, The **32**
lapwing, yellow-wattled masked 46
Larus dominicanus 33
  novaehollandiae 100, 165, 303
Lasiorhinus krefftii 203, 206
  latifrons 319
Lates calcarifer 196
Lathamus discolor 31, 61
La Trobe River 105, 110
La Trobe Valley 53, 110-11
Launceston 24, 28, 29
laurel 201
  camphor 184
  native 48
Lawrencia buchananensis 209
leatherwood 30, 48
Lechenaultia 294
Leeuwin current 289
Leeuwin-Naturaliste National Park 312
Leiolopisma ocellatum 61
Leiopotherapon unicolor 256, 263
Leipoa ocellata 72, 84, 89, 138, 358
Lemonthyme Forest 57
lemonwood 272
Lennard River **266**, 270
leopardwood 138, **138**
Leptolophus hollandicus 195
Leptonychotes weddelli 375
Leptospermum 315
  laevigatum 84, 85, 161
  lanigerum 29
  phylicoides 98
leptospermum 188
Leucopogon microphyllus 161
Leucosarcia melanoleuca 153
Liasis olivaceus 247
libertia 152
Lichenostomus chrysops 165
  flavescens 165
  flavicollis 61
  hindwoodi 201
  leucotis 96, 165, 315
  ornatus 315
  virescens 314
lichens 288, 367

Lichmera indistincta 294, 314
Lightening Ridge 14
lillypilly 109, **109**, 162, 167, 178
Lilly Pilly Gully 109
lily
  garland 88
  native 77
  tinsel 84
Limonium thouinii 345
Limosa lapponica 31
Lincoln National Park 357
Lind National Park 113
Lindeman Islands **200**
Lion Island 157, **157**, 161
Litchfield Park 249- -50
Litoria aurea 103
  citropa 113
  jervisiensis 113
  moorei 305
  verreauxii verreauxii 124
Little Desert **84**
Little Desert National Park 82, 83–4
Little Forest Plateau 131
Little Green Island 60
Little Head **154**
Liverpool Range 170
liverwort 367
Livistona 251
  alfredii 276
  australis 113, 207
  benthamii 248
  inermis 250
  mariae 259
lizard 165, 336, 347
  blue-tongued 153, **165**
  eastern blue-tongued 99
  jacky 99, 102
  legless 101
  shingleback 347, **354**
  stump-tailed 347
Lizard Island **226**
Lobodon carcinophagus 375
Lockerbie Scrub 219, **220**, 221
Logan Lagoon **59**
Logan Lagoon Wildlife Sanctuary 60
logrunner 192, **192**
Lolworth Creek 199
London Bridge 67, **67**, 68
Long Forest Flora Reserve 76
Longreach Waterhole 254
long tom 251
Lophognathus gilberti 329
Lopholaimus antarcticus 184
Lord Howe Island 15, **360**, 361–2, **362**, 363
Lord Howe Island woodhen 362
lorikeet 77, 113, 185, 188, 313, 354
  musk 113
  purple-crowned 313
  rainbow 113, **164**, 165, 251, 262, 273
lotus bird **241**
lotus flower 195
louse, salt lake 326
Lowan Conservation Park 95
Lower Glenelg National Park 69, 71
Lucasium damaeum 337
Lycium ferocissimum 101
Lyperanthus nigricans 83
lyrebird 79, **148**
  superb 103, 130, 148, 314

M

Macalister Range 212
Maccullochella peeli 95, 99
MacDonnell Ranges **8–9**, 13, 252–4, **252**, **255**, 256, 260
mace, reed 344
Mackay 197, 201, 226
mackerel 60
Macquaria ambigua 91
  australasica 89
  novaemaculata 161
Macquarie Harbour 38, 42
Macquarie Island 366–8, **366**, **367**, **368**
Macquarie Island Nature Reserve 368
Macquarie Marshes 137, **137**
Macquarie River 137
Mac. Robertson Land 372
Macroderma gigas 250
Macroglena caudata 110
Macronectes giganteus 165, 367
  halli 165, 367
Macropteranthes leichhardtii 208
Macropus agilis 203, 247
  dorsalis 203
  eugenii 304, 359
  fuliginosus 71, 84, 138, 288, 315, 358
  fuliginosus fuliginosus 294, 358
  giganteus 28, 56, 64, 71, 78, 91, 131, 138, 185, 203, 208
  irma 288, 294, 304
  robustus 140, 203, 258–9, 335, 344
  rufogriseus 28, 36, 139, 203
  rufus 91, 138, 209, 335, 358
Macrotis lagotis 335
Macrozamia macdonnellii 257
  reidlei 302
Madura 321
Magnetic Island 199

magpie 165, 303
  Australian 46, 295
magpie-lark 295
Main Range 117, 122
Main Range National Park 193
Maireana 282, 321
  brevifolia 137
  sedifolia 137
Maitland Bay **158**
Malacorhynchus membranaceus 303
Mallacoota Inlet 113
Mallanganee Flora Reserve 179
mallee 80, 82–5, 89, 91, 93, **93**, 94, 138, 161, 348, 350, 356, 358, 359
  bell-fruited **314**
  bookleaf 282
  coastal 357
  gooseberry 85
  green 137
  Kangaroo Island narrow-leaved 359
  narrow-leaved red 85
  oil 83
  pointed 85, **85**
  red 315
  ridge-fruited 85
  whipstick **79**
Mallee 74, 76, 82– 5
malleefowl 72, 84, **84**, 89, 95, 320
mallet, brown 286, 294
Malurus coronatus 273
  cyaneus 342
  elegans 313
  lamberti 84
  splendens 85, 295
Mammoth Cave 310
manfern 29, 48
mangrove 19, 162, 165, 170, 171, 202–3, 212, 215, 216, 219, 246, 247, 273, 350, 356
  grey 107
Manjimup 306, 312
Manly Beach 162, **167**
Manning River 172
Manorina melanocephala 165
  melanophrys 103
manucode, trumpet 218
Manucodia keraudrenii 218
Marakoopa Cave 47
Marble Bar 276, **282**
mardo 304
Margaret River 310, 312, 313
Maria Island 31, **31**
Maribyrong River 101
Marra Marra National Park 158
marri 291, 292, 293, 300, 312, 315
  mountain 312
marsh-marigold, alpine 117
Marsilea drummondii 85, 327
marsupial mole 335
martin
  fairy 250–1, 257
  tree 61
Mary River 246, 248, **248**
Marysville 77
Mastotermes darwiniensis 249
Mataranka Pool 251
Mawson Peak 369
McArthur River **223**
McDonald Islands 360, 368–9
McIlwraith Range 202, 218, 223
McLeod Morass 111
McPherson Range 181, **186**, 190
Meander Falls **52**
Meander River **52**
medic 20
Meetus Falls **29**
Megalurus timoriensis 153
Melacca Swamp 249
melaleuca 69, 93, 202, 278, 304, 313, 314
Melaleuca 251, 292, 315
  lanceolata 85, 302
  leucadendron 198, 276, 278
  neglecta 83
  uncinata 83, 85
  viridiflora 200, 220, 272
Melbourne 74, 76, 96–103, 104, 106, 114, 116
Meliphaga lewinii 184
Melithreptus affinis 61
  lunatus 165, 294
  validirostris 61
melomys, Cape York 218
Melomys capensis 218
Melophorus bagoti 339
Melopsittacus undulatus 195, 256, 338
Melville Caves **77**
Menura novaehollandiae 79, 103, 130, 148, 314
Merimbula 130
Merops ornatus 295
merrit 315
Merriwa 170
Mersey River 45
Mersey Valley 53
meryta, broad-leaved 363
Meryta latifolia 363
Messent Conservation Park 72
messmate 109
metamorphic rock 390
Michaelmas Cay 233
Michelago 125
Micromyrtus 85
microstrobos conifer **153**

Microstrobos fitzgeraldii 153
Middle Derwent 50
Middle Head **156**
Midland Highway 25
Midland Valley 52
Mid Mount Barren **310**
Mildura 87, 89, 90, 91, 93, 95
Millstream-Chichester National Park 276
Mimosa pigra **243**
Mimosa Rocks 130
Mimosa Rocks National Park 130, 131, **132**
miner
  bell 103
  noisy 165
Miniopterus schreibersii 69
Mirounga leonina 367
mistletoe 78, **78**
  orange 260
mistletoe bird 78, **78**
Mitchell Falls 268, **269**
Mitchell grass 195, 206, 209, 261, 262, 329
Mitchell Plateau **269**, 273
Mitchell River National Park 111
Mogurnda mogurnda 348
Mole Creek 44, 47
Moloch horridus 263, 336
Monarcha melanopsis 184
Monaro Tableland 112, 133
Mondurup Peak 309
monitor
  freckled 257
  lace 165, 342
Monkey Mia 280
monoliths 45, 258, **190**, 358, **358**
Monolith Valley 129
Moona Falls 181
moonah 69, 85, 302
Moondarra State Park 110
Moore River 286
Moore River National Park 301
mopoke 295
Mordacia mordax 98
Morelia bredli 337
  spilota 344
Moreton Island **188**
Morialta Conservation Park 354, **355**
Morton National Park **130**, 131
Morus serrator 60–1, 67, 100, 127
moss 184, 212, 288
  giant **173**
  peat **173**
Mossman 211, 212, 213
moth
  Bogong 118
  cedar-tip 202
Moulting Lagoon 31
mountain bells 309
mountain celery 117
Mount Anne **39**, 42
Mount Arapiles 80, **80**
Mount Babbage 349
Mount Banks 146
Mount Barney National Park 192
Mount Barrington 172
Mount Barrow 309
Mount Bartle Frere 211
Mount Bates 362, 363
Mount Baw Baw 122
Mount Bell 150
Mount Bingar 139
Mount Bischoff 45
Mount Bogong 121
Mount Bruce **276**
Mount Buangor State Park 77
Mount Buffalo 121
Mount Buffalo National Park 120
Mount Caley 146
Mount Canobolas 151
Mount Cavern 343
Mount Cobberas 120
Mount Conner 257, 259, **259**
Mount Cook 291
Mount Coriaday 174
Mount Coricudgy 150, 170, 174
Mount Dandenong 103
Mount Disappointment 103
Mount Dromedary 128
Mount Dryander 200
Mount Eliza 103
Mount Ellery 105, 112
Mount Exmouth 141
Mount Feathertop 121
Mount Fisher 211
Mount Gambier 68, 69
Mount Gardner 313
Mount Gee 349
Mount George 308
Mount Geryon **51**
Mount Gog 309
Mount Gower **360**, 361, 362
Mount Hann 267
Mount Hooghly 105
Mount Hotham 118, 119
Mount Hypipamee National Park 215
Mount Ida **53**
Mount Jagungal 120
Mount Jim 117
Mount Kaputar 141, **141**
Mount Kaputar National Park 141
Mount Kaye 105

Mount Kerry 150
Mount Kiangarow 190
Mount Kosciusko 40, 118, 122
Mount La Trobe 105
Mount Lesueur 287, **287**
Mount Lesueur Reserves 287
Mount Leura 68, **68**
Mount Lidgbird **360**, 361, 362
Mount Lindesay 308, 309
Mount Loch 116–17
Mount Lofty Ranges 92, 350, 352, 353–4, 359
Mount Macedon 103
Mount Magnificent Park 353
Mount Magog 309
Mount Manypeaks 308, 309
Mount Martha 103
Mount Meharry 44
Mount Napier 68
Mount Nibelung **130**
Mount Norfolk 44
Mount Norman 194
Mount Ohlssen Bagge 345
Mount Olga 259
Mount Ossa 55
Mount Painter 349
Mount Ragged 308
Mount Remarkable 340
Mount Remarkable National Park 343
Mount Rescue Conservation Park 72
Mount Richmond 69
Mount Roland 44
Mount Royal Range 170, 171, 172
Mount St Leonard 103
Mount Schank 15, 68
Mount Solitary 146
Mount Sonder **255**
Mount Spec National Park **197**
Mount Stanley 59
Mount Strzelecki 61, **61**
Mount Strzelecki National Park 59, 61
Mount Success 309
Mount Surprise 199
Mount Tempest **188**
Mount Tingaringy 125
Mount Tozer **216**
Mount Trafalgar **267**
Mount Twynam 117
Mount Victoria 29
Mount Vincent 291
Mount Wadbilliga 130
Mount Wareng 174
Mount Warning **180**, 181, 191
Mount Warrawolong 175
Mount Wellington 27, **28**, 32, **384**
Mount William **80**
Mount William National Park 28
Mount Wilson 105, 150, 152
Mount Windsor Tableland 214
Mount Wom)argo 120
Mount Yengo 174, 175
Mount Zeil 254
mouse 108
  ash-grey 304–5
  broad-footed marsupial 71
  fawn hopping- 335
  marsupial 71, 263
  Mitchell's hopping- 358
  narrow-footed marsupial 71
  New Holland 108
  pebble-mound 278
  smoky 113
  spinifex hopping- 278, 335
Mud Island 99
Mud Island Faunal Reserve 100
Muehlenbeckia cunninghamii 209
mugga 136
mulga 21, 137, **137**, 142, 262, 281, 325, 327, 334
  'hard' 208
  'soft' 208
  red 329
mulla mulla 262, 278
mullet 71
  freshwater 161
Murchison 274
Murchison Gorge **282**
Murchison River 45, 281, 282, **282**
Murphys Glen 150
Murramarang National Park 130, 131
Murray Bridge 88, 92, **92**
Murray-Kulkyne National Park 90
Murray River 17, 62, 64, 71, 72, **73**, 80,
  86–95 **87–93**, 136, 142, 181, 194, 196, 272,
  290, 350, 380
Murrayville-Yanac track **83**, 85
Murrumbidgee Irrigation Area 90
Murrumbidgee River 80, 86, 89, **90**, 93, **93**
Mus musculus 108
muttonbird 29, 33, 60, 67–8
Muttonbird Island 68, 185
muttonwood, brush 109
myall 138, 321, 325
Myall Lake **126, 174**
Myall Lakes 170, 171
Myall Lakes National Park 171
Mycorrhiza 152
Myctiris longicarpus 28
Myiagra inquieta 165
Myoporum platycarpum 141
myoporum 321
Myriocephalus stuartii 262

Myrmecodia 220
Myrmecobius fasciatus 294
Myxus petardi 161
Myzomela sanguinolenta 113, 188

N

Nadgee Nature Reserve 130, 131
Namadgi National Park 124
Nambung National Park 289, 301
Namoi River 180
Nandewar Range 141–2, **141**
Nangar-Murga Range 139
Nangar National Park 139
Napier Range 270, 272
Naracoorte 69, 71, 72
Naracoorte Caves Conservation Park 71
Narrabri 141
Narrows, The 344
Nasutitermes triodiae 339
Nelson 69
Nattai River 147
Neck, The **33**
Nectarinia jugularis 203
needle bushes 162
Neerabup National Park 298, 302
Nelson Bluff 321
Nelumbo speciosum 195
Nemadactylus macropterus 128
Neobatrachus centralis 338–9
Neophema chrysogaster 33, 61, 101, 107
  chrysostoma 61
  elegans 282, 295
  petrophila 357
  pulchella 139
Neophoca cinerea 357
Neossiosynoeca scatophaga 221
Nepean Island 362
Nepean River 159–60, **159**
Nepenthes mirabilis 220
Neptune Island Conservation Park 357
Neptune's necklace **129**
Nettapus coromandelianus 199
  pulchellus 199, 248
Newcastle 170, 171, 176
Newcastle Bay 216, 219
Newcastle Harbour 175
New England 176–85
New England National Park 178, **179**, 181, 192
New Guinea 213, 216, 218
Newland Head Conservation Park 353
New Norfolk 24
Ngarkat Conservation Park 82, 84, 85
Ngungun National Park 190
Nightcap National Park 182, 183
nightingale 21
Ninety Mile Beach 105, **105, 110**, 111
Ningaloo Marine Park 279
Ningaloo Reef 279, **280**
Ningaui ridei 141
  timealeyi 141
Ninox boobook 98, 130, 295
  connivens 78, 84
  squamipila natalis 365
  strenua 78, 98, 113
  undulata 363
Nip Nip Lake 91
Nitmiluk National Park 250
Nobbys Beach **175**
Noctiluca scintillans 131
noddy 289
  black 363
Nogoa River 198, 206
noolbenger 304
Noosa **190**
Noosa National Park 190, **190**
Norfolk Island 360, 361, 362–3, **363**
Norfolk Island National Park 363
Norfolk Range 44
Normanby River 220
Norman River **217**
North Esk 29
North Flinders Ranges 353
North Head (Macquarie Island) **366**
North Head (Port Jackson) 156–7, 157, 167
Northiella haematogaster 72, 320
North Keeling Island 365, **365**
North West Cape 280
North West Island 233
Notechis ater 47, 61, 344
  scutatus 99, 165, 295, 299
Nothofagus cunninghamii 29, 55, 110, 122
  gunnii 30, 55, **55**
  moorei 171, 178, 191
Notomys alexis 278, 335
  cervinus 335
  mitchelli 358
Notoryctes typhlops 335
nudibranchs 129
Nullarbor Homestead 316
Nullarbor National Park 320
Nullarbor Plain 15, 92, 274, 316–21, 333
numbat **294**
Numenius madagascariensis 101, 164
  phaeopus 171
Nut, the 45
Nuytsia floribunda 294, 301, 315
Nuytsland Nature Reserve 321
Nyctidorus caledonicus 98

Nyctiphaens australis 131
Nyctophilus geoffroyi 295
  gouldi 295
  timoriensis 141
Nymphaea 206
Nyngan 138

O

oak 103
  bull 195
  desert 262, 334
  river 151, 173
  white 363
Old Mans Hat 128
Olearia argophylla 48
  elliptica 141
  phlogopappa 33
Olgas 14, 252, 257, 259, **259**
Olga Valley 38
Olinda State Forest 103
Olive Pink Flora Park 262
Olive River 219
Ommatophoca rossi 375
Oncopera 27
one-spot puller 128
Onkaparinga River 353
Onychogalea fraenata 203, 206
ooline 208
Orange 151
orange, native 348
Orbost 111, 112, 113
orchid 66, 79, 83, 139, 184, 191, 192, 212, 250,
  288, 342, 344, 353, 354
  double-tailed 101
  golden-flowered king 192
  greenhood 85, 354, **354**
  Gunn's 48
  king **191**
  leek 47
  lizard 66, **66**
  Mackay tulip 201
  orange blossom 192
  parson's band 354
  ravine 192
  red beak 83
  spider 66, 85, 192
  streaked rock 30
  swamp 66
  tailed spider 47
  tea-tree 200
Orcinus orca 375
Ord River 270, 271, 272, 273
Ord River Dam **270**
Organ Pipes National Park 81, 101, **101**
oriole 247, 273
Oriolus 273
  flavocinctus 247
Ormiston Creek 257
Ormiston Gorge **256**, 257
Ormiston Gorge and Pound National Park 257
Ormiston Pound 257
Orthonyx temminckii 192
Oscar Range 270, 272
osprey 247, 289, 359
Otway Light **64**
Otway National Park 64
Otway Range 62, **63**, 64–6
Overland Track 55, 57
owl
  barking 78, 84
  barn 78
  boobook 130
  masked 113
  Norfolk Island boobook 363
  powerful 78, 98, 113
  sooty 78, 107, 113
  southern boobook 98
Oxley Wild Rivers National Park 181, 182
Oxylobium ilicifolium 175
Oxyura australis 289, 303
oystercatchers 172
  sooty 47

P

Pachycephala olivacea 61, 178
  pectoralis 178
Pachyptila 29
pademelon
  red-legged 193
  red-necked 184, 193
  Tasmanian 28
Pages, The 359
Pagodroma nivea 376
palm
  Alexandra 203
  cabbage-tree 113, 207, 251
  Canary Island date 162
  Carpentaria 248
  fan 248, 250
  gebang 220–1
  Kentia 362, **362**
  Millstream fan 276
  red cabbage-tree 259
  thatch 362
  windmill 250
  zamia 302

Palm Beach **154**
Palm Creek 247, 259
Palm Valley 259, **260**
Palmerston National Park 215
Palmerville 218
Paluma 212
Paluma Range **197**
pandanus **40**, 41, **41**, **190**, 250, 251, 272
Pandanus 272
  aquaticus 251
  forsteri 362
Pandion haliaetus 281, 289, 359
Pantoneys Crown 146
paperbark 170, 171, **174**, 175, 198, 200, 212,
  221, **241**, 248, 251, 288, 292, 300, 301,
  broad-leaved 200, 220
  tropical 272
Parachilna Gorge 346
Paralana Springs 349
Paralucia pyrodiscus lucida 98
Paranaspides lacustris 56
Paraplesiops bleekeri 128
pardalote
  forty-spotted 31, 33, 61
  striated 273
Pardalotus quadragintus 31, 61
  striatus 273
Paroo River 194, 195
Parramatta River 157, 162
parrot 77, 89, 91, 195, 200, 313, 320, 342
  Australian king 153
  blue-winged 61, **61**
  double-eyed fig- 215
  eclectus 218
  elegant 295
  elegant grass- 282
  fig- **218**
  golden-shouldered 221
  green 363, **363**
  green ground 66
  ground 185
  hooded 251
  king 313
  mallee ring-neck 348
  mulga 278
  orange-bellied 33, 61, 101, 107
  Port Lincoln 357, **357**
  red-capped 295, 313
  red-rumped 195
  red-sided 218
  red-winged 273
  regent 85, 95, 139
  ring-neck 303
  rock 357
  superb 93, **93**, 95, 139, **139**
  swift 31, 61
  turquoise 139
parrotbush 345
parrotfish **227**, 230
Patersonia sericea 141
Patriarchs, The 60
Pattas Bluff **191**
Paynes Find 284
pea
  bush **75**
  pink Darling 141
  purple Darling 141
  Sturt's desert 263, 321, 327, 329, 345
  yellow 162
pea-flower 356
peat islands 72
Pebbly Beach 130
Pedionomus torquatus 95, 139
Pelagodroma marina 29, 100
Pelamis platurus 165
Pelecanus conspicillatus 71, 98
pelican 31, **72**, 98, 129, 142, 165, 302, 325, 353
  Australian 71, 72
penguin 131
  Adélie **374**, 375, 376, **376**
  emperor 375, 376, **377**
  fairy 68, 161, 172, 353
  gentoo 367
  king **366**, 367, 368
  little 28, 29, 33, 47, 99, 108, **108**
  macaroni 367, 368, 369
  rockhopper 367
Penguin Island 303
Penrith **159**
pepper, mountain 112
peppermint 151, 179
  black 28
  broad-leaved 111
  narrow-leaved 79
  Smithton 49, 61
  Swan River 300
  Sydney 161
  white 33, **33**
Perameles bougainville 281
  gunnii 68
  nasuta 130, 164
Perca fluvialis 91
perch
  butterfly 128
  European 91
  golden 91, 95
  Macquarie 99
  silver 95
  spangled 256, 263
perentie 257, 279, 336

Peron Peninsula 280
Perth 24, 284, 287, 291, 310, 364, 365, 368
Petauroides volans 124, 141, 153, 193
Petaurus australis 103
  breviceps 124, 163, 185
  norfolcensis 185
Pethericks Rainforest 250
petrel
  Antarctic 376
  northern giant 165, 367
  providence 363
  snow 376
  southern giant 165, 367
Petrogale lateralis 256
  penicillata 112, 141, 153
  persephone 200
  xanthopus 142, 206, 347
Petroica goodenovii 315
  multicolor 342
  rodinogaster 31, 61
  rosea 178
Petrophassa albipennis 273
Pezoporus wallicus 66, 185
Phaethon rubricauda 363
Phalacrocorax atriceps 369
  varius 68
Phalanger maculatus 218
  orientalis 218
Phantom Falls 64
Phaps chalcoptera 262, 303
Phascogale 71
Phascolarctos cinereus 78, 99, 141, 152, 162
Philemon argenticeps 273
  corniculatus 165
Philip Island 361, 362, 363
Phillip Island 107, 108
Phillips River 310
Philoria frosti 120
Phoenix canariensis 162
Phylidonyris melanops 29, 313
  nigra 165, 188, 294, 313
  novaehollandiae 165, 313
  pyrrhoptera 29
Phyllanthus thymoides 139
Phyllocladus aspleniifolius 29, 48
Phyllodactylus marmoratus 305
Physignathus lesueurii 111, 165
Phytophthora cinnamomi 293
Picnic Point **132**
Pieman River 44, 45
Pieman River State Reserve 49
pigeon 91
  bronzewing 303
  Christmas Island imperial 365
  mountain brushtail 153
  plumed 278
  spinifex 281, 337
  topknot 184
  Torres Strait imperial 250
  white-headed 184
  white-quilled, rock 273
  wonga 153, **153**
Pigeon House 128, **128**, 129, 131–2
pigface 67, 85
Pilbara 11, 274, 276, **276**
Pilbara ningaui 278
Pildappa Rock **358**
Pilliga Scrub 138, **138**, 174
Pimelea 85
pincushion 288, **288**
pine
  black cypress 139, 140, 174
  bunya 190
  celery-top 29, 30
  cypress 138, 140, 261, 344, 347
  hoop 179, 191, 200, **200**, 214, 218
  Huon **40**
  King Billy **41**, 48
  mallee 85
  Monterey 110
  mountain plum 112–13, 117–18
  native 345
  Norfolk Island 162, 363
  Oyster Bay 31
  pencil 54
  Rottnest Island 302
  slender 84
  screw 272, 362
  white cypress 21, 124, 137, 138, 140, 174, 334
pineapple grass 33
Pine Creek 250
Pinjarra plain 298, 300
Pink Hills 134
Pink Lakes State Park 91
Pinnacles, the 15, 349
Pinnacles Desert **289**
pitcher plant 220, **221**
pitta
  noisy 184, **184**, 192
  rainbow 247
Pitta iris 247
  versicolor 184, 192
pittosporum 321
  sweet 167
Pittosporum phylliraeoides 348
  undulatum 167
planigale, narrow-nosed 342
Planigale tenuirostris 342
Platalea flavipes 289
Platycercus elegans 69, 102, 103, 342, 363

icterotis 295
platypus 48, 99, 101, 359
Platypus Bay **188**
plover 303, 357
  hooded 29, 353
Poa cookii 369
  foliosa 367
Podargus papuensis 215
  strigoides 98
Podocarpus lawrencei 112, 117
Poecilodryas albispecularis 214
Pogona barbata 165
Point Cook 99
Point Labatt 357
Point Lookout 178, 181
Point Nepean 99
Point Nepean National Park 103, **103**
Polblue Tops 172, **173**
Polytelis anthopeplus 85, 95, 139
  swainsonii 93, 139
pomaderris 321
Pomaderris apetala 61
Pool of Memories **50**
Porongurup Range 290, 308, **308**, 309, 312
Porphyrio porphyrio 303
Port Campbell 68
Port Campbell National Park 66
Port Darwin 249
Port Davey 38, **38**, 43
Port Douglas 211
Port Elliot 353
Port Essington **240, 245**
Port Hacking 157, **158**
Port Hedland 279
Port Hunter **175**
Port Jackson 154
Port Kembla 127
Port Macquarie 178, 184, 185
Port Musgrave 222
Port Phillip Bay 62, 96, 99–101, 103, 105, 108
Port Sorell 46
Port Stephens 170, 171
possum 56, 99, 102, 103, 107, 114, 132, 172,
  206
  brushtail 98, 163, 185, 288, 294
  common brushtail 305
  common ringtail 64, 193
  gliding 99, 314
  green ringtail 213
  Herbert River ringtail 213, **213**
  honey-possum 281, 294
  Leadbeater's 81, 96, **98**, 123–4
  lemuroid ringtail 213
  mountain brushtail 193
  ringtail 98, 163
  striped 213
potoroo
  long-footed 113, 124, 132
  long-nosed 47, 64, 108, 113
Potorous longipes 113, 124, 132
  tridactylus 47, 64, 108
poverty bush 282
Prasophyllum brachystachyum 47
Pretty Beach **126**
prickly dryandra **292**
Princess Charlotte Bay 220, 222
Prince Regent River 267, **267**, 268, 273
Pringlea antiscorbutica 369
prions 29
Prion Bay 42
Prionodura newtoniana 213
Probosciger aterrimus 218
Proserpine River 200
Prostanthera striatiflora 347
  walteri 112
Protestors Falls **183**
Psaltoda argentata 166
Psephotus chrysopterygius 221
  dissimilis 251
  haematonotus 195
  varius 278
Pseudalmenus chlorinda myrsilus 32
Pseudantechinus macdonnellensis 335
Pseudechis australis 337
  porphyriacus 165
Pseudemydura umbrins 295
Pseudocheirus archeri 213
  herbertensis 213
  peregrinus 64, 98, 163, 193
Pseudomys albocinereus 305
  chapmani 278
  fumeus 113
  novaehollandiae 108
Pseudonaja affinis 295, 305
  textilis 165, 347
Pseudophryne corroboree 118
Psophodes nigrogularis 313, 356, 357
  olivaceus 103
Pteris vittata 112
Pterodrona solandri 363
Pteropus alecto 248
  poliocephalus 98, 113, 164
Pterostylis 85, 354
  tenuissima 66
Ptilinopus cinctus 250
  magnificus 184, 218
  regina 250
Ptiloris paradiseus 184, 201
  victoriae 213
Puffinus griseus 33

tenuirostris 29, 60, 67–8
puffy pussytail 347
Pulletop Nature Reserve 89, 95
pultenaea **152**
pumpkin flower 362
Purpureicephalus spurius 295, 313
pygmy-possum 288, 320
  eastern 72, 163
  mountain 118–19
  western 84, 294, 304, 353
Pygoscelis adeliae 375
  papua 367
python
  Bredl's 337
  carpet 337, 344
  green **219**
  Oenpelli **244**
  olive 247

Q

quail
  king 108
Quail Creek Gorge **264**
Quail Island 107
Quamby Bluff 44
quandong 85, 201, 278, 348
Queenscliff 99
Queenstown 43
Queens Wharf 175
Queen Victoria Gardens **96**
quenda 305
quokka 299, 304
quoll 180
  eastern 28, 56, 64
  spotted 64
  spotted-tailed 28, 56, 61, **64**, 113, 178
  western 294

R

rabbit **20**, 21, 46, 56, 72, 180, 259, 363, 368
Raffles Bay **245**
rail 303, 362
rainbow bee-eater 295, **295**
Raine Island 232
rainforest 170–2, 172, **212, 264**
  cool temperate 49, 64
  littoral 184
  temperate **36**, 186–191
  tropical 210–15
  warm temperate 178
Rallina tricolor 214
Ranunculus anemoneus 117
Rapanea howittiana 109
raspberry jam 286
rat
  bush 358
  long-haired 261, 335–6
Rattus fuscipes 358
  villosissimus 261, 335
raven, Australian 295
Recherche Archipelago 308, 311
Red Cliffs 93
Red Gorge 72
Red Rock Lookout 72
Red Rocks **150**
Reeve Channel **105**
Regent River **264**
Renmark 88, 91, **92**
Repulse Bay 200, **200**
Restio australis 49
Rheobatrachus vitellinus 201
Rhinonicteris aurantius 250
Rhipidura fuliginosa 184, 295
  rufifrons 192
Rhododendron lochae 212
riceflowers 85
Richea 49
  gunnii 121
  pandanifolia 41
Richmond River 179, 183
riflebird
  magnificent 218
  paradise 184, 201
  Victoria's 213–14
Rip, the 99
Riverina 86-95 **88**, 140
River Torrens 354
robin
  grey-headed 214
  pink 31, 61
  red-capped 315
  rose 178
  scarlet 342
  western yellow 282
  white-breasted 313
Robinson Creek 207
rocket, mountain 30
Rockhampton 201, 203, 227
Rock Nature Reserve 89
Rocky Cape 46–7
Rocky Cape National Park 46–7
Rocky River 359
Roe Plains 317, **321**
Roger River 49
Rokeby-Croll National Park 221
Roper River 251, **251**

rosella 354
  crimson 69, 102, 103, 342, 363
  western 295
Rosetta Head **353**
rosewood 138, 171, 172
  inland 141
  scentless 167
Rotten Point 64
Rottnest Island 298, **299**, 302, 304
Rottnest Shelf 289
Rough Range 279
Royal Cave 112, **112**
Royal National Park 126, 156, 158, **158**, 162, **163**, 165
Rubicon River 46
Rufous calamanthus 84
Ruined Castle 119
Rumex vesicarius 345

S

Sabai Island 360
Sacred Canyon 347
Saddleback Mountain 127
sage, green **368**
St George Basin **267**
St Georges Basin 129
St Georges Head 128
St Mary Peak 345
Sale 107
salinity 19, 20, 94, **94**
Salisbury River 39
sallee
  black 170
  Mount Buffalo 121
  narrow-leaved 125
Salmo trutta 98
salmon, eastern Australian 99
saltbush 93, 107, 282, 288, 320
  bladder 137, 138, 315
Salt Creek Nature Walk 72
salt lakes 91, 136, 322–29, **323, 324–26**, 356
salvation jane 345
samphire 165, 281, 288, 325
sandalwood 278
Sand Bay **197**
sand dunes **70**, 71-2, **71**, 85, 142, 142–3, 186, 202, 296, 298–9, 328, 332
sandpiper 107, 303
  sharp-tailed 101
Sandy Cape **187**
Sandy Creek **249**, 250
Sandy Creek Conservation Park 354
Sandy Hollow 173
Santalum acuminatum 85, 278, 348
  spicatum 278
Sarcochilus australis 48
  falcatus 192
  fitzgeraldii 192
  olivaceus 192
Sarcocornia quinqueflora 67
Sarcophilus harrisii 27, 56, 310
Sarcophyton **229**
Sardinops neopilchardus 99
Sargassum 230
Sarina 200
Sarothamnus scoparius 173
sassafras 152, 162, 171, 178
  southern 29, 48, 106
Savage River 45
sawfish 222
Schouten Island 31
Scleropages leichhardti 196
sclerophyll
  dry 161, 167, 170
  wet 64, 162, 170, 172
Scone 172
Scorpaena cardinalis 165
Scotts Creek **248**
Scottsdale 29
scree 30, 119
scrub-bird 192
  noisy 192, 313
  rufous 192
seabirds 60, 61, 71, 157, 303
seablite 107
sea eagle 31, 47, 247
  white-bellied 31, 281, 289
  white-breasted 248
seagrass 99, 107, 202, 230
sea-heaths 107
seal 61, 375
  Antarctic fur 369
  Australian 32, 61, 99, 165
  crabeater 375
  elephant 369
  fur 367–8
  leopard 131, 165, 375
  New Zealand 357, 359, 368
  Ross 375
  southern elephant 367–8, **368**
  Weddell 375, **375**
sea lavender 345
Seal Bay **352**
Seal Bay Conservation Park 359
sea-lion **359**
  Australian 352, 357, 359
Seal Island 353
sea rocket 67

sea slug 233
sea snake,
  yellow-bellied 165
sea squirt 230
sea stacks 32
sea urchin 231
sea wasp 383
seaweed 230
sedge, brickmakers 106
sedges 137
Senecio spathulatus 161
Sericornis sagittatus 165
Sericulus chrysocephalus 184, 201
Seriola lalandi 166
Serpentine Gorge 257
Serpentine Gorge National Park 257
Serpentine National Park 300
Serra Range **80**
Sesbania formosa 279
Setonix brachyurus 299
Seventy-five Mile Beach **188**
Shackleton Shelf 373
Shady Camp Reserve 248
shag, Heard Island 369
Shannon National Park 312
shark 99, 222
  bull 222
  freshwater 251
  Port Jackson 166
Shark Bay 274, **274**, 279, **279**, 280, **280**, 281, 282
shearwater 167, 185, 289
  short-tailed 29, 60, **60**, 67–8
  sooty 33
sheathbill
  Heard Island 369
Shelburne Bay 219, **219**
shelduck
  Australian 71
  radjah 199
Shelly Beach 64
sheoak 85, 162, 179, 300, 302, 312, 315
  black 33
  drooping 101, 359
  dwarf 85
  swamp 301
Sherbrooke Forest 103
Shoalhaven Delta 127
Shoalwater Bay 201–3
short-headed lamprey 98
shrike-thrush,
  Bower's 214
  grey 295
shrimp **258**
  brine 326
  cave-dwelling 251
  mountain 56, **56**
  shield 259
  Tasmanian mountain 56
silk cotton tree 218
silkworm 20
Sillaginodes punctata 99
Silvan Reservoir 103
silvereye, Christmas Island 365
Simpson Desert 322, 328, 334, 338, 339
Simpsons Gap 256
Simpsons Gap National Park 256
Sir Edward Pellew Group of islands **223**
Sir Joseph Banks Group of islands 357
skink 99, 305, 336, 354
  bobtail 305
  ocellated 61, **61**
  sand-swimmer 337
  shingleback 305
  swamp 107
  yellow-footed 153
skua 165
  south polar 375
Sleaford Bay 357
Sleaford Mere Conservation Park 357
Sliding Rock 345
Smicrornis brevirostris 315
Sminthopsis 71, 304
  crassicaudata 335, 358
snake 165, 336, 337
  black tiger 47, 61, 344
  black whip 247
  broad-headed 165
  brown 347
  copperhead 47, 99
  death adder 347
  desert death adder 337
  eastern brown 165
  eastern tiger 99, 165
  mainland tiger 165
  mulga 337
  red-bellied black 153, 165
  Sydney broad-headed 165
  tiger 299, 305
  white-lipped 47, 99, **99**
snapper 99
snipe, Latham's 99
Snowy Mountains 13, 15, 88, **88**, 89, 117–19, 125, 130
Snowy River 111, **112**, 124
Snowy River Gorge 112
Snowy River National Park 112, 124
sooty oyster-catchers 47
Sorrento 99
South East Point **105**

Southern Forests (Tas.) 41
Southern Highlands 144
Southern Ocean 34, 44, 45, 58, 62, 66, 71, 92, 316, 350, 357
Southern Tableland 125, 126
South Esk pine 29
South Esk River **28**
South Georgia 368
South Gippsland Highway 107
South Head (Port Jackson) **156, 159**, 157
South Point 105
South Pole 372
South West Cape 42
Southwest National Park 39, 43
Southwood National Park 195
Spencer Gulf 340, 342, 344, 349, 350, 356, 357
Sphecotheres viridis 247
Sphinx Rock 194
spider
  daddy long-legs 48
  harvestman 48
  Sydney funnelweb 166
  Tasmanian cave 48
spider flower, grey 167
spike-rushes 137
spinebill
  eastern 61
  red-eyed eastern 46
  western 294, 314
spinefoot fish 230
spinifex 199, 209, 262, 263, 299, 302, 334, 335
spinifex bird 278, 337
Spinifex hirsutus 161
sponges 230
  fossil 347
spoonbill 72, 195, 248, **248**, 303, 353
  yellow-billed 289
Springbrook Plateau 193
Spring Gully Conservation Park 354
Spring Mount Conservation Park 352
spurge, thyme 139
squid 60, 161
Staaten River National Park 221
Standley Chasm 257, **257**
Stanwell Park 126
starfish 231
  crown-of-thorns 233
starling 21, 46
  metallic **219**
Steamers Beach 129
Steep Island 60
Stenocarpus sinuatus 192
Stenochlaena palustris 247
Sterna albifrons 165
  anaethetus 303
  bergii 29, 30, 71, 100, 165, 303
  caspia 29, 100
  nereis 29, 71
Stictonetta naevosa 289, 329
Stilbocarpa polaris 367
stilts 302, 303
stinger 383
stinging tree 172, 184
  giant 191
stingrays 222
stinkwood 272
stint 107, 303
  red-necked 31, 101, 164
Stipiturus malachurus 69, 295
  ruficeps 337
Stirling Range 309, **309**, 310, **313**, 314, 315
Stirling Range National Park 315
Stones Faunal Reserve 68
Stony Creek **211**
stork, black-necked 273
storm petrel,
  white-faced 29, 100
Stradbroke Island 188
Streaky Bay 357, 358
Strepera versicolor 103
Streptopelia chinensis 303
  senegalensis 303
stringybark 41, 179
  Blaxland's 171
  brown 69, 83, 85, 354
  browntop 30
  Darwin 221
  gum-topped 29, 30
  messmate 79, 81, 111, 123, 170, 172, 352
  narrow-leaved 173
  red 101, 122, 139, 179, 354
  silvertop 170
  white 106, 111
  yellow 109, 111
stromatolites 11, **274**, 357
Strzelecki Desert **328**, 329
Strzelecki Ranges 61, 105, 106, **106**, 110
Sturnus vulgaris 46
Sturt National Park 329, **329**
Sturt's desert rose 262, **262**
Sturt's Stony Desert 322, 324, 329, 333–4
Styx Valley 41
Sugarloaf Point **172**
Sula abbotti 364
sunbird, yellow-bellied 203
sundews 77, 161, 302, 314
sunray **263**
surgeon fish 230
Swain Reefs **227**
Swainsona 327

galegifolia 141
swainsonas 321
swales 83
Swallow Cave 250
swamphen 72
  purple 303
Swan-Avon River system 290
swan, black 28, 31, 71, 129, 131, 142, 165, 172, 195, 303, 325
Swan Hill 29
Swan River **29**, 290, 292, 296, 298, 300
Swan River colony 310
Swansea Heads 175
Swan Valley 298, 310
sweet bursaria 98, **99**
swift, needletail 131–2
swordfish 251
Sydney 126, 129, 154–67, 175
Sydney Harbour National Park **156**, 162, 167
Syncarpia glomulifera 162
Syncarids 56
Synoum glandulosum 167

T

Table Cape 45
Tabletop Mountain 117
Tabletop Range 249–50, **249**
Tabot Bay 267
Tachyglossus aculeatus 47, 78, 84, 99, 315
Tadarida australis 84
Tadorna radjah 199
  tadornoides 71
Taeniopygia guttata 256, 338
tallow wood 170, 178
Tamar River 28, 29
tamarind 171
Tambo River 105, 111
Tamborine Mountain 193, **193**
Tamworth 178, 182
Tanami Desert 334, 335
Tandanus tandanus 91, 95
Tantawangalo **133**
Tantawangalo Creek 132
Tantawangalo State Forest 133
Tanunda 353
Tanysiptera sylvia 203
Taree 181, 182
Tarlo River 151
Tarlo River National Park 151
Tarra-Bulga National Park **106**, 110, **111**
Tarra Valley 110, **111**
Tarsipes rostratus 288, 304, 314
Tarsipes rostratus 281, 294
Tasman Arch 32
Tasman Highway 29
Tasman Peninsula 24, **27**, 32
Tasman Sea 104, 111, 124
Tasmania 24-33, 34-43, 44, 58, 64, 214, 367, 368
Tasmanian tiger 49, 56, 142, 310, 320-1
Tasmannia lanceolata 112
teal
  chestnut 71
  grey 71
tea-tree 31, **63**, 131, 161, 170, 315, **320**
  coastal 84, 85
  woolly 29
Tea Tree Bay **190**
Telopea oreades 112
  speciosissima 179
  truncata 30, 49
Telowie Gorge 344
Telowie Gorge Conservation Park 343, 347
Temple Bay 219
Templetonia retusa 345, 356
Tennant Creek 254
Tenterfield 178, 179, 182
Terania Creek 182, 183
Terminalia 273
termite mounds 221, **243**, 246, **249**, 251, 339
termite 165, 339
  soldier 249
  spinifex 339
tern 172, 289, 357
  bridled 303
  Caspian 29, 100
  crested 29, 30, 71, 100, 165, 303
  fairy 29, 71
  little 165
  white 363
Terraces, The 344
Terrible Hollow 150
Tessellated Pavements **32**
Thalassoica antarctica 376
thistle 101
  artichoke 101
Thompson River 322, 327
Thomson River (Vic.) 105
Thomson River (Qld) 205, 209
Thopha saccata 166
thornbill 89
  brown 313
  chestnut-rumped 315
  striated 314
  yellow-rumped 165
Three Hummock Island 60
Three Sisters 147, **148**
Threskiornis aethiopicus 98
  spinicollis 98

Thryptomene maison-neuvii 334
Thunder Cave 67
thylacine 49, 56, 310, 320
Thylacinus cynocephalus 49, 56, 310
Thylogale billardierii 28
  stigmatica 193
  thetis 193, 193
Tia Falls 181
Tibooburra 136, 329
Tibrogargan National Park 190
Tidal River 109
Tiliqua rugosa 305
  scincoides 99
Timor Sea 246
Tinderry Nature Reserve 125
tinsel plant 273
Tintinara 84
Tirari Desert 328, 334
toadlet 305
  warty-skin 344
Tocumwal 93
Todd River 262
Todiramphus pyrrhopygius 338
Toll Peak 309
Tolmer Falls 250
Tonduron 140
Toodyay 294
Toolbrunup Peak **309**
Toolibin Lake 289
Toolong Range 120, 122
Toona australis 152, 171, 184, 191, 202
Torres Strait 213, 218, 226, 360
tors 108
tortoise 251
  Cooper Creek 329
  long-necked 98, 99
Tower Hill 68
Townsville 199, **199**, 203, 210, 213
Townsville Town Common Environmental Park **199**
Towra Point 162, 164
Trachydosaurus rugosa 347, 354
Transantarctic mountains 372, **372**
Trafalgar 267
Treachery Head **172**
treecreeper, rufous 320
tree-fern 61, 64, 79, 129, **133**
  graceful 49
  rough 103
  skirted 110
  slender 110
  soft 103
tree-heath 49
tree-kangaroos 213
tree peach 201
Trefoil Island 60
Trema orientalis 201
Trephina Gorge 257
Trephina Gorge Nature Park 257
trevally 32
Trezona Range 347
Trichoglossus concinna 113
  haematodus 113, 165, 251, 262, 273
Tricholimnas silvestris 362
Trichosurus caninus 153, 193
  vulpecula 163, 185, 288, 305
trigger plant 288
Trigonella suavissima 209
Triodia 199, 334
  plectrachne 262
Triops 259
Tristania conferta 162, 183, 191
tropicbird, red-tailed 363
Tropic of Capricorn 210
trout 21, 56
  brook 56
  brown 98
  coral 229
  rainbow 56
trumpeter 32
tuart 300, 301
Tuckers Creek **89**
Tully 212
Tully River 211
Tumby Bay 357
tuna, bluefin 32
Tunnel Creek 270
Turkey Creek 264
Turnix velox 320
turnstone, ruddy 164, 171
Tuross River 130
turpentine 162
Tursiops truncatus 99, 280
turtle 165
  Australian flatback 232
  broad-shelled 95, **95**
  common snake-necked 95
  flatback 202
  freshwater 165
  green 165, 202, 230, 232, **232**
  hawksbill 232
  leathery 202, 232–3
  loggerhead 165, 202, 232
  long-necked 165, 165, 295
  Macquarie 95
  marine 165
  oblong 305
  short-necked 95
  snake-necked 95
  western swamp 295

turtle-dove
  laughing 303
  spotted 303
Turtle Rock 194
turtle weed 230, **230**
Tweed River 179, 183
Twelve Apostles **66**, 67
Tyers, Lake 111
Tyers Park 110
tymbals 166
Typha domingensis 301
Tyto alba 78
  novaehollandiae 113
  tenebricosa 78, 107, 113

U

Ubirr **237**
Ulan 173
Ulladulla 129, 130, 202
Uluru 12, 14, 257, 258, **258**, 259
Uluru National Park 257
Umbercollie Lagoon 195
Umbrawarra Gorge Park **248**, 250
umbrella bush 260
Umpherston Cave 69
Underbool 91
Underwoodisaurus milii 358
Upper Colo 153
Upper Derwent Valley 53

V

Valley of the Giants 312
Valley of the Winds 259
Vanellus miles 46
Vanishing Falls 39
Varanus giganteus 257, 336
  gouldii 305, 337
  rosenbergi 358
  tristis 257
  varius 165, 342
velvet bush 358
Venus Bay Conservation Park 357
Verticordia mitchelliana 287
Vestfold Hills **374**, 377
Victoria Fossil Cave 71
Victorian Alps 119–20
Victoria Range **80**
Victoria River 246, **246**
Viola hederacea 33
violet
  ivy-leaf 33
  tree 98
  wild 152
volcanoes **68**, **140**
Vombatus ursinus 28, 36, 47, 56, 61, 99

W

Wadbilliga National Park 130, 131
Wagga Wagga 89, 93
Wahlenbergia 88
Waldheim 57
Walcott Inlet 267
Wallabia bicolor 64, 78, 131, 139, 185, 203
wallaby 56, 103, 172, 173, 180, 185, 206, 208, 304, **347**, 353
  agile 203, 247
  banded hare- 281
  Bennett's 28, 32
  black-footed rock- 256, 279
  black-gloved 294
  black-striped 203, **203**
  bridled nailtail 203, 206
  brush-tailed rock 141
  red-necked 28, 36, 139, 141, 203
  swamp 64, 78, 131, 139, 141, 185, 203
  tammar 304, 359
  Tasmanian 30, 32
  western brush 288, 294, 304
  yellow-footed rock 142, 347
Wallaman Falls 211, **211**
wallaroo 140, 141, 203, 258–9
  common 263, 335, 344
Wallis Lake **171**
Wall of China **270**
wallowa 354
'Walls of China' 142
Walls of Jerusalem National Park 54, 57
Walpole-Nornalup National Park 312
Walyunga National Park 300
wanderer, plains 138–9
wandoo 286, 292, **292**, 294, **294**, 300, 315
  powder-bark 286, **286**, 294
Wangi Falls 250
waratah 45, 179
  Gippsland 112, **112**
  Tasmanian 49
  yellow 31
Waratah 45
warbler
  brown 184
  clamourous reed- 303
  speckled 165
Warburton Creek 327

Warialda 136
Warners Bay 175
Warrabah National Park 182
Warragamba Gorge 147
Warragamba River 160
Warrandyte 99
Warrandyte State Park 98
Warrego River 194, 206
Warren National Park 312
Warriup Hill 309
Warrnambool 68
Warrumbungle National Park 140
Warrumbungle Range 138, 140–1, **140**
Warwick Hills **136**
Washpool National Park 182
Watagan Mountains 170, 171
Watarrka National Park 260–1
water buffalo 21, **242**, 248–9
water dragon
  eastern 110, 165, **165**
  Gilbert's 329
  Gippsland **111**
Waterfall Bay 32
waterlily, Undulla 206
water-rat 99, 101, **328**, 329
wattle 31, 77, 88, 124–5, 137, 141, 142, 278, 288, 299, **307**, 312, 314, 334
  coast 161
  creek 348
  dead finish 321
  golden 354, 355
  grey 85
  mulga 208
  sandhill 260
  silver 32, 124
  Snowy River 112
wattlebird
  brush 185, 203
  chestnut-winged little 46
  red 165, 355, 314
Wave Rock 287, **287**
Wave Rock Reserve 287
wax-flower, rock 125
waxlip 139
Weddin Mountains National Park 139
Wedge Island 357
Wedge Light 100
weebill 315
weka 368
Weld River 41
Weld Valley 38
Weldborough 29
Wentworth **89**
Wentworth Falls 144, 146, **146**, 149, 153
Werribee Gorge State Park 74
Werribee Plains 101
Werribee River 74, 101
Werrikimbe National Park 178
Wes Beckett State Reserve 49
West Coast Range **35**
Western Bluff 44
western plains 134– 43
Western Port 107, **107**, 108
Western Tasmanian Wilderness National Parks 43
West Island 353
West Mount Barren 310
wetlands 71–2, 98, 137, 165, 195
wet tussock 367
whale 165, 320
  blue 375
  killer 375
  southern right 32, 68, 131, 321
  sperm 375
whalebacks 358
Whale Beach **155**
Whalers Bay **356**
wheat belt (WA) 284–9
Whian Whian State Forest 183
whimbrels 171
whipbird
  eastern 103
  western 313, 356, 567
whipstick 79–80, **79**, 209
Whipstick Range 76
Whipstick State Park 76, 79
whistler
  golden 178
  olive 61, 178
White Cliffs 136
white dragon tree 279
whitey wood 49
whiting, King George 99
Whitsunday Group 200, **200, 232**
Whoogarup Range 310
Widden Brook 174
wild almond 273
Wildman Reserve 248
wilga 137, 142
Wilkawillana Gorge 346
Willandra Creek 142
Williams River **172**, 173
Willochra Plain 343
Wilmington 342
Wilpena 346, 347
Wilpena Creek 345
Wilpena Pound **341**, 343, 344–5, 347
Wilsons Promontory 59, 105, **105**, 106, 108–9, **109**, 110
Wilsons Promontory Marine Reserve 109

Wilsons Promontory National Park 109
Wimmera 74, **80**
Wimmera River 83
Windjana Gorge **266**, 270
Windorah 205, 327
Wineglass Bay **27, 381, 383**
Wingan Inlet **107**, 113
Wingen 170, 173, **173**
Winton 209
Wisemans Ferry 157
witchetty bush 256, 262
witchetty grub 256
Wittenoom Gorge 276, **277**
Wolfe Creek crater 271, **271**
Wollemi National Park 150, **150**, 153, 158, 171, 174, **174**
Wollombi Brook 174
Wollomombi Falls 181
Wollondilly River 147
Wollongong 126, 127
wombat 28, 36, 47, 56, 61, 72, 99, 173, 359
  fossil giant 71
  giant 142
  northern hairy-nosed **203**, 206
  southern hairy-nosed 319–20, **320**
Wombelano Falls **102**
Wombeyan Caves 118, **150**
wongai ningaui 141
Wongan Valley 149
woodhen, Lord Howe Island 362
woodswallow 263
woollybutt **251**
  Darwin 251
Woolshed Creek 111
World Heritage areas 142, 172, 183, 185, 210, 214
Woronora Plateau 166
woylie 294
wrasse 32
  blue 128, **128**
Wreck Bay 132
wren 78
  black grass- 273
  southern emu 295
Wyalong 138
Wyangala State Recreation Area 151
Wynyard 46
Wyperfield National Park 82, 84 -5

X

Xanthorrhoea 79, 288, 312
  media 161
  quadrangulata 344
Xanthostemon paradoxus 272

Y

yabbies 95
Yacaaba Head 171
yakka 344
Yalgorup National Park 302
Yallingup Cave 310, **311**
Yampire Gorge 276
Yanakie Isthmus **108**, 109
Yardie Creek **278**
Yarra River 96, 98–9, **99**
Yarra Valley Metropolitan Park 98
yarri 312
Yellingbo Faunal Reserve 103
yellow robin, western 282
Yelta 93
Yengo National Park 158, 174
yertchuk 106, 111
York Peninsula 350, 356
You Yangs 101
Younghusband Peninsula **70**, 71, **73**
Yumbarra Conservation Park 320
Yungermere 309

Z

Zanthus 316
Zeehan 43
Zostera muelleri 107
Zosterops natalis 365
Zygochloa paradoxa 143, 334

ACKNOWLEDGEMENTS

The publishers are indebted to the many individuals and organisations who provided assistance during the preparation of this book. They include:
AUSLIG; Australian Capital Territory Parks and Conservation Service; Australian Conservation Foundation; Australian Museum; Australian National Parks and Wildlife Service; Bay Books; Bureau of Meteorology, New South Wales; Commonwealth Scientific and Industrial Research Organisation; Conservation Commission of the Northern Territory; Department of Agriculture and Rural Affairs, Victoria; Department of Agriculture, Western Australia; Department of the Arts, Sport, the Environment, Tourism and the Territories; Department of Conservation and Environment, Victoria; Department of Conservation and Land Management, Western Australia; Department of Parks, Wildlife and Heritage, Tasmania; Department of Primary Industry and Fisheries, Tasmania; Department of Tourism, Sport and Recreation, Tasmania; The Earth Exchange (Geological and Mining Museum), Sydney; Engineering and Water Supply Department, South Australia; Federation of Bushwalking Clubs (New South Wales); Penelope Figgis; Fisheries Department, Western Australia; Forestry Commission of NSW; Forests Department of Western Australia; Great Barrier Reef Marine Park Authority; Murray–Darling Basin Commission; New South Wales Agriculture and Fisheries; New South Wales National Parks and Wildlife Service; New South Wales Tourism Commission; Northern Territory Government Tourist Bureau; Paddy Pallin, Sydney; Queensland Department of Primary Industries, Division of Fisheries and Wetland Management; Queensland National Parks and Wildlife Service; Queensland Tourist and Travel Corporation; Royal Botanic Gardens, Sydney; Soil Conservation Service of New South Wales; South Australian Department of Agriculture; South Australian Department of Fisheries; South Australia National Parks and Wildlife Service; Tasmap, Tasmanian Department of Lands, Parks and Wildlife; Technical and Field Surveys Pty Ltd; Tourism South Australia; Victorian Tourism Commission; Western Australian Tourism Commission.

The following books and journals were consulted for reference:
Antarctica (Reader's Digest); *Australia: A Timeless Grandeur* Helen Grasswill (Lansdowne Press); *Australia: The Land Time Forgot* Geoff Higgins and Neil Hermes (Child and Associates); *Australia: The Untamed Land* (Reader's Digest); *The Australian Encyclopaedia* (Australian Geographic/The Grolier Society of Australia); *Australian Freshwater Fishes* John R. Merrick and Gunther E. Schmida (John R. Merrick); *The Australian Gardener's Wildflower Catalogue* Denise Greig (Angus and Robertson); *Australian Geographic* (Dick Smith); *The Australian Museum Complete Book of Australian Mammals* Ronald Strahan (ed.) (Angus and Robertson); *Australian Native Plants* John W. Wrigley and Murray Fagg (Collins); *Australian Rainforest Trees* W. D. Francis (Australian Government Publishing Service); *Australian Ranger Bulletin* (Australian National Parks and Wildlife Service); *The Australian Wildlife Year* (Reader's Digest); *Australia's Dangerous Creatures* (Reader's Digest); *Australia's National Heritage* (The Australian Conservation Foundation); *Australia's Wilderness Heritage* (Weldon); *Australia's Wildflowers* Michael Morcombe (Lansdowne Press); *The Blue Mountains: Nature's Geological Masterpiece* Jeff Toghill (A. H. and A. W. Reed); *Christmas Island National Parks Plan of Management* (Australian National Parks and Wildlife Service); *Christmas Island – Naturally* Howard S. Gray (Christmas Island National History Association); *The Cocos (Keeling) Islands: Australian Atolls in the Indian Ocean* Pauline Bunce (The Jacaranda Press); *The Cold-Blooded Australians* Gunther Schmida (Doubleday Australia); *The Collins Australian Encyclopaedia* (Collins); *Country Australia* (Reader's Digest); *Discover Australia's National Parks and Naturelands* Michael and Irene Morcombe (Lansdowne Press); *Discover Australia: Our Highways and Byways* Robert Wilson (Runaway): *Discover the Great Barrier Reef Marine Park* (Bay Books); *The Exploration of Australia* (Reader's Digest); *Floods of Lake Eyre:* Vincent Kotwicki (Engineering and Water Supply Department of South Australia); *Flowers and Plants of Western Australia* Rica Erickson, A. S. George, N. G. Marchant, M. K. Morcombe (A. H. and A. W. Reed); *Forest Trees of Australia* (Nelson Wadsworth and CSIRO); *GEO* (Weldon Young Productions); *The Heritage of Australia* (Macmillan); *Key Guide to Australian Palms, Ferns and Allies* and *Key Guide to Australia Wildflowers* Leonard Cronin (Reed Books); *The Living World of Animals* (Reader's Digest); *Native Trees and Shrubs of South-eastern Australia* Leon Costermans (Weldon) *New South Wales Rainforests: The Nomination for the World Heritage List* Paul Adam (National Parks and Wildlife Service of New South Wales); *Plants of Western New South Wales* G. M. Cunningham, W. E. Mulham, P. L. Milthorpe, J. H. Leigh (New South Wales Government Printing Office); *Reader's Digest Atlas of Australia* (Reader's Digest); *Reader's Digest Book of the Great Barrier Reef* (Reader's Digest); *Reader's Digest Complete Book of Australian Birds* (Reader's Digest); *Reader's Digest Guide to the Australian Coast* (Reader's Digest); *Regional Landscapes of Australia* Nancy and Andrew Learmonth (Angus and Robertson); *Reptiles and Amphibians of Australia* Harold G. Cogger (A. H. and A. W. Reed); *Scenic Wonders of Australia* (Reader's Digest); *South Australia's Mound Springs* John Greenslade, Leo Joseph and Ann Reeves (eds.) (Nature Conservation Society of South Australia); *We Were the Christmas Islanders* Margaret Neale (Bruce Neale); *Wild Australia* (Reader's Digest); *Wildlife Australia* (Wildlife Preservation Society of Queensland); *Wild Places of Australia: A Guide to Australia's National Parks* (Bay Books).

Photographs and maps   The publishers give particular thanks to Auscape International (Auscape) and to Australasian Nature Transparencies (ANT).
Positions of photographs on the page are given as: t – top; b – bottom; l – left; r – right; c – centre. RD = Reader's Digest.
Front cover AusChromes background map This topographical map is Crown copyright and has been reproduced with the permission of the general manager, Australian Surveying and Land Information Group, Canberra, A.C.T. Back cover t & c AusChromes, b RD.Endpapers Richard Woldendrop/The Photo Library. Title page Weldon Trannies. 8–9 Michael Jensen/Auscape. 10 Silvestris/ANT. 11 Robin Morrison/RD. 13 t, Technical & Field Surveys P/L; b, Edwin Barnard. 14–5 Ted Mead/ANT. 15 t/c 16 Graeme Chapman. 17 Technical & Field Surveys P/L. 18 Jan Taylor/ANT. 19 tl & tr Jan Mason/Soil Conservation Service of NSW; b, Ralph & Daphne Keller/ANT. 20 Graeme Chapman. 21 Gunther Deichmann/Auscape; b, Kathie Atkinson/Auscape. 22–3 Gunther Deichmann/Auscape. 24 l, P. & M. Walton/ANT. 24–5, 26–7 & 27 The Photo Library. 28 t & b, Otto Rogge/ANT. 29 & 30 t, Grant Dixon/Wilderness Society. 30 b, B. Burton/Wilderness Society. 31 tl, Otto Rogge/ANT; tr, Grant Dixon/Wilderness Society; b & 32 b, Bob Mossel. 32 t, Jean-Paul Ferrero/Auscape. 33 t, Bob Mossel; b, Ian Skinner/Wilderness Society. 35 Wilderness Society. 36 l & 36–7, Ted Mead/Wilderness Society. 37 Jean-Paul Ferrero/Auscape. 38 & 39, Grant Dixon/ANT. 38–9 Robin Morrison/RD. 40 b, Rob Blakers/ANT. t & 41 t, 42 t Ted Mead/Wilderness Society. 42 b, J. Burt/ANT. 43 Jean-Paul Ferrero/Auscape. 45 Weldon Trannies. 46 l, Dave Watts/ANT; r, International Photographic Library. 47 t, Bill Bachman/ANT; b, G. Cheers/ANT. 48 t, Reg Morrison/Weldon Trannies; b, C.A. Henley/Auscape. 49 Rob Blakers/ANT. 51 Grant Dixon/ANT. 52 t & b, Dennis Harding/Auscape. b, John Brownlie/ANT. 54 t, Rob Blakers/ANT; 53 t, Chris Bell/ ANT; c, Dennis Harding/Auscape; b, Grant Dixon/ANT. 55 t, Ted Mead/Wilderness Society; b, Dennis Harding/Auscape. 56–7 Bill Bachman/ANT. 57 Dennis Harding/Auscape. 58 Graham Robertson/Auscape. 58–9 Robin Morrison/RD. 59 John Brownlie/ANT. 60 t, Dave Watts/ANT; b, Ralph & Daphne Keller/ANT. 61 t, Tony Howard/ANT; c, Dave Watts/ANT; r, Robert W.G. Jenkins/ANT. 63 t, Robin Morrison/RD; b, Reg Morrison/Auscape. 64 t, D. Parer & E. Parer-Cook/Auscape; b, Dick Whitford/ANT. 65 P. Jeans/ANT. 66 Dave Watts/ANT. 66–7 Paddy Ryan/ANT. 67 Ralph & Daphne Keller/ANT. 68 J. Burt/ANT. 69 G.D. Anderson/ANT. 70–1 Otto Rogge/ANT. 72 Bill Bachman/ANT. 73 Natural Images/ANT. 74 t, Wild Nature/ANT; b, Bill Bachman. 76 I.R. McCann/ANT. 77 t, Coo-ee Picture Library; b, Bill Bachman. 78 t, James Calder; b, D. & M. Trounson/ANT. 79 t, Coo-ee Picture Library; b, Kathie Atkinson. 80 t, Bob Mossel; b, Glenn Tempest/Winter Light. 81 Reg Morrison/Weldon Trannies. 83 t & b, Otto Rogge/ANT. 84 tl, David R. Austen; tr, Bill Bachman/ANT; b & 85 c & b, Coo-ee Picture Library. 85 t, Otto Rogge/ANT. 87 Leo Meier/Weldon Trannies. 88 t, Robin Morrison/RD; b, Peter Shore/Weldon Trannies. 89 t, The Photo Library; c, Michael & Irene Morcombe; b and 90 t, Ralph & Daphne Keller/ANT. 90 b, The Photo Library. 91 t, Otto Rogge/ANT; b, Robin Morrison/RD. 92 t, J. Burt/ANT; b, Natural Images/ANT. 93 t, Hans & Judy Beste/Auscape; b, Bob Mossel. 94 t & b, David R. Austen. 95 t & b, Gunther Schmida. 97 Leo Meier/Weldon Trannies. 98 l, A.P. Smith/ANT; r, Coo-ee Picture Library. 99 t, Toppix; c, G. Cheers/ANT; r, D. & V. Blagden/ANT. 100 t, J.M. LaRoque/Auscape; b, Ralph & Daphne Keller/ANT. 101 Coo-ee Picture Library. 102 t, Australian Picture Library; b, Bill Bachman/ANT. 103 Bill Bachman. 105 t & b, Ralph & Daphne Keller ANT. 106 P. & M. Walton/ANT. 106–7 Bill Bachman. 107 t, Esther Beaton/Auscape; b, & 108 b, Ralph & Daphne Keller/ANT. 108 t, Otto Rogge/ANT. 109 t, Jean-Paul Ferrero/Auscape; b, J. Burt/ANT. 110 t & b, Ralph & Daphne Keller/ANT. 111 l, W. Farrugia/ANT; r, J.M. LaRoque/Auscape. 112 tl, J. Burt/ANT; bl & r & 113 t, Ern Mainka/ANT. 113 b, G.E. Schmida/ANT. 115 Jean-Paul Ferrero/Auscape. 116 t, Reg Morrison/Weldon Trannies; b, Wild Nature/ANT. 117 t, Glenn Tempest/Winter Light; b, Tony Rodd. 118 t, J.E. & E.S. Baker/ANT; c, Kerrie Ruth/Auscape; b, Jean-Paul Ferrero/Auscape. 119 t, Bill Bachman/ANT; b, Tony Rodd. 120 S. Wilson/ANT. 120–1 J. Burt/ANT. 121 R. Thwaites/ANT. 122–3 J.P. & E.S. Baker/ANT. 123 Bill Bachman/ANT. 124 l, Alan Gibb/ANT; r, P. & M. Walton/ANT. 125 Australian Picture Library. 126 The Photo Library. 127 Bob Mossel. 128 t, Graham Robertson/Auscape; b, H.G. de Couet/Auscape. 129 t, Jean-Paul Ferrero/Auscape; b, Robin Morrison/RD. 130 t, Grant Dixon/ANT; b, P. & M. Walton/ANT. 131 The Photo Library. 132 Grant Dixon/ANT. 133 t, Rob Blakers/ANT; b, Esther Beaton/Auscape. 135 Denis & Theresa O'Byrne/ANT. 136 t, Otto Rogge/ANT; b, Graham Robertson/Auscape. 137 t, Robin Morrison/RD; b, Denis & Theresa O'Byrne/ANT. 138 t & b, Tony Rodd. 139 t, Tony Howard/ANT; b, Kathie Atkinson. 140 A. Fox/Auscape. 141 Robin Morrison/RD. 142 Tony Howard/ANT. 142–3 Reg Morrison/Auscape. 143 B.G. Thomson/ANT. 145 t & b, Ross W. Barnett/Auscape. 146 t, Neville Prosser; b, Ted Hutchison/ANT. 147 Leo Meier/Weldon Trannies. 148 t, G.E. Schmida/ANT; c, Hans & Judy Beste/Auscape; b, Ross W. Barnett/Auscape. 149 t & b & 150 t, David Noble. 150 b, Ken Griffiths/ANT. 151 b, David Noble; t & 152 t & b, Tony Rodd. 152 c, G. Cheers/ANT. 153 t, Tony Rodd; c, Tom & Pam Gardner/ANT; b, Jaime Plazavan Roon/Auscape. 155 Leo Meier/Weldon Trannies. 156 Brett Gregory/Auscape. 156–7 The Photo Library. 157 Leo Meier/Weldon Trannies. 158 t, J. Burt/ANT; b, Rob Little/Auscape. 159 t, The Photo Library; b, Jutta Hösel/ANT. 160 t, J. Burt ANT.; b, The Photo Library. 161 t & b, Jean-Paul Ferrero/Auscape. 162 Rodney Tuck. 163 t, Brett Gregory/Auscape; b, Jutta H-94-sel/ANT. 164 t, Ken Griffiths/ANT; b, pavel German/ANT. 165 t & b, Kathie Atkinson. 166 & 167 b, Jean-Paul Ferrero/Auscape. 167 t, The Photo Library. 169 Australian Picture Library. 170 Denis & Theresa O'Byrne/ANT. 171 t, Brett Gregory/Auscape; b & 172 b, J. Burt/ANT. 172 t, Richard Woldendorp. 173 t, Kathie Atkinson; b, Reg Morrison/Weldon Trannies. 174 t, Coo-ee Picture Library; b, J. & E.S. Baker/ANT. 174–5 Richard Woldendorp. 176 David R. Austen. 177 David Hancock/Auscape. 178–79 P. Jeans/ANT. 179 P. & M. Walton/ANT. 180 t, Garry Werren/ANT; b, Ted Hutchison/ANT. 181 t, The Photo Library; b, J. Burt/ANT. 182 Leo Meier/Weldon Trannies. 183 t, Denise Greig; b, J.P. & E.S. Baker/ANT. 184 t & c, D. & V. Blagden/ANT; b, Ralph & Daphne Keller/ANT. 185 t, Hans & Judy Beste/Auscape; c, Tony Howard/ANT; b, Robin Morrison/RD. 186 Michael & Irene Morcombe. 187 & 188 t, Jean-Paul Ferrero/Auscape. 188 b, Robin Morrison/RD. 189 Natural Images/ANT. 190 t, Robin Morrison/RD; b, Reg Morrison/Auscape. 191 b, Ralph & Daphne Keller/ANT; t & 192 b, Glen Threlfo/Auscape. 192 t, Michael & Irene Morcombe. 193 t, P. & M. Walton/ANT; b, J.P. & E.S. Baker/ANT. 194 Gunther Schmida. 195 David Hancock/Auscape. 196 Natural Images/ANT. 197 l, The Photo Library; r, Michael O'Connor/ANT. 198 t, Frithfoto/ANT; b, Denis & Theresa O'Byrne/ANT. 199 t, R.J. Allingham/ANT; c, Frédy Mercay/ANT; b, J. Burt/ANT. 200 t, leo Meier/Weldon trannies; c, Gordon claridge/ANT; b, Robin Morrison/RD. 201 t, The Photo Library; b, Ben Cropp/Auscape. 202 l, Stirling Macoboy; r, Robin Morrison/RD. 203 t, I.R. McCann/ANT; c, Hans & Judy Beste/Auscape; b, C. Andrew Henley/Auscape. 204 t, Photo Index; b, Jim Gasteen. 206 & 207 b, Michael O'Connor/ANT. 207 t, C. & S. Pollitt/ANT. 208 t, G.E. Schmida/ANT; b, Tony Rodd. 209 t, Jim Gasteen; b, Reg Morrison/Auscape. 211 t, Robin Smith; b, Natural Images/ANT. 212 Michael Cermak/ANT. 213 t, J. burt/ANT; b, Ralph & Daphne Keller/ANT. 214 t, Klaus Uhlenhut/ANT; b, D. Parer & E. Parer- Cook/Auscape. 215 Brett Gregory/Auscape. 216 Hans & Judy Beste/Auscape. 217 l, Bob Mossel; r, The Photo Library. 218 t & b, & 219 t & c, Jim Frazier/Mantis Wildlife Films. 219 b, D. Parer & E. Parer-Cook/Auscape. 220 Leo Meier/Weldon Trannies. 221 t, S. Wilson/ANT; l, Densey Clyne/Mantis Wildlife Films; b, Klaus Uhlenhut/ANT. 222 t, Michael & Irene Morcombe; b, Kathie Atkinson. 223 t & b, Bob Mossel. 224 Natural Images/ANT. 225 t, Eva Boogaard/Lochman Transparencies; b, Ron & Valerie Taylor/ANT. 226 t, Natural Images/ANT; b, D. Parer & E. Parer-Cook/Auscape. 227 t & cr, Ron & Valerie Taylor/ANT; cl, Paddy Ryan/ANT; b, Fenton Walsh/ANT. 228 b, Kelvin Aitken/ANT; t & 229 t, Neil Wehlack/Lockman Transparencies. 229 b & 230 b, Fenton Walsh/ANT. 230 t, G. Saueracker/Lochman Transparencies; c, Kathie Atkinson. 231 Natural Images/ANT. 232 t, Bill Bachman; c, Kathie Atkinson; b, D. Parer & E. Parer-Cook/Auscape. 233 Jean-Paul Ferrero/Auscape. 234 Frank Woerle/Auscape. 235 Neil Morrison/Weldon Trannies. 236 Gunther Deichmann/Auscape. 236–7 Bill Bachman. 237 Reg Morrison/Auscape. 238 Peter Jarver/Auscape. 238–9 J.M. LaRoque/Auscape. 240 Bill Bachman. 241 t, Bob Mossel; b, Glen Threlfo/Auscape. 242 t, P. Jeans/ANT; b, Michael Jensen/Auscape. 243 l, David Hancock; r, Mark Burgin/Auscape. 244 Jean-Paul Ferrero/Auscape. 245 Bob Mossel. 244–5 & 246–7 Bill Bachman. 248 t, G.E. Schmida/ANT; c, Jean-Paul Ferrero Auscape; J. Burt/ANT. 249 t, Bill Bachman/ANT; b, David Hancock; c, Frédy Mercay/ANT. 250 Weldon Trannies. 251 t, Bill Bachman/ANT; b, Denis & Theresa O'Byrne/ANT. 252 Michael Jensen/Auscape. 253 M.W. Gillam/Auscape. 254 David Hancock. 255 t, B.G. Thomson/ANT; b, Grant Dixon/ANT. 256 t, J.M. LaRoque/Auscape; b, David Hancock. 257 Reg Morrison/Weldon Trannies. 258 t, bob Mossel; c, I.R. McCann/ANT; b, Otto Rogge/ANT. 259 t & b, David Hancock. 260 t & 261 t, D. Parer & E. Parer-Cook/Auscape. 260 b & 261 b, Robin Morrison/RD. 262 t, Reg Morrison/Auscape; c, Jim Frazier/Mantis Wildlife Films; b, David Hancock. 263 t, B.G. Thomson/ANT; c, Kathie Atkinson; b, Densey Clyne/Mantis Wildlife Films. 264 Marie Lochman/Lochman Transparencies. 265 Gunther Deichmann/Auscape. 266 Bob Mossel. 267 t, Robin Morrison/RD; b, Reg Morrison/Auscape. 268 t, Hans & Judy Beste/Auscape; b, D. Parer & E. Parer-Cook/Auscape. 269 Photo Index. 270 t, Bob Mossel; b & 271 t, Bill Bachman/ANT. 271 b, Photo Index. 272 r, Jiri Lochman/Lochman Transparencies; l & 273 t, Bob Mossel. 273 b, Hans & Judy Beste/Auscape. 274 Paddy Ryan/ANT. 275 Reg Morrison/Auscape. 276 b, Jiri Lochman/Lochman Transparencies; t & 277 Jan Taylor/ANT. 278 t, Marie Lochman/Lochman Transparencies; b, Frédy Mercay/ANT. 279 t, Kathie Atkinson; c & b & 280 t, Photo Index. 280 b, Robert Garvey. 281 t, J.P. & E.S. Baker/ANT; b, Jan Taylor/ANT. 282 Photo Index. 282–3 Kathie Atkinson. 284 & 284– 5 Jan Taylor Jan Taylor/ANT. 285 Photo Index. 286 t & b, Jan Taylor/ANT. 287 b, J. Burt/ANT; t & c, Photo Index. 288 tr, Jiri Lochman/Lochman Transparencies; cl, Jan Taylor/ ANT; b, J.P. & E.S. Baker/ANT. 289 t, Photo Index; b, Paddy Ryan/ANT. 290 Jiri Lochman/Lochman Transparencies. 291 Marie Lochman/Lochman Transparencies. 292–3 Jan Taylor/ANT. 292 & 293 Frédy Mercay/ANT. 294 t, Jiri Lochman/Lochman Transparencies; b, Frank Park/ANT. 295 t, J.E. & E.S. Baker/ANT; b, Graeme Chapman/Auscape. 296 Photo Index. 297 WA Department of Land Administration. 298 t, Reg Morrison/Weldon Trannies; b & 299 t, Photo Index. 299 b, Jan Taylor/ANT. 300 t, Jirri Lochman/Lochman Transparencies; b, The Photo Library. 301 b, G.E. Schmida/ANT; t & 302 b, Marie Lochman/Lochman Transparencies. 302 t, Jiri Lochman/Lochman Transparencies. 303 b, Michael & Irene Morcombe; t & 304 t, I.R. McCann/ANT. 304 cl, Photo Index; b, Michael Cermak/ANT. 305 t, S. Wilson/ANT; b, Marie Lochman/Lochman Transparencies. 307 Jean-Paul Ferrero/Auscape. 308 t, Robin Morrison/RD; b & 309 Marie Lochman/Lochman Transparencies. 310 t, Reg Morrison/Auscape; b, J.P. & E.S. Baker/ANT. 311 t, Jiri Lochman/Lochman Transparencies; b, Robin Morrison/RD. 312 Kathie Atkinson. 313 t, Jean-Paul Ferrero/Auscape; b, Brett Gregory/Auscape; c & 314 c, Graeme Chapman. 314 t, Frédy Mercay/ANT; b, A. Burbidge/ANT. 315 t, Ralph & Daphne Keller/ANT; c & b, Jiri Lochman/Lochman Transparencies. 317 t, Michael Seyfort ANT; b, J. Burt/ANT. 318 t, Natfoto/ANT; b, Bill Bachman/ANT. 319 b, Jean-Paul Ferrero/Auscape; t & 320 b, Frank Park/ANT. 320 t, Natfoto/ANT; c, John Cancalosi/Auscape. 321 t, A. Burbidge & J. Baines/ANT; b, D. Parer & E. Parer-Cook/Auscape. 322 Robin Smith. 323 Bob Mossel. 324 b, J. Burt/ANT. 324–5 D. Parer & E. Parer-Cook/Auscape. 325 & 326 t, Bob Mossel. 326 c, G.E. Schmida/ANT. 326–7 Photo Index. 327 Hans & Judy Beste/Auscape. 328 l, Bob Mossel; r, Esther Beaton/Auscape. 329 t, Graham Robertson/Auscape; b, David R. Austen. 330 Otto Rogge. 331 Weldon Trannies. 332 t, Reg Morrison/Auscape; b, Bob Mossel. 333 J. Burt/ANT; b, Bill Bachman/ANT. 334 Jiri Lochman/Lochman Transparencies. 334–5 t, M.W. Gillam/Auscape; b, C.A. Henley/Auscape. 336 tl & tr, Jiri Lochman/Lochman Transparencies; b, David Pearson. 337 t & b, Graeme Chapman/Auscape; c, Graeme Chapman. 338 Ted Hutchison/ANT. 339 tl. Jiri Lochman/Lochman Transparencies; tr I.R. McCann/ANT; b, D. Parer E. Parer- Cook/Auscape. 341 Michael & Irene Morcombe. 342–3 Photo Index. 343 Grant Dixon/ANT. 344 t, Bob Mossel; b, Michael & Irene Morcombe. 345 Robin Morrison/RD. 346 t, Ern Mainka/ANT; b, Bob Mossel. 347 t, R. Thwaites/ANT; r, J. Hutchison & M. Pfeiff. 348 Frank Park/ANT. 349 l, D. Parer & E. Parer-Cook; tr & b, Bob Mossel. 350 Jean-Paul Ferrero-Auscape. 351 Leo Meier/Weldon Trannies. 352 t, The Photo Library; b, Bob Mossel; t & 353 t, The Photo Library. 353 b, Bill Bachman/ANT. 354 tl & c, Bob Mossel; r, Otto Rogge/ANT. 355 t & b, Bob Mossel. 356–7 Coo-ee Picture Library. 357 t, D. & M. Trounson/ANT; b, The Photo Library. 358 t, Bob Mossel; b, Jean-Paul Ferrero/Auscape. 359 tl, J. Hutchison & M. Pfeiff; tr, D. & J. Heaton/ANT; cr, S. Wilson/ANT; B, C.A. Henley/Auscape. 360 John Carnemolla/Australian Picture Library. 362 t, John & Val Butler/Lochman Transparencies; c, Grant Dixon/ANT; b, D. Parer & E. Parer-Cook/Auscape. 363 t, Tom & Pam Gardner/ANT; b & 364–5 John Hicks/ANT. 364 Jan Aldenhoven/Auscape. 366 t & b, Chris Bell/ANT. 367 & 368 t, Graham Robertson/Auscape. 368 c, R.J. Tomkins/ANT; b, Chris Bell/ANT. 369 t, John Béchervaise/ANT; c & b, Jonathan Chester/ANT. 370 D. Parer & E. Parer-Cook/ANT. 371 G. McInnes/ANT. 372 t, Jutta Hösel/ANT; b & 373 t, Jonathan Chester/ANT. 373 b, Graham Robertson/Auscape. 374 t, Jonathan Chester/Extreme Images; b & 375 t & b, Tony Howard/ANT. 376 t, D. Parer & E. Parer-Cook Auscape; b, Tony Howard/ANT. 377 t & c, Graham Robertson/Auscape; b, Tony Howard/ANT. 378–9 Photo Library. 381 D. Parer & E. Parer-Cook Auscape. 383, 384 & 387 Jean-Paul Ferrero/Auscape. 388 Reg Morrison/Auscape.